NOEL MALCOLM

Agents of Empire

Knights, Corsairs, Jesuits and Spies in the Sixteenth-Century Mediterranean World

PENGUIN BOOKS

PENGUIN BOOKS

UK | USA | Canada | Ireland | Australia
India | New Zealand | South Africa

Penguin Books is part of the Penguin Random House group of companies
whose addresses can be found at global.penguinrandomhouse.com.

First published by Allen Lane 2015
Published in Penguin Books 2016
002

Set in 8.98/12.24 pt Sabon LT Std
Typeset by Jouve (UK), Milton Keynes
Printed in Great Britain by Clays Ltd, St Ives plc

A CIP catalogue record for this book is available from the British Library

ISBN: 978–0–141–97837–6

www.greenpenguin.co.uk

MIX
Paper from
responsible sources
FSC® C018179

Penguin Random House is committed to a
sustainable future for our business, our readers
and our planet. This book is made from Forest
Stewardship Council® certified paper.

This book is dedicated to Alban, Faruk and Uran

Contents

List of Illustrations

27. Petru Şchiopul, Voivod of Moldavia, with his son Ştefan. Illustration from N. Iorga, *Ospiti romeni in Venezia*, Bucharest, 1932.

28. Martin Kober, *Stephen Báthory, King of Poland*, c.1580. State Art Collection, Wawel Royal Castle, Kraków. (akg-images/Erich Lessing)

29. Turkish school, *A Venetian bailo having an audience with the Grand Vizier, with his dragoman standing behind him*, miniature, 17th century (original destroyed in World War Two). Reproduced in Franz Taeschner, *Alt-Stambuler Hof- und Volksleben*, Hannover, 1925, plate 51.

30. Italian School, *Valletta, Malta*, detail from a fresco, 1580, in the Galleria delle Carte Geografiche, Vatican Museums and Galleries, Vatican City (Giraudon/Bridgeman Images)

31. Coat of Arms of the Bruti family, mounted on a wall at Resslova Ulica 2, Koper, Slovenia. (Copyright © Dr János Korom, Vienna)

32. Three-quarter-length caftan, polychrome silk stuff with gilt-metal thread on brown silk, Ottoman, 16th century. (Topkapı Palace Museum, Istanbul. TSM 13–46)

List of Maps

Preface

Nearly 20 years ago, I was reading a sixteenth-century Italian book about the Ottoman Empire when the hairs began to stand up on the back of my neck. The author had referred to a treatise on the main European province of the empire by a certain 'Antonio Bruni'; then, discussing the Albanians, he said that information about them was available in the work of 'Bruni, their compatriot'. Here was a reference to a text about (or at least partly about) Albania, written by an Albanian – something of special significance to those who study the history of that country, since it would appear to be the first ever work of its kind by a named Albanian author.

I had not seen any reference to this treatise before. Further research quickly established that it was unpublished, unlocated and altogether unknown. One modern Albanian textbook appeared to quote from it, but the quoted material consisted only of a detail given in the sixteenth-century Italian book, at the point where it referred to Bruni's work. As for Antonio Bruni himself: he seemed to be a near-invisible figure, who had left almost no trace of his existence in Albanian history. I could find just one mention of him, in a work by the *doyen* of modern West European writers on Albania, Peter Bartl, who noted that someone of that name had apparently interceded on behalf of an errant priest (who later became an Albanian bishop) in Rome, at an unspecified date in the late sixteenth century. The rest, at that stage, was silence.*

Of course it was quite possible that Bruni's treatise had not survived in any form. But I knew that in Renaissance Italy manuscript treatises of a politico-geographical nature were a popular genre, and that they often circulated in many copies; given the extraordinary wealth of libraries and archives in that country, there was no shortage of places where a copy of this work might conceivably be lurking. As the years went by, I tried many different ways of locating it, some of them methodical (for example: looking for references to other manuscript sources in the Italian book and then hunting for those ones, in the hope that

* Pollo and Buda, *Historia*, i, 366 (textbook); Bartl, *Der Westbalkan*, 90.

Bruni's work had travelled in convoy with them), and some of them more or less random (browsing in the catalogues of Italian manuscript collections at every opportunity). But in the end it was good fortune, rather than skill or effort, that led me to it. In a recent Italian doctoral thesis, the author carefully listed all the contents of a volume of miscellaneous manuscripts in the Vatican Library; reading this, I saw the title of Bruni's work staring me in the face. Within ten minutes I had booked a flight to Rome.*

When I finally had the manuscript of Bruni's treatise in my hands, I found that it was not as long as I might have hoped; nor was it devoted exclusively to Albania, though it did contain many points of interest about that country. Nevertheless it was an unusually fascinating work, with a distinctive character, very different from the normal run of West European writings about the Ottoman territories in this period. Here was a text written by someone with significant amounts of inside knowledge – not a foreign diplomat picking up second-hand information in Istanbul, or a traveller passing through places where he could not communicate directly with the inhabitants. I decided that I would transcribe the work, and find some suitable scholarly venue in which to publish it, with a short introduction.

But there my real problems began. How could I introduce this work without giving an account of who Antonio Bruni was, and of how, when and why he chose to write it? A few hints about his activities emerged from the text itself (including a rather puzzling connection with an exiled ruler of Moldavia), but otherwise the manuscript gave me only two details about him. One was his name, given there as Antonio 'Bruno' rather than 'Bruni'; trying to find more information about him on that basis was almost impossible, as both forms of the name are frustratingly common in Italian culture and history. The other was the name of the city he came from: 'Dolcigno' or 'Dulcigno' – Ulcinj, in present-day Montenegro. I knew that a Giovanni Bruni of Ulcinj had been the local archbishop, and so I began with him, hoping to find a family connection. Gradually, by a combination of more good luck and much time-consuming detective work, I pieced together some of the family history, and began tracing the stories of several of Antonio Bruni's closest relatives – his father, his uncles and his cousins – until, eventually, there came a point where I realized that I had a much larger project on my hands.

* Gennari, '"Milione"', p. viii.

Here was a family story of particular richness, and occasional real drama, which was closely intertwined with some of the major events of sixteenth-century European history, especially where relations between the Christian and Ottoman worlds were concerned. For many years I had been studying the ways in which those two worlds both clashed and connected in the early modern period. The full spectrum of interactions between Western Christians and Ottomans ranged from war and corsairing at one end, via espionage, information-gathering and diplomacy (including the essential work of the 'dragomans' or professional translators), to trade, collaboration and actual employment by the Ottomans at the other. And now I could see that members of Antonio Bruni's family occupied, at different times and in different places, every one of those places on the spectrum. Thus the idea for this book gradually took shape. I had two basic aims: to describe the experiences, adventures and achievements of an unusually interesting set of people; and at the same time to use their collective biography as a framework on which to build some broader, more thematic accounts of East–West relations and interactions in this period. The themes here are many and various, involving not only the large-scale diplomatic and strategic issues that shaped those international relations, but also topics such as the grain trade, piracy and corsairing, the exchange and ransoming of prisoners, galley warfare, espionage in Istanbul and the role of the dragoman. Each time that I turn aside from a biographical narrative to discuss one of these issues, this is not a digression; it is part of the substance of the book.

As I did more research, a tertiary aim also developed. I wanted to shed a little light here and there on the history of the Albanian lands, and to draw attention to the Albanian strand that runs, sometimes in surprising ways, through various areas of European history in this period. Albanian historians themselves have written comparatively little about the sixteenth century, paying much more attention to the era of their national hero, Skanderbeg (1405–68), on the one hand, and on the other hand to the seventeenth century, which is better documented. Only a very small part of this book, admittedly, is devoted to events that took place within the borders of the modern Albanian state. But Albanians had (then as now) a wider presence in the Balkan lands; and besides, they played a role not only in the military affairs of several West European states, but also in the political history of the Ottoman Empire, where many of the most important pashas were Albanian. The fact that Albanians were capable of crossing the cultural and political divide was a key to their usefulness to their Western employers, giving them, at

times, a special salience in the story of these East–West relations. And of
no one is this more true than of the extended family of Antonio Bruni,
whose ability to serve Western powers was sometimes vitally enhanced
by the fact that they were related to one of the most powerful viziers in
the Ottoman government.

Of all the individuals whose life-stories I was trying to reconstruct,
only one, Bartolomeo Bruti, had attracted any attention from historians
in the past. Several Romanian historians (including two of the most distinguished, Nicolae Iorga and Andrei Pippidi) had looked at his career,
with a special interest in his role in Moldavian affairs, and a few Spanish historians had discussed his earlier activities in the service of the
King of Spain – activities which, incidentally, earned him a walk-on part
in the final section of Fernand Braudel's great history of the sixteenth-
century Mediterranean. But the Romanians had left much of his earlier
life unexplored, and the Spaniards had paid no attention to his later
career, noticing him, in any case, only as a secondary figure in a story
with other leading players; so there was still plenty of work for me to
do. Other figures had been extraordinarily neglected: for example,
Antonio Bruni's father, who played an important role as a captain at the
Battle of Lepanto, went unmentioned in almost every one of the standard modern accounts of that engagement. Many works gave lists of the
captains of the galleys, but omitted his name, and one of the very few
works that did name him assumed that he was an Italian nobleman
from the Papal States.*

Much of the research for this book, therefore, consisted of a hunt for
biographical details. When one is trying to rescue an individual from
centuries of oblivion, every surviving fragment of information becomes
precious. This volume does not by any means contain all the material I
have gathered, but I make no apology for including some details that
are there simply to supply the texture and flavour of an individual's life.
The life-stories set out in this book are – I hope – intrinsically interesting; at the same time, they point beyond themselves to the world or
worlds which these people inhabited. To some extent, the task I set
myself here resembled the one accomplished in some well-known works
of 'microhistory': focusing on the story of a hitherto unknown individual, and using it to conjure up a wider social or cultural world. There
are some differences between my approach and theirs, however, arising
partly from the nature of the available evidence. Most of the classic

* Salimei, 'La nobiltà', 14.

works of microhistory have relied on a single underlying cache of rich documentation – typically, a set of dossiers relating to judicial proceedings, conducted by an examining magistrate. My own search for biographical information was never rewarded by any such treasure-trove. The nearest thing to it would have been the detailed manuscript account of the Bruti family (Antonio Bruni's cousins) which was drawn up in the eighteenth century on the basis of many original documents; this was last seen by a local historian of Istria, Domenico Venturini, who published an article in 1905 giving some of the information it contained, but the manuscript itself does not apparently survive.*

My approach has therefore been to try to work out what each of these various individuals was doing at a particular time, and then go to any archive that might contain some documentation of that activity, to hunt for traces of their existence. While such research is labour-intensive, it is also constantly haunted by thoughts of what the researcher may be missing. I have no doubt, for example, that more information about several of these people must exist in the Vatican Archives and the State Archive of Venice. Those are two mighty oceans of papers, in which I have made repeated fishing expeditions; but to trawl them systematically would require many more years of work. I console myself with the thought that if this book places the Bruni and Bruti families on the map, other historians who come across their names in the archives will at least notice them, and may perhaps record what they find there.

I have not ventured upon that other great ocean of documentation, the Ottoman archives in Istanbul. The main reason is quite simple: although I have a basic reading knowledge of modern Turkish, I have not spent the years that would be needed to convert that into an ability to read Ottoman manuscripts, with their appalling mismatch between the vowel-rich Turkish language and the notably vowel-poor Arabic script. (Where Ottoman materials have been published in modern Turkish transcription, I have used them; otherwise I have used a range of translations of Ottoman texts into Albanian, Serbo-Croat, Macedonian, Romanian and various West European languages.) But although some of the people whose stories I tell had dealings with the government in Istanbul, it is doubtful whether the Istanbul archives would yield much information about them – other than brief references in judicial records, perhaps, if they were involved in court cases. While the Ottoman archives are rich in administrative documents for this period, such as

* Venturini, 'La famiglia'.

tax registers, spending accounts and executive decrees, they largely lack
the types of more personal material that are so commonly found in the
records of Western governments: letters and reports from individuals,
discursive policy papers, and so on.

The other, and greater, difference between this book and some of the
well-known examples of microhistory is that many of the people I
describe here were heavily involved in the 'macrohistory' too. To recover
the mental and social world of a peasant or a miller is always a fascinating enterprise, but that world will be necessarily a limited one, having
no contact with international affairs, military leadership or major developments in religion. Taken together, the people whose lives I reconstruct
here were bound up in all of those things – befriended by cardinals and
corresponding with popes and monarchs, including Queen Elizabeth I.
One was an archbishop, active in the reshaping of Catholicism at the
Council of Trent; another was the right-hand man to the commander of
the papal fleet in three campaigns; one was involved in negotiations for
a Spanish–Ottoman truce and a Polish–Ottoman peace treaty, as well as
being chief minister of Moldavia and commander of its army; another
almost succeeded in preventing a particularly destructive Habsburg–
Ottoman war, and yet another went on a dangerous mission to the
Emperor Rudolf in order to end it. So telling the story of these individuals has also meant painting, on quite a broad canvas, the international
history in which they were involved.

This book certainly does not pretend to be a general history of Europe in the second half of the sixteenth century; but it does attempt to
build up an account of the relations – cooperative as well as conflictual,
diplomatic as well as military – between the Ottoman Empire and a
range of Christian powers. As it does so, it tries to challenge some
assumptions, and it also offers one or two new answers to some long-
debated questions. While it contains much new material that may be of
interest to a variety of specialists, everything in it has been written with
non-specialist readers primarily in mind. My hope is that for such readers it will illuminate a vital period of history; cause them to question
some of the things they may have assumed about the relationship
between Christendom and the Ottoman world; and give them a glimpse
of the all-too-neglected Albanian thread that is woven into the history
of sixteenth-century Europe. If I succeed in any or all of those aims, I
shall feel that this was a book worth writing.

My first debt of gratitude is to the Warden and Fellows of All Souls
College, who have not only given me the ideal conditions in which to

research and write this book, but also supported much of the travel to archives which that research required. I am extremely grateful to two distinguished historians, Sir John Elliott and Andrei Pippidi, for their comments on a draft of this work, and to Stuart Próffitt, who has been a wise and constructive editor as well as a sharp-eyed reader of the text. I should also like to thank the copy-editor, Mark Handsley, for his exceptionally diligent work. I am indebted to several friends and colleagues for supplying hard-to-find materials: Daniel Andersson, Bejtullah Destani, Uran Ferizi and Labeate Ferizi Zeneli, Kate Fleet, Eric Nelson, Andrei Pippidi and Oliver Schmitt. Agnieszka Kołakowska gave me not only generous hospitality in Warsaw, but also invaluable help in reading and translating some problematic Polish documents. My thanks go also to Veli and Sahit Ibrahimaj, for hospitality in Topojan and for showing me some of the places traditionally associated with Sinan Pasha there; I thank also Uran Ferizi and Ardiana Ferizi Olloni for making that visit possible. I am very grateful to all the libraries and archives listed in the List of Manuscripts at the end of this book; where most of the libraries are concerned, my thanks go to the staff of the general or rare books reading rooms, as well as of the manuscript collections. In addition, I should like to thank the following libraries: All Souls College, Oxford; the Biblioteca Civica Attilio Hortis, Trieste; the Biblioteca dell'Istituto Italiano per la Storia Antica, Rome; the Biblioteca Giustino Fortunato, Rome; the Biblioteca Nazionale Braidense, Milan; the Biblioteca Universitaria, Padua; the Bibliothèque des Études Turques (Bibliothèque Jean Deny), Paris; the Bibliothèque Jean de Vernon, Paris; Cambridge University Library, Cambridge; Corpus Christi College, Oxford; Heythrop College, London; the Queen's College, Oxford; Rhodes House, Oxford; the School of Oriental and African Studies, London; the School of Slavonic and East European Studies, London; the Skilliter Centre for Ottoman Studies, Cambridge; the Taylor Institution, Oxford (and especially its Slavonic and Modern Greek Library); the Warburg Institute, London; and the Wellcome Library, London.

While mentioning archives and libraries, I should like to comment on two in particular. I am especially grateful to Count Gherardo degli Azzoni Avogadro Malvasia, who welcomed me at the Gran Priorato di Venezia e Lombardia of the Order of Knights of St John of Jerusalem in Venice (and to the Grand Master of the Order, Fra Matthew Festing, for helping to arrange my visit, and to the honorary archivist, Dr Mattiuzzo, for his assistance during it). The documents held there are of

great importance; this is the only historic archive of a Priory of the
Order to survive intact in Italy. But it is badly in need of financial help,
both to repair the physical fabric of the rooms where it is kept, and
to facilitate its study, by digitizing or other means. This would be an
extremely worthwhile project for a philanthropic donor or funding
organization.

My other comment is, alas, less positive. Towards the end of the
Second World War, the municipal archive of the Slovenian city of Koper
(Capodistria) was taken away by the Italian authorities. Since then it
has remained, unconsulted and unconsultable, in a store-room of the
Biblioteca Nazionale Marciana in Venice. Some, but not all, of the manuscripts were microfilmed in the 1960s, and the films were deposited at
the Archivio di Stato in Trieste, where I have tried to study them. The
quality of the filming was exceptionally low; I am full of gratitude to the
staff of the Archivio di Stato in Trieste, who were wonderfully helpful in
trying to find ways to improve the legibility of this material, but the difficulties in some cases were almost insuperable. This archive, consisting
of many hundreds of bound manuscript volumes dating back to the
Middle Ages, represents the greatest single source of potential knowledge about any Venetian-Slovenian city; it is or should be a vital part of
the cultural heritage of the Slovenian people. If it were returned to its
proper home in Koper, or even if it were made available to scholars in
Venice, it could be used to generate much new understanding of both
Venetian and Slovenian history. That the present situation should
obtain, nearly 70 years after the end of the Second World War, is an
absolute scandal.

A Note on Names, Conventions and Pronunciations

Generally, place-names are given in their modern form, i.e. in the language of the country to which those places now belong, though standard English forms such as 'Florence' are used where appropriate. Commonly encountered alternative forms are given in brackets, with simple abbreviations for the language (e.g. 'Ital.', 'Trk.'; note also that I use 'Srb.' as an abbreviation for 'Serbo-Croat', a term which I employ here in a purely linguistic, politically neutral sense). Modern geographical names are used for purposes of location; thus when I write that someone travelled across Bulgaria, I use this term for the convenience of the reader, without suggesting that there was a Bulgarian political entity at that time. It is on that basis also that I refer to Transylvania, Wallachia and Moldavia as 'Romanian' principalities. Similarly, I use 'Istanbul' sometimes as a general term for the conurbation that included Galata (or Pera), just as a historian of this period might talk of someone going to 'London' without thereby distinguishing the city of London from the city of Westminster. (But where Galata/Pera is meant, it is specifically referred to.) The terms 'Greece' and 'Albania' are used in their modern senses; 'Venetian Albania', on the other hand, is a distinct historical territory, as described in Chapter 1. Generally, the context will make clear whether I am using geopolitical terms in the sense they had then rather than now – for example, the 'Poland' ruled by its sixteenth-century king, or the 'Moldavia' governed by its voivod.

For personal names, the general rule is that people are referred to by the name given in the surviving documents. Where there are letters or other papers signed by them, the forms found there are used (e.g. Jacomo, not Giacomo, Bruti; Gasparo, not Gaspare, Bruni). In some cases the documented form of the name has been filtered through another language; where a reasonable guess as to the original form is possible, this is given in brackets, but generally the documented version is the one used. (Thus we have 'Tommaso Pelessa', an Albanian whose name survives only in Italian-language texts; he was probably Toma Plezhë, but that is an inference, not a certainty.) The major exception to this rule consists of some well-known historical figures whose first names are normally Anglicized: popes (e.g. 'Gregory'), Portuguese and Spanish kings (also Don John of Austria), and rulers of Poland and Transylvania. Ottoman names are given in their modern Turkish forms (but with the older forms 'Mehmed', 'Murad', etc., rather than 'Mehmet', 'Murat', etc.), without the diacritical marks that would apply to transliterations from the Ottoman Arabic script.

Where Ottoman terms exist in standard English forms (e.g. 'pasha', 'spahi'), those are used here. Otherwise, the words are presented in italics (with, if necessary, a non-italicized English plural ending). They are explained on their first appearance, and those explanations are recapitulated in the Glossary. Also repeated there are the meanings of other words in West European languages (e.g. 'commenda', 'giovane di lingua') or unfamiliar terminology in English (e.g. 'foist', 'stradiot').

Most Western European languages in the early modern period used a version of the word 'Turk' ('turco', 'turc', etc.) to mean either 'Ottoman' or 'Muslim'. Only rarely was it used to mean what modern English means by 'Turk' (that is, in an ethnic-linguistic sense). I have usually translated it as 'Ottoman' or 'Muslim', in accordance with the context.

All quotations from foreign languages are given in translation in the text, with the original supplied in the end-notes. Those notes are consolidated, normally on the basis of one note per paragraph; guide-words are added in brackets (like the originals of the quotations) to indicate which references correspond to which details in the text. Where supplementary information is given in a footnote to the text, any relevant references will be found in the end-note for the paragraph to which that footnote is appended. Full publication details of the works cited are given in the Bibliography.

For the pronunciation of unfamiliar foreign words, the following equivalent sounds in English (some of which are only approximate) may be noted:

Turkish:

c	'j' (as in 'jam')
ç	'tch' (as in 'match')
ğ	is silent or virtually silent, lengthening the preceding vowel
ı	a light 'uh' (like the 'u' in 'radium')
ö	a long 'uh' (like the 'ur' in 'murder')
ş	'sh'
ü	acute 'u' (as in French 'tu' or German 'über')

Albanian:

c	'ts'
ç	'tch' (as in 'match')
dh	'th' (always voiced, as in 'this'; Albanian writes 'th' for the unvoiced 'th', as in 'thin')
ë	a light 'uh' (like the 'u' in 'radium'; virtually silent at the end of a word)
gj	'dj' (as in 'adjure')
j	'y' (as in 'you')
ll	like 'l', but a slightly heavier, longer sound
q	like 'tch', but a slightly thinner sound
rr	like 'r', but a slightly heavier, more rolled sound
x	'dz' (as in 'adze')
xh	'j' (as in 'jam')
y	acute 'u' (as in French 'tu' or German 'über')
zh	'zh' (as in 'Zhivago')

Romanian:

ă	a light 'uh' (like the 'u' in 'radium')
â	a long 'uh' (like the 'ur' in 'murder')
c	is soft ('tch') before 'e' and 'i'; otherwise hard ('k')
ch	'k'
i	at the end of a word can be virtually silent (e.g. 'Iaşi', pronounced 'Yash')
î	a long 'uh' (like the 'ur' in 'murder')
j	'zh' (as in 'Zhivago')
ş	'sh'
ţ	'ts'

Serbo-Croat:

c	'ts'
č	'tch' (as in 'match')
ć	like 'tch', but a slightly thinner sound
dj	'dj' (as in 'adjure')
j	'y' (as in 'you')
š	'sh'
ž	'zh' (as in 'Zhivago')

Simplified Family Tree

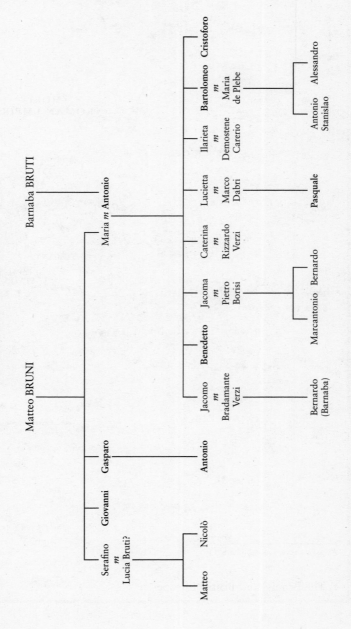

1. The Brunis' and Brutis' Europe

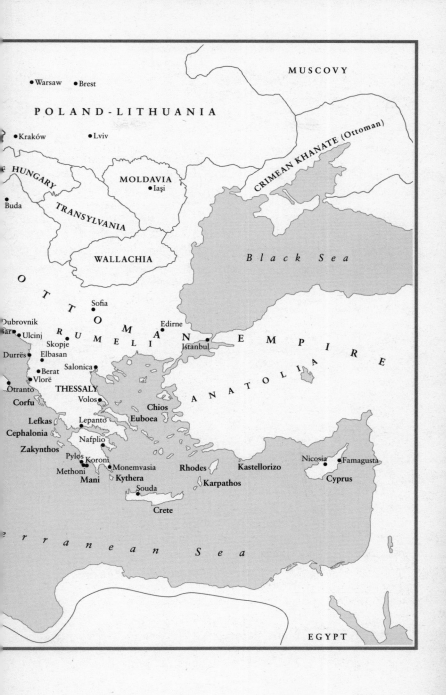

MUSCOVY

POLAND-LITHUANIA

• Warsaw • Brest

• Kraków • Lviv

CRIMEAN KHANATE (Ottoman)

HUNGARY

MOLDAVIA
• Iași

TRANSYLVANIA

• Buda

WALLACHIA

Black Sea

O
T
T
O
• Sofia
M
Dubrovnik
ar • Ulcinj
R
U
M
E
L
• Edirne
I
A
N
• Istanbul
E
M
P
I
R
E
Skopje
Durrës • Elbasan
• Berat
• Salonica
ANATOLIA
• Vlorë
Otranto
THESSALY
Corfu
Volos •
Lefkas
Lepanto
Chios
Euboea
Cephalonia
Nafplio
Zakynthos
Pylos Koroni
Methoni Monemvasia
Mani Kythera
Souda
Rhodes
Karpathos
Kastellorizo
Nicosia
Famagusta
Cyprus

Crete

erranean Sea

EGYPT

I

Ulcinj, Albania and Two Empires

This story begins in Ulcinj, a city on a rocky outcrop overlooking the Adriatic sea, and the home town of the central figures of this book. Located close to the southern tip of present-day Montenegro, it is little visited nowadays by Western Europeans, but has become a popular summer resort for people from Albania and Kosovo; they go there both because of the seven miles of golden beach that stretch below it to the south, and because it is an Albanian-speaking city. Ulcinj (Alb.: Ulqin; Ital.: Dulcigno) is not large – the present population is roughly 11,000 in the town itself, with another 20,000 around it – and has not played a very prominent role in history. To modern historians it is best known for the crisis that arose after the 1878 Congress of Berlin, when the decision to transfer it to the Montenegrin state was opposed by the Ottoman Empire, which had held Ulcinj since 1571, and by the town's inhabitants, who were mostly Muslim Albanians. Before that it had been widely feared, during the seventeenth and eighteenth centuries, as a notorious pirate lair, with a special connection to the 'Barbary corsairs' of North Africa. Its one other claim to fame was that the self-styled Jewish Messiah, Sabbatai Ṣevi, whose proclamations had sent shockwaves through the entire Jewish world, died in exile there in 1676 – after his mysterious (and, to his followers, deeply troubling) conversion to Islam. But, like most cities in the region, Ulcinj had a much older history than that. Originally Illyrian, then Roman, it had been one of a long skein of eastern Adriatic coastal towns, with their own municipal traditions, that were absorbed first into Byzantine provinces and then into Slav kingdoms or principalities. Under its last Slav rulers, the Balšić or Balsha dynasty in the late fourteenth century, it had been an important trading centre, with strong links to Dubrovnik, and had minted its own coins. Ulcinj came under Venetian rule in 1405, and, after some early interruptions, remained under it until the Ottoman conquest in 1571.[1]

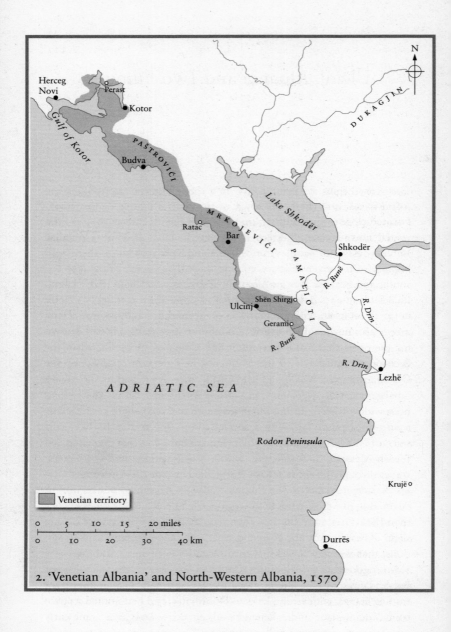

N

Herceg
Novi
Perast
Kotor
Gulf of Kotor
PAŠTROVIĆI
Budva
MRKOJEVIĆI
Ratac
Bar
Shën Shirgjo
Ulcinj
Geramio
R. Bunë
Lake Shkodër
PAMALIOTI
DUKAGJIN
Shkodër
R. Bunë
R. Drin
R. Drin
Lezhë

ADRIATIC SEA

Rodon Peninsula

Krujë

Durrës

Venetian territory

0   5   10   15   20 miles
0   10   20   30   40 km

2. 'Venetian Albania' and North-Western Albania, 1570

The first detailed descriptions of Ulcinj that survive date from the 1550s – the chronological starting-point, as it happens, of this book. At that stage it was quite a small town, of little economic importance. But it mattered to Venice because it stood on a vital frontier: it was the furthest outpost in a long stretch of Venetian territory on the eastern coast of the Adriatic, abutting the Ottoman Empire. A Venetian official who visited Ulcinj in 1553 recorded that it had 300 households, with a total of 1,600 inhabitants, of whom 300 were men of fighting age. He divided them into three categories: nobles, citizens and 'workers' ('lavoratori'), the last-named being those who worked the surrounding land, producing the wine and oil from which 'the nobles and citizens get the main part of their income'. The territory belonging to Ulcinj was small (two miles by six), containing just two or three villages, with 600 inhabitants; yet, as another report of the same year noted, it provided enough grain to feed the city for half a year and enough wine for the whole year, plus the finest olive oil for export. Not every worker went out to tend the crops; a report of 1558 observed that many earned their livings as sailors, and that most of the population was poor. Indeed, the general poverty of this town is something that emerges from all of these documents; recent Ottoman advances had taken over much of what had once been a large and profitable agricultural hinterland, and the modest amount of trade that flowed through Ulcinj was not enough to make up the difference. The city's revenues consisted of up to 700 gold ducats per year of customs duties on goods, and up to 50 on the trade in horses (bought from the Ottomans and sent on to Venice), plus 120 or 130 ducats from a tax on wine, which was used to pay the salary of the city governor. But since the basic defence costs were 1,770 ducats per year, it is clear that maintaining Ulcinj was not a viable proposition without Venetian subsidies. And from the complaint, made in one of these reports, that an ordinary soldier stationed there found it difficult to live on an annual pay of 32 ducats, one also gets a sense of the painfully small scale of the city finances, which, had they been spent exclusively on soldiers' pay, could not have covered the salaries of more than 27 men.[2]

Since Ulcinj was a frontier town, one might expect it to have been maintained as a prominent military stronghold. But Venetian strategy towards the Ottoman Empire was not as confrontational as that, and most military scenarios would involve both the enlistment of local fighters and the rapid reinforcement of the city by sea. So only a small force was kept there, to police the territory and to deal with casual

raiding – some of which took the form of attacks from the sea by pirates.
In 1553 there were just eight soldiers, under a Venetian officer, manning
the castle, plus eighteen infantrymen under a captain from Padua, nine-
teen 'stradiots' (light cavalry) under two Albanian captains, and 24
martolos soldiers (a general term for local Balkan fighters), recruited
from the territory, who were 'extremely fierce men', armed with scimitars, javelins and bows with poisoned arrows. The city as a whole was
described in 1553 as 'un-fortified'; city walls did exist, but this suggests
that they had not been kept in a defensible state. The castle itself may
have looked impressive, with its 'old, high walls'; yet, as the 1558 report
noted, it was overlooked by two points of higher ground inland, and on
the seaward side 'part of the wall looks likely to collapse'. Previous
reports and messages from Ulcinj had also given a poor impression of
the city's defences: in 1531 the governor had warned of the ill condition
of the armaments, saying that 'some artillery pieces and firearms are
completely useless', and the artillery officer who was stationed there
three years earlier had also complained about the Albanians he had to
deal with.[3]

One of the officials who visited the town in 1553 also failed to warm
to the inhabitants: 'These Albanians', he wrote, 'have barbarous customs.' He immediately added – as if this were evidence of their
barbarity – that 'they speak the Albanian language, which is utterly different from the Dalmatian [Slav] one.' But, he noted, 'they deserve
commendation for the fact that they are extremely loyal to their ruler.
There are no extreme persecutions or mutual hatreds among them, but
they are nevertheless very quickly moved to anger; they willingly engage
in slanging matches in public, but this innate sullenness of theirs is also
quickly dispelled.' In some ways, this would have appeared a strange
and remote place to a visitor from Venice – especially one from the
patrician class, as this official, Giovanni Battista Giustinian, was. One
may get a similar sense from looking at one of the city's few physical
survivals from the Venetian period: a stone carving, over the entrance to
a house in one of the old town's narrow streets. 'Nemo profeta aceptvs
est in patria sva', 'No prophet is accepted in his own country', it says
(quoting Luke 4: 24); it was probably placed there by a Venetian citizen
who had been expelled from Venice, nursing bitter feelings about this
distant exile.[4]

And yet the basic conditions of urban life here would not have
seemed so alien to anyone from mainland Italy. While Albanian was
habitually spoken by most of the inhabitants, and the Slav language by

a minority, the language of public life, and of much merchant activity, was Italian. A grand civic building facing the sea, which was probably the city hall, was directly modelled on the Palazzo del Governo (city hall) in Ancona. There was a Romanesque-Gothic cathedral, with its bishop and chapter of canons, plus at least five other churches. Roman Catholicism had a long tradition in this city, and although its medieval Slav rulers had founded or sponsored Orthodox churches, it was significant that the most important of these lay outside the city walls. We know nothing about education in Ulcinj, but there were certainly enough clerics there to guarantee basic schooling in Italian and Latin; a humanist writer, Martino Segono, from the Kosovan town of Novo-bërdë (Srb.: Novo Brdo), had served as Bishop of Ulcinj in the late fifteenth century, and one scholar from Ulcinj, Lucas Panaetius 'Olchin-ensis', published editions of works by Caesar, Plautus and Aristotle – as well as the philosopher Marsilio Ficino and the charismatic preacher Girolamo Savonarola – in Venice in the 1510s and 1520s. Regular connections with Venice must have been maintained not only by trading and administrative business, but also by the significant population of émigrés from Ulcinj who lived and worked in that city. In short: although this was a small-town world, and very much a backwater, to go there from Italy was not to cross some fundamental divide, but rather to move to a distant part of a still recognizably Venetian cultural sphere.[5]

The same could be said of the city of Bar, another Venetian possession, which lay roughly twelve miles to the north (as the crow flies). This was not the modern port-city of that name, but 'Old Bar' (Stari Bar), a walled town located a few miles inland, which survived until the late nineteenth century but was then progressively demolished by artillery bombardment, a colossal munitions explosion and an earthquake. In the mid-sixteenth century Bar was a larger town than Ulcinj (with 2,500 inhabitants rather than 1,600), and a more prosperous one: the agricultural territory that belonged to it was greater, and it was able to export significant quantities of wine and oil. Here too there was a Roman Catholic cathedral, together with other churches, but there was also an Orthodox element in the population. Regardless of religious affiliation, most of the population was Slav-speaking. A study of emigrants from Bar in Venice shows that they associated much more there with émigrés from the towns just to the north – Budva and Kotor (Ital.: Cattaro) – than with those from Ulcinj; language probably played a part in this. But while Albanians were a minority in the population of Bar itself, Giustinian noted in his 1553 report that both languages were used in the nearby villages; this whole area was an interface between the Albanian-speaking and Slav-speaking worlds, and bilingualism must have been common.[6]

As Giustinian observed, some people regarded Bar as the end-point of Albania and the beginning (as one moved northwards) of Dalmatia. But the use of these names was flexible, and they were treated more as geographical terms – albeit on criteria that were obscure – than as linguistic markers. Official Venetian practice usually referred to the whole of this Montenegrin coastal territory, stretching all the way to the northern side of the Gulf of Kotor, as 'Venetian Albania', and the Ottoman definition of Albania also extended that far north; but some writers put the upper limit of Albania at Ulcinj, or even further south, at the mouth of the Drin river. When documents from this period refer to Albanians, they may use the term in a way that broadly corresponds to our modern ethnic-linguistic sense, but they may just mean people from a geographical area, larger than, or at least differing from, the Albania of today.[7]

Visiting the region in 1553, Giustinian thought even less well of the inhabitants of Bar than he did of the people of Ulcinj. While he noted appreciatively that the town could supply 500 fighters who were extremely warlike, he described their customs as utterly barbarous ('barbarissimi'), adding: 'they are sullen and innately hostile to foreigners, and scarcely love one another, being slanderous and extremely irritable.' A certain ethos of violence seems to have been present in this society: a study of violence and the clergy in the late fifteenth century highlights two cases of laymen killing priests in Bar, one case of two priests fighting each other, and one of two priests beating up a deacon. In 1512 a dispute broke out between two clerics who both claimed the nearby Benedictine abbey of Ratac. Each represented an interest-group with its own faction of armed men; by the time they had stopped fighting, 62 people lay dead. (As we shall see, however, there were deeper socio-political reasons at work here than mere ecclesiastical rivalry.) And there was more violence outside the city walls, thanks to the very strained relationship between the people of Bar and the Mrkojevići (Ital.: Marcovichi; Alb.: Mërkoti), a warlike clan or tribe, with 1,000 fighting men, which dominated the countryside round the city. They had been coopted by the Venetian authorities in the fifteenth century, and had done loyal military service. However, much of their territory was later taken over by the Ottomans, and when they then rose up against their new masters they were refused help by the Venetian authorities in Bar, who did not want to violate a recent Venetian–Ottoman peace agreement. That, it was said, was the origin of their fierce hostility towards the city. Nevertheless many urban families continued their traditions of intermarrying with the Mrkojevići; and Bar's rather summary justice system also meant that citizens denounced by the authorities would immediately go off and join these clansmen, instead of lingering in the city with the likely prospect of being hanged. Such was the overall insecurity that the people of Bar could not go out to work on their farms without armed guards, and a senior official such as Giustinian, on his arrival, could not travel from the shore to the city (less than three miles) without an escort of stradiot light cavalry. He was, however, able to see one advantage in this ongoing conflict: it was only their constant 'war' against the Mrkojevići, he said, that prevented the people of Bar from killing one another 'like rabid dogs'.[8]

This situation was not untypical of the messy state of affairs in the Venetian–Ottoman borderlands, or, indeed, in Christian–Ottoman border zones more generally. Often, the endemic source of conflict was not the opposition of one state to another, but local enmities involving groups who shared several features of their identity: the Mrkojevići were Slavs, like most of the inhabitants of Bar, and Orthodox, like some of them. The fact that the main Mrkojević territory lay on the other side of the Ottoman border did not mean that their attacks on the people of Bar were pro-Ottoman (the story of the dispute's origin suggests the precise opposite of that); but it did tend to prolong and reinforce the conflict, as it upped the stakes for any governor of Bar who might be tempted to take retaliatory action against the Mrkojević villages.

A rather similar pattern could be observed further up the coast at the small town of Budva, which was also under Venetian rule. Today this cluster of stone-built, russet-tiled houses, almost surrounded by the sea, is one of the most prized sites in the cultural heritage of the region. In the 1550s it was a poverty-stricken place, commanding a tiny strip of territory in which all agriculture had been replaced by vineyards, to supplement the meagre incomes of the sailors, fishermen and small-scale coastal traders who lived there. The town and territory together mustered only 800 souls, with at most 200 fighting men. Converted to Catholicism (from the Serbian Orthodox Church) in 1521, they did have their own bishop, but he resided mostly in Italy. Giustinian's account of the Budvans may help to explain why: 'they have barbarous customs, and live in a sordid way like Gypsies, staying in one room together with their animals, as do almost all the Albanians [sc. people of 'Venetian Albania'], because of the extreme poverty that exists in that province.' The security problem here did not involve the inhabitants of the nearby Ottoman villages, with whom the Budvans enjoyed very friendly relations. It arose, rather, from the undying hatred between the people of Budva and another powerful clan or tribe, the Paštrovići, who dominated a wide area, with a clan base just to the south-east of Budva. The origins of this hostility were obscure. As Giustinian noted, it persisted despite two common factors: the two groups were related by blood, and they were both 'extremely faithful' to Venice. The Paštrovići had also been coopted as a fighting force by Venice (they could raise 1,200 men), and had been given a variety of privileges to keep them loyal: they had fiscal and trading advantages, and applied their own laws, governing themselves, as the 1558 report put it, 'almost as the Swiss do'. For the Venetians the result was an awkward situation, in which the people of Budva were more directly identified with Venice and better controlled by it, but the Paštrovići were the ones who, for security purposes, mattered more to Venetian interests.[9]

On his way northwards from Budva Giustinian travelled overland, with a guard of stradiot cavalry, passing through the territory of a clan which had switched allegiance to the Ottomans roughly fifteen years earlier. This journey brought him to Kotor, another Venetian-ruled fortified town (with defensive walls ascending a steep mountain-side behind the city, to encompass a small fortress at the top). Kotor stands at the innermost point of the Gulf of Kotor, a huge, irregularly shaped, spectacularly beautiful, fjord-like stretch of water that provides the best deep-water haven on the entire eastern Adriatic coast; not for nothing was it a major Austro-Hungarian naval base during the First World War. Of all the towns mentioned so far, Kotor was the most important. Not only did it have a population of 3–4,000, and a significant tax income from trade with the hinterland; it also controlled a lengthy territory, containing 31 villages, that snaked along the eastern and northern edge of the Gulf. (Though not all the way to the sea entrance: the Ottomans had taken control of a strategically important outpost there, the town and fortress of Herceg Novi (Ital.: Castelnuovo).) Kotor may not have been formally described as the capital of 'Venetian Albania' in this period, but that is how it functioned in most ways: so, for example, while judicial appeals against the rulings of the governors of Bar and Ulcinj went straight to Venice in major cases, those involving claims of less than 100 ducats went to the governor of Kotor instead. The reasons why Kotor stood higher in the pecking order were both military and commercial. But while the military concerns might make one expect that relations with the local Ottoman authorities here were more tense, such worries were more than outweighed, in normal circumstances, by the trading connection, involving a flow of Ottoman wool, hides, wax and horses with an annual gross value of 300,000 ducats. Writing just thirteen years after a major Venetian–Ottoman war which had seen serious fighting in this region, Giustinian was able to declare that 'the people of Kotor and their subjects have extremely good neighbourly relations with the Ottomans.'[10]

Which was just as well, since the Ottoman state which lay beyond these tenuous stretches of Venetian territory, to the east and to the south, was by far the most dynamic power in Eastern Europe. In the previous two centuries the Ottoman Empire had expanded at an astonishing rate. By 1400 the Ottoman Sultans had already taken over Thrace, Bulgaria and Macedonia, seized the major port of Salonica from the Venetians, inflicted a strategic defeat on a Serb-led coalition army at the Battle of Kosovo, and sent large marauding forces through northern Albania as far as Ulcinj. For a short time in the early years of the fifteenth century their advance stalled, or was even rolled back, but they were soon on the move again; most of Albania, with the exception of a handful of Venetian-controlled cities, was conquered – using a combination of direct military action and the coopting, under pressure, of local lords – between 1415 and 1423. Other Balkan territories to the north were already submitting to Ottoman influence or even to vassal status; but after the seizure of Constantinople in 1453 Sultan Mehmed ('the Conqueror') decided to dispense with methods of indirect rule, and sent his armies to incorporate first the Serbian lands and then the kingdom of Bosnia into the Ottoman state. The conquest of mainland Greece was also completed at this time. The next major phase of expansion in Europe came with the Hungarian campaigns of Sultan Süleyman the Magnificent in the 1520s, when a large part of the kingdom of Hungary became Ottoman territory. The Sultan's army now faced the Habsburg-led forces of the Holy Roman Empire – in 1529, indeed, it did so at the very ramparts of the city of Vienna, which the Ottomans narrowly failed to capture. There was little more direct conquest in mainland Europe after that, though the Sultan's power was significantly strengthened over the following decades in the Romanian lands; but the Ottoman state continued to pose a huge military threat to its northern and western neighbours, thanks especially to the financial resources it had gained when, in 1516–17, Süleyman's father had conquered the productive territories of Syria and Egypt.

In their directly governed domains the sultans imposed an effective system of military and civil rule. The administrative system was designed to supply two essential things: men to fight wars, and money to pay for them. Much of the agricultural land was therefore divided into military-feudal estates and placed under spahis or cavalrymen, who collected taxes in peacetime, retaining part of the income for their own use, and brought armed retainers from their estates when summoned to go on campaign. (There was also a standing army based in Istanbul, consisting of cavalry regiments and the regular infantrymen known as janissaries.) Territory was divided into large districts called *sancak*s – from the Turkish for a battle-standard – governed by *sancakbeyi*s, and these were gathered in provinces, some of them as big as modern countries, governed by *beylerbeyi*s. But much of the administering at the local level was done by judges (*kadi*s), who also dispensed Ottoman justice, applying a legal system which combined Islamic principles with sultanic decrees and, in many cases, elements of local traditional law. Non-Muslims could seek justice from the *kadi*, though they suffered some legal disadvantages. They also paid a special poll-tax, applied on a graduated basis to adult males, from which Muslims were exempt. In normal circumstances, however, the Ottoman régime made no attempt to force its non-Muslim subjects to convert to Islam; both the Orthodox Church and the Roman Catholic one continued to function in Ottoman territory. This was partly because of traditional Islamic principles concerning 'people of the book' (a category that included all Christians and Jews), and partly because the public revenues would fall if the tax on non-Muslims ceased to be paid. But an underlying reason was that the Ottoman state, like many pre-modern empires, took only a very limited interest in the lives led by its subjects; it seems to have felt no desire to remould them, so long as it received the money and military manpower – plus some other basic services and raw materials – that it needed. It is true that the exercise of Ottoman power could at times be capricious and authoritarian; but that was also the case in many Christian states. In some parts of the Balkans the conditions of the peasantry underwent a real improvement when they came under Ottoman rule, as the amount of labour they were obliged to perform on the spahi's land was much less than what they had owed to their previous feudal lords. During the fifteenth and sixteenth centuries, indeed, there were many cases of peasants migrating from unconquered areas to settle in Ottoman territory.[11]

Yet, in some areas, there was armed resistance to the Ottomans, long after their administration had been imposed. Religious motives often played a part in this; popular hostility to taxation, and to recruitment for distant campaigns, could also be involved, in areas where the previous rulers had done little of either; and another important factor was the dissatisfaction of local leaders, whether religious or secular, whose social authority greatly exceeded the restricted political power that they were now allowed to exercise. Nowhere in the Balkans was the attempt to throw off the Sultan's rule more strongly and persistently made than in fifteenth-century Albania, where a scion of an important landowning family, Gjergj Kastriota – known as Skanderbeg, from the Turkish 'Iskender Bey', 'Lord Alexander' – led a series of anti-Ottoman campaigns during the 25 years before his death in 1468. Three times the Sultans came in person with their armies to Albania to crush him, and three times they failed to conquer his main stronghold, the fortress of Krujë. Skanderbeg would die of illness, not on the battlefield, and it was only in 1478, a decade after his death, that Krujë was finally taken.[12]

Four cities in Ottoman Albania will feature quite often in this book. Shkodër (Ital.: Scutari), situated at the southern end of the large lake of that name, was just a day's journey to the east of Ulcinj. South of Shkodër, a similar distance from Ulcinj but more easily accessible by sea, was the town of Lezhë (Ital.: Alessio). There had long been close connections, both economic and social, between Ulcinj and these two places. Both were commercial towns, the coastal or near-coastal end-points of a major trade route which brought goods across the mountains of northern Albania from Kosovo – and from much further afield. Shkodër is connected to the Adriatic by the river Bunë (Srb.: Bojana; Ital.: Boiana), and sea-going ships that entered the river mouth could get to within six miles of the town. At that point there was a river-port; long caravans of mules would unload their merchandise there into ships from Venice and elsewhere. Lezhë was very close to the coast, at a point where the river Drin divided into two main branches before entering the sea; it was served both by its own harbour and by a nearby port in a more sheltered bay.* Thirty miles south of Lezhë (as the crow flies) was the coastal city of Durrës (Ital.: Durazzo), and more than 50 miles south of that, also on the shore of the Adriatic, was Vlorë (Ital.: Valona). These two, today, are the main port-cities of central and southern Albania respectively.[13]

---

* Subsequent alluvial deposits have greatly altered the landscape round the mouth of the Drin. The old two-branch arrangement is clearly visible in seventeenth-century maps.

In the 1390s, as Ottoman military and political pressure first began
to disrupt the Albanian lands – which, being divided into a patchwork
of feudal lordships, were ill-equipped to resist – Durrës, Lezhë and
Shkodër were transferred by their local rulers to Venetian control. As
trading cities they had an Italian-speaking merchant class, and Venice
was itself the dominant trading partner; so the arrangement seemed a
natural one, the best way to protect their commercial activities from the
threat of an Ottoman conquest. Throughout the lifetime of Skanderbeg
these three cities remained under Venetian rule, in a greatly extended
version of 'Venetian Albania'. They were thus largely exempt from the
turmoil that was experienced elsewhere in the Albanian lands. But the
Ottoman campaign which finally took the castle of Krujë in 1478 also
saw the capture of Lezhë, and an epic siege by Ottoman forces of the
citadel of Shkodër, begun in that year, achieved its eventual success in
1479. Durrës would remain under Venetian control for another couple
of decades, but fell to the Ottomans in 1501.[14]

The effects of Ottoman conquest on these cities were quite dramatic.
In the case of Shkodër, most of the Christian population fled; so, as
numbers gradually recovered (from c.730 people in 1500 to c.1,410 in
1582, though probably with a higher total before the 1570s), it turned
into a Muslim-majority town. The trade route was eventually restored;
according to Giustinian's report in 1553, the typical goods that passed
through Shkodër were leather, wax, wool, carpets, felt, camlet (a luxury
fabric, made of silk and cashmere) and spices of all kinds, and some of
them came from as far away as Asia Minor and Armenia. A part of this
trade also still came to Lezhë. Here too the Christian population of the
town fled at the time of the Ottoman conquest in 1478, and those who
remained on the so-called 'island' – the triangle of land between the two
river-branches – also left after a failed revolt in 1501–3; by the second
half of the sixteenth century, Lezhë consisted only of the castle and its
garrison, a population of perhaps 400 Muslims, and a small Christian
settlement below it on the river-bank. Despite all these vicissitudes, merchants from Venice and Dubrovnik still came to Lezhë; one report in
1559 said that Persian silk was traded there, though Giustinian's
account emphasized that grain, from the fertile plains of north-central
Albania, was the main commodity.[15]

Durrës also lost its Christian population after the Ottoman conquest
in 1501. A tax register compiled a few years later listed only the 118
members of the garrison in the fortress; travellers who visited the place

in the second decade of the sixteenth century described it as a city in ruins. And yet by the 1550s Durrës was featuring quite often in Venetian reports as a centre of piracy or corsairing. The commander of the Venetian fleet, Cristoforo da Canal, reported in May 1556 that there were eight corsair ships at Durrës, and in the following year a merchant ship from Venice was seized by five corsair vessels just off the coast of Ulcinj and taken straight to Durrës. These were probably Muslim corsairs, and what no doubt attracted them to this port was the presence of an Ottoman-controlled castle under whose artillery they could shelter when pursued by Venetian galleys. (On one occasion, in 1559, a Venetian naval commander called their bluff, bombarding the castle and sinking several of their boats, in order to recover six merchant vessels; this unprecedented action nearly started a war.) But corsairing was, after all, a form of economic activity; the stolen goods were often sold in Durrës, which suggests the functioning of a market economy there, and the town had Ottoman civilian officials, not just military ones. A little later in the century it was also operating, as we shall see, as a centre for the export of grain.[16]

Vlorë too became a corsair base, and was also – on a larger scale – a source of grain for visiting merchants. But although it was often paired in foreigners' accounts with Durrës, and although the two towns had operated quite similarly as commercial centres in the pre-Ottoman period, their recent histories had developed in very different ways. Vlorë was one of the first Albanian towns to be acquired by the Ottomans (as early as 1417), and, since it was peacefully surrendered by its then ruler, there had been much less disruption at the time. The biggest change to the population that occurred as a result of Ottoman rule was the influx of large numbers of Jews, fleeing persecution in Western Europe, who were welcomed there in the late fifteenth and early sixteenth centuries. By 1520 there were at least 2,700 Jews living in Vlorë, settled in quarters that were named after their places of origin, such as 'Ispanyol' (Spain), 'Qatalon' (Catalonia), 'Qalivrus' (Calabria) and 'Otrondo' (Otranto, the port on the heel of Italy). At that time they made up more than a third of the population; the rest were mostly Christians (Greek Orthodox), and the Muslim component was very small. The Jewish population dwindled as the century progressed, but it remained a vital factor in commercial life. Eventually, the growth of corsair activities – again, in complicity with the local Ottoman military – helped to strengthen the Muslim element, but the basis of the economy remained the grain trade (to Venice and Dubrovnik above all), some exports of wine and rock salt, and the local mining of high-quality pitch or bitumen, which was an essential material for building and maintaining ships.[17]

One aspect of these stories needs to be clarified. At first sight, it may seem that an alien element took over at every level – not just where the ruling power was concerned, but with the introduction of Muslim townsmen, and the growing dominance of corsairs. This impression is false. With a few exceptions (soldiers, and some others), the Muslims were not immigrants brought in from distant Islamic territories; they were local Albanians who happened to convert to Islam. Reasons for conversion were various, and in many cases probably had more to do with advancing one's social and economic position than with any religious concerns. But although Muslim Albanians had some legal advantages, they did not form anything like a separate caste, and the strong ties of family loyalty continued to operate across the religious divide. There is more continuity here, and also more cooperation, than at first meets the eye. In the case of Vlorë one can find many examples of Muslims, Christians and Jews working together as traders, ship-owners and ship's captains. (So, for example, in 1567–8 the Jew 'Abraham of Vlorë' and the Muslim 'Captain Sinan' contracted to buy 22½ tons of wheat to sell in Venice; in 1576 a ship owned by 'Mustafa' carried cargo belonging to 'Ioannis Theodorou' from Vlorë to Dubrovnik.) As for the corsairs: small-scale piracy and coastal raiding had long been endemic in these waters, as in many other parts of the Mediterranean. Half-way between Lezhë and Durrës, for instance, was the peninsula of Rodon (Ital.: Redoni), whose men, still Christian in the mid-sixteenth century, went out in their home-made boats to raid other coastal areas. (They were, however, sworn enemies of the corsairs of Durrës.) Examples of piracy in the Rodon–Durrës area can be found as far back as the fourteenth century. And when, as early as 1479, the Sultan issued orders against the corsairs of Vlorë, we may suspect not only that these were men from local families, but also that they were still Greek Orthodox, as the city had no Muslim population at that time.[18]

The stories of Shkodër, Lezhë, Durrës and Vlorë prompt some broader reflections on what had happened to Albania in this period. It is not a coincidence that all four towns were on or close to the coast. Trade was the main factor that had sustained their existence for centuries, and had enabled them to maintain special municipal rights even when controlled by feudal rulers. The coastal and near-coastal network of towns to which they belonged, which was heavily weighted towards the north-western part of Albania, was both a dominant element and, for the same reasons, an untypical one, as there was no urban net-work in the large hinterland of the country on an equivalent scale.* We should not be surprised that many of the Catholic, Italian-using inhabit-ants of Shkodër, Lezhë and Durrës chose to move to other Venetian possessions – including Ulcinj – or indeed to Venice itself. Mass expul-sion was not an Ottoman policy, though it is true that their rules of war did permit the punitive treatment and enslavement of people in towns that had refused to surrender when first invited to do so – a point which increased the desirability of flight for those who could manage it.[19]

But it is also true that in the middle part of the fifteenth century the fierce and recurrent conflict between the Ottomans and Skanderbeg's forces had caused waves of emigration from the hinterland, with many thousands of people passing through the coastal towns and taking boats to southern Italy. (In the Albanian-speaking villages of Apulia, Calabria and Sicily that survive to this day, popular tradition tends to date their arrival to just after the death of Skanderbeg, implying a single tragic exodus; while this dating may be true in some cases, there was clearly a much longer process of emigration, some of it war-induced, with further waves in the 1480s and '90s, but some of it due to long-term economic factors.) Many settled as farmers, and some put to use their skills as stradiot fighters; Albanian light cavalry became a standard component of armed forces in most of Italy, and in other armies too. At the Battle of Avetrana (in Apulia) in 1528, Albanian stradiots recruited by the Kingdom of Naples found themselves fighting against other stradiots, both Albanian and Greek, who had been recruited by Venice. At the siege of Boulogne in 1544 the troops serving under the English King Henry VIII included 'Arbannoises'; a generation later, Albanian soldiers fought in the King of France's army during the French Wars of Religion; the Spanish army in Flanders in the 1570s had Albanian stradiots armed with javelins; and there were Albanian soldiers in Brussels in 1576. One might say that as a result of Skanderbeg's long years of fighting against the Ottomans, two things had spread through much of Europe: his own reputation as a hero of Christendom, and the descendants of his cavalrymen.[20]

The Albanian lands did not suffer equally from destruction and mass

* In the second half of the sixteenth century there were only two major towns in the interior of present-day Albania: Berat and Elbasan. The former had expanded greatly, after an initial decline, under Ottoman rule, and the latter was essentially an Ottoman creation.

emigration during the period of Skanderbeg's revolt. The southern part
of present-day Albania benefited from mostly peaceful conditions under
Ottoman rule from the mid-1430s onwards, and its villages and small
towns enjoyed a healthy rate of growth in population. If it is true – as it
surely is – that the process of being taken over by the Ottomans was
more traumatic for the northern half of Albania than for almost any
other part of the Balkans, the reason is not that the Ottomans applied
any essentially different method there, nor that they imposed a more
repressive system of rule once they were in control. Rather, two different factors seem to have been at work. The people who lived in the main
network of towns, in the north-western corner of the country (including
the three discussed here) had a special connection with a major power,
Venice, to which they could ultimately look for refuge. The flight of
such a commercially active sector of the population could not fail to
have a large and negative effect on the economy. And on the other hand,
in much of the rest of this area the long-drawn-out wars of resistance
wrecked villages and estates – especially when the Ottomans used
scorched-earth tactics – and broke down existing power structures.
Once the opposition to their rule was finally crushed, the Ottomans had
less interest in rebuilding that part of the country precisely because its
economic significance had declined, with reduced agricultural yields,
disrupted trading routes and disinhabited commercial centres. Vlorë, in
the south, fared much better; and while some towns in the north, such
as Drisht (Ital.: Drivasto), collapsed and were reduced to villages, several
places in the south, such as Përmet and Këlcyrë, grew from village-sized
settlements into small towns.[21]

Finally, a few words about the Venetian Empire which had previously
linked Ulcinj with those northern Albanian cities, and to which the
remaining territory of 'Venetian Albania' still belonged. This empire –
differing so greatly in character from that of the Ottomans – had had a
long history. One could say that the 'Big Bang' of the Venetian Empire
came in 1204 when Venice participated in the scandalous Fourth Crusade, which, instead of going straight to the Holy Land, sacked
Constantinople and divided the Byzantine territories among its participants. (The astronomical metaphor is not entirely right, however, as
Venice had controlled some parts of the eastern Adriatic coast before
then.) While feudal lords from other Western European states awarded
themselves unproductive territories in mainland Greece, with pompous
titles attached to them, Venice cannily selected a string of places that
would strengthen its power over trading routes – trade being, then as

later, the life-blood of its economy. Key points in this new sequence of possessions were two fortified ports on the south-western tip of Greece, Koroni (Ital.: Corone) and Methoni (Ital.: Modone), and the island of Euboea (Ital.: Negroponte), on mainland Greece's eastern flank. The smaller islands in the Aegean were also marked down as Venetian; for practical reasons, Venice handed them over to the private enterprise of individual patricians, who became their hereditary rulers. (In the long run this policy did not work out well; some rulers became petty tyrants, and it is said that the islands of Syros and Tinos once went to war over the ownership of a donkey.) In order to fill an important gap in the sequence, and to pre-empt a move by Genoa, its key trading rival, Venice also took Corfu and Durrës at this time, though it did not hold them for long. More importantly, it bought the island of Crete, and successfully fought off some fierce Genoese competition for it. Venice's imperial progress went into reverse in the mid-fourteenth century, when it had to give up (to Hungary) its possessions on the eastern Adriatic coast. But in 1386 it gained Corfu, and the next 34 years would see an extraordinary sequence of additions to Venetian territory: Durrës, Lezhë and Shkodër in the 1390s, the important Dalmatian city of Zadar (Ital.: Zara) in 1409, and several other Dalmatian ports and islands, plus the town of Kotor, by 1420. As we have seen, Ulcinj also fell into Venetian hands during this period – as did Bar and Budva, though local Slav rulers regained them for a while. So, in geographical terms, the mid-fifteenth century was a high point in the story of Venetian power. The loss of Lezhë, Shkodër and Durrës towards the end of the century was a heavy blow; Euboea was conquered by the Ottomans in 1470, and Koroni and Methoni in 1500. But there was one major gain: the island of Cyprus, which became a Venetian possession at first *de facto*, through the political strong-arming of its last queen, and then *de jure* in 1489.[22]

In this whole process of empire-formation, commercial motives were paramount. Venice had no interest in carving out large territories on the Balkan mainland; of course cities came, as we have seen, with their own agricultural domains, for food and income, but these were mostly quite small (with the exception of Zadar's). And although Crete and Cyprus, once acquired, were naturally used as sources of grain, oil, cotton and wine, that was not the prime reason for their acquisition. The first concern was with the practicalities of travel on the long trading voyages to the markets of 'the Levant' – meaning, for the most part, Istanbul, Syria and Egypt. Galleys were used as well as roundships for trading purposes, and they were also the warships which, when necessary, protected the trade. Since galleys, with their banks of rowers, were labour-intensive but had only limited storage, they needed regular replenishment with food and water; frequent halting-places were required. Unpredictable Mediterranean storms were another factor, strengthening that requirement. At its lowest point the side of a galley was little more than a metre above the water, which meant that there was a real danger of being swamped in rough seas; so access to a string of safe havens was a huge advantage. One modern historian has argued that since the navigation methods of this period were already good enough to take mariners across the Mediterranean without hugging the shore, the main reason for acquiring towns on the eastern Adriatic coast must have been to use them as ports for the commodities that came to them overland; this may have been a supplementary incentive in some cases, but the mariners did have strong (non-navigational) reasons for wanting these Venetian bases.[23]

Once they had reached such a haven, they could find it useful for other purposes too, such as recruiting men for their crews. The larger possessions, such as Crete, became important sources of manpower – not just the raw muscle needed to row the galley, but experienced sailors too, and craftsmen with relevant skills. Another advantage of these bases was that they could provide information about conditions ahead. Intelligence of this kind was a vital commodity for captains and traders. Venetian ships returning from the Levant were required to stop at Koroni or Methoni to give whatever information they had about such things as the price of spices and the movements of pirates and corsairs. As Giustinian commented in 1553, one of the reasons why the loss of Ulcinj would be very damaging to Venice was that merchants would become unwilling to risk taking their ships to the Albanian ports; at present, they always stopped in Ulcinj to get the latest information about corsair activities in the area. From his account it is also clear that there was an agreement between Ulcinj and the men of the Rodon peninsula, who, whenever they saw the corsairs of Durrës coming out, notified Ulcinj by means of smoke signals.[24]

Trade needed to be protected and defended, so Venice's trading interests generated security interests too. It developed the doctrine that the entire Adriatic – what it called 'the Gulf' – was a Venetian lake, into which the armed vessels of other powers should not enter without its permission. Dubrovnik, a major trading rival located half-way down the Adriatic coast, was obliged to accept this rule: in 1562, for example, an armed foist (Ital.: 'fusta'; a small galley-style vessel) belonging to it was seized, just outside Dubrovnik, by a Venetian commander who solemnly warned the authorities there that if they armed any ships he would destroy them. And the Ottomans also accepted the rule, most of the time; in their eyes it gave the Venetians a special policing duty, to protect Ottoman traders and their goods in the Adriatic, being part of the web of reciprocal rights and duties on which the Venetian–Ottoman trading relationship was based. Occasionally Vlorë might be visited by Ottoman fleets, for supplies and other practical purposes, but they would not normally proceed any further to the north. Just below Vlorë was the pinch-point of the Adriatic, a strait between Italy and the Balkans only 50 miles wide. And situated just below that strait was Corfu, which, with its fine harbour and well-defended citadel, was one of Venice's most essential strategic possessions. Corfu, Crete and Cyprus acted as bases for squadrons of Venetian galleys that could patrol the seaways, and Venice's Greek territories were also important as sources of military manpower, including stradiot light cavalry. (Most Venetian stradiots were probably Greek; the term comes from the Greek word 'stratiōtēs', soldier, and a series of comic poems written by a Venetian in stradiot dialect is stuffed with Greek vocabulary.)[25]

'Empire' is a historic term, and a very adaptable one, so there is nothing problematic about attaching it to this collection of Venetian dominions. But of course it should not be taken to imply twentieth- or twenty-first-century notions of 'imperialism' – still less of 'colonialism'. The whole Venetian story supplies, in fact, only one significant case of a colonizing programme: that of Crete, where thousands of Venetians settled in the thirteenth century, and members of patrician families acquired large estates on which they lived. In Cyprus there was no mass settlement, but the Venetians supervened on a system where previous rulers had developed a mixed Latin–Greek élite, and some Venetian patricians now joined the mix. Different territories were handled in different ways in this composite and flexible empire. While several Greek islands became petty fiefdoms, Crete, Koroni and Methoni were subjected to something much more like direct rule from Venice. Corfu, Venetian Albania and Dalmatia were governed with a lighter touch, respecting local statutes, and in some minor cases – the Paštrovići, for example – these Venetian subjects were hardly governed at all. It is true that in its Greek territories, and especially in Crete, Venice placed some restrictions on the Orthodox Church, for political as well as religious reasons; the clergy were expected to acknowledge the primacy of the Pope (as agreed, ephemerally, by the Orthodox at the Council of

Florence in 1439), and the priests of Crete were not allowed to have their own bishop on the island. Senior appointments in the Catholic Church, throughout the empire, were also tightly controlled. But more generally there was no programme of Italianization, or of suppressing local languages and customs: schooling, for instance, was a local matter, not directed from Venice at all.[26]

The only general 'Venetianizing' requirements were that Venetian money, weights and measures were to be used; Venetian criminal law applied, at least to major offences (whereas in civil law cases the judges followed or took note of local laws and customs); and the empire was subject to certain general principles of Venetian economic policy. These included treating the production and trading of salt – a vital element in some local economies – as a state monopoly, and (from 1502) a restriction on the size of ships that could be built outside Venice. (There is a record of ship-building at Ulcinj in the 1560s; presumably it involved small vessels of this kind, of less than 80 tons.) The requirement that all Adriatic trade must pass through Venice existed in theory, but was widely ignored in practice; and the traditional rule that only Venetian citizens, as opposed to Venetian subjects, could engage in the Levant trade was abandoned in the early sixteenth century.[27]

This overseas empire was known as the 'Stato da Mar', as opposed to Venice's territories on the Italian mainland, the 'Terraferma'. The distinction was a practical one, used, for example, in the registering of documents in the Venetian chancery, but it had no constitutional meaning. In terms of the Venetian constitution, the one basic difference was between the city of Venice on the one hand and its possessions on the other. Venice was the ruling power, and only members of its own patrician families – a finite group, after the famous 'closure' of the Venetian patriciate in 1297 – could hold high public office; these men were sent to govern Zadar, Ulcinj or Corfu in just the same way that they went to administer Padua, Vicenza or Bergamo. There was another sense in which those Italian cities were theoretically on a par with the towns of Dalmatia and Venetian Albania, as well as Corfu: in each case, the foundational principle of Venetian rule was that the town or community had voluntarily offered itself to Venice, in an act known as 'dedition'. The act had normally included a request that Venice respect the town's existing statutes, a request to which Venice had graciously acceded. Naturally, the workings of those statutes were changed in some ways by the new power-relationship: where the governing council of a town had previously been the legislator, it now turned into a consultative body assisting the Venetian governor. Yet many rights were preserved in this way; judges would be chosen, as before, from the local patriciate, not the Venetian one, and in some cases (including fifteenth-century Ulcinj) the town would jealously insist that it, not the Venetian governor, had direct power over the villages in the town's rural domain. One other consequence of the fact that Venetian rule was theoretically based on a voluntary act of devotion was that these towns could from time to time send 'embassies' to Venice, expressing their loyalty in over-the-top adulatory terms, while requesting special favours or the redress of grievances.[28]

Overall, then, Venice governed its Albanian and Dalmatian possessions with a surprisingly light touch. There would typically be three key Venetian officials in each place: a civil governor (called 'Podestà', 'Conte' or 'Rettore'); a military governor ('Capitano'); and a financial administrator or chamberlain ('Camerlengo'). In smaller towns, such as Ulcinj, the first two positions might be combined. Normally these officials served for a maximum of two years in a particular place, and they did so not as career administrators but as patricians who would perform a variety of public services, on and off, during their adult life. One historian has sharply criticized the system, saying that it was generally corrupt, and that the governors never stayed long enough in one place to gain an adequate understanding of its needs. Such criticism seems to make conflicting demands, since the brevity of tenure was itself an anti-corruption device, aimed at reducing the likelihood that a governor would become enmeshed in webs of local interests. Corruption certainly did occur, as prosecutions of various governors show. Yet at the same time the impressive fact is that there was a powerful system in place to deal with it (involving roving inspectors or 'Syndics', who would hear complaints against the governor *in situ*); corrupt practice was handled more seriously here than in almost any other administration in Western Europe.[29]

Just how strict the rules were can be seen from the set of formal instructions given by the Doge of Venice to Andrea Marcello when he went to be governor of Ulcinj in 1513 (a manuscript which is a lucky archival survival – preserved, apparently, for its pretty calligraphy – as there is otherwise very little documentation for Ulcinj in this period). The injunctions follow a standard pattern. On your arrival, you must not make any speech. You are forbidden to get involved in commerce. You may not give a salary to anyone without our permission. You may not spend a night outside the castle of Ulcinj, on penalty of a five-ducat fine. If you steal money from our dominion, you will have to repay it, and will be permanently stripped of all patrician honours. You must render full accounts within fifteen days of your return to Venice. You may have your coat of arms carved or painted only in one place, simply, at a maximum cost of two ducats. No son, nephew or other relative of yours may sell to any state employee any horse, wool or silk cloth, clothing, or silver, etc.; nor may you, on pain of deprivation of all offices for five years. All fines you impose must be written down and accounted for. And so on. Conditions may well have been more lax in practice than is suggested by this fierce set of injunctions, but it is clear that, in principle at least, the writ of Venetian law ran just as strongly in distant Ulcinj as it did on the Rialto.[30]

Such, then, was the world in which the central characters of this book were born and raised and governed.

2

Three Families

In his report of 1553, having described the nobles, citizens and workers of Ulcinj, Giovanni Battista Giustinian continued:

> Besides those three kinds of inhabitants, there are also the remnants of respected families who have been driven into this city – families from the neighbouring cities, which are now ruled by the Ottomans, such as Shkodër, Lezhë, Durrës and other places. Chief among them is the family of Bruni, Pamaltotti and Brutti, of which only Mr Marc'Antonio is an extremely virtuous gentleman and extremely loyal to the Venetian republic; he is descended from the famous Roman 'Brutus' family. The members of the foreign families occupy themselves mostly with trade, and, doing business in the Ottoman ports, they are rather well off.[1]

Giustinian referred here to three distinct families, and not every detail he gave was correct. 'Pamaltotti' was a slip (perhaps a scribal one) for 'Pamalioti'; 'Brutti' was normally spelt 'Bruti'; 'Marc'Antonio' Bruti was called, in every other surviving document about him, just Antonio; and the story of direct descent from Roman ancestors of the same name is the sort of claim that did not seem surprising to sixteenth-century minds, but can only appear outlandishly far-fetched today. Yet his description of them as a single family appears to have been a sign of knowledge, not ignorance. We do know that the Bruni and Bruti families were closely connected by ties of marriage, so it seems likely that the Pamalioti family was also related to them – though the precise nature of the link, in their case, is not known.

Where the Bruni family is concerned, we have an extraordinarily detailed account of its origins, thanks to a lucky historical fluke. In the mid-seventeenth century a priest with strong antiquarian interests from the city of Vicenza, Francesco Barbarano de' Mironi, compiled a mass of information about the religious history of his home town: churches,

bishops, saints, miracles, and so on. Keen to accumulate as many ecclesiastical dignitaries as possible for the greater honour of Vicenza, he
even included an entry on Giovanni Bruni of Ulcinj, who was Archbishop of Bar from 1551 to 1571, on the basis that his family went back
to a Vicenzan ancestor. And as he wrote about the Brunis, he also mentioned that in 1623 he had met, in the town of Koper (Ital.: Capodistria,
in modern Slovenia), 'a very learned and venerable old man', called
Matteo Bruni – who was one of Giovanni Bruni's nephews. Although he
said that he made no special enquiries of Matteo at that time, it is hard
to believe that the very precise genealogical information in his book did
not derive from that chance encounter with the last surviving member
of the Bruni family.

The account given by Barbarano was as follows. A certain Albino
Bruni lived in Vicenza in the early eleventh century; his great-grandson
Nicolò went to serve at the court of the Byzantine Emperor, and then
established his family in Shkodër, becoming lord of the fortress of
Medun (to the north-east of Lake Shkodër, in modern Montenegro)
'and other castles'; and his descendant Antonio Bruni fled from Shkodër
when it fell to the Ottomans in 1479. Antonio moved to Ulcinj; his son
Giovanni was lord of 'Toscano' – meaning, probably, 'Tuscena', the
Italian name for Tuzi, which is located to the south of Medun, also in
Montenegro. And Giovanni's son Matteo had three sons: Giovanni,
who became Archbishop of Bar and died at the Battle of Lepanto in
1571; Gasparo, who fought at that battle; and Serafino.[2]

The precise dates of birth of these three brothers are not available,
but some estimates can be made. Giovanni, the eldest son, became an
archbishop in 1551, so was probably well over 30 (the minimum age in
canon law) at that time; yet, as we shall see, he was still capable of being
used as a rower at the Battle of Lepanto, so he may have been under 40
when he gained his archbishopric. A date of birth in the early 1510s
thus seems likely. While we know almost nothing of Serafino, we do
know that his son Nicolò, who died with Giovanni at Lepanto, was 29
at the time of his death; if Nicolò was born in 1542, his elder brother
Matteo (the supplier of genealogical information) may have been born
a year or two earlier, in which case the father was probably born before
1515. As for Gasparo, he remained active in his military career into the
mid-1580s, when he might have been in his sixties, so was perhaps born
closer to the year 1520.[3]

One thing is clear enough, though. While the name 'Bruni' had an
Italian origin, Barbarano's notion that all of these people were

Vicenzans was quite absurd: the family had lived in Shkodër for at least a quarter of a millennium, constantly intermarrying, no doubt, with local families. The Brunis were Albanians – albeit untypical ones, if compared with the great mass of the Albanian population, as they belonged to the outward-looking élite of a trading city. Barbarano did add one other useful detail: he specified that the mother of the three brothers was 'Lucia del Nico, an extremely noble lady'. The de Nicho family was indeed one of the most prominent in Ulcinj: when that city came under Venetian rule in 1405, and again when Venetian power was restored there in the early 1420s after an interval of Slav rule, the de Nichos were among the handful of leading families with whom Venice negotiated. Whether the Brunis were themselves accepted into the patriciate of Ulcinj is very uncertain. In most of the Adriatic towns something similar to the Venetian 'closure' had taken place, so that the ranks of the nobility were very hard to join (although the Venetian governor could force the issue). Giustinian's account, quoted above, suggests that this 'foreign' family still retained a degree of outsider status, more than 70 years after its settlement in the town. But the Brunis had certainly enjoyed noble status in the city of Shkodër; as we shall see, Gasparo's career would depend on that fact. So the nobles of Ulcinj – a lesser town – would have treated them with great respect.[4]

In the case of the Bruti family we are also lucky to have an unusual amount of information, thanks mostly to the manuscript history of the Brutis, compiled in the eighteenth century, that was consulted by Domenico Venturini some time before 1903. Here there was no obvious Italian origin – and, we can be fairly sure, no ancient Roman one – to the name of the family; only guesswork is possible. One expert on medieval Albania has pointed out that there was a fashion, in some of these northern towns, for Latin or mixed Albanian-Latin names that seem to have started as humorous nicknames, the humour being affectionate, ironic or even positively abusive: for example, 'Bonushomo' ('good person'), 'Syignis' ('fiery eyes'), or 'Buzolatus' ('thick lips'). In the city of Durrës jokey Italian names were also popular: 'Formica' ('ant'), for instance, or 'Battipiedi' ('foot-stamper'). Since 'brutus' is the Latin for 'stupid' or 'irrational', and 'brutto' is the Italian for 'ugly' or 'nasty', it seems possible that an offensive nickname was somehow taken up with pride.[5]

What we do know, at any rate, is that this family was in Durrës from at least the thirteenth century: a Marco Bruti was born there in 1285. Until the fall of Durrës in 1501 there was an unbroken succession of

Brutis in that city; they intermarried with leading families such as the Dukagjins, who were feudal landowners in northern Albania, and the Spans, who were patricians of Shkodër, as well as Skanderbeg's family, the Kastriotas. Of course the much later account of the family used by Venturini may have exaggerated their status, as family histories often do; we may doubt that Marco became 'lord of Durrës', as it claimed. Some further information can be gleaned from documents in the Venetian archives, which give us details of a Bartolomeo Bruti who served as vice-governor of Durrës in 1429, was vice-governor and vice-captain too in 1432, and was chosen to undertake an important diplomatic mission to the Ottoman Sultan in 1439 because he was 'extremely loyal, and experienced in such matters'. But it is on Venturini's source that we must rely for the story of how the family fared during and after the Ottoman conquest of Durrës in 1501: Bartolomeo's son Antonio, who had married a Kastriota, was either killed or enslaved, with most of his family, but his son Barnaba survived the slaughter and fled to Lezhë, where, living under Ottoman rule, he apparently picked up the pieces of the family's trading business.[6]

It was there that his son Antonio Bruti – one of the significant figures in this book – was born in 1518. And it was Antonio who, after his father's death (the date of which is unknown), came under pressure from the local Ottoman authorities and fled to Ulcinj. There he married Maria Bruni, a sister of Giovanni, Serafino and Gasparo. Nor was this the only linkage between these two families with coincidentally similar surnames. According to Venturini's family tree, a younger sister of Antonio, Lucia Bruti, born in 1524, married a 'Stefano Bruni'. It is quite possible that 'Stefano' was really Serafino; Venturini's source-material was evidently hard to read, and the family tree he drew up contains several garbled names, such as 'Caverio' for 'Carerio' and 'Bensa' for 'Borisi'. Whether it is true that Antonio had been forced to leave 'a huge fortune' behind in Lezhë (as he later claimed), we cannot know; relatively impoverished he may have been, yet he certainly landed on his feet in Ulcinj. In addition to forming those two marital bonds with the Brunis, he also married one other sister to a Dukagjin, and another to a member of the Suina family, who were well established in Ulcinj. No doubt his trading activities in Lezhë had involved frequent contacts with the élite of this neighbouring town. Yet still we may note that the arrival of Antonio and his sisters in Ulcinj took place more than two generations after that of the Brunis. It was the Brunis who had already had time to accumulate a good quantity of 'social capital' in this rather small town; in that sense they were probably, to begin with, the senior partners. But whatever Antonio Bruti lacked at this stage, he quickly made up for by means of sheer dynamism and charisma, as we shall see.[7]

As for the Pamaliotis: here the link with the Brunis and/or Brutis is unknown, but there is some information about the family. 'Pamalioti' itself was not a family surname, but rather the name of a clan or tribe, like the Mrkojevići or the Paštrovići. Like those two clans, the Pamaliotis had a territory containing many villages, and could raise a significant force of fighting men; unlike them, they appear to have had Albanian as their mother tongue.* In the early 1420s, when Venetian power in this region was under serious attack from the ruler of Serbia, the Pamaliotis had been won over – just like the Paštrovići – by Venice, and had played a vital role, since their control of the territory along the Bunë river made it impossible for the Serbs to renew their siege of Shkodër. As a reward for their services, they were given lands in an area which bordered on Ulcinj's domains – immediately prompting complaints from the 'commune' of Ulcinj. In a further round of fighting against a Slav ruler in the 1440s, the Pamaliotis were again recruited and once more rewarded with estates, which in at least one case were confiscated from a landowner of Ulcinj who had rebelled against the Venetians.[8]

When he wrote about the Pamaliotis in 1553, Giustinian had a good idea of the special nature of their story. They were, he said, the only local people, other than the small force of soldiers and stradiots, who received a pension or salary from the Venetian authorities. They were 'feudatori', fief-holders of Venice, 'who came from Shkodër and places round it, and for their merits they have houses and properties which were given to them by Venice; they have also been exempted by Venice from taxation, and they have other special privileges'. But although he must have understood that the Pamaliotis were a tribal group, it seems that when he wrote about the family of Bruni, Pamalioti and Bruti, he was thinking of one prominent Pamalioti family living in Ulcinj. A good

---

* Although a Greek origin has been proposed for their name, it seems more likely to come from 'malok', meaning 'highlander'; but whether the 'Pa-' came from 'Pal' ('Paul'), or whether it came from 'pa' meaning 'without', and therefore meant 'non-highlander', is not clear. The Croatian scholar Milan von Šufflay took 'non-highlander' here to mean 'non-Albanian'. If the Pamaliotis did have a non-Albanian origin, it seems likely to have been Vlach – the Vlachs being a people, formerly widespread in this part of the Balkans, and certainly present in the area around Shkodër during the Middle Ages, who spoke a Latinate language similar to Romanian.

guess can be made as to its identity. Among the first Pamaliotis to be rewarded in 1424 were Niche and Georgio 'Erman' and Duche and Theodorio 'Armenia'; Niche was described as the leader of the Pamaliotis. In 1505 a list of members of the city council of Ulcinj included a 'Georgius Armani vaiyvoda' – 'vojvod' being a widely used term for a military chief. Forty years later, the governor of Ulcinj reported to Venice that Nica Armani, who called himself vojvod of the Pamaliotis, was demanding payment of his salary and threatening to go to Venice to complain about it. Very probably this family, the Armanis, was the one linked to the Brunis and Brutis; and from the fact that George Armani served on the city council, it appears that they had been accepted as one of the leading families of Ulcinj.[9]

So, in terms of status, the Brunis and/or Brutis were not marrying down when they formed a connection with the Armanis; but they were linking themselves to a family with a rather different character and history. It may be that one branch of the Armanis had already settled in the city of Shkodër during the Venetian period (a 'Medono Armano' was living there in 1416 when, in what became a notorious scandal, the Venetian governor put severe pressure on him in order to have sex with his daughter); but the Armanis of Ulcinj owed their special position to the fact that they controlled a large number of loyal followers in the countryside. A fascinating glimpse of the power of the Armanis comes from a sequence of intelligence reports sent by a Spanish agent in Dubrovnik in the summer of 1573. This was two years after the Ottoman conquest of Ulcinj, and it was also several months after Venice had signed a peace settlement with the Sultan – which meant that Spain, not Venice, was now the most likely sponsor for anti-Ottoman activities. According to the Spanish agent, a 'captain of some Albanians who had rebelled against the Ottomans and given their loyalty to the Venetians' said that he had 40 good soldiers in Kotor, and that it would be possible to seize Kotor – from Venice – for the Spanish crown.[10] As the agent later explained:

The man I am dealing with is a noble cleric of Albania, who used to be like a bishop, possessing ten or twelve villages; and his brother was lord of all those Albanians who, in the time of the League [sc. in 1571], were exhorted by the Venetians to rebel against the Ottomans. And when the [Ottoman] fleet came into the Adriatic, this brother of the cleric installed himself with 400 men in Ulcinj, where he and all his men died. He was called Andrea Armani, and the one who is still alive is called Giorgio Armani; their villages were below Shkodër.[11]

According to a further report, in November 1573, this person had 40 or 50 men, and claimed that for a full campaign he could raise between 2,000 and 3,000; the plan to take Kotor seemed feasible, and Armani was certainly worth cultivating, since 'these are important people'. The numbers in their thousands are questionable, like so many of the optimistic estimates made by rebel leaders in Albania during this period. But one significant fact that emerges here is that the Armanis had retained a traditional leadership role not only for members of the Pamaliotis under Venetian rule, but also for ones who lived under the Ottomans (the border having shifted in 1540 westwards from the river Bunë, closer to Ulcinj): those were the ones who had rebelled against Ottoman rule in 1570–1. And this link to a local population, weakened though it must have been by the disaster of 1571, helps to explain why the Armanis did not emigrate far away from the region, in the way that the Brunis and Brutis did. There are some surviving traces of their activities in subsequent years: an 'Arman, the Albanian', based in Budva, was helping to organize the shipment of grain from the Bunë river-port to Dubrovnik in 1580; a 'Giorgi Ermani' (perhaps the 'noble cleric' himself) was financing, from Dubrovnik, similar shipments from the Bunë in 1584; in 1590 a 'Duca Armani', who had spent the previous seven years as parish priest of the river-port, was promoted to Bishop of Shkodër; and 20 years later his successor at that port was a 'Thoma Armani'. But there the trail goes cold. The Pamaliotis cease to be referred to as a significant force and, by the same token, the local importance of the Armanis seems to come to an end.[12]

The account given here of these three families has put some emphasis on questions of status, because they mattered so much to the people involved. Personal trust and family connections may have been the most important things to underpin activities outside one's own local society, but inside it, status and honour – mostly acquired and maintained on a family basis – were of crucial importance. They mattered politically, too. Indeed, the whole story of Venice's relations with its touchy eastern Adriatic towns and communities cannot be understood without constant reference to questions of social status, which interacted powerfully with the Venetian axis itself.

In almost every town and in many of the island communities of the eastern Adriatic, there had already been, before the start of Venetian rule, a social and political division between an élite of noble families, who sat on the governing council, and the rest of the population. Sometimes there was a three-way division, with nobles, citizens, and non-citizens from the countryside; and on at least one island, Korčula, the country people had their own governing councils, which they jealously preserved against encroachment by the city nobles. But almost everywhere the basic difference was between the nobles or patricians, who had power under the local constitution, and the others who did not. In several ways, Venetian rule weakened the nobles' position. It curtailed some of their economic freedoms (as we have seen, limiting the salt trade and ship-building, and at first requiring them to do their trading via Venice). It also undermined whatever economic privileges they had had, as it imposed general taxes regardless of status, and – most importantly – gave everyone, not just the nobles, some of the essential privileges of a Venetian citizen in the conduct of trade. Also, while the local patricians might keep up some role in the judicial system, they were no longer its masters: the Venetian governor was head of the judiciary, and beyond him was the possibility of appeal to Venice itself. So there were many reasons why the non-nobles might welcome Venetian power, and the nobles might resent it. A further reason for resentment was that, in the case of the Dalmatian towns, the previous ruler was Hungary; they had therefore been subjects of a monarchy, which functioned, in a way that Venice could not do, as a fount of noble honour. Pro-monarchist loyalism was a problem which the Venetians had had to deal with when they consolidated their rule in the early fifteenth century, and it was still present in the late sixteenth. And yet, on the other hand, the nobles had good reason to be grateful for Venetian rule. Not only did it provide a security guarantee, of a kind that became essential when, in the fifteenth century, Ottoman armies completed their conquest of most of the Adriatic hinterland. It also locked in the nobles' own local constitutional privileges, which were not negligible: Venice's promise to respect existing statutes meant that the rules and traditions of the city councils, where the noble families held power, would not be altered. From the patricians' point of view that became an ever more valuable guarantee, because their economic power-base was being increasingly eroded. Some non-noble traders and entrepreneurs were becoming rich, while at the same time the patricians' agricultural incomes were falling. A report from Zadar in 1528 said that because most of the nobles there did no work and lived only on the income from their estates, they were becoming poorer all the time, as much of the land was not cultivated, out of fear of the nearby Ottomans.[13]

The overall result was, not surprisingly, frequent social tension and occasional violent conflict. Some of the worst episodes occurred in the early sixteenth century. In late 1510 there were outbreaks of violence between nobility and 'popolari' on the island of Hvar (Ital.: Lesina), and the violence spread to several of the coastal cities, including Zadar, Šibenik and Split, where the commoners demanded that they be given places on the city councils. Before long Kotor was also riven by fighting. Generally, these conflicts were exacerbated both by the activities of pro-Hungarian nobles, who wanted to throw off Venetian rule, and by the fact that Venice was preoccupied with a war on the Italian mainland. By the winter of 1511–12 the situation had become so bad that Venice sent a military commander with two galleys (partly funded by fugitive pro-Venetian nobles) to restore order; he did so not only on Hvar but also in some of the coastal towns, before returning to Venice, where he had to face serious charges over the excessive severity of his actions.[14]

One of the places where the tensions were strongest was Bar, where the commoners had already taken up arms in 1507 to demand representation on the city council. The dispute rumbled on until, in 1512, a compromise solution was found: there would be two councils, one for nobles and one for commoners, meeting on successive days. But in the final months of that year violence flared up again in the dispute over the Benedictine abbey of Ratac; fatefully, one of the two priests competing for control of the abbey was a noble and the other was not.* According to a vivid and quite desperate letter to Venice from the governor of Bar, the non-noble activists threatened to cut the nobles to pieces, and fighting quickly ensued 'with firearms, bows and arrows, and various weapons'; altogether, 62 people were killed. The Venetian authorities feared that Bar might become so weakened that it could easily be taken by the Ottomans; so they sent the governor of Kotor to pacify the situation. Almost immediately after his arrival, on 20 December, the non-noble faction attacked the nobles again, wounding several and killing two; the governor of Kotor was reduced to taking refuge, with his Bar counterpart, in the castle. Eventually he was able to broker an agreement under which the new, non-noble council would be accepted by the patricians, and would make half of all appointments to civic offices. But the underlying hostility did not go away. Giustinian's comment in 1553 about how the people of Bar would kill one another like rabid dogs has already been quoted; he described the hatred between commoners and nobles as 'ancient and inextinguishable'. One or two years later, according to a subsequent account, the noble priests even

* See above, p. 6.

came to blows with the non-noble ones at the Good Friday service, in a dispute about who had the right to raise the ciborium (the vessel containing the eucharist) in front of the congregation. Similar tensions were observed by Giustinian in Kotor, where two councils, noble and non-noble, had also been introduced; the patricians still retained power over the key appointments, and the hatred was unabated.[15]

The only places where, according to Giustinian, these socio-political disputes were largely absent were Budva and Ulcinj. Budva was too small and too poor to support a noble élite; the communal government had been formalized only 60 years earlier, and it did not even distinguish between citizens and non-citizens. And although Ulcinj did make the classic three-way distinction between nobles, citizens and non-citizen 'workers' (as we have seen), the nobles were by now so few that they did share most of the city's offices with the citizens, reserving only the judiciary for themselves. Giustinian was expressing genuine relief when he made the comment, already quoted, that 'there are no extreme persecutions or mutual hatreds' among the people of Ulcinj; but this relatively good state of affairs may have been due much more to the weakness of the patrician families than to their benevolence. In fact, since the city council had been thoroughly penetrated by non-nobles, it is difficult to work out who the noble families of Ulcinj actually were. One listing, drawn up by the Venetian governor in 1505, gives just eleven people, two of whom belonged to the same family; only one of the ten surnames, 'Dabre', had any known connection with the Bruni or Bruti families. In 1544 the governor reported to Venice that there were only two noble families left, with just five (adult male) members, and that he was using his powers to add several families to the ranks of the nobility; frustratingly, however, he did not name the new additions. They did not include the Brutis, for it was only in 1562 that the Doge of Venice issued a special decree making Antonio Bruti a nobleman of Ulcinj. Whether, by that stage, the nobility also included Brunis or Armanis, we do not know. But we can at least say that the relative flexibility of the system in Ulcinj made that a less vital question than it would have been elsewhere.[16]

One other aspect of social conditions in Ulcinj deserves some comment. It has already been pointed out that the language of public life, and of much merchant activity, was Italian. This was a practical fact, but it may also have had a symbolic value for the old urban families, acting as a kind of 'marker' for the deep-rooted difference which they felt to exist between them and the rural population. In almost all

of the historic towns on the eastern Adriatic coast, including the northern Albanian ones, a Latinate language had been spoken until the
eleventh or twelfth century; in Dalmatia the city-dwellers were called
'Latini' in the Middle Ages, as opposed to the rural 'Sclavi' (Slavs). No
doubt they also knew the language of the surrounding population; but
it took time for the flow of incomers from the countryside – greatly
accelerated by the Black Death in 1348 – to make the local languages,
Slav and Albanian, the ones generally spoken within the city walls. By
the fifteenth century, even the proud citizens of Dubrovnik had lost their
Latinate 'Old Ragusan' language. Throughout this period there were
increasing commercial and political contacts with Italy, so the use of
Italian was a growing phenomenon. While there was certainly no linguistic continuity between the use of the old Latinate language and the
adoption of Italian, there may still have been some psychological linkage: the special nature of city culture, in contrast with that of the
surrounding peasantry, was thereby preserved. By the sixteenth century,
the noble élite and the non-noble merchants in a town such as Ulcinj
were fully bilingual. Their education, indeed, would have involved
learning to write in Italian, and to some extent in Latin too, whereas
there seems to have been very little practice of writing in Albanian.
Some uncertainty applies, though, to the women in this society, whose
chances of receiving any kind of education were much more limited. In
Dalmatian cities such as Split and Dubrovnik, travellers commented on
the fact that while the men spoke Italian as well as Slav, the women had
only the Slav language. Was the equivalent true of the Albanian towns-
women of Ulcinj? Perhaps it was, for some of them. But it is a striking
fact that when the surviving members of the Bruti family moved, after
the Ottoman conquest of Ulcinj, to an Italian-speaking town much
closer to Venice, several of the young women were quickly married off
to local men who were Italian-speakers and certainly not speakers of
Albanian. So it seems very likely that these women already had at least
a good working knowledge of Italian. This may reflect the relatively
high social standing of the Brutis in Ulcinj – rather in the way that aristocratic Russian women in the novels of Tolstoy might converse in
French, as the wives of more humble merchants might not.[17]

   The most famous member of the Bruti family, Bartolomeo, has been
described by almost all of the historians who have written about him as
an 'Italianized Albanian'. The phrase is not directly false, but it may
be misleading, or even prejudicial, suggesting that his linguistic or cultural Italian-ness was a mere surface layer – and therefore, perhaps, a

deceptive one. Members of the Dubrovnik élite spoke Italian, recorded
their government business in Italian, and even wrote works of literature
in Italian; we do not refer to them suspiciously as 'Italianized Croats'.
Bartolomeo Bruti was certainly an Albanian, but he had an Italian cultural identity too, which was much more than skin-deep. The Brunis
and the Brutis were genuine linguistic and cultural amphibians. And
that, as we shall see, was essential to their success in the wider Mediterranean world.[18]

3

Antonio Bruti in the
Service of Venice

In 1560 Antonio Bruti sent a long petition from his home in Ulcinj to the government of Venice, listing the various loyal services he had performed. It is missing from the relevant file of petitions in the Venetian archives, but a copy was included in the manuscript family history seen by Domenico Venturini, who noted many of its details. This is an unusually rich source – and, despite the obvious purpose of self-glorification, probably a reliable one, as it fits with all the other evidence we have of Antonio's activities.[1]

It begins with the Ottoman–Venetian war which broke out in 1537 and lasted until 1540. The precise origins of the conflict are rather obscure. Sultan Süleyman the Magnificent was apparently spoiling for a fight with Venice, and may even have welcomed an incident in early 1537 when a hot-headed Venetian naval commander, Alessandro Contarini, attacked three Ottoman ships and sank two of them, thereby giving Süleyman a pretext for war. Yet the large army and fleet which the Sultan took to Vlorë in 1537 were aimed not at Venice but at southern Italy, which belonged to the Ottomans' primary enemy, the Habsburgs. A joint Franco-Ottoman pincer-campaign had been planned, with French armies attacking the Habsburgs' northern Italian territories. Although the Ottomans did mount a large raid on Apulia, seizing thousands of captives, the French king failed to keep his part of the bargain, so the strategy had to be changed. With ships, soldiers and artillery all to hand, Süleyman decided to take the opportunity to attack Corfu. His siege of the citadel there failed; but Venice was now at war with the Ottomans. (Other Venetian territories were also attacked: Bar and Ulcinj were both besieged for a while by local Ottoman forces.) In 1538 the Venetians joined in a 'Holy League' with the Habsburgs, brokered and supported by the Papacy. The best-known battle of the war was the naval engagement of Preveza, off the north-western coast of Greece, in

September 1538. In strict military terms this was not very conclusive: the Christian fleet, under the famous Genoese commander Andrea Doria, suffered some losses but remained a serious fighting force. It was Doria's decision to retreat, and his refusal to re-engage with the enemy, that turned it into a decisive victory for the Ottomans – one that is officially celebrated by the Turkish navy to this day, even though a large part of the Ottoman fleet was destroyed by a storm off the Albanian coast immediately afterwards. Otherwise the fighting during this war was generally inconclusive; Spanish forces did seize the town and fortress of Herceg Novi, guarding the Gulf of Kotor, but a massive siege by Hayreddin Barbarossa then took it back. By the time Venice sued for peace in 1540 it had lost many of its smaller Greek islands, as well as two of its footholds on the Greek mainland, Nafplio (Ital.: Napoli di Romania) and Monemvasia (Ital.: Malvasia); and it was during this war that the Ottomans made further encroachments on the territories of towns in Dalmatia and Venetian Albania, including Bar and Ulcinj, weakening their local economies.[2]

From Antonio's petition it seems that he made the move from Lezhë to Ulcinj at or soon after the beginning of this war (when he was nineteen years old, and had presumably taken over from his late father as head of the family). Perhaps the Ottoman authorities in Lezhë drove him out because they discovered that he was working for the Venetians. Soon after his arrival in Ulcinj he was put in charge of a brigantine – a swift, low-lying, galley-style vessel, smaller than a foist – by the Venetian commander Alessandro Contarini, and sent on missions to reconnoitre the coastal waters of Albania which, from his family's trading activities, he already knew so well. Soon he was sending information about the movement of Ottoman forces to the military headquarters in Kotor; and at the same time, it seems, he was buying much-needed grain in Albania (perhaps from places such as the Rodon peninsula, where the inhabitants paid little attention to their Ottoman masters) and bringing it to Kotor too. Other services listed in his petition included assistance to the people of Bar, who were under attack from the Mrkojevići, and fighting under a Venetian commander to defend the territory of Ulcinj from an Ottoman offensive.[3]

After the conclusion of peace in 1540, Antonio Bruti was not needed as a fighter – at least, not until 30 years later. But two of the types of service performed by him in this earliest period of his work for Venice would remain important: gathering intelligence, and obtaining grain. And, as he gained experience, he would also be valued as a negotiator with Ottoman officials and others in the Albanian lands. Each of these three categories of service was significant in its own way.

It would be difficult to exaggerate the importance that attached to information and intelligence in this eastern Mediterranean world. The general concern of the Venetians to find out about corsair or pirate activities, and to gather commercial information, has already been mentioned briefly; the desirability of military intelligence during a war is obvious enough; but the need for news extended much further than that. This was a news-hungry world in which information was power, and where, precisely because much of the news was inaccurate or fragmentary, with irregular time-lapses in its transmission, it was vital to accumulate as many overlapping reports as possible in order to sift out the truth, or something close to it. Every naval commander, and indeed every corsair or pirate, would send a small boat ahead to 'pigliar lingua' – literally, to take tongue. This involved landing on the coast, or on an island, and questioning (or sometimes abducting, in order to question) local fishermen and sailors about conditions, the movement of other ships, and so on. Indirect evidence could often be crucial: when the Venetians or Spaniards were analysing Ottoman military intentions, they paid much attention, for example, to news about the increased production in places such as Vlorë of 'biscotto' (biscuit), the durable and relatively light ship's tack, made of twice-baked bread, that was the essential human fuel for a naval campaign. And Ottoman political news of all kinds, both local and imperial, was also highly valued. Elaborate measures were taken to ensure a flow of information from Istanbul – not only from merchants and diplomatic sources, but also, as we shall see, from espionage networks in that city.[4]

At some time in the period 1555–62, Antonio Bruti was asked by the Venetian naval commander, Cristoforo da Canal, to send 'the fastest possible reports' to Dalmatia about the movement of the Ottoman fleet; the fear was that instead of passing westwards to engage with Spanish forces it would enter the Adriatic and attack Venetian territory. Antonio was even given 'a new kind of cipher' in which to send his messages. While the use of ciphers was common in high-level diplomatic correspondence, it was an unusual requirement for this sort of task, indicating both the sensitivity of the information and the fact that Antonio was meant to transmit information from a fixed position, not to sail back with it himself. The precise date is not given in Venturini's account, but a document in the Venetian archives may supply some of the background to this episode. In mid-April 1558 the Venetian government

wrote to da Canal, explaining that it had previously written (in early
March) to say that it feared the intentions of the Ottoman fleet, and that
it was now sending reinforcements to Cyprus, Crete and Corfu. It urged
him to do everything possible 'to get information about the movements
of that fleet', and that it had arranged, via the governor of Corfu, for
Antonio Bruti to be placed in the Ottoman port of Vlorë, so that the
naval commanders 'could be informed of every development'.[5]

Antonio performed another valuable service some time after this,
when he was asked to organize on a regular basis the transmission of
letters, both official and private, from Corfu to Venice and vice-versa.
The problem here was apparently that they were being intercepted
by ships (presumably pirate or corsair ones) off the Albanian coast;
Antonio found a safe way of getting them from Corfu to Ulcinj, after
which they were sent on Venetian naval vessels to Kotor. And one other
piece of evidence, from 1567, sheds light on a different aspect of his
work in relation to getting and sending information. In April of that
year the Venetian government gave him the special privilege of being
able to export from the territory of Ulcinj 12 'botte' (7½ metric tons) of
wine and 8 botte (5 tons) of oil, without taxes or other restrictions. The
purpose of this, it explained, was to give him 'an easier opportunity
to have friendly dealings with the officials of the Sultan in this border
region, and to make new contacts, which he could make use of in
the service of our state'. This was a marvellously practical way (and,
we may suppose, a financially advantageous one for Antonio – had he
suggested it himself, perhaps?) of combining commercial activity with
intelligence-gathering and cultivating 'agents of influence'.[6]

In their dealings with Ottoman officials and others in the Albanian
lands, the Venetian authorities made much use of Antonio Bruti as a
negotiator, local diplomat and all-purpose 'fixer'. Negotiating for the
release of merchant vessels (and merchants) captured by the corsairs of
Durrës or Vlorë was a typical task. On one occasion, during a dispute
between Ulcinj and Lezhë, corsairs working for the latter town seized,
emptied and then sold a cargo vessel belonging to an eminent Venetian
patrician, Alvise Vendramin; Antonio somehow persuaded them to
hand over the cost of the ship. Soon afterwards he was taken by Cristoforo da Canal to Durrës, where he obtained a declaration by one corsair
captain, sworn in front of the *kadi* (judge), that he would not attack
Venetian citizens; he also got back another Venetian cargo ship, and
secured the release of three Venetians who were held captive in Vlorë.
An account of this sort of work is given in a narrative by another

Venetian naval commander, Filippo Bragadin. In the last week of March 1563, he wrote, 'having gone to Ulcinj, I took the cavaliere Bruti on board my galley, as he is a person with much experience of the ports of Albania, and of dealing with the Ottomans, and went to Durrës and Vlorë to recover the two cargo ships belonging to Morosini, laden with oil, which were seized by foists off Ostuni [a town in Apulia].' In Durrës they found that the oil had already been sold 'to various local people', and that the ships had been drawn up on land and half taken apart; so they proceeded to Vlorë to speak to Hüseyin, the port *emin* and *nazır* (both terms mean superintendent) there. Conveniently for the corsairs, Hüseyin produced sworn testimonies saying that the ships had belonged to merchants from Ferrara, and/or Apulia (non-Venetian territories), which, if true, would mean that there was no obligation to restore them or offer a recompense. As Bragadin wrote: 'since he was thick as thieves (as the saying goes) with the corsairs, I made a strong complaint about his injustice, and left him.' Although this mission was a failure, Antonio Bruti was sent again to Vlorë just a few months later, in June, to work for the recovery of more stolen cargoes and the release of captive Venetian subjects.[7]

As Bragadin's experience shows, there was no guarantee that a local Ottoman office-holder would be persuaded merely by official protests or by appeals to the rules – which, given the reciprocal agreements between Venice and the Ottoman Empire, did indeed dictate that each should respect and protect the other's merchant shipping. Other, less formal methods were needed. One was to give presents. Any request to an official for a special favour would normally be accompanied by a gift; this could consist of gold or silver coins, but high-prestige objects such as lengths of expensive fabric, pieces of fine glass, silver cups, high-quality wax candles or sugar-loaves (or an assortment of the above) would always be acceptable. Western travellers in the Ottoman Empire often commented resentfully on the hunger of officialdom for such sweeteners: 'whoever wishes to dwell amongst the Ottomans', one wrote, 'as soon as he enters into their territories, must immediately open his purse, and not shut it till he leaves them again . . . for the Ottomans are shameless and immoderate in taking money and presents.' Yet the practice of gift-giving to officials was commonplace in West European societies too: in France during this period, an officer of the Crown might expect to receive from the towns under his jurisdiction 'wines of the region, olives, sweets, spices, candied fruits, cheeses, grains, game, fish, heavy wax torches, silver and golden cups, golden chains', and suchlike.

Present-giving was not just an *ad hoc* affair to lubricate special requests; across the Venetian–Ottoman border there was a regular flow, which was important for keeping up amicable relations between the two sides. As early as 1506 we find a report by the governor of Ulcinj on the money spent 'to maintain good neighbourly relations with the *sancak-beyi*s [district governors] and *voyvoda*s [local officials – normally tax-collectors, though the term was also used for the managers of large Ottoman estates]', and Giustinian noted in 1553 that the nearby Otto-man *voyvoda*s came often to the city 'on the pretext of conducting public business' in order to be showered with gifts, the total cost of which came to 600 ducats a year. Each time a new *sancakbeyi* was installed in Shkodër, he wrote, the city would send him a present of 80 scudi (66.6 ducats). Giustinian disapproved of this practice, viewing it as a 'tacit tribute'. Others complained both about the high cost (one report calculated in the early 1550s that Venetian officials in Dalmatia had given 30,000 ducats in presents since the end of the war in 1540 – a rate of more than 2,300 per year) and about the opening this gave for other corrupt practices: some governors were giving their own goods and then charging inflated prices for them on their expenses, while others were thereby greasing the palms of their counterparts on the other side of the border in order to engage in the lucrative export of fine horses from Ottoman territory.[8]

While the evidence from Venetian sources is of an efflux of money and goods in one direction only, there is reason to think that some pre-sents did travel the other way – if only to elicit even more largesse. In Dubrovnik (a state which, from the Ottoman point of view, was actu-ally part of the Ottoman Empire, but which differed so much from the neighbouring territories under direct Ottoman rule that it also needed the constant upkeep of good relations with local officials), the registers of the city council record a regular flow of gifts from the Ottoman side. In August 1567 the authorities of Dubrovnik received livestock and cheese from the *voyvoda* of Trebinje; in December, two carpets and two sets of horse's harnesses from the two *emin*s of Vlorë; in March 1568, a carpet from Kara Hoca, the much feared corsair captain of Vlorë; in February 1569, twelve cheeses and 122 pounds of butter from the *voy-voda* of Trebinje, and a carpet and a horse's harness from the new *emin* of Herceg Novi; and so on. In each case, the gift prompted a monetary present in return. The sharp-eyed merchants of Dubrovnik assessed very precisely the value of the gift they had received; they usually responded with a larger sum, but the increment varied greatly. We can assume that it depended on their valuation of each Ottoman official's good will, and that this was no less carefully calculated.[9]

Thus, present-giving was an 'informal' matter when viewed from a strictly legal standpoint, but could be a seriously formalized one in practice. Other ways of lubricating relations between the two sides of the Venetian–Ottoman border were more genuinely informal, depending as they did on personal bonds, whether of friendship or of relatedness by blood and marriage. The imposition of that border had not eliminated many kinds of economic and social contact, and the fact that the frontier had moved over time made it even less likely to be reflected in any clear division between the two societies. Many families straddled the border; even if one branch had converted to Islam, that in no way eliminated the familial bonds of mutual duty and respect. The result was a far-reaching web of Christian–Ottoman personal connections. So, for example, the *beylerbeyi* (provincial governor) of Buda wrote to the Venetian authorities in 1550 asking them to give a prebend to his cousin in Dalmatia, a Catholic priest called Antonio of Šibenik. In 1591, when a Venetian envoy had to travel overland from Lezhë to Istanbul, he considered employing a Christian caravan-leader called Žarko who was based in Dubrovnik and happened, rather usefully, to be the nephew of the Ottoman *aǧa* (military commander) of Herceg Novi. Six years later, when an Italian count was being held as a prisoner of war in the Bosnian town of Banja Luka, his family sought the help of a senior priest in Split, who was described as the vicar of the Archbishop there; the priest wrote that he was making enquiries both in Banja Luka and among his own Muslim relations in Sarajevo. He added as a postscript: 'Today one of my relatives came here, a Muslim who is a man of authority, and, on a personal level, a benevolent man'; this relative too had promised to take up the search. Such examples, involving family ties, could easily be multiplied, and there must also have been many cases of friendship based on trade relations and other long-standing links.[10]

In this world of cross-border connections, where personal trust could easily trump official enmities, an intermediary such as Antonio Bruti could be particularly useful to the Venetians. In his petition he reminded them both of his many important 'aderenze' (connections or contacts) in Ottoman Albanian territory, and of his high-placed friends, most of them converts to Islam, in Istanbul. There may have been an element of boasting here, but the basic claim he made was no fantasy; as we shall see, one of his sons would later make use of a very high-level family connection of this kind. So the fact that Venice employed Antonio on some important local diplomatic missions is probably a reflection not only of his personal qualities but also of his valuable local relationships and contacts. In 1568, for example, the Venetian authorities became concerned at a local *sancakbeyi*'s increasingly hostile attitude. Hasan Bey, the governor of the northern Albanian and Montenegrin *sancak* (district) of Dukagjin, had begun demanding that some of the people on the Venetian side of the border should acknowledge Ottoman sovereignty and pay tribute to him; so Antonio was asked to go and persuade him to respect the existing frontier, which had been agreed between Venice and the Sultan after the 1537–40 war. This was potentially a dangerous task, as local Ottoman governors could act with capricious malevolence, and a fair degree of impunity, when their wishes were crossed. Just six years earlier, when another *bey* (lord) had put similar pressure on the borders of the territory of Ulcinj, that city had sent 'an honourable and experienced man' to negotiate with him as its ambassador; the *bey* had flown into a rage with the man, having him and his companion strangled and buried, as one report put it, 'in a certain disgraceful place' – meaning, probably, a dung-heap.[11]

The instructions given to Antonio by the Doge of Venice were curiously circumspect. He was to approach the *sancakbeyi* of Dukagjin, at first, only on the subject of a specific and relatively minor issue, a dispute concerning the village of Gerami or Gerano. This was a village on the coast, belonging to the territory of Ulcinj and lying to the south-east of the city: Giustinian described it, in untypically lyrical terms, as a place that enjoyed cool and pure springs, pleasant pastures, and dense woods abounding in game. It seems that Antonio had developed a special connection with it; in his petition he emphasized that he had helped to save 'the territory of Ulcinj with the village of Gerano' during the 1537–40 war, and in 1553 he obtained a long-term lease on some potentially productive land close to the village, belonging to the nearby abbey of St Nicholas on the bank of the Bunë river. Probably he was trying to set up a family estate there, and had become a sort of patron or protector of the village. So Antonio's first task was merely to remind the *sancakbeyi* of a promise which he had apparently made to the Venetian representative in Istanbul concerning this village, and which he had so far failed to fulfil. Only then, after gaining the *bey*'s confidence, should he broach the much larger subject of his attempt to usurp Venetian territory, suggesting to him that if he agreed to desist, he (Antonio) would be able to persuade Venice to give the *bey* a large present as an expression of its gratitude. Antonio was to take with him a copy of the existing border agreement, which clearly stated which places lay on which side of the frontier; at a certain point, he would offer to send a man to the chancery of Kotor for this document, and would then wait for the man to return, whereupon he would give the *bey* the paperwork, pretending to have only just received it. (The reason for this piece of pantomime was evidently to conceal the fact that Antonio had been sent by the Venetians with the frontier business as his main task, at the same time avoiding the risk that his man might be robbed of the papers en route.) And, all the while, Antonio was authorized to distribute liberal gifts to key figures in the *bey*'s entourage, in order to ensure a favourable attitude to his requests. In his petition he proudly recorded not only his success in these negotiations, about both the village and the frontier, but also the fact that he obtained the freedom of an Italian, Marco Baroci, who was one of the *bey*'s slaves. What this whole episode demonstrates is not just Antonio's skill as an operator, but, even more significantly, the nature of his personal standing. Remarkably, the Venetian authorities accepted that if he went to negotiate in his own right, using his own authority and no doubt his own contacts, he could achieve much more than if he went arrayed with all the official dignity of a Venetian representative.[12]

The other major area of Antonio Bruti's service to Venice was his work in getting supplies of grain. At first sight, this might seem not so much a special service as a general and ordinary aspect of his business as a merchant. Giustinian, as we have seen, noted that the Brutis made a comfortable living from their trading, but did not specify the merchandise. Another report, perhaps also from 1553, said that the refugees from Durrës and Lezhë (and other cities) in Ulcinj traded in two things, horses and grain; the former were brought in overland, but the latter came from the ports of the Albanian coast. (Giustinian recorded that horses were brought to the city by 'Turks', but not openly, as their export was forbidden by the Ottomans.) Another commodity was mentioned in passing in Antonio's petition, where he wrote that one of his nephews once returned from Venice with 1,500 ducats, having sold wool there on Antonio's behalf. Wool from the Balkan interior was also to be purchased in the ports of Albania, especially in Lezhë: for instance, in 1577 a cargo of wool from Lezhë was shipped to Dubrovnik and then on to Ancona, and in 1594 a Muslim merchant from Skopje called Rizvan was writing letters to a Florentine trader in Dubrovnik about the bales of wool which he had brought to Lezhë for onward shipment. No doubt Antonio and his family traded, whenever there was a profit to be made, in the various other goods that were available in the Albanian ports: hides, leather, wax, oil, wine and – if they could obtain it, despite the Ottoman ban on the export of military matériel – pitch. But grain was special.[13]

The purchase and sale of cereals were supervised and regulated like those of no other commodity. Governments had to take the grain supply very seriously indeed, as human life depended on it. Two studies of Genoa in the early seventeenth century have shown that for the members of the affluent family of Spinola, cereals provided 52 per cent of the calorific value of all the food they ate, while for the paupers in a city hospital the figure was 81 per cent. For rowers and crew in the Spanish fleet in 1560, it was over 70 per cent. The standard measure of grain in the Venetian world was a 'staro' (or 'staio'), which contained 62 kg; it was estimated that each person would consume 4 stari per year (just under 250 kg) – which may seem excessive, but after allowing for the milling process, and for wastage, it represents something like one large loaf per day. In the European history of this period, one of the fundamental drivers of economic change was the steady growth of the population, which in some areas may have doubled during the course of the sixteenth century; towns which had previously fed themselves with grain from the surrounding countryside found that they needed to develop new sources of supply far away. As Fernand Braudel pointed out long ago, that is one major reason why nearly all the cities that grew spectacularly in this period were either on the coast or connected to it by water, as the overland long-distance transportation of a bulk commodity such as grain was prohibitively expensive. When the population of Venice reached 158,000 in 1552, the city needed roughly 108 tons of cereals per day; less than half of this could be supplied by the Venetian Terraferma, so it is likely that at least 60 tons per day had to be shipped in from elsewhere. A list of the large merchant ships (with a minimum cargo of 240 tons) that came to Venice in the period 1558–60 shows that just under a quarter of their entire tonnage consisted of grain. Big cities were not the only places that needed imports, of course. Giustinian reported that the Venetian possessions in Dalmatia, with a population of 100,000, needed 450,000 stari per year (a figure which may include animal feed as well as grain for human consumption), and that they were able to grow only 100,000 stari – partly because of the Ottoman inroads into their territory, but also because land had been given over to the production of wine, which was more profitable. Crete, once a significant producer of grain, similarly went over to wine production during the sixteenth century, by the end of which it was importing a quarter to a third of all the grain it consumed. But cities were where the problem was felt most acutely, and the larger (and more fast-growing) the city, the greater the problem: Istanbul, by far the biggest city in the sixteenth-century Mediterranean world, with a population of roughly 500,000 people in the middle of the century, needed something like 340 tons of grain every day.[14]

In almost every city, accordingly, elaborate measures were taken to maintain and control the supply of cereals. In Istanbul grain storage was organized by the state, and all food supplies were under the authority of the Grand Vizier. Genoa had an 'Ufficio dell'Abbondanza' which arranged the import and storage of grain, and regulated prices. (The rather upbeat name, 'Office of Plenty', was a medieval inheritance; several other Italian cities used the same phrase.) In Dubrovnik a huge municipal grain store was built in the period 1541–57, as part of a similarly regulated system; known as 'Rupe' ('The Pits'), it now houses the city's history museum. In 1557 a so-called 'Prefecture of the Annona' (using a Latin word for the price, and/or supply, of grain) was set up in Rome, to organize imports, fix prices, stockpile the cereals and distribute them to bakers. And in Venice a 'Magistrato alle biave' or 'Zonta delle biave' (Grain Commission) performed a similar range of tasks, publishing at regular intervals a tariff of the prices it would pay to merchants who brought grain to the city, and also commissioning particular traders to buy large quantities on its own account. Such was the need for this type of import that the city authorities were quite indiscriminate in welcoming any merchants, Venetian or foreign, who brought it; most of those who did were non-noble general traders, and many were foreign subjects – including Ottoman ones. In April 1559, for example, the Venetian government authorized a payment 'to those Muslim merchants who have sold their grain to Venice'; in July 1562 it accepted an offer by the ship-owner 'Cagi (or 'Cogia') ferruch Turco' (Hacı Faruk, or Hoca Faruk, the Muslim) to go to Durrës and Vlorë for grain. But, not surprisingly, Venice's own maritime subjects featured prominently – Greeks from Corfu being especially active in this trade.[15]

That Dubrovnik built a new grain store in 1541–57, and Rome put its provisioning system on a new basis in 1557, are not coincidental facts. For the middle of the century was the period in which supply problems in the Mediterranean grain market really began to pinch. And when such difficulties arose, at least for any large city (a category that did not include Dubrovnik, with its population of roughly 6,000), they could not be solved by storage facilities alone; some kinds of 'soft' wheat lasted less than a year, and in any case the sheer scale of a big city's needs necessitated a regular supply. Another factor exacerbating the problem was that in the case of any particular grain-producing region – Sicily and Apulia, for example, which were the two major suppliers to Venetian and other Italian consumers – the exports came only from what was surplus to that area's own needs, which remained at a fairly constant level; so if overall crop yields fell by 20 per cent, the amount available for export might fall by 40 per cent or more, with a dramatic effect on prices. Starting in the late 1540s, poor Italian harvests caused a rolling crisis in the provisioning of several cities: Florence and Siena experienced serious difficulties in 1548, Venice in 1549 and Dubrovnik in 1550. By 1551 Zadar was suffering a famine. After a respite in the early 1550s, these problems soon recurred: a graph of grain prices in Palermo and Malta shows a steep rise in the years 1553–6. That a poor harvest in Apulia eliminated its wheat exports in 1555 was bad enough; but in the same year, for the first time, the Sultan issued a general ban on exports of grain from the Ottoman Empire, following the outbreak of famine in Egypt and a three-day period when no bread was available in Istanbul. Over the next two years, Dubrovnik had to take a series of special measures to avoid starvation, cadging cereals from sources in the Ottoman Balkans and giving special privileges to ship-owners who brought grain to the city. In 1560 exports from Sicily slumped, and at the end of that year another shortage of cereals in Istanbul led the Sultan to ban Ottoman exports again; he even sent galleys to the coast of Greece to intercept those Western cargo ships (from Venice and Dubrovnik) that had already been loaded with grain, and to take them by force to Istanbul. And there were other periods of crisis, each more severe than the last: 1568–9; 1573–5; 1588–90.[16]

As some of these details already indicate, the Ottoman Empire had become an important source of grain for Venice and Dubrovnik (and others too, including Genoa). Some records can be found of such transactions from the first part of the century: the Venetian fleet was buying grain from the Ottomans in 1505, for example, and Florence made a formal request for grain at Istanbul in 1528. But the flow increased greatly from the mid-century onwards. There were three major cereal-growing areas in the Ottoman Empire: Egypt, the Romanian territories of Wallachia and Moldavia, and the broad stretch of fertile land that extended from Thessaly (in north-central Greece) up through Macedonia and Thrace to Bulgaria. All three were increasingly aligned towards the provisioning of Istanbul and other places in the Ottoman heartland. Venetian ships were able to get grain from Varna, on the Black Sea coast of Bulgaria, in the early 1550s, but thereafter most foodstuffs that came from Romanian and Bulgarian territories to the Black Sea proceeded to Istanbul and no further. Venice also sent ships to Egypt (and Syria) for cereals in the late 1550s, but this supply also seems to have dried up thereafter. Luckily, Thessaly was so productive that in most years it had a surplus to sell (usually via Volos, its main port), and there was also grain to be had from the Peloponnese, the larger Greek islands, and the Albanian lands. The further away these were from Istanbul, the less likely their products were to be swallowed by that city's almost insatiable demand; and this was especially true of grain that was traded in the western ports of Greece, and on the coast of Albania.[17]

Venetian merchants were both hindered and helped by the Ottoman regulation of the grain trade. Officially, a sultanic permit known as a *hüküm* (Ital.: 'cochiumo') was needed to authorize the export of any large quantity of grain. Dubrovnik, as a tributary state within the Ottoman Empire, was usually able to obtain these, on the strict condition – which it sometimes broke – that the cereals were for its own use and not for resale. But the Venetian representative in Istanbul could encounter political difficulties, and after the general prohibition of 1560–1 was lifted the Sultan continued to turn down Venetian requests. However, many of the leading pashas had large agricultural estates of their own, so it was sometimes possible to deal directly with them for the cereals they produced. And in one important way the Ottoman system actually helped the Western purchasers. It imposed a *narh* or fixed maximum price for grain, which was enforced by the local judges; since the *narh* was often below the natural market rate – both to assist state purchasing, and to serve social justice – it could create a large incentive for under-the-counter sales to outside buyers, and for smuggling. In 1563 one Ottoman report complained that people in Greece were selling grain to foreign buyers for almost twice the official price. Later in the century, another factor was added to this price differential: devaluations of the Ottoman coinage made people even more eager to find foreign buyers, since they paid in stable currency. So, although the Venetian representatives in Istanbul received no formal *hüküm*s for the export of cereals between 1560 and 1590, many shipments did make their way, directly or indirectly, from Ottoman territory to the Serenissima. In these conditions the local knowledge and local contacts of intermediaries, such as the Albanian merchants of Ulcinj, could only become more important. Overall, then, Venice was locked in an economic relationship with the Ottoman Empire which, although less glamorous (and much less discussed by historians) than its well-known trade in pepper, spices, silk, mohair and other luxury goods, was of vital importance to its survival as a functioning state.[18]

There was one other way in which Venice could obtain grain: letting others obtain it first, and then seizing their ships. The main victim of this practice was its great trading rival in the Adriatic. In September 1562 the Venetian commander Filippo Bragadin seized a Ragusan ship – i.e. a ship from Dubrovnik (Ital.: Ragusa) – which had been loaded with grain at the Apulian port of Barletta, and sent it under armed guard to Corfu to feed the town and the galley-crews stationed there; a year later, after his abortive trip to Durrës and Vlorë with Antonio Bruti, he captured another Ragusan ship off Budva, loaded with 5,000 stari of wheat and 7,000 of barley. More such episodes occurred in 1565 and 1566. There was no attempt to justify this by arguing that the Ragusans should not be trading with the Ottomans; as the example from 1562 shows, grain from Italy was just as likely to be targeted. The only justification given was sheer need. And that was thought sufficient – by the aggressors, at least – since these were not intended as acts of piracy. Reimbursement for the value of the cargo was always promised, and mostly delivered, though often after long delays, and at a low rate. (The Knights of Malta were said to follow the code of conduct a little more scrupulously, by stopping ships and forcing them to sell their grain at the price they would have received at their destination.) Very occasionally, Dubrovnik adopted such a tactic itself. In the late summer of 1569 it seized a ship which had just been loaded with cereals in Apulia and was en route to Naples. Its explanation was that the ship had been blown by a storm into Ragusan waters; that it was in any case a Ragusan vessel; and that its captain had taken refuge in Dubrovnik to evade being seized by prowling Venetian galleys. But still the Ragusan authorities felt obliged to send copious apologies to the Viceroy of Naples, with a promise to make up the loss with the next delivery they received, and with the statement that they had been forced to act in this way by 'the general famine everywhere, especially in Dalmatia'. Usually, though, it was Dubrovnik that suffered from this kind of treatment. The instructions it issued to its mariners and merchants in the crisis year of 1569 are full of warnings about the predatory Venetians: to one captain it wrote that he should stay far from the waters of Corfu, 'steering absolutely clear of all the other Venetian possessions, and of their warships', and to another it suggested giving a present to the commander of the Ottoman fortress at Durrës (in front of which it would load its grain), as 'he could do you a favour, against the Venetian galleys'. Such tactics were not always successful; the Venetians seized one Ragusan grain ship in August 1569, three (on their way from Vlorë) in September and another one in November.[19]

It is from the Ragusan archives that we get the most detailed picture of the business of grain-buying in the Albanian ports in this period – a time when Antonio Bruti and other Venetian subjects were just as active, but less apt to leave written traces of their work. The authorities of Dubrovnik were major purchasers of grain from Albania in the 1560s and '70s. They took care not only to get appropriate sultanic *hüküm*s through their representatives in Istanbul, but also to deal with those pashas who had large estates; in October 1569, for instance, they were paying the *Kapudan Paşa* (head of the Ottoman navy) for wheat and millet bought from his agent in Vlorë. Just one month earlier, they wrote to one of their merchants in Durrës, who was trying to deal with the obstreperous agent there of the chamberlain of the Grand Vizier, Mehmed Sokollu (Srb.: Sokolović). They enclosed a letter to the agent (a Christian, called Simo) in which they loftily informed him that the chamberlain, his master, had asked them to take the produce of his estates, and that they had agreed to do this, 'even though we had no particular need of it' – a wonderfully brazen example of mercantile guile, at a time of famine in Dubrovnik. Sometimes these arrangements with the large estates were covered by *hüküm*s. In 1565, for example, a sultanic order to the officials of Vlorë permitted the Ragusan purchase of grain from three estates in the region: the Sultan's, Sokollu's, and that of another vizier, Pertev Pasha. But much of the negotiating of particular purchases seems to have been done on the spot by people working for the Ragusan authorities. Apart from their merchants and captains, who might stay for several months in order to accomplish such a deal, they also had a network of agents *in situ*, who had to deal with many predictable problems: slow delivery, sub-standard grain, and so on. There was also an official 'consul' in Vlorë (for most of this period, a Jew called Jacopo Coduto); his duties extended not only to organizing purchases of grain, but also to dealing with the robbery and enslavement of Ragusan subjects by the corsairs of Vlorë – a growing problem in the 1570s.[20]

One of the most active agents was an Albanian Catholic priest, Giovanni Gionima, presumably a member of the famous Jonima family who had been patricians of Shkodër. In the late summer of 1569 the Ragusan government wrote to him: 'in the name of God and the Virgin Mary, go to those parts of Albania, in whichever places seem most suitable, and busy yourself with your usual diligence in buying on our account what grain you can find, whether wheat or other kinds, and at the lowest price possible.' He was to spend up to 1,000 ducats, for which he would be reimbursed by another Ragusan agent, Elia Suina, who was a member of a prominent family in Ulcinj. (Elia and Lauro Suina – who, incidentally, had married Antonio Bruti's sister Bona – performed various services for Dubrovnik, including buying oil in Ulcinj, sending couriers from there to Lezhë, and forwarding letters to Coduto in Vlorë.) Gionima quickly responded that he had bought 3,000 stari (222 metric tons) of millet and 1,000 of sorghum, as well as 205 of beans which he had obtained on the Rodon peninsula; the next instruction given to him, in Lezhë, was that he should send whatever he had on Ottoman vessels – which, the Ragusans knew, Venice would not dare to seize. The work of this Catholic priest continued for many years: in late 1579, for example, we find him bringing grain to a Ragusan vessel on the beach at Durrës, and hiring another Ottoman ship to take an extra 2,000 stari which he had managed to obtain.[21] But four years later, when he was again supervising the loading of cereals onto a ship there, he and the Ragusan sailors on the beach were attacked by 'a large number of Muslims of Durrës', who beat and wounded the sailors, tore the clothes off their backs, seized the payment for the grain (more than 2,600 ducats) from Gionima, and murdered him. As the Ragusan government noted, this was not the only case of its kind; in the same year violent crowds of 'insolent people' had attacked its merchants and mariners in Vlorë, preventing them from taking any grain over a period of three months. The underlying reason for such resentment is not difficult to guess: bulk purchases of grain by outsiders were pushing up the local prices, and most of the people in these ports were consumers, not producers. As the governor of Ulcinj wrote to the Ragusan authorities in January 1570: 'your agent has been the main reason why grain prices have greatly risen in this area, with the result that the people here have been reduced to extreme misery.'[22]

This, then, was the complex and demanding market in which Antonio Bruti operated for many years. No doubt he was already an experienced trader in 1553, by which time Ulcinj was playing a key role in the extraction of Albanian grain. Giustinian's report of that year said that the merchants of Ulcinj brought 150,000 stari (9,300 tons) of cereals each year from the ports of northern Albania; for a small trading centre, that is an impressive figure – roughly a quarter of the annual consumption of the city of Venice. In his petition Antonio mentioned that in 1556, when there was a serious grain shortage on Corfu (following the Sultan's ban on exports), he was given three ships by the Venetian authorities, which he managed to fill with millet from the Albanian mainland; this service, he said, was performed at his own expense, out of sheer devotion to the Venetian state. Soon afterwards, more services were required of him. For two years he was stationed in Ottoman Albania as a resident Venetian agent, charged principally with getting supplies of grain – a task which, he wrote, he performed despite 'very great dangers and difficulties'. (His petition does not specify the dates, but a despatch from the Venetian representative in Istanbul does refer to him as the agent in Lezhë in the summer of 1558.) In the slightly vainglorious account he later gave, he said that because of his local popularity he was somehow able to force the Ragusan merchants there to let him take whole ship-loads of grain which they had arranged; such was his prestige that, despite this treatment, they still courted and favoured him. Even if he embroidered a little, the essential story here may well have been true; he had a huge advantage over them in terms of local knowledge and connections, since Lezhë was the town in which his family had lived throughout his childhood. By 1559, when he was back in Ulcinj, Antonio seems to have been that city's most prominent grain trader. In that year a Venetian official recommended building a mole or jetty to give Ulcinj a proper harbour, explaining that 'then it would be possible to bring a large quantity of wheat from Albania, with the certain help of Mr Antonio Bruti and his partners'. When Antonio visited Venice in the summer of that year, he was given 3,000 ducats by the Grain Commission to spend on cereals, and in the following year they sent him 6,000; he was now their chief buyer of grain from the Albanian ports.[23]

Antonio Bruti's visit to Venice in 1559 was made in order to receive a signal honour from the Venetian state: on 30 June, in a ceremony conducted by the Doge, Lorenzo Priuli, he was made a 'cavaliere' (knight) of the Order of St Mark. This was Venice's only order of chivalry, and it was, by the standards of other European orders, rather an anomalous one: it had no Grand Master, no statutes, no headquarters, and no general activities or ceremonies in which its members would gather. Yet, as membership of this order was the only honour of its kind dispensed by the Republic, it was held in very high regard. There were three kinds of recipient: those who acquired it *ex officio*, by serving as Grand Chancellor of Venice or by performing foreign embassies; members of a handful of noble families in which the honour was hereditary; and individuals who had done some exceptional service to the state. Most knights were in the third category. In time of war the number of appointments would rise, but in peacetime they were few: Antonio Bruti was one of only three people to be made a cavaliere in 1559, and the annual total in the 1550s ranged from one to thirteen. The formal citation, entered in the records of the Senate, praised Antonio's services as follows:

> On various occasions we have seen how much service and benefit to our affairs has been performed by our most faithful servant Mr Antonio Bruti of Ulcinj among the Ottoman officials on our borders, given that he has much experience and familiarity with some of them, and much reputation and credit with all of them, in the affairs which happen from time to time – not only concerning the freeing of ships, and Venetian subjects, and their goods, and the purchasing of grain, but in other no less important dealings.[24]

Quite a detailed description has survived of the usual investiture ceremony, which took place in the Audience Hall of the Doge's Palace, in front of members of the 'Collegio' or ruling council. The Doge would make a speech, honouring the recipient and exhorting him to further service; he would touch him on both shoulders with a large ceremonial sword; then he would place a gold chain round his neck, while another official attached gold spurs to his boots; and then, to the music of the Doge's pipers, there would be a triumphal exit from the palace, and the new knight would be accompanied in great style to his home or lodgings. There were some costs to the recipient: various fees and tips, to the pipers among others, came to a total of 57 ducats. But on the other hand the solid gold chain was more than a symbolic gift; Antonio's was valued at 100 scudi (83.3 ducats), and one surviving example from the following century weighs no less than 600 grams. The knight also received a fine diploma signed by the Doge; in Antonio's case, the text declared that he 'had never been reluctant to accept any task, had spared no effort or expense, and had never shrunk from any mortal danger' in the service of the Republic of Venice.[25]

This was the high point of Antonio Bruti's career in that service; as we shall see, his sons would never fail to draw attention to his knighthood when seeking to emphasize their own loyalty to the Venetian cause. But it was not the only sign of recognition he received. His accession to the nobility of Ulcinj, decreed by the next Doge in 1562, has already been mentioned.* So too has his privilege of exporting wine and oil tax-free, awarded – albeit with mixed motives, in part at least to assist his work as a Venetian agent – in 1567. Two years later he sent another request to Venice, asking that the next two lucrative public offices to become vacant in Ulcinj should be assigned to his nine sons; the nature of the offices was not stated, but he did mention the annual income of each, which was 150 ducats. That request too was granted.[26]

Antonio's energetic grain-buying for the Venetian authorities continued all through the 1560s. The lack of sultanic *hüküm*s does not seem to have been a major obstacle – though it is noteworthy that one instruction he received from Venice, in October 1569, authorized him to spend between 200 and 300 ducats on bribing the local *sancakbeyi* and other Ottoman officials. His final purchases of Albanian grain probably took place in the first half of 1570. In the middle of May of that year – some months after the outbreak of war between Venice and the Ottoman Empire – the governor of Budva wrote a rather craven letter to the Venetian government, explaining that he had seized a brigantine full of wheat which the cavaliere Antonio Bruti had sent to Budva on its way to Venice. He had done this, he admitted, in contravention of an explicit order that the cities of Istria, Dalmatia and Venetian Albania should not detain shipments of cereals that were intended for the metropolis; he was forced to do so by 'utterly extreme necessity', having to feed 4–5,000 people 'in these times of war, plague and famine'. Perhaps Antonio decided at this point that he could no longer contribute to the Venetian cause by means of merchant activities. Shortly afterwards, he made a grand offer to the government of Venice: he would like to join the Venetian navy with two of his sons, and would bring, at his own expense, a corps of ten Albanian archers. The offer was gratefully accepted, and recorded in an official letter to the Venetian naval commander on 7 June. Towards the end of that month the commander took his fleet of galleys to Corfu, and it was probably there that Antonio joined it, with his archers and his sons Marco and Jacomo; such was Antonio's prestige that they were all placed on the flagship. But in late July, just before the galleys sailed for Crete, Antonio was asked by the commander of all the infantry forces aboard the fleet to return to Ulcinj. As one of that city's most charismatic and practical figures, he was

* Above, p. 32.

needed for its defence; and it was, after all, his home. He had devoted his life to rebuilding the fortunes of his family in that city, and he had done well: he had made money, he had a country property nearby, he was a noble of the city, he was even a knight of St Mark, and he had been making arrangements there for the future status and income of his children. This whole structure of security and prosperity, which he had laboured so hard to build, would come crashing down in the late summer of 1571, and Antonio Bruti would meet his own death as it fell.[27]

4

Giovanni Bruni in the
Service of God

Of Antonio Bruti's three Bruni brothers-in-law, one, Serafino, has left almost no traces of his existence. We know only his name, and the identities of his two sons: Nicolò, who became a captain of stradiot cavalry in Ulcinj and was killed at the end of the Battle of Lepanto, and Matteo, who will feature to a small extent in these pages. As Serafino was certainly not a priest and apparently did not have a military career, it seems most likely that he entered the family trading business; perhaps he was one of the 'partners' of Antonio Bruti mentioned by the Venetian official in 1559. But nothing further is known about him. The story of this family continues, rather, with the lives of his two brothers, Giovanni and Gasparo.

Giovanni Bruni was born in Ulcinj, and probably received his early education there. His later career suggests that he had much more than elementary schooling: at the Council of Trent he would make lengthy impromptu speeches in Latin to an unusually demanding audience, citing from memory works by St Thomas Aquinas. It is quite possible that he went to university in Italy; if so, the most likely candidate is Padua, which functioned as the local university for Venice, but its detailed matriculation records for this period do not survive. Neither is it known when, or where, he was ordained a priest. The first definite information we have about Giovanni Bruni is that, before becoming Archbishop of Bar in 1551, he was a canon of the cathedral of Ulcinj. The bishop under whom he served there was Jacopo Dalmas, a member of a noble family of the city of Bar, who had been appointed in 1536. The eighteenth-century historian Daniel Farlati, who studied a mass of documents about the Catholic Church in this region, called Dalmas a virtuous man; but an angry letter from the governor of Ulcinj in 1544 took a very different view, complaining that he had plunged his clergy into 'confusion and division'. It seems that the Bishop supported two of his relatives in Ulcinj who were bitterly resisting the governor's attempt to bring new families into the ranks of the city's nobility, and that this – in the governor's view, at least – was creating the sort of dispute between noble and non-noble clergy from which Bar had suffered badly, but Ulcinj had been mercifully free. Five years later, another possible source of division emerged: the Archbishop of Bar wrote to the Inquisition in Venice saying that, according to a report he had received, 'Lutheran heretics' were causing 'great scandal and confusion' in Ulcinj. But nothing more is known about these people; the term 'Lutheran', as used by an Italian Catholic in this period, meant 'Protestant' in a very general sense, and might be applied to people who voiced almost any kind of criticism of the Papacy or the Roman Catholic Church. Given Giovanni Bruni's later career, as a defender – and definer – of Catholic orthodoxy, we can be confident that he was not one of them.[1]

The Archbishop of Bar who wrote that letter in 1549, Ludovico Chieregatto, did so from the comfort of his residence in his home town, Vicenza. Appointed to Bar in 1528, he had spent very little time there. Nor was such absenteeism at all unusual. Many Italian ecclesiastics, especially from the patrician families of Terraferma cities that were excluded from high government office in Venice, were given bishoprics in the Stato da Mar without any real expectation that they would reside there, and the revenues of those sees were in many cases so small that they were treated merely as supplementary incomes. When Chieregatto attended the Council of Trent for a couple of months in 1546 he persuaded the Papacy to give him a special subsidy of 50 scudi (41.6 ducats) because of his poverty. Not long afterwards he tried to resign his archbishopric, appointing a Franciscan from the island of Korčula to administer it in his place; but the Venetian authorities fiercely objected to that person, so Chieregatto was forced to withdraw his resignation. Instead he wrote to the Pope in 1547 saying that old age – he was 65 – prevented him from living in his archdiocese. Four years later, in May 1551, the Pope appointed Giovanni Bruni Archbishop of Bar, on the grounds that Chieregatto had 'abdicated'; Giovanni travelled to Rome, and received the pallium – a special vestment for senior archbishops – in person on 21 June. But there were two unwelcome provisos: Chieregatto would retain the honorary title of Archbishop of Bar, and would receive a pension of 65 scudi (54 ducats) from the revenues of the archdiocese. The income of the new Archbishop would thus be even lower than that of his poverty-pleading predecessor.[2]

For such an ill-funded position, the responsibilities were extraordinarily large. First there was the diocese of Bar itself. There were eighteen

churches in the city, including the cathedral, as well as a Franciscan friary and a nunnery; Bar had quite a large clerical community, and in the
early sixteenth century there were at least ten priests from Bar in Venice
itself. Outside Bar there were 48 churches in the rural parts of the diocese, which extended into Ottoman territory, far beyond the relatively
recent frontier. Within the archdiocese were not only the neighbouring
sees of Ulcinj and Budva, but also seven other bishoprics. And besides
governing the archdiocese, the Archbishop of Bar also had the position
of 'Primate of Serbia' – a historic title which had long belonged to the
Archbishop of Split, but which, for reasons that remain mysterious, had
been transferred to Bar by the early sixteenth century. It was by virtue
of being a primate that the Archbishop gained the pallium; he also had
the unusual privilege of wearing purple robes, like those of a cardinal.
According to a later account, 70 sees in Serbia, Albania and Macedonia
came under the jurisdiction of the Primate of Serbia. That number seems
implausibly high, even though many of these may have been historic
entities that had become – thanks to the lack of actual Catholics in
them – merely notional ones, little more than lines on an ecclesiastical
map of the Balkans. But there were major populations of Roman Catholics in the northern Albanian lands (including Kosovo), and smaller
numbers of them in many of the towns of the entire region, especially in
those that contained so-called 'colonies' of merchants from Dubrovnik.
So there were real duties here for the Primate to perform, relating to
a very large area. The fragmentary evidence that has come down to
us suggests that the new Archbishop of Bar took those duties very
seriously.[3]

Giovanni Bruni seems to have resided full-time in Bar, except for the
period when he attended the Council of Trent. When Giustinian entered
the city of Bar in 1553, he and his companions were 'met by the most
Reverend Archbishop and by the honorable governor, and saluted with
a great pealing of bells and with a tremendous firing of artillery'; with
the Archbishop they visited the cathedral first of all, before they went to
their lodgings. Also in 1553, the Pope wrote to Giovanni in Bar, and to
Bishop Dalmas in Ulcinj, asking them to investigate the proposed grant
of land by the abbey of St Nicholas to Antonio Bruti; Antonio had asked
for papal confirmation of this (so that his heirs would hold the estate
with greater security), and the Pope wanted to be sure of the facts before
he gave it.* In 1557 Giovanni visited Laç, a Catholic village to the south

* See above, p. 42.

of Lezhë, north of Krujë, to consecrate a newly built church there; the Latin inscription recording this – 'Hoc templum consecravit R. D. Ioannes Brunnus Archiepiscopus Antibarensis' ('The reverend lord Giovanni Bruni, Archbishop of Bar, consecrated this church') – was noted down in the early twentieth century, but the church itself was destroyed by explosives in 1967, during the Communist campaign to make Albania an 'atheist state'. No doubt there were many other visits, over the years, to Catholic parishes inside Ottoman territory. The Ottoman authorities generally made no difficulties about this, and serious tensions between them and the Roman Catholic Church were usually confined to the periods when they were at war with Catholic powers (though it seems that, after the Venetian–Ottoman war of 1570–3, they did remain suspicious of clerics based in Venetian territory for quite a long time). One of Giovanni's bishops, Antonio Ciurleia, Bishop of Budva, told a story at the Council of Trent of how he had visited Ottoman territory 'in disguise, because he could not travel there in any other way, since it is in the power of the Turks'. But this was surely an exaggeration – as was, no less surely, the story he related, which involved a 100-year-old 'Greek' who met him, immediately divined that he was a bishop, asked for the sacrament of confirmation, and promptly died in his arms.[4]

Specific details of Giovanni Bruni's work for his far-flung flock have not survived. Indeed we know little about the conditions of the Catholics of the region in this period; detailed documentation by the Church began only in the following century, after the creation of the 'Propaganda Fide' (an organization to support the faithful in non-Catholic territories) in Rome in 1622, and the introduction of Franciscan missionaries to Albania in 1634. But the basic problems reported in the early seventeenth century were very probably the same as those that faced Archbishop Bruni in the sixteenth: Catholicism was declining because priests were either entirely absent or, if present, of poor quality and ill-funded. The result was a slow but steady flow of conversions to Orthodoxy or Islam. (Or at least, inertial acceptances of those faiths and practices – to modern minds, the term 'conversion' suggests a strenuous process of changing one's theological beliefs, which may not be applicable in many of these cases). So, for example, a report from Bar in the 1630s said that most people there had become Orthodox or Muslim 'because they do not have good pastors'; and in the same period Franciscans observed that large numbers of Catholics in the area of Krujë were turning to Islam 'because of their ignorance of the mysteries of the faith, and because of the lack of those who could explain those things to them'.[5]

Giovanni Bruni seems to have striven hard against these dangers. An idea of his work is given by some general comments made by Catholics in the region in the years after his death. In 1578 a group of Roman Catholics in distant Kosovo sent a letter to Rome in which they said that under Bruni they had at least received some spiritual consolation, and that his vicar had sent them priests, albeit ill-educated ones; after his death the supply of priests had failed, with the result that many people had joined either the Orthodox Church or Islam. A more whole-hearted tribute came at roughly the same time from an anonymous writer to Rome on behalf of 'the people of Serbia and Macedonia'. While Giovanni Bruni was Archbishop of Bar, he declared, 'all the Christians in Ottoman territory who follow the faith and rites of the holy Roman Church – not only those of the [former] kingdom of Serbia, but also all those of Macedonia, and their bishops too – had recourse to him in their times of need; he visited them in person, and to those who were far away he sent bishops, providing them with preachers and confessors.' Memories of his work would take a long time to fade. Nearly half a century after Giovanni's death, a Catholic priest who travelled from Bar through northern Albania to Kosovo found 'several paintings' of archbishops of Bar clad in their purple vestments, 'especially Giovanni Bruni'.[6]

That the Ottoman régime was generally tolerant not only of the presence of Catholics among its subjects, but also of visits to them by Catholic clerics from foreign territories, is in a certain sense surprising, since it must have been aware of the Papacy's deep hostility – political as well as religious – to the Ottoman Empire. Some of the popes of the sixteenth century devoted huge energies to planning the destruction of that empire, whether by internal revolts, warfare by Western rulers, geopolitical strategies involving other powers such as Muscovy (or even Persia), or any combination of the above. The term 'crusade', for most historians, seems to lose its meaning after the end of the Middle Ages; it is seldom used to describe these later papal plans. If the word were taken to apply only to a war for the recovery of the Holy Land, that would imply a real difference, since the sixteenth-century projects were aimed above all at smashing Ottoman power in Europe. Another difference would arise if the word applied only to cases where armies were raised primarily by appealing to the religious feelings of the general population. But 'crusade' has, and had, a much broader sense, meaning any religiously motivated and formally declared war by Christians against infidels; and that is just what the sixteenth-century popes continued to urge the rulers of Christendom to undertake against the Ottoman Empire. They themselves did use the term, and they were right to do so.[7]

Grand geopolitical plans were seldom absent from their thinking. In the second decade of the century, for instance, three years before the outbreak of the Reformation, Pope Leo X sent an envoy to Moscow in the hope of organizing a coordinated campaign to conquer Istanbul; that envoy never got there, but one sent by Pope Clement VII in 1525 did, with a similar anti-Ottoman proposal. Of course there were mixed motives in such cases, involving the hope (a painfully naïve one, as we now know) that by means of such collaboration the Orthodox Russians could somehow be brought to accept the primacy of Rome. The crusade project was both an end in itself and a means to other ends, the common factor being the long-term strengthening of Catholic Christendom. Something similar is true of the way in which these crusading ideas were developed further in response to the Reformation and its divisive consequences. At several key moments – especially the Diet of Speyer in 1526 and the Diets of Regensburg in 1532 and 1541 – the Emperor Charles V was obliged to make concessions to the German Protestant princes because he desperately needed their support against the Ottoman threat; this, more than any other single political factor, made it possible for the Reformation to establish itself in Central Europe. To eliminate the Ottoman threat would radically alter the situation, so that a Catholic *reconquista* in the German lands would become a much more attractive option. And that was not the only major intra-European problem to which an anti-Ottoman crusade might provide the solution. The popes were dismayed by the inveterate conflict between the kings of France and the Habsburgs – not least because so much of it had been fought out on Italian soil. These were the two greatest Catholic powers; it was scarcely tolerable that they should war so frequently between themselves, but the situation became even harder to bear when, from approximately 1530 onwards, King François I developed a geostrategic alliance with the other major anti-Habsburg power, the Ottoman Empire. That alliance could take quite startling forms, such as the combined military operations of 1543–4, when a fleet of Ottoman warships wintered at Toulon as guests of the King of France. Some of the Christian powers who professed to be scandalized by this sort of collaboration were being hypocritical, as the principle that 'my enemy's enemy is my friend' was one that they themselves might happily apply, if opportunity arose, to their dealings with the Sultan. But the Papacy's dismay was more obviously genuine. To settle the French–Imperial conflict would be a means towards creating a broad European alliance against the Ottomans; and, at the same time, to create such an anti-Ottoman league, if it included both Habsburg and Valois, might be a means towards settling the conflict at the heart of Christendom.[8]

As the century developed, one important difference did emerge between these crusading plans and those of the Middle Ages. The geopolitical strategies of the sixteenth century became bound up with a much larger project of restoring, strengthening and extending the influence of the Roman Catholic Church. This project was truly universal in its scope. It looked both inwards, to the ordinary Catholics whose understanding and practice of their own faith were in need of instruction and improvement, and outwards, at three principal targets: heretics (above all, Protestants), who had to be confuted and repressed; nonheretical but 'schismatic' Christians, such as the Greek Orthodox and other Eastern Churches, who must be persuaded to end their schism by accepting the primacy of Rome; and non-Christians, who needed to be converted. If those non-Christians ruled over Christian subjects (as the Ottomans did), or if they were at war with Christian states (as the Ottomans frequently were), the Church must be involved in organizing the struggle against them. The long-term goal was to defeat them and win their lands and people for Catholicism, while the medium-term benefit was the re-establishment of a moral and spiritual leadership role for the Papacy in the affairs of Europe.

This whole project of strengthening the nature and role of the Roman Catholic Church can be referred to as the Counter-Reformation. The term is an ambiguous one, since its original meaning, self-evidently, was something rather narrower: the move by the Catholic Church to counter Protestantism. For quite a long time, historians tried to distinguish between Catholic Reformation (eliminating abuses, improving education, and so on) and Counter-Reformation (enforcing orthodoxy); in some accounts, the former had been making great progress until it was constrained by the intolerant rigidities (Inquisition, Index of Prohibited Books, etc.) of the latter. It is now more common to accept that these various strands were intertwined and interconnected almost from the start; the history of an order such as the Jesuits – the Counter-Reformation order *par excellence* – cannot be told on the basis of any clear separation between them. Yet still the standard accounts tend to concentrate on the interplay between Catholic reform and the fortifying of the Church against its heretical foes within Christendom. If a more outward-looking dimension is added to the story, it usually involves the sending of missionaries to evangelize in distant parts of the world. What is still not fully recognized is the importance of the crusade against the Ottomans, and the larger geopolitical schemes that surrounded it, as a key element in the entire Counter-Reformation project.

In 1536 Pope Paul III announced his intention to hold a General Council of the Church in the Italian city of Mantua, with three main aims: to extirpate Protestant heresy, to create peace in Christendom and to organize an anti-Ottoman crusade. The council never took place, but he did achieve his third end, to some extent at least, two years later when he assembled a 'Holy League' of the Papacy, the Holy Roman Empire and Venice to fight against the forces of Süleyman the Magnificent. As we have seen, that war ended inconclusively in 1540, after what was widely regarded as a serious defeat for the Holy League's navy. Two years later, Paul III issued a papal bull proclaiming a new General Council, to be held at Trent. In it, he set out the story of his previous attempt to call a council, and his reasons for doing so: he had hoped to put an end to the religious disputes between Christian princes in Europe, because he 'wanted the commonwealth to be safe and protected against the weapons and stratagems of the infidels', and knew that peace was necessary to free the commonwealth 'from many impending dangers'. He rehearsed the history of recent defeats at the hands of the Ottomans: the loss of the island of Rhodes in 1522, the conquest of much of Hungary in the mid-1520s, and 'war by land and sea, conceived and planned against Italy, and against Austria and Illyria [sc. Croatia, Dalmatia and Venetian Albania], since the Sultan, our impious and merciless enemy, never rested, and took our mutual hatreds and disagreements as a profitable opportunity for himself'. After the failure to hold a council at Mantua, there had been more attacks by 'the Sultan, our savage and perpetual enemy'. Now it was time to act.[9]

The political difficulties involved in organizing a General Council were huge; not surprisingly, there were more delays before the Council of Trent actually began its work in 1545. The location itself was a political compromise between the Papacy and the Emperor Charles V: the city of Trent (Ital.: Trento; 'Tridens' or 'Tridentina civitas' in Latin, hence the adjective 'Tridentine') was an autonomous prince-bishopric, within the Holy Roman Empire in jurisdictional terms, but geographically in Italy, where it usefully lay on one of the most important routes

between the German lands and Rome. The French king was ...
let the council happen at all, as he feared that it would solve the ...
or's domestic problems and give him a free hand for his wars again...
France; here the compromise was forced out of him by an Imperial invasion of his territory, though French participation in the Council would
be at a token level until its final phase. The only people who seemed
unwilling to compromise at all were the Protestants, who declined to
take part. And so, as the Council got under way, its work fell into two
main categories. One was reforming the practices of the Catholic
Church; the other was clarifying and strengthening its doctrine in those
areas where Protestants disagreed with it. Gradually, with long delays
between its sittings, it worked through some of the most contentious
subject-matters: the theology of justification and some of the sacraments in its first session (1545–9), and the eucharist, and other
sacraments, in its second (1551–2). (A few Protestant theologians did
appear at the second session, but only to make demands about voting
rights that the Council could not possibly accept; they had no influence
on the substantive issues.) By the time the Council was set to work
again in January 1562, most of the difficult doctrinal questions had
been dealt with, but there were important issues of practice – notably,
ones concerning the powers and duties of bishops – that still waited to
be resolved.[10]

Given the nature of its work, the Council of Trent had no direct concern with Ottoman affairs; there was no need, for example, to have any
discussion of the theology of Islam or of missionary activities towards
Muslims. But the Ottoman threat was a background condition that
would not go away. In 1551, one might almost say, it came to the Council. The Orthodox Archbishop of Salonica, Makarios of Chios, turned
up at Trent and asked to be admitted – a request which the authorities
would not grant, unless he made a profession of Roman Catholic faith
and accepted the primacy of the Pope. Privately, Makarios was letting it
be known to agents of Charles V that he could act as an intermediary
between the Empire and three of the most important pashas in Istanbul,
who, he said, might be persuaded to come over to the Christian side. He
was also claiming that he could help to set up contacts with the great
enemy of the Ottoman Empire on its eastern flank, the Shah of Persia.
As it happened, one of the Imperial agents in Trent was an experienced
intelligence-gatherer, Girolamo Bucchia, originally from Kotor, who ran
a network of informants in Venetian Albania and was well informed
about Ottoman matters. It was Bucchia who, as he wrote to one of the

Emperor's chief ministers, eventually discovered that Makarios was a spy, sent by the Ottomans in order to find out how far the plans that he put forward were already being developed by the Imperial side.[11]

The idea that such a General Council could play an important role in the Papacy's anti-Ottoman geopolitical schemes was another thing that did not go away. In the run-up to the third session one of the papal secretaries, listing the central aims of the Council, included 'putting down that enemy of Christianity, the Sultan'. During the long wait between the announcement of the third session in late 1560 and its eventual start in 1562, Pope Pius IV sent agents to potential anti-Ottoman allies such as the Shah of Persia and 'Prester John', the Christian ruler of Ethiopia; he invited the ruler of Moldavia (an Orthodox Christian principality which formed part of the Ottoman Empire, and was a potential participant in any grand project to overturn Ottoman rule) to attend the Council; and he also despatched an envoy to Ivan the Terrible in Moscow, with the request that he send some prelates and an ambassador. (The King of Poland refused to let the papal agent pass through his territory, but the Pope found a more secret way of sending another representative to Russia.) As his special envoy to the King of Spain explained, Pius IV wished to 'arrange the affairs of Christendom against the Ottomans, in order – if it please God – to recover Constantinople and the Holy Sepulchre and to root out the Muhammedan faith'; to achieve this, he emphasized, the Pope would 'make every effort and use all his power, not sparing any expense'.[12]

Once the third session was under way, Pius soon became impatient with its slow progress; in May 1562 he sent a letter from Rome to his legates (the papal representatives in Trent who directed the business of the Council), urging haste. 'The Sultan cannot live long,' he wrote, 'as he suffers from dropsy and is thoroughly worn out in mind and body; Monsignori, let us try to bring this Council to a speedy and productive conclusion, really uniting all of Christendom, so that we can turn our weapons against the infidels, heretics and schismatics. That is the aim which we must all keep in our sights.' Similar sentiments had already been expressed on the floor of the Council itself. In February the Bishop of Castellana had made a speech referring to the rumour that Sultan Süleyman was dying, predicting a civil war between his sons and arguing that this would be an opportunity for a pan-Christian alliance (including even the Protestants) to conquer the entire Ottoman Empire. A few days later the Bishop of Pécs (in Hungary – a diocese under Ottoman rule) made a passionate oration praising the Emperor for having saved Europe from being overrun by the Ottomans; in April a message was read out from the Archbishop of Esztergom, a city which was also in Ottoman hands, saying that the constant danger in which his archdiocese stood made it impossible for him to come to the Council. And there were other reminders of the various forms that the threat could take. In May 1563 the Bishop of Bova (an impoverished see in Calabria, on the toe of Italy) asked for permission to leave the Council, in order to organize the ransom of several relatives who had been seized by 'the Turks' – meaning the corsairs of North Africa, who were formally under Ottoman rule. In July the Council held a special Mass to celebrate the victory of Spanish forces over those pro-Ottoman corsairs at the Algerian port of Oran. And in September 1563, as the Council was heading towards its close, it heard a long and eloquent speech by the representative of the Knights of Malta, who described how his order defended Italy against the infidels: if Malta fell, he said, 'it can scarcely be doubted that this would strike a very great wound – perhaps an incurable one – in the whole body of Christendom.'[13]

So when Giovanni Bruni arrived at the Council of Trent in early 1562, he would have encountered much interest in, and sympathy with, his position as a prelate from the Ottoman borderlands. Apparently he missed the opening of the new session on 18 January; his name is absent from the initial roll-call. But he must have got there not long afterwards, as his first recorded intervention in a debate was on 10 February. It seems likely that, instead of taking the direct route via Venice, he had gone first to Rome to consult with senior members of the hierarchy – and, probably, report on conditions in his archdiocese. On 10 January one of the Pope's right-hand men, his nephew and secretary Carlo Borromeo, wrote to a legate in Trent, asking him to pay a monthly subsidy of 30 gold scudi (25 ducats) to Giovanni Bruni, 'starting on the day when he gets there' – a phrase which suggests that Borromeo was sending him on his way. From other evidence it is clear that a real bond of friendship developed between these two men; the eighteenth-century historian Daniel Farlati would describe Bruni as 'extremely dear to Carlo Borromeo'. In his later years Borromeo would become one of the towering figures of the Counter-Reformation, an exemplary archbishop and a man of great moral and spiritual authority; but at this stage he was only 23 years old, not yet a priest (though already, thanks to his uncle, a cardinal), nor yet the transformed person he became after a spiritual crisis in late 1562. During the third session of the Council of Trent he would be one of the key intermediaries between the legates and Pope; he acted

mostly as a faithful transmitter of papal instructions, and if he inter-
posed any preferences of his own, they were aimed at defending the
position of the Papacy. Whether he had any continuing contacts with
Bruni during the work of the Council is not clear; the main evidence of
their friendship comes, as we shall see, from after its close.[14]

Giovanni Bruni needed that subsidy. He was one of only a few prelates to receive 30 scudi per month; most of the people who were given
such help got only 20 scudi at first (rising to 25 a little later). If that was
all they had to live on, they could not live well; in 1563 the Huguenot
diplomat Hubert Languet commented scornfully that in Trent, 300
scudi per year was 'hardly enough to feed a servant and a donkey'.
Those who held sees in Dalmatia and Venetian Albania featured prominently on the list of the subsidized: they included the bishops of Zadar,
Rab, Senj and Budva. A special commission, set up by the Council in
early 1562 to investigate the reasons why so many bishops failed to reside in their sees, began its report with the problem of episcopal poverty,
singling out the six worst cases: three Italian sees, plus Rab, Budva and
Bar, which, it said, 'have nothing'. And while Giovanni was particularly
poor, the prices in Trent had become unusually high. This small sub-
Alpine city, with a normal population of approximately 8,000, had to
accommodate a huge influx of people. By March 1562 there were 131
cardinals, patriarchs, archbishops and bishops, plus fifteen theologians,
four ambassadors and seven other delegates. Each of these brought his
own entourage. The Archbishop of Segovia arrived with 33 people, the
Polish Cardinal Stanislaus Hosius with 60, and Cardinal Ercole Gonzaga with 160, as befitted his status as a prince. The average for the
patriarchs, archbishops and bishops was just over nine servants and
retainers each; Giovanni Bruni brought four. We know the identity of
one of them, his nephew Matteo (son of Serafino), who, as a very old
man in Koper in the early 1620s, would impress Francesco Barbarano
with his personal memories of the Council. Giovanni thus had his own
secretary; his other employees would have included a manservant to
cook for him, and a stablehand. Some records survive of his servants'
purchases of grain, at roughly four stari per month. The rate of consumption seems high for five people, even allowing for the use of some
of it as animal feed; possibly the servants were taking advantage of the
price of this commodity (subsidized for participants in the Council), to
sell some of it on at market rates. For although merchants were flocking
to Trent from as far afield as Germany to sell their provisions, feeding
the city with more than 1,000 head of cattle every two or three days,

prices remained very high. It also seems that the formal instructions to the Council, issued in January, that the participants should eat modest meals and forgo 'sumptuous dinner parties', were not universally obeyed.[15]

It is not possible to say where Giovanni Bruni lived in Trent. The inadequate stock of great houses – some of which, still with the exuberant polychrome designs that were painted on their façades, can be seen to this day – must have been entirely taken up by the time he arrived. An interesting letter from Borromeo to Ercole Gonzaga in December 1561 stated that the papal commissary in Trent was distributing housing according to the 'nations' (and, at the same time, trying to evict the impecunious Archbishop of Naxos from a house that was too grand for him); as Borromeo explained, the Pope was worried that such an arrangement might lead to national groupings forming 'secret conventicles', and many other undesirable consequences. By modern criteria there were at least thirteen nations at this session of the Council: Italians predominated by a very wide margin (coming eventually to a total of 195), but by the end of the session the participants also included 31 Spaniards, 27 Frenchmen, and a smattering of Greeks, Flemings, Hungarians, Portuguese, Irishmen, Poles, Germans, Czechs and Croatians. (The fact that one prelate was an Albanian has been omitted from all accounts of the Council of Trent, thanks to the ignorance of some of the Council's official record-keepers, who twice listed Giovanni Bruni as 'Greek'.) But what Borromeo and the papal commissary meant by nations was probably something different; in their view, the Venetian bishops might have counted as one nation, regardless of ethnic origin. Among the members of that group, Giovanni would certainly have known the Bishop of Budva, Antonio Ciurleia (an Italian from Bari), but may not have wished to associate closely with him; with his whimsical, jocular speeches, Ciurleia quickly developed a reputation as a maverick lightweight, causing amusement to some and irritation to many. No doubt Giovanni had personal knowledge of some of the other bishops from the Stato da Mar. But although he followed – as we shall see – a distinctively Venetian line on some points, the detailed evidence of the debates and votes at the Council gives little sense that those bishops were hunting as a pack.[16]

The Council's debates were held in the city's cathedral, a massive Romanesque building of pearl-white and rose-tinted stone. In the previous session the participants had fitted into the choir, but now there were so many that – as a famous sketch once attributed to Titian shows – the whole nave was used. People spoke more or less in order of seniority, and Giovanni Bruni, not only an archbishop but also a primate, was in one of the highest categories. He quickly got to work, becoming a regular and conscientious attender of the debates. When he arrived in February the Council was discussing improvements to the upkeep of the Index of Prohibited Books, and drafting a decree that would both set up a body to examine all previous indexes and judgments, and invite any interested parties to come, with a safe-conduct, to the Council to make representations. Giovanni gave this his approval. Then, on 11 March 1562, just before it wound down for an Easter break, the Council plunged headlong into what would be by far the most contentious issue of the entire session: the question of episcopal residence. The initial draft proposal that was circulated seemed unobjectionable enough. It merely stated that archbishops, bishops and all priests with 'cure of souls' (direct pastoral duties) should reside where their churches were, and not be absent 'unless for reasons that are just, virtuous, necessary and in the interests of the Catholic Church'. Almost everyone could agree that this was a good thing, even if many who did so were being hypocritical where their own practice was concerned; no fewer than 80 absentee bishops had been residing in Rome in 1561, and the issue was being promoted now at the Council by a group of reformists who feared that if absenteeism were not firmly dealt with, the Protestants would triumph in most of the German lands. But the bitter dispute which broke out during the Easter recess was about whether the fundamental requirement to reside was a matter of divine law or merely human law. What made this issue so difficult to handle was its potential implication for the power of the Pope: it seemed clear that in a matter of human law (an area that included most of the arrangements set out in the canon law of the Church) the Pope could issue a dispensation, but it was much harder to see how papal authority could extend to permitting someone to break a law of God. And beneath that problem there lurked a verit-able ticking bomb, left over from previous General Councils of the Church: the question of whether bishops received their powers from the Pope, or directly from God Almighty.[17]

When the session resumed on 7 April, Archbishop Bruni was one of the first to speak. He argued that residence was necessary, whether by divine or by human law, and that 'there is no need now to declare by which law we are required to reside; instead, we should give the reason why bishops ought to reside.' This was an attempt to be both non-confrontational and practical; he went on to say that the important thing was to eliminate those problems that made bishops feel that they were unable to live in their sees with dignity (a transparent reference to their insufficient incomes). He did not take part in the long and heated debate, over the next two weeks, on the question of divine and human law. On 20 April, when a vote was held on a proposal to declare that residence was indeed required by divine law, he adopted the moderate but clearly pro-papalist stance of saying that the answer should be 'no', unless the Pope decided otherwise. In subsequent months, on several other issues relating to parish priests and bishops, Giovanni Bruni spoke in favour of reforms (especially ones that would make their positions more viable financially), but with a particular emphasis on strengthening the powers of bishops; he was keen, for example, that a bishop should have a supervisory authority over all the religious bodies in his diocese, including monasteries, friaries, schools and confraternities. In a debate in September on a proposal that cathedral churches with incomes below 500 ducats should not in future have those incomes reduced by the assignment of special pensions, he said that the first thing to do should be to remove the pensions from which they already suffered. Clearly the deduction of 54 ducats for Chieregatto out of his own meagre income still rankled. And when, in December, the question of episcopal residence came up once more, he again expressed his own belief in the importance of residing, and then added a more personal point: as the minutes record, 'he said that he himself does not refuse to reside, even though he has a diocese in Ottoman territory, is in constant danger of death, and is very heavily burdened by a pension.' (Perhaps the minute-takers got a little carried away here; while some parts of the diocese were on the Ottoman side of the border, Bar itself was, as we have seen, in Venetian territory.)[18]

In some ways, then, the positions Giovanni Bruni took can be related quite directly to his own experiences. The same is true of his stance on issues that were of special concern to Venice because of its Greek Orthodox or Serbian Orthodox subjects. In July 1562 some draft canons (rules) were put forward, with the aim of opposing Protestant claims about the eucharist – especially their claim that it was wrong of the Roman Catholic Church to give communion to lay people in one 'kind' only, bread, reserving the wine for the clergy. One canon stated that if anyone said that God required the use of both kinds, he should be anathematized (i.e. fully excommunicated); another decreed the same penalty for anyone who denied that Christ was entirely present in each kind; and another for anyone who claimed that divine law required giving communion to children. The Patriarch of Venice argued that the wording of the first of these should be made clearer, 'so that the Greeks are not included in it'; he said that the second should also be clarified, and that the last was acceptable 'so long as the privileges of the Greeks are not abolished by it'. When Giovanni Bruni spoke, it was to express his agreement with the Patriarch.[19]*

Another potential conflict with Eastern Orthodoxy arose in the following year during the debate on new canons about marriage. One draft canon declared that if anyone said that marriage could be dissolved because of adultery, and that the innocent party could remarry during the lifetime of the previous spouse, he should be anathematized. To this the Venetian ambassadors at the Council expressed a strong objection: they said it would cause a scandal in Crete, Cyprus, Corfu and other islands, since the Greeks had long permitted divorce in cases of adultery, without ever being condemned for it in any General Council of the Church. Here too Giovanni Bruni expressed his support for the Venetian position. He was one of many prelates who thought that whilst the Roman Catholic Church should have a legal decree against divorce, the Council should not make it a theological rule that anyone who approved of divorce in these circumstances was a heretic.[20]

Marriage itself was one of the major topics discussed by the Council during 1563, and Archbishop Bruni was an active participant in the debates about it. He argued in favour of stronger punishments for clandestine marriages (which, it was said, were often used for second, bigamous unions); he proposed that bishops should have the power to give dispensations from the 'forbidden degrees' of marriage; but he also argued against a suggestion that people should be allowed to marry those who were related to them in the fourth degree, i.e. third cousins. Possibly he was influenced here by his Albanian background: in the mountain areas of northern Albania, Catholics maintained a strict taboo on marriage to any relative through the paternal line, up to the twelfth degree.[21]

In February 1563 Giovanni was nominated to a small committee

---

* Note, however, that the canons did not say that it was positively wrong for the laity to enjoy both kinds. In the following month, the Emperor sent a formal request to the Council to permit the use of both kinds in Bohemia and Hungary, a measure he judged essential to recover people who had been switching to Protestantism; Giovanni said that they should be allowed this only if they reverted fully to the Catholic Church and accepted all its doctrines. He also said that the matter should be remitted to the Pope; eventually the Pope did make this concession, but it became a dead letter after a fairly short time.

whose task was to gather evidence of abuses of the sacrament of ordination; other members included the Patriarch of Venice and the
Archbishop of Sens. It met in the house of the Polish Ambassador, presented an interim report to the Council in April, and continued to meet
until July. Otherwise, most of Giovanni's interventions during this final
year of debates were on subjects relating to the rights of bishops, which
he wanted to strengthen against those under them, and the rights of
archbishops, which he wanted to strengthen against the bishops. The
latter point seems to have taken on a particular importance for him. So,
for example, when a draft canon stated that a primate should perform
visitations of his own cathedral city, but not of the churches below that
level unless his bishops requested it, he objected that the rights of archbishops would be undermined by such a rule. In November, just one
month before the end of the Council, that canon came up for discussion
again, together with two others that also displeased him: one of them
said that while primates should call provincial councils at regular intervals, monks and nuns could be exempted from their jurisdiction, and
the other proposed that serious charges against bishops, such as accusations of heresy, should be heard and judged not by their archbishops but
only by the Pope. Bruni was so offended by these three proposals that
he read out a formal statement of dissent, declaring that they were
incompatible with 'the good and ancient rights of archbishops', and
that they would harm those rights so much that 'that whole ecclesiastical hierarchy [sc. the archiepiscopate] would be almost destroyed.' As
he pointed out, the majority of voters in the Council were bishops; so in
any dispute of this kind they were both parties and judges. His conclusion was that the whole matter should be remitted to the Pope, and not
decided by this innately biased assembly. This was the strongest speech
he ever made at the Council; and by this time, after all his conscientious
work and assiduous attendance, he had earned the right to be listened
to with respect.[22]

The Council of Trent was brought to an end on 4 December 1563. In
the final weeks some issues had been rushed through, and some ready-
made decisions rubber-stamped. On the great question of the duty of
residence a compromise formula had been found, referring to the divine
'precept' that pastors should look after their sheep, but not actually saying whether residence was required by divine law or not. Despite, or
indeed because of, its various compromises, the Council of Trent had
done something quite remarkable: it had put the whole structure of
Roman Catholic doctrine and practice on a new basis, which would last

unaltered for three centuries, and still sets the essential rules for many
areas of Catholic life and thought today. The achievement was immense,
and all the participants knew it. After the presiding legate had pronounced the Council closed, a Te Deum was sung. And then, in the
words of one of the Council's chief legal advisers (who was keeping a
diary), 'I saw so many grave and distinguished prelates, with tears of
happiness flowing from their eyes, congratulating even those with
whom they earlier were at odds ... There was no one who did not
express ... the very height of happiness, praising God.' Among them,
too, greeting and thanking both friends and foes, was the Albanian
Archbishop of Bar.[23]

Giovanni Bruni's movements immediately after the Council are not
known; perhaps he spent some time in Venice. By May he was in Rome,
where he probably renewed his acquaintance with Borromeo. While he
was there, he persuaded the Commissary General of the Franciscans to
let him have one of their most experienced friars, the 70-year-old Fra
Silvestro of Verona, who had worked in Dalmatia and spoke the Serbo-
Croatian language fluently. As the Commissary General wrote, Giovanni
wanted someone who could 'instruct his flock by preaching and reading, not only in the city of Bar, but also in every place in his diocese, as
the most Reverend Archbishop thinks fit'. Giovanni then travelled with
Fra Silvestro to Bar.[24]

Archbishop Bruni seems to have returned from Trent filled with
reforming zeal. Not long after his arrival, he began to put pressure on
the abbot of the Benedictine monastery of Ratac, which was located on
the coast, four miles to the north-west of Bar. Evidently the monastery
enjoyed a good income – as we have seen, it had been the object of a
murderous struggle for control in 1512 – and its church may have had
some pastoral responsibilities towards the local people.* Since 1554 the
abbot had been Lorenzo Marcantonio Pisani, a member of a Venetian
patrician family; although he was a Benedictine, he seems to have
treated this position as a mere sinecure. Giovanni wanted to make him
reside at Ratac, but Pisani would not accept the Archbishop's jurisdiction. So Giovanni tried to launch legal proceedings against him at the
Roman Curia. The Pope took advice from a special congregation of
cardinals which he had set up to deal with cases involving the interpretation of the Tridentine decrees; and eventually, in March 1565, the
secretary of that congregation sent a letter to Giovanni in Bar, telling

* See above, pp. 6, 31.

him to suspend all action in the matter unless and until he received further instructions. Bruni was learning the hard way, perhaps, the difference between reform in theory and reform in practice.[25]

However, this rebuff from Rome did not mean that the Pope no longer trusted his judgement. When the Bishop of Ulcinj, Andrea Giubizza (successor to Bishop Dalmas), died in 1565, the Pope decreed, by a formal letter of 30 October, that Giovanni should administer that diocese; and at roughly the same time he also made him the administrator of the see of Budva, because its maverick bishop, Ciurleia, had travelled from Trent to his family home in Bari and had not budged from there. Immediately, Giovanni found himself embroiled in another clerical dispute. While Bishop Giubizza was alive, the canons of the cathedral of Ulcinj had chosen another eleven priests from that city and added them to the cathedral chapter, without his permission; the city's nobles protested that not one of the eleven was from a noble family, and Giubizza also opposed their appointment, which he regarded as invalid. Giovanni Bruni took the same position as his predecessor. The cathedral chapter appealed to the papal envoy in Venice, who handed the matter to the Bishop and Archdeacon of Kotor; a formal hearing was held there, in which one lawyer appeared on behalf of Bruni and the nobles of Ulcinj, while another represented the canons. The two judges failed to agree, and sent the whole matter back to the envoy in Venice. What the final result was is not known. Nor can we tell whether Giovanni Bruni was acting here strictly on his understanding of canon law, or whether he was also influenced, to some extent, by his own close connections with the noble and governing families of Ulcinj. But the general evidence of his activities in this period, limited though it is, does strongly suggest that he was motivated by the good of his flock, and of the Catholic Church.[26]

In December 1564, exactly a year after the end of the Council of Trent, Giovanni Bruni wrote from Bar to Cardinal Borromeo, asking for his help. Since there had been a change in the generalship of the Franciscans, he was worried that the new General might recall Fra Silvestro; he enclosed a testimonial from the chapter and clergy of Bar, and asked Borromeo to intercede with the Franciscans in Rome. At the same time he also asked that permission be renewed for an 80-year-old friar, Marco Pasquali (a member of one of Bar's most prominent families), to live in the nunnery of Poor Clares in the city in order to hear the nuns' confessions. As he put it in his letter to Borromeo, 'I have always made a great effort to keep these poor people in the Catholic faith, even though this poor province is oppressed by schismatics [i.e. Orthodox] and Muslims.' The letter from the chapter and clergy of Bar confirmed this, testifying not only to the work of Fra Silvestro but also to that of their tireless prelate. From the day that he had first come to Bar as Archbishop, they wrote, 'he has ruled and governed his flock in the most peaceful way, demonstrating that he is not only a good pastor, but a father and brother to everyone.'[27]

There is one other piece of evidence – a tantalizing one – of Giovanni Bruni's conscientiousness as pastor to his flock. On 13 August 1568 Pope Pius V sent him a letter, thanking him for a report which Bruni had recently submitted about his visitation of the city and diocese of Bar. This is tantalizing because the report itself has not apparently survived; if it could be found, it would be an unusually rich source of information from a period in which such detailed accounts are almost entirely absent. Bruni was certainly acting in accordance with the decisions of the Council of Trent, but the record-keepers in Rome seem to have taken much longer to appreciate the importance of visitation reports. As it is, we have only the Pope's rather short letter to guide us. He praised Bruni for his 'diligence and piety', and urged him to keep up his work, since the Catholics of that region were in great danger, being 'in the jaws of the infidels'. Above all, he insisted, 'the seeds of superstition should be completely plucked out from those people, and that horrifying and savage way of behaving towards the bodies of the dead which they used to practise should henceforth be removed from them and utterly abolished.' The most likely explanation of this rather troubling sentence is that Bruni had commented on the practice of mutilating the bodies of enemies killed in fighting. This may serve to remind us that his diocese was indeed in a frontier zone, and that low-level conflict, of a sometimes brutal kind, was almost endemic in the region.[28]

A final document sheds a gentler light on Giovanni Bruni's work, and on his dealings with both Carlo Borromeo and the Papacy. In September 1565 he wrote to Borromeo from Ulcinj, saying that – as he had mentioned in a previous letter – he had managed to buy three very fine horses for the Pope, thanks to the help of his brother, who had gone to a horse-fair in Ottoman territory to get them. He explained that this was a commission given to him by the Pope when Giovanni had an audience with him and received his blessing on the way back to Bar. Now, he wrote, 'I have put them on a ship to take them to Ancona, with my nephew Matteo, whom I take this opportunity to send in my place to kiss His Beatitude's most holy feet and your most holy hands.' The horses were, he said, young and beautiful, each with an excellent gait. If there were any other services that he could perform, he would be happy to do whatever was in his power, 'together with my aforementioned brother, and relatives'. This was a particularly well-chosen present, since the neighbouring Ottoman territories were famous for the quality of their horses: as one sixteenth-century treatise on horsemanship noted, the purest-bred ones came from Anatolia, but those were often crossed with local Albanian or Slav breeds to create horses that were less nimble, but 'gagliardi' – 'vigorous' or 'robust'. As we have seen, importing horses was a major activity of the merchants of Ulcinj, but also a rather clandestine one, since their export was forbidden by the Ottoman authorities because of their military value. Just five months after Giovanni Bruni wrote this letter, the Sultan issued a formal order to the *bey* of Shkodër, complaining that Muslims were selling horses 'to the unbelievers in the enemy castles' (i.e. Ulcinj and Bar), and demanding that the practice be halted. So Giovanni Bruni and his brother had done well. His devotion to the Papacy was deep and genuine; but at the same time we can see, in this letter, some devotion to the long-term interests of his family too. The sending of Matteo to accompany the horses was a shrewd move, which may have paid off. According to Barbarano, who met him nearly 60 years later, Matteo 'served for a long time at the Curia in Rome, where he had honorable employments, as befitted his worthy merits'. It is only reasonable to assume that, like his brother-in-law Antonio Bruti, Giovanni Bruni would have done what he could to secure the future of his family. For they lived in a world where the bonds of family duty were stronger than any others – save only one's duty to God.[29]

5

Gasparo Bruni and the
Knights of Malta

Nothing very definite is known of the life of Gasparo Bruni until October 1567, when he became a Knight of Malta – or, to use the full title, a Knight Hospitaller of the Order of St John of Jerusalem. It was suggested above that he was born close to the year 1520, and that he was probably the youngest of the three brothers.* In view of his subsequent military career, we may guess that he would have fought in the war of 1537–40, so long as he was old enough to do so. His later career also suggests that he spent part of his early life becoming an experienced ship's captain; so, given Giustinian's comment about how the Bruni and Bruti families supported themselves by trade, we may assume that he was involved in transporting grain and other commodities, perhaps in collaboration with his brother-in-law. And there is at least a 50 per cent chance that Gasparo was the brother who obtained those three fine horses for the Pope in 1565 – perhaps more than 50 per cent, since Giovanni's phrasing in his letter to Borromeo ('my aforementioned brother, and relatives') might be taken to imply that by this stage he had only a single brother left. The one other thing that can be said about Gasparo before he became a Knight of Malta is that he fathered a son, Antonio, in c.1557–8 – but that boy would go unmentioned in any document for well over a decade. It is only with his entry into the Order of the Knights of Malta that Gasparo Bruni steps into the historical record.[1]

As their official title suggested, these Knights had their origin in Jerusalem, when that city was held by the crusaders. At first they ran a 'hospital' – not a medical institution in the modern sense, but a hospice or resting-place for pilgrims, in which the needy and the sick were also looked after. Before long they were combining their hospitaller duties with those of a military order, similar to the Knights Templar and the

---

* Above, p. 24.

Teutonic Knights; in their heyday the Knights of St John controlled nearly 50 castles in the Middle East, including the grandest of them all, Crac des Chevaliers. After the final destruction of the Latin Kingdom of Jerusalem at the end of the thirteenth century, they found a new home on the island of Rhodes. There they turned themselves into a maritime power, their main targets being the galleys and merchant ships that plied the trade route (and, for Muslims, pilgrimage route) between Ottoman territory and Egypt. In 1480 they withstood a major Ottoman attack; soon afterwards they signed an agreement not to molest Ottoman ships or territory, but their attacks on other vessels using the trade route continued, and they also became a sponsor of Christian corsairs in the region. After the Ottoman conquest of Syria and Egypt in 1516–17 the trade in these waters became an intra-Ottoman affair, and the government in Istanbul grew much less willing to tolerate such a thorn in its own side. In 1522 the recently enthroned Süleyman the Magnificent brought a huge force to the island and, after a siege lasting nearly six months, captured the city of Rhodes. The Knights were allowed to leave honourably with their weapons, their sacred relics, and – luckily for historians – their archives. Eight years later the Emperor Charles V granted them the island of Malta.[2]

From that moment onwards the Knights had a dual allegiance: as a religious order they were subject to the Pope, but in legal and political terms they held Malta as a fief from the crown of Aragon. They were thus subject to the Emperor – or, after Charles V's division of his empire between his successors in 1554–6, to the King of Spain, who also ruled Sicily and the Kingdom of Naples. This connection mattered to the Knights in practical terms: much of their island's food supply came from nearby Sicily (including more than 6,000 tons of grain per year), and they depended on the Spanish governors of Sicily and Naples for other kinds of practical help, including the recruitment of soldiers. In turn, it mattered to Charles V and his heir, Philip II of Spain, to have this military force occupying such a strategic position in the Mediterranean. At its narrowest, the gap between Sicily and Tunisia is less than 100 miles wide; this is the choke-point that divides the two halves of the Mediterranean, and Malta is close enough to guard its eastern approaches. The main problem here was not the threat of a large Ottoman fleet proceeding all the way from Istanbul to attack the Spanish mainland, though that was at times a genuine fear. Rather, the constant concern of the Spaniards was with the passage to and fro of the corsairs of North Africa – above all, of Tripoli, Tunis and Algiers.[3]

In the late fifteenth century Spain had begun to acquire 'presidios' or fortified outposts on the Moroccan Mediterranean coast. (Melilla, seized in 1497, is still held by Spain to this day – as is Ceuta, an earlier Portuguese acquisition, later transferred to Spain.) In the sixteenth century it began extending this policy eastwards, seizing key positions on the Algerian coast and even taking the distant port of Tripoli. The main aim was to suppress, or at least develop a systematic defence against, the actions of the local Muslim corsairs, who raided Spanish shipping and territory. But it was Spain's misfortune that this policy initiative coincided with the rise of two of the most talented and charismatic corsair leaders, the brothers Hayreddin (also known as 'Barbarossa') and Oruç, who swiftly took control of the city of Algiers. When Spanish forces put more pressure on them there, and succeeded in killing Oruç, their actual achievement was to create the connection that Spain had most reason to fear: in 1518 Hayreddin placed himself under the formal protection of the Ottoman Sultan. In the following years, as Charles V poured more blood and treasure into a series of North African expeditions, he merely strengthened that link, and gave Hayreddin the motives – political as well as economic – to step up his raiding activities. Then, in 1532, when Charles sent a fleet to the Peloponnese to conquer the fortress and town of Koroni (which, as we have seen, had been taken from Venice by the Ottomans in 1500), the final stage in this sequence of counter-productive policies was reached: the Sultan, desperate to acquire the services of a really experienced naval commander, summoned Hayreddin to Istanbul and put him in charge of the Ottoman fleet. It was Hayreddin's tactical skill that gave the Ottoman side the victory at the Battle of Preveza six years later. After his death in 1546, the Ottoman navy would continue to make use of large contingents of North African corsairs; and, when they were not assisting in this way their political patrons in Istanbul, they continued to carry out their raids on shipping and coastal territories.[4]

In theory, the prime purpose of the Knights of Malta was to counter this threat. Indeed, when they were first given Malta they were also put in charge of the fortress at the Libyan port of Tripoli, which was then in Spanish hands; they maintained a garrison there for two decades, abandoning it only in 1551. The Knights took part, of course, in major naval expeditions mounted by their own political masters – they were a component of the force that took Koroni in 1532, for example. It is true that they did attack the vessels of the 'Barbary corsairs' when they encountered them at sea, and they also raided the North African coast from time to time. The instructions of the Grand Master of the Order to one of his Knights in 1536 seem clear enough: 'our profession is primarily to fight infidels, and to drive the corsairs away from the coasts and seas of the Christians.' But an analysis of their regular expeditions between 1532 and 1574 shows that, out of the ones where a specific destination was entered in the records, only five were to the 'Barbary' coast, while eighteen were to 'the Levant' – meaning the waters of the eastern Mediterranean. The richest pickings were still on the Istanbul–Egypt trade route, or on the coastal route which took traders and pilgrims from the Maghreb to Egypt. The Greek archipelago, in which so many of the islands were now Ottoman territory, also provided a good hunting-ground, with the added advantage that the Knights could often find refuge, food and water at those islands that were still in Venetian hands – however unwelcome they were to the authorities there. What emerges from this whole pattern of activities is that the prime motivation, in most cases, was booty: merchandise, people (for enslavement or ransom) and ships. Harming 'the infidels' was an important consideration; the booty was taken, in theory at least, only from them. But the prospect of inflicting harm without gaining any profit was much less motivational.[5]

In modern terminology there is a clear distinction between a pirate and a corsair. A pirate will rob and raid indiscriminately, complying with no law and recognizing no superior authority. A corsair acts with the authorization of his ruler, targets particular enemies, follows a code of conduct – for example, about how to proceed if enemy personnel or merchandise are found on a non-enemy vessel – and may be subject to more rules when he returns to his home port (concerning the distribution of the booty, and, often, the payment to his ruler of some sort of tithe of it). In the sixteenth-century Mediterranean, the word 'corsair' (Ital.: 'corsaro', from 'corsa' or 'corso', meaning a raiding voyage) was widely employed in its various forms; the word 'pirate' (Ital.: 'pirata') existed, but was much less commonly used. In Ottoman Turkish, *korsan* (adapted from 'corsaro') could mean either type, and so could *levend* (derived either from 'levantino', Levantine, or from a Persian word for a free soldier), which also had a wider meaning, including brigands on land. One reason, perhaps, for the relative lack of distinct references to pirates is that most of the people engaged in these activities were at least claiming to be corsairs. Real piracy certainly existed; one Ottoman writer referred to the pirates of the Kaz Dağ region (on the Anatolian coast of the Sea of Marmara), who attacked all kinds of Ottoman subjects, including Christians, Jews and Muslims. (The term *harami lev-end*, 'robber levend', was used for these.) Most real piracy, however, was small-scale and local. Once the activity got above a certain level, the pirates would need the help and approval of whoever it was that held political power – who, in turn, might also find them useful. But the transition to full corsair status was a blurred one, as there were gradations of power and different kinds of approval, some more tacit than others. The rather piratical corsairs of Durrës and Vlorë, for example, did enjoy the connivance and protection of the local Ottoman authorities, but could sometimes be called to account by Istanbul. They broke some of the Sultan's rules, by preying on Venetians and Ragusans, yet they could not be described as pirates in the fullest sense, as they did not normally attack Muslims, or ships from directly ruled Ottoman territory.[6]

Reading traditional accounts of these matters by Western European historians, one might almost think that the only pirates and corsairs operating in the Mediterranean were Muslim ones. But there were many Christian corsairs too; those of Valencia were very active in the 1560s, when they even mounted a daring attack on Algiers itself. The greatest Christian corsairs of them all, however, were the Knights of Malta, who fully satisfied the definition of the term. The political ruler in this case, for all practical purposes, was the Grand Master of the Order, and it was he who issued the formal authorization, both to his own Knights and (increasingly, in the late sixteenth and early seventeenth centuries) to private entrepreneurs. These corsairs did have a code that made some targets legitimate and others not; booty captured by the Order's ships belonged to the Order, and the private corsairs paid the Order a proportion of theirs. It must be noted that the same, generally speaking, is true of the 'Barbary corsairs' in this period, at least in the main ports, such as Algiers: a tithe of what was gained was paid to the pasha, and the choice of targets was constrained, to some extent, by the policies and international agreements of the Ottoman state, which, for instance, exempted the French. The old histories, which portrayed a black-and-white conflict between the Knights as noble policemen of the seas and the Barbary captains as indiscriminate brigands, were very wide of the mark; both sides were corsairing in surprisingly similar ways.[7]

Yet still one must wonder whether, from the point of view of their victims, there would have seemed to be much difference between being targeted by a corsair or by a pirate. The many Jews who were captured on Ottoman ships, brought to Malta and reduced to slavery, may have asked themselves that question. (For example: in 1594 a safe-conduct was issued by the Grand Master for 'Sion son of Samuel, of Safed, a short man with a black beard, roughly 30 years old, our Jewish slave', to go and raise the ransom for himself and eight other captive Jews. The Order's archives contain many such records.) Much depended, too, on how the official codes of conduct were interpreted, and how strictly they were adhered to. The Knights would happily seize not only the vessels of Greek Orthodox Christians who were Ottoman subjects, but also, occasionally, those of Dubrovnik; the Ragusans paid a tribute to, and were at least arguably the subjects of, the Sultan, but they were also Roman Catholics. It was claimed, too, that the Knights would seize Christian ships and torture crew members to make them say that the cargo belonged to Muslims or Jews, thereby entitling the Knights to take it. Various Christian powers objected to the Order's actions from time to time, but the one that resented them most fiercely was Venice. It constantly feared that its own trading relations with the Ottoman Empire might be undermined by incidents involving the capture of Ottoman ships by the Knights off Crete or Cyprus; not unreasonably, the Sultan held the Venetians responsible for patrolling the sea round their own possessions. The complaint just mentioned, about the torture of Christian crews, came from the Venetian government; many of their ships did in any case carry goods owned by Jews and Muslims. In fact Venice had a long history of distrust and distaste for the activities of these knightly corsairs: during the siege of Rhodes in 1522 it had stopped volunteers from going to help them, and when the Knights finally surrendered it sent a special envoy to congratulate the Sultan. In 1536 and again in 1553 it announced a 'sequestro', a freezing of all assets and revenues of the Order in Venetian territory, as a way of strengthening its demand that the Knights stop plundering Venetian and Ottoman ships. Occasionally Venice may have found them useful, but mostly there was little love lost betweeen these two sides. It was the Venetian government that, in its complaint to the Pope, called them the 'cavalieri ladri' – the thieving knights.[8]

There were certainly good profits to be made. In June 1564 one of the most skilful and adventurous knights, Mathurin de Lescaut Romegas, seized a large galleon that belonged to the *Kapu Ağası*, a senior official who was head of the white eunuchs at the Sultan's court. Its cargo was said to be worth 80,000 ducats. Three months later he engaged with another big merchantman; it eventually sank from the effects of his cannon-fire, but he was able to rescue several important passengers, who would command very high ransoms. These actions seem to have been

the trigger that persuaded Sultan Süleyman to undertake, in the following year, a project that he must have been contemplating for some time:
the complete conquest of the island of Malta. When ordering the governor of Algiers to muster ship's captains for the campaign, the Sultan
gave two simple justifications for it: Malta had become 'a headquarters for infidels', and the Knights had 'blocked the route utilized by
Muslim pilgrims and merchants in the East Mediterranean, on their
way to Egypt'. Probably there were more strategic calculations at work
too: the conquest of part or all of mainland Italy had been a serious
Ottoman long-term goal since the 1480s, and Malta would make a
useful stepping-stone towards Sicily and the Kingdom of Naples. But
destroying the Order was the principal aim.[9]

The story of the massive siege which took place between mid-May
and mid-September 1565 has been told many times, and need not be
repeated in any detail here. The Order's main stronghold, the town of
Birgu (later renamed 'Città Vittoriosa'), was on one of the small fingers
of land that project into Malta's Grand Harbour from the southern side.
The large peninsula on which Valletta now stands was at that time just
a barren hillside, with a recently constructed fortress, Sant'Elmo, at its
tip, commanding the entrance to the harbour. A courageous and, at the
end, utterly suicidal defence of this fort gained valuable time for the
defenders in Birgu. Although the Ottoman land forces under Lala
Mustafa Pasha were hugely superior in numbers, they were gradually
weakened by disease, and by September they were both low on supplies
and fearful of sea conditions for the voyage home if they stayed much
longer. They also feared the arrival of a Spanish relief force from Sicily;
this came, after a long delay, only as they were on the point of abandoning the siege, with the consequence that the Spanish commander, García
de Toledo, was widely blamed for sloth or timidity (though a modern
military historian has argued that he acted with justified caution and
good strategic sense). By the time the Ottomans had finally left, roughly
300 Knights were dead or missing in action – more than half of all those
who had been present at the start, and almost a third of the entire membership of the Order. Much rebuilding was now needed, both physical
and metaphorical. In March 1566 the elderly Jean de Valette, the Grand
Master of the Order who had commanded the Knights and their auxiliary forces throughout the siege, laid the first stone of what was to be an
entire new fortified city, named Valletta in his honour. Donations flooded
in from the Catholic rulers of Europe, and the Order itself dug deep
into its own resources to fund a rapid and vastly ambitious building

programme. Speed mattered, because it was widely expected that Otto-man forces would return within a few years. And for the same reason it was important to recruit more Knights, to fill the Order's very depleted ranks. This, then, was the state of affairs when Gasparo Bruni became a Knight of Malta in 1567.[10]

A brief sketch of the structure and ethos of the Order may help to explain the procedures that were involved in joining it. The Knights were divided into eight quasi-national sections, known as 'langues' ('tongues' or 'languages'): Provence, Auvergne, France, Italy, Aragon, Castile (which also included Portugal), England and Germany. (In effect, how-ever, there were now only seven: the English properties of the Order had been confiscated by Henry VIII, and just a handful of English Knights survived.) Each langue represented both a geographical recruiting-ground for new Knights, and an administrative area – divided into units called Priories – for the huge quantities of manors and other properties which the Order had accumulated in Europe over the centuries. Those proper-ties were typically bundled up into individual estates called 'commende', which were handed out to senior Knights as a reward and/or a pension for their retirement. The Knights did not enjoy the whole income them-selves, as 15–20 per cent of it went, via the officials of the Priory, to the central finances in Malta; and in many cases Knights were expected to make some 'miglioramenti' or 'improvements', by purchasing extra land and adding it to their estates. In the early 1580s it was estimated that the Order itself received 100,000 scudi (83,000 ducats) a year from these properties. It also got four fifths of the personal estate of every Knight on his death, plus the high fee of 150 scudi paid by every new Knight who entered the Order; the total income available for the Grand Master in Malta was at least 200,000 scudi, not counting the booty gained by the Order's galleys and the tithes paid by the private corsairs it licensed. Assisting the Grand Master in Malta was a Council consisting of the heads of the langues (each of whom had a historic role *ex officio* – the head of the langue of Italy was the Admiral, for example) plus a few other officials; and this could be expanded into a Grand Council by the addition of two representatives of each langue. The larg-est body, the Chapter General, containing many more Knights, met to consider changes to the statutes, and to choose a new Grand Master, who was elected for life.[11]

As the list of langues shows, this was a very international organiza-tion, albeit one in which Frenchmen were over-represented quite heavily, and Spaniards to a lesser extent. Given the sometimes bitter political conflicts between Spain and France, between France and the Holy Roman Empire, and between all manner of Italian states and statelets, it is remarkable that the Order was never torn apart on national-political lines. The main reason was that it focused on an external enemy; in this sense it was a rare living example of the intra-European cooperation that the sixteenth-century popes hoped to achieve. But another reason was that the Order had undergone, since the Middle Ages, a process of 'aristocratization', so that its members were now connected by what might be called caste solidarity – plus, in some cases, the remarkably far-reaching links of relatedness through blood and marriage. Over time, the qualifications needed for entry into the Order became more and more demanding. In the sixteenth century, the requirement for applicants from Italy was four quarters (i.e., all grandparents), each representing 200 years' nobility in the male line; for France it was eight noble quarters, and for Germany sixteen. Thanks to pressure from the Spanish langues, it was also agreed in 1555 that anyone of Jewish or Muslim ancestry must be excluded. Normally, an applicant had to be of legitimate birth, but illegitimate sons of 'high' nobles, such as princes or dukes, were admitted if they could show that their great-grandfather had also been a high noble. And, since the Middle Ages, the Order had excluded anyone who worked in the typical 'bourgeois' occupations of banking or the wool trade, or who earned money as a scribe or notary; generally, having a father who had engaged in trade was a disqualification.[12]

These were some of the rules that governed the admission of full Knights, the 'Knights of Justice'. There were also men known as 'servienti d'arme' or 'fratres serventes' ('servants in arms' or 'serving brothers' – the English word 'sergeant' is derived from a version of this term, and some Italian writers called them 'sergenti'), who formed an important element in the Order's fighting force; until the rules were tightened even further in 1603, these men were not required to be noble. Nor were the chaplains, who, unlike the Knights, were ordained priests; in Malta, where each langue had its own 'auberge' or hostel for accommodation and meals, the serving brothers and the chaplains sat at a separate table. But there was one exceptional category: non-noble individuals who had performed special services for the Order (such as the painter Caravaggio in 1608) could be made 'Knights of Grace' by a special dispensation or 'grace' of the Grand Master, and a similar by-passing of the rules could take place at the direct request of the Pope. Since the Pope's main reason for doing this was to confer a valuable commenda on the beneficiary, turning him into a rich 'commendatore', this practice was much resented by the rest of the Order: in theory, only the Knights of Justice were entitled to hold commende. A fascinating mid-sixteenth-century text about the Order, written in dialogue form, contains some bitter remarks on this subject. Although the Pope regularly confirms the Order's statutes, one of the speakers says, nevertheless, 'overcome by the importunity of cardinals and others, he gives commende to whomever he pleases, to the great prejudice of the poor Knights.' What is worse, 'he also creates these Knights without any proofs of nobility, and without any other ceremony.' But, he adds, 'this happens only in the poor langue of Italy.'[13]

If Gasparo Bruni entered the Order by the normal route, the procedure would have been as follows. First, he must apply in person to the relevant Priory – in his case, the Priory of Venice. He had to satisfy the officials of the Order there that he was of sound mind and body, and that he was not of notorious reputation (for example, someone expelled from the army), heavily in debt, a homicide, a man condemned by the Inquisition, a married man (even if now a widower), or a member of another order. The Order would then send two Knights to his birthplace, with a notary, to take sworn testimonials from up to six witnesses about his family's reputation and noble ancestry. Those documents, if satisfactory, were then signed and sealed and given to the applicant to take with him to Malta. On his arrival, he would pay the entry-fee of 150 scudi, and present himself and his documentation to the langue – which, if it were satisfied, would recommend his admission to the Grand Master.[14]

There is good reason to think that Gasparo did follow this route, though the process was not absolutely problem-free. Sadly, the dossier which the Order compiled on him, containing detailed accounts of his family background, has not survived either in the archive of the Order in Malta or in that of the Priory of Venice. The first reference to him in Malta – indeed, the first specific mention of him in any surviving document – comes in a minute of a meeting of the Council on 14 October 1567. 'In the case concerning the reception of Gasparo Bruni into the venerable langue of Italy in the rank of Brother Knight', it recorded, the Council had listened to submissions from two opposing parties: Bruni himself, through his legal representative, and two Italian Knights, Girolamo Avogadro and Francesco Cataneo, who were 'contradicentes' – opposing his admission. The Council set up a commission consisting of two other Knights (one Portuguese or Spanish, the other

French) to investigate, saying that they should consider only 'the main question of his admission, not the dispensation ['gratia'] which is claimed'; they should 'hear the parties, inspect the documents, and, if necessary, examine witnesses'.[15]

The two objectors were Knights of some standing: Avogadro, from Piedmont, had joined the Order in 1541, and Cataneo, from Lombardy, in 1553. The precise nature of their objection is not known, but it failed to convince the investigators. On 28 October a meeting was held of the langue of Italy, with its head, the Admiral, presiding. As its minute recorded: 'a special dispensation ['gratia spetiale'] was made to Gasparo Bruni, after scrutiny of the ballot (in which there were no objections), concerning only the fact that he was outside the borders; and thus he is understood – with his consent – to be accepted from today.' The reference to the 'borders' ('limiti') is easily explained: by a statute of the 1550s, each applicant had to be born within the geographical borders of the langue, and by a more recent statute the borders of the Italian langue were defined as those of the provinces of Italy plus Sicily. People from the Venetian Stato da Mar had been admitted in the past, however – one, Cesare Morizzo of Šibenik, had entered the Order in 1566 – and this was a straightforward dispensation to make. So the nature of the Italian Knights' objections remains obscure. They cannot have complained that Gasparo had not spent a probationary year in Malta, as that became a statutory requirement only later in the century. We do know that Gasparo had a young son; yet so long as he had not actually married the boy's mother, that would have been no impediment. We can also be fairly sure that both Gasparo and his father had engaged in trade; but that exclusion had never been applied in the Priory of Venice, as it would have eliminated the entire Venetian nobility. The only dispensation or 'grace' mentioned here is the one concerning borders; it is absolutely clear that Gasparo was admitted as a full Knight of Justice, so he cannot have been one of the people forced on the Order as a 'Knight of Grace' by the Pope.[16]

Given the reference to inspecting documents in the instructions to the two-man commission, the most likely explanation is that the objectors doubted the validity of Gasparo's noble status. The nobility of Shkodër and Ulcinj, though taken very seriously in those places, may have seemed a paltry and rather dubious affair in the eyes of some noble Italians, especially non-Venetian ones. Nevertheless, on 30 October the langue of Italy met again and, as its minutes record, 'the proofs of nobility of Gasparo Bruno were accepted as valid, with no one objecting, and he

was accepted as a Knight, as decided above.' Overall it may seem hard
to believe that the Order should have continued to scrutinize promising
candidates so severely, at a time when it was desperately in need of
new recruits; immediately after this episode, on 1 November, the Grand
Master issued a general plea to the nobles of France, Spain and Portugal,
urging them to come to Malta during the following six months – before
the start of the next Ottoman campaigning season – to join the Order.
(He promised that they would be allowed two years in which to settle
their proofs of nobility, and that their seniority would nevertheless start
from the moment they arrived.) And yet the criteria themselves were not
relaxed at all. Just three months earlier, when a certain Cesare Ferretti
was admitted with incomplete documentation, the Order sent two
Knights all the way to Lombardy to get further witness statements
about his grandmother; a similar enquiry about a new Knight from
Pisa, Lelio Lucarini, which began just a few days after Gasparo's admission, would end with his ejection from the Order.[17]

On 31 October, in the chapel of St Catherine, the patron saint of the
langue of Italy, Gasparo Bruni underwent the solemn ceremony of
induction into the Order of the Knights of St John. First he attended
Mass, kneeling in front of the altar and holding a torch, to signify the
burning flame of charity, in his hand. Then the officiating Knight,
Admiral Nicolò Orsini di Rivalta, asked him formally whether he was a
member of another order, or married, and so on; he replied 'no'. Gasparo placed his hands on the Missal, and took the three vows: of
obedience, chastity and poverty. Showing him the habit of the Order,
with its prominent white 'Maltese' cross, the Admiral told him that he
must take special care of widows and orphans, and never abandon the
cross (as displayed on the Order's flag) in battle, whatever the peril to
his life. Then Gasparo put on the habit, and was dubbed three times on
his left shoulder with a great sword. He was now Fra Gasparo, a member of a religious order, and thus a member of the clergy – though one
whose *raison d'être* was to fight.[18]

Was Gasparo Bruni the first native speaker of Albanian to become a
Knight of Malta? This seems quite possible, though it would require an
exhaustive search of the previous records to prove it. What can be said,
though, is that there was already a partly Albanian or at least symbolically Albanian presence in the Order when he joined it. Costantino
Castriota – whose surname declared his connection with Gjergj Kastriota, also known as Skanderbeg – had become a Knight in 1561, and
had played a prominent role during the siege four years later. At a

crucial stage during the prolonged Ottoman assault on the outpost of
Sant'Elmo, when the Knights defending it had sent a desperate message
to de Valette saying that further resistance was impossible, Castriota
was one of three Knights sent by the Grand Master to report on the
situation there; the other two concluded that the fort could not be held,
but he disagreed, and volunteered to lead a new contingent of Knights
and soldiers to man it. Cannily, de Valette let it be known that he would
accept this offer, and that the existing defenders would be free to leave,
but that if they did so they would be regarded as cowards. As a result,
the defenders stayed in place, and held Sant'Elmo for another two
weeks. By his bravado Castriota may have guaranteed the deaths of
those proud Knights, but he probably also saved the Order from total
defeat.[19]

Costantino Castriota's behaviour was perhaps influenced by the fact
that he bore the name of one of the most famous military heroes of
recent history, even though he could not claim to be descended from
him. Some of Skanderbeg's children had settled in Italy after his death,
and the family name was so highly honoured that even people related
to him only by cousinage and marriage were pleased to adopt it. In
Costantino's case, the relationship was quite distant. He was an illegitimate son of Alfonso Granai, the Marchese (Marquis) of Atripalda, and
Alfonso's father had been the son of Bernardo Granai or Branai, the son
of one of Skanderbeg's most important Albanian companions in arms,
Conte Vrana. Alfonso's mother was a cousin of the mother of Skanderbeg, and it was to honour that connection that Alfonso and his brothers
also adopted the 'Castriota' surname. The Albanian link still resonated
quite strongly in Alfonso's generation: Alfonso not only led a force of
local stradiots but also maintained an active spy network in Albania
and Greece, and his brother Giovanni, Duke of Ferrandina, is known to
have spoken Albanian. The connection mattered to people on the Albanian side too. In 1532 the leaders of the Himarë region of Albania wrote
to Alfonso, addressing him as 'captain of Himarë and of Albania'; and
in 1551, when a Habsburg agent (from the city of Bar) went to Rodon
in Albania for a secret meeting of local notables who were planning an
anti-Ottoman revolt, one of the men he encountered there was 'Dimitro
Massi, son of the late Andrea Massi, who was a relative of the much
lamented Marchese of Atripalda'.[20]

Costantino Castriota kept up some Albanian connections of his own.
He corresponded with the so-called Prince of Macedonia, Arianitto Arianiti, a commander of papal troops in Rome, whose grandfather had

been an organizer of anti-Ottoman resistance in Albania and a key supporter of Skanderbeg; and one of the witnesses consulted by the Order
about his noble status was Costantino Musacchi, a member of another
aristocratic Albanian family which had settled in the Kingdom of
Naples. It is not known whether Castriota (who had a literary career as
well as a military one, producing several belle-lettristic works in elegant
Italian) actually spoke any Albanian. But although he described himself
as a Neapolitan, the suggestion, made by one modern historian, that he
had no awareness of his Albanian origin seems very unlikely – after all,
his very name proclaimed it. He was in Malta in 1566, when he was
fined for drilling newly recruited soldiers too severely (the Grand Master stepped in and paid the fine, saying that although he was a 'capricious'
character, he had done great service during the siege); he was presumably there when Gasparo Bruni was inducted; he was given a position
in Valletta in 1569, and was still resident there in 1581. So although
Gasparo, as an Albanian-speaker born in Albanian territory, was an
oddity in the Order, it seems likely that the Knights of Malta during
this period had, thanks to Castriota, some reason to associate Albanian ancestry with the qualities they most prized: martial valour and
daring.[21]

It is hard to judge what Gasparo's motives might have been for this
great change in his life. Religious faith may well have played a part (he
was, after all, the brother of an archbishop); but on the other hand there
were many Knights, especially young ones, who took their religious
duties very lightly indeed. Disciplinary decrees of 1567–8 condemned
the wearing of fancy clothes ornamented with gold and silver thread,
firing arquebuses for amusement after sunset, and playing bowls during
the times of Mass or the Sunday sermon. During that period a group of
young Spanish Knights were accused of singing satirical songs, both
about senior Knights and about the ladies of Malta; at the moment
when their formal indictment was being drawn up, they barged into the
Council chamber, seized the pen from the hand of the Vice-Chancellor
of the Order and threw his ink-pots out of the window. This organization was not something to join in pursuit of a purely religious vocation.
Nor was becoming a Knight a natural step for an ambitious subject of
Venice; although some Venetian families kept up long-standing connections with the Order, the government generally discouraged its citizens
from applying.[22]

A more likely explanation is that Gasparo had been encouraged to
take this step by the Papacy – which, as we shall see, swiftly became

involved in his deployment as a Knight, and would take charge of much
of the rest of his career. Perhaps, while performing more services after
the purchase of those three horses, he had visited Rome and been talent-
spotted by one of the secretaries of state, or even by the Pope himself.
Pius V, who was elected in January 1566, was a crusader in every fibre
of his being, and men of fighting spirit who had some detailed knowledge of the Ottoman world were just the sort of people he wanted.
Three decades later the Venetian writer Lazaro Soranzo would write, in
his treatise on the Ottoman Empire and how to resist it, of the need for
men who were familiar with the territory, knew local languages, had
judgement, credit and intelligence, and were keen to defend Christendom. Giving examples of the employment of such people, he noted that
'Pius V summoned from Ulcinj Fra Gasparo Bruni, commendatore of
the Order of St John of Jerusalem, in order to make use of him, both in
the fleet prepared against the Ottomans and in other important matters
pertaining to that war.' This might refer only to the events of 1570 (the
first year of the war against the Ottomans), when Gasparo was indeed
summoned to join the fleet; but the claim could be a more general
one – written, so many years later, without chronological precision – that
related also to his initial employment in 1567. And this evidence has
real importance since, as we shall see, Soranzo must have derived his
information here directly from Gasparo's son.[23]

Less than two weeks after his entry into the Order, Gasparo Bruni
was sent on an important mission. In the summer of 1567 the Grand
Master had learned from the Order's 'amici' in Istanbul (literally,
'friends' – a word used in the world of sixteenth-century espionage to
mean trusted informants) that the new Sultan, Selim II, was planning to
send out a major naval expedition in the following spring. This seemed
very likely, since Selim was in the process of winding down the Ottoman–
Habsburg land war begun by his father, Süleyman, in the previous year;
two Habsburg peace envoys arrived in Istanbul in August 1567. Even
before then, Venetian intelligence had noted intensive work on building
new galleys in the Istanbul Arsenal. The ports of Libya and Tunisia,
reportedly, had also received large orders for biscotto from the Ottoman government. With his Order still heavily depleted and his new city
only just begun, the Grand Master feared a fresh assault which his
Knights would not be able to withstand. On 24 October he wrote a
document saying that he had sure news of Ottoman preparations from
'the letters of many people, and envoys, and our spies'; that day he sent

a 'bull' (formal decree) to the Priors of Spain and Portugal, requiring them to send money to strengthen Malta's defences, and explaining that 'every day letters arrive saying that Selim is preparing a much more powerful fleet and a much more numerous army to invade this island.' On 1 November, as we have seen, he made a general appeal to the nobility of France, Spain and Portugal; at the same time he sent out ten Knights to recruit soldiers. And on 11 November he despatched three senior Knights as ambassadors to the Pope and the Kings of France and Spain; they were all to go first to Rome, where the Pope would add his own letters to those two kings, pleading for help.[24]

Travelling with them to Rome was Gasparo Bruni, with a special assignment of his own. In the words of the first historian of the Order, Giacomo Bosio (who himself became the Order's agent in Rome in 1574): 'Fra Gasparo Bruni, an Albanian, was also sent by the Grand Master to reside in the city of Dubrovnik, to receive the letters which came from the "amici" in Istanbul, who normally wrote to the Grand Master in cipher.' Why had the Grand Master selected for such a sensitive task this hitherto unknown and untested man, who had been a Knight for just a few days? It is hard to avoid the conclusion that his employment in this role already had papal approval, being probably a papal initiative in the first place.[25]

By 6 December Gasparo was in Rome, and on that day the Pope wrote a formal 'breve' or letter to the government of Dubrovnik:

> Beloved sons, greetings. I am sending to you the bearer of this letter, my beloved son Gasparo Bruni, for the sake of certain affairs of mine, and of the Apostolic See. I have instructed him that, if need be, he should ask you in my name for your help and favour. For although I do not doubt that, for the sake of your habitual and particular reverence and devotion towards me and the Apostolic See, you will assist the said Gasparo promptly and generously, nevertheless I want you to be fully assured that any exertion or assistance towards him would be very highly appreciated by me; and, when opportunity arises, I shall liberally reward you for your obedience in this matter.[26]

That was a strong recommendation, but also a rather unspecific one, so far as the actual purpose of Gasparo's mission was concerned; and it notably failed to mention that he was a Knight of Malta, or even that he had any connection with that Order. Also noteworthy is the fact that the Ragusan authorities, who were normally so proud of receiving papal

breves that they copied them out in honorific large script into their official records, preserved no trace of this one; indeed, its original text is
not extant in their archive, although many others are. The Ragusans
were extremely well informed, and must quickly have discovered the
real nature of Gasparo Bruni's employment, if they did not know it even
before he arrived. In deference to the Pope, they could not reject or
expel him; but the fact is that his arrival must have placed them in an
extremely awkward position.[27]

To explain this, it is necessary to say a little more about the peculiar
status of this small but highly prosperous Adriatic city-state. Its wealth
came originally from being an export centre for commodities from the
Balkan interior, especially the silver and lead of Bosnia and Kosovo.
When the Ottomans took over the Balkans, they understood that the
presence of this trading city, with its active network of merchants
throughout the region, was advantageous to them; so they allowed it to
continue to run its own affairs and govern its own small strip of coastal
territory, never subjecting it to direct conquest. In 1442 Sultan Murad II
confirmed that in return for an annual gift of 1,000 ducats from
Dubrovnik, he would give its merchants a preferential customs rate and
would respect the laws and liberties of the city. Over the next half-
century, however, this 'gift' was both increased in quantity (to 12,500
ducats) and increasingly interpreted by the Ottomans as *haraç* – an
annual tax paid by the non-Muslim inhabitants of a territory which had
been acquired by the empire by an agreement or treaty. So far as the
Ragusans were concerned, paying a tribute of this kind did not involve
acknowledging an ultimate political authority; and they had good reason to think so, since at various times both Venice and Austria made
similar annual tribute payments to Istanbul. Yet in the eyes of the Sultans, Dubrovnik was an integral part of the 'well-protected domains' (to
use the official Ottoman term) of their empire. The Sultans accepted
that this Christian city-state did have its own laws, its own administration and its own rulers; in this it was not exceptional, since three much
larger European territories – the Romanian principalities of Transylvania, Wallachia and Moldavia – enjoyed similar autonomy within the
Ottoman system. Dubrovnik's relationship with Istanbul was significantly looser than theirs, with the result that it could continue to present
itself to the rest of Christendom (and even, apparently, to itself) as an
independent state that just happened to have a close commercial and
political relationship with the Ottoman Empire – like Venice, so to
speak, only more so. But the reality was that, unlike Venice, it was

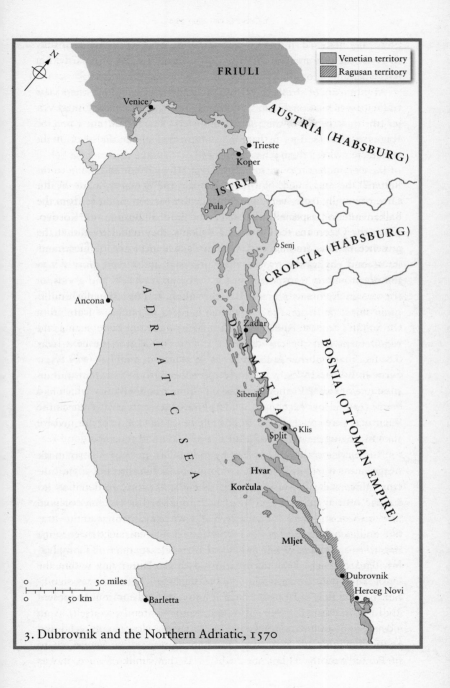

FRIULI

Venetian territory
Ragusan territory

Venice

AUSTRIA (HABSBURG)

Trieste
Koper
ISTRIA
Pula

Senj

CROATIA (HABSBURG)

Ancona

A D R I A T I C   S E A

D A L M A T I A

Zadar

BOSNIA (OTTOMAN EMPIRE)

Šibenik

Klis
Split

Hvar
Korčula

Mljet

Dubrovnik
Herceg Novi

0   50 miles
0   50 km

Barletta

3. Dubrovnik and the Northern Adriatic, 1570

physically hemmed in by Ottoman territory, it had no serious capacity to resist the Ottomans militarily, and it depended not just partly, but overwhelmingly, on the Ottoman lands for its supply of food.[28]

At moments of stress, the Ottoman authorities could put their view of the power-relationship in stark terms. In August 1568 the Grand Vizier (the most senior of the Sultan's ministers) flew into a rage when the Ragusan ambassadors in Istanbul complained about the level of the tribute, and asked them what right they had to make demands on behalf of the city, its territory or its inhabitants: 'Does it not all belong to the Sultan?', he exclaimed. Normally, though, the demands made by the Ottoman régime were very light. The most important difference between Dubrovnik and the Romanian lands was that the Ragusans did not supply military forces to the Ottoman Empire; nor were they required to let any Ottoman soldiers be stationed on their land or even pass through it. Beyond paying the tribute, their practical duties were mostly very minor: providing transportation for Ottoman travellers and goods, or for foreign diplomats accredited to the sultan, and occasionally sending grain-ships, or (from 1580 onwards) cargoes of pitch, to Istanbul at the Sultan's request. And some duties were purely symbolic, such as the requirement that the city celebrate major Ottoman victories in war. The fact that Dubrovnik could act as an almost neutral half-way house between East and West was clearly appreciated by the Ottoman authorities: one of the tasks they gave the city quite frequently was to act as a venue for prisoner exchanges. And its liminal status was also relevant to what was perhaps the most important practical task it performed for the Ottomans: the supply of information and intelligence.[29]

This service was highly valued by the sultans. In 1541 Süleyman the Magnificent wrote to Dubrovnik: 'do not cease to write and submit the true information that appears and that circulates ... in detail to my Court.' And again in 1547: 'you shall not interrupt the flow of your information, and shall not cease to find out from the troops of the dust-like infidels and from their fleet what in fact their absurd thoughts and intuitions are about.' While that last demand clearly referred to military intelligence, much of the information sent from Dubrovnik to Istanbul was general political news, the value of which was not that it was secret, but that the European network of Ragusan merchants could supply it ahead of any other system of transmission. So, for example, in April 1568 the government of Dubrovnik resolved to write to the authorities in Istanbul with the latest news about an agreement between the King of France and the Huguenots; and in December of that year, when sending a letter (in Italian) full of recent news to its own ambassadors in Istanbul, it decided to enclose a translation 'in the Serbian language', for the benefit of the Grand Vizier, Mehmed Sokollu (Sokolović). But sometimes the intelligence it sent was sensitive, and potentially damaging to Christian states. In August 1565, while the fate of Malta hung in the balance and the Viceroy of Sicily, García de Toledo, gathered his relief force, a Habsburg agent in Dubrovnik reported that news from Messina came there every ten days, 'particularly regarding what Signor Don García, General of His Majesty, does ... When he washes his face, soon the news of it arrives here, and then a Turk leaves the city, carrying the news to Constantinople.' In September 1568, similarly, the Ragusans gave the Grand Vizier precise information about the size and location of the Spanish fleet. Dubrovnik did not cease to perform this service after the Ottoman–Venetian war got under way in 1570: it sent the Sultan details of the Venetian fleet's numbers and movements in the summer of that year, it informed him about the Spanish fleet in 1571, and it wrote again about the movements of the naval commander Don John in 1572. The Ragusans were well aware of the value of this kind of intelligence-giving to the Ottoman state. In 1590 their ambassadors in Istanbul told the Grand Vizier: 'We pay two tributes, not just one, in view of the large and constant expenditures we make in maintaining people in every part of the world, in order to know what is being done and discussed, so that we can then inform the Ottoman government about it.' And they quoted what another vizier, Ferhad Pasha, had recently said to them: 'The Sultan does not need your tribute, as you are poor, but he does need to be informed by you every day of the affairs of the world, so take care to do him that service.'[30]

An intelligence agency is not ultimately to be relied on, however, if it is at the same time supplying intelligence to one's enemies; and that was what Dubrovnik was also doing. As loyal sons of the Church the Ragusans sent information regularly to Rome, and from 1551 onwards they transmitted a steady stream of news about the Ottoman Empire, including military intelligence, to the Spanish authorities in Naples. (Spain's good will mattered for a special reason to the Ragusans: as the ruler of southern Italy it was a major power in the Adriatic region, and therefore a much-needed counterweight to Dubrovnik's often hostile rival, Venice.) At the same time, Dubrovnik's position as a communication hub between East and West made it a natural destination for the intelligence agents of various Christian powers. In the 1530s one prominent Ragusan patrician was working for Spain, while the Archbishop of Dubrovnik,

an Italian from Milan, was active on behalf of the King of France; and
for much of the century there was a network of Venetian intelligence-
gatherers in the city, even though Venice was the one power whose
agents the Ragusans tried consistently to exclude.[31]

Such was the general state of play when, in 1566, Dubrovnik received
some shocking news. The son of the commander of the fortress at Barletta (a port in the Spanish-governed territory of Apulia) had gone to
Istanbul, converted to Islam, and denounced the Ragusans for sending
intelligence reports to Naples – a matter about which he was very well
informed, as they had passed through his father's hands. This coincided
with the enthronement of the new Sultan, Selim II; the privileges of
Dubrovnik had to be renewed by each sultan on his accession, and there
was suddenly a risk of serious harm to its traditional rights. So on 11
November 1566 the Ragusan government issued a stern decree: henceforth no one would send any news or information to the West; members
of the government, if found to be doing so, would be fined 1,000 ducats;
ordinary citizens would be executed; if a foreigner did it, the Senate
would decide what action to take; and no private person was to travel
to the West without the government's permission. This was no cosmetic
exercise to lull the Ottomans – it was meant very seriously. In June 1567
a member of the government was found to have infringed this law, and
was condemned to eight years' exile, with the proviso that if he set foot
on Ragusan soil he would be fined 1,000 ducats and lose all his patrician rights. When the Viceroy of Naples sent a new agent, the government
of Dubrovnik expelled the man; and when the Viceroy protested, it
decided, on 4 October 1567, to send a special envoy to explain why it
simply could not allow such a person to reside in the city. Twelve days
later it issued another decree, restating the penalties of the previous one.
It declared that 'if any foreigner here in our city and dominion should
have presumed and had the audacity to transmit such news to any
prince or indeed to his ministers, or to other private individuals, or
should have received or delivered such letters', he must be strictly inves-
tigated; no foreigner was to send ships of any kind with such news, or
people bearing news, 'without the knowledge and express permission of
the Magnificent Rector and his Council'.[32]

It was thus with extraordinarily bad timing that the Grand Master of
Malta and the Pope should have sent Gasparo Bruni to Dubrovnik, as
an intelligence agent, within just a few weeks of the promulgation of
that decree. As there is no mention of him in the Ragusan records, it is
impossible to say how he was received, but we can be sure that it was

his papal credentials that made all the difference; for Dubrovnik very much appreciated the fact that the Pope was whole-heartedly pro-Ragusan. In the following summer, when there were real fears in the city that the Ottomans would send their fleet to seize Dubrovnik by force, it was the Pope who offered to send them soldiers. They also knew that the Pope was the only person who might be able to persuade other Christian powers to come to their aid. So, however reluctantly, Gasparo Bruni was accepted there. The account given in Bosio's history of the Order makes it clear that he did stay in Dubrovnik for quite a long time, and that he was able to do his work: 'the said cavaliere Bruni had the job of sending mail frigates [small, swift oared vessels], whenever necessary, and taking delivery of the spies, and the intelligence reports, that came from Istanbul and went there, without sparing any expense or effort in the matter.' Bosio appears to have seen some of the reports from Istanbul; he noted that they were written in cipher and addressed on the outside to 'Vittorio Belforte', meaning 'victorious fine fortress' – a not very subtle allusion to the Order's military success in 1565 and its building of Valletta. But none of these documents appears to have survived. From other evidence we have some indications of the kind of information that was transmitted in this way. Some of it involved counter-espionage; in December 1567, for example (just before Gasparo's arrival in Dubrovnik), the Grand Master informed the Spanish authorities of the activities of three brothers, Muslims from Malaga, of whom one was in Istanbul, and one was working as an Ottoman spy in the presidio of La Goletta, an important Spanish stronghold just outside Tunis. Mostly, though, the concern was with discovering Ottoman strategic plans and military intentions.[33]

The few details given by Bosio concentrate on the much-feared threat of an Ottoman intervention to help the Moriscos of Spain; this was becoming a major security concern for the Spanish authorities just at the time when Gasparo Bruni took up his duties in Dubrovnik. The Moriscos were people who had been converted from Islam to Christianity, at least in official terms – but in reality the 'conversions' had been perfunctory and/or forcible, so that a great many Moriscos were in fact crypto-Muslims. In late 1566 Philip II of Spain prepared a decree that was calculated to destroy, with brutal thoroughness, the remnants of Islamic culture among them all. Moorish dress, music and dancing were to be banned, bathhouses destroyed, the Arabic language abandoned, and all Arabic books burnt within three years. The decree came into effect on 1 January 1568, and well-grounded rumours soon began to

circulate of preparations by radical Moriscos for a full-scale rebellion.
In April the authorities in Granada intercepted a letter from one rebel to
the corsair leader Uluç Ali in Algiers; and shortly afterwards Uluç Ali
was appointed *beylerbeyi* (provincial governor) of Algiers by the Sultan.
While the Spanish government had long been fearful of sporadic contacts between its own Muslims and the North African corsairs (whose
ranks did contain many embittered Spanish Muslim émigrés), it was
much more worried by the thought of a rebellion on its soil being
backed up by an Ottoman expeditionary force that would also com-
prise a large corsair fleet; the prospect of a full-scale Muslim *reconquista*
of southern Spain was a genuine fear. And when the long-expected
Morisco rebellion did break out in December 1568, leading to a lengthy
and bloody war in the region of Granada, the fear of such intervention
could only seem more well-grounded, as many volunteer fighters did
come from North Africa, and Ottoman policy-makers seriously discussed going to the Moriscos' aid.[34]

The Grand Master, Jean de Valette, died at the end of July 1568.
According to Bosio, he had been sending vital information to Philip II,
having been 'secretly informed by letters in cipher from the spies whom
he kept in Istanbul on regular salaries, who penetrated and got knowledge of the negotiations of the ruler of Algiers, and of other captains of
the Moors of Barbary, with the Ottoman government, when they begged
and pleaded with the Sultan to give support, help and encouragement to
the people of Granada'. Just one of de Valette's agents can be identified:
Giovanni Barelli. He was a Venetian subject from a noble family of
Corfu (in Greek: 'Varelēs'), members of which were active in the grain
trade and prominent in the Greek community in Venice. When he was
made a 'Knight of Grace' by de Valette in 1566 he was actually described
as 'from Constantinople', which suggests that he had been living there
as a merchant; and in late 1569, when he was volunteering to go on
another mission there for the King of Spain, it was noted that de Valette
had previously made an arrangement via Barelli 'with two leading Ottomans, whose job is to govern and direct the entire Arsenal, to burn all
the Sultan's ships'. Even a Knight of Malta, an openly avowed enemy of
the Sultan, could visit Istanbul and other places in the Ottoman Empire
if he were engaged (ostensibly, at least) in organizing the ransom or
exchange of captives; as we shall see, Barelli would do this on subsequent occasions. So it seems quite likely that reports written by him,
among others, passed through the hands of Gasparo Bruni during this
period. Whether Gasparo used his own family and mercantile connec-

tions to develop a more local intelligence network of his own, extending to such places as the Ottoman port of Vlorë, is not known. All that we do know, from Bosio, is that Philip II thanked the Grand Master for the reports he had sent, which, he said, had greatly helped him in his fight against the Moriscos.[35]

Today we look on the plight of the Moriscos with much sympathy – even though the methods they adopted in their revolt were sometimes brutal, and despite the fact that, in hindsight, it is obvious that they could not succeed. But Gasparo Bruni had his own particular experiences and loyalties. He was a subject of Venice, from a frontier zone where the Ottomans represented a constant threat; he was a member of a Roman Catholic order, owing special loyalty to the Pope; and, through that order, he also owed allegiance to the King of Spain. Within a short time, those three powers would come together in a Holy League, creating a combined navy to oppose the Ottoman fleet; and Gasparo Bruni would have an even more important role to play.

6

Galleys and Geopolitics

On 25 March 1570 the Ottoman *çavuş* Kubad arrived in Venice. A *çavuş* was an imperial messenger, but his status was higher than that description might imply; within the Ottoman Empire these were the men who transmitted the will of the Sultan directly to officials, and outside it they were much used as envoys and *ad hoc* ambassadors. Kubad knew Venice well. He had been there on missions in 1567 and 1569; he was made very welcome each time, and on the latter occasion he enjoyed a special concert for violin and harpsichord in his lodgings on the Giudecca. Kubad also enjoyed a cordial friendship with one of the city's chief translators of Oriental languages, the Cypriot Michele Membré – who, like him, came from a Circassian family. But on this occasion he had a sombre duty to perform. He presented the Doge and government of Venice with an ultimatum, issued by Sultan Selim II in the first half of February, which demanded that they hand over the entire island of Cyprus to the Ottoman Empire. If they did, the inhabitants would have their security guaranteed, being free to stay or leave with their possessions, and Venice's trading privileges in the empire would be renewed. If they did not, the two states would be at war, and the Sultan would conquer the island by force. This news was profoundly unwelcome, but it did not come as a surprise; the Venetian representative in Istanbul, Marcantonio Barbaro, had been told of the Sultan's intentions on 29 January, and had managed to transmit the information to Venice, despite a vigorous attempt by the Ottomans to intercept all his outgoing mail. For more than a month before Kubad's arrival, therefore, the Venetian government had been making energetic preparations for war. Its response to Kubad's ultimatum was a largely ceremonial affair. A solemn vote was held in the Senate; of the 220 who voted, 199 were in favour of war, 5 were against, and there were 16 annulled votes. The Doge gave a brief and unyielding written reply to the Sultan, for

Kubad to take back to Istanbul; its proud tone, and deliberate omission of many of the Sultan's grand titles, would cause intense irritation there. On 27 March, which was Easter Monday, the Doge gave Girolamo Zane his baton as captain-general of the sea, and Zane then proceeded to his galley with the war-standard of St Mark. Three days later he set off with a small fleet of galleys; there were 2,000 soldiers aboard, and their destination was Cyprus.[1]

The Sultan's ultimatum began with a litany of grievances. Venice had been illegally building castles in Dalmatia, beyond the previously agreed borders; on two recent occasions Christian corsairs had been fed, watered and protected by Venice when they used Cyprus as a base to attack Egyptian shipping; Venetians killed *levend*s when they captured them, instead of delivering them to the Ottomans; the Venetians had wrongly condemned and executed the father of an Ottoman Christian or Jewish merchant; and an Ottoman Muslim merchant called Hacı Ali who traded at Kotor was not compensated after he had been robbed at sea. This was a rag-bag of complaints, hardly justifying an all-out war of conquest – with the exception of the details about the use of Cyprus by Christian corsairs, which suggested an underlying parallel between this case and that of Rhodes in 1522. In his conversations in Istanbul, the representative Marcantonio Barbaro also encountered another component of the Ottoman claim, which was that Cyprus had long ago been under Muslim rule (briefly), and that there were remains of mosques on the island, which meant that the Sultan was under a religious duty to recover it for Islam. This too was, rather obviously, an argument cooked up to justify a decision that had already been taken on other grounds. So what were the real reasons for the targeting of Cyprus? Popular belief, then and for centuries thereafter, attributed the decision to the sinister influence of Joseph Nasi, a rich Jewish merchant who was a confidant of Sultan Selim. In one version of the story the motive was to obtain the wines of Cyprus for the Sultan (Nasi being already the tax-farmer for all wine imports to the Ottoman Empire, and Selim 'the Sot' being notoriously fond of his drink), while in another it was Nasi's hatred of Venice. Neither stands up to serious scrutiny, and there is no evidence that the Cyprus policy was directed by Nasi, even though it is true that he knew the Sultan and the senior viziers. The foreign policy of the Ottoman Empire in this period was driven not by personal whims but by some large-scale geostrategic concerns; it is to these that we must look for the underlying reasons for Selim's decision.[2]

Since the Ottoman takeover of Syria and Egypt in 1516–17, the most important axis in the empire was that connecting Istanbul and Cairo. Over the following 50 years, it was the huge revenues from Egypt that kept the imperial finances in surplus and, in effect, funded the Ottomans' many campaigns elsewhere. Moreover, the fact that the Sultan had at the same time become the guardian of the Holy Places of Mecca and Medina stimulated Ottoman ambitions to enjoy leadership of the Islamic world; it also made the Sultan responsible for the safety of the Hajj (the pilgrimage to Mecca), which for many Muslims began with a sea voyage to Egypt. These two facts alone would have sufficed, probably, to make the elimination of Christian rule in Cyprus a long-term goal; for the island was in practice (as the ultimatum said) a resort for corsairs, and could in theory become a stepping-stone for an offensive Western campaign against the Ottoman heartlands.[3]

But there was a larger background to Ottoman thinking on this issue. During those same 50 years, the Ottomans had made great efforts to extend their power and influence southwards and south-eastwards from Egypt, through the Red Sea, out into the Indian Ocean, and even further, as far as the Muslim Sultanate of Aceh in Sumatra. Their aims were partly commercial, to stop the valuable East Indian trade from being diverted by their new rivals in that region, the Portuguese; but commerce and politics went hand in hand here, as success in this strategy would greatly weaken the Ottomans' major eastern rival and enemy, Persia. The scale of Ottoman ambitions was astonishing. In 1568 the Grand Vizier, Mehmed Sokollu, ordered the governor of Egypt to commission a study by architects and engineers of the feasibility of digging a Suez canal. One year later, troubled by the advance of Muscovite power towards the Caspian Sea, he sent an army to seize the town of Astrakhan, on the Volga delta, and to begin excavating another canal, linking the Volga and the Don. That Astrakhan campaign was a failure on both counts. But if it had succeeded, and if the canal had been dug, the Ottomans would have achieved several policy goals: creating a security cordon between their Russian and Persian enemies; gaining direct access to their distant anti-Persian Sunni allies in Central Asia, the Uzbeks; and acquiring the capacity to send galleys to the Caspian, thus developing a naval route towards the Persian heartlands. This would not only bring about the conditions for a giant anti-Persian pincer movement; it would also set up a route for Central Asian Muslims to come on an Ottoman-guarded Hajj all the way from the shores of the Caspian to Mecca, creating long-term bonds of amity and possible allegiance. For both of these schemes, the maritime passage down the eastern side of the Mediterranean, past Cyprus, formed a central component. One modern study argues that Mehmed Sokollu was reluctant to attack Cyprus because he preferred to concentrate on his grand geopolitical plans. Yet the evidence of his reluctance is rather uncertain; he may have given some Western diplomats the impression that he was opposed to the war, but he was, after all, a consummate bluffer and dissembler. Even if he was against the attack in 1570, that was surely just a disagreement about tactics and timing; his own long-term policy demanded the closing of this strategic loophole.[4]

Several factors of a more short-term kind may well have played a part. In 1566 the Ottoman admiral Piyale Pasha (a Croat, originally from Ragusan territory) seized not only the Genoese-ruled island of Chios, but also four of the small Greek islands which had been owned by Venetian noble families since the thirteenth century. His action, although economically damaging to the Ottomans where Chios was concerned (it harmed a valuable trading entrepôt), was very well received in Istanbul. This may have weighed in the minds of the Sultan's advisers three years later; after the disastrous Astrakhan venture of 1569, and with another problematic campaign in the Yemen still hanging in the balance, they probably wished for a popular success of the same kind. What made the Cyprus campaign a practical option was the establishment of a new treaty with the Holy Roman Emperor in early 1568, which freed up men and matériel for a new European operation. Another relevant consideration was the fact that in the latter part of 1569, when the decision to target Cyprus was finally taken, Spain was bogged down in two conflicts: the war against the Moriscos in the mountains of Andalusia, and the Dutch Revolt. Some observers might have thought that this increased the chances of a direct Ottoman attack on Spain, in support of the Moriscos; but although Mehmed Sokollu dropped many hints about that – presumably for the benefit of Western ears – he was a good enough strategist to rule out any major invasion of a powerful state at the opposite end of the Mediterranean. The significance of Spain's military distractions was, rather, that they made a Venetian maritime target much more attractive; the Ottomans were confident that they could defeat a Venetian navy on its own, but not if it were combined with a Spanish fleet, and Spain was surely too preoccupied now to go to Venice's aid. Their confidence can only have increased when they learned that most of the munitions stores at the Venetian Arsenal were destroyed by fire in mid-September 1569. But although there may have been some opportunism in the decision to aim the next campaign at Cyprus, the general tendency of Ottoman policy in that direction had already been obvious for some time. It was clear enough, certainly, to the Knights of Malta, who wisely liquidated their estates on Cyprus in 1567.[5]

In retrospect the Venetians seem to have been slow to see where Ottoman policy was heading. That is partly because they had experienced false alarms in the past, and partly because they were equally worried about the Ottomans' intentions for Crete and Corfu. It is true that there was a current of opinion among them which held that the Ottoman Empire would not start a war against Venice because it would lose the huge customs duties paid by Venetian traders; the classic statement of this argument had been made by a Venetian 'bailo' in Istanbul (in effect, the resident ambassador, though also with powers over the Venetian community there), Marin Cavalli, on his return to Venice in 1560, when he went so far as to claim that a year's boycott of the Levantine trade by Venice would leave the Ottoman Empire begging for assistance. But at the same time he had also expressed an even more fundamental Venetian principle: 'we should proceed, with great dexterity and prudence, between the two paths – of making war and not making war against them. Most certainly we should not make war, but not on the grounds that they think us incapable of it.' Now, despite the fact that Venetian–Ottoman trade had boomed in the 1560s, the time had come to show that Venice was indeed capable of making war.[6]

Venice knew that it could and should fight, but it was also aware that victory against the Ottoman Empire was unlikely unless it had allies fighting with it. The most important of these, in the Mediterranean arena, was Spain. As late as January 1570, the Venetians' policy – as transmitted to their ambassador at Madrid – was merely to prod King Philip II in a more anti-Ottoman direction by warning him of the Sultan's plans to aid the Moriscos; it was only in early March, as Kubad rapidly approached, that they told their ambassador to seek a formal alliance. So, up until the last minute, Venice was in the grip of its traditional policy of coldness towards Spain as a Mediterranean power. There were many reasons for such an attitude. They included the failure of the last alliance with Spain in the anti-Ottoman war of 1537–40, and specifically the fact that it was the commander of the Spanish fleet, Andrea Doria, who was blamed for the defeat at Preveza. (That Doria belonged to the leading Genoese family did not help; the republic of Genoa, which had become a satellite of Spain in the late 1520s, was a traditional competitor and enemy of Venice.) Spain also represented, via the Kingdom of Naples which it ruled, a potential rival to Venice in any future carve-up of Balkan territory. Since Spain had virtually no commercial links with the Ottomans, it was happy to sponsor corsairing activities – not just of the Knights of Malta, but of other so-called 'Ponentini' or Westerners – which put much strain on Venetian–Ottoman relations. And above all there was the fear that if Venice became involved in a formal anti-Ottoman alliance with Spain, its forces would be diverted to the defence, or even the offensive pursuit, of Spanish interests in North Africa, which were of no strategic concern to Venice. What was of great concern to Venice, in normal circumstances, was Ottoman good will. So it was in keeping with the logic of their situation that, as recently as 1568, the Venetians had actually been sending the Ottomans information about the movements of the Spanish fleet.[7]

Venetian *froideur* towards Madrid was fully reciprocated. In Spanish eyes, the Venetians were unprincipled collaborators with the enemy, who would not lift a finger to aid even a defensive operation against the Ottomans unless it brought them profit. As a papal diplomat at the court of Philip II reported in April 1570: 'there are few friendly feelings towards the Venetians, as they have never been willing to go to the help of others, and there is very little confidence that they will not gladly drop out of the war whenever they can, leaving the task to others and thinking only of their own interests.' Throughout the 1550s and 1560s Spain's sporadic warfare in North Africa had continued – without the slightest help from the Venetians – against the Ottomans and their protégés. After Hayreddin Barbarossa's death, another talented corsair commander had come to the fore, Turgud Reis (*reis* means captain). With his help the Ottomans took Tripoli in 1551; an energetic ruler of Algiers, Salih Reis, captured the Spanish presidio of Bougie in 1555; and Spanish forces suffered a huge defeat near Oran in 1559. Then came a much greater disaster for the Spanish. At the end of that year the King of Spain sent a combined fleet of approximately 50 warships, including Genoese, Maltese and papal vessels, to seize the Tunisian island of Djerba; the aim was to make it a military base for further campaigns, which would drive out Turgud Reis from Tripoli and establish control over the Tunisian and Libyan coasts. It is estimated that 12,000 soldiers went out on this expedition, and only a very few returned. Many died of disease; the rest were killed or captured in a counter-attack by a large Ottoman fleet under Piyale Pasha and Turgud Reis, which sank many of the Christian galleys, took possession of roughly 20 of the rest (including the papal flagship), and pinned down the remnants of the Spanish force in an 82-day siege which ended when they were beginning to die of thirst. The Ottomans built a 'pyramid of skulls' on Djerba to mark this victory; it was still to be seen in the nineteenth century. At this deeply traumatic moment in Spanish military history, Venice expressed commiserations, but offered no help of any kind, and instructed its own naval commanders to steer clear of any encounters with the Ottoman fleet.[8]

If there was a long-term benefit to the Spanish from this disaster, it was the fact that it forced them to devote more energies to building up their naval resources, especially in southern Italy. The fleet of the Kingdom of Naples had been growing in the 1550s; now efforts were redoubled to increase the number of ships. Other shipyards were also put to work, such as that of Barcelona; by the mid-1560s the numbers of galleys had been restored to their pre-Djerba levels, though Don García still had to exercise great caution in risking an operation against the Ottoman fleet at Malta in 1565. Much of the Spanish ship-building programme was funded by special ecclesiastical taxes agreed by the Pope, which paid tithes and other sums to the Spanish crown from the revenues and properties of the Church in Spain. There were some tensions between Rome and Madrid over these; the papal suspicion was that the monies were not always used for religious purposes – i.e. war against heretics and infidels. But when Pius V became Pope in January 1566 he was quick to renew the largest tax, known as the 'subsidio'; for Pius was obsessed with the idea of an anti-Ottoman crusade, and he knew that Spanish naval power would have to play a vital role in it.[9]

From Spain's point of view, the main purpose of its fleet was to pursue anti-Ottoman and anti-corsair policies in North Africa and the western Mediterranean. It had no interest in going to the defence of the distant island of Cyprus. But it would not be true to say that the Spanish authorities had no interest in any part of the Ottomans' European domains. The sheer closeness of south-eastern Italy to the Balkans meant that some strategic interests were always potentially in play. As we have seen, Costantino Castriota's father, the Marchese of Atripalda, had an intelligence network in the Balkans. (His informants included several Christian Albanians and a Muslim called Mustafa.) This was not a private hobby; as governor of the territories of Otranto and Bari in the 1530s he sent regular reports to the Viceroy in Naples, summarizing the Levantine news he had obtained, and the work would be continued by his very active successor in the 1550s. Nor had people in the Kingdom of Naples forgotten their previous dynasties' involvements in the Balkans, which could be taken to generate some ghostly legal claims. An interesting text survives, drawn up by a government lawyer in Naples in 1567, discussing the ancient possessions of the kings of Naples in the former Byzantine Empire. Among other things, it argued that the 'duchy' of Durrës had passed from the Norman ruler Robert Guiscard to the Angevin kings of Naples, and cited a fourteenth-century document declaring that 'the whole kingdom and province of Albania' had belonged to King Charles I of Naples. On the duchy of Durrës the lawyer commented, significantly: 'I believe that it includes Vlorë.' His text was not a policy proposal for an invasion of Ottoman Albania, but it indicated a line of justification for possible future use; and that future was in fact not very far away. Within a few years, as we shall see, the King of Spain's half-brother, Don John of Austria, would be pursuing strategic connections with the Balkans, and even possible territorial plans, quite seriously. Yet although in one sense this tendency might align Spanish interests more closely with Venetian endeavours against the Ottomans, it had the effect of making them potential competitors for the same Balkan prizes. Venice had not forgotten the unpleasant experience of 1538, when, albeit for only a short time, the newly cap-tured stronghold of Herceg Novi was occupied by an Imperial (in effect, Spanish) garrison – a very unwelcome insertion of a Habsburg wedge between Venetian Dalmatia and Venetian Albania.[10]

Pius V's repeated pleas to King Philip II of Spain to join in a Holy League had fallen on stony ground in the late 1560s, and Spanish atti-tudes towards Venice were just part of the reason for this. Some of Philip's advisers believed that a Catholic alliance, set up by an ascetic crusader-pope whose zeal was directed as much against heretics as against infidels, would be a red rag to European Protestantism – especially in the Netherlands, where Spain's official line was that it was suppressing a secular rebellion, and not (as Philip himself increasingly felt) fighting a religious war. Also, in 1570 Philip still had the Morisco revolt to deal with; he had put his charismatic young half-brother, Don John of Austria, in charge, but the fighting would not be over until late in the year. Nevertheless, the Pope's special envoy received a sympa-thetic hearing when he arrived at the Spanish court in April, and less than a month later, on 16 May, Philip wrote to Pius V agreeing in prin-ciple to join a league with Venice, the Papacy and others. Why this major – and, for a notoriously ruminative decision-maker, rapid – change of position? It is possible that some of Mehmed Sokollu's bluff and misdirection may have backfired rather badly; Spain did take seriously reports from its own intelligence agents suggesting that the Sultan might also send a fleet to attack the Spanish coast. The papal envoy's fundamental argument, that neither Venice nor Spain could defeat the Ottomans in the Mediterranean without the other's help, was hard to gainsay. His confidential assurance that the Pope would favour Spain over Venice must have been welcome, as was the Pope's offer of a massive increase in ecclesiastical taxes. And no less important was the fact that Philip's acceptance came with a key condition: that the league would be directed not only against the Sultan but also against the rulers of Tripoli, Tunis and Algiers. Philip cannot seriously have expected Venice to divert its own forces, in the current circumstances, to those targets, but he wanted the assurance that if he diverted his own, no one could accuse him of abandoning the fundamental purposes of the league.[11]

Pius V was enough of an idealist to hope that other major Catholic powers might be persuaded to join. But there was little chance of that. The Holy Roman Emperor, Maximilian, had secured a peace treaty with the Ottomans, valid for eight years, as recently as 1568. He was sceptical about the feasibility of the league, he had his own disagreements with the Pope, and he had also had quite frosty dealings with his cousin Philip during 1569. Poland's relations with the Ottomans – their direct territorial neighbours – were too sensitive for any Polish ruler to contemplate going to war for the sake of a quarrel in the far-off Mediterranean. (However, with undying optimism Pius V did tell the papal nuncio in Poland to go to Moscow to persuade Ivan the Terrible to join the league – and, for good measure, to offer him priests to 'instruct his peoples in the ceremonies of Rome'. The nuncio had to explain to Pius that Ivan had just made peace with the Sultan, and that there was not the slightest chance of converting him to Catholicism.) France had been an ally of the Ottomans, on and off, since the 1530s; although the young king and his mother (Charles IX and Catherine de' Medici) were trying to distance themselves a little from the Sultan at this time, in order to placate the more hard-line Catholic elements in France's own internal conflicts, the long-term position had not changed. In a letter to Catherine de' Medici, the French Ambassador in Venice put a very reasonable gloss on French policy, reminding her that François I – the founder of the Franco-Ottoman alliance – had said that he would not join a defensive league to help those who had always acted as his enemies, and that this applied to any league called offensive that was in reality defensive. If all Christendom united for a genuine offensive league to regain territories conquered by the Ottomans, of course France would wish to take part. But in the present circumstances joining would be pointless, serving merely to alienate Ottoman good will for no lasting benefit; Cyprus was already as good as lost, and the Venetians would eventually make peace with the Sultan to save their other possessions.[12]

Those were arguments which could all be made in public. Less openly avowable was the basic idea that France needed the active engagement of the Ottomans in order, as a French envoy to Istanbul would put it in 1572, 'to act as a counterweight to the excessive power of the house of Austria [i.e. the Habsburgs]'. Any development that reduced the power of the Austrian or Spanish Habsburgs was potentially good for France, and this principle applied especially to Spanish defeats in the Mediterranean and North Africa. As a later French ambassador to Istanbul, François Savary de Brèves, would write, referring to the King of Spain: 'when we have been at war with him, and when he has used his forces and means to stir up our internal quarrels, it is certain that he would have fared altogether differently were it not for the trouble and expense that he was obliged to go to in order to defend his sea-coasts, both the Italian ones and the Spanish.' In particular, de Brèves noted, the territories of Algiers and Tunis 'are so necessary and important to him, because if he had them he could pass from Spain to Italy with full security and total freedom, and as a result he would be much better enabled to make himself master of the whole of Italy' – another long-standing concern of the French. Counter-Reformation religious zeal may have burnt fiercely in the heart of Pius V, and it was certainly not absent from that of Philip II; but in the minds of French policy-makers it was wholly eclipsed by political calculations of this kind.[13]

So the most that Pius V could muster for his grand coalition, in addition to Venice and Spain, was a handful of minor powers. The participation of Malta – a separate polity, though not quite a sovereign state – was of course guaranteed. Genoa came automatically as a Spanish satellite, and the Duke of Savoy was also firmly within the orbit of Spain. More problematic was Cosimo de' Medici, the ruler of Tuscany. In theory he too was strictly beholden to the Spanish crown; after his forces had conquered the neighbouring territory of Siena in 1555 it had been transferred first to the Holy Roman Emperor and then, via Philip II, back to Cosimo, who thus held it as a vassal of Spain, with military obligations attached. But Cosimo had greater ambitions. In 1561–2 he set up his own order of maritime knights, the Cavalieri di Santo Stefano, partly modelled on the Knights of Malta, in order to play a larger role on the Mediterranean stage. Pius V was impressed by this, and by his other signs of religious enthusiasm (loans of money and men to France to combat the Huguenots), and in 1569 he granted Cosimo, unilaterally, the title of 'Grand Duke'. The fury and rancour this caused in both Philip II and the Emperor Maximilian, on whom the bestowal of such a title should have depended, were on a scale almost unimaginable to modern minds. Maximilian seriously contemplated a punitive military expedition against Florence, and Philip was against admitting Cosimo to the anti-Ottoman league at all, lest the formal documentation should use his new title. Tuscan galleys would eventually play an important role in the war against the Ottomans, but only after many long and wearisome diplomatic tussles between Spain and the Papacy.[14]

From the early summer of 1570, then, negotiators in Rome were beginning to hammer out the details of a deal between Venice, the Pope and Philip II; the formal negotiations would begin on 1 July. The template they had to work on was the Holy League of 1538, which had been based on a simple formula for who contributed what, but there were many other matters to settle, including vital ones such as a Spanish pledge to provide grain from Sicily for the Venetian forces. Agreeing all the details of a Holy League was a long-drawn-out task, the practical aim of which was to set up a combined operation for the following year's campaigning season, beginning in the spring of 1571. But in the mean time the Ottoman invasion force was massing for the attack on Cyprus. So, from late April 1570 onwards, the Pope was also hard at work organizing military support for Venice. It was the traditional practice of the Venetians to maintain quite a small active navy in peacetime, keeping a large reserve of galleys mothballed but, in principle, ready for use. In the 1560s there might be roughly 50 galleys at sea, and more than 70 laid up. To activate the reserved galleys required fitting them with all kinds of equipment, and finding the large numbers of sailors, rowers and soldiers that would man them – which in turn meant getting the money to pay for it all. At first, Pius V grandly offered to man and equip 24 galleys; but the scale of the operation proved too daunting (despite his strenuous efforts to raise funds, including the appointment of sixteen new cardinals who had to pay handsomely for the privilege), so the figure was reduced to twelve. This force was to constitute a distinct papal fleet, working alongside the Venetian fleet under its own papal commander – a plan which pleased the Venetians, as they thought it would give them a sympathetic high-ranking figure to turn to in case of any disagreements with the commander of the Spanish forces.[15]

The task of this papal commander would in fact be diplomatic as much as military; the combined fleet of the 1570 campaign was to be an *ad hoc* alliance of forces, not the navy of a formal Holy League, and therefore might be vulnerable to political and psychological frictions of all kinds. Pius needed someone with tact, intelligence, courtliness and considerable personal authority. The person he chose was the 35-year-old Marcantonio Colonna, Duke of Paliano, a leading member of Rome's greatest noble family. This was an ideal choice in almost every respect. Colonna was a subject of the Pope, and – despite a serious clash with the previous pope but one, which had led to the temporary confiscation of his lands – a loyal son of the Church; one close relative, also called Marcantonio, was a cardinal. But Colonna's large estates in southern Italy also made him a feudal subject of the King of Spain, to whom he was distantly related (via his mother, a granddaughter of King Ferdinand of Aragon), and he had spent some time at the Spanish royal court in the 1560s. While the Venetians may have had some misgivings about his Spanish links, their more serious worry was that he was not an experienced naval commander. He was certainly no such thing by the standards of that maritime republic; but in the papal territories he was one of the few people with relevant experience. In the early 1560s, after the papal navy had been completely lost at Djerba, Colonna's small private fleet had been the only one available to protect the coast (and, probably, engage in corsairing activities). In 1563, or shortly before, he bought three galleys from Cardinal Borromeo; he sold one of them to a Genoese ship-owner, but was still active as a galley-owner in 1565, and his fleet is believed to have contained seven galleys at its peak. It is also thought that he had spent some time on board one of his ships – enough, at least, to get his sea-legs.[16]

On Sunday 11 June 1570, in a ceremony in the Sistine Chapel, Pius V gave Marcantonio Colonna his commission and handed to him the papal battle-standard. Losing no time, Colonna began that day to issue 'patenti' or formal commissions to the men who would captain the twelve galleys. (As commander of the entire fleet, he would have larger responsibilities, and would need someone under him to be captain of his flagship.) The list of names contained several prominent members of the Roman nobility, including his brother-in-law Orazio Orsini, his brother Prospero Colonna and his cousin Pompeo Colonna – an experienced fighting man, who had pursued a military career partly to earn papal forgiveness for the fact that he had murdered his own mother-in-law. Being captain of a galley was a different matter from being captain of the soldiers who would be embarked on it, but in three cases Marcantonio Colonna did combine the two jobs. One of these double captains was the man he chose to be captain of his flagship, Cencio (short for 'Innocenzo') Capizucchi, a member of an old Roman aristocratic family that was loyal to the Colonnas; his commission was also issued on 11 June. Five days later Colonna left Rome for Ancona, where one of his captains had already brought eight of the galleys from Venice, with a view to completing their fitting-out and crewing in that port. After four days in Ancona he went on to Venice, to obtain the other four galleys, and to discuss the planned campaign with the authorities there. While he was in that city he received assistance from the papal nuncio, who reported on 6 and 13 July that Colonna had made most of the advance payments for the rowers promised by Venice, and that he had taken 'the very greatest care' over the whole business; once the rowers had been provided, Colonna left Venice with the four galleys on 23 July, to rejoin the others at Ancona. For his own flagship, the Venetians had taken out of storage a famous vessel, a large experimental quinquereme (with five men on a bench, each with his own oar), designed by a classically-minded naval architect in 1529; it had performed well in the past, but by now it had been laid up for 30 years.[17]

Soon after his arrival in Venice, Colonna received a letter from Gasparo Bruni, written in Ancona on 30 June. 'This morning', it began, 'I arrived here with an armed frigate, with 36 men and 3 officers.' He had spoken to Pompeo Colonna, who told him to write immediately to Marcantonio with details of the naval officers he had brought with him – which he now did. But he added: 'by this letter I also wanted humbly to inform you of this: that I have already sent word to Venice, to a nephew of mine, a son of the cavaliere Bruti, that he should find a way of getting the officers for me; therefore I am telling you that he should also let Your Excellency know what kind of officers he has found.' Evidently this message crossed with one from his nephew in Venice reporting that he had failed to obtain any suitable men – which is hardly surprising, since the Venetian authorities had been scouring their own city and territory for weeks in search of people with naval and military skills. So on the following day Gasparo Bruni wrote again to Colonna, to say that 'as my nephew has not provided officers', he had chosen 12 of the 36 men to serve as sailors, and the other 24 to be officers.[18]

There is much that is unclear here, including the identity of the nephew (as we have seen, Antonio Bruti had nine sons). It is not easy to say where Gasparo had come from on his frigate; that was the type of vessel he had used for sending his despatches from Dubrovnik, but it is very unlikely that the Ragusan authorities would have allowed him actively to recruit men from among their subjects. Perhaps he had travelled from another port on the eastern coast of the Papal States, though it is not clear why he should have been used as a recruiter in a place where he had no special contacts of his own. It is not impossible that he had come from Ulcinj, having been summoned – as Lazaro Soranzo would later write – by the Pope. What is noteworthy, though, is that when Gasparo signed both of these letters he gave himself the title of 'governor [i.e. captain] of a galley of the Pope'. It seems that he had been sent to Ancona, by a papal command, with the specific purpose of taking over the naval captaincy of the flagship from Capizucchi. A possible scenario might be that Capizucchi had decided to confine himself to the infantry captaincy, but that he had communicated this decision to the Pope just after Colonna's departure from Rome on 16 June; the Pope had then swiftly instructed Bruni to go to Ancona as his replacement, gathering sailors and ship's officers as he did so. But the timetable for this seems very tight, if it did involve communicating with Bruni in Ulcinj – from where, in addition, he would have had to send a message to his nephew that reached Venice before the end of June. So perhaps Bruni's services had been activated by the Pope, in some capacity at least, already, bringing him from the eastern to the western shore of the Adriatic.[19]

Marcantonio Colonna reached Ancona by 26 July. This was probably his first meeting with Gasparo Bruni, who quickly slipped into his role as Colonna's right-hand man. An order to the other captains of that date, issued by Colonna on his flagship, says: 'The cavaliere Fra Gaspar Bruno [sic] will tell you in my name what orders you have for loading various essential provisions; so do not fail to obey them.' (There followed a list, with quantities given: biscotto, wine, rice, flour, oil, vinegar, sardines, etc.) The very next day, Gasparo received his formal 'patente' from Colonna, appointing him captain of the flagship:

> Because it befits the service of His Holiness, and our own honour and satisfaction, to have a person of experience and valour in charge of our flagship, and knowing that such qualities are to be found in the magnificent and much honoured signore Fra Gaspar Bruno, Knight of Jerusalem, given the trustworthy account we have received of his virtue and merits, we have chosen him, as by this commission we choose and depute him, to

be governor and captain of our said galley with all the usual authority, power, honours, importance, prerogatives and emoluments; therefore we expressly order that all the men who serve on that said galley should obey, respect and revere him as they do me.[20]

However, these were mostly formulaic phrases, to be found in other commissions of this kind; so there is not much here to shed light on the true origins of Gasparo's selection for this highly prestigious position. What we can be sure of is that this was not an appointment Colonna would ever regret; he would retain Gasparo as the captain of his flagship for three campaigning seasons.

Gasparo Bruni spent just over five weeks in Ancona, from his arrival on 30 June to the departure of the fleet in early August; he was an energetic man, and there was plenty of work to do, making the arrangements for the complex fighting machines that were early modern Mediterranean galleys. A typical galley was 41–43 metres long and 5–6 metres wide; usually it would have 24 or 25 benches of oars on each side, with three, four or five men to an oar. (The practice of giving each rower an individual oar, as embodied in Colonna's antique flagship, had been gradually abandoned in the first half of the sixteenth century – the new system was simpler, and required only one of the men on each oar to have real skill.) A larger type of galley, known as a 'lanterna' or lantern galley, would have more benches, and got its name from the three big glass lanterns that were suspended at its stern, for leading and signalling to other galleys at night; these larger vessels were often used as flagships. Every galley had two masts with lateen (triangular) sails. Long-distance travel depended primarily on wind-power, but the oarsmen could keep up a steady pace of 3–4 knots over many hours, if needed; when pursuing or escaping from the enemy, a speed of 12 knots was attainable, but only for a maximum of 20 minutes, causing extreme exhaustion even in hardened crews.[21]

Physically, at least, a galley was dominated by its benches of rowers, which took up most of the deck. On the galleys of Venice the rowers had traditionally been free men from the republic's own territories, especially people from Dalmatia and the Greek islands, who had plenty of maritime experience. Over time, as conditions worsened and the rate of pay lagged behind, this supply became inadequate, and many of the benches were filled with 'forzati', meaning 'forced men' – usually convicts from the prisons. Other states, such as Tuscany, the Papal States and Naples, made use of these, and of free men (known as 'buonavoglie' or 'volunteers', who were described by one source as 'vagabond people, whom hunger or gambling has forced to sell themselves, or wager themselves, into the galley'); Naples was especially dependent on 'forzati', who formed roughly 60 per cent of its rowers. But those other states also had access to a kind of manpower which the Venetians, because of their agreements with the Ottomans, could not use: Ottoman slaves. In the Neapolitan fleet slaves made up 11 per cent of the rowers in 1571, and the figure would rise to 21 per cent by the end of that decade. A handbook written by an officer of the papal navy in 1601 advised that 'Moors [i.e. North Africans] taken from their foists are better than those who are taken from the land.' But many came from elsewhere in the Ottoman Empire: a list of the slave rowers on one of the Borromeo galleys acquired by Colonna includes 'Hüseyin son of İbrahim, of Durrës', 'Hüseyin son of Mustafa, of Vlorë', 'Pervan son of Hasan, of Durrës' and 'Hasan son of Ali, of Bosnia'. The Knights of Malta relied almost entirely on slaves they had seized. This made for cheap labour, but could entail other problems. It was said to have contributed to the major disaster the Knights suffered in late July 1570, when three of their galleys were captured at sea by the corsair commander Uluç Ali: apparently the Muslim rowers, anticipating liberation, simply stopped rowing, so that the Knights were reduced to taking the oars themselves even though their own numbers were utterly inadequate for the task. And, as both Christian and Ottoman naval commanders well knew, volunteers and convicts could also be trusted with weapons in battle (the former as loyal subjects, the latter as violent men who were motivated by a promise of pardon), whereas slaves could not.[22]

In this as in so many other areas of Mediterranean maritime practice, there were strong similarities between the two sides. While the North African corsairs depended, like their Maltese counterparts, on slave rowers, the Ottoman fleet used a mixture of free men (typically recruited by a conscription system which demanded a fixed number of rowers per village), prisoners and slaves. The account given by one Westerner who served as a slave on an Ottoman galley can stand for the experiences of many thousands: 'thus fettered hand and foot the captive must row day and night, unless there is a gale, till the skin on the body is scorched like that of a singed hog, and cracks from the heat. The sweat flows into the eyes and steeps the whole body, whence arises excessive agony ... When the superintendent of the boat sees anyone taking breath, and resting, he immediately beats him ... till he makes abundance of bloody weals over his whole body.' If there was any difference between Christian and

Ottoman practice, it was, according to one Western observer in the 1580s, that 'as I have seen and experienced, the slaves on the Ottoman galleys have much better conditions than those on the Christian or Spanish galleys; for when I travelled by galley from Naples to Sicily, I myself was shocked by how tyrannically and horribly the slaves were treated.'[23]

In addition to the rowers, there were two other bodies of men. A war galley would typically carry 100 soldiers, under their own commander. And there was also the crew of sailors with their officers. Serving under a ship's captain such as Gasparo Bruni was a 'comito' (approximately: first lieutenant, but with special responsibility for directing the rowers), with a 'sottocomito' under him; a secretary or purser, who kept accounts and supervised the stores; a pilot; three master-workmen, such as ship's carpenters, each with an assistant; six bombardiers to operate the ship's artillery; a chaplain; a barber-surgeon; eight first-class sailors and thirty ordinary sailors. Those details come from a list of the monthly wages for a galley (ranging from 7 scudi per month for the comito to 2.5 for an ordinary sailor), drawn up for Colonna in late June; the flagship probably had a larger complement, in view of its greater importance and physical size. One addition was made on 12 August, when a special commission was issued by Colonna to 'Francesco of Korčula' as an expert adviser on navigation.[24]

There would also have been several 'nobili in poppa' or 'gentiluomini di poppa' (literally, nobles or gentlemen of the stern), men of some social standing who could perform officerial tasks. This was the capacity in which young men might, by the favour of a captain or ship-owner, receive their first experience of naval life. A report commissioned by the Vatican on the moral failings of the Christian fleet in 1571 had a whole section on the sin of sodomy, singling out the presence of these young 'gentlemen' as a key part of the problem, since the practice made it possible for officers to bring their favourite youths aboard: 'they pretend that this is done to give them experience, and that they are their relatives; it is true that they get experience, of a devilish kind; they are not their relatives but their wives.' The other main concern of that report was blasphemy. As the author put it, 'on a galley it seems that people forget the normal way of blaspheming on land, and adopt a new way, at which hell itself is thunderstruck.' The moral tone of life on board the papal fleet was a matter of real concern to Pius V: while Colonna and Gasparo Bruni were at Ancona, he sent a Jesuit to distribute copies of a little treatise by an influential Jesuit writer, Antonio Possevino, entitled

Il soldato christiano ('The Christian Soldier'). Published in the previous year, this was a Counter-Reformation classic which would go through many editions; it was aimed at inspiring Catholic soldiers to fight against heretics and infidels, urging them to purge themselves of their sins in order to do so. The book had a special section on blasphemy, but it also inveighed against duelling, 'slander, lying, luxury, greed, gambling and ostentation'. Its suggestion that soldiers should spend their time reading the works of St Augustine, Orosius and Bede does seem rather unrealistic, even without taking into account the conditions of life on a crowded war galley. There is no reason to think that either Colonna or Bruni was particularly lax in his Christian devotion or general moral standards (leaving aside the small matter of Bruni's illegitimate son, a common phenomenon for a man of his class); but on the other hand, since Colonna's personal accounts while at Ancona include an entry for money spent on gambling, we may assume that he did not meet all of Possevino's high standards either.[25]

In early August the small papal fleet left Ancona and travelled down the coast to Otranto, on the heel of Italy, reaching it on the 6th. On his arrival Colonna found a letter from Philip II, saying that he had ordered his own naval commander, Gian Andrea Doria (a great-nephew of Andrea Doria), to proceed there with part of the Spanish fleet. A previous negotiation between Philip and the Pope had resulted in a Spanish commitment to treat Colonna as the overall commander of their combined forces; but in this letter Philip requested that when it came to the actual fighting, Colonna should take Doria's advice in all things. While it was certainly true that Doria had much more naval experience, this was a troubling request, since it carried the possible implication that Philip had told Doria that he expected his advice to prevail – in which case, Colonna's position as overall commander would be fatally undermined. In fact, the secret instructions Philip had given to Doria were worse than that: he had told him to proceed with caution, and to aim above all at preserving his galleys (which meant, if possible, not risking them in battle at all). Doria felt the awkwardness of his situation, but he was happy to follow the drift of Philip's policy, not least because twelve of the galleys in his fleet were his own property, rented out to the King, and he would not be adequately compensated if they were lost in battle. So he sailed with deliberate slowness from Sicily to Otranto, making Colonna wait there for two weeks. When he finally arrived, Colonna concealed his irritation at this obvious foot-dragging and treated him with special honour. But at the council of war which Colonna then held, he found that the Genoese commander was sceptical about undertaking any action in the eastern Mediterranean. At the most Doria accepted, somewhat grudgingly, that the combined fleet should proceed to Crete, and consider its options once it got there. On 22 August the two forces, totalling 61 galleys, left Otranto; they arrived at Souda (Ital.: Suda), a port with a fine natural harbour on the north-western side of Crete, on the last day of that month.[26]

They were greeted by Girolamo Zane, the naval commander who had left Venice with the standard of St Mark just after the rejection of Kubad's ultimatum. Things had not gone well for him since his departure. He had been obliged to spend two months in Zadar, waiting for other elements of his fleet and infantry force to assemble, and while he was there a serious outbreak of typhus began to ravage his men. In late June he took his fleet of 70 galleys to Corfu, where he waited again for more forces to arrive; during the month that he spent there, the deaths from typhus continued. (It was there that, as we have seen, Antonio Bruti's sons Jacomo and Marco joined the fleet, with their company of ten Albanian archers. Jacomo survived the campaign, but Marco Bruti disappears from the historical record at around this time; if he did not die during the following year at the Battle of Lepanto, he may well have fallen victim to typhus on a Venetian ship.)* Zane finally brought his galleys to Crete in early August. Hasty recruitment among the Cretan population could not make up for all the losses; although the addition of other squadrons would bring the total of Venetian warships to 148, they were badly undermanned. By early October Zane would put the total Venetian losses of rowers and soldiers from typhus and dysentery at over 20,000.[27]

On 1 September Marcantonio Colonna called a meeting of the commanders and selected senior officers (at the level of general command – not including ship's captains such as Gasparo Bruni) to discuss their options, and another high-level meeting was held two days later. We know quite a lot about these discussions, because subsequent bitter recriminations would give rise to several retrospective – and, no doubt, to some extent self-serving – accounts of them. Colonna, faithful to his master, the Pope, urged that the whole fleet proceed as soon as possible to attack the Ottoman fleet at Cyprus; he was supported by Zane and by one senior Spanish officer, and opposed not only by Doria

* See above, p. 53, and p. 458, n. 27.

but also by some of the Venetians.* With Doria insisting that he must start the homeward journey by the end of September, the wrangling continued until the 13th of that month, when Colonna finally persuaded his colleagues to set off in the direction of Cyprus. Doria managed to delay them a little further by demanding a formal review of the fleet at the eastern tip of Crete; this did reveal serious weaknesses in the manning of some ships, and several galleys were set aside, with their crews and soldiers distributed among the others. One of the papal vessels was 'disarmed' in this way; a disgruntled later memorandum by the papal commissary who accompanied the fleet complained that Colonna did this suddenly by means of 'an order he gave to a certain cavaliere Bruno of his', without taking proper account of the papally owned assets on board. The memorandum also recorded that at the time of departure, Colonna 'sent the cavaliere Bruno to notify each ship of its place in the order of sailing'; the commissary complained when he found that his own galley was in fifth place, and Colonna lost his temper, threatening him with his life. Marcantonio Colonna had clearly had enough pressures and frustrations to deal with, without having to put up with a status-obsessed ecclesiastical bureaucrat. At least Gasparo Bruni was a man he could rely on to get things done.[28]

As they departed eastwards on 17 September, their combined force came to a total of 192 warships. The allied commanders had quite good intelligence about the Ottoman fleet, and knew that it was smaller than theirs. There was also an Ottoman land army on Cyprus, which they understood to be engaged in the siege of Nicosia, the heavily fortified capital city at the heart of the island. If the allies had been quicker, and luckier, they might have been able to attack the Ottoman fleet at the time when its commander had sent many of its own soldiers to reinforce the land army at the siege. But luck was not on their side, and Doria's procrastinations had done their work. When Colonna and the other commanders left Crete they were unaware that Nicosia had in fact fallen to the Ottomans on 9 September. This news reached them on 21 September, by which time they had got as far as the little island of Kastellorizo, just off the Anatolian coast to the east of Rhodes. They were

---

* The commander of the Venetian infantry, Sforza Pallavicino, had an alternative plan: to attack the Dardanelles, heading for Istanbul, and thereby draw the Ottoman forces away from Cyprus. Although the choice of target was audacious, the general idea was not as wild as it may seem; as recently as late July, the Venetian government had told Zane that he could either engage with the Ottoman fleet at Cyprus or make a diversionary attack on 'some important place'.

now half-way on their voyage from Crete to Cyprus; but although the large fortified port of Famagusta was still holding out, they knew that the fall of Nicosia must change their plans decisively, as it would free large numbers of Ottoman soldiers for galley service. Only Zane was still in favour of proceeding to Cyprus, and he was outvoted. Some proposed an attack on Euboea (the former Venetian possession of Negroponte, off the eastern coast of mainland Greece); Doria rejected this, as it was too close to the Ottoman heartland, and airily suggested choosing some other target, such as Vlorë, Durrës or Herceg Novi. But when they met again a few days later at Karpathos (Ital.: Scarpanto), the island between Crete and Rhodes, he simply announced that he was taking his entire contingent back to Sicily forthwith. A bitter quarrel now broke out between Colonna and Doria, with the former insisting that he was in command of the whole fleet, and Doria refusing to obey him. Any further chances of combined operations were clearly at an end, so they all returned to Crete in a mood of intense mutual hostility. As they did so, a severe storm sank one Venetian galley and two of the papal ones; another papal vessel, captained by Domenico de' Massimi, was overwhelmed (together with three more Venetian galleys) by a storm while riding at anchor off the Cretan shore.[29]

For a few weeks the papal and Venetian commanders kept their fleets at Crete, organizing the redistribution of men and supplies, and arranging for an infantry force to stay there over the winter as the nucleus for a future expedition to Famagusta. On 24 October Gasparo Bruni wrote from Souda to Marcantonio Colonna, who had gone to the nearby city of Chania (Ital.: Canea). He reported that he had discussed with Zane the problem of redistributing men among the galleys, and that he was still waiting for a full register of Zane's troops. He had received Zane's instruction that Domenico de' Massimi was to go with 40 men on board a Dalmatian galley; and he added the rather cryptic information that he had given orders for Nicolò Centurione (a captain from a famous Genoese family) to be put in irons. He ended: 'I paid honour in Your Excellency's name to the General [Zane], who slept badly last night, and still suffers from a painful colic.' There were worse problems than that, however, awaiting these already tattered remnants of the allied expedition.[30]

The nautical handbook by Bartolomeo Crescentio summed up the standard Mediterranean wisdom as follows. 'From 24 September to 22 November sailing is not completely safe, but not completely dangerous; and in this period prudent rulers bring their fleets back into harbour';

the entire period from 23 November until 20 March was, on the other hand, 'extremely dangerous'. Colonna and Bruni were to find out the truth of these principles the hard way. They left Crete on 10 November, heading for Corfu. By the time they reached the island of Cephalonia, many of the soldiers and crew were dying of disease (probably typhus again); they spent some time there washing the galleys with vinegar and fumigating them, before moving on to Corfu, where Colonna decommissioned another of his ships. On 28 November they set off again, but were pinned by fierce northerly winds to the little port of Kassiopi (Ital.: Casopo), on the northern tip of the island of Corfu, for a month. When they managed to proceed from there to Kotor a new disaster struck: while sheltering from another powerful storm just in front of the city, their flagship was struck by lightning. With its old wood, preserved during the long years of storage by regular applications of pitch, the vessel went up like a torch. A later narrative, celebrating Colonna's achievements in a very laudatory way, stated that he personally released the rowers, took the papal standard, and was the last to leave the ship; but the account given by Bosio, historian of the Knights of Malta, specifies that Colonna was actually in the city of Kotor at the time. According to Bosio, the ship was destroyed 'but with all the men, standards and valuables saved by the effort and diligence of Fra Gasparo Bruni, who nevertheless was at extreme risk of being killed in the flames or in the water – insofar as, while he was on the galley, busying himself with rescue work, and with organizing the most important matters, he was forced by the flames to hurl himself into the sea'.[31]

Colonna and Bruni then borrowed a Venetian galley and proceeded up the coast, but the next night they were driven ashore and shipwrecked, a few miles from Dubrovnik, by another violent storm. They and their men took refuge for the rest of the night in a mill-house, whose inhabitants told them that there was a force of Ottoman soldiers nearby; they posted guards until dawn, when they returned briefly to the wreck in order to burn it, and then marched as swiftly as they could to Dubrovnik itself. According to one later account, the Ottomans demanded that they be handed over, but the Ragusan authorities 'denied knowing anything about them, keeping them hidden'; this sounds like a later embroidery (probably put about by the Ragusans themselves), as the arrival of such a large party could hardly be concealed. At any rate, they were safe in Dubrovnik, and among friends. Gasparo Bruni must have had many acquaintances from his recent prolonged stay in the city, and Marcantonio Colonna would have been given a special welcome as a representative, in effect, of the Pope. For the Ragusans' greatest fear, ever since the outbreak of hostilities in the spring, had been that Venice would use the war as a pretext to seize their city. Their envoy to Rome, a skilled diplomat called Francesco Gondola (Frano Gundulić), had begged the Pope for protection against the Venetians. In May he was able to report that when the Venetian Ambassador in Rome accused the Ragusans of being close allies and informants of the Ottomans, the Pope replied that they were not their allies, but merely people obliged by necessity to maintain amicable relations with them, as Venice itself had long tried to do. (And on the question of giving the Ottomans information, Gondola was able to point out that official documents by the Venetians showed that in the past they had done this too.) But this issue would not go away; in September the Ragusan government sent a letter to the Pope complaining of the 'calumnies' reported to them by Gondola, and Pius V was still defending Dubrovnik against Venetian criticisms during the negotiations over the Holy League in November. So Colonna was treated with honour and respect. On 2 January he was given, on credit, some of the equipment he needed to fit out a small vessel, and he was also loaned 1,011 gold scudi (which, as the Ragusans would remind him, he had still not repaid seven years later). That money was spent on pay and food for Colonna's men, and on the hire of a ship to take them to Ancona. He himself – with, presumably, his faithful captain Gasparo Bruni – also travelled to Ancona, and thence to Rome.[32]

No one had come out well from this expedition. Altogether, Colonna had laid aside or lost nine out of his twelve galleys. Many men had died of sickness, while there had been no combat of any kind. Cardinal Granvelle, Philip II's ablest and most cynical diplomatic agent, commented humorously that Colonna knew as little about naval affairs as he did. Colonna himself would later complain to Philip about another of Granvelle's reported *bons mots*: he had said that 'it doesn't mean much to say that the King can trust Marcantonio; he can trust his own sister even more, but still he wouldn't give her a military command.' But behind Granvelle's joking there lay a considerable amount of bad faith and, perhaps, bad conscience; for he must have been well aware that the fundamental reason for the failure of this campaign, and indeed for the lateness of Colonna's return voyage, with all its attendant risks, was that the whole enterprise had been sabotaged from the outset by Doria, acting on Philip's direct orders. This did not bode well for the formation of the Holy League, or for its campaign prospects in the following year.[33]

7

Rebellion and Ottoman Conquest

In the early months of 1570, even before the formal outbreak of the Ottoman–Venetian war, the *sancakbeyi*s of the Balkan hinterland began sending irregular cavalry forces to raid the Venetian territories on the eastern Adriatic coast – both Dalmatia and Venetian Albania. The city of Zadar, which had the largest inland area of its own, was particularly badly hit. These attacks, which consisted mainly of burning villages and seizing livestock and other property, do not seem to have been part of any proper strategy of territorial acquisition. The military aim was merely to force Venice to send soldiers to the region, thus reducing the number available for any expedition to Cyprus (and in this the Ottomans were successful: 1,000 men were quickly sent from Venice to Dalmatia). But there was also, clearly, a larger psychological purpose: to make life miserable for the Venetians, and to show them that they needed the amity of the Ottoman Empire for normal conditions to be possible throughout their own extended domains.[1]

This was a game that two could play, however. Not in the sense of mounting equivalent raids in the opposite direction: the local stradiot forces, which could engage in that sort of warfare, were too small, and were needed for defensive operations. But rather, Venice might retaliate in a way that similarly involved extending the conflict far beyond the island of Cyprus, and making conditions difficult for the Ottoman authorities in other parts of their empire. For there was one basic asymmetry between the two sides that could work to the Venetians' advantage. Venice did not rule over a Muslim population, but the Ottomans did have many Christian subjects, who might be persuaded to rise up in rebellion in order to acquire, or regain, a Christian ruler. (Even here, however, the situation was not black-and-white. Some of Venice's Orthodox Cypriot subjects did apparently welcome the overthrow of their Catholic feudal master, even though they had not plotted to bring it about, and there would be some local rumblings of pro-Ottoman revolt in Crete during this war.) In the circumstances, the only surprising thing is that it took Venice so long to adopt this strategy.[2]

A word of caution is needed when approaching the subject of anti-Ottoman revolts. Because the first phases of modern history-writing in every Balkan state, in the nineteenth and early twentieth centuries, were bound up with the process of acquiring independence from the Ottoman Empire, the national history of each country has focused eagerly – obsessively, even – on any past episodes that could be described as struggles for liberation from Ottoman rule. As a result, some things have been put in this category that do not belong there: the activities of gangs of brigands, for example, or tax rebellions that were aimed only at getting the authorities to restore the previous level of taxation. Large-scale peasant revolts, of the kind that afflicted many Western European societies, were very rare in the sixteenth-century Ottoman Balkans. Thanks to general economic growth, the relatively low level of feudal dues in the Ottoman system and the regional political stability that was guaranteed by imperial rule, the basic conditions of life ranged broadly from the tolerable to the positively good. Nevertheless, it is true that some people, in some places, were animated by what can be called political or politico-religious motives to engage in acts of rebellion.

In Ottoman Albania there were two main centres of resistance: the 'Dukagjin' territory of high mountains to the north and north-east of Shkodër, and a rugged stretch of the southern coast – lying mid-way between Vlorë and the Corfu Channel – known as Himarë. In these areas, while the Ottoman invasion had destroyed the previous structures of rule by regional lords, it had failed, thanks to the hostile terrain, to impose a viable system of administration of its own. The incentive to do so may not have been strong enough to outweigh the difficulties, given the low level of economic return that could be expected from such territories. To fill the vacuum, local power structures had developed, which had become robust and very hard to dislodge: a system of clans in the mountainous north, and a quasi-federation of villages, with what might be called quasi-clans, in Himarë. These areas developed a martial culture, necessary for self-defence in the absence of government-provided police or justice; and this, combined with a gradual growth in population that could not easily be sustained by the area's own agriculture and stock-breeding, led to raiding – and, on the coast of Himarë, some piracy. That in itself could cause serious clashes with the Ottoman authorities in the region. But what sparked large-scale rebellion was any

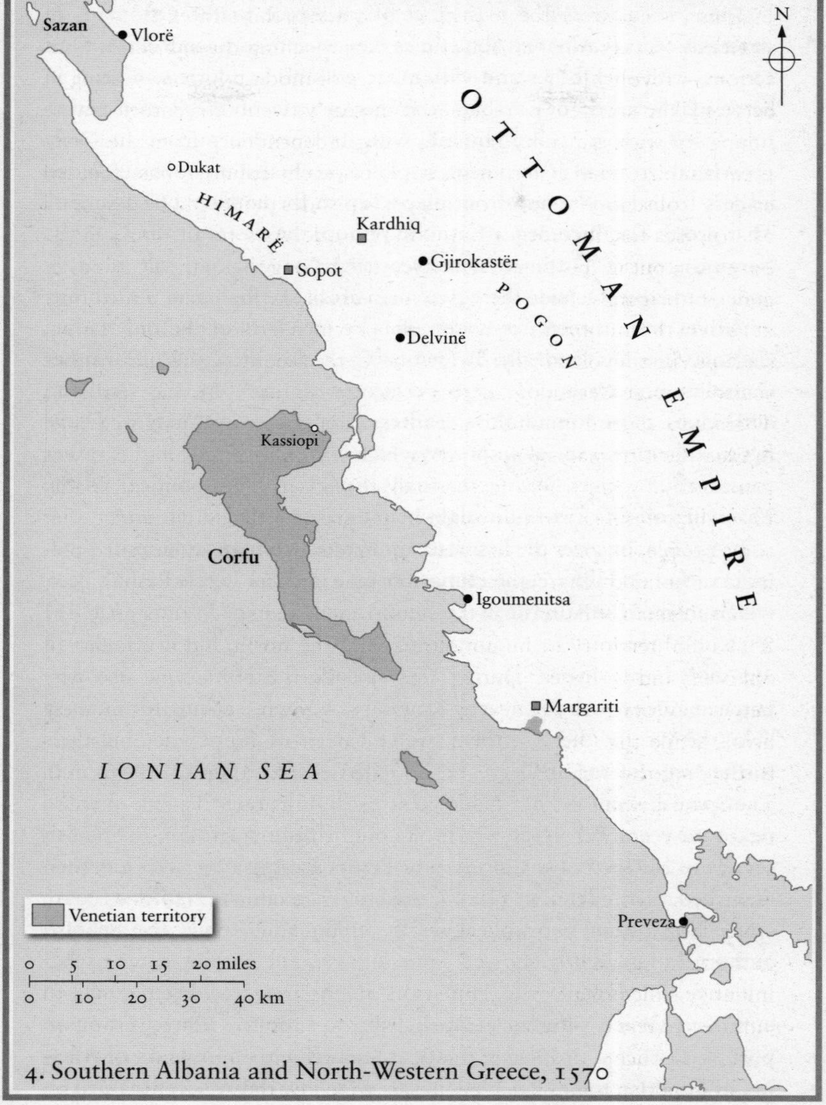

N
Sazan
Vlorë
OTTOMAN EMPIRE
Dukat
HIMARË
Kardhiq
Gjirokastër
Sopot
POGON
Delvinë
Kassiopi
Corfu
Igoumenitsa
Margariti
IONIAN SEA
Venetian territory
Preveza
0 5 10 15 20 miles
0 10 20 30 40 km

4. Southern Albania and North-Western Greece, 1570

attempt by those authorities to impose the sorts of taxation and military recruitment that were accepted as normal in most other areas.[3]

These, then, were the main foci of resistance to the Ottomans in sixteenth-century Albania. Sometimes they even tried to coordinate their actions, with each other and with other possible supporters in areas in between: the group of notables who met in 1551 on the Rodon peninsula (itself almost a mini-Himarë, with its seaborne raiding and only superficial Ottoman government) to plan a pro-Habsburg revolt included leaders from Himarë and from places 'up to the country of Dukagjin'. That group also included a Catholic bishop; the desire of the Catholic clergy to replace Ottoman with Neapolitan or Venetian rule is easily understandable. Outside these two main areas of Albania, anti-Ottoman initiatives were sometimes undertaken by members of the old leading Catholic families, and also by senior Orthodox clergy. While neither Catholics nor Orthodox were persecuted as such by the Ottoman authorities, those communities' leaders or representatives may well have felt that their own social authority, which was slow to fade in this rather conservative society, was increasingly dislocated from political power. Throwing off Ottoman rule might help to reverse that situation.[4]

In 1566, soon after the first attempt by the Ottomans to impose regular taxation on Himarë, the Himariots rose in arms. Piyale Pasha's fleet, which entered the Adriatic in the summer, sent an expeditionary force of 8–10,000 men into the mountains to quell the revolt, but it was driven out with heavy losses. During this episode the Himariots also despatched an envoy to the nearby Kingdom of Naples, asking for military help; the Viceroy did give them twelve barrels of gunpowder, but their further request for artillery and an experienced captain was ignored. The Spanish seem to have made no effort to maintain this link over the next four years. When the war broke out in 1570, a stradiot in Spanish service in Milan, Pietro Ciucciaro or Petros Tsountsaros (who has been described as an 'Albanian Vlach'), tried to reactivate the Naples–Himarë connection, using two colleagues in Milan and Rome; the Spanish authorities apparently showed some interest, but nothing came of this initiative. Meanwhile the Himariots themselves had been quick to approach Venice, offering in April 1570 to seize the nearby Ottoman port of Vlorë and proposing to act as 'escorts' for an invasion of Albania by Venetian forces. Such proposals were invariably accompanied by requests for large quantities of firearms and other munitions. That, presumably, is the reason why the Venetians did not act on the offer, though they expressed general encouragement.[5]

Two months later, however, the Venetian military governor of Corfu, the energetic 70-year-old General Sebastiano Venier, did send an infantry force, with artillery, to attack the fortress of Sopot (Ital.: Sopotò), in the southern part of Himarë. This was a medieval fort which the Ottomans had strengthened in the mid-sixteenth century; it had walls described as two palms thick (its ruins, near the village of Borsh, can be visited today), and it had been the only Ottoman position to hold out against the Himariot revolt in 1566. The Ottoman garrison fled, and Venier installed there a small Venetian force under a Greek or possibly Albanian officer, Emanuele Mormori, who had used his local knowledge to help plan and execute the attack. Encouraged by this success, Venier then launched a similar assault on another Ottoman fortress, Margariti (Alb.: Margëlliç), which lay about eight miles inland below the southern tip of Corfu; despite the deployment of 5,000 men and four large artillery pieces, he was unable to take it. Nevertheless, at a time in the Venetian–Ottoman war when nothing seemed to be going right for Venice, the small victory at Sopot in early June 1570 was a great boost to morale. It may also have helped to stimulate the policy which, up to that point, seems to have been only embryonic in the minds of the Venetian government, of encouraging revolts in the Ottoman territories of Albania.[6]

Soon after this, in the last days of June, another such episode occurred on the peninsula of Mani (Grk: Manē; Ital.: Maina), at the southern tip of the Peloponnese. This mountainous area had also been a very tough nut for the Ottomans to crack. The Maniots were similar to the Himariots in their recent history, social organization, way of life, and attitude to the Ottomans; there were also Albanian families among them, as there were in very many parts of the Peloponnese. After suppressing a rebellion in the Mani in 1568 (enslaving 200 women, children and old people, while the Maniot men retreated into the mountains), the Ottomans built a fortress at a place known – using a general term for the Mani peninsula – as Braccio di Maina (modern Porto Kagio). On the night of 29 June 1570 Marco Querini, the captain of Venice's Cretan squadron, who was bringing his galleys to Corfu to rendezvous with Zane, landed a detachment of arquebusiers to take a position overlooking the fort, and the next day he began bombarding it with his ships' artillery; unable to man their own guns under withering arquebus fire, the small garrison quickly surrendered. This stimulated a new general revolt in the Mani peninsula, which would continue for the next two years. Possibly the Venetians were acting here in response to specific requests from the Maniots; a self-styled representative of the Peloponnese, Gregory Malaxas, had appeared in Venice in April, asking for help. The general idea of raising a revolt in southern Greece was certainly not absent from the Venetians' minds. Two months earlier they had sent an agent, a Greek from the formerly Genoese-ruled island of Chios, to Istanbul to seek the help of the Orthodox Patriarch in organizing a large-scale rising in the Peloponnese, to be coordinated with a Venetian landing. Proposals of this kind were in the air: when Giovanni Barelli, the Corfiot-Venetian Knight of Malta, was sent to Istanbul in late 1569 on a mission for the King of Spain, one of his tasks was to talk to two of his contacts there who claimed to be able to raise 50,000 men in a southern Greek revolt. Yet there is little sign, at this stage, of such a strategy being seriously adopted by the Venetians. Querini's attack on Braccio di Maina looks quite opportunistic, even though it wisely focused on an area with a strong record of anti-Ottoman resistance.[7]

In the northern Albanian region the story is quite similar. There had been a large-scale rebellion in the mountainous Dukagjin area in 1565–6; the export trade from Shkodër had been completely paralysed by it. And in late 1568 there was another revolt in the same location, when the Ottomans tried to collect the poll-tax on non-Muslims. The strategic importance of this area was not in doubt; a major revolt there would not only pin down Ottoman forces, but also protect the landward approaches to Kotor, an important Venetian naval base. (Eventually, in late 1571, collaboration between rebels in the Dukagjin mountains and the authorities in Kotor was established, and it caused the Ottomans much disquiet.) Yet, for quite some time after the outbreak of the war, there was no Venetian strategy. Everything seems to have depended on local initiatives of various kinds. In the first half of 1570 there was little scope for any such initiative-taking, as the local Venetian officials struggled with such basic practical issues as the problem of feeding their people: as we have seen, the governor of Ulcinj complained to Dubrovnik in January that high grain prices were causing 'extreme misery' in his city, and in May the governor of Budva detained Antonio Bruti's consignment of wheat on its way to Venice.* In late May or early June the *sancakbeyi* of Dukagjin brought a force of 700 men to attack Ulcinj and Bar, but without artillery he had no chance of taking the cities, and at Ulcinj his men were routed by a sortie of stradiots – led presumably by their 28-year-old captain, Nicolò Bruni,

---

* Above, pp. 50, 53.

the nephew of Gasparo and Giovanni. At some point, before or soon after that attack, there was a much larger incursion by an Ottoman force, under the command of three *sancakbeyi*s, which spent its time burning villages and destroying property throughout the Venetian territory. Large numbers of country people took refuge within the walls of Ulcinj. Before long the city's stores of grain were almost exhausted, but conditions in the countryside were still too dangerous for anyone to try to harvest the crops that remained.[8]

Those last details come from a long and unusually interesting text, written in 1570 during the harvest-time – probably in July. Entitled 'An Account of Albania and its towns, rivers, mountains, lakes, plains, borders, etc.', it not only discusses the situation in Venetian Albania, but also ranges widely over the whole territory of Ottoman Albania, describing its economic resources, political organization and military preparedness. The text's comments on the resources of the country were clearly written by an experienced merchant: it discusses, for instance, the leather and silk produced in Elbasan and Berat, and the fine pitch brought from the Dukagjin mountains to the port of Lezhë, where 'I have seen it sold at three or four pounds' weight for one soldo [half a ducat].' There is also much emphasis on the production of grain, including the 'great quantities of wheat and millet' that were grown in the area between Ulcinj and Shkodër and sold secretly, because of the Ottomans' export ban. If Venice sent two or three armed galleys, it argued,

> the men of Ulcinj could go to Rodon, where they are received very amicably by those Albanians, in spite of the Ottoman war, because they do not fully obey the Ottomans, and they could get from Rodon all kinds of grain in large quantities, not only for the benefit of the people of Ulcinj but also in order to feed the city of Bar, which is virtually under siege because it does not lie on the coast, and to feed Budva, Kotor and Dalmatia, given that in peacetime we were obtaining 50,000 stari of all kinds of grain from the Gulf of the Drin to send to the city of Venice.[9]

The author had travelled widely: he reported, for example, that the water in the Ottoman military-administrative centre of Krujë was excellent 'to my taste'. He seems to have had some experience, or at least some memory, of the 1537–40 Venetian–Ottoman war. And he had a very practical turn of mind, especially where military matters were concerned. In his detailed account of the city of Ulcinj – the one place, it seems, with which he was most familiar – he gave a searching analysis of the strengths and weaknesses of the castle there, pointing out that the sea-facing side was the least secure part; it was at present in an 'extremely dangerous' state, but could be made 'unconquerable' if proper work were done on it. Above all, he analysed the military weakness of the Ottomans in Albania. Of the five *sancakbeyi*s, he wrote, those of Vlorë, Elbasan and Ohrid had left with all their spahis (military-feudal cavalry-men, who raised contingents of men from their own estates) to take part in the Cyprus campaign. So only two, the *sancakbeyi*s of Shkodër and Dukagjin, were left. Among the major cities in the north, Durrës would be hard to capture; while the walls of its castle were weak, there were two strong artillery bastions, and it was guarded by 700 men, in readiness for an attack by Venetian galleys. Shkodër, on the other hand, might well be taken even though its castle was situated on a high rocky outcrop, since the physical position of the castle was its only real strength. Whilst the surviving manuscript of this text is anonymous, all aspects of the evidence encourage the strong suspicion that he was none other than the cavaliere Antonio Bruti, whose profile matches every detail of this author's experiences and interests; the likeliest scenario is that Antonio wrote this while he was with the naval and infantry commanders of the Venetian fleet at Corfu during July 1570, so that they could forward it to the authorities in Venice.* If that identification is correct, this is the earliest surviving description of the country of Albania written by an Albanian. (If it is not, then the earliest such description is one written, as we shall see, by his nephew.) But its significance here is that it shows how a local Venetian loyalist and activist was trying to stimulate a policy of military engagement in the Albanian lands, both by signalling Ottoman military weakness and by suggesting the long-term economic benefit to be gained from a takeover of Albanian territory.[10]

Another such activist was the Venetian governor of Bar, Alessandro Donato (or Donà). In September 1570 he wrote to Venice, proudly announcing that he had managed to win over two villages of the Mrkojevići, the aggressive clansmen who had been in conflict with the people of Bar for so many years.† He was confident that he could gain

---

* For Antonio's stay on Corfu see above, p. 53. Antonio evidently had good personal relations with these commanders; he would write letters to both of them from Ulcinj later in the year, receiving a respectful reply from the infantry general. In those letters he explained that a Venetian offensive in northern Albania could make use of the two ports that served Lezhë: one was San Giovanni di Medua (given as 'della Medoa' by Antonio; Alb.: Shëngjin), and the other was the 'Sacca' (Italian for a small bay or inlet) of Lezhë itself. The only other text of this period to use the latter place-name is the anonymous work of 1570, which refers jointly to San Giovanni 'della Medoa' and the 'Sacca'.

† See above, pp. 6–7.

the support of 'other villages, which are many, and which are extremely important, since they provide the security for the fortress of Shkodër'; his only problem was that he needed money to give them. Donato's letter was tremendously optimistic. 'With the uprisings and rebellions of these warlike men,' he wrote, 'and with the news, just arrived, of the victory of your fleet against the enemy [a false report], this whole province is so changed, so that they look only for the sight of half a shadow of the battle-standard of St Mark to take up arms in your service.' There was an element of self-aggrandizement too, which, after Donato's unimpressive performance less than a year later, would make painful reading in retrospect: 'And I myself, if only I had had the soldiers whom I have so often requested, would have given such a demonstration of my desire to serve my country, that Your Serenity would not think me an unworthy citizen.' Another account, published in 1581 by the historian Natale Conti, who lived in Venice and had many sources of information there, puts Donato's activities in a rather different light. According to Conti, Donato obtained the submission of the Mrkojevići by attacking one of their villages with a troop of arquebusiers, massacring its men, women and children, and burning it down; he also bribed people to kill some of the Mrkojević captains, to sow mutual distrust among them. By these methods he gained the submission of roughly 80 villages.[11]

At the same time, Conti noted, other peoples also pledged their loyalty, in the area between the mouth of the river Bunë and the outskirts of Shkodër. A large element among these must have been the Pamaliotis, recruited to the Venetian cause by the Armani family of Ulcinj (which was related to the Brunis and Brutis); as we have seen, the leading member of this family would later be described as 'lord of all those Albanians who, in the time of the League, were exhorted by the Venetians to rebel against the Ottomans'.* Here the method used was not coercion but the deployment of personal and familial leadership – although, in keeping with the traditional practices of the region, those who pledged future military support would send sons or brothers as hostages, to guarantee fulfilment of their promise. In the area round the river Bunë, and in a broader stretch of Ottoman territory from just outside Ulcinj to Shkodër and Lezhë, Donato's bullying tactics were not needed, as there was much genuine enthusiasm for an anti-Ottoman revolt. By mid-October 1570 Hieronimo Venier, the governor of Ulcinj, was reporting that 'the leaders of the Albanian villages on this side of the river Drin' were

* Above, p. 28.

asking for his support in anti-Ottoman operations, and that 28 villages had already come out publicly for Venice. By the end of the month another nine were added to his list. And it was not only Christian Albanians who were eager for change: in early October Donato wrote that 32 local Muslims had come to Bar in order to convert to Christianity. They had been baptized, and were now receiving religious instruction from the Archbishop.[12]

Giovanni Bruni was actively involved in more than one anti-Ottoman initiative. In the first week of October 1570 he received a letter in Albanian from the Catholic priest of Briska, a village in Ottoman territory to the east of Bar, towards the shore of Lake Shkodër, which had just declared its allegiance to Venice.* The letter was an invitation to the Archbishop to come and discuss important matters with 'some elders'. When he went to Briska he found that those elders were representatives of several villages near Shkodër; they told him that the inhabitants of that city were keen to rebel, and that the Ottoman presence there was heavily depleted, as the *sancakbeyi*s of both Shkodër and Dukagjin had taken their forces to southern Albania in order to help quell the revolt in Himarë. The castle of Shkodër had been left under the command of the *sancakbeyi*'s steward or deputy, Mustafa Bey, who had reportedly told the few remaining members of the garrison that if they came under a major attack they should surrender rather than risk their lives. As it happened, this Mustafa Bey was already in contact with Donato, to whom he had just transmitted a message asking what sort of payment he would receive if he delivered the castle into Venetian hands. Donato sent Mustafa a valuable diamond to show his good intentions, but he entrusted the actual negotiation to Giovanni Bruni. And he did so for a good reason: Mustafa Bey was in fact related to the Archbishop. Giovanni wrote a friendly letter, which began with the words 'Greetings in the Lord to you, Mustafa Bey, my dearest relative', promised a pension of 3,000 ducats a year, and ended: 'May Our Lord Jesus Christ give you the light by which to recognize the true and safer path.' Nothing had come of these dealings by early November, when the return of the *sancakbeyi* seemed to eliminate the possibility of a straightforward handover of the castle of Shkodër. In the middle of that month, however,

---

* The letter was later forwarded by Donato to Venice. Sadly, however, only an Italian translation of it survives. Albanian-language texts from this period are extremely rare; this evidence does at least show that the practice of writing in the language was not unknown among educated Albanians.

Giovanni Bruni went on another mission into Ottoman territory, to the little port on the river Bunë, in order to meet some disaffected Albanian Muslims from Shkodër who said that they could show the Venetians the most vulnerable point at which to attack the castle. They also said that the *sancakbeyi* was about to leave the city, on a journey to Istanbul; so the Archbishop's negotiations with Mustafa Bey were resumed. At some point during the next couple of months there was even a secret nocturnal meeting between these two relatives. But in the end the governor of Ulcinj became convinced that Mustafa was a double agent, trying to set a trap at Shkodër for the Venetian forces. A similar conclusion was reached by the acting governor of Kotor, Bernardo Contarini, who would later write a very negative account of all these initiatives. According to Contarini, when the governors of Bar and Ulcinj both urged him to support the idea of an attack on Shkodër, he found that they had quite different plans, and were working in competition with each other; in his opinion there was no chance of success, and the raising of open revolt among the local Albanians might prove dangerously counterproductive, attracting a larger Ottoman military force to the area. With the benefit of hindsight, the truth of that criticism would be impossible to deny.[13]

While the Archbishop worked hard for the Venetian cause in Bar, his brother-in-law Antonio Bruti was no less active in the city of Ulcinj. Having returned there from Corfu in mid-August, he had spent his time (as he later put it) 'forming and strengthening the minds of these Albanians of ours in their loyalty to the Serenissima'. By 'these Albanians of ours' he meant ones in nearby Ottoman territory who were now coming over to the Venetian side, and thus, in historical terms, reverting to their old allegiance. Writing to the Doge on 1 November, he declared that 'I have so thoroughly formed the minds of our Albanians that nothing more is needed to complete the business, and to make Albania return to the Venetian flag, than [for you to send] galleys, and a captain with a certain number of soldiers.' Indeed, his main fear now was that his efforts might have been all too successful:

> Because Albania is my homeland, and they have much faith in my promises – which are that you have no intention of ever abandoning them, and that you will, rather, maintain them as your subjects and your grateful servants – they are so filled with anti-Ottoman zeal that it will be more difficult to stop them from making some furious but premature attack than it will be to encourage them to take up arms against the Ottomans.

I promise you that the minds of the Albanians are made up to come under your authority, and I offer you my own life, my sons' life and my property, in your honour and service.

Six weeks later, on 13 December, Antonio sent personal letters to the naval and infantry commanders of the Venetian fleet, begging them to send galleys and soldiers. He explained that such help, combined with the efforts of the local Albanians, would make it possible to seize the castles of Lezhë and Shkodër – so long as the soldiers came with 'a courageous captain who knows how to besiege places using artillery, ladders and mines'. While he wrote confidently that now was the time to achieve 'the conquest of Albania', his evident fear was that without such help all the efforts of the local people would be in vain.[14]

When Antonio Bruti sent off those letters, the limitations of the local forces had just been amply demonstrated. During the previous weeks a certain Bartolomeo Dukagjin (a member, presumably, of the patrician Dukagjin family from whose ancestor the northern mountain region got its name), had been begging the governor of Ulcinj, Hieronimo Venier, to attack the Ottoman castle in Lezhë – which was Bartolomeo's home town. In the end the governor agreed to do so, despite being advised by Antonio Bruti that he should wait for assistance from Venice. As Antonio reported to the Venetian government on 15 December, the expedition reached Lezhë on the 8th of that month, 'where our men immediately conquered the town, and the Muslims fled and blockaded themselves inside the castle. On the 9th the *sancakbeyi* of Dukagjin came with 200 cavalry to help them, but we defeated him and forced him to flee. And because our men lack skill, and the weather was bad, when they had looted and burnt down the town they came home again.' (Another account of this episode specifies that the raid was carried out by a force of stradiots from Ulcinj – so perhaps they were under Nicolò Bruni's command.) The 'lack of skill' here was, self-evidently, a complete inability to engage in any kind of siege warfare. Antonio Bruti commented that whilst it was good for morale to attack the Ottomans and avenge the burning of villages in the territory of Ulcinj, much more significant gains could be achieved during the winter months if only Venice would make the necessary investment: once more he urged the government 'to send soldiers, weapons and galleys, so that we may seize not only the castle of Lezhë but also the fortress of Shkodër, and the enemy's other possessions'. However, while the raid achieved little in Lezhë, its psychological effects did extend further afield. As Venier reported in early

January, news of this exploit inspired a revolt in the Mat region of north-central Albania, which spread fear among the Ottomans as far as the important fortress of Krujë; the rebels sent envoys to Ulcinj, begging for help, but Venier could not spare any soldiers. Meanwhile, in another opportunistic and uncoordinated initiative, Girolamo Zane had stopped with his galleys at a point opposite southern Corfu on his return from the abortive 1570 naval campaign, and had sent an infantry force to attack Margariti – again, without success.[15]

These initiatives, while doing little to achieve their avowed ends, did have one large and fateful consequence: they seriously alarmed the authorities in Istanbul. In late December 1570 the Sultan sent an order to the *beylerbeyi* of Rumeli – the major Balkan province of the empire, to which all the Albanian *sancak*s belonged – telling him to proceed urgently to Skopje to put together a force of janissaries and cavalry, and send it to Lezhë. The Sultan explained that, according to a message from the *sancakbeyi* of Dukagjin, thousands of men from Ulcinj, Bar and Kotor had gathered to attack the town again, and that Christian Albanian rebels from the sub-district of Krujë were destroying the property of Muslims in the area from there to Lezhë and collaborating with the invaders from Venetian Albania. In mid-February 1571 the Sultan sent an urgent order for the supply of munitions and equipment to the castle at Shkodër; eight days later he transmitted a message to the *beylerbeyi* of Rumeli emphasizing the importance of the castles of the Shkodër region and Hercegovina (a reference primarily to Herceg Novi) as the eyes and ears of the empire, and singling out the fortress of Lezhë as a place in need of special protection. On 4 March he wrote again, this time to the *kadi* of Krujë, expressing concern at reports that rebels had come several times to Lezhë, burning houses, sacking the surrounding villages, blocking the road between Lezhë and Shkodër, and performing acts of devotion to Venetian flags. Nine days later another order to the *beylerbeyi* began by reporting information derived from an Ottoman spy who had been in Corfu; it commented on the recent reinforcement of Margariti, saying that that stronghold was now in a better position, but insisted that the *sancakbeyi*s of Shkodër and Dukagjin should take more measures to protect the fortresses of Lezhë and Durrës, given that 'the unbelievers of the castles of Bar and Ulcinj are leading astray the Albanian rebels.' By not only linking Margariti (which lies some way to the south of the modern Albanian–Greek border) with the northern Albanian forts, but also referring to problems in both Herceg Novi and the Peloponnese, this order showed – perhaps for the first time – that the various local pin-prick assaults had become, in the eyes of Istanbul, a single strategic issue.[16]

Meanwhile the activities of local rebels did not cease. In March 1571 Bartolomeo Dukagjin and other Albanian leaders met a Spanish agent on the Rodon peninsula, and explained their requirements: 35 Spanish galleys with men and equipment, including artillery pieces and 4,000 arquebuses for the Albanians to use, plus 2,500 trained arquebusiers, of whom the majority could be stradiots from the Kingdom of Naples. For their part they would raise 12,000 local men, and the number would rise to 80,000 once they got going. The request was exorbitant – Philip II must certainly have thought so, as he turned it down – and the projected number of rebels probably over-ambitious, but the fact that such a meeting took place testifies to continuing unrest in the area. Also in March, a Venetian naval commander, Agostino Barbarigo, who was travelling southwards to join Sebastiano Venier on Corfu, stopped at Bar to discuss the possibility of an attack on Shkodër. The governor of Bar, Alessandro Donato, insisted that the castle could be taken so long as the Venetians sent galleys up the river Bunë and supplied a force of soldiers. Writing a little later to Venice, Donato exclaimed that once Shkodër had fallen it would be easy 'to conquer all Albania, Serbia, Hercegovina, and many other places, as there are no more fortresses all the way to Istanbul'. Despite the somewhat megalomanic strain in Donato's thinking, Barbarigo was sufficiently impressed to send a captain, Nicolò Suriano, with four galleys to the mouth of the Drin to reconnoitre and to talk with local leaders (perhaps some of the same people who met the Spanish agent); Suriano did what he could to encourage them, by promising that they would receive military supplies from the Venetians.[17]

Gradually, it seems, these miscellaneous enterprises were beginning to be merged in a more general Venetian policy, though much still depended on local initiative and on sheer chance. In April it was the Albanians who lived near Margariti that came to Corfu, asking for assistance in seizing it, and offering to leave hostages as proof of their sincerity; a Venetian captain who went there decided that these local volunteers were insufficient for the task, as they had only 200–250 men armed with swords and spears. But shortly after that, Emanuele Mormori, the commander of the recently conquered fortress of Sopot, took his soldiers and 'a large number of Albanians' to attack the small Ottoman fortress of Nivica, at the southern end of Himarë, which they managed to seize and sack. Encouraged by this success, which helped to cement the alliance with the local Himariots, Mormori then asked the authorities on Corfu to send him more men so that he could attack another Ottoman fort, at Kardhiq. This was a much tougher proposition, being a five-cornered castle on the summit of a steep hill, located inland, ten miles from Sopot (as the crow flies) over very rough terrain; but Mormori said he had good information about it, and that he had taken hostages from Albanian families in the vicinity, so Sebastiano Venier brought him the soldiers he requested. After doing that, Venier continued with his galleys up the coast – partly because he wanted to hunt down an Ottoman corsair captain who was said to be on his way to Durrës, and partly for the simple reason that there was a strong southerly wind. Summoning more galleys, he decided rather impulsively to launch a full-scale naval attack on Durrës. But the city turned out to be well defended (just as the anonymous text on Albania had said), and the Venetian force of 22 galleys was forced to retire when it ran out of ammunition for its artillery. When Venier returned to Corfu he found that Mormori's attack on Kardhiq had also been a failure.[18]

It was the mounting worry caused by these operations that led the Sultan, finally, to send a large military force to the region; although the modern historian can see how tentative and ill-coordinated these combinations of local revolt and Venetian intervention were, that may not have been so obvious to the Ottoman ruler, despite his spies in Corfu and elsewhere. During the winter months he had been accumulating troops at Skopje, a strategically located city at the heart of his Balkan domains. By early April there were said to be 30,000 infantry and cavalry there. One report, sent from Istanbul on 4 April, suggested that this army would be divided into three forces, to proceed to northern Albania, Himarë and the Mani peninsula – a reasonable guess in the circumstances. But there was much uncertainty, even among well-informed observers. A news report from Dubrovnik in early March said that the army would go to besiege Zadar; another bulletin, in mid-April, said that its destination was utterly unknown. On 4 May the Venetian bailo in Istanbul, who was managing to smuggle messages back to Venice despite being under strict house arrest, wrote that the Third Vizier, Ahmed Pasha, had left the capital on 29 April to take command of the army, and that its destination was quite unclear: 'it seems that the dominant opinion is that he is going to Dalmatia', though a march to Transylvania (where the ruler had just died, and some political instability could be expected) was also widely mooted. Possibly the Sultan was keeping several of these options open, including the Transylvanian one;

that might help to explain why Ahmed spent some weeks at Skopje after he got there. But when he finally set off with his army, the destination was Venetian Albania, and the purpose was a war of conquest, to eradicate the sources of Venetian support for the northern Albanian rebels.[19]

While the Ottomans readied their forces, Venice had also been engaged in some military preparations of its own in relation to Venetian Albania, though on a smaller scale. On 9 April it appointed the 41-year-old Count Giacomo Malatesta as governor-general of Kotor and of 'all the militia of Albania'; in late April he sailed for Kotor with 2,500 men, arriving there in early or mid-May. Malatesta came from a branch of the famous noble family that had ruled Rimini in the late Middle Ages. He had the classic curriculum vitae of a noble 'condottiere', a freelance military commander who could be hired, with the men he recruited, by different rulers. A tough and impulsive man, he had served Cosimo de' Medici in the 1550s, been imprisoned by the Pope, worked for the Venetians on Cyprus, and lost his position there after he had arbitrarily executed people he suspected of involvement in the assassination of his brother; he had then become a colonel of cavalry of the papal guard, in which capacity he led the 200-strong escort that accompanied Cosimo de' Medici when he received the title of Grand Duke from the Pope. Although Venice could raise thousands of men from its own dominions, it had always depended on condottieri and their mercenary troops to build up its armed forces in times of war; by this means it acquired soldiers from many areas outside Venetian territory, including central Italy (Malatesta's main recruiting-ground was the Romagna), Tuscany, Liguria, Savoy and Corsica. Sometimes Swiss fighters were hired, or wandering companies of French or Spanish soldiers. For its intra-Italian conflicts, in periods when it was at peace with the Ottomans, Venice even made arrangements with the *sancakbeyi*s of Bosnia to employ Croatian light cavalry to supplement its own stradiots. (In the crisis year of 1509, when most of the Terraferma fell under enemy occupation, there were serious discussions in the Venetian government about hiring an Ottoman army of 15–20,000 men; according to the diarist Girolamo Priuli, this caused concern to those who said it would destroy Venice's image as a defender of Christendom, 'as though a man were to cut off his penis to spite his wife'.) Wherever they came from, mercenaries were not cheap; so the despatch of this large contingent to Kotor shows that Venice had finally begun to take seriously the proposals of its officials in Venetian Albania for a more active anti-Ottoman policy in the region.[20]

Immediately after his arrival, Malatesta had a meeting with the three key figures in Kotor: Zaccaria Salamone, who was the 'provveditore' (overseer or governor-commander) of Dalmatia and Albania; the acting governor of Kotor, Contarini; and the naval captain Nicolò Suriano, who had negotiated with Albanian rebel leaders at the mouth of the river Drin. He then went with Suriano to reconnoitre the area, and to talk to other local Venetian officials; he visited Bar, and also Ulcinj, where he met Antonio Bruti and 'the leaders of the Bunë district' (probably meaning, above all, the Armani family). According to one report, he went to the mouth of the Bunë, 'in order to fortify the loyalty of the Albanians who had newly become subjects of Venice', and also to encourage the men of Dukagjin to join in. The plan he discussed with Bruti involved seizing Lezhë, using that position to take control of the southern approaches to Shkodër, and then rousing the local Albanians against the Muslim population – and garrison – of Shkodër itself. At long last, it seemed, Antonio Bruti's prayers for galleys and soldiers had been answered, and his firm conviction that the castles of Lezhë and Shkodër could be conquered was about to be put to the test.[21]

Malatesta returned to Kotor convinced that the plan was workable, and persuaded Salamone and the acting governor of Kotor to let him have, in addition to his own forces, all their cavalry and 2,000 experienced soldiers. Preparations were made, but an extra delay was caused by waiting for the arrival of the hostages promised by the Albanians of the area between the Bunë and the Drin. On 30 May, just a few days before he and his men were finally due to set out from Kotor, Malatesta decided to mount a little local punitive expedition of his own. The surviving accounts differ in the details of what he intended. According to one early report, he sent 200 men to burn down a nearby Ottoman village, while he took 500 soldiers across the Gulf of Kotor to the Venetian-controlled town of Perast; his plan was to sack another Ottoman possession, the small trading entrepôt of Risan, and then return with his men over the mountains, rejoining the other 200. Another report has him simply leading 200 men up the coast, burning and pillaging a six-mile-long stretch of Ottoman territory. Whatever the plan, it failed devastatingly; marching with his soldiers back to Kotor along a mountain path, he was ambushed by local fighters who hurled heavy stones at them from the heights above. As many as 100 of his men were killed or badly wounded. Malatesta received a head wound and a broken leg; he was captured and taken to Risan, whence he was sent off in chains to Istanbul. His planned expedition to Lezhë was then abandoned, and his soldiers were distributed to the garrisons of various places in Venetian Albania. As Alessandro Donato reported, the 160 Albanian hostages who had gathered in Bar were now reduced to 'extreme despair'.[22]

The news of this disaster reached Venice in mid-June. Before the end of the month, the government sent out a replacement for Malatesta as military commander of Venetian Albania: another condottiere, Count Sciarra (or Sarra) Martinengo, who came from a famous noble family of Brescia, in the Terraferma. His father, an officer in the French army, had been killed by a member of a rival Brescian family, the Avogadros; Sciarra, an illegitimate son who had followed his father into French military service, had returned to Brescia with a group of French soldiers and tried to kill his father's murderer in broad daylight in the main square. When that man escaped, he killed another Avogadro in his place, and was sentenced to perpetual banishment. But on the outbreak of war he made a deal with Venice to supply troops, in return for a lifting of the ban (though he was still forbidden to enter Brescia itself). The soldiers he recruited were French Protestant mercenaries from Gascony – a troublesome set of people, it seems, even by the standards of sixteenth-century military men. While stationed in Chioggia, just to the south of Venice, before their departure for Albania, they got into a fight with a much larger force of Italian soldiers, who killed two of their men. As the Italians advanced, Martinengo put his troops into battle order; they charged their opponents, killed 100 of them, and drove many into the sea. The acting governor of Kotor would later write that having these men in his city was almost as bad as having the plague.[23]

Nevertheless the arrival of 600 men with Martinengo was appreciated in Venetian Albania, because, by the time they reached Kotor in early July, it was known that a large Ottoman army was approaching. Venetian spies – presumably, Albanians who could pass unnoticed in the region – had tracked Ahmed Pasha's movements, and it was now clear that he was heading for Ulcinj and Bar. An urgent request was sent to Kotor by Hieronimo Venier, Antonio Bruti and the leaders of the rebels in the Bunë district, asking for galleys and soldiers to defend the river-port of the Bunë, Sveti Srdj (Alb.: Shën Shirgj or Shirq; Ital.: San Sergio). They were sent the forces they asked for, not because it was imagined that a large army could be held back for long at the river-bank, but merely to gain a few more days for the preparation of Ulcinj's defences. The Venetian captain Nicolò Suriano, who visited Sveti Srdj on or just before 9 July, found a battle raging between the Ottoman army on the eastern side of the river and the Italian garrison troops from Ulcinj, 'together with Albanians', on the western bank, who were supported by two Venetian galleys. He noted, however, that the Ottomans were building a bridge further up the river, over which they would soon transport their army with its 44 artillery pieces, four of which were heavy cannons; his fear was that the Italian soldiers would soon find their path back to Ulcinj cut off. The whole situation of Venetian Albania had dramatically changed: whereas Malatesta's mission had been ambitiously offensive, Martinengo's had suddenly become a matter of defence against huge odds.[24]

Ahmed Pasha's army was not the only hostile force approaching the area. During April and May the Ottomans had assembled a very large fleet, under two commanders: the Second Vizier, Pertev Pasha, who was in charge of all the soldiers, and Ali Müezzinzade Pasha, the admiral of the fleet. After raiding Crete in June, it had proceeded up the western coast of the Peloponnese, devastating Venetian possessions such as Cephalonia and heading for Corfu. The squadrons of Crete and Corfu, which were much too small to oppose it, were withdrawn, heading westward to join the allied navy that was assembling at Messina. The primary aim of the Ottoman fleet was to block, and engage with, any large fleet that might be sent out by the Christian allies. But its other aims were various: to strike a psychological blow by wreaking havoc on Venetian territory, to capture thousands of men for use as galley-slaves, to seize booty more generally, and also, apparently, to go up the Adriatic coast as far as Zadar and conquer that city. It did not pause on its way to undertake the siege of any major town or castle, but when it reached Himarë the commanders did take a force of several thousand men ashore to capture the fortress of Sopot. According to one account, Emanuele Mormori rejected the demand that he surrender, but many of his soldiers began secretly to flee; the fortress was seized, and he was taken as a prisoner to Istanbul.[25]

By this stage Ahmed Pasha's army had already reached Shkodër. Some of its men were left there, to guarantee the security of the city. He then advanced on Ulcinj; the line of resistance at the river Bunë did not detain him for long. Estimates of the size of his army vary wildly. Some accounts put it at 15,000 men, which seems low, given that earlier reports said that 30,000 had assembled at Skopje, while other sources and early chroniclers, implausibly, say 70,000 or even 80,000. Nicolò Suriano's initial report gave the figure of 30,000; Sciarra Martinengo would later specify 80,000 – but by the time he wrote, he would have reason to reach for the highest possible figure, in order to exonerate his own conduct. The precise number of defenders – including able-bodied citizens of Ulcinj – is not known, but it was certainly tiny in comparison; a report of February 1571 had observed that while the garrison there had been strengthened, many of the inhabitants had left, either to seek safety or to serve in the Venetian fleet. To the defenders of Ulcinj, the odds must have seemed overwhelming. On 18 July, as the Ottoman army came close to the city, Hieronimo Venier sent a message to Kotor saying that in the opinion of the soldiers' captains, and of Antonio Bruti, Ulcinj could not be defended – especially as they believed that an Ottoman fleet would soon be attacking them from the sea. He therefore requested four galleys to take away all the remaining citizens and the soldiers, plus their artillery pieces, so that the whole city could be consigned to the flames. The acting governor of Kotor replied that the rumour of an approaching Ottoman fleet was known to be false, and ordered him to remain at his station. Venier's next message, written on 20 July, was a little more positive in tone, while still giving a sense of the extreme difficulty of the situation. He wrote that the citizens of the town showed a good willingness to fight; he had just sent a number of arquebusiers and local Albanians out of the city to engage in combat with the skirmishing forces that formed the advance guard of the Ottoman army, after which his men had succeeded in killing many of Ahmed Pasha's soldiers by firing from the battlements. But he complained of a shortage of gunpowder, and declared that he had barely 300 soldiers (meaning, presumably, the Italian garrison, which had recently been strengthened by men from Malatesta's force). Moreover, 80 of them were useless for combat purposes: whenever they were called to arms, 'they pack up their things and hide.'[26]

By 29 July Ahmed Pasha's men had constructed a bastion for the four large cannons which they had brought with great difficulty from Shkodër, and the bombardment commenced. Sciarra Martinengo was at or near Kotor when he was brought this news, and was told that the people of Ulcinj, together with Venier and Bruti, were contemplating flight, as they could no longer believe that their little garrison was capable of defending the city. So Martinengo immediately went to Ulcinj with his 600 Gascon soldiers. Since Ahmed's forces were only on the landward side, access to the city by sea was still possible, and for a few days it was serviced by Venetian galleys which brought supplies of food and barrels of fresh water drawn from the river Bunë. But the defenders were struck by two heavy blows in succession. Soon after his arrival in Ulcinj, Martinengo was hit by a piece of masonry (or, in one account, part of a bell from a bell-tower) which had been shattered by Ottoman artillery fire. He was 'carried away as if dead', and seems to have been incapacitated for several days; his deputy was similarly wounded soon thereafter, and was taken on one of the last galley trips back to Kotor. Although morale was badly damaged by this, the Gascon and Italian soldiers continued to fight for a few days more; then, however, the fleet of Ali Müezzinzade Pasha and Pertev Pasha appeared in front of the city. This second blow transformed the situation for the defenders. Not only was their supply route cut off, but the Ottoman galleys' own artillery could bombard the sea walls of Ulcinj – the very part of the defensive system which the anonymous writer in 1570 (probably Antonio Bruti) had described as weak and 'extremely dangerous'.[27]

The broad outline of what happened next is known. Martinengo and Venier made a deal with Pertev Pasha, surrendering the city in return for a promise of safe passage to Dubrovnik for all the French and Italian soldiers, plus any inhabitants who wished to leave. The safety of those who remained was also guaranteed. The departing soldiers and inhabitants then embarked on Pertev's galleys; Ahmed entered the town, and the pledge of safety was apparently broken straight away, as many people were killed and part of the city was burnt down. But within this broad outline there are many details that are uncertain.

From an early stage, there was controversy about the decision to surrender. In the brief report which he sent on 16 August, soon after he had been delivered to Dubrovnik, Sciarra Martinengo simply stated that it had become necessary to seek honourable terms because of the arrival of the Ottoman fleet, and 'because the city was weak, with a shortage of ammunition, and of materials for repairing the walls'; both the people and the soldiers had, he said, been 'filled with fear'. According to a well-informed Ragusan report, Martinengo later blamed the decision to surrender on his officers, who had made it because their ammunition had run out; the officers, while insisting that that was the genuine reason for their decision, claimed that Martinengo had himself wished to flee or surrender even when ammunition stocks were high; whereas the local inhabitants said that there was plenty of ammunition, since the Venetian galleys had been bringing it with the food and other supplies, and that the soldiers could and should have continued to fight. Another report, compiled in Kotor in September, attributed the decision to a lack of water. The well-informed Venetian chronicler Fedele Fedeli, on the other hand, claimed that the key factor was fear of the ships' artillery, which could quickly breach the sea-facing walls and also destroy the houses in the city; that was the point emphasized in Hieronimo Venier's report to Venice soon after the surrender, in which he said that Ulcinj could not be defended against an attack from that side. The most likely explanation is that all these factors were involved, but that all of them – not just the fear of ship's cannons – operated in a prospective way: water and ammunition had not run out, but it was expected that they would do so before long. The decision to surrender was, so to speak, brought forward, and the obvious reason for that was that the arrival of the Ottoman fleet created a new opportunity for a deal. Standard practice dictated that if a city or an army refused to surrender when it was called upon to do so and was offered terms – as Ulcinj had refused Ahmed Pasha, over several days – the city could be sacked and the people, both military and civilian, might be seized and enslaved. Dealing separately with the Ottoman fleet, the defenders could start the procedure from stage one and negotiate for safe passage; if they continued to hold out against the fleet too, there would be no escape, at the end, from pillaging and enslavement.[28]

All accounts emphasize that the defenders were keen to negotiate with Pertev Pasha, the infantry general of the fleet, and not with Ahmed. Presumably, the reason for approaching Pertev rather than the admiral, Ali Müezzinzade, was that Pertev, as a vizier, outranked his colleague and was in overall command. Possibly another factor was also at work here: Pertev was an Albanian, unlike Ali (a Turk), and also unlike Ahmed Pasha, who came from an Orthodox Serb family in Hercegovina. Whatever the reason, discussions were opened with him, using the dragoman (interpreter) whom he had brought with him from Istanbul, an Italian from Lucca who had converted to Islam and was called Hürrem Bey. According to the report drawn up six weeks later in Kotor, Pertev felt the awkwardness of his situation vis-à-vis Ahmed, and told the defenders that he would wait one more day, to give Ahmed the chance to take Ulcinj himself; he sent the same message to Ahmed. Consequently Ahmed redoubled his efforts, sending three major assaults against the city, each of which was repelled with serious losses. (From this it is clear that the defenders' ammunition had not run out yet.) On the following day – the exact date is not known, but it may have been 3 or 4 August – the defending soldiers and many of the inhabitants went down to the shore and were taken aboard the Ottoman galleys. They included Nicolò Bruni, his uncle Antonio Bruti, and perhaps some other members of their family. One report (by Contarini, the acting governor of Kotor) states that Antonio Bruti had participated, with Venier and

Martinengo, in the decision to surrender. Perhaps he did in the end, believing that many lives would be saved thereby. But the only account of his final actions that has come down to us gives a very different impression of his underlying attitude. According to the Venetian historian Andrea Morosini, who had access to many sources and may have spoken to eye-witnesses:

> The cavaliere Antonio Bruti of Ulcinj, who had performed exceptional services for the Republic [of Venice] in Albania, had opposed the surrender and had resisted Ahmed's attempts on the city; he feared the extreme hostility of the people against him, and, having boarded a brigantine, he threw himself off it into the depths when it was about to leave for Apulia. He was intercepted by an Ottoman galley and taken as a captive to Ali [Müezzinzade] Pasha.[29]

Some of the details here are puzzling, including the reference to Apulia; passage had been promised to Dubrovnik, not to Spanish-ruled territory. The Ragusan report indicated that many of the inhabitants of Ulcinj had been keen to continue fighting, so they are unlikely to have felt 'extreme hostility' towards Bruti; given that evidence, and given also the apparent sequence of ideas in Morosini's writing here, it seems that the 'people' whose hostility he feared were the Ottomans. In that case, however, a decision to abandon the boat, where he had a guarantee of safe passage, and return to Ulcinj, which was now coming under the control of Ahmed Pasha, would be very hard to comprehend. At a guess, the best explanation of his action may be that he jumped from the brigantine not at the point of departure, but when it had proceeded some way up the coast. Perhaps he hoped to swim to land, make his way to Bar and continue the resistance from there. But his decision proved fatal. Whether he was executed on the spot by Ali Müezzinzade Pasha, or whether he was held as a galley-slave for some time before his death, is not known; family tradition would merely record that he was condemned to death by the Ottoman conqueror at the fall of Ulcinj.[30]

Almost every account of the seizure of Ulcinj simply says that the guarantee of safety for those who stayed behind was broken by Ahmed Pasha, who allowed his men to loot, burn and kill. In the words of the report from Kotor: 'when the general of the land army entered the city, he made his men cut to pieces all those who had remained and set fire to some houses which were full of women and children.' The explanation given for this was partly psychological: he resented the fact that the inhabitants had done a deal with Pertev Pasha, and regarded the city as his own conquest, not his rival's. But since these accounts also say that he took men, women and children from Ulcinj as slaves, and that he placed a substantial garrison in the city before moving on, it is not clear why he should have wished either to kill large numbers of people or to burn down much of the housing. Only the Ragusan document offers an entirely plausible explanation of what happened. According to this account, the Albanian anti-Ottoman rebels of the area between Ulcinj and Shkodër had agreed with the governors of Ulcinj and Bar that they would raise their whole population in support of the Venetians – initially, with the intention of seizing Shkodër. The 300 rebel leaders had said that they could raise 6,000 fighting men. That agreement was a conditional one, however. While the Venetians promised to send them weapons and supplies (a promise which was apparently not fulfilled), in the mean time they handed over 200 of their brothers and sons as hostages, who were held by Venier in the city of Ulcinj. Since the revolt of the local Albanians, actual or planned, was the main reason for Ahmed Pasha's expedition, and since non-citizens of Ulcinj who were Ottoman subjects might well expect to be punished, regardless of any guarantees to Ulcinj itself, these 200 men were not inclined to give themselves up when Ahmed's troops entered the city. (These Albanians, whose numbers perhaps underwent some subsequent inflation, may have been the people referred to in the later account given by Giorgio Armani of his brother Andrea, who, as we have seen, 'installed himself with 400 men in Ulcinj, where he and all his men died'.)* Ahmed Pasha, according to this Ragusan report, did indeed intend to execute the hostages; so, 'having withdrawn into some houses, they defended themselves very courageously; the houses were set on fire; some of the hostages were burnt, and the others were killed, but not without the deaths of many Ottoman soldiers.' If the fires then spread, and the killing too – given that the Ottoman troops had not expected their takeover of the city to be contested – those facts become a little more comprehensible on this account.[31]

After Ulcinj, Bar was next. Here too there were hostages, thanks to Alessandro Donato's heavy-handed enlistment of the Mrkojevići; and for a while, according to Morosini, the Mrkojević clansmen outside the city did resist the advancing Ottoman army. But soon the people of Bar found themselves in the same pincer-grip, with Ahmed's troops

* Above, p. 28.

approaching their city and the Ottoman fleet cutting off any possibility of support from the sea. Very quickly, the city of Bar surrendered. In this case too there is a simple story, widely accepted in the early accounts, and a slightly more elaborate explanation. The simple version was the one given by Contarini, the acting governor of Kotor, in his narrative, where he scornfully declared: 'then Bar, which was supplied with food-stuffs, weaponry, soldiers and other courageous fighters, surrendered itself or was surrendered in an utterly disgraceful way, before the army had arrived under its walls and before the fleet had shown any sign of disembarking its men.' The report compiled in Kotor in September was no less contemptuous of Alessandro Donato: 'the governor of this place surrendered to the admiral without waiting for a single arquebus shot, even though the soldiers, it is said, wanted to fight, and to wait until at least one or two assaults had taken place.'[32]

The Venetian government certainly accepted that version of events; on 5 November it condemned Donato to perpetual exile, with a threat of execution if he were captured, and a reward of 1,000 ducats to any-one who caught him. But a more detailed account is given by Natale Conti, which may help to explain Donato's action: in Bar, unlike in Ulcinj, opinion was strongly divided, with many of the townspeople opposed to the idea of fighting at all. According to Conti, as soon as they received Pertev's offer of the same terms of surrender, some said they wanted to defend the city, while others were keen to accept. For three days there were arguments; 'one part of the citizenry began to riot, saying that they did not want to take the risk of fighting when they had such an extreme lack of provisions.' In Morosini's account, one of the leading opponents of surrender was their Archbishop. 'Giovanni Bruni, the Archbishop of Bar and relative of Antonio Bruti, a man of extreme piety in religion and great loyalty to Venice, urged them with vehement eloquence to resist bravely the enemy's attack, and not to sur-render to the enemy through fear or cowardice.' The commander of the garrison, an officer from Lucca called Giovanni Vidaccioni, was eager to fight, even though he described the city's position as 'weak'; we know this from a set of later affidavits he obtained in Dubrovnik from people who had taken part in the crucial decision-making meeting called by Donato. In the end, it seems, the opposition to continued fighting was too great, and Donato agreed to accept the offer of safe passage in return for surrender. That offer had been brought to Bar by Hürrem Bey, Pertev's Italian dragoman. Hürrem and Vidaccioni, who were both a long way from their native town of Lucca, probably met during the negotiations. Such encounters were not as rare as one might think in the interactions between the Western Christian and Ottoman worlds.[33]

Donato, the garrison soldiers and some of the people of Bar went down to the coast and embarked on the Ottoman galleys. (Again, the precise date of this exodus is not known, but it may have taken place on 8 or 9 August.) But more than one early account emphasizes that a large part of the population preferred to stay; the report from Kotor even states that 'the local people all remained in their houses', though it is clear from the affidavits that at least two noblemen did leave. According to the Ragusan report, as soon as the Ottomans took over, 'immediately, many families of the inferior class denied Christ [i.e. converted to Islam], taking that wicked opportunity to get their revenge for the ancient enmities which they had with the nobles.' Here, perhaps, we find the essential reason for the difference in conduct between the people of Ulcinj, who had not been badly divided in the past by such socio-political disputes, and those of Bar, who had. In the latter, while the nobles, led by Giovanni Bruni, adopted a position of Venetian ultra-loyalism, many of the townsmen took a different line, envisaging a future in an Ottoman city where the old noble oligarchy would no longer have any power over them at all. As in the case of those Orthodox Cypriots who welcomed the ending of rule by Catholic Venetians, it is necessary to bear in mind that Ottoman conquests were not always a matter of simple *force majeure*; sometimes there were local reasons, whether religious, political or social, for acquiescence and cooperation.[34]

After Bar, the next target was Budva. A large number of its people had fled to Kotor after the arrival of the Ottoman army at the gates of Ulcinj; that city rejected them, and many who went back towards their homes were killed by roving Ottoman units. For those who were in Budva when Pertev's fleet arrived, a surrender was quickly negotiated.* A large part of the fleet then proceeded to the Ottoman port and stronghold of Herceg Novi, near the entrance to the Gulf of Kotor; 80 vessels were reported to have arrived there by 11 August. Here Pertev took aside Sciarra Martinengo and a dozen of his officers and men, plus the Venetian dignitaries of Ulcinj, together with their equivalents, military and civilian, from Bar and Budva, and put them on a boat for Dubrovnik.

---

* Soon afterwards, noticing that the Ottomans had left it almost unguarded, the acting governor of Kotor sent galleys and men to reoccupy the town; but later that year it would be lost to the Ottomans for a second time.

(The dignitaries did not include Giovanni Bruni, who was kept in chains on an Ottoman galley.) Pertev had already shown great hostility to Martinengo's Gascon soldiers, denouncing them as rebels and traitors on two counts: as Huguenots (i.e. Protestants) they had rebelled against their king, and as mercenaries fighting the Ottomans they had been in breach of the French–Ottoman alliance. That he broke his promise where they were concerned, condemning them to the galleys as slaves, thus had some specious excuse. But there was no justification for his decision to do the same to the Italian soldiers and the civilian inhabitants who had put their trust in him, other than sheer military necessity – for his fleet had been depleted over the summer months by sickness and desertion. Even that need, however, would not explain his retention of the women, with the evident idea of selling them as slaves on his return; many of these would be freed by the allied forces at the end of the Battle of Lepanto two months later. As with the whole campaign of the fleet so far, from Crete northwards, the essential principle seems to have been to destroy the morale as well as the resources of the Venetians. For that reason it is not impossible to accept the claim, made in one early report, that Martinengo and his colleagues were delivered to Dubrovnik naked.[35]

The news of the conquest of Ulcinj was received with great jubilation in Istanbul. One might almost suspect that its significance was exaggerated there for public relations purposes, were it not for the evidence, from earlier in the year, of the Sultan's serious strategic fears for his northern Albanian domains. He was determined to eliminate the threat to those possessions, and this meant taking permanent control of Bar and Ulcinj. According to the Ragusan report, Ahmed Pasha left a garrison of 500 men in Ulcinj and a similar force in Bar. Those soldiers came, evidently, from his own land army. Many historians have claimed that Ulcinj immediately received a garrison of 400 North African corsairs, which may perhaps have seemed plausible in the light of two facts: a corsair squadron from Algiers, under Uluç Ali, had joined the Ottoman fleet, and in later years Ulcinj would become known as a corsair or pirate centre with a strong North African connection. But the corsairs were the most skilled sailors and maritime fighters in the entire Ottoman fleet; it would have been madness to remove them from it for routine garrison duty on land. Nor could the corsairs have spared 400 men, let alone the 1,000 placed in Ulcinj and Bar, without seriously depleting their force, which came to only 20 galleys. In any case, Ulcinj did not become known as a corsair centre until much later than this.

With the exception of a single reference to people from Ulcinj attacking Venetian shipping in 1592, there are not even sporadic mentions of corsairs from that city until the early seventeenth century, when one visitor noted that they used small foists to prey on merchant shipping; this was described as an activity of local inhabitants, with no mention of North African involvement. Overall, the corsairs or pirates of Ulcinj became a significant factor in the region only from the 1630s, or even later.[36]

The effects of conquest on the population (devastating in Ulcinj, less serious in Bar) were soon exacerbated by plague – brought, probably, by the army or by the fleet, from which many soldiers deserted when they reached this part of the coast. By early January 1572 a French diplomat would write from Dubrovnik that the plague which had spread throughout Albania, the neighbouring Slav lands and much of the Peloponnese was 'so contagious and severe, that almost no one remains, so that the towns of Ulcinj, Bar, Budva, Herceg Novi, Durrës and innumerable others are almost abandoned, both by their inhabitants and by the soldiers'. The local economy also suffered badly from the conflict; the olive-groves of Ulcinj and Bar were cut down or burnt by the Ottoman invaders, and there would be no harvest from them until 1582. Ulcinj seems quickly to have become an almost completely Muslim city, dominated by its garrison of Ottoman soldiers. Bar retained a strong Christian element in the population, both Orthodox and Catholic, but between 1610 and 1618 the overall majority would tip from Christian to Muslim. The cathedral was turned into a mosque soon after the conquest, and the grand residence of the archbishop, where Giovanni Bruni had lived for the best part of 20 years, was given over mostly to stables and hay-storage, with just one part of it inhabited by the city's *kadi* (judge). Of the seventeen other Catholic churches in the city only two were still in use in 1618, one of them having been taken over by the Orthodox. Yet the wider population in the countryside had not been eliminated, and some deeper continuities remained: the linguistic frontier between Albanian and Slav would remain roughly where it had been for several hundred years to come. What changed was that the special synthesis of these languages and societies with the Venetian cultural world had gone. It was to be replaced by another imperial synthesis, of a different kind.[37]

8

The Lepanto Campaign

The primary reason for the presence of a large Ottoman fleet in the waters between Crete and Venetian Albania in the summer of 1571 was to counter any naval offensive by the Christian allies. As the campaigning season got under way in the spring of that year, the siege of Famagusta – the last but also the most important Venetian stronghold on Cyprus – was still in progress, and there was a possibility that Venice and its allies would send a relief force. That possibility became much stronger when, in late May 1571, the long-awaited Holy League was formed at last. A large-scale naval engagement between Christian and Ottoman forces somewhere in the Mediterranean was now a positively likely event.

The negotiations over the League, which had dragged on since July 1570, had been troublesome and fractious, and the recriminations that followed the abortive campaign of that year had added to the difficulties. (Nor were the recriminations only between the different allies; Venice started legal proceedings against its own commander, Girolamo Zane, and also spent some time investigating the conduct of its infantry general, Sforza Pallavicino.) Marcantonio Colonna's own position was quite insecure. Spanish hostility to his re-appointment, expressed by Cardinal Granvelle's gibes and stimulated by Doria's critical account of the 1570 campaign, was at first a powerful factor; but Colonna benefited from the lobbying activities of his cousin Cardinal Marcantonio, who had important contacts in Madrid. He was eventually accepted by Spain for fear that if he were dropped as papal commander, his place might be taken by the son of Cosimo de' Medici – the man whose papally derived title of 'Grand Duke' stuck so uncomfortably in the craw of King Philip.[1]

Pope Pius V, meanwhile, was tireless in his efforts to make the projected League a reality. In this he had the strong support of the Venetians, who were keen to do whatever it might take to save Famagusta and recover Cyprus – though there was a growing opinion among some of the Venetian patriciate that they should cut their losses and negotiate peace with the Sultan. The main obstacle to the formation of the League was Spain. The Spanish diplomats in Rome, Cardinal Granvelle and Juan de Zúñiga, raised one difficulty after another. They were acting according to the spirit of their King's instructions, but one could scarcely say that they did so according to the letter, as months went by without Philip instructing them at all. When he did in February 1571 it was to emphasize two points: that the Spanish commander should have authority over the entire fleet of the League, and that the primary objective of the campaign should be Tunis. His nominee for Spanish commander was his half-brother, Don John of Austria, a young man (aged only 23 at the beginning of that year) who had previously served briefly as captain-general of the Spanish Mediterranean fleet, and had acquitted himself well in the bloody land campaign against the Moriscos. The Pope and the Venetians agreed to his role as overall commander, but baulked at the additional demand that in his absence the command should pass to his Spanish deputy; Philip eventually accepted that at those times Marcantonio Colonna would take charge of the whole fleet. As for the choice of Tunis as primary target: here it seems that the Spanish envoys in Rome decided not to press the issue, as they were aware that to insist upon this demand would mean ending the negotiations. In the early months of 1571 they had real fears that, unless Spain made some concessions, Venice would make a separate peace with the Sultan; and they knew that if that happened, Spanish interests in North Africa and the western Mediterranean would be at much greater risk.[2]

Those Spanish fears were not unfounded. In March 1571 Venice sent an envoy to Istanbul, Giacomo Ragazzoni – a merchant and, as it happened, a brother of the Bishop of Famagusta – with the ostensible mission of negotiating a prisoner exchange, and an end to the impounding of Venetian merchandise in Istanbul and of Ottoman merchandise in Venice. His underlying purpose (admitted two years later by the Venetian authorities, but ferreted out at the time by the intelligence network of the Grand Master of the Knights of Malta) was to discover what sort of peace settlement the Sultan might be willing to accept. Since the Grand Vizier, Mehmed Sokollu, had sent one of the Venetian dragomans to request such an envoy, it was assumed that a reasonable offer might be on the table. But when Ragazzoni met Sokollu at the end of April, he received no such encouragement. He was informed that the

Sultan was deeply offended by the response which Venice had sent to the ultimatum, and that 'for that reason he [the Sultan] was intent on making large-scale war against Venice, and would take Crete too, and Corfu.'* When Ragazzoni replied that there would soon be a league of Christian states which would radically alter the balance of the war, Sokollu's response was a mixture of bravado and well-informed cynicism: he said that 'his lord had strength enough to resist all of them, and to make war in many places at the same time; and besides, he knew perfectly well how little trust Venice could put in Christian princes.'[3]

Over the following weeks Sokollu had more meetings with Ragazzoni, and with the Venetian bailo, Marcantonio Barbaro, who was allowed out of his house arrest to take part in the discussions. What brought the negotiating to a virtual end was the fact that in early May the Venetian government sent Ragazzoni a message full of optimistic news about the war: it announced that Albania had risen against the Ottomans, that Durrës had already fallen (a false report), and that there was a good prospect of taking Vlorë too. Importantly, it also stated that Marcantonio Colonna had come to Venice and had been promised Venetian support for the League. Colonna had in fact spent many days using his Venetian contacts and his considerable diplomatic skills to strengthen pro-League sentiment among the patricians. In a speech to the Venetian government on 14 April he declared that if the League negotiations ended in failure, that would be the greatest victory the Sultan had ever had; in another address to them, on 6 May, he urged them to accept Don John of Austria as commander in chief on the grounds that he was 'a young man who desired glory', and would therefore be eager (unlike the previous Spanish commander, Doria) to fight the enemy. Throughout his time there, Colonna was also acting as an intermediary for a final wave of requests and demands put by the Venetians to the Pope and, through him, to the Spanish representatives in Rome. Mutual distrust between Venice and Spain was still strong, and Colonna played a vital role in overcoming it.[4]

On 20 May 1571 the official document establishing the Holy League was signed in Rome by the Pope and the representatives of Venice and Spain. Its first article declared that the League would be perpetual, and that it would be offensive as well as defensive, with Algiers, Tunis and Tripoli among its potential targets. Articles 2 and 4 said that every spring it would assemble 200 galleys, 100 transport ships, 50,000

* On the Venetian response to the ultimatum see above, pp. 100–1.

soldiers and 4,500 light cavalry, and every autumn the ambassadors would meet in Rome to plan the following year's campaign. Article 7, on cost-sharing, was based on the formula used in the League of 1538: Spain would pay half, Venice one third, and the Papacy one sixth. Two articles, 11 and 12, dealt with the thorny issue of Spain's North African concerns. If Spain were attacked by Ottoman or Barbary forces, Venice would send 50 galleys to help (and Spain, likewise, would send 50 if Venetian territory were invaded); if Spain should undertake action against Algiers, Tunis or Tripoli in a year when there was no League campaign and no definite threat from the Ottoman fleet, Venice would contribute 50 galleys. Article 14 represented a surprising concession by Spain. It decreed that the three commanders (Spanish, Venetian, papal) would form a council of war, which would make decisions by majority vote; these would then bind the commander in chief, Don John, even if he had been in the minority. To the immense relief of the Ragusans, article 19 stipulated that Dubrovnik and its territory must not be molested in any way. And article 21 said that none of the parties could act independently to negotiate peace.[5]

While it is easy in retrospect to identify which of these pledges were dubious or empty, the scale of the diplomatic achievement should not be underestimated. After nearly eleven months of alternately rancorous and stagnant negotiations, the sense of relief was intense. Pius V, who had been campaigning for a Holy League almost since the day he became Pope, was jubilant. Venice too was deeply relieved; when the League was formally promulgated there at the beginning of July, the centre of the city was taken over by euphoric celebrations. After Mass in St Mark's cathedral (presided over by the Spanish Ambassador, who was also a member of the clergy), there was a grand parade of floats with symbolic tableaux. One had three youths representing the Doge, King Philip and the Pope; another consisted of a dragon with a crescent moon over its head (symbolizing the Sultan) being repeatedly struck by three young men with swords; one had a naked 'Moor' with wings and horns, representing Charon, the boatman of the underworld, with a Turk in his boat. Then came the priests in procession, the Spanish Ambassador, the prelates, the Doge, and more than 200 patricians dressed in their finest crimson. In the words of one observer: 'I shall not describe the noise, the pealings of bells, the cannon-fire, and the shouts of the people; as soon as the League was read out and proclaimed, almost everyone was crying, and laughing with joy at the same time.'[6]

While the diplomatic work on finalizing the arrangements for the

League had gone on, many practical matters had also required negotiation. One of the most important, from the Pope's point of view, was the provision of a papal fleet. Venice preferred to keep all its galleys for its own navy; one might suppose that it resented the destruction or abandonment of most the ships it had provided to the Pope in 1570, but there are no signs of recriminations on that score, and it seems to have been Colonna who dissuaded the Pope from approaching Venice again – perhaps because of the poor quality of the vessels it had supplied. The Pope had another option. Grand Duke Cosimo of Tuscany, whose direct participation in the League had been emphatically ruled out by Philip II, was eager to make himself indispensable, and he did possess, thanks to the recent creation of his own Tuscan order of maritime knights, a small fleet of war galleys with experienced crews. From the summer of 1570 Pius V had been investigating the possibility of hiring twelve Tuscan galleys, and had encountered fierce Spanish opposition to the idea. But since Spain also blocked his alternative plan, which involved getting ships from Genoa, and since Cosimo was keen to be of service, and willing to supply rowers, sailors and officers for all the galleys, the Pope pressed ahead. A last-minute sticking-point was Cosimo's demand that he should appoint all twelve of the galley captains; his idea, evidently, was to make the fleet as visibly Tuscan as possible, in order to reinforce the impression that he was a *de facto* participant in the League. But Colonna's adroit diplomacy reduced that figure from twelve to ten, with the other two appointed by the Pope. One of these would be the captain of Colonna's flagship, Gasparo Bruni.[7]

The contract that was finally signed between Cosimo and the Pope on 11 May specified that twelve galleys would be delivered to the papal port of Civitavecchia, fully armed and crewed, with 60 officers and sailors per ship. Eleven of them would have three rowers to an oar, with at least 24 benches, whereas the flagship would have five rowers to an oar in the section from the stern to the main mast, and four from the main mast to the prow. (Figures for the previous year indicate the greater size of the flagship: it had 269 rowers, while a typical galley in this fleet had 210. They also show that 69 per cent of its rowers were prisoners, and 31 per cent were slaves.) The flagship would be a lantern galley, complete with 'a set of trumpeters, and all the other things that are normally carried on other flagships'; only the banners would be provided by the Pope. The wages of half the crews would be paid by Rome, with Cosimo covering the other half; otherwise the main papal contribution would consist of the infantry soldiers on board each ship. Marcantonio

Colonna put Cencio Capizucchi in charge of raising the troops, and appointed Onorato Caetani, who was Duke of Sermoneta and Colonna's brother-in-law, 'captain-general' of the infantry aboard the fleet, with Bartolomeo Sereno (who later wrote a detailed account of the campaign) as his lieutenant. Pompeo Colonna was installed as Marcantonio's own deputy. Some modern historians have supposed that Pompeo was captain of the flagship, while others have given that role to Orazio Orsini or Cencio Capizucchi; the standard histories hardly mention Gasparo Bruni, but there can be no doubt that he captained the flagship throughout this campaign – as he did in the one before, and the one after.[8]

On 13 June Marcantonio Colonna left Rome and travelled to Civitavecchia, where – with Bruni, probably, at his right hand – he spent a week inspecting the assembled forces. Many Roman nobles and other prominent figures had volunteered. Some were rejected because they were too young (the Pope, determined to ensure that his own fleet would be free of the sin of sodomy, gave a strict order that 'beardless boys' must be excluded), but the final list did include some famous names, several of whom had to be placed, for honorific reasons, on the flagship. The most troublesome of these was Michele Bonelli, a 20-year-old great-nephew of the Pope, who had been appointed captain-general of the papal military forces while still a teenager – Pius V, despite his asceticism and reforming zeal, was an old-fashioned nepotist when it came to the interests of his family – and had schemed to supplant much more experienced people, such as Caetani, on this expedition. There was also Paolo Ghislieri, a son of Pius's brother, who had begun a military career in Rome and had then been expelled for immoral behaviour; now he hoped to regain his uncle's favour by acquitting himself well in battle. More reliable, probably, were Orazio Orsini, Antonio Carafa (who was Duke of Rocca Mondragone and Colonna's son-in-law), Cencio Capizucchi and his two cousins, Biagio and Camillo, and the Bolognese nobleman Pirro Malvezzi, who was a colonel of the papal infantry; all of these were on the flagship. The most distinguished military man aboard at this stage – he would later transfer to a Spanish galley – was the 62-year-old Gabrio Serbelloni, a Milanese nobleman with a long and highly successful record as a condottiere, artillery commander and expert on fortifications. He had fought the Ottomans in Hungary 29 years earlier, served as governor of Antwerp, redesigned the Castel Sant'Angelo in Rome during the papacy of his uncle, Pius IV, and been made a senior Knight of Malta; he joined this campaign in his capacity as general of the Spanish artillery. Finally, the flagship also carried one of the most experienced Knights of Malta, Mathurin de Lescaut Romegas – the person whose seizures of Ottoman ships had triggered the Sultan's decision to attack Malta in 1565. According to dal Pozzo, who wrote the continuation of Bosio's history of the Knights, Romegas had a general role as superintendent of the galleys in the fleet, while Gasparo Bruni (who, we may guess, had much less experience as commander of a warship) captained the ship on which Romegas sailed; although there is no particular reason to think that these men clashed, subsequent evidence does not suggest, as we shall see, that any great warmth developed between the two.[9]

On 21 June 1571 Colonna and his men left Civitavecchia and sailed to Naples. They waited there for almost a month, partly because the Spanish galleys were not ready, and partly because of strategic uncertainties about the feasibility of the original plan, which was to rendezvous with the Venetian fleet at Corfu: news of the huge Ottoman fleet's progress north-westwards from Crete had suddenly made that very problematic. The stay in Naples was not without its difficulties. Cardinal Granvelle, the newly appointed Viceroy, was positively obstructive, and when a fight broke out between papal troops and local Spanish forces it took all of Colonna's diplomatic skills to placate the Cardinal (whose viceregal palace the papal troops had at one point attempted to storm). Eventually the papal fleet set off, together with the three galleys from Malta which had joined it, for Messina, entering that port on 20 July. Three days later the Corfu squadron of the Venetian fleet arrived there under its commander, Sebastiano Venier, who had been put in general command of the Venetian navy, replacing the disgraced Girolamo Zane. With a heavy heart he had abandoned Corfu to the oncoming Ottoman fleet, knowing that his own squadron (of between 50 and 60 galleys) could do nothing to protect the island against such odds. For a whole month these assembled forces were obliged to wait in Messina as the news came in of the Ottoman fleet's progress up the eastern Adriatic coast: it was probably while he was there during August that Gasparo Bruni learned of the fall of Ulcinj and Bar. Nor were those the last places to be targeted; one part of the Ottoman fleet attacked the Venetian island of Korčula, beyond Dubrovnik, where it was said that the women of the city donned military uniform to deter the invaders, and it went on to mount an assault on the island of Hvar, even further to the north.[10]

At long last, Don John arrived on 23 August with 44 galleys, having spent time at Genoa and Naples en route from Barcelona. He summoned the leading commanders and asked for their opinions; some spoke against an offensive campaign, but Colonna and Venier were in favour. They discussed the idea of attacking Ottoman ports in Greece and Albania, with the aim of denying the Sultan's fleet any bases on the western coast of the Balkans; according to one Spanish report, Colonna and Don John were privately in favour of this, but the Venetians were strongly opposed, both because their primary aim was still to save Famagusta, and because they feared the establishment of a Spanish base in Greece. Just over a week later, the remaining squadron of 70 Venetian galleys sailed into port, having made the strenuous non-stop voyage direct from Crete. At roughly the same time, Gian Andrea Doria also arrived with the Genoese galleys, and a few days later the Neapolitan squadron of 30 ships came in, under its experienced commander, Álvaro de Bazán, the Marquis of Santa Cruz. On 8 September Don John held a review of the entire fleet, which now numbered 209 galleys and six galleasses (extra-large three-masted galleys with decks over the rowers and built-up 'castles' for artillery), as well as a quantity of transport ships and smaller vessels. Two days later he called another council of war, at which several of the Spanish officers still argued against mounting an offensive campaign. But the original purpose of the Holy League prevailed; Colonna and Venier were keen to set off, and Don John was indeed, as Colonna had assured the Venetians, 'a young man who desired glory'. The fleet finally left Messina on 16 September. As the last preparations were being made for its departure, the papal nuncio positioned himself with a group of Capuchins on the quayside, preventing 'beardless boys' from embarking; and each of the papal galleys was given a Capuchin or Dominican chaplain. The last few days had been spent in an atmosphere of intense religious fervour: on 8 September (the feast of the Nativity of the Virgin) the nuncio had begun a three-day programme of fasts and Masses, which culminated in a grand procession to the cathedral, led by the Archbishop carrying a fragment of the True Cross. He was accompanied through the streets of Messina by 'countless knights' – including, we may reasonably assume, Fra Gasparo Bruni, praying for victory and for the safety of his family.[11]

The fleet of the Holy League arrived at Corfu on 26 September. It was greeted with jubilation by the inhabitants, who had suffered badly during the summer, coming under renewed attack by Ottoman forces at the beginning of that month. By this stage in late September the Ottoman fleet had finished its Adriatic excursion. Within a few days, the League commanders learned that it was now in the Gulf of Patras (the outer part, facing Cephalonia and Ithaca, of the long stretch of sea dividing northern Greece from the Peloponnese). That information came from a scouting expedition which Don John had sent out; despite his public image as a romantic knight of chivalry and/or young hothead, Don John did have a shrewd grasp of the importance of intelligence, and while he was at Corfu he also sent spies into the Greek mainland to get more information. For several days, much of the fleet was stationed in the bay of Igoumenitsa (Ital.: Gomenizza), opposite the southern part of Corfu. Parties from the galleys landed in order to get water; some were attacked, and there were other encounters too. An Albanian on a horse who claimed to have come to sell them food was identified as a spy and seized, to be interrogated by Colonna; possibly the questioning was conducted by the Albanian-speaking captain of his flagship. And at the same time, some members of the landing parties were captured by Ottoman forces and taken overland for interrogation in Lepanto (Grk: Nafpaktos), the port where Pertev Pasha and Ali Müezzinzade Pasha were sheltering their fleet.[12]

Intelligence about the enemy was the most vital commodity in such a campaign, and both sides made special efforts to get it. One daredevil Ottoman corsair, Karaca Ali, had even penetrated the port of Messina to count the Christian fleet there, and another, Kara Hoca (commander of the corsairs of Vlorë), shadowed it off Corfu. For more than two months the Christian powers had been gathering and analysing reports about the strength of the Ottoman fleet. In July a Venetian slave who managed to escape from it had reported that it had 193 galleys and galiots (small galleys), and roughly 107 smaller ships; he also said that although it was generally free of infectious disease, people were dying from many other causes, including poor supplies of food and drink. With a few exceptions, the fleet was 'very badly manned, both with soldiers and with oarsmen, because this year their equipping of the galleys has gone extremely badly, because of a lack of people'. A similar report had reached Messina by early August: 180 galleys, 100 other vessels, and all inadequately manned. Later that month a Spanish slave who escaped at Herceg Novi gave the totals as 155 galleys and 80 smaller ships, while another informant put it at 150 galleys but up to another 150 small (and poorly manned) vessels. The Christian commanders had pored over these and other reports, but without reaching any definite conclusions. A paper written for Don John by one of his advisers, the battle-scarred one-eyed Marquis Ascanio della Corgna, observed that while the League's Spanish and Italian troops were mostly inexperienced, 'and the Germans [sc. two infantry regiments in Spanish pay] are of little use at sea, and are lacking in arquebuses', nevertheless 'I do not think the enemy's men can be very good, or better than ours . . . and as for the number and quality of the ships in the Ottoman fleet, the reports are so various that I cannot judge very well if it is smaller or greater than ours.' Until the eve of the battle, when Kara Hoca performed another surreptitious count of the Christian vessels, the Ottomans were convinced that the League fleet was much smaller than it actually was; the League commanders would think the two were quite evenly matched, with the Ottomans possessing more vessels but fewer full-size galleys, and that seems to have been the truth.[13]

Sailing southwards from Igoumenitsa to engage with the enemy, the Christian fleet reached the island of Cephalonia on 4 October, where it received some dismal news, brought there from Crete: Famagusta had fallen. It is a sign of how thoroughly the Ottoman actions had disrupted communications in the eastern Mediterranean that this news had not come sooner, since the surrender had taken place on 1 August. The report also described how the victorious Ottoman general at the siege, Lala Mustafa Pasha, had turned against the Venetian commander, Marcantonio Bragadin (whom he accused of killing Muslim prisoners), and had ordered the execution of many of the Italian, Greek and Albanian soldiers who had laid down their arms. Bragadin himself was subjected to humiliating treatment before being flayed alive; his skin, stuffed with straw, was then sent on a tour of Ottoman territories as a trophy of the victory. While in one sense the news from Cyprus eliminated the main *raison d'être* of the League's expedition, its immediate effect was to strengthen the resolve of the allied soldiers – especially the Venetians, who were eager for revenge. They would have their chance three days later, when the two fleets finally faced each other just inside the entrance of the Gulf of Patras, close to the northern shore.[14]

The Battle of Lepanto (as it is traditionally called, after the rather distant naval base from which the Ottoman fleet set out) of 7 October 1571 is one of the most famous sea-battles ever fought. To the modern mind, influenced by a continuous history of naval warfare from the eighteenth century to the twentieth, a sea-battle depends heavily on the use of artillery broadsides, the main aim being to sink the enemy's ships. Galley warfare in the sixteenth century was, however, quite different. The ships were primarily platforms for soldiers, who fired at their opponents and then boarded the enemy's vessels and fought at close quarters. The long ram or beak at the front of each galley was there not for sinking enemy ships, but for spearing them and then acting as a gangway for soldiers to cross. And while galleys did have artillery pieces, their main purpose in battle was not to sink an enemy vessel but to mow down the men on deck, or disable the ship by smashing its oars or rudder. Heavy cannons (of the sort that could be used to attack fortifications in amphibious assaults) were mounted only at the prow; small swivel-guns, with anti-personnel shot, could be placed elsewhere, though there was very little room for them on a normal galley. And while the skilled Venetian gunners could hit a galley at up to 500 yards, most artillery fire between ships was at what the Spanish called 'clothes-burning' range ('quemaropa'). The other main weapons used before it came to hand-to-hand fighting were arquebuses and their heavier relatives, muskets; an arquebus fired a half-ounce bullet, and a heavy Spanish 'mosquete' fired a ball of two ounces, which could penetrate armour at 100 yards and kill a horse at 500. Also employed were the crossbow, whose bolt could penetrate light armour, and the traditional bow; no one thought that these had been rendered obsolete by the invention of firearms, since traditional bows had a much faster rate of fire, and both types were unaffected by rain. Devices for hurling 'fire-balls' and containers of the fiercely burning viscous preparation known as 'Greek fire' were also used. At Lepanto both sides had arquebuses, but the League possessed them in much greater quantities; the Ottomans relied more on the traditional composite bow, which was ineffective against good armour. And while both sides had artillery, it was more sparsely distributed among the Ottoman galleys. However, while all of these weapons were important in thinning the ranks of the enemy, the final stage of any encounter between two galleys consisted of boarding and hand-to-hand fighting, with swords, daggers, spears and – the most effective of all, in the hands of Spanish-trained infantry – pikes. In the words of Miguel de Cervantes, who fought on a Genoese ship at Lepanto, in the end everything depended on the courage of the individual soldiers crossing onto the enemy's galley:

> When ships are locked and grappled together, the soldier has no more space left him than two feet of plank on the beak-head. But though he sees in front of him countless pieces of artillery threatening from the enemy's side . . . nevertheless . . . he exposes himself as a mark for all their shot, and endeavours to pass along that narrow causeway into the enemy's ship. And, most amazing of all, no sooner does one man fall, never to rise again this side of Doomsday, than another takes his place – the greatest display of valour and daring to be found in all the hazards of war.[15]

The prospects of such fighting must have filled the minds of the more than 40,000 Christian and Ottoman soldiers who prepared for battle on the morning of 7 October. For several hours, the two fleets faced each other at a safe distance, each stretching itself into a north–south line one galley deep and more than four miles long, with a reserve group of vessels behind the central part of the line. In each case the line was divided into three sections; on the Christian side Don John commanded the centre, Gian Andrea Doria the right wing, and the Venetian quartermaster-general, Agostino Barbarigo (who had taken over some of Venier's functions after a serious dispute between Venier and Don John a few days earlier), the left wing. The tip of that wing, at the northern end of the line, came close to land: not the modern coastline, which is the product of later alluvial deposits, but a group of islands, called the Echinades in Greek and the Curzolari in Italian, most of which have now been incorporated in the mainland. Don John took some care to intermingle Spanish, Venetian and other ships, so that the line did not consist simply of national blocks, but the left wing was heavily dominated by Venetian galleys (especially from Dalmatia and Crete), and the right was, beyond a certain point, mostly Genoese. Don John's own flagship took the central place, with the papal flagship on its right and the Venetian one, under Venier, on its left. Most of the flagships were concentrated there, for reasons of prestige and honour: that of Genoa, with the Prince of Parma on board, for example, and that of Savoy, with the Prince of Urbino. Similarly, the centre of the Ottoman line contained the flagship galleys of Ali Müezzinzade Pasha and Pertev Pasha, as well as the lantern galleys of other dignitaries. These ships also had the greatest concentration of janissaries (members of the Sultan's standing army of infantry), who were equipped with arquebuses and skilled in their use.[16]

The one obvious difference between the two fleets – though the Ottoman commanders realized its significance only at a very late stage – was that the League had six great Venetian galleasses, which it towed out to positions well ahead of the line of galleys. The importance of these became clear when, some time shortly after noon, the Ottoman fleet finally attacked. A galleass rode too high in the water to be boarded; each was a floating fortress armed with, on average, 31 artillery pieces, and some of these were arranged for lateral fire. As the Ottoman galleys approached, the fire they came under was powerful and accurate; having assumed that the galleasses would have artillery only in the prow, they received a second shock as they went past them. Some galleys were

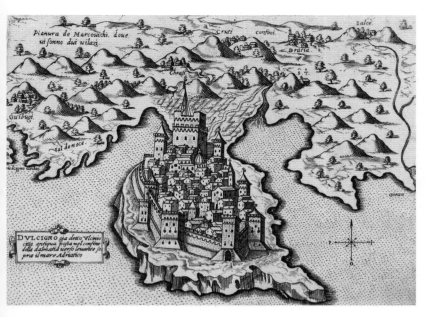

1. View of Ulcinj (1571, representing the city under Venetian rule).

2. Ulcinj today (seen from the north-west).

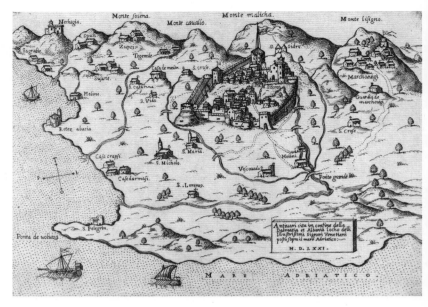

3. View of Bar (1571, representing the city under Venetian rule).

4. The Council of Trent during its final sessions, 1562–3 (a sketch formerly attributed to Titian).

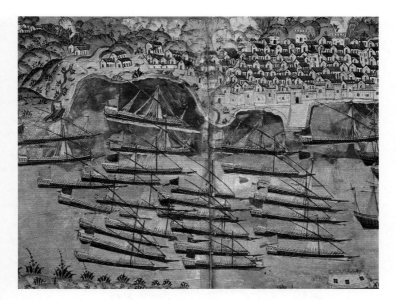

5. The North African corsair fleet under Hayreddin Barbarossa, in front of the town of Nice (from an Ottoman illustrated manuscript made in 1558, twelve years after Barbarossa's death).

6. Dubrovnik: the Sponza Palace, built in the early sixteenth century and used as a government building. (One of the few buildings from this period to have survived the devastating earthquake of 1667, it now houses the State Archives.)

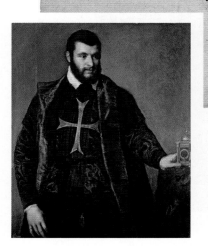

7. Gasparo Bruni's first letter
to Marcantonio Colonna,
from Ancona, 30 June 1570
(see p. 112).

8. A Knight of Malta (identity unknown), by Titian (c.1550).

9. King Philip II of Spain, by Sofonisba Anguissola (1565).

10. Pope Pius V, by El Greco (who was in Rome during the last two years of Pius V's papacy; but this is a retrospective portrait, painted in c.1605).

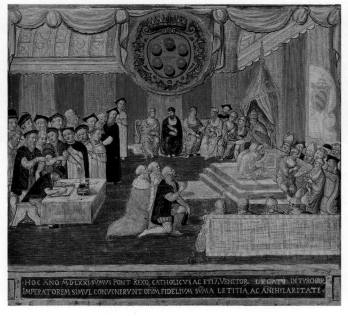

11. Pope Pius V concluding the Holy League, 20 May 1571 (a contemporary painting).

12. The Battle of Lepanto, by Giorgio Vasari (1572–3), with an angel (*upper left*) hovering just above the papal flagship, where Gasparo Bruni was directing the crew.

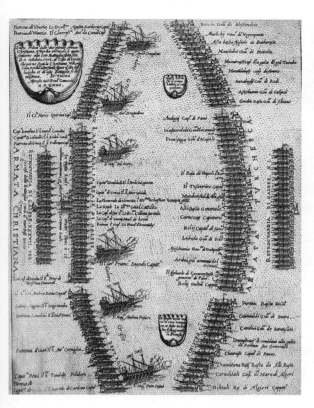

13. The Battle of Lepanto, with the Christian fleet on the left, and the six galleasses in front of it (a plan published in late 1571 or 1572).

14. The three commanders at Lepanto: (*from the left*) Don John, Marcantonio Colonna and Sebastiano Venier (by an unknown artist, 1575).

15. A 'lantern' galley, with twenty-seven banks of oars, and cannons in the prow (an engraving of 1629).

16. A galleass, with thirty banks of oars, a covered deck, artillery 'castles' and lateral cannons (an engraving of 1602).

sunk, and great damage was done both to the morale of the Ottoman combatants and to the physical arrangement of their attack, which lost much of its coherence. Ali Müezzinzade Pasha pressed on, engaging directly with his counterpart, Don John, while Pertev Pasha rammed Colonna's flagship. Other galleys clustered round in support, and intense fighting followed. At any given time the papal flagship was engaged with several Ottoman vessels; these included a lantern galley which had been put under the command of the two teenage sons of Ali Müezzinzade Pasha. According to Caetani's lieutenant, Bartolomeo Sereno (who was with Caetani on a nearby papal galley), the Pope's young great-nephew acquitted himself well, resolutely firing his arquebus while others around him were felled by enemy fire – including Colonna's major-domo, whose head was blown off next to him. In these circumstances there was little manoeuvring to be done, and Gasparo Bruni may well have found himself mostly employed as a director of the fighting by his sailors and crew, and as a fighter himself – hence the serious wounds which, as we shall see, he sustained during the battle.[17]

In every section of these extended lines, the combat was intense. On the left wing Agostino Barbarigo struggled to prevent Ottoman galleys from slipping through the coastal shoals and encircling the League ships; his own ships were still relatively undermanned so far as fighters were concerned, and this group suffered the heaviest losses of the League fleet. As time went by, however, he benefited from the fact that some Ottoman crews were tempted to beach their vessels and escape the fighting. (It may be relevant that 30–40 per cent of the crews were Greek, even though few were from this particular part of Greece.) On the right wing the League galleys had to contend with the most experienced fighters in the Ottoman fleet, the corsairs brought from Algiers by their commander Uluç Ali; a dozen Christian vessels here had their entire complements killed. One of the most famous cases was that of the Venetian ship named *Cristo Sopra il Mondo* ('Christ Over the World'), which fought off five Ottoman galleys and was then attacked by four more, with the loss of almost all its men. In one version of the story it was its wounded captain, Benedetto Soranzo, who waited until many Ottoman soldiers had swarmed aboard and then ignited the remaining powder-barrels, blowing the ship sky-high; another attributed this action to the 'scrivano' or purser, who had just seen Soranzo decapitated. Uluç Ali managed even to outwit Gian Andrea Doria, drawing him out of position and then slipping through the gap thus created; at the end of the battle, as the irreversibility and scale of the defeat was becoming clear, he led his corsairs to the open sea, and was the only Ottoman commander to retain a significant group of vessels. The turning-point of the battle came at its very centre, where the flagships of Don John, Colonna and Venier were caught up for several hours in a vicious mêlée. (As we have seen, the fighters on Venier's flagship may have included Antonio Bruti's son Jacomo, and perhaps also Jacomo's brother Marco, nephews of Gasparo Bruni.)* Extra soldiers brought in from the reserve by Santa Cruz were put on the Spanish and papal flagships, and some of them managed to penetrate Ali Müezzinzade Pasha's ship and kill him. According to Ferrante Caracciolo, who was on a papal galley a little to the left of the central group, a Spanish soldier cut off Ali's head and brought it to Don John, who was disgusted by this unchivalrous conduct; nevertheless, it was put on a pole at the stern of the ship, and the sight of it apparently caused dismay among the remaining Ottoman fighters. With the killing of several other Ottoman commanders the battle drew gradually to its close.[18]

In his analysis of the victory Ferrante Caracciolo attributed it to four particular factors: the role of the galleasses, the fact that the League ships began firing their artillery sooner than the Ottoman ones, 'the trust which the enemy had in the terrain' (meaning, apparently, their willingness to desert the battle because the nearby land was home territory), and the League's superiority in arquebuses. Modern historians have added to this list. One writer, Ricardo Cerezo Martínez, broadly accepts Caracciolo's four claims (while emphasizing the greater accuracy, rather than priority, of the artillery fire), mentioning also the more efficient reserve squadron and the more experienced soldiers. That last point seems uncertain, however; half of the Spanish infantrymen were new recruits, and Ascanio della Corgna's comment (quoted above) suggests that most of the Italians were too. The naval historian John Guilmartin stresses three things: the role of the galleasses; the greater weight of the League's centre, which it owed largely to the superior strength of its reserve; and the skill and determination of Barbarigo in making sure that the Christian line was not outflanked. The most thorough account of the Lepanto campaign, by Alessandro Barbero, puts special emphasis on two other factors. Overall, he notes, the League had a greater number of fighting men, including the sailors and non-slave rowers who could be given weapons; the Ottoman fleet was depleted by deaths and desertions after a sea-campaign of more than five months,

* See p. 458, n. 27.

and may have had as few as 20,000 fighters in total, whereas the League had 23,000 soldiers and another 13,000 crew members who could be used in combat. And while the Christian soldiers had a much greater number of arquebuses, which they wisely used to eliminate as many of their foes as possible before boarding an enemy ship, they also had efficient armour, which protected them from the arrows of the Ottoman archers. The result was, Barbero concludes, an 'inevitable' victory. The points he makes are good ones, and yet the conclusion still surprises; when one looks at how finely balanced the combat was, for a long time, in almost any part of the battle, one has to marvel at the tenacity of the Ottoman fighters who came in fact quite close to winning against those superior odds.[19]

All accounts of this battle draw almost exclusively on Western sources. The Ottoman chroniclers passed over it, understandably, as swiftly as they could. Standard modern accounts do record that an argument took place before the battle among the Ottoman high command about the advisability of engaging with the enemy fleet; this is briefly described by the historian Peçevi, but most of the available detail is drawn from Western sources which got their information from the subsequent interrogation of prisoners. Yet there is in fact a contemporary Ottoman account of the Battle of Lepanto, written by someone who was either a participant himself or an acquaintance of many people who were there: the Persian poet Mohammed ibn 'Abd Allah Zirek el-Hoseini. He took part in the Cyprus campaign, and completed his Turkish-language narrative, 'Fethname-i Qibris' ('History of the Conquest of Cyprus'), in 1574; his account of the Lepanto campaign comes in a supplementary text, written in Cyprus later in the 1570s, which is mainly concerned with the subsequent Ottoman attack on La Goletta and Tunis. Surprisingly, this account seems to have been ignored by all modern studies of Lepanto.[20]

Zirek's narrative describes the fleet's devastation of Crete in the summer, and its sacking of Cephalonia, Corfu, Sopot and Budva, where 'the soldiers, not content to seize the inhabitants' property, carried off the women, girls, boys and old men.' It gives quite an accurate account of the League's fleet, saying that it contained 25,000 fighting men; it notes that Kara Hoca (the corsair captain from Vlorë, who died in the conflict) captured a Christian sailor shortly before the battle and forced him to give the location of the fleet; and it confirms that there was disagreement among the high command, blaming Ali Müezzinzade Pasha for not having taken the advice of experienced sailors. (Ali would be much vilified by the Ottomans: the seventeenth-century writer Katib Çelebi would comment that this recently appointed admiral 'had not commanded a single rowing boat in his life'.) Zirek supplies some details about the battle itself. He writes that 40–50 Ottoman ships went too close to land and were unfortunately grounded, thus putting a gloss of innocence on what may have been a less accidental outcome in many cases. On the actual conditions of the fighting, he confirms the picture drawn in several Western accounts, which emphasize the dense pall of smoke from the constant artillery fire: 'on all sides the cannons firing were like thunderclaps, and the noble fleet was surrounded by a thick smoke which covered the sky.' He also stresses the effect of the superior arquebus fire from the Christian galleys: 'the men succumbed to a hail of bullets.' Inaccurately, he says that Ali Müezzinzade Pasha took his galleys to attack the galleasses. But his account of the dramatic effect of Ali's death does, despite its consciously poetic language, ring true: 'At this news the Ottoman army became like a garden ruined by hail, or a city taken by siege; the soldiers lost their strength, people abandoned the ships which they had seized from the enemy, and each man sought his own safety in flight. The infidels, who had scattered like rabid dogs, regained courage, and became more enraged than a dragon with seven heads.'[21]

The battle ended in the late afternoon. As the fighting died down and the clouds of acrid smoke began to clear, the scene that greeted the survivors was one of devastation on a huge scale. In Ferrante Caracciolo's words, 'the sea was full of dead men, of planks, of clothing, of some Ottomans, who were fleeing by swimming, and of other Ottomans who were drowning, of many shattered remains of ships that were burning, and of others that were sinking.' Bartolomeo Sereno painted a similar picture: between the burning wrecks the water was 'full of tunics, turbans, quivers, arrows, bows, drums', and other objects, plus large numbers of men, still alive but dying of their wounds, whom the Christian soldiers finished off with 'arquebus shots and pike-thrusts'. Of those Ottoman soldiers and sailors who managed to swim to the Christian ships and cling to their sides, some had their hands chopped off, while others were hauled aboard in the hope of obtaining either a ransom or a profitable sale as a slave.[22]

For many people on the Ottoman galleys, on the other hand, the end of the battle brought longed-for freedom: 12,000 or more Christian slaves were liberated. Some were women and children, captured by the Ottoman forces in raids on Venetian territory earlier in the year – including people from Ulcinj and Bar, who had been retained in breach of the agreements made when those cities were surrendered. Many were galley-slaves, who sat chained to their benches, in miserable conditions, rowing the galleys; of these, several thousand had been in the fleet since it had set out from Istanbul at the beginning of the campaign, but a large number had also been acquired by raiding, being made to fill the ranks of galleys depleted by sickness and desertion. In the words of one early chronicler, 'when they heard the cry "Victory, victory!", they broke their chains and, with the weapons that had been scattered by the Ottomans, made much havoc and butchery, taking their revenge for the abuses and acts of cruelty they had suffered.' If they succeeded in killing the last remnants of the Ottoman soldiers and crew, the next step, naturally enough, was to go through the galley – and the clothes of the dead Ottomans – hunting for valuable items. But in this they faced fierce competition from Christian soldiers who were now pouring onto the enemy ships in search of whatever booty they could find. (And not only the enemy ships: from one Venetian galley, where the entire complement had been wiped out during the fighting, Spanish soldiers removed all the valuables, including even the flag of St Mark, which was later bought off them by a scandalized Venetian merchant in Messina.) These were the spoils of war, and the officers knew better than to interfere: the aristocratic Ferrante Caracciolo recalled that the grandees did not dare leave their own galleys, unless the men invited one of their captains to join them so that he could take their loot into his safe-keeping.[23]

It was in these circumstances that one of the worst incidents in the entire story of the Battle of Lepanto took place. Among the slaves on the Ottoman galleys was Archbishop Giovanni Bruni, who, like so many of his flock, had been denied his promised freedom. His new masters had been well aware of his status, but they also knew that he had strongly opposed the decision to surrender the city of Bar, so they had decreed the public humiliation of putting him on a galley bench (together with his nephew Nicolò, the stradiot commander of Ulcinj) and making him row. It was on that galley that Giovanni and his nephew met their deaths. One early Venetian report stated that they were 'killed by the Ottomans'; a later account, sent to the Jesuits in Rome, said that they had both been executed by the Ottomans while the battle was still raging. But in fact they were killed by Christian soldiers. By the late seventeenth century some knowledge of this had percolated into the region: the Archbishop of Skopje wrote that 'in the first attack' Bruni was decapitated by soldiers who mistook him for an Ottoman. Later, the family tradition of a Dalmatian nobleman told a similar story: Bruni was killed by mistake 'at the moment when the galley was seized'. The true story, however, was much worse than that.[24]

After the battle, the Pope commissioned an investigation into the moral failings of the Christian fleet. Many general problems were discussed, such as the maltreatment of Orthodox Christians, or the prevalence of blasphemy, sodomy and gambling.* But the most shocking part of the whole dossier was a report on the death of Giovanni Bruni, compiled – apparently after speaking to eye-witnesses – by the Bishop of the southern Italian see of Nardò. Once the Ottomans had been defeated, he wrote,

> many Spanish soldiers, who were fully armed, killed many poor Christian slaves in order to rob them and to take from them what little booty God had granted them. Among others they killed the poor Archbishop of Bar, who had been made a captive of the Ottoman fleet in the previous August, when that city was taken; although he shouted 'I'm a bishop, I'm a Christian', they refused to believe him, and instead they killed him with a pike. It would not have been so bad if this had happened during the fighting, but it was a long time afterwards.[25]

The death of an archbishop in these circumstances was terrible enough. What made it tragic, however, was the fact that if only Giovanni Bruni had survived, he could have been united almost immediately with his brother – in a reunion that would have made a novelistic scene worthy of Cervantes.† Gasparo Bruni was probably aware that his brother had been taken away after the surrender of Bar, and might have guessed that he would be on one of the Ottoman ships, though he could not have known on which one. Nor is this knowable with any certainty today; but a good guess can be made. The Archbishop was the most distinguished of all the captives, so one would expect him to have been held on the galley of the overall commander of the campaign, Pertev Pasha. (Subsequent letters from two senior Venetian officers said that Giovanni Bruni and his nephew had been made prisoners or slaves of 'the Pasha'; Pertev was not the only bearer of that title at Lepanto, but he is by far the most likely candidate.) Pertev's galley, the *Sultana* – very

---

* See above, p. 116.

† Cervantes himself was now lying in great pain on the deck of his Genoese galley, close to the central group of ships, having received an arquebus shot which shattered his left hand.

possibly with Giovanni Bruni among its rowers – had rammed Gasparo Bruni's ship, and there had been fierce fighting between their soldiers before Pertev turned it aside to give support to the Ottoman admiral. At that point his ship was attacked by two galleys, one Venetian and one Genoese; Gasparo Bruni's ship engaged for a while with another Ottoman galley, but then returned to the attack on the *Sultana*. Pertev's remaining men were mown down, and he himself escaped in a small rowing boat, whose rower, an Italian convert to Islam, passed through the Christian line shouting 'Don't shoot – we're Christians.' The fighting continued, so we cannot simply assume that the soldiers who neutralized Pertev's ship were the ones doing the looting at a later stage. One early source says that Pertev was defeated by the Spanish captain Juan de Cardona, which is certainly not true; the origin of that story may be that it was Cardona who took possession of Pertev's galley at the end of the battle – in which case, it may have been soldiers from his ship (belonging to the pike-wielding *tercio* or regiment of Sicily, which was half Sicilian and half Spanish) that murdered Giovanni Bruni. In any case, neither Pertev's galley nor Gasparo Bruni's had moved far; at the moment of Giovanni's death, his brother may have been less than a hundred yards away.[26]

News of Gasparo's loss quickly circulated. In a formal letter to the Doge of Venice, written a few weeks after the battle, the Venetian commander, Sebastiano Venier, declared that it moved him to 'compassion'; he also wrote that Gasparo Bruni 'did us the greatest service and assistance in important matters to bring about that day of victory – in which, also, he was badly wounded'. As he nursed his wounds and absorbed the terrible news of his brother's pointless death, Gasparo Bruni must have had many cares weighing on his mind. He had lost not only his brother and his nephew, but also his brother-in-law, and probably many other members of his extended family; of his own generation he seems to have been the sole survivor. He had been deprived of his home, and all his property. The place in which he was born and bred was now an Ottoman town – or perhaps little more than the shell of one, charred, partly ruined and heavily depopulated. There were many other Venetians, especially subjects of the Stato da Mar, whose relief at the outcome of the battle would have been tempered by feelings of loss and bereavement; but few, perhaps, had lost as much as he had.[27]

While the deaths among the Christian soldiers, sailors and rowers came to nearly 8,000 (with a larger number of wounded men), the figure for the Ottoman side is thought to have been much higher. The

psychological effect on opinion in Istanbul – where news of the defeat
arrived on 23 October – was dramatic, not just because of the scale of
likely bereavement, but because the sudden loss of most of the Ottoman
fleet caused an unprecedented feeling of defencelessness. A Venetian
diplomat who was there less than two years later heard that 'many
people in Istanbul got ready to flee to Anatolia, and many commended
themselves to Christians and converts from Christianity, expecting the
arrival of the Christian fleet from day to day.' According to one Ottoman chronicler, the Sultan, who was at his palace in Edirne, was so
shocked that he could not sleep for three nights; he returned to Istanbul
to stabilize the situation, after hearing that the city was full of rumours
about the impending arrival of the League's armada. As soon as he
heard the news of the defeat, Sultan Selim began to issue a flurry of
orders to governors and commanders in northern Greece, the Peloponnese and the Greek islands, including Cyprus and Rhodes, warning of
possible attacks. The mood in Istanbul did not settle until the beginning
of December, when the corsair captain Uluç Ali arrived. One of the Sultan's first orders, on 28 October, had instructed him to gather all the
ships he could find and bring them in the direction of Istanbul; he had
managed to pick up 40 more Ottoman vessels from the Aegean islands,
which enabled him to make a grand and reassuring entrance into the
Golden Horn with a fleet of 87 ships. The Sultan had already appointed
him *Kapudan Paşa* (admiral of the Ottoman navy); now he also gave
him, with honorific word-play, the title 'Kılıç Ali' ('kılıç' meaning sword
or sabre).[28]

In fact the commanders of the League had thought only briefly about
the idea of pressing on to Istanbul, before dismissing it as utterly imprac-
ticable. Years later, the writer Francesco Patrizi would record that when
he asked one of the senior figures – who, given Patrizi's Roman connections, may have been Colonna – why they did not follow up Lepanto
immediately with an offensive campaign, he was told that too many of
the League's men had been injured. But that was not the only reason. As
Onorato Caetani, the papal infantry commander, wrote in a letter to
Rome two days after the battle, 'I think we shall find that we have so
many wounded men that we shall not go on towards Istanbul, as we
were thinking of doing, having provisions for only one month, and not
being able to winter away from home.' He added that 'I think we shall
return to the Adriatic to seize Vlorë, Durrës and Herceg Novi'; but even
those plans were quickly abandoned. So too, after a brief reconnais-
sance operation by the expert on fortifications Gabrio Serbelloni, was

the idea of capturing the fortress on Lefkas (Ital.: Santa Maura), the island south of Corfu which was an Ottoman possession and a centre for Muslim corsairs. The only stronghold to be seized from the Ottomans would be Margariti, after a four-day siege by Sebastiano Venier. The Ottomans also abandoned Sopot, which was swiftly occupied by the Himariots and handed by them to the Venetians. But those actions would take place in November, after the League fleet had dispersed.[29]

The days after the battle were taken up – first in the harbours of nearby islands, then at Corfu – with tending the sick and dying, making essential repairs to the ships, and dividing the spoils, of which there were many. Each papal galley, as Caetani reported, had towed back at least one enemy ship (with the exception of one galley, the *Fiorenza*, whose complement had been almost completely wiped out). Marcantonio Colonna's papers contain lists of slaves captured in this way: the majority were Turks from Anatolia and Istanbul, but there were also some black Africans, 'Marin of Ulcinj, a renegade Christian, aged 40', 'Martino, a Calabrian renegade, aged 30', 'Hüseyin, an Albanian renegade soldier, aged 30', 'Cafer, a renegade German', 'Yusuf, an Albanian volunteer rower', 'a Gypsy mute from Istanbul', and 'George son of Manoli, a Cypriot renegade boy'. Don John gave slaves, as tokens of his appreciation, to various dignitaries for their personal use; the recipients included senior officers and galley captains. It is not known whether Gasparo Bruni received one, but if he did, he presumably sold him when he returned to Italy, at the going rate of up to 100 ducats for an able-bodied man. As commander in chief, Don John was personally entitled to one tenth of all the booty, regardless of the proportion that went to his half-brother, the King of Spain. Sebastiano Venier complained bitterly about the distribution; earlier feelings of rivalry were resurfacing now, and Venier did not help matters by sending news of the victory to Venice ahead of the official despatch from Don John. It was with some ill-feelings, then, that the allied forces went their separate ways in the last week of October. The bulk of the Venetian fleet headed northwards; the papal and Spanish ships sailed to Messina, arriving there on 1 November, and two weeks later the papal galleys were at Naples.[30]

Colonna and the other dignitaries proceeded quickly to Rome. There, with the Pope's encouragement, the municipal authorities decided to stage a 'triumph', modelled on the practice of the ancient Romans. The participants were almost entirely confined to the Roman noblemen and gentlemen who had been at the battle – with the predictable result that Spanish observers were deeply offended, claiming that Marcantonio

Colonna was being presented as the sole victor. Just a handful of non-Romans were invited to walk with him through the streets lined with cheering crowds. They did include the French Knight of Malta Romegas, who had been on Colonna's flagship; whether the captain of that ship was also present is not known.[31]

Of course Rome had good reason to be joyful. So did Venice, where the festivities went on for days, with High Masses, bell-ringing, tableaux and fireworks. There were celebrations in many parts of Western Europe, and the battle would be commemorated in art and literature for years and decades to come. And yet the question has inevitably been asked: did Lepanto achieve anything in the long term? As we shall see, the Ottoman navy was quickly rebuilt; the plan to follow up with an offensive campaign was abortive; and Venice's eventual peace settlement with the Sultan would be so humiliating as to merit Voltaire's remark that it was as if the Ottomans had been the victors at Lepanto. The standard reply to the question is that while the battle made little or no practical difference, it was very important psychologically, as it showed Western Christendom that the Ottomans were not invincible: in Fernand Braudel's words, 'The spell of Turkish supremacy had been broken.' But this is not a strong argument, both because there had been other famous Ottoman defeats or, at any rate, failures (the siege of Vienna in 1529, for example, or that of Malta in 1565, which had been a colossal humiliation for the Ottomans), and because set-piece naval battles were a very unusual form of warfare; the defeat of a large Ottoman army in pitched battle on land would have been much more relevant to the Western Europeans' fears.[32]

A more useful way of considering the significance of the Battle of Lepanto is to ask what might have happened if the Ottomans had won. This does of course involve counter-factual speculation; but the assessment of what the Ottoman strategy would have been is not dependent on pure guesswork. Just after the fall of Nicosia, Sultan Selim II sent a letter to his vassal the Voivod of Wallachia, telling him to rejoice at the news and to help prepare an army and navy to capture Corfu. This chimes with Mehmed Sokollu's remark to Ragazzoni that the Sultan would take both Corfu and Crete. Corfu was one of the two linch-pins of the Venetian maritime system (Crete being the other), but it was also more than that. With it, the Ottomans could plan a major invasion of Italy across the Straits of Otranto with great confidence; without it, any such plan would be open to serious disruption. Although the idea of an Ottoman conquest of southern Italy looks strange and far-fetched to the modern eye, it is only in retrospect that it can seem natural that Ottoman westwards expansion should have ended at the Balkan coast and the plains of Hungary. There had been a premonition of possible future plans in 1480–1, when a large Ottoman force occupied Otranto and its territory with the clear aim of establishing long-term dominion there. Süleyman the Magnificent's grand strategy of 1537, involving an invasion of southern Italy coordinated with a French attack from the north, has already been mentioned.* The repeated attacks on southern Italy in the 1550s were mostly raiding expeditions, as was Piyale Pasha's attack on Apulia in 1566, but three years later the French Ambassador in Istanbul was reporting that the Sultan planned an invasion of Apulia with 60,000 cavalry and more than 200,000 infantry. At the end of December 1571, Mehmed Sokollu sent a message to the governor of Lepanto saying that he was going to launch 50,000 Tatars and 40,000 auxiliary troops against Apulia in the coming year; he added that the necessary transport ships 'have previously been constructed in those regions for the siege of Corfu' – thus showing how seriously that Venetian stronghold had featured in the Ottoman plans. In 1573 the Sultan informed the King of France that he intended to invade Apulia in the following year with 150,000 infantry and 50,000 cavalry, and Spanish intelligence agents in Istanbul still thought that such an attack was imminent in the summer of 1574. Two years later the Venetian bailo in Istanbul reported that Kılıç Ali was setting out with a fleet of 100 ships for two purposes: to raid Calabria, and to reconnoitre Corfu for a future siege. Similar plans and similar fears would be revived in the 1590s: in the middle of that decade it was the Ottomans' ally Henri IV of France who offered to share the Kingdom of Naples with them if they invaded it.[33]

What was worse, from the point of view of the rulers of Italy, was that an Ottoman invasion might not be unwelcome to some of their subjects. As the Huguenot diplomat Hubert Languet wrote to Augustus of Saxony in late 1572: 'if the Ottomans should happen to seize some port-town of Apulia or Old Calabria and convey strong forces there, which would not be difficult, in view of the short voyage from Albania and north-western Greece, I do not doubt that many inhabitants of the Kingdom of Naples, infuriated by the Spanish tyranny, which is extremely harsh, would defect to them.' Even if they did not expect the Ottomans to be milder rulers, he added, they would still like the

* Above, p. 35.

satisfaction of seeing the ruin of their actual oppressors. Such attitudes would become plainly visible in Calabria in the 1590s, when a pro-Ottoman conspiracy did take place, involving the philosopher (and Dominican friar) Tommaso Campanella. There were always some people who would happily invite the Ottomans in, to discomfort their own enemies. In 1551–3 the exiled Prince of Salerno was said to be scheming, with the French, to bring 15–20,000 Ottoman Albanians and Slavs to foment an anti-Habsburg revolt in southern Italy; part of his plan, apparently, was to hand over the Apulian port of Trani to the Ottoman navy. And in 1573 a conspiracy was discovered, involving Count Giovanni Aldobrandini of Ravenna and some Dutch Protestants, to deliver the papal port of Ancona into the hands of the Sultan.[34]

The counter-factual proposition, then, is as follows. Had the Ottomans been victorious at Lepanto, they would have returned in the following year to undertake a major siege of Corfu. And had that in turn been successful, they would have had the confidence, and the ability, to mount not just a raid on southern Italy, but an invasion of it. The remnants of the Venetian fleet would have been bottled up in the northern Adriatic, and a depleted Spanish–Genoese–papal fleet would not have been sufficient to oppose the Ottoman landing force. In the end, of course, this never happened. But it was the logic of this scenario that linked the fates of Venice and Spain at the deepest level. Their relations generally may have been rivalrous or resentful, and neither had any interest in the wider strategic aims of the other in the Mediterranean region; indeed, each would usually feel some private satisfaction when the other underwent defeat or humiliation at Ottoman hands. But the Venetians knew that an Ottoman conquest of southern Italy would pose a fatal threat to their own power in the Adriatic. They were aware that in an all-out war against the Ottomans, they would need Spanish help; and the Spanish knew that if they did not help, and if Corfu fell, their southern Italian dominions would be next. Such was the tie that bound these mutually hostile allies inexorably together.

9

War, Peace and Ottoman Resurgence

In many ways, the system of government, taxation and military organization developed by the Ottoman Empire in the fifteenth and sixteenth centuries was the envy of Western Europe. Few episodes give more striking confirmation of its strength than the extraordinary reconstruction of the Ottoman navy after the disaster of Lepanto. Within one week of the news of the defeat, Grand Vizier Mehmed Sokollu had decreed that 200 new galleys were to be built for the next campaigning season. Many of these would be made in the Istanbul Arsenal, but there were 21 other ship-building sites, mostly on the coasts of the Sea of Marmara and the Black Sea. A stream of orders instructed regional Ottoman governors to round up all available carpenters, rope-makers and other relevant craftsmen and send them to the shipyards; janissary soldiers were also put to work as manual labourers. When Sokollu was told in early December that a prisoner from Cyprus, now converted to Islam, was a ship-builder who knew how to design a galleass, he immediately ordered seven of them. Here, as in most other areas of military technology, the Ottomans were quick to adopt whatever new models they encountered. Of the skilled craftsmen in the Istanbul Arsenal and gun-foundry, many were, in any case, Christians; for simple economic reasons Venetian subjects from Crete would go to work there, as did people from France, Genoa, Sicily and Spain.[1]

A famous story, told by the later chronicler Peçevi, has it that the newly appointed admiral Kılıç Pasha informed the Grand Vizier that although the shipyards were able to build the hulls of 200 galleys, it would be impossible to manufacture all the other items needed, such as anchors (three per galley) and sails. Mehmed Sokollu allegedly replied: 'this state is such that if it wishes, it can make all the anchors out of silver, the thick ropes out of silk, and the sails out of satin, without any difficulties.' Behind this hyperbole lay the largely accurate claim that the

Ottoman Empire had all the material resources it needed. The primary requirement, of course, was timber; it has been estimated that to make one galley it was necessary to fell seven acres of hardwood (of different varieties – oars, for example, were made of hornbeam) and five of pine. Timber supplies were carefully managed, bringing wood from areas as far afield as Moldavia and the southern Black Sea coast. Sail-cloth came from Greece, Anatolia and Egypt, hempen rope from the northern Anatolian port of Samsun, pitch from Vlorë, and huge quantities of tallow (cattle-fat, for greasing hulls below the water-line) from the Romanian lands. Iron was produced above all at the great state-run metallurgical complex at Samokov, in western Bulgaria, though minor manufacturing centres existed also in Bulgaria, Serbia, Bosnia and northern Albania. But metal production was the weakest element in the system; as a well-informed French diplomat reported from Dubrovnik in January 1572, there was 'an extreme lack of bronze for making the artillery for the galleys, and of iron to make the anchors'. Where bronze was concerned, the Ottomans may have suffered from their decision six years earlier to conquer the island of Chios, which had functioned as an entrepôt for English traders to sell tin. (As we shall see, England would later renew its role as an important supplier of raw materials for the Ottoman armaments industry.)[2]

Astonishingly, this new fleet was built, almost in accordance with the Grand Vizier's orders and only slightly behind schedule. It was finally assembled in its entirety at Istanbul in mid-June 1572. Giacomo Malatesta, the military commander whose punitive raid near Kotor had ended so badly in the previous summer, had just been released from his imprisonment in Istanbul, but was required to stay there a few days longer so that he could witness the grand review of the fleet and report its size to Venice and the Pope; when Malatesta reached Venice in late August, he said that he had counted the galleys (at Sokollu's request), and that the total came to 244. Modern research suggests the figure of 225 galleys and five galleasses. Some of these galleys would have been pre-existing ones, but not very many: out of the 87 ships brought to Istanbul in December 1571 (many of which were not galleys), some would have gone back to Algiers, and some, by June, would have been at their stations in the Greek archipelago. So it seems likely that at least 180 new ships had been built in eight months – a rate of production that was far beyond the capacity of any Western power, or indeed of all Western powers put together.[3]

There were, however, problems and deficiencies. It was reported that the ship-builders had used 'green', unseasoned timber. In fact this seems to have been a common practice: in 1558 a Venetian bailo had noted that because of it, Ottoman galleys had very short life-spans, with many of them becoming unusable after only one year. (However, a report from Dubrovnik in 1572 said that the Ottomans had now developed a technique of heating the wood, as a substitute for natural seasoning.) There was a shortage of artillery, despite the fact that the Ottomans had captured many Venetian bombardiers at Famagusta and had put them to work in the Istanbul gun-foundry. But perhaps the most important problems concerned the supply of manpower for the fleet – problems both quantitative and qualitative. Mass conscription was needed to supply the rowers, in the face of much reluctance to serve; Sokollu also ordered the governors of provinces to send the criminals from their prisons. Of the 20,000 troops needed, roughly a third were janissaries and spahis, and the remaining ranks were partly filled – unusually for the Ottomans – by volunteers. A French diplomat noted that the Sultan had lost 10,000 men at Lepanto, and that the losses in Cyprus had been much greater, so that neighbouring areas of Anatolia were 'almost depopulated and disinhabited'. Sokollu had decreed that the proportion of arquebusiers should be raised from one in three to two in three of all infantrymen aboard ship. He also ordered that spahis must learn how to use firearms; according to one Venetian report, the persistent problem here lay not with the manufacture of arquebuses (Istanbul produced large quantities, 'made by renegades, Jews and Muslims'), but with the lack of people who understood how to use them. No less important, finally, was the elimination of so many skilled mariners at Lepanto, and the understandable reluctance of others to take their places. Very unusually, the Sultan even asked Dubrovnik to supply 30 captains and 200 sailors – a request which the Ragusans gracefully declined. One French diplomat who also saw the grand review of the Ottoman navy in June 1572 described it as 'a fleet made of new ships, built from green wood, rowed by crews who had never held oars before, topped off with artillery made from hastily founded metal which in many cases was mixed with acidic or rusted material, a fleet with apprentice pilots and mariners, and with soldiers still in shock from the last battle, who had to be beaten to come aboard'.[4]

Whatever its deficiencies, though, this was still a fleet on roughly the same scale as the previous year's, and it did carry up to 20,000 soldiers. But what was it for? Because traditional naval history tends to pass from one great battle to another, it has become easy to assume that such

engagements were the *raison d'être* of navies of this kind. In fact, major
set-piece battles at sea were very rare in the sixteenth-century Mediterranean; there is no need to imagine that this fleet was created in order
to bring about a second Battle of Lepanto with an opposite outcome. To
deter or block an enemy fleet's advance was in itself a valuable achievement; but the point that needs to be emphasized is that any such advance
by a large war-fleet was assumed – if it had an aim that went beyond
mere raiding – to be directed at the conquest of ports or territories.
Naval strategy was organically connected with strategies of territorial
conquest. After Lepanto the Ottoman Empire was in defensive mode,
contemplating possible attacks on its territories in Greece and the western Balkans. In fact the basic assumption of the Ottomans during the
late summer and early autumn of 1571 had been that the League fleet
would be used to seize some of the strongholds on the western coast of
Greece or Albania; special care had been taken to strengthen the defence
of Patras, Preveza, Delvinë (in southern Albania), Vlorë and Durrës, and
Ahmed Pasha's army had continued, during September and October, to
act against actual or potential rebels in the Albanian lands. The combination of a local rising and an invasion by the forces of the League was
what the Ottoman authorities were most afraid of – in 1572, as in the
previous year.[5]

   Their fears were quite well founded. As we have seen, soon after the
Battle of Lepanto the Himariots were actively collaborating again with
Venice, and rebels in the northern Dukagjin area were coordinating
their actions with the Venetians in Kotor.* Another revolt had broken
out just before the battle, in the east-central Albanian region between
Elbasan and Ohrid; this area would remain in a state of instability for
months to come, and Ottoman sources would note with real concern in
January 1572 that these rebels had been in touch with the Venetians in
Corfu. In Greece, several new risings took place both on the mainland
and in the archipelago. Some senior figures in the Orthodox Church
now became very active. In January an Ottoman investigation found
that the Metropolitan of Salonica had not only made contact with the
League, but also sent priests further afield for help; two were arrested in
the Romanian territory of Wallachia, apparently on their way to Poland
and Russia. And in March another senior cleric, appointed by the Archbishop of Ohrid, was in Warsaw, engaged in a similar mission; from

* Above, pp. 128 (Dukagjin), 171 (Himarë).

there he sent a detailed proposal to the Pope, setting out a three-pronged strategy for the destruction of the Ottoman Empire. One Western army would seize Ulcinj, Durrës and Vlorë, uniting with the Himariots and then advancing on Salonica; one would invade the Peloponnese, join the Maniots and also march to Salonica; a third army, under the Habsburgs, would proceed through Hungary, Serbia and Bulgaria; and all three would finally converge on Istanbul. This was not the first and by no means the last of many such fantasy-strategies, combining invasion and mass rebellion.[6]

When the Orthodox envoys were arrested in Wallachia, they were probably seeking support there too. The Romanian principalities of Wallachia and Moldavia were within the Ottoman Empire, but they had their own Orthodox Christian rulers, plus a rich land-owning class of Orthodox nobles whose help or patronage was often sought by their co-religionists under direct Ottoman rule. From the Sultan's point of view, the prospect of a three-way linkage between rebels in the southern Balkans, supporters of them in Romania and invaders from the Christian West would be particularly worrying. A similar constellation of forces emerged, at least potentially, in March 1572 when Sebastiano Venier reported from Corfu that he had received a message from the people of Pogon (Grk: Pōgóni), a large district straddling the modern Albanian–Greek border, saying that their 98 villages had held a meeting and had agreed to rise up in support of Venice. He described them – referring, it seems, to the representatives who conveyed this message – as 'extremely rich', adding that 'they used to be among the leading figures associated with the Lord of Wallachia'; many of the inhabitants of Pogon were probably Vlachs (whose language is very close to Romanian), and there is good evidence of personal and cultural links between the Pogonians and the Romanian lands – an example of the intra-Balkan connectivity that not only survived the advent of the Ottomans, but may in some ways have been stimulated by the fact of being united in a single empire. The message that came to Venier was brought by two men, one of whom was called 'Pano Stolico'; this was probably the person called Panos who had been 'Stolnic' (Steward) at the court of the ruler of Wallachia in the 1560s. He said that the people of Pogon were ready to rebel, but that they needed the help of 20,000 Venetian infantry and 5,000 cavalry. Such a level of support was simply not available; nevertheless it is clear that a rising did take place, as a desperate letter to 'Panos stolnicos' from the Pogonians in July 1572 said that the Ottomans had destroyed their finest monastery, and that 'if they [sc. the League] are unwilling to give any help to us Christians, we shall all be taken as slaves.'[7]

The Venetians were not the only ones in contact with anti-Ottoman elements in the Balkans at this time. Don John maintained a very active network of spies and informants in many parts of North Africa and Ottoman Europe, including Koroni, Rhodes and Istanbul. In December 1571 he spent the huge sum of 30,000 scudi (25,000 ducats) – one quarter of his entire military budget – on espionage. Some of his agents not only collected information, but made contact with potential or actual rebels. At the end of 1571 he sent an artillery officer, named in Spanish documents as 'Juan de Stay', to talk to the leaders of the revolt in the Mani; at a meeting in a monastery near Kalamata in late February 1572, it was agreed that a general rising would begin when the League's fleet approached. Reportedly, various Greeks had proposed that Don John should become king of a liberated Greece – an idea which may well have appealed to this bastard son of an Emperor, lacking as he did any dynastic territories of his own. Regardless of any such personal dimension, the Venetians would still have been suspicious of Don John's intentions, seeing him as a Spanish meddler in Balkan affairs. His envoy de Stay was detained, on his way to the Mani, by the Venetian authorities on Corfu. And a later report to Don John by the Knight of Malta Giovanni Barelli would say that when, after the Battle of Lepanto, some leading Greeks and Albanians had written letters to Don John and sent them to the Venetian governor of Zakynthos (Ital.: Zante), 'inviting Your Highness to come and liberate them, and promising to take up arms to drive away the Ottomans and to give themselves to Your Highness', that Venetian official had decided not to forward the letters to their intended recipient.[8]

Had he known all the details of his half-brother's interests in the Balkans, Philip II might also have expressed some opposition. His basic view had not changed: Spanish anti-Ottoman aims must be pursued above all in North Africa, not in what was generally called 'the Levant'. He allowed his representatives in Rome to sign, at the end of 1571, an agreement for the following year's campaign which stated that the Spanish and papal fleets would meet in March at Messina and then sail east to join the Venetian navy at Corfu. But he continued to argue for a North African campaign, not a Balkan or Aegean one. On 1 January 1572 the Venetian Ambassador to Spain gave Philip a memorandum insisting that the League must attack the European 'centre' of Ottoman

power and not the African 'periphery'. 'The movements and uprisings of
the Greek and Albanian peoples, and of other Christians,' he wrote,
'would have their hopes denied if, instead of being fortified by the forces
of the League, they saw our captains employed in North Africa.' Yet in
the end it seems to have been the Spanish diplomats in Rome, not the
Venetian one in Madrid, who persuaded Philip that he must agree to a
Levantine campaign, as a failure to do so would cause the rapid break-
up of the League. Recognizing the need to keep the formal alliance
going, Philip told them that if European targets had to be accepted, they
should be places such as Preveza, Vlorë and Herceg Novi which would
be useful for the Kingdom of Naples; it was left to his envoy Luis de
Requesens to point out to him that if those places were taken, they
would belong to the Venetians. Instead, Requesens suggested attacking
Euboea, or islands in the Aegean, or the Peloponnese, in order to encourage a Greek rising which might interfere with the Sultan's efforts to
assemble a new fleet. But Philip had little real interest in any of those
possible targets. His mind was still focused on North Africa, and on
other more pressing concerns in his own domains.[9]

   The gathering of the League's fleet got off to a slow start. Don John
spent the spring of 1572 shuttling between Messina, Naples and
Palermo, trying (unsuccessfully) to collect money and supplies for a
quick expedition to North Africa before the agreed rendezvous at Corfu.
The papal fleet – this year, a composite force, partly Tuscan but also
including the old papal flagship which had been seized by the Ottomans
at Djerba and taken back at Lepanto – took time to assemble; the agreement with Cosimo de' Medici was signed in mid-April. By that stage,
however, it was clear that Pius V was mortally ill, which meant that one
of the key components of the League was about to undergo an unpredictable change of leadership. After his death on 1 May, an exceptionally
brief conclave elected the Bolognese nobleman and cardinal Ugo Bon-
compagni, who became Pope Gregory XIII. A serious-minded reformist
(whose name would be for ever associated with the new calendar which
he introduced in 1582), he had served as a papal diplomat at the Spanish court, and was liked and trusted by Philip II. That personal
connection may have been just sufficient to keep Philip in the Holy
League – which he had been planning to abandon as Pius lay on his
sickbed, instructing his ministers that they should withdraw from it on
the Pope's death and prepare an attack on Algiers. But it was not enough
to guarantee the continuation even of Philip's rather nominal adherence
to the League's agreed aims. On 20 May he sent a message to his

half-brother, Don John, commanding him to postpone his departure for
Corfu and the Levant. His orders were to keep his galleys in Messina
until further notice.[10]

Immediately after his election, Gregory XIII summoned Marcantonio Colonna, confirmed his appointment as commander of the papal
fleet, and sent him to Naples. The papal galleys assembled there in the
second half of May, and on the 29th of that month Colonna set off, with
Gasparo Bruni, for Messina. They arrived on 3 June. On the following
day Colonna wrote a note to the papal paymaster: 'you will pay the
cavaliere Bruno, captain of our flagship, his salary as it was paid last
year, that is, you will pay what he is owed from the 1st of December last
year until the end of May, and make sure it continues to be paid to him
in the future in the same way, getting a receipt from him.' Once again
Colonna had Cencio Capizucchi as his infantry commander; there had
been a successful recruitment drive in the papal territories, and Colonna
had so many troops that he was able to put some of them aboard Venetian ships, which were sent to Messina for that purpose. The mood in
Messina in early June was positive. Some representatives of the rebels in
the Mani had just arrived there, and after his discussions with them
Don John issued a grand proclamation to the people of the Peloponnese
on 9 June, urging them to rise up and promising help. By now the Spanish and papal galleys were ready to sail. The final target of the campaign
had not been decided, but Colonna was keen to seize territory in the
Peloponnese, and had the impression that Don John favoured this too.
There was at least no doubt that a suitable target could be found, once
the combined fleet was assembled at Corfu. And yet, against mounting
protests from both Colonna and the Venetian commander, Don John
kept deferring the order to leave Messina. Finally it emerged that Philip
II was forbidding him to move; the official pretext was a fear of some
new French military aggression, which made it necessary to keep the
Spanish infantry on stand-by in Sicily for possible deployment in north-
western Italy, but the truth was that Philip still had his mind set on a
North African campaign. On 1 July Colonna gave Don John an ultimatum: if he did not send galleys to Corfu, the League would be
considered as dissolved. To save the League, Don John offered a portion
of his navy: 22 galleys and 5,000 soldiers. With this Spanish rump fleet,
plus 13 papal galleys and 19 Venetian ones, Colonna finally set sail, in
an understandably bitter mood of anti-Spanish resentment, for Corfu.[11]

Venice's main fleet of roughly 70 galleys, under Giacomo Foscarini,
had been waiting rather uselessly in the southern Adriatic since April.

Just one significant enterprise had been attempted, an attack on the Ottoman stronghold of Herceg Novi in late May and early June. This had been proposed and led by Sciarra Martinengo, the noble condottiere who had surrendered at Ulcinj, but it had ended in failure, either because of his over-confidence or because (reportedly) Ottoman intelligence had known about the attack for months in advance. Colonna stopped briefly at Corfu but then, fearing another typhus outbreak, took all the galleys to Igoumenitsa, where once again the local Albanians came to sell them food. In Don John's absence, Colonna was commander in chief of the entire fleet. Under his command he now had 128 galleys, 20 smaller craft and six galleasses; the latest news reports informed him that Kılıç Ali had left Istanbul on 12 June, and that his war-fleet came to 130 galleys and three galleasses. (Other parts of the Ottoman navy were deployed on guard duty elsewhere.) Before long, probably, the Ottomans would have an accurate account of the size and composition of the League's fleet; during its stay at Igoumenitsa, not only were some of the League's soldiers captured, but also a Muslim slave who served in Marcantonio Colonna's cabin took the opportunity to flee. This gave, in the words of Ferrante Caracciolo, 'the greater advantage to the enemy of having certain information about the Christians'. From the game of naval cat-and-mouse that followed, it seems likely that Kılıç Ali did indeed become aware that the Christian fleet was better equipped and stronger than his; for his main tactic was to avoid any direct engagement with it at all.[12]

While they were at Igoumenitsa, Colonna and Foscarini received the surprising news that Philip II had agreed that Don John could join the Levantine campaign with most, though not all, of the rest of the Spanish fleet. It seems that pressure, both moral and fiscal, from Gregory XIII had had some effect; and Philip probably calculated that some benefit might be had from the League in future years, when the pledge of Venetian support for a North African expedition could be called in. With this news came an order from Don John that the fleet should wait in Corfu until he arrived. It was a moot point, however, whether Colonna's position as commander in chief in the physical absence of Don John could be trumped by an order of this kind from a distance. News was coming in of raiding actions by Kılıç Ali's fleet against Venetian islands to the south; Colonna, Foscarini and the commander of the Spanish contingent were all eager to confront it. So on 29 July they sailed southwards; they reached Zakynthos four days later, having been joined en route by twelve galleys from Venice's Cretan squadron. There they

heard that the Ottoman fleet was off Monemvasia (Ital.: Malvasia), a
port on the easternmost of the Peloponnese's three peninsulas, so they
set off in pursuit. On 5 August the two fleets came within sight of each
other, at a distance of twelve miles; Colonna drew his up in battle array
and began to advance, but Kılıç Ali fell back. At dusk the League galleys
retired to the island of Kythera (Ital.: Cerigo), to get water. For several
days both sides played a waiting game; during this time a Cypriot slave
escaped from the Ottoman fleet and reported that it had 140 or 150
galleys and 50 smaller vessels, with 'rowers in a poor state, but plenty of
soldiers, among whom there is much disease'. On 10 August the League
fleet found Kılıç Ali's ships taking water on the tip of the Mani peninsula and immediately attacked, but as soon as they got within arquebus
range the Ottoman galleys swiftly fled. A careful assessment now put
the Ottoman fleet at 120 galleys and 100 smaller ships, as opposed to
Colonna's 140 galleys and six galleasses. Victory still seemed possible;
but the duty to return to Corfu and unite with the rest of the Spanish
fleet could not be put off any longer.[13]

Don John had reached Corfu with his 53 galleys on 4 August, and
had exploded with rage when he found that Colonna and Foscarini
were not there. Equally, Colonna had written bitterly from Kythera
about the absence of Don John: if only he had been with them, they
could have hunted down and destroyed Kılıç Ali's fleet, and then gained
'almost all of the Peloponnese, since the Christians are standing armed
and ready, awaiting the conclusion of this business'. So when the two
men finally met on Corfu at the end of August it took all of Colonna's
powers of self-control and diplomacy to patch up both their personal
relationship and the alliance itself. After a week of deliberation, the
combined fleet went to Igoumenitsa and then set off southwards, having
learned that Kılıç Ali was now at the port of Pylos (Ital.: Navarino),
north of Methoni, on the west coast of the Peloponnese's western peninsula. The voyage to Pylos took longer than expected, thanks to some
hesitations by Don John and a serious navigational error by his pilot. By
the time they approached their destination, on the morning of 17 September, Kılıç Ali had spirited away most of his fleet to the heavily
fortified port of Methoni. Colonna urged Don John to send 20 galleys
to chase the rearguard group of Ottoman galleys, which was still in
sight; Don John refused, on the grounds that those Ottoman ships were
advancing, though Colonna's look-out was certain that the opposite
was the case. Then, extraordinarily, Don John suggested that Colonna
take the papal flagship, on its own, to get a closer view: he was to fire

two cannon shots if he found that they were retreating, and one if they were advancing. As Colonna put it in a later narrative of these events – written with audibly gritted teeth – 'it seemed strange to the papal commander that he should advance, with the papal standard, on his own'; he also wrote that other galley captains who volunteered to accompany him were forbidden to do so by Don John, though one Venetian simply disobeyed that order. Colonna duly advanced, saw that the enemy ships were retreating, fired his two shots, and, in the words of Ferrante Caracciolo (who was present on one of the Spanish galleys), 'sent the cavaliere Bruno to inform Don John that the enemy had left that night'.[14]

Over the next few days there were occasional skirmishes, but the great bulk of the Ottoman fleet remained safely protected by the fortress of Methoni, and there was nothing that the League could do to winkle it out: attempts to bombard the fortress, or to take it by land, had to be aborted. By 5 October the League fleet was back at Pylos, with its food supplies running low. Colonna sent a dispirited letter to Rome, saying that they did not know where Kılıç Ali's fleet was now, as the supply of intelligence from renegades escaping from it had dried up – whereas, he noted, 'many Spaniards and Dalmatians have gone over to the enemy, and have become Muslims, if they were not such already.' The lack of food, and the approach of autumnal storms, rendered a further campaign unviable. By 19 October the allied fleet was back at Corfu, having lost one papal galley in a bad storm en route. The campaign was over, and the ships returned to their Italian harbours.[15]

No one was happy about this outcome (with the possible exception of Philip II), but the people who were most dissatisfied were the Venetians. They, after all, were the ones whose territories were directly under Ottoman attack; they had fulfilled their obligation to the League, and had been kept waiting for months by Spain. The Venetian military leaders were still keen to fight back against the Ottomans; even as Colonna and Don John prepared to depart from Corfu, Foscarini was trying to persuade them to mount another attack on the Ottoman island of Lefkas. Sebastiano Venier, the military governor of Corfu, had not ceased to be active. In September he had become involved in a plan to recapture the city of Bar: a refugee patrician from that city, Marco Samuele (*alias* Calogianni) had persuaded him that this was feasible, using a Mrkojević chief and a blacksmith who had a house just outside the city walls. The idea was to land 500 soldiers at night, and take them secretly to the smith's house and a nearby church; the Mrkojević leader would trick his way through the city gate, kill the guard, and open it; a priest would ring a church bell as a signal, and the soldiers would enter. This plan was fixed for a day in late September, but then abandoned because of bad weather, and never resumed thereafter – which was perhaps just as well, as a later account of Samuele would describe him as a fraudster and alchemist who 'lives only by means of tricks and roguery'. As autumn turned to winter, the chances for any further direct action dwindled. Early in 1573 an order from the Sultan did refer to a revolt by Albanians in the *sancak* of Ohrid (in east-central or south-eastern Albania), who were receiving active Venetian support. But that was evidently a minor affair, at least from a Western point of view, and the Venetians who encouraged it were, as soon became clear, unaware of the drift of their own government's policy.[16]

By the beginning of 1573 Venice had been at war for the best part of three years. Out of three major allied naval campaigns two had been utterly ineffectual, thanks primarily to Spanish foot-dragging, and Cyprus was irrecoverably lost. During 1571 Venice was estimated to be spending 250,000 ducats a month on the war; by the spring of 1573 it was thought to have paid out 10 million, though one later report (inflated, probably, by the Venetians) put it at 14 million.* Apart from the mounting governmental debt, there were also the huge losses to patrician merchants from the suspension of their Levantine trade; what made this harder to bear was that some of the business was taken over by their hated rivals, the Ragusans, whose commerce boomed during these war years. During October and November 1572 both the Spanish Ambassador and the papal nuncio in Venice reported on a growing willingness among members of the Venetian élite to come to a settlement with the Sultan; according to the nuncio, they had concluded that the Ottoman Empire could not be defeated without a land war, which the League's present membership was insufficient to wage. In fact Venice had sent an envoy to the King of France, Charles IX, in September to explore the possibility of using the French Ambassador in Istanbul to negotiate favourable terms – begging him, all the while, to keep this a secret from the other members of the League. The French envoy to the Ottoman Empire, François de Noailles, Bishop of Dax, was a very skilled diplomat; he had been in Istanbul since 1571, and had kept up

* The total state income of Venice ranged in peacetime between 1.4 million ducats in 1555 and 1.9 million ducats in 1579; the wartime income would have been significantly lower, because of the contraction of trade.

the friendly relationship between his master and the Sultan, while deftly parrying Sokollu's suggestion in the summer of 1572 that France should join the Ottomans in a coordinated anti-Spanish campaign. Earlier that year the French were also seriously considering a proposal from Algiers that they take the port of Algiers under their military protection, to pre-empt any Spanish attack. France did have some influence in Istanbul, and it also had a clear interest in arranging a Venetian–Ottoman peace treaty: by breaking up the League, this would make Spain a more iso-lated and vulnerable target for future Ottoman campaigns.[17]

Yet, in the end, the Bishop of Dax played only a minor role in the negotiations. Having left Istanbul for Dubrovnik in November 1572, he was ordered by Charles IX to return to the Ottoman court; by the time he got there, on the last day of February, most of the negotiating had been done by the captive bailo, Marcantonio Barbaro, with the help of a well-connected Jewish physician and merchant, Solomon Nathan Ashkenazi. The French Ambassador helped to thrash out the final agree-ment, which was concluded on 7 March 1573, but he was clearly dismayed by how humiliating the terms were. The basic template for this treaty was the agreement which had ended the Venetian–Ottoman war in 1540. Now as then, Venice was obliged to pay a lump sum of 300,000 ducats, and the previously agreed annual tribute for the island of Zakynthos was now to be increased. The formal text of the treaty specified that Venice would hand back the castle of Sopot (without which the Ottomans could not hope to control the Himarë region), restoring the artillery which it held when it was captured. Otherwise it said that in 'the Albanian lands' ('Arnavudluk' in the Turkish text) and in the *vilayet* of Bosnia (meaning the Dalmatian hinterland), each side would regain the possessions which it had held before the war. Yet, as Dax knew, there were other provisions and obligations, not specified in the text itself, which contradicted and superseded it. Despite what the treaty said, he understood that the Ottomans would keep 'the towns taken by them in Albania', meaning Ulcinj and Bar. Venice was obliged to hand back not only Sopot and Margariti, as stated or implied in the text, but also the fortress in the Mani, within one month of the publication of the treaty (which took place in Istanbul on 22 March). And there was also an understanding that Venice would make a per-sonal payment of 50,000 ducats to the Grand Vizier, Mehmed Sokollu; such was the way of doing business in Istanbul. Dax commented that the Venetians would not want the provisions of the agreement to be known. Indeed, the bailo's negotiations had been authorized only by the inner core of the Venetian government, the Council of Ten, keeping the matter secret from the Senate, which still contained supporters of the war. But when the bailo's son arrived in Venice on 3 April, bearing the document, the terms of the agreement quickly became public knowledge.[18]

Five days later, when the Venetian Ambassador in Rome broke the news to Gregory XIII, the Pope reacted with fury, immediately ordering him out of the room. Twice the Ambassador asked to be heard further, and twice he was told to get out. Then the Pope went to the window, turning his back on him, and, 'completely incandescent', ordered him once more to leave, telling him as he did so that he was excommunicated. Gregory had put much effort into continuing his predecessor's work with the League; representatives of the three powers had met in Rome over the winter, and a formal agreement to conduct another Levantine campaign had been signed by all parties (including the Venetian envoy) in February. The precise target had not been settled, but one possibility was a major attack on Albania. A manuscript proposal, preserved in the Vatican Library and entitled 'For the campaign against the Ottomans, 1573', argued that a land campaign needed the cooperation of the local inhabitants, which would be best obtained in Albania. It recommended starting not at Bar or Ulcinj, where the territory had been devastated and much of the Christian population had disappeared, but further down the coast. The 'island' of Lezhë would be a possible entry-point, but since, 'so far as I am told', the air there was malarial, it would be better to begin by seizing the port of Durrës, where the League army could also make agreements with local leaders for a general rising. It would also be important to meet the chiefs of the Rodon peninsula, not least because they had special links with the people of Krujë, an important military target inland. Having taken Krujë, the League would rouse the warlike people of Dibër and Mat, further to the east; and at the outset it would also be necessary to contact the chiefs of 'those people of the Dukagjin mountains', to urge them to revolt. The degree of local knowledge in this proposal is remarkable; there is a reference, for example, to sending small warships up the river Shkumbin to attack a minor Ottoman fort that was three miles inland. The author's full name is not given, the text being merely described as 'dil S. P. C.' – 'by the Signore P. C.' One possible candidate is Prospero Colonna, the brother and comrade-in-arms of Marcantonio; a much later document by the allegedly fraudulent but ever-active Marco Samuele of Bar would record that 'il s.r Prospero Colona' had once taken a special interest in a plan to seize Shkodër. If this identification were correct, it would raise the strong possibility that one of Prospero's main informants was Gasparo Bruni, with whom he had had many opportunities for detailed discussions of these issues.[19]

All such plans were now in permanent abeyance, however. The only significant military force that was left to conduct anti-Ottoman operations was the Spanish navy (and army), and there was no possibility that Philip would use it to attack any part of the Ottomans' European territories. The King of Spain was now free to pursue his North African strategy, as he had always wished – which may help to explain his famously impassive reaction to the news of the March 1573 peace treaty when the Venetian Ambassador gave it to him. Or at least he was relatively free; while the large Ottoman fleet roamed unpredictably during July, August and September from Preveza to Igoumenitsa to Vlorë, briefly raiding the Italian coast near Otranto, Philip's Neapolitan and Sicilian squadrons could not possibly leave their stations for an African campaign. But once that threat had passed, Don John went to Sicily, where he had been gathering forces over many weeks, and, with the full agreement of Philip and the royal council in Madrid, took an invasion force – of 104 or 107 galleys and more than 100 other craft – the short distance to Tunis. The city itself had been taken less than four years earlier by one of Uluç Ali's officers from its previous Arab ruler, and placed under Ottoman control. When Don John's fleet arrived on 8 October the Ottoman governor and many of the inhabitants fled, and two days later the Spanish troops entered the city unopposed; at the port of Bizerte (Arab.: Banzart; Ital.: Biserta), further up the coast, the local people overthrew their Ottoman ruler and offered the town to the Spanish. The oddity of the situation at Tunis was that since 1535 Spain had held a fortress just outside it, at La Goletta (Arab.: Halq al-Wadi); this guarded the seaward entrance of the large lagoon or Lake of Tunis, on the other side of which the city stood. Philip's orders were that the city of Tunis should be destroyed, but they seem not to have reached Don John, who – perhaps because of the presence of the permanent garrison at La Goletta – decided to fortify Tunis and hold it for Spain. He left a force of 8,000 men for this purpose, under the command of Gabrio Serbelloni, the distinguished expert in fortifications and artillery, and returned after just one week to a triumphant welcome in Palermo. Even the usually cynical Cardinal Granvelle was elated at the news, writing that Don John could say 'veni, vidi, vici' like Julius Caesar, and could take, like the great Roman general Scipio, the title 'Africanus'.[20]

Granvelle's confidence continued into the spring of 1574: discussing a possible Ottoman counter-attack in March, he told the papal nuncio in Naples that both La Goletta and the new fortress which Serbelloni had built just outside Tunis had 'splendid provisions' and were 'extremely well armed'. The truth was quite different; Serbelloni's operation was starved of resources, as Philip II turned all his attention to the Nether-lands and other trouble-spots in Western Europe. In late May, when there were clear signs that the Ottomans were preparing a large naval force, Granvelle assured Philip that Tunis and La Goletta were relatively safe, as the Ottomans could not attack them from the landward side and a fleet could not stay there for long. A month later, when, as he noted, 'common rumour' had it that the Ottomans were planning an assault on Tunis, he insisted that southern Italy and Sicily were more likely targets. If there was such unconcern on the part of a well-informed officer of the Spanish crown, we can imagine how little thought Philip himself gave to the matter, given his other worries and the fact that he had never wanted the occupation of Tunis in the first place. To Sultan Selim II, on the other hand, the recovery of that city was of the highest priority, as it would salvage and strengthen the prestige of the Ottoman Empire throughout North Africa. Great efforts were made to put together a powerful expeditionary force in the early months of 1574; in April, for instance, orders were sent to the *sancakbeyis* of Kjustendil (in western Bulgaria), Skopje, Prizren, Shkodër, Dukagjin and Elbasan to provide thousands of rowers for the fleet. There is some evidence, too, that Selim tried to turn Philip's attention further away from North Africa, by sending agents to make contact with his Dutch rebels and encourage their revolt. No trouble was spared, certainly, in preparing this campaign. When the Ottoman navy finally appeared off La Goletta in the second week of July 1574, it consisted of between 250 and 300 ships, and carried more than 40,000 soldiers. This was the largest com-mitment of Ottoman forces since the great land campaigns of Süleyman the Magnificent.[21]

As soon as he knew of the approach of the Ottoman fleet, Serbelloni sent his nephew and lieutenant, Giovanni Margliani, in a light vessel to give the alarm to Don John. Since the royal half-brother had been sent to Milan to supervise overall Spanish policy in Italy, this involved an epic journey at high speed; Margliani reached Don John near Milan in less than two weeks, and then resolutely returned to what he regarded as almost certain death or captivity, taking even less time to do so. Don John threw himself into the task of organizing a relief force, arriving at

Naples with 27 galleys on 17 August and summoning more. But the huge superiority of the Ottoman besieging force was already taking its toll, especially since the new Spanish fortifications were still far from complete – the moat around the new fort, for example, had been dug only to knee-depth by the time the Ottomans arrived. The old fortress of La Goletta fell, to the fifth general assault against it, on 23 August. By that stage, out of the 4,500 men who had been with Serbelloni in the new fort outside Tunis, only 2,500 were left; and by the second week of September the figure was down to 700, most of whom were sick or injured. On 13 September 1574 it was finally overwhelmed, and Serbelloni was captured; his son, Giovanpaolo, had been with him until the previous day, when he was killed by an arquebus shot to the head. There were few survivors, and most of them were wounded, including Giovanni Margliani, who had been shot in the face. In the words of the Ottoman writer Zirek, who may have been a participant in this campaign too, 'there were only 100 people who survived, all the rest having been conquered by the sabres of the Muslims.'[22]

The Ottoman victory at Tunis caused immense rejoicing in Istanbul, and deep dismay in Rome and Madrid. It vindicated the colossal efforts that the Ottoman régime had put into the reconstruction of its navy. Kılıç Ali's cat-and-mouse game in 1572, when he took the role of the mouse, had suggested that the new fleet was mainly for show and that its weaknesses would be quickly exposed in any Lepanto-style engagement. His 1573 campaign, which consisted mostly of parading up the Balkan coast, gave a similar impression. But in 1574 he demonstrated that the Ottomans could perform one of the most essential naval tasks, the projection of power – in the form of a land army – to a distant shore. With the collapse of the League, the Ottoman navy was now the dominant force in the eastern half of the Mediterranean. And yet the curious thing, which has long puzzled historians, is that the Sultan did not take any steps to exploit this superiority in the following years. On the contrary, the Ottoman navy was allowed to decline, while the Spanish also turned their attention elsewhere. The Mediterranean, which had been such a central conflict zone for Eurasian geopolitics in the early 1570s, passed rather quickly into a condition of stasis, punctuated only by the renewed activities of Christian and Muslim corsairs.

'Was the Mediterranean no longer sufficiently interesting a prize?', asked Fernand Braudel. 'Whatever the reason, it is a fact that left alone in the closed vessel of the Mediterranean, the two empires no longer blindly clashed with each other.' To talk of the Mediterranean itself as a prize to be won is potentially misleading, however; as the naval historian John Guilmartin has pointed out, the modern notion of 'control of the seas' is barely applicable to sixteenth-century strategies or realities. It is true that phrases such as 'lords of the sea' were used from time to time, but what they normally meant was an ability to mount a superior fleet, if needed, for a specific purpose, not a system of permanent domination and control; the Venetian claim to perpetual dominance over the Adriatic was exceptional. More generally, Venice was the only power whose naval policy was primarily concerned with the protection of trade routes; and since the trade in question was with the Ottoman Empire, the usual policy involved cooperation, not conflict. (Venice reverted to this position in 1573, and would remain at peace with the Ottomans for the next 72 years.) To understand the fundamental reason for the stasis that developed after 1574, it is necessary to remind oneself of the basic purpose of a war-fleet. Naval ships or squadrons might perform a variety of regular tasks (the transportation of important officials, patrols to catch or deter corsairs, and so on), but the primary purpose of a major war-fleet was usually to take an army to seize territory. After 1574, Spain was too preoccupied with its other problems – especially in the Netherlands – to contemplate any large-scale actions of that sort against the Ottomans. For his part, the Sultan had no obviously attainable targets left for amphibious conquest; the most alluring prize, southern Italy, was also the most problematic, as an attack on that territory was the one thing that might bring Venice back into an anti-Ottoman military league, and such a league was the one thing that might defeat the Ottoman forces. Otherwise the most attractive prize was probably the non-Ottoman territory of Morocco. But mounting a campaign there, at the far end of the Mediterranean, would involve huge logistical problems, plus the risk of intervention by a Spanish fleet close to its own home ports; the game might not be worth the candle.[23]*

The answer to Braudel's question, then, is that with the retaking of Tunis, the Ottoman Empire completed its hold over what it could reasonably expect to possess on the shores of the Mediterranean; whilst there were other territories that it could consider or covet, it could not be at all confident of obtaining them. Navies were colossally expensive, and needed constant upkeep; even the Ottoman state, with its huge

---

* There was one other potentially attractive target in the Mediterranean: Crete. But the island contained several well-fortified positions; when the Ottomans eventually attacked it, in 1645, the war of conquest took 24 years to complete.

surpluses pouring in from Egypt, could not afford to run a large-scale naval campaign for more than a few years in a row. Land campaigns, on the other hand, could be undertaken regularly, and could result in much greater gains of territory. In 1578 the Sultan embarked on a war of conquest in the east, encompassing Mesopotamia, north-western Persia and the Caucasus region, which would absorb immense resources for more than a decade. Shortly before the start of that war – and in order to pave the way for it – his Grand Vizier negotiated a naval armistice with Spain, which would later be renewed more than once. The Spanish–Ottoman truce may have been as much a symptom as a cause of the emerging condition of stasis in the Mediterranean, but it did shape the geopolitics of the rest of the century to a significant extent. And in the making of that truce, as we shall see, another member of the Bruni–Bruti family was intimately and controversially involved.[24]

10

The Brutis and Brunis in Istria

The Venetian–Ottoman war of 1570–3 had taken a heavy toll of the Bruni and Bruti families. Gasparo Bruni had lost both his brother Giovanni and his nephew Nicolò. If Nicolò's father, Serafino Bruni, was still living by 1571, it seems likely that he died at the fall of Ulcinj. (There is no particular record of this, but a document issued by a papal secretary at the end of 1572 stated in general terms that Gasparo had lost 'his brothers, his relatives, and everything he had' when Ulcinj was conquered.) It appears that other members of the family also died at that time: in a letter written two weeks after Lepanto, the Venetian naval commander, Sebastiano Venier, referred to Gasparo and remarked that 'many of his honorable relatives were killed by the Ottomans in the city of Ulcinj.' The death of Antonio Bruti, immediately after the surrender of the city, was another blow; whether his wife, Gasparo's sister Maria, survived is not known, but there is no mention of her thereafter. As we have seen, Marco Bruti, one of the two sons of Antonio who went to fight for Venice in 1570–1, appears to have perished. There may well have been other deaths on the Bruti side of the family; of the nine sons mentioned by Antonio in his petition to Venice in 1569, three are otherwise entirely absent from the historical record, which suggests that they did not live much beyond that date.[1]

Nevertheless, Marco's brother and companion in arms Jacomo did survive, and so too did at least seven other siblings. Jacomo himself apparently took part in the Battle of Lepanto; how his brothers and sisters escaped from Ulcinj, if they were there when it fell, is unknown. Perhaps their father had already sent most of them away; it is also possible that some of the younger sons were attending schools in Venice or elsewhere. What is clear is that Jacomo – who was 29 years old in 1571 – now took up the role of head of the Bruti family, and arranged their move to the city of Koper (Ital.: Capodistria) in the Venetian territory of Istria, in the north-eastern corner of the Adriatic. In the absence of any evidence of previous links between the family and Koper, it is impossible to say why they decided on that particular destination; a Venetian decree of 1575, responding favourably to Jacomo's request for noble status in Koper, would simply state that that town was 'chosen' by Jacomo and his brothers 'as their place of permanent residence after the loss of their homeland'. But it is clear, at least, that the Bruti siblings did not come as indigent refugees; they rapidly married into some of the city's most prominent noble families, and it was partly on that basis that Jacomo's request for noble status was granted. From the fact that one of these marriages produced a child in 1572 we may deduce that the move to Koper took place soon after the fall of Ulcinj. At some point, the Brutis were joined there by a member of the Bruni family – Matteo, the elder son of Serafino, who had previously accompanied his uncle Giovanni Bruni to the Council of Trent. Gasparo Bruni's illegitimate son, Antonio, would also become a resident of Koper, probably living in his cousin Matteo's house. Thus it was that, after all the upheavals and bereavements of the war, the remnants of the Bruti and Bruni families were once again united in a small Adriatic town under Venetian rule.[2]

Koper may have been 450 miles from Ulcinj (in a straight line; perhaps ten days' travel by boat), yet the similarities between the two places would have struck anyone who moved from one to the other. Here too was an ancient city, known to the Romans as 'Capris' (from the Latin for 'goat' – hence the Slovenian 'Koper') and to the Byzantines as 'Justinopolis', which had been under a variety of rulers, including the Holy Roman Emperor, before it fell to Venice in 1278–9. It was presided over by a Venetian governor, with a handful of other Venetian officials; under him was the noble Council of the town, which prepared legislation, advised the governor, sent 'embassies' to Venice with special requests, and appointed members of the city's leading families as judges and administrators. Like other communities in the Stato da Mar, Koper was governed in accordance with its own statutes. It was untypical in one way, however. While many cities of Istria, Dalmatia and Venetian Albania cherished the memory of their original autonomy, emphasizing that Venice's power derived only from the voluntary act of 'dedition' by which the city had put itself under Venetian rule, Koper had been more thoroughly Venetianized: after a failed rebellion in the mid-fourteenth century its Council had been abolished by Venice, and when it was reconstituted it was made to consist only of pro-Venetian elements, who based their rights not on the act of dedition but on grants from the

Doge. Thereafter, in the words of one historian, the governing nobility of Koper was 'more Venetian than Istrian, and more bureaucratic than aristocratic'. But if the result was a community that was deeply loyal to Venice, and largely free of the social conflicts that had so badly divided Bar and many of the Dalmatian cities, that too suggests that settlers from Ulcinj might have felt pleasantly at home there.[3]

Koper was the most significant city of the Istrian peninsula; its Italian name, Capodistria, meaning 'head of Istria', seems generally to have been taken as referring to its importance rather than its geographical position. Venetian Istria was not a province in any administrative sense, and did not possess a capital; each town, with its agricultural territory, had its own governor, on an equal footing. Nevertheless, from 1584 Koper was the seat of a special court with jurisdiction over the whole of Istria, so in that specific way it was recognized as the pre-eminent city. It was also the largest. In mid-1553 its population had been more than six times that of Ulcinj; Giovanni Battista Giustinian, who visited Koper in May of that year before travelling down the coast to Venetian Albania, recorded that it had 10,000 inhabitants. He noted approvingly that the population was 'extremely devoted' to Venice, and observed: 'all the inhabitants, both nobles and commoners, are arrayed in the most beautiful clothes; they dress in the Italian style, and there are many Doctors and educated men among them, but the territory is entirely inhabited and worked by Slavs.' Within months of his visit, however, Koper was devastated by plague. More than three quarters of the city's population died or fled; by the end of the epidemic barely 2,300 souls remained, and by 1560 that figure had risen only to 3,600. When the Bruti brothers and sisters arrived there in the early 1570s, they found that this once teeming city had a population only twice that of their native Ulcinj. By 1577 the total had increased to 4,000, but the governor reported that Koper was experiencing 'a greater calamity' than in the immediate aftermath of the plague, 'because of the unceasing famines and storms, and the poor production of salt' – salt being one of the mainstays of the city's economy. Malaria was also a problem; an energetic governor in 1579–80 encouraged the Council to send an ambassador to Venice, requesting engineers to plan the draining of the 'very dense and utterly foul-smelling marshes' that lay just outside the city, and some drainage operations were carried out in the next few years. Subsequent reports show the population rising to 4,800 in the early 1580s, but then sinking as low as 3,500 by 1593; in that year Koper was described as 'thinly inhabited, with many houses in ruins'. Of the 200 members of the city's nobility, it was said, 'some, because of their poverty, engage in farming, some in fishing, and some in shipping; among these nobles extreme poverty is almost universal, as they do not apply themselves to commerce, or to any profession.'[4]

Outside the city of Koper, the territory it controlled had 42 villages, with a population that was in gradual decline throughout this period, from 6,000 in 1560 to 5,000 in 1596. Conditions here too were very poor; in 1577 the governor wrote that 'the cowsheds on the Terraferma, where brute animals live, are much more fine and comfortable than the little hovels made almost entirely of straw in this territory, where the people live.' Before the plague of 1553 this had been a major wine-producing area; Giustinian reported that its wine sold for between 25,000 and 30,000 ducats a year. The main market for it was the Habsburg territory to the north – the border lay only a few miles from Koper, with the Imperial city of Trieste just beyond it. A general report on Istria in 1591 would state that much wine was exported to 'Germany' (meaning the Holy Roman Empire), and that there was also a small amount of silk production in Koper. Grain and oil were also produced, but, according to this report, only for local consumption. The area was never self-sufficient in grain; oil production seems to have grown, however, and in 1598 the governor of Koper noted that oil and wine were two of the three main products sold there to purchasers from the Habsburg lands. The third, and the most important, was sea-salt, which was produced in large quantities along the coast near Koper and sold to the Habsburg hinterland, Dalmatia and Venice. The discovery in 1578 that people from Trieste were setting up their own salt-works caused huge concern to the Venetian authorities, who feared that this development would undermine the entire Istrian economy; Venice ordered its naval commander in the Adriatic, and the governors of Koper and the nearby town of Muggia, to destroy the offending salt-pans, which lay just outside Trieste's jurisdiction. Thirteen years later the governor of Koper was still commenting on the threat that such rival production would pose; salt was sold to Habsburg traders in return for grain, without which the city and territory of Koper might starve.[5]

From Venice's point of view Istria was a strategic bulwark, blocking both Habsburgs and Ottomans; it was a reservoir of manpower, with its total population of 50–70,000; and it was an important source of timber for the fleet. Many writers also noted its agricultural potential. Yet rural Istria as a whole was under-populated and under-developed; a

report in 1560 commented that much of it was 'neither inhabited nor
cultivated as it should be, partly because of the small number of people,
and partly because of their innate negligence, so that the harvest is
roughly half what it should be'. Conscious of this, the Venetian authorities had made great efforts to encourage immigration to the region.
Refugees from territories newly conquered by the Ottomans were
diverted to Istria in 1540; by 1554 more than 15 per cent of the Istrian
population were immigrants; in 1556 all abandoned lands in Istria were
declared state property, so that they could be redistributed; and in the
1560s a colonization programme was set up, transferring families from
the Bologna region to uncultivated areas of southern Istria. There was
an irregular but frequent incoming flow of Vlachs, Slavs, Albanians and
Greeks, including, after 1571, many refugees from Cyprus; the evidence
suggests that the Greeks often gave up and moved elsewhere, while the
Albanians were better able to adapt to their new conditions. The Bruti
and Bruni families belonged to a different category; they were not peasants being settled in an empty countryside, but nobles with significant
amounts of social capital (and, probably, some actual capital, banked in
Venice) choosing a new urban home. Nevertheless these general conditions, with a depleted population and a relatively high level of
demographic flux, may in some ways have made Istria an easier place to
enter as a migrant than some other areas under Venetian rule.[6]

Many of the noble families of Koper had migrated there in earlier
periods, and several had come from Albania. The Albanese family,
whose name proclaimed their origins, had made the move by the fifteenth century, and were incorporated in the city's nobility by 1432; the
Brati family (who pose a constant problem for the historian searching
for 'Bruti' in the manuscript records of the city) had come from Albania
as early as the thirteenth century. Another prominent family was called
Ducain, and was presumably an offshoot of the Dukagjin family of
northern Albania. But the Brutis did not marry any of these, noble
though they all were. Instead, Jacomo quickly formed a double alliance
with the most powerful family of the city, the Verzis, who claimed descent from the old Venetian patrician family of Giorgi or Zorzi and had
been feudal landowners in Istria for more than 300 years. Jacomo himself married Bradamante Verzi, and his sister Caterina married Rizzardo
(or Ricciardo) Verzi. (Whether those two Verzis were siblings or cousins
is not clear.) Jacomo's sister Ilarieta, who was five years younger than
Caterina, married Demostene Carerio, a member of another well-
established noble family which was also closely related to the Verzis;

her son Benedetto was born in 1572, and one of her five other children, Laura, would later marry a Nicolò Verzi. The Brutis were lucky that their move to an entirely new environment happened at the stage when several of them were of marriageable age, since nothing could be better calculated to create strong and immediate social bonds. It seems that only one of the siblings was already married before the move: Jacoma Bruti, born in 1549, whose husband was Pietro Borisi, from Bar. The Borisis were one of the leading noble families of that city, with a strong tradition of pro-Venetian activity; indeed, in 1450 Venice gratefully recorded that a Marco Borisi had been 'the cause of the handing over of the castle of Bar to our rule'. A later document drawn up in Koper would record that Jacomo Bruti 'drew them [sc. the Borisis], likewise, to come and live in this city, because of the loss which they had also experienced of their homeland of Bar'; whether this happened soon after the fall of Bar, or some time later, is not known, though one source describes Pietro and Jacoma's son Bernardo as having moved to Koper in 1590.[7]

The Doge's decree of 3 September 1575, granting noble status in Koper to Jacomo and his brothers and all their legitimate sons, makes it clear that the Brutis' most important piece of social capital was the glowing reputation of their father. 'The Bruti family has always shown itself to be so loyal and well-disposed towards Our State; in particular, the extremely loyal and honoured cavaliere Antonio Bruti, of blessed memory, gave such diligent and fruitful service throughout his life ...', and so on. But it is also clear that the value of this intangible asset had to be cashed, so to speak, in Venice rather than in Koper itself. On 26 December 1575 the Council of Koper decided to send a formal protest to the Doge: it noted that the city's statutes required a three-quarters majority vote in the Council to admit anyone to the nobility, and complained that 'for that reason Mr Jacomo Bruti of Ulcinj and his brothers decided to try a different way of being made members of this Council.' The request to the Doge was that Jacomo be required to go through the normal procedure; but since there is no subsequent record of that happening in the minutes of the Council, it seems that Venetian authority carried the day. If this caused a blow to local pride, no doubt it was eventually softened by the efforts of the Brutis' various marital allies among the Capodistrian patriciate.[8]

How the Brutis supported themselves financially in this period is not at all clear. Jacomo may possibly have engaged in trade, using another important inherited asset, his father's network of contacts; but Jacomo would complain of poverty in his old age, and his four sons all pursued

careers as dragomans (interpreters), which does not suggest that they
had a paternal business to keep up. Nevertheless, whatever his financial
position may have been in these early years, Jacomo did eventually
become an accepted and valued member of the Capodistrian community. In November 1583 the Council selected three of its leading figures
to go as ambassadors to Venice, in order to plead for the lifting of export
taxes on wine and salt (taxes that were applied when those goods were
not exported via Venice); the third ambassador was, in the words of the
Council's own minutes, 'the distinguished Mr Jacomo Bruti'. Five years
later he was elected as one of the overseers of the Fonteca, the municipal
grain store (an important institution, described by one writer as 'the one
and only sustenance of the poor'); his brother-in-law Demostene had
become an overseer just three months earlier. In late December 1589
Jacomo was appointed one of Koper's four judges, stepping into Demostene's place; and a week later, when the city's Grain Commission
selected two out of the four to act for special purposes on its behalf, he
was one of the two so chosen.[9]

Demostene Carerio, on ceasing to be a judge, was elected ambassador to Venice, and in early January 1590 a formal statement by the
four judges and the two syndics of the city described his mission: he was
to tell the Venetian authorities of 'the utterly miserable state in which
this poor people finds itself, together with the entire territory, because of
the two Jewish banks which have been in this city for 70 years, and
which, with an interest rate of 12½ per cent, have reduced every rank
and condition of person to extreme misery'. He was to ask Venice to
dismiss the Jews, and to set up instead a 'Monte di Pietà' – a charitable
institution which lent money to the poor on a pawn-broking basis. The
municipality of Koper owned 113 salt-pans, and the idea was to pledge
these as security to Venice, which would send the sum of 4,000 ducats
to form the opening capital of the Monte di Pietà.* Six weeks later, the
Council sent another instruction to Carerio: he was to ask Venice for
help, once more, in stopping the creation of rival salt-works by the
people of Trieste. 'The commerce and trade in salt', it declared, 'between
this city of Koper and the subjects of the Archduke is the sole support
of all the poor citizens, and the basis of the taxes paid to Venice, since

---

* Neither of these proposals was implemented. A previous Monte di Pietà had got into debt,
being bailed out by the governor of the city in 1579–80 but later collapsing; the people of
Koper were not, it seems, very credit-worthy. The Jews successfully resisted the pressure
against them, and their rights to lend money were eventually renewed.

in this way we send salt, and receive in return wheat, wool, cheese, and cereals of every kind.' This was not a good year for the city of Koper. In August 1590 Carerio was sent again, with another ambassador, to beg Venice for 6,000 stari (372 tons) of grain: 'in these calamitous times, the poverty of this utterly loyal population, and the extreme want in which we now find ourselves, are such that we do not have enough bread for one week, so that there is a very clear danger that the people will rise up and the city will be totally ruined.' Rather grudgingly, Venice's response was to supply the city with 300 stari of flour on credit, and permit it to buy 500 stari of grain. The people did not rise up, and Koper somehow survived.[10]

Jacomo Bruti served again as an overseer of the grain store in 1593, and as one of the two 'giustizieri' (magistrates responsible for executing punishments), together with a Francesco Carerio, in 1597. But his most important appointment was as 'Capitano degli Schiavi', 'Captain of the Slavs', which took place in September 1593. This position, which had been a vital component of the system of government since the mid-fourteenth century, was a kind of magistrature over all the inhabitants of the villages in Koper's territory; the Captain organized and commanded the local militia which was formed from the village men, but he also acted as a protector of their interests. One necessary requirement, evidently, was the ability to communicate with them. The local so-called 'Slavs' included Slovenes, Croats, and Vlachs who were probably also Serbo-Croat-speakers (a report in 1561 had referred to 'a sort of mixed population of Istrians and Morlachs' – 'Morlach' being a general term for the increasingly Slav-speaking Vlachs of the Dalmatian hinterland), and while Jacomo would probably have been fluent in Serbo-Croatian from his upbringing on the Slav–Albanian linguistic frontier, it may have taken him some time to adapt to the Slovenian language. The number of men who received military training under the Captain of the Slavs had recently been raised from 400 to 500. But the Captain's formal responsibilities also extended to all the adult males who formed the pool of manpower from which the militia was drawn. As the governor of Koper noted in 1598, the villages contained 1,235 men aged between 18 and 50: 'all these are called "Slavs", and, by a privilege of the citizens [of Koper], they have a Captain, a gentleman of the city, who is chosen by their representatives when there is a vacancy . . . He is responsible for protecting and defending them, making sure that they are not subject to any extortion, and he receives 156 ducats a year from the city treasury; at present the Captain is Mr Jacomo Bruti, who carries out his

responsibilities to universal satisfaction.' Presumably Jacomo was satisfied too. He had attained both a viable income and a central position in
the life of the city and its territory – a position that would still be filled
by him at the time of his death in 1618, when he was 76 years old.[11]

One other member of Jacomo Bruti's extended family had a similar
career, being closely integrated into the civic life of Koper: his first
cousin Matteo Bruni, son of Serafino. We last encountered Matteo in
1565, when he accompanied the three fine Ottoman horses sent by his
uncle Giovanni from Ulcinj to the Pope; thereafter (according to Francesco Barbarano, who got to know him in Istria towards the end of his
life) he had 'served for a long time at the Curia in Rome, where he had
honorable employments'.* How long he stayed in Rome is not known,
but he must have been well established in Koper by 1587, when he first
appeared in the records as the holder of a civic office – one of the two
'soprintendenti sopra la sanità', or health inspectors. He was made an
overseer of the grain store in 1589, and again in 1591. In the following
year he became one of two officials who maintained the physical fabric
of the city's cathedral, managing the funds of a special endowment set
up for that purpose. Two other appointments swiftly followed: as judge,
also in 1592, and as city advocate in 1593. The judges had no formal
legal training, but the advocate was probably required to have some
expertise; it may also be significant that in 1608 Matteo appeared in
court as the official representative of a Venetian merchant, Benedetto
Tiepolo, in a case against those Jewish bankers who had so successfully
resisted the city's attempt to close down their business eighteen years
earlier. So it seems possible that Matteo's duties at the papal Curia had
involved some sort of legal work. No doubt his Roman credentials
stood him in good stead as he gradually climbed the ladder of civic
employment in Koper. But one other thing may have counted more
powerfully: the fact that he too had married a member of the Verzi family. When his first wife, Camilla, made her will in 1602, she left bequests
to her sisters Veronica and Giulia Verzi, her nieces, the daughters of
Pietro Verzi, and her nephew, the son of Agostino Verzi. The obvious
conclusion is that Jacomo Bruti had acted as match-maker for his
cousin, deftly easing him into his own familial and social network.
Admission to the nobility of Koper had followed; the Brunis would later
be recorded as one of the noble families of the city.[12]

Although Matteo Bruni remained a layman, his experience and

---

* Above, p. 75.

contacts at the Roman Curia would probably have given him a special *entrée* into the ecclesiastical life of Koper; but no light can be shed on this, since, unfortunately, only the civic records, not the ecclesiastical ones, survive. In the decades before the arrival of the Bruti family, Koper had been riven by fierce theological hostilities: the Bishop of the city, Pietro Paolo Vergerio, a brilliant intellectual and high-flying papal diplomat, had been convicted of Protestant heresy in 1549, and defenders of Catholic orthodoxy had done their best to hunt down his sympathizers, real or imagined. (Leading the pack was Koper's most prominent writer, Girolamo Muzio, who is best remembered as a poet, but was also a heavyweight polemicist of the Counter-Reformation; he led a vindictive campaign to eject from the cathedral the tomb of Vergerio's blamelessly non-heretical brother.) The effort to stamp out heterodoxy seems to have been quite successful: of the twelve people tried for 'Lutheran' heresy in Istria in the period 1558–91, not one was from Koper, and when Cardinal Agostino Valier arrived in Koper in early 1580 to conduct a visitation, the most the Bishop could say was that 'he does not know for certain that there are any heretics in this city, though he has suspicions about some people.' Other findings of this visitation paint a rather depressing picture of the conditions of religious life in Koper. The Bishop's revenues came to less than 400 ducats (well below the protected minimum of 500 ducats proposed at the Council of Trent); the eleven canons of the cathedral had incomes so pitifully low (roughly 20 ducats) that they were quite nominal; and the Bishop did not preach, because a serious illness had almost deprived him of his memory. The Tridentine principle that every diocese should set up a seminary had not been followed here, as there was no money to pay for it; there had been one public schoolmaster, but he had left two months previously, and it was hoped that the Jesuits might be able to supply a replacement for him. The judges and syndics of the city said that they had long wished that the Jesuits would set up a college in Koper; but that wish – striking testimony to the rapidly growing reputation of the Jesuits as an educational order – was not to be fulfilled. The visitation report also recorded that there were no printers or booksellers in Koper. This was not intended as a negative comment, meaning only that there was no need to monitor or search any such establishments for 'prohibited books'; yet, to the modern eye, it cannot fail to add another detail to an almost relentlessly negative picture of the overall conditions of life in this city.[13]

The grimness can be exaggerated, however. This was a city with a real cultural life, capable of some spirit and style. When Cardinal Valier arrived to begin his visitation, he was taken through the city under a baldacchino (an ornamental canopy) borne by eight Doctors of Theology, Law or Medicine; they passed under three triumphal arches specially erected for the occasion, decorated with mottoes, coats of arms and pictorial scenes, before proceeding to the cathedral to hear a 'most beautiful motet'. The city's churches contained works by famous painters including Cima da Conegliano, Palma Vecchio and Paolo Veronese, as well as several by Vittore Carpaccio (whose family was closely connected with the city, though it remains a matter of dispute whether Vittore himself was born there). According to one later description, the church of the Dominican friary in Koper had two paintings by Titian, at least one of which may be completely unknown to modern Titian scholarship. That church, with its fine coloured marble, was 'extremely beautiful'; there were five other monasteries and nunneries, and 33 other churches in addition to the cathedral. As for the Bishop, Giovanni Ingegneri, who served in Koper from 1576 to 1600: he may have had problems with his memory, but he was still a highly educated and cultured man. A jurist from Venice, he had been a professor at the University of Pavia, and was the author of a treatise on physiognomy which was published after his death. The person who arranged its publication was his nephew Angelo Ingegneri, a friend of the poet Torquato Tasso; when Angelo published an edition of Tasso's *Gerusalemme liberata* in 1581, he said that if he had not been forced by a pirated edition to hasten the publication of it, he would have retired to Koper in order to prepare an elaborate set of literary annotations on Tasso's work with the help of his uncle the Bishop, who was a man of 'universal erudition'. Capodistrians did make contributions to intellectual life more generally. A Cristoforo Verzi, for example, had been a lecturer in logic at the University of Padua; the physician Santorio Santorio (born in 1561) would be a professor there in the early seventeenth century, famous for applying the principles of Galilean physics to human physiology. And in the city itself, the 'Accademia Palladia' (an 'academy' in the Renaissance Italian sense – not an institution of higher learning, but a convivial society in which dining and socializing were combined with intellectual debate and the performance of literary exercises) flourished from the late 1560s until well into the following century. Several of its members wrote significant works of literature, including Marc'Antonio Valdera's free translation into Italian of Ovid's *Heroides* (edited posthumously by Santorio Santorio); and a published collection of pieces in poetry and prose by many members of the Accademia Palladia would include, as we shall see, a literary composition by Gasparo Bruni's son, Antonio.[14]

So, despite the depleted population and malarial conditions, the low public and ecclesiastical revenues, the occasional near-famines, the recurrent threats to its main industry, the constant reports of poverty, and the lack of a college or seminary or even a bookshop, Koper was not such a bad place to live in. We should not forget that many of those complaints could be duplicated or even exceeded, at various times, in other parts of the Venetian domains. It is true that people found guilty of serious offences in Venice were sometimes sent into exile in this Istrian city: in 1581, for example, a Carlo Durazzo was sent to Koper for four years for trying to shoot someone with an arquebus in Venice, and in 1589 the secretary of the Council of Ten was sentenced to ten years there for the crime of sodomy. But any town in the Stato da Mar could be used by the authorities for such exilic purposes. The most obvious thing that distinguished Koper from most of those other destinations was its closeness to Venice: with a favourable wind, the voyage could be made in less than two days. Naturally, the élite families of Koper were proud of their close relationship with the mother-city. Like every other small-town élite in this Adriatic world, they were at the same time very proud of their own civic community and institutions. This was a place where a family such as that of the Brutis and Brunis, once accepted and established, could put down roots. But on the other hand it was not a place in which it was easy to pursue a profitable career. So while some members, such as Jacomo Bruti and Matteo Bruni, acted as anchor-men in Koper, sustaining the social position of the family, nurturing its civic respectability and cultivating its connections by blood and marriage, others went out to make their fortunes. The most distinguished of these, Jacomo's younger brother Bartolomeo, would have one of the most adventurous careers of any Venetian subject in this period.[15]

11

Bartolomeo Bruti and the
Prisoner Exchange

In June 1573 Bartolomeo Bruti sent a petition to the government of
Venice. He was just fifteen or sixteen years old – not the youngest of
Antonio Bruti's children, but a full fifteen years below his brother
Jacomo, the new head of the family. He explained that he was fluent in
Italian, Albanian and the Slav language, and that he had studied Latin
and Greek at a school in Venice; his request was that he be allowed to
become a trainee dragoman, or interpreter, in Istanbul. Since the 1550s
the Venetian authorities had operated a formal system of training young
men, known as 'giovani di lingua' (literally, 'language youths'), for this
purpose at the house of the bailo, who was in effect the resident ambassador of Venice in the Ottoman capital. The pay was not good during
the apprentice years, but a fully-fledged dragoman would occupy an
important position in the bailate (the bailo's house), with many opportunities for involvement in lucrative side-business of his own, including
commerce, so the position was certainly a desirable one. And Bartolomeo's request was well timed, coming as it did just three months after
the Venetian–Ottoman peace agreement and the resumption of normal
relations. The Senate had apparently received positive information
about this young supplicant. In its response it called him – probably
with his late father in mind – 'such a deserving person of our state', and
declared that 'given the mental quickness and facility which he shows,
he will make himself a very suitable servant of our government in a
short time once he has mastered the Turkish language and idiom.' Bartolomeo Bruti was duly sent to Istanbul.[1]

There are various uncertainties about Bartolomeo's early years in the
Ottoman capital, and the puzzles are unlikely to prove soluble, as he
was too junior a figure to leave more than the tiniest trace in the records.
What is known is that in early September 1574, roughly one year after
his arrival there, the Venetian government gave the bailo permission to

dismiss him from Istanbul, and that in late October he was sent on his way with a payment of 50 ducats for his travel expenses. Apparently it had been decided that he was not suited after all to the life of a trainee dragoman; we may guess that the problem was one of temperament or interest rather than linguistic aptitude, as his later career indicates that he did eventually become fluent in Turkish. Within a couple of months, however, he was back in Istanbul again, and was either working for the bailo or, at least, in contact with him. At the end of November 1574 Gabrio Serbelloni, the artillery general who had been captured at the fall of Tunis in September, was transferred from an Istanbul prison to the house of the Grand Vizier, Mehmed Sokollu, and in mid-January he was allowed to visit the bailo, Antonio Tiepolo. In his report of 15 January Tiepolo gave details of some possible improvements to the fortifications of Corfu which had been suggested to him by Serbelloni, and added: 'that is what Bruti was unable to tell me when he [sc. Serbelloni] sent him to speak to me on his behalf.' Soon after this, Bartolomeo Bruti was despatched to Rome on an important mission (described below) to help arrange a prisoner exchange; as we shall see, this kept him occupied for a large part of 1575. In January 1576 he returned to Istanbul and announced, somewhat to the surprise of the new bailo, Giovanni Correr, that he had been authorized by Venice to resume his linguistic studies. But less than seven months later he was allowed to leave the city again, at his own request; his days as a giovane di lingua were over. Correr reported that 'leaving aside the matter of his paying attention to learning the language as planned, to which his mind is not inclined, I have otherwise always known him to be of good will and full of desire to serve our most illustrious state.' What Correr did not know was that Bartolomeo Bruti had been recruited to work for the Spanish intelligence service, and that he had probably been doing so ever since his most recent return to Istanbul. Far from being a loyal servant of the Venetian republic, he had become a secret employee of one of its chief rivals.[2]

But first, the matter of the prisoner exchange – which raises the larger issue of how the whole system of captivity, exchange and ransom functioned in the early modern Mediterranean world. Throughout this period, warfare, corsairing, piracy and terrestrial raiding generated huge numbers of captives in both the Ottoman domains and the territories of Christendom. Many of these were held on a long-term or permanent basis as slaves: every Mediterranean state with the exception of France had a significant slave population (though France would also use them on its galleys). In Italy there were 40,000 or 50,000 Muslim slaves; the total in Spain may have been similar, though they were greatly outnumbered there by black Africans. The 'Barbary' states of Algiers, Tripoli and Tunis held at least 35,000 Christian captives (one recent estimate is 38,500); the slaves formed a significant percentage of the total population of those territories, and played an essential role in their economies. Domestic and agricultural slavery was also common in the heartlands of the Ottoman Empire. Huge numbers of Poles, Ukrainians and Russians, captured by Tatar raiding expeditions, were shipped across the Black Sea to Istanbul and other trading centres; in 1578 alone, 17,500 such slaves were sold through the Crimean port of Feodosiya (Ital.: Caffa; Trk.: Kefe). In 1584 the former Venetian Ambassador Giacomo Soranzo estimated that there were 10,000 Christian slaves in Istanbul, of whom 3,000 belonged to the Sultan and another 3,000 to the admiral of the fleet; a study of domestic slavery in Istanbul earlier in the century suggests that roughly 40 per cent of the city's slaves may have been so-called Russians, i.e. Slavs from north of the Black Sea. Slavery was a fact of life which affected people from the Ukrainian steppes to the Atlantic coasts of Portugal and Morocco. Its basic features – acquisition by raiding or war, public and private sales, the economic and military function, its legal status, the possibility of manumission – were the same on either side of the Christian–Muslim divide. And, thanks to the attempts of captives to return to their homes, and of families to recover their lost members, that divide was constantly criss-crossed by individuals and agents of many kinds, seeking to organize an exchange or a ransom.[3]

It may be tempting to suppose that there was a clear distinction between those who were treated from the outset as long-term slave material, and those who were set aside for ransom; one might also imagine that only an élite, consisting of nobles, military officers, rich merchants and the like, would be placed in the latter category. Yet in many cases the distinction was not at all clear. Of course the rich and prominent were destined for ransom, as they could raise a much higher sum than their slave-price as physical labourers; generally, those who were obvious candidates for ransoming were better treated. It is also true that the prospects of being redeemed must have been very bleak for peasants from remote Ukrainian villages who had no way even of contacting their families – if, that is, any members of their families had escaped the raiders. The ransom price for an able-bodied male Christian captive in this period was typically between 80 and 100 ducats (though in wartime, with a glut on the market, the ordinary sale price of a slave, which underpinned it, could fall as low as 30); that could represent four, five or six years' earnings for an Italian peasant or unskilled worker. Nevertheless, many Western Europeans from quite ordinary backgrounds were bought out of slavery, and the same kind of release from captivity was certainly possible in the other direction, from Europe to the Ottoman world.[4]

At its simplest, the ransom system could work almost instantly: Barbary corsairs would raid an Italian village, move a few miles down the coast, set up a white flag on the beach and invite the remaining villagers to come and buy back the ones who had just been seized. In these cases, we may assume, prices were very low, unaffected by – to put it in drily economic terms – subsequent overheads or wastage. Sometimes, where a group of people (soldiers, for example, or members of the same family) had been captured, one of them would be permitted to go home to raise a ransom, with the others acting as guarantors for him; in the Ottoman system the guarantee was given on pain of severe punishment, such as the loss of an ear or a nose. An example of this kind of conditional release has already been mentioned, the 30-year-old Jewish captive who was allowed to leave Malta in order to raise a ransom for himself and eight other captive Jews; the Knights of Malta were particularly inclined to this practice, and it has been calculated that in the period 1544–80 more than half of all ransomings of slaves on the island were arranged by the slaves themselves.* In some cases a slave was allowed to go home to raise his own ransom, on condition that he got a family member to come and take his place as a hostage. And on the Ottoman–Hungarian frontier, where border raiding was endemic, there seem to have been 'professional prisoners' who would allow themselves to be captured in order to act as guarantors for others; on the basis of their guarantee, a captive would go and get a ransom, gain freedom for himself and for them, and then pay them a premium for their service.[5]

The practice of arranging an exchange of captives between the two sides allowed more flexibility than the straightforward payment of a fixed sum. In 1597, for example, a Sicilian woman who was a slave in the Tunisian port of Bizerte wrote to a female friend in Palermo, asking her to beg the commander of the Sicilian fleet to free from the galleys – in exchange for her own release – the brother of her Tunisian owner. This woman might have been unable to raise her own ransom price, but she could make use of a personal connection, while also

---

* For the Jewish captive see above, pp. 80–1.

exploiting the special value placed by her owner on his own brother. Sometimes family members would buy a slave with the express purpose of exchanging that captive for their own relative; here the advantage would presumably have lain in the price differential, though if prices differed significantly between the two sides they might find that a one-for-one exchange was not accepted. (Because of the superior cost of labour in Western Europe, the prices of slaves were generally higher there, and the predominant Western tendency was to keep able-bodied captives for slavery, instead of touting them for ransom.) The reports of the Venetian bailo in Istanbul in 1578 include the sad complaint of an Albanian Muslim, Hüseyin, son of Abdullah, of Elbasan, whose son had been captured at Lepanto and was now a galley-slave in Corfu. Hüseyin had bought a Christian slave, 'Pietro da Liesena' (Pietro or Petar from Hvar, the Venetian Dalmatian island) in order to make an exchange. He had approached the Venetian diplomat Giacomo Soranzo in 1575, when the latter was in Lezhë; Soranzo had told him to take Pietro to Venice, and had given him a letter of safe-conduct. But when he went there and handed over his Christian captive, 'after a month, during which he thought he would have his son in exchange for the said Pietro, he was told by those signori that if he wanted his son he should give them another Christian.' He returned to Ottoman territory and took his grievance first to the sancakbeyi of Delvinë and then to the Grand Vizier, who transmitted the complaint to the bailo. The end of this story is not known, but we may suspect that it did not go well for Hüseyin and his son; the bailo noted that Hüseyin was unable to return to Venice, because of physical infirmity and other problems.[6]

In addition to such do-it-yourself exchangers and ransomers, there were also many active intermediaries. Merchants whose normal business involved trade between the two sides could easily become involved in these transactions; Jews were prominent as ransom agents, and in Malta the visiting merchants who performed this task included Jews, Muslims, Armenians, Greeks and Maronites (Christian Arabs). From the Barbary states, Muslim merchants would travel to Florence, Rome and elsewhere, offering deals to free Christian captives by ransom or exchange, or seeking the payment promised by captives who had been allowed home in order to raise it; these merchants were often 'renegades', converts to Islam who might have Italian or Spanish as their native language. Sometimes, in a more speculative way, a Christian merchant would buy Muslim slaves and take them to their home territories, where relatives or other benefactors would pay for their freedom.

Occasionally there were individual acts of entrepreneurship: in 1568, for example, a janissary recovered a Ragusan boy who had been captured by Montenegrins and brought him back to Dubrovnik, receiving a payment of 3,000 *akçe*s (50 ducats) for the service he had rendered. There were many ways of working the system, and some were less morally admirable than others; in 1578 several Ragusan sailors, captured at Lezhë, were made by the *emin*s (superintendents) of that port to sign documents falsely stating that the *emin*s had paid a ransom of 400 thalers (266 ducats) for them, which Dubrovnik was then required to reimburse.[7]

Other types of third-party involvement were more systematic and wide-ranging. Official ransoming projects took various forms. A major city such as Marseille, or one of the smaller towns on the coast of Provence, would gather funds and send an agent to redeem its citizens in North Africa; Dubrovnik similarly sent an officially sponsored mission to Algiers in 1568. Thirteen years later, the Kingdom of Naples raised 10,000 ducats for a 'general ransom' of its subjects in Istanbul. There was nothing equivalent to this from the Ottoman or Barbary side at this time; the pashas and senior corsairs of Algiers did sometimes send envoys with lavish gifts to Western rulers (Francesco de' Medici got two horses, two lions and an ostrich in 1586), but the main purpose of maintaining such high-level contacts was not to win back their own subjects from slavery, but to encourage the Westerners to step up the flow of ransom payments. A significant development during this period was the increasing role of Christian religious organizations in redeeming captives – especially the lay confraternities in Italian cities, and the two major 'redemptionist' orders in France, Spain and Portugal, the Mercedarians and Trinitarians. This was very much a Counter-Reformation phenomenon, as it channelled what could have been purely secular charitable impulses into an overtly religious form; and the captives who were ransomed in this way were often put to work, marching on long ceremonial progresses through European cities in a series of consciousness-raising displays and religious performances. Not every pious redemptionist project went according to plan, however. In 1580 a Spanish Trinitarian friar, Cristóbal Pérez, sent on papal authority to organize the ransoming of Christian slaves in Istanbul, decided to convert to Islam. He had fallen heavily into debt, having apparently spent on credit moneys deposited with the Venetians, some of which had already been used for ransom payments by the bailo; a desire to spite the bailo seems to have been his main motive for apostasy. He was bundled into the house of the Spanish envoy, kept under lock and key there, and eventually sent back to Italy.[8]

In theory at least, Venice did not need to maintain an official ransoming programme of its own, since its long-running agreements with the Ottoman Empire stipulated that neither side would seize or enslave the subjects of the other. Genuine attempts were made, under normal conditions, to follow that rule, and Venice would routinely free enslaved Ottoman subjects if it found them on any Western ship in its jurisdiction. But the steady depredations of pirates and corsairs ensured that many Venetians – especially inhabitants of the Stato da Mar – did fall into captivity; sometimes the Ottomans would claim legalistically that they could hold Venetian slaves so long as their original enslavement had not been carried out by Ottoman subjects. (And on the other side, as the case of the son of Hüseyin of Elbasan shows, not all Ottoman prisoners of war were returned at the end of hostilities in 1573.) Trying to assist, and to free, Venetian slaves was therefore a regular part of the bailo's duties. Until the mid-1580s only *ad hoc* funding was available for this: in 1571, for instance, while himself under house arrest, Marcantonio Barbaro received 1,000 ducats to relieve the sufferings of slaves, and in 1580 the bailo was using, as we have seen, some of the funds associated with Pérez's mission. In 1586 a more regular system was instituted, partly on the basis of moneys raised by a confraternity in Venice, but the amount was never enough. Two years later the bailo Giovanni Moro reported that 'there are a great many slaves here, some seized while serving Venice in various places in wartime, and many in time of peace'; he had only 590 ducats to spend on them, of which 500 were in a fund restricted to Venetian citizens and subjects – thus excluding many foreigners who had fought valiantly for the Serenissima.[9]

The fate of non-Venetians who had fought for Venice was an issue which had loomed large in the aftermath of the war of 1570–3. For a long time the baili struggled to secure the release of all those people, both military and civilian, who had been promised safe passage at the surrenders of Ulcinj and Bar, but who had then been taken off into slavery. The French envoy, the Bishop of Dax, had tried to intercede for the Gascon soldiers in 1572, without any success. When the baili demanded the release of all these prisoners in 1574 they were told that the Ottoman admiral needed them for his galleys. A further attempt in January 1575 seemed on the point of success, until the Grand Vizier said that he would free only Venetian subjects, not all the others who had fought for Venice; but with the help of a bribe to the Grand Vizier, a formal petition to the Sultan and the intercession of Ahmed Pasha (who had been the land commander at the fall of Ulcinj and Bar), the promise of safety given in 1571 was at long last fulfilled.[10]

For those slaves who were not ransomed or exchanged, there were two other ways of regaining their freedom. One was to be manumitted by their master; this was not uncommon in the Ottoman world as a reward for many years of good service, and if a slave had converted to Islam the master might give orders in his will that the slave be freed – as a meritorious act – after his own decease. (Conversion in itself, however, did not bring an end to slavery.) The other method of gaining freedom was to flee to the West. Although the practical difficulties were huge, many escapes did take place, and some were quite dramatic, involving large numbers. In 1550 a group of eighteen or 20 Christian slaves seized a small boat in the Bosphorus and made their way to freedom; in 1572 a number of slaves escaped on a nineteen-bench galiot from Vlorë; and in the most spectacular exploit of all, in 1581 no fewer than 283 Christians managed to take a corsair galley from Istanbul and sail all the way to Sicily. According to Stefan Gerlach, the well-informed and omnivorously curious Lutheran who served as chaplain at the Imperial embassy in Istanbul in the mid-1570s, small-scale escapes by sea took place every year. But that was not the only method. As he also recorded, secret agents (whom he called 'spies') would come from Spain and Italy to Galata, the merchant area of Istanbul, to make contact with slaves and plan their escape. After fleeing his master's house, a slave would be kept in hiding for two or three months while his beard and hair grew; he would then be dressed as an Albanian, and led, with the other 15 or 20 slaves gathered by the agent, away from Istanbul by secret routes at night. Each slave would pay up to 20 ducats, and on reaching Spanish territory the agent would receive a reward of 12 ducats per head. This escape method was beset with dangers. In 1576 the Ottoman authorities caught a group of six slaves, disguised as Bulgarians, together with their three Greek guides; an Italian dragoman at the French embassy was condemned to death because he had allowed them to hide in his house. And in the previous year an internal investigation by the Venetian bailo discovered that four of his Albanian couriers had taken a group of slaves out of Istanbul on this basis and murdered them for their money.[11]

Those whom Gerlach, in this context, called 'spies' were probably not engaged primarily in espionage; but the two lines of business could easily be combined. It would have been odd if the Spanish government,

conscious of such clandestine activities, had not sometimes used these
people for other purposes, especially in view of their expert knowledge
of routes out of the Ottoman Empire. (The Venetian baili also sometimes smuggled slaves out of Istanbul by boat, using methods and routes
that were betrayed to the Ottoman authorities in 1574 by a disgruntled
Venetian dragoman who had converted to Islam; it was probably thanks
to such secret methods, at least in part, that the bailo had been able to
send messages to Venice in 1570–3 while he was held under close house
arrest.) But there was another, less fraught way of combining slave-
freeing and espionage. Because the ransoming of captives was universally
recognized as a necessary and important matter, it was easy for people
engaged in such a task to obtain safe-conducts. Thus equipped, an agent
could travel quite openly to the heart of the enemy's state and spend a
long time there, meeting both public officials and private individuals.
This was the perfect 'cover' for an intelligence mission – less restrictive
than diplomacy, and less time-consuming (or less hard to fake) than
commerce.[12]

It was on this basis that Giovanni Barelli, the Corfiot-Venetian Knight
of Malta, went several times to Istanbul; in 1575, for example, he spent
some months there, and on his return he wrote a very detailed and well-
informed analysis of the Sultan's likely military and geopolitical strategy
for the following year. No category of person was more hated by the
Ottoman authorities than the Knights of Malta; for such a man to be
allowed a prolonged stay in Istanbul was rather as if a KGB general had
been permitted to install himself in a Washington hotel at the height of
the Cold War. Yet Barelli was not only tolerated, but appreciated, by his
Ottoman hosts. As he put it in a memorandum for his Spanish masters
in 1574, 'I have gained great fame among the Ottomans by having a
reputation for doing them a service by ransoming Ottomans who are
slaves.' This method was widely adopted. When the Spanish were building up their intelligence network in Istanbul in the 1560s, two of their
key agents, Adam de Franchis and Giovanni Maria Renzo, used ransoming captives as their cover. In 1572 Don John sent a spy to Tripoli, with
six North African captives whose exchange or ransom he was ostensibly
seeking to arrange. Such an initiative in the middle of a war was a little
too blatant, and he was promptly arrested, before himself being released
for a ransom (and bringing back valuable intelligence on his return). It
was well understood that the Ottomans used the same methods; the
difference seems to have been that the Western powers were sometimes
much less tolerant of such missions in their own territories. When an

Italian renegade known as Mustafa dei Cordovani (who may possibly have been from a merchant family resident in Koper) came to Venice on official ransoming business in early 1574, the Venetian authorities identified him as a spy and decided to have him poisoned. Luckily for him the poison, supplied by the director of the botanical garden at the University of Padua, was ineffective; only on his next visit to Venice, in 1576, was his assassination finally accomplished.[13]

One other aspect of the business of ransom and exchange deserves mention: the special role of Dubrovnik. As a Christian state nestling on the edge of Ottoman territory, practically autonomous but regarded by the Sultan as part of his empire, Dubrovnik was the ideal venue for this kind of East–West transaction. Its cordial relations with the neighbouring *sancakbeyi*s and military commanders meant that it was trusted by the Ottomans; sometimes, to please them, it would return Christian slaves who had escaped and sought refuge in Ragusan territory. Quite often it was asked for help in finding and ransoming Ottoman captives in Italy: in 1568, for example, the Ragusan authorities wrote to Kara Hoca (the corsair commander in Vlorë) promising to do what they could to release one of his men from prison in Apulia, as he had requested. Later that year they decided that, having restored several Muslim captives to the Ottomans, they should take the opportunity to ransom four Christian slaves from them at the bargain price of 50 ducats. Once the Ottoman–Venetian war had broken out in 1570, Dubrovnik's role in these matters was hugely enhanced. In late 1571 Venice agreed to release the Ottoman merchants whom it had interned at the start of the war, swapping them for Venetian merchants similarly treated in Istanbul; these exchanges took place in Dubrovnik. A stream of Christian military captives followed, while the Ragusan authorities made great efforts, at the request of senior figures in Istanbul, to track down and ransom prominent Ottoman prisoners in Italy. Other Christian powers besides Venice were happy to make use of the Ragusan government's services: in 1573, for example, the Grand Master of Malta sent it a letter requesting help for one of his Knights, Fra Pedro de Cisneros, who was coming to Dubrovnik with an Ottoman captive called Cafer in order to exchange him for his brother, Fra Cristoforo. Four years later the Ragusan authorities wrote to their ambassadors in Istanbul, asking them to arrange the ransom of a Spanish slave, Juan de Agreda, who had been captured at La Goletta, and explaining that 'our help has been sought by someone whom we wish to oblige' – perhaps the Viceroy of Naples.[14]

Such, then, was the general background to the prisoner exchange in which Bartolomeo Bruti became involved in 1575. On both sides the prisoners were 'prominenti', men with a high ransom value. Most of the Christians were soldiers who had fought at Nicosia and Famagusta in 1570–1 (including several Albanian officers, such as 'Georgio Vhelmi' (Gjergj Helmi?), the stradiot commander at Famagusta), but they also included Emanuele Mormori, who had been captured at the fall of Sopot in July 1571, and Giovanni Tommaso Costanzo, who, aged only seventeen, had fought valiantly when his galley was seized by the Ottomans off the Albanian coast at roughly the same time. The most prominent of all was Gabrio Serbelloni, who was not only a senior general but also the brother of a cardinal and a cousin of the late Pope Pius IV; he was taken to Istanbul after the fall of La Goletta and Tunis. The Ottoman prisoners, on the other hand, were all men captured at Lepanto. Immediately after the battle, Don John had tried to gather together the *beys*, ship's captains and senior officers, removing them from the general distribution of prisoners. He had faced some opposition; Sebastiano Venier, the Venetian commander, managed to spirit several Ottoman captains away to Venice, where they were never heard of again. (The Venetian government was keen to prevent the Ottomans from ever recovering the skilled manpower they had lost. As soon as it learned of the victory, it sent Venier an order forbidding him to release any captains, and the Doge began to press for a policy of killing all captive Ottoman sailors.) Don John managed to assemble 42 important prisoners, whom he took to Naples on the basis of an agreement that they would be handed to the Pope for safe-keeping. Two of these were the teenage sons of Ali Müezzinzade Pasha, who had commanded their own galley in the battle; the elder brother died in Naples, but the younger one would later be released by Don John, at the request of their sister Fatima, in what was presented as a grandly chivalrous gesture of compassion. One other captive went no further than Naples: an Ottoman military officer called Mustafa, who was originally Gregorio Bregante, from Genoa. He had been on the payroll of Spanish intelligence in Istanbul, and was detained by Cardinal Granvelle, who suspected his loyalty. So the prisoners who finally travelled to Rome in the spring of 1572 came to a total of 40. The most important among them was the *sancakbeyi* of Euboea, Mehmed Bey, whose value was raised by two things: the fact that he was very rich, being the son of the former ruler of Algiers, Salih Bey; and his good personal connections with the Ottoman imperial family. Described as 'of medium height, with a sparse chestnut-coloured beard, and a slight squint', and roughly 40 years old, he was valued at the huge sum of 20,000 scudi (16,666 ducats).[15]

Once they were comfortably installed in a Roman palazzo – in contrast to the Christian prominenti in Istanbul, who were held in the notorious prison-tower of the Yedikule fortress and subjected to fierce beatings – the Ottoman captives soon became a bone of contention between the Papacy and its allies. At first Venice urged the Pope to kill the lot of them. When he declined to execute prisoners in cold blood, the Venetians asked that they be shared out between the allies, so that they could at least kill a third of the total. That idea too was rejected; the Pope valued these captives too highly, as assets and as bargaining-chips. In March 1573 Giovanni Barelli was allowed to take one prisoner, at Don John's behest, for ransoming purposes; in reality this was 'cover' for an intelligence mission to Ottoman territory, aimed at investigating the prospects of a revolt in the Peloponnese. (His plans were altered by the news of the Venetian–Ottoman peace agreement, but he did travel as far as Salonica, and he managed to ransom his charge for 1,000 ducats.) During that year the Pope came under some pressure from the Spanish, who resented his desire to exchange the captives only for his own subjects, and urged that the most valuable ones, including Mehmed Bey, should be handed over to Spain.[16]

Moral pressure came also from one individual who could speak with personal authority in these matters: Giacomo Malatesta, the noble condottiere whose hapless punitive expedition near Kotor in 1571 had ended in his own capture and incarceration, in the same tower and under the same harsh conditions. Thanks to his high-level personal connections, especially with the Medici family, there had been an extraordinary international campaign for his release. (This risked becoming counter-productive, by giving the Ottomans an exaggerated idea of his importance: at one point the Grand Vizier was said to be demanding Zadar, Šibenik and Kotor in exchange for Malatesta.) While the Duke of Urbino begged both Dubrovnik and Philip II to intercede for him, King Charles IX of France and his Medici mother used their influence in Istanbul to obtain Giacomo's freedom; he was back in Venice by late August 1572. But his own son Ercole, who had been captured by the Ottomans in Cyprus, was still locked up with the other prominenti in Istanbul. In late 1572 or early 1573 Giacomo addressed a strongly worded memorandum to the Pope, urging him to organize an exchange of the two groups, and arguing that although some of the

Muslims in Rome had a high ransom value, none of them was of any real military significance. If the Pope did not go ahead with such a scheme, he wrote, the prospect of being left to rot in an Ottoman prison would make Christian soldiers reluctant to go to war in future. Eventually, by the summer of 1574, Pope Gregory XIII did come round to the idea of a general exchange of captives. Spanish pressure also intensified after the fall of La Goletta and Tunis in September of that year, though Philip II was now hoping to obtain a very different set of prisoners from the ones that were finally agreed on: he complained bitterly at the idea of exchanging Ottomans captured by the Holy League for Venetians who had been taken at the fall of Nicosia, before the Holy League had even been created.[17]

The deal that emerged in the early months of 1575 was negotiated by the Venetian bailo. Presumably Venice was operating (as the Spanish Ambassador in Rome surmised) on secret instructions from the Pope. Venice's own attitude had become much less uncompromising after its peace with the Sultan – as well it might, given that the Christian captives involved in the exchange were mostly Venetians who had been excluded by the Sultan from the general Ottoman–Venetian return of prisoners in 1573. But it is not at all clear whether the idea of asking Bartolomeo Bruti to play a part in the process came from the Venetian bailo. His name first cropped up in a formal letter about the exchange from the Sultan to the Doge of Venice, dated 28 January 1575, which said that it would take place in a few months' time in Dubrovnik, and that 'Bartolomeo Bruti, the bearer of this imperial letter, will bring the Ottoman prisoners from Rome'; on this basis it has even been supposed that Bartolomeo was now an employee of the Sultan, though that is certainly not a necessary implication of the wording. On 31 January the bailo reported to Venice that Bartolomeo, 'the son of the late cavaliere Bruti of Ulcinj', would take the official letters, adding in cipher: 'and signor Gabrio wants the same Bruti to go to Rome with my letters'. On 2 February Gabrio Serbelloni also wrote a letter to the Doge, in which he described Bartolomeo as the bearer of his letter and asked that Bartolomeo be allowed to go on from Venice to Rome to ensure that the whole business would reach a satisfactory conclusion. Two days later, Bartolomeo left Istanbul. By 19 February he was in Dubrovnik, where he had a long conversation with Cesare della Marra, who resided there as an intelligence agent for Spain. Della Marra not only reported that 'the son of the cavaliere Bruti' had come to arrange the swapping of Gabrio Serbelloni for Mehmed Bey, but also gave some of the Istanbul news and gossip that Bartolomeo had imparted to him: there would be no great naval expedition that year; the deposed King of Fez was asking the Ottomans to restore him to power and promising a huge annual tribute; the Grand Vizier, Mehmed Sokollu, was still in great favour with the Sultan; and Sinan Pasha, the victor at Tunis, 'gives Mehmed [Sokollu] all the money he makes, for which Mehmed favours him greatly'. By 26 February Bartolomeo was in Venice; the authorities there sent him on, with their blessing, to Rome.[18]

One or two years later, when Bartolomeo Bruti was fully employed by the Spanish authorities, he sent a long memorandum to the King of Spain about his own conduct. In it he described, among other things, how he had been recruited. 'I found myself in Istanbul in 1574', he wrote, 'working for the Republic of Venice – instructing and training their baili and ambassadors in the customary ways of proceeding at the Ottoman court when doing the republic's business there.' That absurdly vainglorious statement tells us much about his desire to impress his new masters, but nothing about the reality of his status in late 1574, which was that he was a teenaged ex-giovane di lingua who probably had no formal position at the bailate at all. He went on to explain that he had got to know Giovanni Margliani, one of the captives from Tunis, and had had some conversations with him in the bailo's house. Margliani was the nephew of Serbelloni who had made an epic voyage to warn Don John of the Ottoman attack on Tunis, and had returned there to face what he regarded as almost certain death or capture.* He was not in the group of prominenti that formed the subject of the prisoner exchange, being one of many captives from Tunis and La Goletta (including eight priests and two women, wives of La Goletta garrison soldiers) whose release had already been negotiated, piecemeal, with the bailo's help. 'One day', Bartolomeo wrote, 'I was entreated by him, in a favourable way and with telling arguments, to make up my mind to serve Your Majesty.' At first he hesitated, thinking of 'the honourable position in which I found myself with the Venetians'. But then, overcome by Christian zeal, a desire to serve the King who was the greatest enemy of 'the Muhammedan sect', and a longing to 'avenge to some extent the injuries which my entire family had suffered from that accursed sect', he began to favour the idea. When Margliani asked him again a few days later, 'I allowed myself to be easily overcome by his arguments; and so, using a good pretext, and in order to serve Your

* See above, p. 190.

Majesty, we arranged that I should be sent to Rome to urge the Pope to undertake the prisoner exchange.'[19]

If we can assume that the basic story told here was true, this information provides an essential piece of the jigsaw: Margliani and – no doubt on his advice – Serbelloni nominated Bartolomeo Bruti as the courier for this mission. (The bailo's ciphered comment of 31 January, quoted above, also tends to confirm that.) Yet still we are entitled to ask whether these men had the power simply to arrange such a thing at their own volition, and why they were so keen to obtain the services of such an inexperienced youth. A clue to the answer may lie in one of the fragments of information relayed by Cesare della Marra, quoted above: the news, reported to him by Bartolomeo, that Sinan Pasha was earning the favour of the Grand Vizier by giving him all the money he acquired. On the one hand, that might have been just a piece of external gossip. On the other hand, it might have been something derived from a conversation with Sinan himself, or at least with someone close to him in his household. There is good reason to think that it was the second of those alternatives; for, as we shall see, Bartolomeo was to enjoy a particularly strong connection with Sinan Pasha, to whom he was in fact related. Bartolomeo's father, Antonio, had boasted in his 1560 petition to the Venetian government that he had many 'aderenze', connections or contacts, in Ottoman territory, and that he had high-placed friends in Istanbul; this was an advantage that Bartolomeo would have taken great care to exploit when he went to live in that city. The decision to abandon the post of trainee dragoman, made by early September 1574 – and thus unrelated to any approach by Margliani or Serbelloni, who were still defending Tunis at that time – most probably arose from the fact that Bartolomeo had found other methods of supporting himself, using his father's contacts and relations. This does not mean that he had entered Ottoman service, or even the personal employment of Sinan Pasha (who might well have suggested that Bartolomeo build an Ottoman career for himself, but would in that case have required him to convert to Islam); the simplest scenario is that he was finding ways of turning his contacts to profitable use, perhaps on behalf of Western merchants in the city. The fact that he relayed some information from Serbelloni to the bailo, when the former was lodged in the Grand Vizier's house, suggests two things: that he was keeping in with the Venetians, and that he had easy access, perhaps as a protégé of Sinan Pasha, to Mehmed Sokollu's residence. It was surely the nature and quality of his contacts, not the limited range of his experience, that made him a

desirable catch for the Spanish. And when his name was floated as a
suitable courier for the prisoner exchange business, it would have ticked
every box: trusted by the Venetians, liked and accepted by the Ottomans, and – secretly – engaged by the Spaniards.[20]

Bartolomeo Bruti reached Rome in early March, and the papal
administration quickly made the necessary preparations. On 12 March
1575 he left Rome with 34 Ottoman prisoners – all that remained of the
original 40. He wrote that evening to the Doge, explaining that he was
taking them to Fermo (a town in Papal territory, close to the Adriatic
coast); from there, he said, he would not move them without instructions from the Venetians, whose task it would be to ferry them to
Dubrovnik for the exchange. Bartolomeo signed himself 'Your Serenity's most devoted subject and servant' – which, in view of his agreement
to work for Spain, involved some bending of the truth. He also enclosed
a letter in Turkish, with Italian translation, from Mehmed Bey, to be
forwarded to the Sultan; this was important, as the Ottoman ruler
would not let the Christian prisoners set out from Istanbul until he was
assured by Mehmed himself that the Ottoman ones were on their way.
Once they were settled in Fermo, Bartolomeo wrote to the papal secretary of state Tolomeo Gallio, Cardinal Como, saying that his charges
were anxious at the fact that they had not been taken to Ancona, as
originally promised, and that they were still under lock and key; but,
said Bartolomeo with his characteristic tendency to self-promotion, 'I
reassured them, speaking to them at length in an extremely skilful way.'
He also warned the Cardinal about a new problem, concerning one of
the prisoners, Mehmed *Subaşı* (a *subaşı* was a military officer who acted
as a district's chief of police). One of this man's relatives in Istanbul had
bought a valuable Italian captive and had sent him to Dubrovnik to be
swapped one-for-one; it was feared that this would undo the entire collective exchange that was now in train. (Two months later, while they
were still waiting, that problem was solved, but in a way that must have
seemed even more problematic, when Mehmed *Subaşı* was stabbed to
death by one of his colleagues. Bartolomeo quickly organized the writing of affidavits by the others, testifying to the blamelessness of the
Christian authorities.) During the long wait at Fermo, Bartolomeo must
have become well acquainted with Mehmed Bey, the most prominent of
all the prisoners, and the one who, it seems, was most inclined to complain that the promise made to them about their release was not being
kept. A letter to Rome from the papal commissary, who was looking
after the practical arrangements, described his handling of this awkward

customer in terms that suggest that Bartolomeo's self-praise was not altogether unjustified. 'Since our arrival in Fermo, signor Bartolomeo Bruti has never ceased to give him [sc. Mehmed Bey] earnest assurances of that promise; but he is a bone-headed man, and it is hard to satisfy him, or to do business with him.'[21]

At long last, in late May, things began to move. On the 29th the bailo handed in an official petition to the Sultan, asking for the release of the 39 Christian prisoners, stating that there were 33 Muslims awaiting the exchange, and promising to find another six to make the numbers equal. In early June the Sultan sent an order to the government of Dubrovnik, in which he said that the 39 Christians were now en route from Istanbul; he required the Ragusans to hold them securely until the Muslims were there, to check the number and identities of the Muslims when they arrived, and, if everything was in order, to make the exchange. On 15 July Venice sent three galleys to take Mehmed Bey and his fellow captives across the Adriatic; at the same time the Venetians supplied the six extra prisoners, as arithmetic required. The exchange was finally effected, in a ceremony presided over by the Ragusan authorities, on 22 July. On the 27th they wrote to their ambassadors at the Ottoman court, recording that it had gone smoothly, and also specifying that they had lent 1,000 ducats to Mehmed Bey, which he had promised to repay on his arrival in Istanbul. Mehmed Bey himself, meanwhile, sent a gracious letter to the Doge of Venice, thanking him for his help and praising the conduct of Bartolomeo Bruti. This had been one of the largest and most important formal exchanges of captives in recent Mediterranean history; its memory would live on for a long time. Eighteen years later, when Archduke Matthias of Austria wrote to the Pasha of Buda with a proposal to swap prisoners, he would suggest that the arrangements be modelled on this famous exchange. Bartolomeo Bruti could reasonably claim some of the credit; although he had not been at all involved in the diplomacy that had made the deal possible, he had acquitted himself well in the difficult and sensitive task of handling the Ottoman prisoners during the last four months of their captivity. He had also got to know at least one person who might become a valuable high-level contact in Istanbul: Mehmed Bey, the rich son of the former ruler of Algiers. Bartolomeo's career as a Spanish agent was just beginning.[22]

12

Espionage and Sabotage in Istanbul

Intelligence-gathering and espionage are not quite the same things, though much of the latter does consist of the former. As we have already seen, the sixteenth-century Mediterranean was a news-hungry world, where information of many kinds – about commodity prices, for example, or the movements of corsairs – was highly valued. The compiling of 'avvisi' (news-letters) was a widespread practice, serving both private individuals and states. While the things written about in such reports were in many cases objects of public knowledge in their place of origin (the fall of a minister, the outbreak of famine or flood, and so on), to have reliable information about these matters, at a great distance, was still worth taking some trouble over. And although a government could expect its own diplomats to report such news in their despatches, there were some advantages in receiving multiple, overlapping accounts of the same things, especially when those things were rumours rather than known facts. So outside the embassies there was often a penumbra of information-gatherers – agents, in some sense, but not spies in any strong meaning of that term. It is surprisingly difficult, though, to determine at what point an intelligence-gatherer turns into a spy. To say that spies gather the sort of information that the host country would want to stop them from having, or transmitting, is not to put forward a very clear criterion; for the range of topics coming under that heading will increase at times of tension between the two states, and can become very general in wartime.

Merchants were natural information-gatherers, whose services were much in demand by governments. One of the earliest detailed intelligence reports in the Ottoman archives was prepared by an official in Durrës in 1530, using information supplied by a merchant called 'Dhuka' from the southern Albanian town of Gjirokastër. Dhuka, who was evidently fluent in Italian, had recently returned to Ottoman

territory from Genoa, having spent three years in the mohair trade in
Italy, France and Spain, and he supplied much information, albeit of a
non-secret kind, about the state of Western Europe. The great advantage of merchants was that they could travel without arousing suspicion;
in 1567 Girolamo Bucchia, the Habsburg intelligence agent from Kotor
(who, as we have seen, had rumbled an ecclesiastical spy for the Ottomans at the Council of Trent), advised the Pope that he should send
traders from Dubrovnik, Kotor, Bar or Ulcinj 'under the pretext of commerce' to assess the prospects of an anti-Ottoman revolt in Albania. On
the other hand, those traders who were long-term residents in foreign
cities were good sources of political gossip, which they would anyway
acquire in the pursuit of their own business interests. The Spanish
authorities made much use of merchants, and would offer them special
trading privileges in return for their services. Sometimes a merchant
would have become so embedded in the local society that he had sources
of information that few outsiders could hope to match. In September
1575 the two baili and the special Venetian ambassador in Istanbul,
Giacomo Soranzo, reported that they had received a visit from a Venetian merchant, Lorenzo di Scudi, who had married a Christian woman
from the Galata district of the city. He said that his wife was a close
friend of the 'Sultana', who was the widow of the former Grand Vizier
Rüstem Pasha, and that she had heard several of the women in the Sultana's household say that 'an extremely large naval expedition would
take place in the following year', with Venetian territory as its target.[1]

If intelligence-gathering was second nature for merchants, it was a
primary part of the job description for diplomats. Their aim in these
matters, above all, was to winkle out the secrets of the host government,
particularly where its own diplomacy was concerned. The Western
envoys in Istanbul devoted much effort and ingenuity to this. Unlike
ambassadors elsewhere, they enjoyed one huge advantage: in the upper
reaches of the Ottoman administration there were many 'renegades'
(converts to Islam), from Italy, Croatia, Hungary, Austria and elsewhere,
whose native language and mental formation were Western – or, at
least, Christian and non-Ottoman – European. It was a basic feature of
the Ottoman system that the government consisted primarily of slaves
of the Sultan, who owed him their undivided allegiance because they
had been uprooted from, or had never belonged to, any local interest-
group within the empire. The classic method of recruitment was the
devşirme or 'collection' (sometimes more dramatically described as the
'blood tribute'), which took teenaged boys from Christian families in

the Ottoman Balkans, gave them the status of sultanic slaves, converted them to Islam, and raised them to be janissaries or palace servants; but many foreign-born Christian boys or young men who were captured in war could, if they became Muslims, also rise high in the administrative system. And for obvious linguistic reasons the Ottoman government's dragomans, and the secretaries it used for diplomatic correspondence, were often of Italian, Austrian or Hungarian origin. The system was riddled with such people; some may have become super-loyal to their new masters, but there was always the possibility that a Western diplomat could play on their residual affection for their homeland (where, often, they still had family members), or at least develop a personal friendship with them on the basis of their common language, shared mentality and, in some cases, undiminished fondness for alcohol.[2]*

Once a link was established, and a flow of confidential information (or other forms of help, which could include exerting an influence on Ottoman policy) had begun, it was not difficult to find ways of paying these people for their services. The gift culture of Ottoman society was especially strong at court and in the higher reaches of the government. A document of 1594 in the Venetian archives lists all the people who would receive gifts on the arrival of a new bailo in Istanbul: they included not only the Sultan, the Grand Vizier and the other viziers, but also the *Kapudan Paşa* and his officials, the Chancellor and *defterdar* (state treasurer) and their dependants, the *ağa* of the janissaries and his chief officers, the judge and *subaşı* of Galata and their subordinates, the customs *emin* and his officials, and so on. In such a culture, a payment to an Ottoman dragoman or secretary would hardly arouse suspicion. And quite apart from these formal present-givings, there was a constant flow of largesse: as the previous bailo wrote in 1592, 'the bailate is commonly visited by many Ottomans who are looking for gifts, and are like bees round a honey-pot.' It was worth paying those who could perform some favour or supply valuable news, he advised, but the bailo had to reject all the others, as 'otherwise his house would have more customers than a shop on the Rialto bridge.'[3]

One other category of people played a special role in Istanbul and at the Ottoman court, which made them valued sources of information:

---

* Alcohol was widely available in Istanbul in most periods, but Western embassies were appreciated for their liberal dispensing of it; the Dutch traveller Joris van der Does, who was there in 1597, wrote that he seldom saw a Muslim able to walk unassisted after a meal at the English Ambassador's table.

the Jews. Many of the major trading families among them had branches in Venice, Vienna or elsewhere in the Christian world; this raised the possibility of multiple or flexible loyalties. Thanks to their wealth, the most prominent Jews had access to senior viziers and pashas (or, in the well-known case of Joseph Nasi, friendship with the Sultan), and were prized by them in turn for their foreign contacts and international outlook. One of the most active was David Passi, a Jew of Spanish origin who was living in Dubrovnik in 1569, when he warned the Venetian government about the Sultan's plan to attack Cyprus. He moved to Venice in 1572, possibly to assist with secret peace initiatives towards the Ottomans, but, unhappy at his treatment by that state, volunteered to work for the Spanish intelligence service in the following year. He was described as having a wife in Ferrara, a brother at the royal court in Poland, a father in Salonica, and an uncle who was a physician to the Sultan in Istanbul. By the early 1580s he was resident in Istanbul, and before long he became one of the Sultan's confidants; now it was the turn of the English Ambassador to seek his services, as he was said to be both anti-Venetian and anti-Spanish. Jewish physicians, such as Passi's uncle, also enjoyed privileged access to senior Ottomans. In many cases they had studied medicine in Padua or at other Italian universities, and had their own cultural and familial links with the West; a web of connections might exist that could be utilized for various purposes. Dubrovnik, for example, was happy to exploit the fact that one of its municipal physicians, Samuel Abeatar, was the brother of Rabbi Abeatar, who served as personal physician to the chief *defterdar* in Istanbul. Perhaps the most influential figure in this period was Solomon Nathan Ashkenazi (or, as he signed his name, 'Salamon Natan Ascanasi'), a Venetian subject, born in Udine, who had studied medicine in Padua and practised at the Polish court before settling in Istanbul, where he quickly acquired many high-level contacts and patients. By 1576 he was described by Stefan Gerlach as 'in such favour with the Grand Vizier that he is his confidential adviser on French, Venetian, Polish and Hungarian affairs'. Solomon always kept up his links with Venice, not least because he had five sons there, for whom he sought special privileges from the Venetian authorities; his services were highly appreciated, and in late 1576 Venice resolved to pay him a pension of 300 ducats a year. But at various times he also acted as a source of information for, and an agent of influence on behalf of, the Empire (where he had a brother, resident in Vienna), Spain and France. Writing to Henri III of France from Istanbul in 1580, he felt able to call himself 'your most faithful servant';

he told the King that he had always given him his help, 'above all in the election when Your Majesty was elected King of Poland [in 1573], where I was behind everything that was done here – even though I think the Bishop of Dax took all the credit for himself'.[4]

Using renegades, Jews and others, the most skilled Western diplomats commanded an extraordinary range of sources. As Lazaro Soranzo wrote in his very well-informed book about the Ottoman Empire (published in 1598), the rulers of Western Europe 'keep many paid spies in Istanbul, while also paying salaries to Jews and Muslims who are among the most intimate and confidential people of the leading pashas'; he added that the servants of those pashas would sell secrets to the Western diplomats, and so too would the women of the Sultan's court. This was no exaggeration. Reporting on his tour of duty from 1585 to 1587, the bailo Lorenzo Bernardo wrote that he had 'flattered and gratified many captains and other seamen' in order to obtain inside information about the Arsenal, and that one of the secretaries there regularly told him of the orders that went out for provisions – a useful way of assessing the scale of impending naval campaigns. The Sultan's chief dragoman, Hürrem Bey, who was originally from Lucca, was on the Venetian payroll; as he was also working secretly for Spain, he was able to supply Bernardo with valuable information about Ottoman–Spanish relations. Details about the Sultan himself, and about events in the closed world of his Istanbul residence, the Topkapı Palace, came via an intermediary from the Jewish woman who worked in the palace as the trusted agent of the Sultana. For news of the ongoing campaigns in Persia, Bernardo relied on the three secretaries of the Ottoman Chancellor; they also gave him the originals of many letters from European rulers to the Sultan (which, once translated by them into Turkish, were usually discarded). And the agent whom, he said, he was most proud to have recruited was Ali Ağa, originally from Ancona, who was one of three young men who waited constantly on the Sultan. There is plenty of other evidence to confirm this picture of far-reaching penetration. To give just a few examples: in 1579 the bailo was able to transmit to Venice confidential letters sent by the Grand Duke of Tuscany to the Grand Vizier and *Kapudan Paşa*; his successor in 1588 had copies of a letter from the Grand Vizier to the Sultan about a revolt in Tripoli, and of one to the Grand Vizier from the Ottoman general at the Persian front; and in 1596 the bailo was able to see all the confidential papers sent by the Grand Vizier to the Chancellor of Poland before they were despatched.[5]

The Venetians may have been the best at this game, but they were not
the only ones playing it. In 1575 Stefan Gerlach noted that his master,
the Imperial Ambassador, David Ungnad, spent large sums of money on
obtaining information about 'Venetian, Polish, Transylvanian, French,
Spanish and Hungarian affairs from many Muslims'. The Istanbul agent
of the pasha of Pest – the Hungarian town, at that time distinct from
Buda – gave Ungnad copies of all the official papers that were sent out
to his pasha; also in Imperial employ were a janissary and a spahi in
Pest itself, who would secretly forward Ungnad's own letters to an official in the nearby Habsburg town of Komárno (Hung.: Komárom). In
February 1576, when a çavuş (messenger of the Sultan) was sent to Pest
with orders for military preparations against the Habsburgs, Gerlach
gleefully recorded not only that the contents of those orders were
known, but also that 'he is carrying, unwittingly, my master's letter,
since the agent enclosed it in his own, telling his friends in Pest that they
should immediately send the enclosure to Herr Kielman in Komárno.'
Such practices were continued by Ungnad's successors. Seventeen years
later, on the eve of the Ottoman–Habsburg war in 1593, another Imperial ambassador 'induced', in the words of one of his staff, 'by many gifts
and payments, the *aǧa*s, or imperial chamberlains, to send him, by an
old woman, information of the intentions of the Ottoman court'.[6]

There was a real asymmetry between East and West in these matters.
Not only did the Ottomans not maintain any resident ambassadors in
Christendom (sending, instead, *ad hoc* envoys, especially to Venice and
Poland), but also there was nothing in the Western system equivalent to
the high-ranking 'renegades' in Istanbul. The situation with the Jews,
while certainly more of a two-way affair, was not at all equal, as they
seldom held such high positions of trust at Western courts. It is true that
Pope Sixtus V (r. 1585–90) enjoyed the company of two Jewish doctors
and an influential Portuguese Jewish banker, Giovanni Lopez; Soranzo
would confidently write that 'it is known for certain that Giovanni
Lopez passed to Sultan Murad many of the secrets of Pope Sixtus V,
which he spied out while living in Rome.' Even if Soranzo's claim were
correct, this would be an exceptional case; but there are grounds for
doubting it, since it fits so neatly into a wider pattern of paranoid hostility towards Jews, as exemplified also by the popular belief that Joseph
Nasi maintained a huge spy-ring in the West. The most that can reasonably be assumed is that information did flow in both directions through
Jewish trading networks; one bailo complained in 1585 that the Levantine Jews in Venice were sending to Istanbul 'the most detailed news

reports of everything that happens', and that too often their accounts were, in his view, 'false', and damaging to the reputation of the republic.[7]

As for the renegades: while there were no equivalents to them on the Christian side – no converts from Islam installed in sensitive governmental positions – the fact that the Sultan had many loyal servants who were native-born Italians, Austrians and others was still of real value to the Ottomans for espionage purposes. In some cases these people were sent to the West under deep cover, pretending to be ordinary Christian Europeans. The Western intelligence services in Istanbul made every effort to warn their governments about them. In 1572, for example, the Spanish network told its masters in Naples of the advent of four Ottoman renegade spies: a 35-year-old Florentine with reddish skin, a dark-haired elderly Neapolitan, and two Genoese, one of them with a red beard. Two years later the Venetian bailo reported that the Grand Vizier had just sent a renegade to spy in Venice. The man was from Rome, and had converted to Islam just one month earlier; he was, wrote the bailo, 'roughly 40 years old, of reasonable height, with skin more light than dark, and a rounded black beard; but I am not happy with this description, as many people will be found to match it'. In 1579 the Imperial Ambassador likewise warned that a Flemish renegade, called Mehmed Abdullah Frenk, was being sent as a spy to Spain. The Ottomans certainly sent many such agents to the West, though the scale of the operation may sometimes have been overestimated by nervous Christian powers; the claim that there were 30 Ottoman spies in Venice in 1570 was perhaps exaggerated, and there was surely a touch of paranoia in the suggestion, made by one intelligence expert to the authorities in Naples in 1559, that all Greek sailors arriving at that port should have their foreskins examined to make sure that they had not become Muslims. Aside from spies under deep cover, there were other renegade agents whose Ottoman provenance was not concealed, but who could still benefit from their familiarity with the West. In 1574, for instance, two renegades were sent from the Balkan mainland to Corfu and then to Apulia; officially they were engaged in slave-ransoming, but their real mission (as the Spanish learned from one of their own secret informants, an official of the *sancakbeyi* of Delvinë) was to spy on fortifications, as they were both experienced engineers. A more ambitious plan involving a known renegade was Grand Vizier Sokollu's idea of sending a Transylvanian, Markus Benkner, who had taken the name of Ahmed, to the West on the pretence that he had fled the Ottomans and wished to give his services as a translator to King of Spain; according to one report, it was even agreed that he would send back secret messages to Sokollu using a cipher – a common practice among Western powers, but a very rare one in the Ottoman world. In the end, Benkner's mission was terminated after barely six weeks, because efficient counter-intelligence work by the Imperial embassy in Istanbul had blown his cover.[8]

Gathering information was not the only purpose for which an agent might be employed. As we have seen with the envoys sent by the Marquis of Atripalda and Don John to the Balkans, one important task was to make contact with potential or actual rebels. This was a major concern of Western powers, who could aim such missions at various different categories of people: the local community leaders in districts that were prone to rebellion, such as Himarë and the Mani peninsula; the hierarchy of the Orthodox Church, which was generally assumed to be seeking liberation from Ottoman rule; and, above all, renegades in positions of power who, it was believed, could be 'turned' if given the right inducements. Here too the situation was asymmetrical; there were no candidates for 'turning' in Western governments, and the only significant known example of Ottoman support for rebels involved sending agents to the Moriscos in Spain.* Another role for secret agents was the carrying out of actual hostile acts, such as sabotage or assassination. When Giovanni Barelli first attracted the attention of the Spanish authorities in 1569, it was as someone who offered to organize the burning down of the Istanbul Arsenal and the capture or murder of Joseph Nasi, as well as a number of risings in the Peloponnese. (Another idea mooted at the same time, but which Philip II found less appealing, was the assassination of the Sultan's son; a version of this plan, including the Sultan himself as one of the targets, was reactivated by Spain in late 1571, and received some encouragement from Venice.) In the summer of 1574 a Greek from Chios offered his services as an arsonist to the Spanish; his plan to burn the Istanbul Arsenal was abandoned because the fleet had left it, but he did set fire to the Sultan's palace, causing some damage and the deaths of several janissaries. The Ottoman authorities seem to have been less adventurous in such matters; although the great fire in the Venice Arsenal in late 1569 was popularly attributed to agents of the Sultan, no evidence to that effect was ever discovered. In 1577, indeed, the bailo reported that the Grand Vizier

---

* Occasionally there were reports of Ottoman agents going to the Netherlands during the Dutch Revolt, but those were more like diplomatic envoys.

had driven away a disgruntled Venetian who had offered to burn down the Doge's Palace. How or why a large fire did in fact break out there one year later remains entirely unknown.[9]

For all these purposes, the Ottomans may have been somewhat disadvantaged by not having resident embassies to use as centres of operations. But, if so, the same is true of the Spanish with respect to the Ottoman Empire, where they had no official diplomatic representation. In the 1540s and 1550s it was the Spanish embassy in Venice that ran the few agents they had in Istanbul. That embassy retained some involvement in these matters for the rest of the century; but when, from the early 1560s onwards (after the terrible defeat at Djerba), Philip II became more actively interested in anti-Ottoman operations, more was done through the Kingdom of Naples. The essential breakthrough came in 1561, when an enterprising man from the Genoese town of San Remo, Giovanni Maria Renzo, recruited a group of agents in Istanbul, including several renegades. (The person who would later be detained in Naples after Lepanto, Mustafa 'Genovese', né Gregorio Bregante, was one of these; another was a janissary commander, Murad Ağa, who was also of Genoese origin.) Philip II took an immediate interest, and ordered the Viceroy in Naples to set up communications systems via Corfu, Dubrovnik or Otranto. At first the emphasis was on planning a revolt in the Ottoman fleet and the burning of the Arsenal, but gradually, as the group expanded, it turned into an all-purpose intelligence network, providing safe houses for visiting agents and transmitting a stream of 'avvisi' and intelligence. One of the most important recruits was a Venetian merchant, Aurelio di Santa Croce, who had resided full-time in Istanbul since 1552. From 1564 onwards he was sending regular reports with news of Ottoman naval preparations; he seems to have become the resident head of the network, responsible for distributing payments and recruiting new members, so that by the mid-1570s he could be described by one Spanish operative as 'Capo degli Oculti' in Istanbul – chief of the secret agents.[10]

As with any such operation set up rather quickly and maintained at a distance, there was scope for inefficiency or even fraud. Some of the men recruited may have been mere sleeping partners, taking the money for no work; some may have been simultaneously employed by other Western powers (an accusation that would be made against Santa Croce himself at a later stage); but none, it seems, was working for Ottoman counter-intelligence – which does at least attest to the basic competence of Renzo and Santa Croce. There were also the potential inefficiencies and confusions generated by the fact that different chains of command, and even different groups of agents, might be controlled by different people: the Viceroy of Naples, the Viceroy of Sicily, King Philip (who sometimes by-passed his own viceroys), the ambassador in Venice, and, most actively for a time, Don John. This was a somewhat dysfunctional system, and much of the intelligence that came from Istanbul was disregarded. Renzo was described by one of Philip's ministers as 'a chatterbox and a liar'. Cardinal Granvelle complained in 1571 that Renzo's avvisi were concocted from tavern gossip, and again in 1574 that the spies in Istanbul just wrote out old news with a false date on it. 'They send me old and general things, and, so that they can say that they have hit the mark, they put forward all possibilities, including contrary ones, so that one of those things cannot fail to happen.' Perhaps the Cardinal had good reasons for his scepticism; yet we should not forget that when Giovanni Barelli returned to Naples in early 1574 with accurate warnings of the Ottoman preparations to attack La Goletta and Tunis, it was Granvelle who brushed Barelli aside as a person of 'little or no credibility'.[11]

Such, then, was the world into which Bartolomeo Bruti entered in 1575 – though the real nature of the network he had joined may not have become known to him for some time. After the conclusion of the prisoner exchange in July 1575, he met up again with Giovanni Margliani, who had apparently travelled to Dubrovnik from Istanbul with the captives. Margliani then accompanied Gabrio Serbelloni to Naples, taking his young Albanian recruit with him. There, in the words of Bartolomeo's later autobiographical memorandum addressed to the King of Spain, 'I was brought to kiss the hands of the most serene lord Don John, who welcomed me benignly, and with whom I discussed many things relating to Your Majesty's service.' Don John was pleased with the answers Bartolomeo gave to his questions; 'so, shortly afterwards, I was ordered to return to Istanbul, and I was given by Giovanni Margliani a way of returning honourably with a set of instructions signed at the bottom by Don John, in which I was given the details of the service that I was to perform for Your Majesty.' It seems that he did not go back to Istanbul immediately, but spent some time in Venice (and, presumably, Koper). Quite how he arranged with the Venetian authorities the resumption of his training as a 'giovane di lingua' is not explained, though his prominent role in the prisoner exchange must surely have helped; but anyway it was, as we have seen, on that basis that he returned to the bailo's house in January 1576.[12]

Giovanni Correr, the bailo, noted Bartolomeo's arrival in his report of 23 January. Just six days later a grand wedding took place in Galata of Matteo del Faro, who was one of the dragomans at the Imperial embassy. A member of a Perot family ('Pera' being another name for Galata), del Faro was an Italian-speaking Greek Orthodox man who had worked for the Imperial embassy since 1559. His bride – a second wife, after the death of his first – was a daughter of Aurelio di Santa Croce, the chief of the Spanish secret agents; and at some stage between 1571 and 1575 Matteo del Faro had himself joined the payroll of the Spanish network. Stefan Gerlach, who attended the wedding, noted the presence there of a group of Venetian and Ragusan guests, including a number of merchants and the bailo's secretary. Several of the names are recognizable, but one of them is the puzzling 'Mr Bruli'; later on, this person is described as the groom's 'best man', the person who, at a crucial moment in the ceremony, passed the ring to the bride. Gerlach's text was edited long after his death by his grandson, who may not always have read his handwriting correctly. No one called 'Bruli' is known of in Istanbul in this period. But since Bartolomeo Bruti was, as we shall see, clearly acquainted with Aurelio di Santa Croce by the summer of 1576, and since he would also marry a close relative of Matteo del Faro within roughly three years, there are strong reasons for thinking that it was Bartolomeo who acted as best man. It does not necessarily follow that Bartolomeo already knew of Aurelio's secret role. This was a small world, in which coincidental linkages were possible. There is no special reason to think that Aurelio di Santa Croce was directing Bartolomeo's work, and it is not even clear what that work was, though it is likely to have included picking up information that passed through the Venetian bailate. It was only in the summer of 1576 that Bartolomeo Bruti would be – to use what may perhaps be an overly dramatic term – activated, and the cause was a rather contingent one, involving the mission of a more temporary Spanish agent to Istanbul.[13]

For several years, Spanish emissaries or agents of various kinds had been making visits to the Ottoman capital. Because the most important development in Spanish–Ottoman relations in the later 1570s was the negotiation of a truce between the two powers, modern historians (starting with Fernand Braudel) have tended to see most or all of those earlier visits as aiming ultimately at that outcome. Such a view has been reinforced by comments drawn from the despatches of the French envoy in Istanbul, the Bishop of Dax, who was very suspicious of any possible Spanish initiatives; the French dreaded the prospect of a

Spanish–Ottoman rapprochement, as it would make it much easier for Spain to concentrate its forces against France. Yet there is no clear evidence of any serious attempt by Spain to negotiate such a deal with the Ottomans in the first half of the decade. That is not to say that the Spanish emissaries never tried to discover how willing the Ottomans might be to make a truce; to find out your enemy's readiness to negotiate is always worthwhile, as you thereby gain valuable information about his own sense of strength or weakness. But all the evidence suggests that these were general intelligence missions, not peace initiatives.[14]

They began almost immediately after Lepanto, when Don John sent one of his secretaries to Istanbul with a special captive, the tutor of the two teenaged sons of Ali Müezzinzade Pasha. (The Bishop of Dax wrote ominously about this mission, seeing it as a continuation of Spanish negotiations that had begun, in his opinion, even before the war – though evidence of those is also lacking.) In the summer of 1573 Don John made his grand chivalrous gesture of releasing the one remaining son, whom he sent off with fine horses, gold coins, beautiful clothes, and 40 ordinary Muslim captives for good measure; while this did astonish and impress the Ottomans, its main purpose may have been to make possible the prolonged visit to Istanbul by two trusted agents, the Spaniard Antonio Avellán (or 'Avellano') and the Florentine Virgilio Polidori, who accompanied the boy. Avellán, who had been recruited by Renzo in 1568, knew Istanbul well, having spent a long time there as a slave of the former naval commander Piyale Pasha, and spoke fluent Turkish. After his arrival in July 1573 – which provoked an immediate and passionate complaint to the Grand Vizier by the Bishop of Dax – he stayed for a total of fifteen months, cultivating personal contacts of all kinds and sending reports back to Naples and Spain. While he was there, another Spanish agent, Juan Curenzi, made a brief and clandestine visit to the city in early 1574. He took letters to Aurelio di Santa Croce, meeting him secretly at the house of a friar, Benedetto Carantino, from whom he got information about the Ottoman fleet; and he was probably also the agent responsible for an explosion in an Istanbul powder magazine at that time.[15]

In May 1575 yet another emissary, Jaime de Losada, arrived in Istanbul, having been sent by the Viceroy of Sicily. He had previously been a slave of the corsair chief and naval commander Uluç Ali (now Kılıç Ali), who had taken a liking to him and placed him in a position of trust; the main aim of his mission now was to deal with his former master about ransoming people who had been captured at La Goletta and Tunis. In the long report which he later wrote, Losada described how Kılıç Ali took him to see the Grand Vizier, Mehmed Sokollu, who wished to question him about Spanish naval intentions. From Losada's account it becomes very clear that it was Sokollu who, more than once, raised the possibility of an Ottoman–Spanish truce: 'the Sultan's Porte was always open', he said, 'and anyone who came to it would not go away disappointed.' This chimes with a comment made by Avellán to the Venetian bailo when he came back to Istanbul in early 1576: he said that during his previous stay, in 1573–4, he had had several meetings with Sokollu, who had told him that the Porte was always open (the very phrase quoted by Losada) and that 'a small token of good will' – i.e. a large payment – might lead to a truce which would save the King of Spain much more money. And a similar picture of Sokollu's manoeuvring emerges from an account given by Giovanni Barelli in 1575, after he had returned from Corfu to Naples. Barelli wrote that one of the important Ottomans he had ransomed, a certain Memi Çelebi of Athens (*çelebi* being an honorific term for a cultured gentleman), had told the Grand Vizier that he should make a peace agreement with the Spanish for two reasons: ordinary Ottomans were now terrified of serving in the fleet, and peace would bring a very profitable growth in trade. Sokollu had apparently favoured the idea, and had sent a *çavuş* to Barelli in Corfu on the pretext of some Ottoman–Venetian tax business; he had invited Barelli to go to Istanbul to negotiate a peace settlement, and had promised a safe-conduct for that purpose. What all these stories suggest is that Braudel had it the wrong way round: it was the Grand Vizier, not Philip II, who was trying to get negotiations going. Naturally, when a Spanish envoy did eventually appear for that purpose, Sokollu would pretend that Spain was and had been the suitor. But there was a clear reason why he should wish for peace: any prolonged military stand-off against Spain in the Mediterranean would involve maintaining the fleet at something near its renewed, post-Lepanto strength, which was a massive drain on the Ottoman finances. And once La Goletta and Tunis were secured, the reason became clearer still: there was little left for such a fleet to do.[16]

Spanish intentions, meanwhile, remained essentially offensive. In the summer of 1575 the Viceroy of Sicily encouraged a volunteer agent who had offered to burn down the Istanbul Arsenal and assassinate Kılıç Ali using poisoned fruit preserves and sweetmeats. Meanwhile Avellán had gone to Madrid and persuaded King Philip to back a plan of his own, which involved 'turning' an important Ottoman called Murad Ağa – not the Genoese renegade of that name who was already in Spanish service, but the major-domo and trusted right-hand man of Kılıç Ali. This Murad Ağa, who was originally from Lucca, had already indicated his willingness to come over to the Spanish side; Avellán proposed getting the help of his fellow-Luccan Hürrem Bey, the dragoman, in order to bring this about. And the higher goal at which he aimed was the turning – through the persuasion of Murad Ağa – of Kılıç Ali himself, the Ottoman admiral, who was an Italian from Calabria. In late 1575 Avellán went from Apulia to Dubrovnik, and travelled from there (despite the attempts of the suspicious Ragusan authorities to stop him) overland to Istanbul. His ostensible mission was to ransom slaves; not surprisingly he stuck to that story when interviewed by the Grand Vizier, who seemed disappointed that he had not come to negotiate a truce on behalf of Don John. (Later on, he was denounced to Sokollu by Ottoman agents who said that he had been seen at the Spanish court; the Grand Vizier said that he would respect his safe-conduct as a ransomer this time, but threatened to enslave him again if he ever came back to Istanbul.) Avellán's real mission, however, ran into difficulties, as it quickly became clear that Murad Ağa had got cold feet. So he turned to the resident head of the network, Aurelio di Santa Croce, for help and advice.[17]

It was at this point that Bartolomeo Bruti became involved, according to his later autobiographical memorandum. This document gives what may well be an inflated impression of Bartolomeo's own importance; nevertheless, it is the only specific account we have of what happened next. Aurelio decided that 'there was no other solution but to deal with me, Bartolomeo Bruti, and see if they could persuade me to take on such a great and difficult task.' Together, they spoke to Bartolomeo at length; Aurelio showed him the letter he had received from the King, telling him to give Avellán all possible help, and Avellán produced the royal letter to Murad Ağa. Having considered the matter, Bartolomeo proposed a better idea. The invitation that had been designed for Murad Ağa should be redirected to Mehmed Bey, the dignitary whom he had escorted from Rome to Dubrovnik in the previous year. 'I knew that he was much more suitable for performing some services [for Christendom], both because he had become very well informed about Christian matters [during his stay in Italy], and because of the poor reward that he gets from the Sultan for his services to him.' We are entitled to wonder whether this really was Bartolomeo's idea, or whether it was with precisely this alternative in mind that Aurelio had come to him. But one thing at least is clear: only Bartolomeo knew Mehmed Bey well enough to make the approach. This he now did; Mehmed was at first astonished and alarmed, but gradually – 'sometimes threatening me, sometimes agreeing with me' – he came round to the idea of working for the King of Spain. His one strict condition was that Bartolomeo himself would take a letter from him to the King, and negotiate with Philip in person on Mehmed's behalf. And so it was that in early August 1576, having obtained permission to depart from the bailo on the pretext that one of his brothers had died in Koper, Bruti boarded a Ragusan ship, together with Avellán, and sailed from Istanbul.[18]

By now Bartolomeo Bruti was fully in Spanish employ; but it is not entirely clear what had happened when he had his dealings with Aurelio di Santa Croce and Antonio Avellán in July. Avellán claimed to have enrolled him there and then in the service of Spain. Aurelio, writing to the King just after this episode, declared that he had 'now recruited to your service Bartolomeo Bruti, an Albanian cavaliere, who still has the credit accorded to his ancestors in his homeland, and has important relatives in Istanbul'. And Bartolomeo himself would shortly produce another account for King Philip in which these versions of events were somehow combined with the other version that featured Margliani and Don John. On this account (written in the third person), both Avellán and the 'oculti', the secret agents in Istanbul, had begged Bartolomeo to leave Venetian service and come to work for Spain:

> having well considered that it was the right thing to do, and that he could serve Your Majesty whether as a soldier or in secret matters of Ottoman business, thanks to the great experience and many connections that he has in those parts, and his many relatives who are in positions of authority, and also because he had already given a definite promise to His Highness [Don John] through Giovanni Margliani to serve Your Majesty at the next honourable opportunity that should arise, he put himself at Your Majesty's service.

Perhaps this was just a compromise story, devised to make Aurelio gain a little more credit or seem a little less ill-informed. But still it is worth noting, not least because of the emphasis it puts on Bartolomeo's high-level connections in Istanbul.[19]

Bruti and Avellán finally reached Naples in mid-October 1576. Giovanni Margliani, who was in military service there, introduced Bartolomeo to the Duke of Sesa, the commander of the Neapolitan fleet; told that Bruti had urgent business to conduct in Madrid, the

Duke promised to send him on a galley as soon as possible. Meanwhile Bartolomeo had some other matters to deal with on behalf of Aurelio, who had given him a letter to hand to the Viceroy, the Marquis of Mondéjar. Its subject was the need to set up a new secure communications route for messages, and people, travelling between Istanbul and Naples. The previous route had gone overland to the coast of Epirus (modern north-western Greece) and thence to Corfu. As it happens, we know a little about two of the people who helped to run this system. The key figure on the coast of Epirus, at Bastia, a little port just to the north of Igoumenitsa, was an Albanian called Dulis; a figure of some substance, favoured by the *sancakbeyi*s of Vlorë and Delvinë, he had been recruited by Renzo in 1566, and, as he himself explained in a letter to King Philip, had looked after all the servants of Spain who passed through Bastia on their way to and from Istanbul. The other important operative, during the previous two years, was a young Corfiot nobleman, Petros Lantzas, who would transfer agents from Corfu to Otranto on his fast frigate.* But the system had been compromised by its Greek and Albanian couriers, who had developed a side-line in smuggling fugitive slaves from Istanbul; the Grand Vizier had imposed extra guards and controls to stop this, which made the route unusable. Before he left Istanbul Bartolomeo Bruti had written a paper at Aurelio's request, describing how to set up and run a new network; this was enclosed in the letter from Aurelio which he now gave to the Marquis of Mondéjar.[20]

In his paper, Bartolomeo suggested sending the despatches from Istanbul to Budva, Kotor and Dubrovnik, to be taken by frigate from there to southern Italy. Each of those three places should have a resident local agent; they would be chosen and paid directly by Naples, and kept in ignorance of one another's identities. It would be best to use the regular Venetian couriers who went from Istanbul to those places, as they were reliable and did not get involved in the fugitive slave business; they were 'of the Slav nation' and would need to be paid 'trip by trip'. As they approached Istanbul they should go to the house of a priest, eighteen miles outside the city, and give him the letters. The priest (who should be paid a salary) would pass them on to the 'oculti', whose identities would thus remain unknown to the couriers. Above all it was

---

* Lantzas was a dynamic military leader who had been in Venetian service until 1574 when, unhappy with the Venetian–Ottoman peace settlement, he transferred to Spanish service. In 1576 he organized, with the help of a large group of fighters from Himarë and a Spanish engineer, the demolition of the fortress of Sopot, which Venice had given back to the Ottomans after the war.

necessary to have one paymaster for the whole system. In the past, Bar-tolomeo wrote, couriers went with memorandums of their services from person to person, demanding payment, and the 'oculti' did the same, with the result that secrecy was broken. The natural conclusion to the paper duly followed: Bartolomeo Bruti should be given a royal patent to set up and run the entire system. Although an element of self-promotion was clearly present, this paper was a serious piece of work, demonstrat-ing a good grasp of the problems involved. Bartolomeo was, after all, the heir to something of a family tradition in these matters; his father had organized the transmission of news from southern Albania to Ven-ice, and his uncle Gasparo had been a resident intelligence-gatherer in Dubrovnik, receiving information from the Maltese Order's own secret agents in Istanbul.[21]*

At first, Bartolomeo's proposal succeeded almost too well: when the Viceroy read it, 'he liked it very much', and ordered him to start work immediately on setting up the new system. Bartolomeo replied that he had to go to the Spanish court on other business, and, when Mondéjar asked what business that might be, said he had been forbidden to tell anyone. The Viceroy responded angrily: 'Don't you know that I am the King in this kingdom?' Bartolomeo returned to his lodgings in dismay, wondering whether he would ever be permitted to travel to Madrid. Soon after this, another potential obstacle arose, caused by the arrival in Naples of a Spanish agent called Martín de Acuña. This man, who had spent some time as one of the slaves of Kılıç Ali's right-hand man Murad Ağa in Istanbul, had yet another plan for a sabotage attack on the Istanbul Arsenal; the King had given it his blessing, and Acuña had now come to Naples with a royal instruction to Mondéjar to assist him in preparing his mission. Chancing upon Bruti in the street one day, and recognizing him from his time in Istanbul, Acuña told him about his plans and urged him to come with him as a local guide and fixer. Barto-lomeo declined the invitation, but that evening he was summoned by the Viceroy, who demanded that he accompany Acuña. Again Bartolo-meo refused; when he said that the mission was doomed to failure, Mondéjar asked him to write a memorandum setting out his reasons. This document too shows that Bartolomeo possessed mature judgement and a good knowledge of conditions in the Ottoman capital. First of all, he pointed out, by the time Acuña arrived after a slow overland journey, the galleys would be at sea, 'consigned to individual captains', so there

* See above, pp. 37–8 (Antonio Bruti), 97 (Gasparo Bruni).

would be no chance of destroying them *en masse*. Acuña's plan involved ransoming two particular slaves of the Sultan for use in this exploit; he was apparently unaware that 'the Sultan's slaves cannot be freed for money, but only in an exchange, and you have to spend months negotiating their freedom with petitions to the Grand Vizier.' (It seems that slave-ransoming was a line of business in which Bartolomeo had already taken an interest, or been actively involved.) As for Acuña's idea that he, Bartolomeo, would buy sulphur, saltpetre, gunpowder and other ingredients for 'fire-balls' from shops in Istanbul, such a task must be divided among several people. Acuña claimed to know many renegades in Kılıç Ali's household, but the only one he mentioned, 'Süleyman the Venetian', would be of little use: 'I know him, he is very young, and has little experience.' In sum: the mission would fail, causing the deaths of many Christians, and 'shattering the plans of many important men who have undertaken and arranged many things for the service of God, the service of His Majesty, and Your Excellency's own reputation'.[22]

The Viceroy's mind, once made up, was not easily changed. Besides, he had an order from the King to help Acuña on his way. At his insistence, Bartolomeo gave Acuña advice on the route to take, wrote letters recommending him to some of his acquaintants, and provided a man who could act as his guide. But when he refused yet again to go with him, pleading that he had business with the King, Mondéjar flew into a rage: 'Either you tell me what this business is, or I shall have you put in the depths of a prison where you will stay until you die.' Four halbardiers took Bartolomeo off for detention in the office of Mondéjar's secretary, while the secretary himself was sent to seize all the documents that could be found in Bartolomeo's lodgings. Only when Mehmed Bey's confidential letter to Philip was opened and read did the Viceroy's attitude change. The next morning he spoke to Bartolomeo with 'friendly words and offers of help'. Nevertheless, for reasons which remain obscure, there were serious delays before Bartolomeo was able finally to leave Naples. On 16 February 1577 a senior official there, the auditor-general of the fleet, wrote a letter to the King's secretary saying that Bartolomeo had waited for a long time for galleys to take him to Spain, and that he was now setting off overland for Genoa to take a boat from there. 'I know that he is a very good and honest man, and that he is a noble person who can do much service for Christianity in his homeland; and in Istanbul, whence he has come, he has important and reliable sources of information, with which he has served and will serve His Majesty.'[23]

ESPIONAGE AND SABOTAGE IN ISTANBUL

At long last, in the spring of 1577, Bartolomeo Bruti reached Madrid. It is not known whether he had a personal audience with Philip II, but he certainly dealt directly with Antonio Pérez, the King's powerful secretary of state. The proposal he brought from Mehmed Bey was welcomed enthusiastically; for at its heart was a bold plan to deliver the city of Algiers into the hands of the Spanish. Mehmed was confident that if he gave the Grand Vizier a present of 25,000 scudi (nearly 21,000 ducats), he would be appointed *beylerbeyi* of Algiers. Once installed there, he would send a messenger to Philip to arrange the details of a Spanish-assisted anti-Ottoman coup. He would then rule Algiers as a vassal of the King, handing over one of the city's forts to a Spanish garrison, and eliminating the anti-Spanish activities of the corsairs. The only condition on which he insisted was that if the scheme failed and he had to seek refuge in Philip's territory, he should be permitted to continue to practise Islam, as had been allowed in the case of the exiled son of the former ruler of Tunis. The Spanish Council of State considered his proposal carefully, consulting those whom it regarded as experts in Ottoman affairs, including Giovanni Margliani, who had been summoned to Spain; Philip II also took a personal interest. At a special meeting in Aranjuez on 10 May 1577, the Council approved the plan. The risks were obvious, but the potential advantages hugely outweighed them: such a coup, if successful, would transform the entire security situation of the western Mediterranean.[24]

But then there came a bombshell. Martín de Acuña returned from Istanbul, bearing extraordinary news: he had made some kind of preliminary deal with the Grand Vizier for a formal truce between Spain and the Ottoman Empire, and the Vizier had given him a letter to Philip, asking him to send an ambassador to negotiate. To show his good faith, Sokollu had even promised that there would be no naval expedition against the Spanish during that year. How had a secret sabotage mission taken such an unexpected diplomatic turn? The real story – key parts of which Acuña concealed from the Spanish authorities – was as follows. When he arrived in Istanbul in late February, Acuña had been accompanied by some dubious Albanians (including, perhaps, the man supplied by Bartolomeo Bruti), who were involved in the smuggling of fugitive slaves. One of them was identified by Ottoman counter-intelligence, arrested, and tortured. Aurelio had arranged for Acuña to stay secretly in the house of Matteo del Faro, Aurelio's son-in-law; now he was holed up there in fear of his life, as the Ottoman authorities knew from their tortured prisoner that there was a Spanish 'caballero' at large in the city.

At this point Aurelio hit on a desperate but ingenious piece of improvisation. He recalled being told by Jaime de Losada in the summer of 1575 that the Grand Vizier had asked him why Philip did not send anyone to negotiate a truce; now, he decided, the only way to save Acuña was to pretend that he was just such an envoy. Luckily, Aurelio had in his possession one letter from Madrid (addressed in fact to Joseph Nasi, another candidate for 'turning'), bearing the authentic seal of Philip II. Using this, he forged an official letter of introduction to Sokollu for Martín de Acuña and sent him, with the help of Sokollu's chief dragoman, the Luccan renegade and Spanish agent Hürrem Bey, to meet the Grand Vizier. The trick worked; even the well-informed Stefan Gerlach recorded, on 9 March, that 'the Spanish envoy went to the Grand Vizier and handed over his letters of credence from his King.' An amicable discussion took place; the imprisoned Albanian was released; and Acuña was sent back to Naples bearing Sokollu's offer of formal negotiations leading to a two-year- or even six-year-long truce in the Mediterranean.[25]

Martín de Acuña reached Naples in late April and gave the news to the Viceroy, who immediately wrote to Madrid about it, before sending Acuña on to be questioned in person. Spanish policy-makers went into a flurry of debate about the possible advantages and disadvantages of a formal armistice. The huge savings in money and manpower were very attractive, especially since the royal finances had reached the point of bankruptcy in 1575. Also highly desirable were the benefits such a deal would bring if the North African corsairs were obliged by their Ottoman masters to honour it. The main drawback was the possibility that the Sultan would use the truce to mount a campaign against Corfu – which, if successful, would pose a grave threat to the Kingdom of Naples. (As we have seen, the mutual dependence, in security terms, of southern Italy and Corfu was a fundamental feature of both Spanish and Venetian strategic thinking.)* Giovanni Margliani warned of this danger; so too did the secretary of state, Antonio Pérez, who advised that Venice must be included in any such truce. Other disadvantages were also considered: Mondéjar warned that Spain would lose 'reputaçion', and that the Pope might be so offended by such dealing with the enemy of Christendom that he would withdraw the ecclesiastical subsidies, on which the royal finances were still heavily dependent. The King's final decision reflected his careful thinking about those risks. His

---

* Above, pp. 172–4.

envoy would be authorized to negotiate a truce of two or three years, in which Venice and the Pope (and the minor Italian states, and the Empire) would also be included. It would be a 'dissimulated' or secret truce; for reasons which are not entirely clear, the letter to Philip from the Grand Vizier had been brought by Acuña in a doctored translation, in which Sokollu appeared to offer Philip the choice between public and secret diplomacy – a choice that the original Turkish text simply did not contain. As for the envoy who would do the negotiating: Acuña was heavily criticized by Mondéjar for financial irregularities, and he did not help his cause by writing intemperate letters when he found that he was being sidelined. (One historian has called them 'a minor literary monument of expressivity, mental instability and impertinence'.) What Philip eventually decided, in late June 1577, was that Giovanni Margliani and Bartolomeo Bruti should take over the mission. Margliani would be the principal negotiator; Bartolomeo was instructed not only to help him in that task, but also to continue his own quite separate dealings with Mehmed Bey.[26]

A formal truce on the one hand, and an audacious plan to wrest Algiers from the Ottoman Empire on the other: at best this might be described as keeping options open, at worst as a contradiction. It would not be the only problematic thing about this mission, as Bartolomeo Bruti embarked on his new role as a secret envoy, entrusted with the task of helping to guarantee – or, alternatively, disrupting, in a novel and daring way – the peace of the entire Mediterranean.

13

Secret Diplomacy and
the Grand Vizier

The serious tensions that would trouble the mission of Giovanni Margliani and Bartolomeo Bruti began long before they reached Ottoman soil. Most probably the arguments started while they were still at the Spanish court. Evidence for this comes in a long letter written in 1580 by Bartolomeo to Philip II, in which he said that the problems they encountered on their arrival in Istanbul vindicated all the doubts he had expressed at the outset. 'At Your Majesty's court I told the secretary Antonio Pérez that what Don Martín [Acuña] said about a secret truce could not be true; I declared that Don Martín had altered the translation of the letter which Mehmed [Sokollu] Pasha wrote to Your Majesty, but no one listened to me.' And when he was instructed that he must act with the utmost secrecy and not even inform the Viceroy in Naples about the true nature of this mission, he had said to Pérez that 'it is not the practice, nor the desire, of the Ottomans to make any secret negotiation with any ruler, and especially not with Your Majesty.' It may be understandable that Philip, who had no experience of dealing directly with the Ottomans, did not know this; what is harder to comprehend is his belief that such negotiations, once under way, could ever be kept secret. Most difficult of all to understand is his decision to keep his own Viceroy in Naples in the dark. It is true that Mondéjar had behaved in a hostile way towards Bruti, and he had also advised against negotiating a truce with the Sultan; but he was, after all, subject to Philip's commands, and could have been ordered to comply with the new policy. Instead, the King sent him a letter telling him to pay a monthly salary of 30 scudi (25 ducats) to Bartolomeo Bruti 'because, in view of the good account we have received of his person, and of the experience and knowledge which he has of Levantine affairs, we have sent him to go and live in Istanbul. He is to stay there under cover, as he has done up until now, so that he may take care to send such news and warnings of the Sultan's actions as he may think fit.'[1]

A further complication arose while Margliani and Bruti were on their way from Spain to Naples (via Genoa) in early September 1577, when they learned that Aurelio di Santa Croce had arrived in Naples in August, bearing another letter from the Grand Vizier. Margliani, apparently determined to follow the order that he must keep the mission secret, wanted to avoid letting Aurelio know that he and Bartolomeo Bruti were travelling together for the same purpose. On the galley from Genoa, he told Bartolomeo that when they reached Naples he would meet Aurelio first, and that when Aurelio asked after Bartolomeo he would say that he had left the galley at Civitavecchia (the main port for Rome) and was going to complete the journey to Naples overland; Bartolomeo would lie low in Naples for some days, before making his appearance. Margliani was indeed sought out by Aurelio, and he did utter this fiction; but shortly afterwards he found that 'Bruti told Aurelio how he had arrived, and he came to see him and they went out to dinner together.' When he complained to Bartolomeo, the answer he received was that Aurelio was travelling with Bartolomeo's brother Benedetto, 'whom he had not seen for many years', that his feelings of fraternal love made it impossible to wait, and that he had tried to impart the news of his arrival only to his brother. (This, incidentally, is the first mention of Benedetto Bruti, an elder brother whose career up to this point is entirely unknown; it seems that he had gone to Istanbul after Bartolomeo's departure from that city in August 1576.) Margliani thought – correctly, we may presume – that this was mere excuse-making. But, having lost faith in Bartolomeo's reliability, he then began to suspect that he had 'revealed everything' to Aurelio – though Bartolomeo insisted that he had told Aurelio only that he was going to Istanbul to pursue the project of turning Mehmed Bey.[2]

Reading the long, angry letter which Margliani wrote to Antonio Pérez about all these matters from Naples on 25 October 1577, in which he exclaimed against Bartolomeo's apparent betrayal of the mission and described him as an 'evil man', it is hard to tell whether Margliani was apprised, at this stage, of the real nature of Aurelio di Santa Croce's role in Istanbul. He certainly knew that he was more than just a Venetian merchant who happened to be bringing a message from the Grand Vizier; he was apparently aware that Aurelio had been involved in the targeting of Mehmed Bey, and he may have known that he had helped

Martín de Acuña. Yet we may doubt whether Margliani understood – as Bartolomeo surely did, by the time he left Istanbul – that Aurelio di Santa Croce was the resident head of the entire Spanish network. Giovanni Margliani himself had not been an intelligence operative, and had spent only a short time in the Ottoman capital; if he had in some sense recruited Bartolomeo, it is clear that he did so without having any dealings with Aurelio about the matter. As his encounters with Aurelio in Naples continued during late September and October, he seems not to have realized that the man had a special importance, continuing to treat every contact between him and Bartolomeo as suspicious. When Bartolomeo said that he would not undertake the journey unless he received a safe-conduct, for both of them, from Aurelio, Margliani was merely irritated by that request, because it forced him to tell Aurelio that he was travelling on the same mission with Bartolomeo; but when Bartolomeo said that he wanted not only the safe-conduct itself but also the 'secret marks' or 'secret tokens', Margliani just told him that Aurelio could not possess any such things.[3]

Eventually, feeling compromised by Bartolomeo, Margliani decided to explain the true nature of the mission to Aurelio, and to seek his advice. It was at this point that Aurelio revealed what it was that Acuña had actually negotiated with the Grand Vizier; Aurelio had a copy of the letter to Philip which Sokollu had written after that meeting, with an accurate translation of it – unlike the doctored one provided by Acuña himself. On learning from this that Sokollu had never offered the possibility of a secret truce negotiation, Bartolomeo said to Margliani: 'now you see that what I predicted at court has turned out to be true.' He urged Margliani to send this information to Madrid and wait for further instructions before leaving Naples, as they would otherwise be in great danger when they appeared in Istanbul; but he was met with a blank refusal. Margliani's own later account of this argument makes no mention of the real reason for their disagreement, presenting Bartolomeo Bruti simply as a coward who was reluctant to go on a risky mission. According to him, Bartolomeo just said that 'he was not willing to go to his death for the sake of anyone'; Margliani wrote that he was so enraged that he thought of asking the Viceroy to imprison Bruti and supply a substitute guide for the journey – until he recalled that he was meant to keep the mission a secret from the Viceroy himself.[4]

Whilst Aurelio did give the two would-be negotiators some important and troubling information of this kind, it is doubtful whether he explained to what extent the whole affair was founded upon the forging of documents – something he had actually done more of, as the situation in Istanbul had worsened during the previous months. After Acuña's departure from Istanbul, the Grand Vizier Mehmed Sokollu had become increasingly mistrustful. Sokollu expected a rapid formal reply from Spain, but heard nothing; Acuña's first letter from Madrid, vaguely assuring him that Philip was in favour of pursuing the negotiation, was sent in July, and had not been received by the time Aurelio left Istanbul. Another reason for suspicion was that King Sebastian of Portugal was known to be preparing a major campaign against the new ruler of Fez and Morocco, who was a protégé of the Sultan. The Ottoman authorities feared that Spain would be involved in the campaign, or that it might launch a coordinated attack on Algiers; if either or both of those things happened, the apparent Spanish truce initiative would turn out to have been a mere feint. (This fear was strengthened in late July when an Ottoman spy returned from Naples and reported that Acuña was a fraud; according to this source, Acuña had talked about his adventure when he got back to Naples, saying that his real mission was to discover whether the Ottomans would send out a large fleet that year, and that his negotiation with Sokollu was aimed at reducing its strength 'because his master the King wanted to attack the Moors of Fez and Morocco'.) As early as mid-April, the dragoman Hürrem Bey told Aurelio that the Grand Vizier, determined to get to the bottom of the matter, was planning to open an investigation into the Albanian agents who had accompanied Acuña. There was a danger that the whole Spanish network would be uncovered. So, in desperation, Aurelio forged two more letters from Philip, to Hürrem Bey and to the Grand Vizier, in which the King said that he was keen to pursue the negotiations and asked that a Christian be sent to Spain to advise on how to conduct business with the Ottoman authorities; this Christian – helpfully, the letter put forward the name of Aurelio di Santa Croce as a very suitable person – should also bring a safe-conduct for the envoy who would be sent to negotiate the truce. Sokollu fell for this forgery too, and duly sent Aurelio as the go-between.[5]

On his arrival in Naples in August 1577 Aurelio went to see Mondéjar, who forwarded to Spain copies of all the documents he brought. (Evidently Aurelio kept the original of the Ottoman safe-conduct, which he would fill in with the names of Margliani and Bruti.) A letter of 27 August to his brother in Istanbul, which was intercepted by the Imperial embassy there, shows that he was in high spirits, being well treated by the Viceroy, and confident that he would be nominated ambassador to negotiate the truce: 'I hope to return victoriously to Istanbul with the task of finishing the negotiation, which I think will be entrusted to me, since there are no other people in Spain with the experience to conduct such business.' While he stayed in Naples he got on with his usual trade of ransoming Muslims, writing in September that it would bring 'greater honour and fame to the ambassadorial mission' to bring them back to Istanbul with him. But his hopes were to be doubly dashed – first because, as he now learned, Margliani and Bruti had been chosen to undertake the mission, and secondly because the contents of Sokollu's latest letter, which he had brought, made Philip aware that Acuña's negotiation had been based on a forgery, so that Aurelio himself now fell under a large shadow of suspicion. (Summoned to Spain towards the end of 1577, Aurelio would spend some time in prison there, thanks also to information supplied by Mondéjar that he had grossly over-charged for his expenses.) Yet at the same time Philip was also able to see from the Grand Vizier's letter that Sokollu was keen to proceed towards a truce, and that it was necessary to choose between support-ing King Sebastian's Moroccan project and going ahead with a truce negotiation. He chose the latter.[6]

Giovanni Margliani and Bartolomeo Bruti left Naples at the end of October 1577. With them went Giovanni Stefano de Ferrari, a young man from a well-known Milanese family, who had previously served as Margliani's 'alfiere' or lieutenant at Tunis, and had been captured and freed together with him. They sailed to Brindisi, and embarked on a frigate (a small, fast, oared vessel) on 4 November. Their first attempt to cross the Adriatic was defeated by strong contrary winds, and they returned to Brindisi. Setting off again, they were caught by a severe storm; when they finally saw land, on 8 November, the sailors thought at first that they were off Ulcinj, or even further north, but then they recognized the little island of Sazan (Ital.: Saseno) and realized that they were just outside Vlorë. This caused serious disquiet among the crew, who recalled that in the previous year some official frigates from the Kingdom of Naples had been attacked and robbed when they had escorted a trading ship to that port. The reputation of Vlorë as a nest of violent corsairs was well developed by this time – and, it seems, well deserved. Less than two years later, a Frenchman and a German trav-elled on a Venetian ship which stopped a few miles off Vlorë to let some merchants do business there. When the merchants set off from the ship in a frigate they were pursued by corsairs; they beached the frigate and fled inland, but were chased and captured, regaining their liberty only on paying an instant 'ransom' of 50 or 60 ducats. The travellers then went to Vlorë to find out what had happened to those men. As the Frenchman noted, this was a dangerous thing to do; he and his companion were not dressed in the Venetian style and might have been mistaken for Spanish subjects, who 'were seized and enslaved, or indeed executed, if they were suspected of being spies'. While they were there they observed a captured merchant vessel being escorted into the port by three foists, and the French traveller recorded that 'you see booty brought there every day.'[7]

After discussing the idea of sailing up the corsair-infested coast to Lezhë, Margliani and Bruti decided after all to go straight to Vlorë. Two miles from the town, they picked up a local man from the coast and used him as a pilot. On their arrival, as Margliani wrote in a letter from Vlorë on 11 November, they were quickly surrounded by a mass of people; 'signor Bruti and my lieutenant immediately disembarked, and went together to the *kadi* [judge] with the safe-conduct which we got from signor Aurelio.' The *kadi* sent them to the *nazır* (superintendent) of the port, whom Margliani described as the deputy or representative of the *sancakbeyi* (district governor); the *nazır* invited them to his house, and sent an armed guard to watch over their frigate. At this point Margliani must have felt the advantage of travelling with someone who not only spoke Albanian but knew how to deal with this sort of local Ottoman official. According to Bartolomeo's own account, the advantage was even greater than that: in Vlorë, he wrote, 'we were in danger, were it not for the fact that I found the Viceroy of that province, who was a relative of mine; he received us very politely, and rescued us from the fury of the *levend*s, who had risen up against us, Vlorë being a nest of corsairs.' As it happens, we know the *nazır*'s name, Mustafa Çelebi; unfortunately there is no independent information about his family background. This claim of relatedness may have been an exaggeration, as was the description of the *nazır* as a 'Viceroy', but Margliani himself recorded in his letter from Vlorë that Bartolomeo Bruti 'has friends to visit everywhere'. From this it would seem either that Bartolomeo had spent some time in Vlorë in his early teens, probably with Venetian traders, or that he was able quickly to reactivate some of his father's personal contacts.[8]

As Margliani saw it, however, the fact that Bartolomeo had many local friends was a liability, not an asset: his worry was that the secret of their mission would be leaked. He was taken aback to find that some people in Vlorë had already been expecting a Spanish ambassador to arrive; this was the first sign that the Ottoman authorities adopted a very different line on the question of the secrecy of the negotiations. On Aurelio's advice, Margliani asked the *nazır* to say that he was an emissary of the Grand Duke of Tuscany. Arriving several days later at the town of Berat, he met the *sancakbeyi* of Vlorë there and had to reveal the true nature of his mission to him, while also asking him to go along with the Tuscan story. By 25 November Margliani and Bruti had reached the Macedonian town of Bitola (Alb.: Manastir), and from there the brother of the *sancakbeyi* of Vlorë set off to Istanbul bearing a confidential letter from Margliani to Hürrem Bey. In it he explained that he had come to 'finish the business that was started a few months ago with signor Don Martín de Acuña'; he begged Hürrem to treat the news as strictly confidential, and he asked him to find a place where he could live in secret, either in Hürrem's own house or near to it. (He also wrote that Bruti had arrived by chance in Naples when he was there, and had joined the mission only at that stage.) After a slow journey through the snows of Macedonia and Bulgaria, the travellers finally reached Küçük Çekmece (Ital.: Ponte Piccolo), the last way-station before Istanbul, on 14 December. Hürrem Bey sent a messenger to take them into the city in the dead of night; when they reached the house which had been arranged for them, the landlady refused to let them stay, so they were forced to go to the messenger's own house and wait there. It was not a good beginning, and things were about to get much worse.[9]

At two hours before dawn, Hürrem Bey came to see them. When he learned of the terms on which Margliani had been sent to negotiate, he exclaimed: 'If I were a Christian I would make the sign of the cross! Where did Don Martín [Acuña] dream up such falsehoods? The Grand Vizier is expecting an ambassador, as that is what he wrote in the letter sent with Don Martín. The Grand Vizier will strongly resent this turn of events, and I hope to God that he does no irreparable harm to your persons.' The next day Hürrem Bey returned, saying that he had spoken to Sokollu; the Grand Vizier was, as he had expected, very angry, insisting that if Margliani was not a proper ambassador he should go back to Spain immediately. When Margliani said that Sokollu had given the King of Spain a choice between open negotiations and 'dissimulated' ones, Hürrem said that he absolutely denied having done that. Nevertheless, Sokollu did offer Margliani and Bruti an audience on 16 December. On their way to his house – their first venture into the streets of Istanbul in daylight – they happened to encounter Melchior (or 'Marchiò') Spinelli, a young Venetian dragoman who had trained as a giovane di lingua in 1574–5 and knew Bartolomeo Bruti well; so the secret of their mission had already begun to be compromised, so far as the other European representatives in Istanbul were concerned. At the entrance to Sokollu's house they met Hürrem with Solomon Nathan Ashkenazi, whom Margliani had previously got to know at the bailo's house when he was staying there after his release from captivity. Sokollu was too busy to see them that day, so Margliani returned home, while Bartolomeo (a more recognizable figure in the city) waited until night-fall so that he could do so unobserved.[10]

Finally, on 17 December, the promised audience took place. Mehmed Sokollu was an imposing figure, now in his early seventies; a Serb from south-eastern Bosnia, he had been taken by the *devşirme* (the 'collection' or so-called 'blood tribute') at the age of eighteen, when he was serving as an altar-boy at the Orthodox monastery of Mileševa. After a distinguished career as both an administrator and a military commander, he had been promoted to the position of vizier (senior minister and member of the Sultan's small *divan* or governing council) in 1555, and had become Grand Vizier in 1565. The relatively inexperienced Sultan Selim II, who succeeded his father, Süleyman the Magnificent, in the following year, tended to leave more decision-making to his Grand Vizier, so that Sokollu's power to determine strategic policy increased significantly. When the bailo Marcantonio Barbaro returned to Venice in 1573, he included in his report an admiring portrait of Mehmed Sokollu. 'He alone takes care for and orders all things, especially the most important things, and in fact all civil matters, criminal matters and state affairs pass through his hands; in dealing with them, he has no other adviser than his own mind. He is pious, sober-minded, inclined to peace, and neither vindictive nor grasping. He is in good health, with a good complexion, a solemn presence, tall, with a good figure, and an excellent memory.' The next bailo, Antonio Tiepolo, commented three years later that 'he seems extremely skilful, since he listens quietly and then replies without any change in his manner'; negotiating with him, Tiepolo observed, 'you might think you were dealing with a Christian ruler rather than with an Ottoman one.' Not every Western diplomat agreed with this characterization, however. The Imperial Ambassador, Joachim von Sinzendorf, complained in 1579 that 'when you negotiate with him about something today, he categorically promises, accepts, and comes to an agreement; but the next day, or even the same day, he denies, contradicts or changes it.' The idea that he was not 'grasping' was not universally held; Gerlach noted that when a vizier died he would appoint a successor on payment of a bribe of 50–60,000 ducats, and even Tiepolo, who admired him, commented on 'the extremely strong desire he has to accumulate treasure'. Sokollu also became famous for his nepotism: one Ottoman chronicler totted up seven viziers and ten *beylerbeyi*s who were members of his family. Perhaps the main reason for the positive portrayal of him in the Venetian reports was that he was regarded as sympathetic to Venice; the Ragusans similarly thought well of Sokollu, as they saw him (with better reason, probably) as their friend and protector. But the idea – expressed by one Venetian envoy – that he was generally pro-Christian was surely based on nothing more than his own skills in diplomacy and opinion-management; all the evidence indicates that he was a devoted servant of the long-term interests of the Ottoman Empire.[11]

When Giovanni Margliani met Mehmed Sokollu on 17 December 1577 his experience of the man was far from that of the admiring Venetian baili. The Grand Vizier made clear his extreme displeasure, saying that he was 'amazed and offended' by the nature of this surreptitious mission, and demanded to know why they had not brought the usual lavish presents. (It also did not help that Margliani was disfigured by the arquebus shot he had received at Tunis, and wore a large black patch under one eye to hide the scarring; Sokollu would later say that the Sultan wanted an ambassador who was not hideously blemished.) Margliani tried hard to defend his position, insisting on King Philip's bona fide wish for an armistice, and pointing out that not only had the Spanish fleet remained in its ports during that year, but also the King had refused to send soldiers from Flanders to join Sebastian's proposed Moroccan campaign. Sokollu's scornful reply was that the Ottoman Empire enjoyed such military strength that it needed no concessions from Spain: he boasted that it had restored its entire fleet in one year, and forced Venice to make a humiliating peace with the sacrifice of Sopot, Ulcinj, Bar and much of the territory of Zadar. And yet there was, beneath all this bluster, a genuine desire on Sokollu's part to reach an agreement. A further meeting was held on 23 December, and another on the 28th. While the Grand Vizier still affected to believe that Spain was a desperate suitor in these matters – at one point he said that Venice had paid 300,000 ducats for its peace agreement, and that if Philip did not want to give such a sum of money, he should hand over the Algerian port of Oran instead – he was in fact patiently working out what the limits of Spain's negotiating position might be. On 3 January 1578, at his request, Margliani wrote a document setting out the Spanish terms.

It specified that the other powers to be included in the armistice were the Papacy, the Empire, Portugal, Venice, Malta, Genoa, all Spanish territories in Italy, and a number of smaller Italian states; and it also made clear Philip's desire to maintain, in the eyes of the world, a sort of cold war between Spain and the Ottoman Empire. 'His Majesty also requires that no communication or traffic of any kind should follow such a truce, except with a permit or safe-conduct from both sides.'[12]

Gradually, and surprisingly, a provisional deal was hammered out. Margliani was helped both by Hürrem Bey and by Sokollu's confidant Solomon Ashkenazi, whom he invited to talk to him on the pretext that he needed his medical advice. At one point in January the Grand Vizier threw a large spanner into the works by proposing that the Prince of Orange – leader of the revolt against Philip in the Netherlands – should also be included in the truce; but this seems to have been little more than a piece of psychological warfare. The final document on the Spanish side was drawn up by Margliani with the help of Hürrem Bey and Solomon Ashkenazi on 4 February; three days later those two intermediaries told him that the Grand Vizier had accepted a modified version of its terms. The countries to be included in the truce would be the Papacy, Malta, Genoa and the smaller Italian states on the Spanish side, and Fez, France, Poland, Venice and the Empire (those last two being, in the Sultan's eyes, Ottoman tributaries) on the Ottoman side. The Grand Vizier promised that the Ottoman fleet would not be sent on an offensive campaign during 1578. In return, he required both a promise not to deploy the Spanish fleet against any Ottoman possession in that year, and an undertaking that a proper ambassador from Madrid would come to Istanbul, with due public ceremony and presents, to finalize the armistice within three months. Margliani was not in fact empowered to make either of those pledges, and he was doubtful about whether any embassy could be sent within that time-limit; nevertheless he gave his word, and offered himself as a hostage until the new ambassador arrived. On 8 February Sokollu wrote a formal letter to King Philip, setting out his terms and complaining that 'undercover negotiations are contrary to the practice of our great and magnificent sultans.' Four days later, Margliani's loyal assistant, Giovanni Stefano de Ferrari, was sent to Madrid with this and his master's own despatches. It seemed that Giovanni Margliani had triumphed – thus far, at least – over all the odds.[13]

The physical conditions in which Margliani had been working were peculiarly uncongenial. An obscure lodging had been found for him and his two companions; as Bartolomeo Bruti wrote in a letter to Antonio Pérez on 11 February, 'we have spent all the time in one small room, where we had to prepare food and sleep in the same place – a pitiful situation, since we could not light a fire because of the smoke, and without a fire we were dying of cold.' (When Margliani summoned Solomon as a doctor, he told him that he was ill from the cold, 'not having the possibility of making a fire, nor of taking exercise'.) It is hard to understand why such an effort to maintain secrecy was still being made, when Sokollu's distaste for it was already fully apparent. If Margliani thought that he was keeping his activities from the prying eyes of the other Western diplomats in Istanbul, he was being woefully naïve. On 26 December 1577 the Imperial Ambassador wrote a report including a detailed account, given to him by Sokollu himself, of Margliani's mission and its aims – and since one of those aims was to include the Empire in the truce, it is not surprising that the Grand Vizier had discussed it with him. Two days later the new bailo, Nicolò Barbarigo, wrote to the Venetian government about the recent arrival of Margliani and Bruti, saying that it was rumoured that they had come as ambassadors for Spain. While the bailo did not yet know the details of their quasi-embassy, the authorities in Venice did: they had recently received an anonymous intelligence report from Spain which described Margliani's mission very accurately, saying that he carried papers describing him as an ambassador but was under orders never to use that title in practice.* And on the same day that the bailo sent his despatch, the French Ambassador, Gilles de Noailles, the abbé de Lisle (brother of the Bishop of Dax), wrote to Paris with the news of Margliani and Bruti's arrival; in a later report, of 22 January, he commented also on the Grand Vizier's desire to include France in the truce. By this stage, Margliani seems to have been almost the only person to think that his negotiations were still a secret affair.[14]

While he was cooped up with Bartolomeo Bruti in a small, freezing room, Giovanni Margliani's hostility to his companion intensified and festered. As we have seen, the fundamental breach between them had occurred in Naples, when he decided that Bartolomeo was cowardly and treacherous. Writing to the secretary of state Antonio Pérez on 11

---

* Some of the details in this report make it seem likely that it was written by a person who had been in Naples with Aurelio di Santa Croce – or even by Aurelio himself, who had been accused in 1573 of working simultaneously for Venice, and was certainly playing such a double game by 1585.

SECRET DIPLOMACY AND THE GRAND VIZIER   255

February, he exclaimed that 'Bruti is the greatest traitor, the greatest coward, the most insolent and most spineless man alive. Is this not one of the worst calamities in the world, that a well-intentioned knight should have to live for years on end with a man of such wicked and evil quality, and, in order not to breach the terms of his service, that he should have to yield to him all the time, and be patient?' He continued: 'When I had to send this despatch, he was so insolent as to tell me to my face that it was his job to take it, and that he had as great a role in this business as I did, and that he would speak to the Grand Vizier in such a way as to ensure that he would take it' – which, since we know that the despatch was taken by Giovanni Stefano and not by Bartolomeo, shows that Margliani did not in fact yield to the latter all the time. As he later wrote to Philip, Margliani was convinced that in his own luggage he had unwittingly brought some kind of secret message from Aurelio to Hürrem Bey; having been suspicious of Bartolomeo's closeness to Aurelio ever since the first days in Naples, he persuaded himself that all three of those people were jointly conspiring against him. A version of this story appears also in a report by the two Imperial ambassadors, Ungnad and Sinzendorf, of 17 January, who had been told that Aurelio had hidden in Margliani's luggage a letter to Hürrem written in lemon juice. Motivated allegedly by jealousy, as he thought he should have been made ambassador himself, Aurelio was said to have informed Hürrem that Margliani's mission was 'merely fraudulent' and that he was there 'only to gain time with the Ottomans, and to prevent the deployment of this year's fleet'. Even if Aurelio had sent such a message, it seems highly unlikely that Hürrem acted on it, since all the evidence shows that he worked hard to salvage the negotiation. But the belief in a conspiracy obviously became well entrenched. The Imperial ambassadors also noted: 'Apparently someone called Bartolomeo Bruti, who came with Margliani, is likewise manoeuvring to get himself sent to the King of Spain, with Margliani staying here; it is thought that Bruti is also working surreptitiously with Aurelio and Hürrem Bey. So Margliani keeps his negotiations very secret from Bruti, and because Bruti is a Venetian citizen, it seems that he absolutely refuses to let him go to the King.'[15]

Some of Margliani's suspicion towards Aurelio may have been justified. It is very likely that the long-established intelligence chief resented the fact that he had not been put in charge of these negotiations. Another cause of resentment comes to light in one of Margliani's later reports, where he wrote that Aurelio warned Hürrem Bey in a letter that Margliani had been given the task of reforming the intelligence system in Istanbul and investigating its finances. It is certainly possible that Aurelio was working for Venice too; such parallel service was not unusual in the world of early modern espionage. But Venetian allegiance would not in itself have given Aurelio a reason to sabotage this project, so long as he knew that Venice would also be covered by the truce. (Two years later, when the French Ambassador in Istanbul asked the Venetians to help obstruct the truce negotiation, they answered that they had not worried about it previously since they assumed it would fail, and that now they thought it would go ahead, they were simply asking Spain to make sure that they were included in it.) The Venetian archives do not supply any evidence that Bartolomeo Bruti was working for Venice in this period; so there is no apparent reason to doubt his statement, in his letter to Pérez of 11 February, that 'I am being persecuted by the Venetians, who cannot stop persecuting me out of their displeasure at the fact that I abandoned their service.'[16]

From Bartolomeo's point of view, there were many reasons for dissatisfaction with Margliani's mission. He had warned of the severe problems they would encounter, and had been disregarded. He believed that he had an equal role in the enterprise, but was treated as something more like a servant. (Later he would complain to the King that he could not write confidentially to him because 'I do not have the cipher, and Margliani has refused to let me have the one which, on Your Majesty's orders, was given to both of us together.') His own mission to turn Mehmed Bey had had to be abandoned, since he found in Naples that the Viceroy had told Acuña about it, and Acuña had 'revealed it to many people'. His request to act as courier for the despatches and documents relating to the provisional agreement was rebuffed – not so much, we may suppose, because he was a Venetian as because Margliani did not wish the King to briefed by someone whom he regarded as his personal enemy. In a later letter to Philip, Bartolomeo mentioned another cause of disagreement: when he learned that two galleys of the Sicilian fleet had been seized by Barbary corsairs, he wanted to present a formal protest to the Ottoman authorities, but Margliani refused to do so. 'After that', Bartolomeo wrote, 'his suspicions towards me grew larger every day, perhaps as he suspected that I was writing secretly to Your Majesty about what happens and was happening here; seeing how suspicious he was, I thought it best to leave his company.'[17]

There was one other reason for the growing estrangement between Bartolomeo Bruti and his companion: unlike Margliani, he seems not to have believed that the mission had any chance of success. Some of the

grounds for such disbelief can be guessed at. It was obvious that Philip
would be very reluctant to send out a high-level embassy, with the eyes
of the world upon it, to plead for peace at Istanbul. It was hard to
imagine that the Ottomans, having invested so much effort after 1571
in developing a huge war-fleet, would agree to lay it up for many
years – especially when they had such a dynamic naval commander,
Kılıç Pasha (who did in fact lobby hard against the truce). On the other
hand, it was easy to suppose that the well-known Portuguese plan to
conduct a major war in North Africa – against a Moroccan ruler who
was a protégé of the Sultan – would draw in the Spanish. If that happened, any Spanish–Ottoman armistice would quickly become a failure
or an impossibility. But what Bruti may not have known was that since
at least the beginning of 1577 Mehmed Sokollu had been planning
a war against Persia; so when the Shah, Ismail II, died in November
of that year, the Grand Vizier saw a not-to-be-missed opportunity to
intervene there before the next ruler had time to consolidate his
power. Historians have long understood that the 'great powers' of early
modern Europe were locked in a system which set the two Habsburg
powers, the Holy Roman Empire and Spain, against the two anti-
Habsburg ones, France and the Ottoman Empire. Yet they often forget
the involvement of a fifth great power in what was, in reality, a Eurasian
dynamic: power-relations in Europe could at times be decisively influenced by Ottoman concerns about Persia. What Sokollu now envisaged
was a large-scale, multi-year campaign, which would seize territory
from the Persians and build fortified positions in it, creating an entire
new geopolitical settlement on the Ottoman Empire's eastern flank.
This would involve sending armies to occupy broad stretches of land
continuously, not just sallying forth each spring for a limited campaigning season; in such conditions, security against any large-scale military
threat on the European side of the empire would become much more
important. It was this requirement, arising from Sokollu's ambitious
vision of the future of the empire in Asia, that made the Grand Vizier
stick with the policy of the Spanish truce, even when the King of Spain
gave him more than enough reasons to renounce it.[18]

The three-month time limit, set in early February 1578, came and
went. More months went by, without any news from Madrid. In mid-July
the Portuguese army, led by a stubborn young king whose head was filled
with ideas of crusading piety and chivalric glory, landed on the Atlantic
coast of Morocco. It consisted of between 8,000 and 10,000 inexperienced Portuguese soldiers (including much of the nation's nobility, dressed

in all their finery), a few thousand northern European mercenaries, a force of 6–700 English and Irish Catholics and Italian bandits who, recruited by Thomas Stucley in Italy to launch an invasion of Ireland, were fatefully diverted by Sebastian when they reached Lisbon, and, finally, between 1,600 and 2,000 Spaniards – whose participation Sokollu either did not know about or chose to overlook. On 4 August, at the Battle of Alcazar (Arab.: El-Ksar el-Kebir), King Sebastian and his local ally, a claimant to the throne of Fez, engaged with the forces of Abd el-Malek, the ruler of the country, and were crushingly defeated; Sebastian and the other two leaders died in the battle, and thousands of Portuguese survivors were taken off for slavery or ransom. News of these developments took some time to reach Istanbul. So, throughout the summer, Margliani remained in his lodging, isolated and apprehensive. As he later wrote to Philip: 'I stayed about fifteen months in two rooms, having no other pastime than going to a window. When the King of Portugal went over to Africa, because I had appeared at that window, my house was stoned. Every time Your Majesty sent out the fleet, I found myself in danger, because the French Ambassador persuaded them that you were planning a campaign against Algiers.' On 4 September 1578 he wrote to Antonio Pérez that he had still heard nothing from Spain, seven months after sending Giovanni Stefano, and that meanwhile he had learned that Bartolomeo Bruti was taunting him with the words: 'what excuse will Giovanni [Margliani] give to Mehmed [Sokollu] for this voyage to Barbary by the King of Portugal?'[19]

In the same letter, Margliani also wrote that Bartolomeo Bruti had told Hürrem Bey that he, Margliani, was planning to flee the city. Whether Bruti was acting here on sincere beliefs, or engaged in sheer mischief-making, is hard to tell; what is clear is that relations between the two men had broken down entirely. In late October 1578 Bartolomeo and the Imperial dragoman Matteo del Faro went to see Sokollu at night to warn him about Margliani's conduct. In the words of Margliani's later account (which was at second hand, and no doubt deeply biased), Bartolomeo declared 'that he had been sent jointly with me by His Majesty to negotiate this truce, and that I had excluded him from the business so that I could destroy the negotiation, because, as I had been employed in the navy, I did not want the truce to come about, since, if it did, His Majesty would not maintain a fleet, and if he did not maintain it I would be out of a job'. When Sokollu seemed sceptical, Bartolomeo assured him that his own word could be trusted, as he was planning to settle in Istanbul, where he was going to marry a niece of

Matteo del Faro. Asked why he had come at night, he said he had done so to avoid Solomon Ashkenazi, who, on the promise of a large gift from Margliani, was also trying to sabotage the negotiation. At this point the Grand Vizier became angry and dismissed him. On the following day Sokollu asked Solomon if he knew Bartolomeo Bruti, and received, in Margliani's words, 'extensive information about him, which was not at all good'. Hürrem and Solomon had joined Margliani in a firm alliance against Margliani's former colleague.[20]

It was only in mid-October 1578 that King Philip at last decided to send an ambassador, as Sokollu had requested, and chose the man for the job: Juan de Rocafull, a nobleman with a distinguished military career who had fought at Lepanto. His instructions were to go to Istanbul, give substantial presents to the Sultan and the Grand Vizier, and obtain a truce for up to 20 years. On 22 October Philip sent a letter explaining this to Bartolomeo Bruti – which, since the tone of the letter was perfectly normal, suggests that some of Margliani's heated criticisms of him may have been discounted at the Spanish court. But travel between Madrid and Istanbul was slow, and it was not until mid-January 1579 that these messages were finally brought to Margliani by the faithful Giovanni Stefano de Ferrari. (Bartolomeo would later complain, however, that Margliani did not pass on the King's letter to him.) The news was that Rocafull would travel from Naples via Dubrovnik, in order to reach Istanbul within the next two months. Margliani therefore asked the Grand Vizier to send a çavuş to Dubrovnik to wait for him. This was duly done; but in late March word came back from that city that Rocafull was nowhere to be found, and the same was reported two months later. In June 1579 Margliani received a letter from Naples saying that Rocafull was 'a little indisposed'. During July and early August Margliani's position in Istanbul deteriorated, as rumours began to spread of Spanish naval preparations for an attack on Algiers; he nervously asked Solomon whether he could expect to enjoy diplomatic immunity. In late August the rumours were dispelled, and another letter arrived promising that Rocafull would soon come to Istanbul. Yet that promise too was broken.[21]

Finally, on 4 October 1579, a Spanish agent appeared: an army officer called Antonio Echevarría, who had previously been a slave in Istanbul and had acquired fluent Turkish. For some time he had been waiting to travel to the Ottoman capital as an assistant to Rocafull. But his task now was to confer the ambassadorial credentials on Margliani, and to give him the King's instructions, which were that he should conclude the negotiation himself; if he could not persuade the Ottomans to abandon the idea of open diplomacy, he should ask them to have the truce document, once agreed, brought to Dubrovnik for a formal signing ceremony between a Spanish envoy and an Ottoman one. To Margliani's intense relief, Sokollu accepted this arrangement. The reasons for Philip's long prevarication – and for the patently fictitious illness of Rocafull – were various; apart from his general tendency to drift or drown in the huge sea of his own administrative paperwork, they included the shifting prospects of military success for the Spanish in Flanders on the one hand, and for the Ottomans in Persia on the other, as well as the problems caused by Pope Gregory XIII's extraordinarily hostile reaction to the news of these negotiations. The upheavals generated by Philip's order to arrest his secretary of state Antonio Pérez in July 1579, on a charge of judicial murder, also did not help. Sokollu was probably aware of all these factors. Margliani may not have been. What he did know was that after eighteen months of tension and often severe anxiety he was now back, more or less, where he had started. But he had at least survived, and there was everything still to play for.[22]

14

Sinan Pasha and the
Moldavian Venture

For much of 1578 and the first half of 1579 there is little information about Bartolomeo Bruti's activities. Presumably he was cultivating his personal connections in Istanbul; since many of these would have been with traders, he may well have been engaged in commerce – or, perhaps, slave-ransoming – himself. No doubt he found some way of supporting himself financially; Margliani's accounts show that Bartolomeo received money from him in March, April and June 1578, totalling 134 scudi (111½ ducats), but those were loans, to be repaid, and he received nothing over the next twelve months. The one major event in his personal life during this period was his marriage, which was described in October 1578 as about to happen 'soon'. Unfortunately there is very little information about his bride; we know only that she was a Perot (inhabitant of Pera or Galata), a niece of the dragoman Matteo del Faro, and that her name – according to the family tree drawn up by Venturini – was Maria de Plebe. Foreign visitors to Istanbul often commented on the charms of the Perot women. A French traveller, Jean Palerne, who was there in 1582, wrote that the girls wore their hair long, spread over their shoulders, 'which is very graceful', that they darkened their eyebrows and eyelashes with dye, as the Muslims did, and that they had 'certain little languid mannerisms, and such a sweet and attractive look that it is very hard to escape their snares'. Another visitor, Pierre Lescalopier (1574), was somewhat less captivated: 'the women seem prettier than they are, because they use as much make-up as possible and spend all their money on dressing and adorning themselves with great quantities of rings on their fingers and precious stones on their heads, most of which are false.' What struck all observers was the luxurious way in which these women dressed whenever they appeared in public; as both Palerne and the German slave Michael Heberer noted, even a woman of lowly social status would wear satin, damask, velvet or silk, with multiple chains and bracelets of gold or silver. And nowhere was this love of magnificent display more apparent than at a Perot wedding.[1]

In 1573 the French traveller Philippe du Fresne-Canaye attended an Orthodox marriage ceremony in a merchant's house in Galata, where, as he put it, all the women were dressed like royal princesses in France. The bride sat, in a dress of crimson velvet with a gold crown on her head, under a baldacchino, and 'I was dazzled by the splendour of her pearls, rubies and jewels.' While wines and sweetmeats were served, the groom came and sat next to his bride, and both were covered with a scarlet veil; the mother of the bride received presents placed in a silver basin; then a man began playing a Greek harp, and dancing began. But the fullest description we have is Stefan Gerlach's account of the wedding in 1576 of Matteo del Faro, where Bartolomeo was apparently the best man; perhaps it was on this occasion, indeed, that Bartolomeo first glimpsed his bride-to-be. It is not known whether Maria de Plebe was Roman Catholic or Greek Orthodox. Mixed unions were anathematized, in theory at least, by the Orthodox Church; but Jean Palerne noted that in Pera such marriages were common, 'with each person following his or her own religion, as happens here in France with a Huguenot woman and a Catholic man'. If Maria was, like her uncle, Greek Orthodox, the ceremony described by Gerlach in 1576 may possibly serve as a model for Bartolomeo's own wedding to a member of the same family two or three years later. The bride sat under a golden canopy, flanked by her two bridesmaids; covered with gold and precious stones, and wearing a golden crown, 'she looked like a lifeless image, and could not say a word.' The priest placed the hands of the bride and groom together, and performed the marriage; the best man then gave the ring to the bride. Some of these details would have been different at a Catholic wedding, but what followed was the general custom of the Perot community. After the ceremony, the guests gave their presents to the bride, before going to another room for muscatel wine, sweetmeats and fruit. They moved to a different house for a musical performance, and were then given dinner with malmsey wine; here too Gerlach was struck by the number of richly dressed girls, some wearing silver slippers. After the dinner, music was performed by three Jews, singing in Turkish and playing a violin, a small drum and a tambourine. Gerlach admired the Perots' way of dancing, which seemed to him more chaste and virtuous than the Western European style: it was performed mostly by the women, and a man who danced with a woman would touch not her body but only the delicate handkerchief which she held in one hand. He was less pleased, though, by the 'Mumerey' or comic dumb-show that followed, which involved a Venetian merchant grandee tangling with two prostitutes, and a crudely enacted scene of homosexual lust. The dancing and dumb-shows went on through the night; at a rich family's wedding, he noted, the festivities could continue for up to a week.[2]

When Bartolomeo told Sokollu in October 1578 that he was going to marry Matteo's niece, he reportedly said that he planned to do so in order to be able to live 'piu quietamente' – in a calmer or more untroubled way. That phrase may have referred not so much to attaining domestic bliss as to regularizing his position in Istanbul; by marrying into a Perot family he would acquire a permanent base there, and might find a way of extricating himself from the powers exercised by the bailo over the Venetians. Bartolomeo was a young man with a career still to make, and his chances of advancement in Spanish service had apparently been blighted by the row with Margliani. It is not at all surprising that he should have regarded the Ottoman capital as a place teeming with opportunities; it was. But there was very probably a special reason in his case for planning a career within the Ottoman Empire: his link with Sinan Pasha, whose personal protégé he seems to have become during this period.[3]

That these two men were related was a fact which became known in later years; the papal nuncio in Poland, for example, who had many dealings with Bartolomeo, would write in 1589 that Sinan was his 'cousin'. But no details of the nature of the family connection have ever been known. A little light can be shed on this, by putting together two documents, one in Venice and one in the Spanish archives. In January 1576 the Venetian authorities recorded information given to them by an Alessandro Giubizza of Ulcinj, now resident in Kotor. He said that he had come in 1575 from Istanbul, where he had been 'at the court of Sinan Pasha, who is the first cousin of my mother, being an Albanian'. Having been taken captive at the fall of Ulcinj, Giubizza had managed to get himself ransomed; he had then gone back to Istanbul to release from slavery a sister and a nephew, whose freedom Sinan Pasha obtained for him without payment. 'So, as I stayed in that city, and often spent time with Sinan's nephew Mehmed Bey and with his steward, when I left, because I had become very close friends with them, we agreed that whenever anything arose that was against Venetian interests, especially concerning the city of Kotor and these border areas, they would willingly send news of it all to me, at my expense'; in return, he would buy luxury goods, such as glass and silken garments, for Mehmed Bey in Venice.* The Giubizzas had been a well-established Ulcinj family: in 1555 a Marco 'Gliubizza' was a grain merchant there, and, as we have seen, Andrea Giubizza had served as Bishop of Ulcinj from 1558 until his death in 1565, when Giovanni Bruni was put in charge of that see.† In the autobiographical text which he submitted to the Spanish authorities in 1576, Bartolomeo wrote that he wished to avenge himself against the Muslims because 'they cut off the heads of my father and two of my uncles by blood, one being the Archbishop of Bar, the other being the Bishop of Ulcinj, and they tyrannized my poor homeland.' While Bartolomeo was undeniably inclined to exaggerate, it seems unlikely that he would have turned his uncle Giovanni into two separate people merely to increase the number of episcopal victims in the family; most probably, Bishop Andrea Giubizza (the circumstances of whose death are not recorded) was the second uncle referred to here. What he might have meant by calling him an uncle by blood ('carnale') is not clear; perhaps Andrea's mother was a Bruti, or possibly this phrase was itself an exaggeration, arising merely from the fact that a Bruti had married one of Andrea's siblings. The neatest way of joining together all this evidence would be to suppose that Alessandro Giubizza's father, a brother of Andrea, had married a Bruti who was herself a cousin of Sinan Pasha. The truth may have been much less neat than that, of course. But at least there is the clear basis here for Bartolomeo's connection with Sinan Pasha: the Brutis were related to the Giubizzas, while the Giubizzas had a close family tie to Sinan. And that, in a world where personal bonds played such a powerful role, would have been quite enough.[4]

Sinan came from a small village in north-eastern Albania. As the writer Lazaro Soranzo put it, very probably deriving his information from Bartolomeo's cousin Antonio Bruni, he was 'an Albanian from Topojan in the *sancak* [district] of Prizren'. Attempts by some Serb historians to claim a Serbian origin for him are unconvincing. While the group of villages around Topojan was ethnically mixed at this time, probably with a Slav predominance, Topojan was mainly Albanian, and there is good evidence that Sinan's family background was neither Slav nor Orthodox. From the fact that documents from the latter part of his

---

* Alessandro Giubizza seems to have developed a taste for intelligence work. He would later offer his services to Pope Gregory XIII; the Pope sent him to Spain, where he was imprisoned as a suspected spy, but eventually released, and he ended his life farming land in the Kingdom of Naples.

† Above, p. 73.

life refer to his father as 'Ali *bey*', some have supposed that he was born a Muslim; but it is much more likely that he came from a Catholic family (as the relationship with the Giubizzas strongly suggests), and that once he and his brothers had prospered in their Ottoman careers they persuaded their father to convert, the better to share in that success with them. A Ragusan document of 1571, listing all the 'renegades' in the Sultan's governing council, described Sinan as a 'Catholic Albanian' by origin. He seems to have been born in 1519 or 1520, and to have been taken as a boy to Istanbul. (There are various legends about this, involving an improbable encounter as a shepherd-boy with the Sultan, but the most likely story is the one heard by a Venetian writer in Istanbul in 1582: that he and several brothers were fast-tracked into the Sultan's service by an influential relative. As one Italian account of the Ottoman system put it, 'some boys are put into the palace training centres by favouritism, as all the important figures at the Porte who have Christian relatives get them to become Muslims, and put them in.' At least four of Sinan's brothers became high officials of various kinds.) The tradition that he then caught the Sultan's attention when working in the palace kitchen is not implausible, as he did become a *çaşnigir*, one of the élite corps of butlers or food-tasters who, dressed in brilliant uniform, took dishes to the Sultan's table. In 1556, when he was chief butler, Sinan was appointed *sancakbeyi* of Tripoli in Syria; a series of regional governorships followed, culminating in his appointment as *beylerbeyi* of Egypt in 1567.[5]

It was after his arrival in Egypt that Sinan began to exhibit the qualities that would take his career to the very highest level within the Ottoman government: political and military skill, ostentatious piety and ruthless ambition, especially when it came to elbowing rivals out of his way. In 1568 Sokollu ordered Lala Mustafa Pasha – the man who had led the unsuccessful siege of Malta but would later triumph at Famagusta – to assemble an army in Egypt in order to crush a revolt in the Yemen. Sinan, who had a grudge against Lala Mustafa (holding him responsible for the death of one of his brothers), obstructed his work, briefed against him to Istanbul, and brought about his recall. Possibly this clash had been planned by Mehmed Sokollu, who, although Lala Mustafa was a fellow-Bosnian and perhaps even a distant relative, wanted to make either or both of these potential rivals more dependent on his own favour. (The bailo commented: 'this was all done by Mehmed, to show how great his power is.') Sinan was put in charge of the Yemen campaign, and did a very effective job there, earning himself the title

'Yemen Fatihi' or 'Conqueror of the Yemen'; on his way back he also
burnished his Islamic credentials by performing the Hajj at Mecca,
rebuilding and improving some of the facilities around the Kaaba there,
and setting up an endowment to have the Koran read aloud, in both
Mecca and Medina, by 30 koranic readers throughout the year. His
next military success was the seizure of La Goletta and Tunis in 1574,
from which the title 'Tunis Fatihi' duly followed.[6]

According to a widely circulated story, Sinan had an argument with
the wounded captive Gabrio Serbelloni on board ship on the way back
to Istanbul and struck him, whereupon he was reproved by Kılıç Ali for
his improper behaviour. Certainly Sinan Pasha developed a reputation
as both a hot-tempered man and a passionate enemy of the Western
Christian powers. Earlier in 1574 the Bishop of Dax had described him
as 'a very severe, cruel and anti-Christian man'. Two years later the
bailo Antonio Tiepolo wrote to the Doge that Sinan was 'uncouth, arro-
gant and proud by nature', and that 'he makes threats indiscriminately
against Your Serenity, the Emperor, and everyone', being 'utterly hostile
to all Christians'. Some of this may have been bluster. Reading the many
accounts of his unnervingly hostile responses to Western diplomats, one
begins to sense that a routine 'spiel' was being deployed; this seems
to have been especially the case during the normally sedate ritual of
present-giving, when such hostility could be maximally disconcerting.
Thus, when the Imperial Ambassador gave him fine gifts including two
silver drinking-cups in 1575, he exclaimed: 'What are you giving me
those for? You know well that I drink no wine. If you wish to honour
me, give me guns, armour and other weaponry, so that I can fight your
people.' Once in the early 1590s, when the Imperial Ambassador was
waiting for an audience with him, a shepherd appeared with a live sheep
on his shoulders as a gift for Sinan; in the words of one of the Ambassador's scandalized retinue, 'The pasha immediately ordered him to be
admitted, sheep and all, into his presence, thankfully received the sheep,
and gave audience to a shepherd in preference to the Imperial Ambassador.' Yet that story can also be read the other way, as testimony to
some of the qualities that made Sinan popular with the Sultan's subjects.
There were several such qualities. As one bailo's report would put it
towards the end of Sinan's life, 'they say that he is much valued in the
ordinary governing business of the Porte, as he is tireless in both acting
and listening, remitting legal cases to the competent judges; and takes
extreme care in providing plentiful supplies for the city.' Sinan's reputation has suffered from the fact that one of the most influential Ottoman

historical writers of the period, Mustafa Ali of Gallipoli, was a protégé of Lala Mustafa and a bitter opponent of Sinan Pasha; his criticisms were also repeated by the chronicler Peçevi, who was heavily dependent on Mustafa Ali's work. Mustafa Ali, who prided himself on his high literary culture, satirized Sinan as an uncouth man who used long words which he did not understand; he also wrote that all the poets rejoiced when he died. Yet Sinan was in fact a patron of writers and artists (at one point he even gave work to Mustafa Ali), who, at his death, owned 89 volumes in Turkish, 117 in Arabic and 128 in Persian. At least seven illustrated Persian manuscripts that belonged to him are in the Topkapı Palace collections today. Sinan endowed pious foundations (*vakıf*s) on a massive scale, in Cairo, Damascus, Istanbul and many other places (such as the small town of Kaçanik, in southern Kosovo, not far from his birthplace); these included three *medrese*s (institutions of Islamic higher education), and his own memorial tomb was also equipped with a library.[7]

In 1577, when Sokollu was planning – many months before the actual death of Shah Ismail – the military campaign against Persia, he appointed Lala Mustafa commander of the northern part of the front, in Azerbaijan, and Sinan commander of the Iraqi section to the south. During that year, however, the rivalry between the two commanders became so disruptive that he decided in January 1578 to give sole responsibility to Lala Mustafa, dismissing Sinan from his post. This seems to have completed the breakdown in relations between Mehmed Sokollu and Sinan which had been under way for several years. Sinan had benefited from the Grand Vizier's patronage, and, as we have seen, in 1575 Bartolomeo was able to report that Sinan kept his patron sweet by giving him money; but after his triumphant success at La Goletta and Tunis he had enough prestige to establish a power-base of his own. In 1576 the bailo Antonio Tiepolo wrote that relations between the two men had cooled since that victory, and a later Venetian report would even comment that Sinan was encouraged to oppose Sokollu by the Sultan, who wanted a counterweight to the Grand Vizier's excessive power. One other factor may have been at work here: the Albanian dimension. The Sultan's favourite consort, Safiye, who had great influence over him, was Albanian, and a supporter of Sinan; in 1585 the bailo would report that Sinan was 'much loved' by her (and by her son, the future Sultan Mehmed III). One of the criticisms made of Sinan repeatedly by Mustafa Ali of Gallipoli was that he promoted an Albanian clique in the military and the government administration; Mustafa Ali wrote admiringly of Bosnians, such as his patron Lala Mustafa and Mehmed Sokollu, and scathingly about Albanians. So possibly this too was an element in the estrangement between Sokollu and Sinan, as the latter gradually replaced some of the former's clients and protégés with his own. It would be anachronistic to talk here about 'national' consciousness in the modern sense. Nevertheless, historians have observed a kind of ethnic-regional solidarity emerging in the Ottoman system in the early modern period, and it is not surprising that a powerful man should have wished to surround himself with people whose underlying culture he shared, and with whom he could talk easily in his mother tongue. Bartolomeo Bruti would perhaps have been a beneficiary of this, even without his special family connection.[8]

This hostility between the Grand Vizier and Sinan Pasha forms part of the background to the crisis which occurred in the summer of 1579, when Bartolomeo Bruti came very close to losing his life. In mid-July Margliani reported that on the 8th of that month Hürrem Bey had been sent to him by Mehmed Sokollu, to ask 'whether I knew Bruti, whether he lived in my house, and why he did not live in my house, given that he had come with me'. Margliani told him to say that Bartolomeo had married a niece of Matteo del Faro and gone to live in Pera, and to explain that the King had sent him to accompany Margliani on his mission 'because he had the Albanian language and had experience of this Porte'. The next day Hürrem told him that Sokollu had announced that he was going to arrest Bartolomeo. When he had done so he would ask Hürrem and Solomon to testify that, as they had previously said, Bartolomeo had urged Margliani to flee from Istanbul. Margliani declared that he had a duty to the King of Spain to protect his former colleague, and begged them not to testify; but three days later Hürrem told him that the Grand Vizier had made a formal request to the Sultan to have Bartolomeo executed, by impalement, for his 'evil behaviour'. Margliani's response was to threaten that if that happened, he would be obliged to end his mission and leave Istanbul.[9]

Both Giovanni Margliani and Mehmed Sokollu were engaged in pretext-making here. As the former admitted, his motive for protecting Bruti was not mere solidarity with a fellow servant of the Spanish crown. 'In reality,' he wrote, 'I suspected that once this man were in prison he might convert to Islam [to save his life]', whereupon he might give the Sultan sensitive information about the background and nature of the Spanish dealings with Sokollu. If such matters were revealed, Margliani feared, 'the intelligence operation would at the same time be destroyed' – meaning, probably, that the role of Hürrem and some others would be exposed. As for the Grand Vizier's accusation about encouraging Margliani to flee: this may possibly have been true. We know that Margliani and Bruti had met, perhaps for the first time in a year, on 29 June, when Bartolomeo borrowed some more money, and we also know that at just that time Margliani was anxiously discussing his diplomatic immunity, or lack of it, with Solomon, as rumours spread of an impending Spanish attack on Algiers. Margliani may well have been contemplating flight himself. But the real reason for Sokollu's desire to get rid of Bartolomeo was quite different. As Margliani himself reported, the Voivod (princely ruler) of Moldavia – one of the quasi-autonomous Romanian principalities within the Ottoman Empire – was a client of Sokollu's who had paid him a huge sum of money for his position; a plan was now afoot to get him displaced by a rival claimant to the throne, and Bartolomeo was deeply involved in it. 'Certain Greeks' who were related to the rival prince had employed a Perot drag-oman called Ambrosino to help organize their project, and Ambrosino was a friend of Bruti's. Bartolomeo's role was to enlist the powerful assistance of Sinan Pasha, offering him a large payment and annual gifts thereafter; in return, Bartolomeo would receive 2,000 ducats for his ser-vices. The identities of the 'Greeks' – meaning, probably, members of the Orthodox Church – are not known; Ambrosino was Ambrosio Grillo, a Catholic Perot who worked as a dragoman for the Tuscan envoy (secretly sending copies of Tuscan documents, a little later, to the Ven-etian bailo); and, according to another report, Bartolomeo was also working with 'some renegade Albanians, his compatriots'. Here we catch just a glimpse of the circles in which Bartolomeo was moving. But in his own rather self-aggrandizing account of the matter, written later to the King of Spain, he gave the impression that he had managed the entire business himself, and put all the emphasis on his high connec-tions: he had operated 'with the favour of Sinan Pasha and of the Sultan's wife, who is of my nation and homeland'. As he explained: 'when I had offered in the name of the [claimant] prince 80,000 ducats to the Sultan, besides many very valuable presents for his wife, and had concluded the whole business, news of this reached Mehmed Pasha [Sokollu], who immediately had me arrested.'[10]

Bartolomeo Bruti was seized on 19 July 1579, and spent just under a month locked up in a building belonging to Sokollu. The public justifi-cation for this, put out by the Grand Vizier, was that he had been sending detailed intelligence to Naples, not only about Istanbul politics but also about the war in Persia. (As we shall see, there may have been some truth in that.) Margliani made strenuous efforts to have him released, using both Hürrem Bey and Solomon, who visited Bartolomeo and gave him money. Also involved was Bartolomeo's younger brother Cristoforo, who had recently come to Istanbul to study as a giovane di lingua in the Venetian bailate; Margliani's accounts show that on 10 August Cristoforo received on credit from one of Solomon's nephews some quantities of fine Venetian crimson damask cloth, which were probably intended as presents to Bartolomeo's gaolers. The real battle to save Bartolomeo's life, however, was conducted not by Margliani but by Sinan Pasha. According to the Imperial Ambassador, Mehmed Sokollu and Sinan clashed openly at the Sultan's *divan*: 'Mehmed Pasha spoke strongly to the vizier Sinan about it, since Sinan apparently wanted to treat Bruti as a friend because he was an Albanian, asking what he was doing with such a friend, who was an arch-traitor to Sinan's lord and Sultan.' In the end, according to Bartolomeo's own account, it was Sinan's intercession that obtained an order from the Sultan to free him. This took place on 13 August. But the compromise was that he should be expelled from Ottoman territory – as Margliani himself had suggested. So on the following day Bartolomeo was sent off with an escort to Dubrovnik, with a message from the Grand Vizier to the authorities there saying that he must be given a boat to Barletta (on the Apulian coast) because he had important business to conduct in Spain. Ten days later, it occurred to Sokollu that Bartolomeo might meet the incoming ambassador Juan de Rocafull in Dubrovnik and, being 'so impudent and wicked', might try to return to Istanbul in his retinue, so he told Margliani to send orders to prevent that. And to make doubly sure, Sokollu also instructed the Ragusan ambassadors in Istanbul to write to their government saying that Bartolomeo must be put on a boat to Barletta as soon as he arrived.[11]

Bartolomeo Bruti managed to thwart the Grand Vizier's plans not once, but twice. When he reached Dubrovnik at the end of August he found Giovanni Stefano de Ferrari and Antonio Echevarría, and learned from the latter that, because of Rocafull's continuing 'illness', the ambassadorial credentials were to be bestowed on Margliani. Bartolomeo now decided to accompany Echevarría on his way to Istanbul; and the Ragusan authorities did nothing to stop him, as Sokollu's message had asked them only to help him pursue his important Spanish business, without explaining the real nature of his ejection from the Ottoman Empire. Rather surprisingly, Bartolomeo also sent a messenger ahead to

Margliani with a letter announcing his return. Echevarría, Bruti and the çavuş who had been waiting for Rocafull in Dubrovnik set out together for the Ottoman capital. But after several days' journey, when they were at the small town of Novi Pazar, just to the north-west of Kosovo, they met a courier bearing further messages from Margliani, one of which informed Echevarría of the Grand Vizier's determination to have Bruti expelled. So, at Echevarría's insistence, Bartolomeo went back to Dubrovnik. By this time the Ragusan authorities had received their instructions. They quickly found a boat that was going to Barletta, put Bartolomeo on it (refusing his request that he be allowed to stay one day in Dubrovnik to write letters to the King of Spain and the Viceroy of Naples), and told the captain and a Spanish passenger to guard him until they reached their destination. But as luck would have it, soon after they set off they were driven by a contrary wind to Mljet, a Ragusan island to the north-west of Dubrovnik. When they landed there, Bartolomeo managed to escape from his custodians and went to the nearby island of Korčula, which was Venetian territory. He was now a free man again.[12]

Bartolomeo's determination to go back to Istanbul may seem surprising, given the evident willingness of the Grand Vizier to have him either expelled again or put to death. It is very hard to accept his claim, in his later letter to King Philip, that he was motivated only by a desire to continue serving the Spanish crown; if Rocafull had gone to Istanbul as the ambassador Bartolomeo might conceivably have tried to start on a new footing with him, but the knowledge that Margliani was to play that role must have made all thoughts of further Spanish service impossible. The only reasonable explanation for his return to the Ottoman capital – apart from the fact that he now had a wife and home there – is that Bartolomeo felt very confident about the power of Sinan Pasha to protect him.[13]

From Korčula Bartolomeo took a ship to Lezhë, in Ottoman-ruled Albania. According to his own account, he wrote from there 'to certain gentlemen, my friends' in Dubrovnik, and to the Ragusan government, explaining his actions. While in Lezhë, he also offered his services to Giovanni Gionima, the Catholic priest who worked as a grain buyer for Dubrovnik (and who, as we have seen, would be murdered on the beach at Durrës four years later).* It seems that Bartolomeo badly underestimated the seriousness with which the Ragusan authorities took their

* Above, p. 50.

instructions from Mehmed Sokollu. Replying to Gionima's letter of 13 October 1579, they warned him 'not to share this business with him [Bartolomeo] in any way, nor to trust him in anything else, but to avoid him like fire'. On 15 October they asked their ambassadors to apologize to Sokollu for Bartolomeo's escape, and to assure him that 'with great diligence we have sent couriers to Lezhë to get him arrested and held by force.' By the 27th those couriers were back in Dubrovnik, reporting that they had persuaded the *kadi* (judge) of Lezhë to arrest Bruti, and that the *kadi* had handed him over to the two *emin*s (superintendents) with instructions to hold him until they received further orders. The Ragusan government duly reported this news to Istanbul. But events now took a very dramatic turn. In Bartolomeo's own words: 'when the sister of Sinan Pasha learned of my detention in Lezhë, she sent one of her sons with a squadron of 25 men, all well armed and on horseback, who took me from Lezhë by force, and set me at liberty, giving me men, with the things I needed, to go with me to Istanbul.' Biographers of Sinan have speculated that he had a sister; this passage confirms it, while also suggesting that she lived in Albania, not Istanbul. For, as Bartolomeo also explained, Sinan heard about his arrest only from the Ragusan report; when he did so, he immediately got an order to have him freed, and sent it by a *çavuş*, who was accompanied by Bartolomeo's brother Cristoforo, to Lezhë. Only on arriving there did they learn of his escape; according to Bartolomeo they then imprisoned the Ragusan officials who had arranged his arrest. (This may be embroidery on Bartolomeo's part, as we know that the couriers had returned safely to Dubrovnik; but it might refer to some resident senior Ragusans, through whom the couriers had approached the *kadi*.) Cristoforo and the *çavuş* returned to Istanbul, arriving there one day after Bartolomeo himself.[14]

While Bartolomeo Bruti was in Lezhë, one surprising event had taken place in Istanbul that would greatly improve his own prospects: on 11 October Mehmed Sokollu was assassinated. He was receiving petitioners in his own residence after lunch when a man dressed as a dervish approached him, drew a knife, and stabbed him in the chest; Sokollu died two hours later. The killer was beaten so badly that, when brought before the Sultan for questioning, he was incapable of speech. Various theories circulated: that he was a religious fanatic who regarded the Grand Vizier's policies as too pro-Christian, that he was a lone individual seeking revenge for having been made a galley-slave by him, or (improbably) that he was an assassin hired by Sokollu's wife after she had caught her husband *in flagrante* with a young man. The truth may never be known, but one modern historian plausibly suggests that the murderer was a genuine fanatic who had been put to work by Sokollu's political enemies – a group of leading pashas that included Sinan. The person who was appointed Grand Vizier in Sokollu's place, however, was not one of those, nor was he an Albanian (his parents were Orthodox Serbs from Herceg Novi). He was Ahmed Pasha, the man who had commanded the land army at the fall of Ulcinj and Bar; he had been the next most senior vizier, and enjoyed high status because his wife was the child of a still very influential daughter of Süleyman the Magnificent. Ahmed's relations with Mehmed Sokollu seem to have been good; but he had not been involved in the Spanish truce negotiation, so there was much fresh work to be done by Margliani, Solomon and Hürrem.[15]

One of the first tasks they addressed was that of dealing with the problem of Bartolomeo Bruti. It was only on 5 November that Margliani learned from the Ragusan ambassadors that Bartolomeo had jumped ship, escaped to Korčula and travelled from there to Ottoman territory. On the 17th they told him that the *emin* of Lezhë had written to the Ragusan government to say that Bartolomeo was in his custody, and to ask whether he should send him back to Dubrovnik; the government wanted to know what the Grand Vizier's wishes were. At Giovanni Margliani's request, the Ragusan ambassadors went to see Ahmed Pasha the next day, taking Solomon and Hürrem with them; Margliani knew that these two were very keen that, whatever happened, Bartolomeo should not be allowed to return to Istanbul. When the new Grand Vizier asked what Bartolomeo had done, the Ragusans replied that they had no idea; they had merely been ordered to arrest him by the Porte. Then Hürrem approached Ahmed and spoke into his ear 'for a long time', after which Ahmed said: 'If that's how it is, let us carry out the wishes of my brother [Sokollu], and send him to Apulia.' (Hürrem later told Margliani that he had explained that Bartolomeo had shown disrespect to Sokollu and had plotted to replace the Voivod of Moldavia; perhaps he added other accusations too.) The Grand Vizier announced that he would have an official order drawn up to that effect, and told the Ragusans to send their dragoman later to collect it. But when the dragoman did so, he saw that it was an order that Bartolomeo should be set free, on the grounds that he was from Ulcinj and therefore an Ottoman subject who could not be forced to go to Italy. He consulted Hürrem, who, thinking this was just an error by the scribe, went to see Ahmed again. The Grand Vizier declared that, after reading the documentation from Lezhë forwarded from Dubrovnik, which described Bruti as from Ulcinj and a subject of the Sultan, he could not fail to command that he be freed. When the Ragusan dragoman remonstrated with him, he said: 'What has this man done? Has he killed anyone? Who is bringing a case against him? Who accuses him? My job is to do justice, and not to concern myself with anyone's passions.' It is possible to see this as an example of the rule of law in action; but it is also possible to suspect that the Grand Vizier had just been nobbled by Sinan Pasha.[16]

Margliani's despatches portrayed Hürrem and Solomon as in a state of panic, and explained (in cipher) the reasons for it. Acting on a special request in the royal instructions to Rocafull that were brought to Istanbul by Echevarría, they had altered the text of the truce as previously agreed by Sokollu, surreptitiously inserting the Emperor and the Archdukes of Austria, and the King of France, into the agreement. What terrified them was the idea that this falsification – for which they might well be executed – would be exposed by Bartolomeo, who, as they believed, knew how the text had previously stood. Moreover, according to Hürrem, Bartolomeo had also told the *çavuş* with whom he travelled to Novi Pazar that Hürrem and Solomon were secret Christians, and that when they were in Margliani's house 'they both lived like Christians' – an accusation that would seem quite plausible in the case of Hürrem, a former Roman Catholic from Lucca, but very surprising in the case of Solomon, who was commonly referred to as a rabbi. Underlying all these fears was the knowledge that Bartolomeo had a special relationship with Sinan Pasha. On 14 October, just after Ahmed's appointment as Grand Vizier, that same *çavuş* (the one who had waited so long in Dubrovnik for Rocafull) had been questioned by Ahmed and Sinan Pasha, who asked him what he knew about the truce negotiation. Among other things, Sinan demanded to know Margliani's social status; the *çavuş* said that he believed he was a great *bey* like Don John. As Margliani later reported, 'Sinan answered that he understood the opposite to be the case from Bruti, who told him the truth; and in connection with this the *çavuş* told me that Sinan said so many things which he said he had learned from Bruti that I was horrified.' On 8 November the *çavuş* visited Margliani again and said that 'Sinan Pasha had asked him whether he knew that the Albanian (meaning Bruti) had escaped; he had answered that he did not know. Sinan had said that he had escaped, and that he would learn from him the truth about what had been negotiated with Mehmed Pasha [Sokollu], adding: "we can't be deceived any more, as he will tell me the truth about everything." '[17]

What exactly Bartolomeo Bruti told his powerful relative when he finally appeared in Istanbul, we do not know. But whatever it was, it did not derail the truce negotiation; nor is that surprising, given that the Ottoman Empire was now heavily committed to its Persian war, which would continue – with massive loss of blood and treasure – for more than a decade. In March 1580 a document was signed by the Grand Vizier and Margliani, renewing the provisional armistice for another year. During the latter part of 1580, just as the Ottoman authorities became more keen to finalize a long-lasting truce, Philip engaged in further foot-dragging; it seems to have been a desperate plea from Margliani, saying that he feared impalement, that persuaded Philip finally to clinch the deal. In February 1581, three years and two months after his arrival with Bartolomeo Bruti in Istanbul, Giovanni Margliani signed a three-year truce – in which both Venice and the Knights of Malta were included – with the Ottoman Empire. At last, he was given the Sultan's permission to leave Istanbul. He reached Naples in May, bringing with him as his prisoner the disgraced friar Cristóbal Pérez, whose conversion to Islam had been so narrowly averted.* A month later Margliani was in Rome, where he had the delicate task of explaining his actions to the Pope; the French Ambassador there described him, not without reason, as 'a very clever negotiator'. Further negotiations in Istanbul, conducted mostly by Giovanni Stefano de Ferrari, would take place in later years: the truce was renewed for one year in 1584, and again (after a period of expensive compromise, when Spain paid a high sum for a quasi-truce that could be terminated at six months' notice) in 1587. In the winter of 1589–90 de Ferrari was still trying to get the Ottomans to accept a temporary truce of one or two years, until they could receive a new Spanish envoy: Count Ruggiero Margliani, Giovanni's son. But by then the exhausting conflict with Persia was coming to an end, so that peace in the Mediterranean arena was no longer imperative for Ottoman policy-makers.[18]

As for Bartolomeo Bruti: the next chapter in his life was already beginning to open, even before he reached Istanbul. Giovanni Margliani, writing the long despatch on 23 November 1579 in which he described the panic of his colleagues at the thought of Bartolomeo's reappearance, added almost as a postscript: 'they have given Moldavia to the person for whom Bruti was negotiating, for a certain amount of money.' The Ottoman system operated as follows: first the Sultan would

---

* On Pérez see above, pp. 211–12.

nominate the new voivod, then that person would go to see the Grand
Vizier, who would carry out the investiture, informing him of his duties
and giving him various symbolic gifts, including ceremonial robes and a
cylindrical hat with a heron feather. (This type of feather, which featured also in the Sultan's own turban, had a talismanic significance; it
symbolized the legendary *hüma* bird, an all-powerful royal vulture,
from which the Ottoman word *hümayun*, 'imperial', was derived.) With
an honour guard of janissaries, the new voivod then went to the Patriarchal church in Istanbul to be anointed. Within a few days he had an
audience with the Sultan, who did not look at him and spoke only via
the Grand Vizier; shortly thereafter, he travelled to Moldavia. In the
case of the voivod whose appointment Bartolomeo had helped to
arrange – Iancu Sasul ('John the German') – the investiture by the Grand
Vizier took place on 21 November, and the meeting with the Sultan on
the 26th. It is known that Iancu Sasul left Istanbul for Moldavia on 8
December. But it is far from clear whether Bartolomeo had returned to
the Ottoman capital by that date; if he got back just one day ahead of
the *çavuş* sent (with his brother Cristoforo) by Sinan Pasha, we may
doubt whether he arrived before mid-December, as that *çavuş* can have
left Istanbul only in mid-November, and surely took at least four weeks
to go to Lezhë and come back again in winter conditions.[19]

   Bartolomeo Bruti's prospects were now utterly transformed. The
appointment of Iancu Sasul gave him not only the promised fee of 2,000
ducats, but the possibility of some lucrative office in Moldavia itself. In
Istanbul Bartolomeo's chief enemy was dead, and his relative and patron was in a more powerful position than ever before. On 25 January
1580 he wrote a long, self-confident letter to King Philip, explaining his
own conduct and blaming Margliani's; he said that on his return to
Istanbul he had visited Margliani and asked him to forget the past, but
had been treated in a cold and hostile manner. Assuring the King that he
was still his faithful servant, awaiting his orders, he also took care to
remind him that he had served for three years at his own expense, and
asked to be reimbursed. Nevertheless, he wrote, 'my service to Your
Majesty is not based on my personal interest; rather, I glory to call
myself a servant of the greatest king in the world.' He asked Philip to
send any letters to him not through Margliani but via the Imperial
embassy in Istanbul, with orders to give them in his absence to his
brother Cristoforo. For, as he explained, 'I have been summoned by the
Prince of Moldavia, and urged by Sinan Pasha to go there, with the title
of general of all his men, a rank which I have not refused; but I did not

want to go there without first taking leave of Your Majesty, having sworn loyalty to you, since wherever I am, I shall always call myself a servant of the Catholic King.' He did not leave Istanbul immediately, however, and this was not his last letter to Philip. On 10 February he wrote again, saying that Margliani had spoken that day to Grand Vizier Ahmed Pasha in the presence of Kılıç Ali (the admiral, who was adamantly opposed to a Mediterranean truce), and had been treated with great scorn. 'Certainly', Bartolomeo affirmed, 'I believe that there will be no peace, and that everything Margliani has negotiated up until now, at a cost to the reputation of Your Majesty, will come to nothing, because they did not listen to me at your court.' It can easily be imagined that these missives did not go down very well in Madrid. In late May one of the officials there wrote to Margliani: 'nothing has been done about Bruti's salary, nor will he be paid unless you advise that it is necessary in order to avoid the things that this traitor has done and will wish to do. We must just play for time with him until you personally are safe.'[20]

By the end of May 1580, Bartolomeo had left Istanbul. As the French Ambassador wrote from that city on 2 June: 'Bruti, having negotiated at the Porte the restoration of the Voivod of Moldavia who is now ruling, and having gone to see him thereafter, was generously rewarded by that voivod a few days ago; he was made general of his cavalry and infantry, and given a port or the customs duties of a port worth 3,000 ducats a year, and the income from the estate of a lord who had been executed.' The transformation in Bartolomeo's fortunes was now almost complete. Although the death of Ahmed Pasha in April 1580 had led to the appointment of Lala Mustafa Pasha, Sinan's old rival, as Grand Vizier, after only four months Lala Mustafa would die and the new Grand Vizier would be none other than Sinan himself. Bartolomeo Bruti rapidly became the second most powerful man in Moldavia; his relative and patron became the most powerful minister in the whole of the Ottoman Empire.[21]

15
Gasparo Bruni and the Huguenot War

When the young Bartolomeo Bruti applied to become a trainee dragoman in 1573, he was not the only member of his family seeking a new
position. His uncle Gasparo Bruni was also in need of employment, or
at least of an income. At the end of the previous year Pope Gregory XIII
had made an effort to ensure that Gasparo would be rewarded for his
labours with a 'commenda' (income-yielding estate) from the Order of
the Knights of Malta. On 19 December 1572 Gregory's secretary of
state wrote a note to the Grand Master of the Order, Jean Levesque de
La Cassière, to accompany the papal 'breve' or formal letter:

> The cavaliere Fra Gasparo Bruni, an Albanian, has served continuously
> during these three years of warfare against the Ottomans as captain of the
> papal flagship; during this time he has lost his homeland, his property, his
> brothers, his relatives, and everything he had, which all fell prey to the
> Ottomans last year. His Holiness, wishing to make provision in some way
> for the needs and necessities of the said cavaliere, who has deserved well
> of this Holy See, requests by his breve that your most illustrious lordship
> should provide him with the first discretionary commenda that shall fall
> vacant.

This letter, and the Pope's formal breve, were sent to the French knight
Romegas, who had served with Gasparo on the flagship at Lepanto.
Romegas himself was a beneficiary of papal favour. Earlier in December
Pope Gregory had used his own power to grant him the Priory of
Ireland – a position, within the virtually defunct 'langue' of England,
which brought its holder no income but did give him the higher rank of
Knight Grand Cross, with a seat on the Council of the Order. Gregory
had sent Romegas to Malta bearing not only the document that awarded
him the Priory, but also a letter asking that he be made 'Turcopilier',
which was the honorific position of head of the entire English langue.

The Council accepted the appointment as Prior of Ireland as gracefully as it could – it had no choice in the matter – but firmly resisted the Turcopilier suggestion, saying that there were many Knights who were more senior and better qualified. This was not a good augury for the papal request to give a commenda to Gasparo Bruni.[1]

With its highly aristocratic ethos, the Order was obsessed with titles and privileges, and peculiarly reluctant to have its distribution of honours dictated from outside. During this period there were several fierce internal disputes about absurdly small points of honour. The French and Spanish langues argued bitterly about which had the privilege of being served first in the meat market, while the langue of Aragon denounced the head of the Italian langue for usurping its right to drive the symbolic silver nail into the poop of a new galley built by an Italian officer of the Order. But there were special reasons for coolness towards papal instructions about the Order's internal affairs; for relations between the Knights of Malta and the Pope had deteriorated badly in the summer of 1572, and were still in a poor state. At Marcantonio Colonna's request, Pope Gregory had written a stern breve to the Grand Master in early June of that year, demanding that he send the Maltese galleys to join the papal fleet; the Grand Master's rather supercilious reply said that he was surprised that the Pope did not know that his galleys were already promised to the King of Spain. Later that month, when Colonna, fretting in Messina at the Spanish failure to set sail, demanded that the Maltese knights come with him on the campaign, they simply refused, even when he got the papal nuncio to threaten them with excommunication. Eventually they were included in the group of galleys which Don John allowed to sail eastwards under Colonna.* But after the end of the campaign, in November 1572, a special commission was set up in Malta to investigate 'the grumbling and imprudent speech of certain brother Knights who openly said that they did not want to set out on the expedition against the savage Ottomans together with and under the command of the illustrious lord Marcantonio Colonna'. Within the Order, which was often anti-Venetian, there was evidently a significant current of anti-papal feeling too; this was not a good time to seek favours for a man such as Gasparo Bruni, a Venetian subject who had been Colonna's right-hand man. Even Romegas, who enjoyed much personal prestige in Malta, may have been a little tainted by his closeness to Colonna.[2]

* Above, p. 182.

When the papal secretary Tolomeo Gallio, Cardinal Como, sent Romegas the Pope's letter requesting that Bruni be given a commenda, he wrote: 'since you know the merit and goodness of that cavaliere, and the state in which he finds himself, robbed by the Ottomans of everything he had in the world, I shall not ask you to use diligence and loving kindness in this matter, as I am utterly certain that you will do so of your own accord.' On 8 March Romegas reported that he had given the letter to the Grand Master, 'and, in addition, I spoke to him, telling the story of the services which this signor Brul [sic] had done for His Holiness.' The misspelling of Bruni's name (which occurs twice in Romegas's letter) makes one wonder how much he knew or cared about his colleague, even though they had spent many weeks on board the same ship. But however much diligence and loving kindness Romegas used, or however little, the result would probably have been the same. On 25 March Grand Master La Cassière wrote to Cardinal Como saying that he had already assigned all the commende that came under his own discretionary power: 'I cannot in any way obey His Beatitude in this matter, as it is something completely impossible for me to do.' By the time Gasparo Bruni received this dispiriting news – perhaps in April 1573 – the Venetian peace agreement had made it clear that there would be no further need for him as captain of the Pope's flagship. It is not known how he spent the rest of that year; perhaps he stayed mostly in Rome, or else retired for a while to Koper. He would later write that he had served the Pope 'continuously', so it seems that there was no formal intermission in his service; and after six months he reappears in the records in October 1573, when he was gathering soldiers for a new military campaign. Here too his task would be to defend and promote the interests of the Papacy against a religious enemy. This time, however, the foes were not the infidel Ottoman Muslims, but the heretical French Protestants or 'Huguenots', who were threatening the papal enclave of Avignon.[3]

That papal possession consisted of two conjoined territories in the south of France, centred on the city of Avignon and surrounded by lands belonging to the French crown. The larger of the territories was the Comtat Venaissin ('comtat' or 'comté' meaning county, land ruled by a count); ceded to the Pope in 1229, it was governed by a papal Rector and represented by its own 'estates general' which met in the town of Carpentras, fifteen miles to the north-east of Avignon. Like so many feudal possessions, this county was not a neat geographical unit. Some of its outlying areas were not connected with it, and at its heart there was

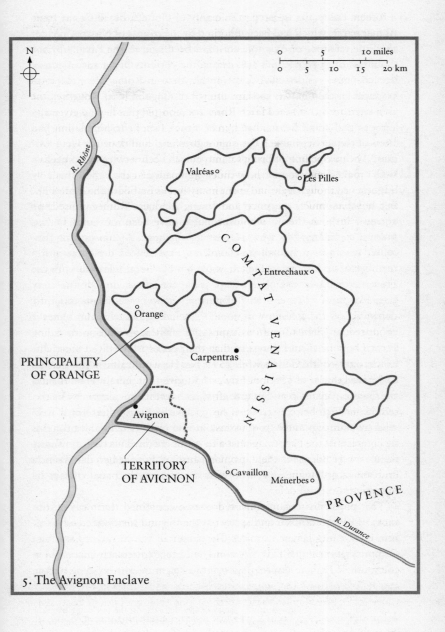

N

	5			10 miles
0	5	10	15	20 km

R. Rhône

Valréas ○

○ Les Pilles

C O M T A T   V E N A I S S I N

Entrechaux ○

○ Orange

Carpentras ●

PRINCIPALITY OF ORANGE

Avignon ●

TERRITORY OF AVIGNON

○ Cavaillon

Ménerbes ○

PROVENCE

R. Durance

5. The Avignon Enclave

a foreign entity, the isolated principality of Orange, based on the town of that name, which had been inherited by the counts of Nassau.* As for the little territory of Avignon: this had been sold to the Papacy by the Countess of Provence in 1348, during the period when a succession of French popes resided in Avignon rather than in Rome. Here the local political institution was the city council of Avignon itself. Together, the two territories contained fewer than 100,000 people; there were many villages and small towns, but by the 1590s (after the population had been depleted by plague) the only significant conurbations were Avignon, with 4,000 or more people, Carpentras, with 2,500, and Cavaillon, with 2,000. Avignon and its territory were ruled in the Pope's name by a legate or vice-legate; in the mid-1560s the King of France, Charles IX, insisted that the Pope appoint Cardinal Charles de Bourbon (the King's cousin), but since the Cardinal was mostly absent from Avignon he was given a co-legate. This was Georges d'Armagnac, Archbishop of Toulouse, who was a humanist scholar, an experienced diplomat and a member of an important French noble family. Good relations with the French crown were essential, since this papal enclave could not possibly be held against a French war of conquest; and in peacetime its economy depended on the free flow of goods – including the excellent wines it produced, at Châteauneuf-du-Pape and elsewhere – to the surrounding French territories and towns, and to the port of Marseille, a short distance to the south. Generally relations had been amicable in this period, and a succession of kings of France had given the inhabitants of both the Comtat Venaissin and Avignon (which together, for simplicity's sake, will henceforth be referred to as the enclave of Avignon) not only freedom from import and export taxes, but also all the essential legal rights of French subjects. Yet the possession of this enclave was always something of a problem for the Papacy, because of its geographical position and the fact that the revenues from it never covered the costs of its administration and defence.[4]

The problems became much more severe from the early 1560s onwards. Protestantism had spread in the Comtat Venaissin, and hardline Protestants began to reject the temporal as well as the spiritual authority of the Pope. This new creed had been particularly successful in the south of France. Several important towns in the surrounding region,

---

* Hence the princes of Orange in the history of the Netherlands: the title came from the French town, whose Latin name was Arausio, and had nothing to do with the fruit or the colour.

such as Montpellier and Nîmes, already had Huguenot majorities – as did the little city of Orange, which became a militant Protestant stronghold. For the Papacy, the issue was not just one of securing its own territory; as the Council of Trent reconvened for its final session, Pope Pius IV felt that the eyes of the Christian world were upon him. It was essential to set an example: the Counter-Reformation, as we now call it, would seem feeble indeed if it could not even eliminate heresy in the Pope's own domains. Pius revived the long-extinct post of general of the troops in the territory of Avignon and gave it to his cousin Fabrizio Serbelloni (brother of Gabrio), who turned Avignon into a well-fortified city. Serbelloni also seized from the Huguenots first the little town of Mérindol and then the city of Orange, which was sacked and (perhaps because of one soldier's negligence) mostly burnt down. Avignon was saved for Catholicism, but opinion in the enclave was radicalized. The houses and estates of many Protestants were confiscated; and it was this, more than anything, that both spread the mood of militarism on the Huguenot side, and made the local Catholics – who benefited from the property bonanza – reluctant to accept any compromise with the Protestants thereafter.[5]

These events took place against the background of the French Wars of Religion, which convulsed the country for most of the period between 1562 and 1598. The French kings were Catholic, and their primary opponents on the battlefield were Protestant; but such was the strength of the Huguenots, both militarily and in French society, that any peace agreement necessarily involved making concessions to them, and this in turn provoked the growth of a hard-line Catholic movement, hostile to royal policy. One such agreement was the Peace of Saint-Germain of 1570, which ended the Third War of Religion (a war in which papal forces had participated, sent from Italy with a posse of Jesuit chaplains to assist King Charles IX: the Huguenot battle-standards they captured would be proudly displayed in the church of St John Lateran in Rome until they were confiscated by French soldiers in 1798). That peace agreement's provisions included a marriage between the young King Henri of Navarre, who had emerged as the leader of the Protestants, and Marguerite, King Charles IX's sister. It was during the marriage celebrations in Paris in August 1572, when many Huguenot leaders were present in that fiercely Catholic city, that an assassination attempt on one of the Huguenot military commanders precipitated an extraordinary outbreak of religious violence. The King and his council decided that their best option was to use this opportunity to eliminate the

Huguenot leadership altogether, while mobs began to hunt down Protestants in the streets. These murders and pogroms, which began on St Bartholomew's Day, spread to other towns in France; the Fourth War of Religion swiftly followed.[6]

In the enclave of Avignon – where, as in Rome, the St Bartholomew's Day massacre was treated as a cause for public celebration – the situation rapidly deteriorated, and co-legate d'Armagnac ordered all the Protestants to retire from the enclave to the territory of Orange. During 1573 attacks by Huguenots continued, unaffected by the settlement which ended the Fourth War elsewhere in France in the summer of that year. The enclave's forces were commanded by Marcantonio Martinengo, an experienced military man (and cousin of Marcantonio Colonna) who had fought at Lepanto; but the troops available to him were few and utterly inadequate, so in July he pleaded with Rome to send more. While he was waiting for these reinforcements the Huguenots struck a significant blow: on the night of 2–3 October 1573 they seized the stronghold of Ménerbes, a small but well-nigh impregnable castle which dominated the little town of that name, just 21 miles south-east of Avignon. This was partly an act of retaliation, since the master-mind of the operation, Scipion de Valavoire, wanted to avenge the death of his brother on St Bartholomew's Day. It was also intended as a bargaining-chip: the man de Valavoire put in charge of the castle, Captain Ferrier, let it be known that Ménerbes would be handed back only when the Protestants' confiscated properties were returned to them. That did not happen, so Ménerbes now became a base for frequent raiding expeditions, not only in the Avignon enclave, but also in parts of the French territory of Provence. By early October the papal secretary of state Cardinal Como was already planning to send reinforcements to Martinengo; on the 5th of that month he wrote to the papal nuncio at the French court, asking him to get a passport or permit for them to cross French territory. Two weeks later, having received the news of the seizure of Ménerbes, he wrote again, saying that the Pope could not wait but was already sending 100 cavalry overland, via Piedmont; 'and 600 infantry will set out from here within three days.' Again he asked for a passport for these soldiers, who would need to march across Provence. They were divided into three companies of 200 men, under the commands of three officers: Pompeo Catilina, Camillo della Penna and Gasparo Bruni.[7]

After some further delays, the secretary of state wrote to Gasparo Bruni (who was probably in or just outside Rome) on 31 October 1573.

He told him that four galleys were heading for the Papal port of Civitavecchia, and that Gasparo and the two other officers should take their men there as quickly as possible. The weather was good for sailing, and if they lost this opportunity they might have to wait a long time, while 'every day the needs of the garrison in Avignon become greater.' Another letter from Cardinal Como four days later said that the galleys had arrived and were waiting; and by 16 November Gasparo Bruni was at Civitavecchia and ready to embark – after a dispute with the quartermaster there, who refused to pay for extra body-armour for his men. It is not clear to what extent he had been personally responsible for recruiting his soldiers. In the old 'condotta' system, a condottiere would receive a monetary advance from the ruler who wished to engage him, and would use that money to go out and hire men for his force. But in recent decades the Papacy had shifted to a more integrated system, in which the captain was not an independent contractor but an employee of the state, earning a salary from it; and the development of a regular militia in the Papal States meant that some of the manpower may have been readily available. At all events, Gasparo certainly received an advance, which was used to give the soldiers a first instalment of their salary; without it, they would never have boarded the ships.[8]

The little fleet of galleys, with its complement of just over 600 soldiers, arrived at Marseille on the morning of 27 November 1573. Immediately, the difficulties began. The governor of the city refused permission to disembark, and told the officers that they must speak first with a representative of the governor of Provence, who was several miles away. The three captains drew lots; it fell to Gasparo Bruni to make the trip, but the permission he requested was not given. Then they sent a message to the governor himself at Aix, only to be told that he would seek the King's instructions before allowing them off their ships. During the following days they approached various other dignitaries, asking just to be let ashore, as men were beginning to die of fever on board; these efforts too were unsuccessful. In fact the papal nuncio had spoken to the King on 26 November, and had received a promise that they would be allowed to disembark and given food. Yet at the same time Charles IX had refused to grant a passport for them to go to Avignon, on the grounds that the arrival of such a large Italian force would inflame the situation and reduce the chances of a settlement with the Huguenots in the south of France. Finally, on 19 December, after more than three weeks confined to their fever-infested galleys, the three captains decided to resolve the matter themselves: after dark they beached the ships, landed the soldiers, and began the trek to Avignon. In the words of a hasty note written by Gasparo Bruni to Cardinal Como in a jerky, angular hand as he left his galley: 'tonight we managed to disembark all the men, and I pray to God that he guide them safely.' On the following evening the papal commissary and military paymaster in Avignon, Antonio Monterentio, was astonished to see Gasparo Bruni and Pompeo Catilina lead 550 exhausted men into the city of Avignon. They had walked more than 35 miles. Roughly 80 men had disappeared en route, including the other officer, Camillo della Penna, who was feared captured by Huguenots; and most of their equipment had been left on the galleys, so that there were only 100 arquebuses between the 550 soldiers. 'It is pitiful to see them, indigent and unarmed', wrote Monterentio. Nevertheless, they had arrived, and Gasparo Bruni's new life in the enclave of Avignon had begun.[9]

Marcantonio Martinengo, the general of the papal forces, distributed these soldiers around the territory as best he could. He kept 100 from della Penna's company in the city of Avignon itself, which also had some Swiss troops and local French levies; Pompeo Catilina's company, of 202 men, was scattered among many towns and villages, with the largest unit in the city of Cavaillon; and Gasparo Bruni's company, with a total of 190, was spread around various settlements in the Comtat Venaissin, with 97 men in Carpentras. Bruni himself resided there, as military governor of the city. His prime responsibility was to keep Carpentras safe from attacks, but he was also on call for military action elsewhere in the Comtat. In mid-March 1574, when the Huguenots seized the little town of Sérignan-du-Comtat, just to the north-east of Orange, Martinengo ordered him to take his men to a position one mile away; when he did so he found that the Protestants had quickly abandoned the fortress at Sérignan, so he left a garrison of 20 men there to hold it. Soon afterwards he was ordered to join a larger force which went to attack the city of Orange itself; a peace agreement was made at the last minute, so the papal forces retired 'with', as Gasparo put it in a letter to Cardinal Como, 'the extreme dissatisfaction of all the soldiers at having lost such a fine opportunity to fight the rebels'. In the following month Gasparo Bruni had to go to the town of Beaumes-de-Venise, just to the north of Carpentras, where intelligence had revealed that some local French soldiers were planning to hand over the castle to the Huguenots, for money; those soldiers fled at his approach, and he left a small group of Italians to guard the place. The French troops were, it seems, doubly unreliable: they had little military experience, and their local ties of kinship and friendship could make it easy for the Protestants to approach and suborn them. In July 1574 the Bishop of Carpentras, Jacopo Sacrati, wrote to Rome saying that he could not trust French soldiers in his city as he could the Italian ones, 'and especially signor cavaliere Bruno, whom I know in this matter to be a man of very good spirit and much courage'.[10]

Although Gasparo Bruni did not have any major military engagements to deal with, his life was far from problem-free. The little force under his command was gradually eroded, not only by mortality but also by desertion; conditions were not attractive, and the cost of living was high. Gasparo's own pay was also unsatisfactory. As he wrote to Cardinal Como, in February 1574: 'It greatly pains me that, having unfortunately lost my property together with my homeland, I now cannot maintain my rank and condition in this governorship on this pitiful amount of pay; so I beg your most illustrious lordship to be so gracious as to help my cause with our lord the Pope, when any opportunity for a commenda arises.' In September he complained that the paymaster, Monterentio, had contested his accounts, refusing to accept his evidence that he had paid out the advance given to him in Rome; Como replied emolliently, assuring him that his honesty was not in question, and that Monterentio was just doing his job. By the spring of 1575 Bruni had another grievance, in which the paymaster was also involved. Pompeo Catilina had volunteered to go to Piedmont and find another 300 infantry; on his return, with the approval of both General Martinengo and Monterentio, Pompeo would be raised to the rank of colonel, with three companies totalling 500 soldiers under his command. Gasparo Bruni (whose company had by now shrunk to only 135 men) complained bitterly about his own relative demotion, saying that it contravened the original orders they were given in Rome; reminding Cardinal Como on 14 April that he had served the Holy See 'for five years continuously', he said that this affair was causing 'the total eclipse of my reputation'. Two weeks later he wrote again, claiming that what lay behind this development was Pompeo's personal friendship with Monterentio, and once more begging the Cardinal to preserve his 'reputation'. By early June he learned that Como had issued an order saying that half the men recruited by Pompeo Catilina should be assigned to him; but nothing had yet been done to implement this. And when the transfer was finally carried out in August 1575, there was another unwelcome surprise: he was expected to reimburse Pompeo for the travel costs of those soldiers from Piedmont to Avignon, to the tune of 200 ducats. Once again

Gasparo sent an embittered complaint to Cardinal Como: he had not been allowed to argue the matter, he had already paid 380 ducats to Rome, for which he had had to borrow money off his friends, and in any case many of the Piedmontese recruits had already run away, taking their weapons and their advance payments with them. (A little over a year later, he had just 50 Piedmontese soldiers left, and Pompeo only 70 – but Pompeo still had the rank of colonel.) The whole affair gives some sense of the awkward nature of this kind of command, at a messy stage of transition between the medieval entrepreneur-condottiere and something more like the modern army officer.[11]

For a few weeks in the winter of 1574–5, Avignon was visited by the new King of France, Henri III. A younger brother of Charles IX, he had been elected King of Poland – with the support of the Ottomans, which was brokered at least in part, as we have seen, by Solomon Ashkenazi – in 1573, and had been crowned there in February 1574.* But less than four months later, when he learned of Charles's death, he had slipped secretly away from the royal castle in Kraków and returned to France, to claim the throne. His visit was aimed at gaining support, and negotiating with Protestant leaders, in nearby Provence and Languedoc. For a short time Avignon was the centre of the French world, with the King being attended by the Queen Mother and many dignitaries, including Cardinal de Bourbon and the military commander Albert de Gondi (the future maréchal de Retz). When he travelled through the enclave in December and January, Henri was attended by three companies of cavalry and 400 arquebusiers; Gasparo Bruni may have commanded some of these. In January 1575 a council of war in Avignon discussed the problem of Ménerbes; de Gondi and others were convinced that it would succumb to an artillery bombardment, arguing that the Protestants holding it could not last more than six weeks. However, they calculated that to besiege it properly would involve building two forts, and deploying 2,500 infantry and 700 cavalry: such manpower was not currently available, and the cost would run to 25,000 ducats per month – a sum which the Papacy was unable or unwilling to pay. So the problem of Ménerbes remained.[12]

Once the King and the other grandees had left, Avignon relapsed into its previous state of tension and fear. In late January 1575 the municipal officials wrote to the Pope, saying that since many 'recatolezati' ('re-Catholicized' people, returning from Protestantism) had entered

---

* On Solomon's role, as described by him, see above, pp. 226–7.

Avignon, they suspected a conspiracy to seize it; they had appointed an officer to check all strangers found in the city's streets and taverns, and were mounting a special guard of the weapons store at night. A few weeks later, the city council resolved to ask the Pope for 200 more Italian troops to protect the city from 'the eminent danger in which it finds itself'. Gregory XIII did agree to send 300 Italians to replace the local soldiers; his fear was not that Protestants would seize the city, but rather that there was a conspiracy to hand it over to the French, as some of the citizens thought their chances of both peace and prosperity would be much greater under French rule.[13]

Avignon did not rise, and the situation in the rest of the enclave remained the same, with sporadic moves in a complex game of military manoeuvres and counter-manoeuvres. In June, for example, Gasparo was sent by the Bishop of Carpentras to the nearby village of Venasque, on intelligence that the Huguenots in Ménerbes were planning to capture it; he went to Martinengo to propose setting an ambush for them, but the general, having at first approved his design, then countermanded it. (As Gasparo wearily wrote to Cardinal Como: 'thus my plan was abandoned, to the great irritation of all of us. My superiors can do whatever they like, and I just have to content myself with whatever pleases them.') At the end of 1575 a six months' truce was agreed in Paris; yet although the enclave of Avignon was included in it, the fighting there continued. When that rather notional truce lapsed in the summer of 1576, some more solid efforts were made to reach a settlement. Gregory XIII issued a papal bull granting the restitution of the Protestants' estates, on condition that they be administered by Catholic procurators, and in September a peace agreement was actually signed in Avignon. Nevertheless several of the local Huguenot commanders simply refused to recognize it, and would not give up their strongholds; one went on the offensive, capturing a military position near Saint-Léger, but was quickly driven out of it by a force of 400 men under Gasparo's command. An anonymous informant in Avignon, writing to Cardinal Como in December 1576, said that the situation was now as bad as it had ever been; and two months later it got significantly worse, when the local French officer in command of the castle of Entrechaux (nineteen miles north-east of Carpentras) betrayed it to the Protestants. General Martinengo immediately began to besiege the castle, taking troops from Carpentras, but Huguenot forces broke through to bring it food and ammunition, so the siege was called off at the end of March 1577. It was on the 28th of that month that Gasparo Bruni penned the most negative and depressed of all his letters to Cardinal Como. 'I know', he wrote, 'that on many occasions that have arisen I have not been able to do anything to serve our lord the Pope, or to benefit this poor country, still less to gain any honour – rather, to lose it heavily.' So he humbly begged his patron: 'if I am capable of serving you in some other place, please remove me from this one.'[14]

Something was about to change, however. In the spring of 1577 the authorities in Avignon, led by d'Armagnac, finally decided to mount a full-scale siege of the castle of Ménerbes, and obtained the agreement of both the Pope and the King of France. Henri III promised to send soldiers and artillery from Provence. Gregory XIII appointed a well-known military expert, Vincenzo Matteucci, to command the enclave's forces while Martinengo went to Rome on a basis which, though temporary at first, proved permanent. Matteucci had had a long career serving Venice, France, the Papacy and, most recently, Dubrovnik, where he had been general of the minuscule Ragusan army. At almost the same time Gregory sent a highly respected military organizer, Domenico Grimaldi, to be the Rector of the Comtat Venaissin (the territory that contained Ménerbes). A churchman from a famous Genoese family, he had served as papal commissary during the naval campaigns of 1571 and 1572. At the Battle of Lepanto this reverend warrior had put on a cuirass and waded into the thick of the fighting, wielding a great sword; in the aftermath of the battle he had ended up in the water clutching a captive, and would have drowned if that man had not been a strong swimmer. Although he was not on the papal flagship, Grimaldi's official duties meant that he must have had many dealings with Gasparo Bruni. So, when he reached Avignon on 27 April 1577 and then went straight to Carpentras the next day, there would have been a meeting of old acquaintances. Matteucci arrived a little later, in mid-May. After months of preparations, the promised troops marched from Provence to the territory of Avignon in August, and combined with the enclave's own forces outside Ménerbes on 1 September. In total they had 12,000 infantry, 1,200 cavalry and 22 artillery pieces; their overall commander was the Grand Prior of France, Henri de Valois, a half-brother of the King. Believing that the Huguenot defenders of the fortress had no artillery, de Valois and his fellow commanders assumed that Ménerbes would quickly fall. That assumption would prove to be a very costly mistake.[15]

On 1 August 1577, while general preparations for the siege were under way but before the arrival of the troops from Provence, Gasparo

Bruni wrote a letter to Cardinal Como. He did so from Entrechaux; the Protestants had vacated that position in June, on payment of a large sweetener, and he had been put in command of the new garrison there.

> Your lordship knows very well that I was driven out of my homeland by the Ottomans, those enemies of the true Christian faith for which many of my ancestors at various times have shed their blood; and since there remain some of my nephews and other miserable relics of my family, all of them scattered, who live in the same [Christian] spirit, among whom there is my only son, who has been in the Collegio Germanico for six years, and since I wish to gather them together and put my affairs in some order (which they very much need), I humbly beg your most illustrious lordship to obtain permission from our lord [the Pope] that, once the grape harvest and the grain harvest are finished, I may come [to Rome], stay and return, all within two months. I would leave my company under my lieutenant, who is a brave, diligent and loyal person, and come to Rome, to put my affairs in order, as they are in a very poor state.

The 'scattered' nephews and other 'relics' are hard to identify, though they probably included Matteo Bruni, the surviving son of Gasparo's brother Serafino, who is known to have spent some time in Rome; otherwise, most of his Bruti nephews were already gathered in Koper by this stage. In the same letter, Gasparo also reported that in the recent attack which had driven the Huguenots out of the fortress of Les Pilles 'a brave young man, a relative of mine', having climbed the walls, had received an arquebus shot in the chest and had died a week later. The identity of this person is impossible to establish. The forces in Avignon did include a young infantry captain from Koper, Paolo Emilio Carerio; he was perhaps a younger brother of Demostene Carerio, who had married Gasparo's niece Ilarieta Bruti. But although Paolo Emilio did die while serving in the Avignon enclave, he did not do so in 1577: he would be commanding a company there eleven years later.[16]

This was not the first request for leave that Gasparo had made. Two years earlier he had written that he wanted, once the harvest was in, to 'come and arrange some little affairs of mine in Rome', also for a maximum period of two months' absence. It is not clear why he did not go then; but his reason for wanting to visit Rome now may have been connected with the fact that his son, Antonio, was just about to leave the Jesuit seminary (incorrectly described by Gasparo as the Collegio Germanico) where he had been studying. Cardinal Como's reply was that the Pope did not want Gasparo to abandon the enclave 'now that your work is perhaps more useful and more necessary than ever', but that on reflection he had agreed to permit two months of leave, between mid-October and Christmas. However, by the time Gasparo received that reply he was fully engaged as one of the infantry officers at the siege of Ménerbes. Writing back to Como from the besiegers' camp on 13 October, he thanked him for the decision, but explained that 'even though I have a pressing need to come away, I wish to see this engagement at Ménerbes to the end, now that it has started.' And then he added, cautiously but ominously: 'I do not want to say anything about the method adopted and the progress achieved in the siege up until now, except that I pray to God that it turns out well in the end.'[17]

Six weeks of siege warfare had already passed, and things had not gone well. The artillery bombardment had been intensive, reaching almost 1,000 shots in one day. But although the walls were holed in several places, the defenders included many skilled arquebusiers, who drove off the besiegers with heavy losses. In the words of one early historian: 'when the first breaches were made, assaults took place with the loss of the best soldiers, especially from the Italian companies; those in the castle defended themselves with such determination that when one fell, another took his place, and men wounded by splinters of masonry threw back the stones stained with their own blood.' Those arquebusiers were ever-vigilant: one night they managed to shoot Pompeo Catilina in the shoulder as he was taking a group of men to poison a well. The Huguenot commander, Captain Ferrier, resisted all calls to surrender until late September, when the use of red-hot cannon-balls caused some serious fires inside the castle. On the 23rd of that month he did agree to relinquish Ménerbes; the women and children were allowed to leave immediately, and the formal handover was fixed for the 27th. Merchants from Avignon quickly flocked to the castle to buy up all the valuables which the Protestant raiding parties had looted over the years. But some of the Huguenot soldiers did not want to surrender; hearing of this, a Protestant military leader from the Dauphiné, Jacques Pape, lord of Saint-Auban, slipped into the castle at night, arrested Ferrier, and seized the merchants (and some members of the besieging force) who were within the castle walls. The artillery bombardment was resumed on 28 September. On the following day a large assault was made on a fortified house, known as 'le Castellet', which overlooked the castle; if the besiegers held it, they would be able to train their fire on the defenders when they went to fetch water. This attack, led by two Capuchins bearing crucifixes, was repulsed with heavy losses. Two more attempts to seize le Castellet in October failed, with the loss of 300 men each time; on the fourth occasion it was taken, but the soldiers sent to occupy it were driven out on the following night. When Henri de Valois tried a general assault on the castle a few days later, that too failed.[18]

During October, news arrived of a peace treaty recently signed by King Henri III of France and the King of Navarre. As leader of the Huguenots throughout France, the King of Navarre sent a message to the defenders of Ménerbes, telling them to yield, but Jacques Pape ignored it. On 3 November 1577 Henri de Valois published the peace treaty and, using it as a pretext, withdrew all French forces on the next day, leaving only four artillery pieces. He had lost 1,500 men, to absolutely no effect. Only the papal troops now remained; so Matteucci and the military churchman Domenico Grimaldi (who, as Rector of the Comtat Venaissin, was the higher authority) were left in charge. Knowing that this engagement had become a matter of international prestige for the Papacy, Grimaldi was determined to do the job properly. His first task was to stop the resupplying of the defenders: it seemed scandalous that, during the siege, parties of Huguenots had been passing in and out of the castle at night. By mid-December Grimaldi had constructed four forts around Ménerbes; several others were built in the following months, and by early May 1578 he had created a large trench connecting all the forts, and protecting passage between them from enemy fire. (The protection was not total, however: while inspecting the trench, Grimaldi himself was shot in the mouth by an arquebusier. Luckily for him the bullet passed through one cheek and out of the other, and he made a rapid recovery.)[19]

It was during this period that Gasparo Bruni finally made his long-delayed visit to Italy. He left in the last days of November 1577, bringing letters from General Matteucci and the paymaster, Monterentio, and reached Rome in the second half of December, where he met Cardinal Como and had an audience with the Pope, briefing him on the situation. He returned to the enclave of Avignon, but by late February was planning to go to Rome again; that trip was deferred, since his services were needed at Ménerbes. However, in April Cardinal Como wrote urging him to come back, as the papal authorities were raising new troops and he wished to put some of them under Gasparo's command. Seeing the opportunity, at long last, to improve his own rank and standing, Gasparo travelled to Rome as quickly as he could. He spent some time there in May, and went back bearing instructions to Matteucci to put one or two of the new companies under him, and to raise him to the rank of

colonel. Having nursed his grievance about the matter of his 'reputation' for more than three years, Gasparo must have felt satisfied at last;
and, for good measure, he also brought an order to Monterentio to pay
him the sum of 45 scudi (37½ ducats), which the paymaster had quib-
bled over on his first arrival. But nothing went smoothly for Gasparo
Bruni. He was delayed on his return journey by a 'misfortune', arriving
in Avignon only in early July; Monterentio still refused to make the payment; and at the end of the month Gasparo had to inform Cardinal
Como that the order to put other companies under his command had
not been carried out, because Matteucci was seriously ill. He asked
Como to send another order, addressed to Grimaldi and d'Armagnac;
meanwhile he was on his way back to the siege of Ménerbes, where he
had been asked to take command of one of the new forts. Vincenzo
Matteucci died in Avignon just two days later.[20]

The siege continued for several months, and in October it was
strengthened by the arrival of a new commander, Montacuto Montacuti, with 500 fresh Italian soldiers. Yet it was diplomacy, not war, that
ended it. Under a peace agreement, signed by Jacques Pape in early
November and ratified by King Henri III later that month, a general
amnesty was declared, the expelled Protestants were allowed to come
back to the Comtat Venaissin, and the confiscated properties were to be
returned. Pape marched his men out of Ménerbes on 10 December
1578; as d'Armagnac reported a week later, many of those who watched
them leave were surprised that 132 well-armed soldiers, who apparently had supplies for another nine or ten months, had abandoned such
an impregnable fortress. Still, the siege was over; the forts were disman-
tled, the trench was filled in, Montacuti returned to Italy (to be replaced
by a Bolognese commander, Pirro Malvezzi, who had served on the
papal flagship during the Lepanto campaign), and Domenico Grimaldi
was given a gold chain by the grateful representatives of the Comtat
Venaissin. A few months later, when d'Armagnac was sent by the King
of France to quell disorders in Provence, Grimaldi was made acting co-
legate by the Pope; very unusually, he thus exercised governmental
power over both parts of the Avignon enclave.[21]

The people he governed must by now have been yearning for a period
of peace and prosperity. Their prayers were not to be granted. Violence
continued, with sporadic Huguenot raids from Orange, and a miserable
harvest pushed up the price of food. In January 1580 the captains of all
the Italian infantry companies sent a protest letter to Rome saying that,
given the cost of foodstuffs and other necessities, their soldiers could

not live on the pay they received. Two months later Grimaldi himself was almost murdered by a gang of armed men, the retainers of a local nobleman whom he had offended. He was travelling on horseback with his brother and a few companions when they were attacked; he managed to fight off the assailants with his sword, but not before they had killed his brother. Shaken by this experience, Grimaldi travelled to Rome in May 1580 to offer his resignation. But the Pope asked him to return, and sent with him another military commander, Biagio Capizucchi, to assist Malvezzi. (Biagio was a first cousin of the Cencio Capizucchi whom Gasparo Bruni had replaced as captain of the papal flagship; Biagio, Cencio and Biagio's brother Camillo all served as infantry officers on that ship at Lepanto.) Before long, Grimaldi probably wished that he had refused to come back. During his absence Pirro Malvezzi had had to deal with a threatened uprising in Avignon, which involved both a secret plot to hand the city over to the Protestant King of Navarre, and much popular hostility towards the Italian soldiers stationed there. Then, in September 1580, plague came to the enclave; it was the worst outbreak in living memory, and would last just under a year. Within the first two months the mortality rate in the city of Avignon had risen to 100 per day. A plague journal, compiled from original reports, makes horrifying reading; the authorities had to harden their hearts to carry out whatever measures seemed necessary to control the spread of the disease. To pick just one example: when a woman was found to have concealed the death of her child for three days, she was stripped, whipped, and then made to walk through the city, still naked, carrying her child's body to the burial ground. By July 1581 the city's representatives were reporting to Rome that half its population had died, and that there were 1,500 destitute people who had to be fed at public expense, though the city had completely run out of money.[22]

A further misfortune struck the administration of the enclave in January 1582, when the paymaster, Antonio Monterentio, killed himself: having spent days in his room writing letters, he locked the door, drank poison, lay on his bed and fired an arquebus into his stomach. A rambling suicide note, addressed to Cardinal Como, accused Pirro Malvezzi of having ruined him by making unauthorized spending, but the more likely explanation was that Monterentio had been guilty of embezzlements that he could no longer conceal. Writing to Como immediately after this event, Gasparo Bruni noted that he had not received his pay from Monterentio for two months running. 'I was sorry to hear of the miserable story of Monterentio, and I pray God to have mercy on his soul', he commented; but the man had been a thorn in Gasparo's side, and his real feelings may have been altogether less generous.[23]

Gasparo's own life had not seen any great improvement since the ending of the siege. In the summer of 1579 he was complaining again about his pay, pointing out that other captains were receiving the higher rate of 35 ducats a month because they had more men; this was unfair because his company had served non-stop at Ménerbes, 'where many of my soldiers died, some in the fighting and some of disease'. He begged Como to do something about this 'insult' to his honour. (The accounts show that when he made that complaint he had only 105 men under his command; the figure rose to 152 in the following spring, before jumping to nearly 200 at the end of 1582.) For much of this period Gasparo was stationed in Valréas, a small town in the far north of the Comtat which had been particularly exposed to Huguenot attacks; in early 1581 he referred to it as 'this district surrounded by enemies'. Reporting on an incident there in May 1582, the new papal general, Giovanni Vincenzo Vitelli, described it as a town of 700 households, garrisoned by 70 soldiers, which was 'full of extremely ill-natured people'. The incident had begun with a quarrel between some of the Italian soldiers, in which three were killed; the four malefactors fled to the Franciscan friary, and when Gasparo Bruni followed them there with a few of his men they retreated to the bell-tower. As they refused to give themselves up, Gasparo prepared to take them by force – whereupon they used the bell to ring the alarm. 'At the sound of it, all the men of the town came out, some with weapons, some without; the cavaliere Bruni had to talk to them with fine words, and he did it so well that he got them to go home, as he is much loved in that place. Otherwise they could easily have cut to pieces most, perhaps all, of the garrison.' After this, Gasparo again called on the four soldiers to surrender; again they rang the bell, and the whole episode was repeated. The situation was saved only 'with the greatest difficulty, by the patience and prudence of the cavaliere Bruni'; he kept them surrounded in the bell-tower and despatched a messenger to the general, who sent the captain of his guard there the next day.[24]

In the spring of 1583 Gasparo Bruni was ordered to take his men to Ménerbes; that summer there were rumours of a possible uprising, and he posted extra sentries at the castle walls. In October severe tensions developed in Avignon, after one of the local guards was badly beaten by an Italian soldier, so Gasparo was told to bring his company to the Avignon garrison. He was probably being sincere, not ironic, when he wrote about this move to Cardinal Como: 'I'd like to hope that I am destined always to go wherever disorders spring up, as I was sent to Valréas, and recently to Ménerbes.' But during the spring of 1584 there was a significant change in Gasparo's circumstances. In April he wrote to Como from Avignon, thanking him for securing a continuing subsidy for the education of his son, Antonio. Until then, that education had taken place in Italy; but now, he explained, 'he has come here to see me, and I do not want him to go back just now to Italy, but rather to stay with me in this city, for the opportunity he will have to study, and, if opportunity arise, to serve the Holy Apostolic See.' Antonio Bruni enrolled at the University of Avignon, and Gasparo now had a strong reason for wanting to remain in that city himself; this was his first chance in very many years to spend a prolonged period in the company of his own son. In July 1584 he wrote anxiously to Cardinal Como, saying that the authorities wanted to move him back into the countryside to make way for Pompeo Catilina, even though Catilina had enjoyed six years in the comfort of Avignon already. Two months later he pleaded that he should not be sent back to Ménerbes but rather allowed to stay in Avignon, 'if not for a year, then at least for this winter, so that no one should get the idea that I have been driven out of this city because of some fault of mine'. For once, fate smiled on Gasparo Bruni. The commander of the papal forces in the enclave, Baldassare Boschetti, fell ill and died; confirmation of the order to move could not be obtained, and so he was able to dig in his heels, until in late November the Pope nominated Boschetti's successor – Domenico Grimaldi. Favoured, it seems, by his former comrade-in-arms at Lepanto, Bruni remained in Avignon throughout the winter.[25]

Some important changes took place in 1585. In April Pope Gregory XIII died; he was succeeded by one of his personal enemies, Cardinal Montalto, who took the name of Sixtus V. Gasparo's employer and patron, Cardinal Como, who, as a loyal supporter of Gregory, had often clashed with Montalto, now resigned from the papal secretariat. Writing to Como's successor, Cardinal Rusticucci, in May, Domenico Grimaldi explained that Bruni and Catilina had 200 men each in Avignon; he commended them and the third infantry captain, Ludovico Manari, as 'good servants of the Pope'. Three months later Grimaldi wrote that he had heard reports from Rome that the Pope was sending a new military commander, Captain Odoardo, with orders to replace the three captains; he said that this news was having an unsettling effect, and that many of the soldiers might leave if their officers were dismissed. In a succession of further letters he begged Rusticucci to retain the services of those three captains. What exactly Odoardo decreed when he finally arrived in November is not known. At some point during the next six months Gasparo went to Rome; he returned to Avignon at the beginning of May 1586 bearing a letter from Rusticucci to Grimaldi. That is the last trace of his presence in the city. Later evidence makes clear that while the other two company commanders, Catilina and Manari, kept their positions, Gasparo Bruni's company was transferred to his relative Paolo Emilio Carerio, who was commanding it by September 1586, and may have been doing so for several months before then. It is hard to believe that Gasparo's service was thought less valuable than that of his two fellow officers; in 1587 Domenico Grimaldi would wistfully remark that 'I never felt so reassured in this administration as I did during the time when there were those three old and experienced captains, Cavaliere Bruno, Colonel Ludovico Manari and Colonel Pompeo Catilina.' Most likely it was Gasparo himself who decided, in late 1585 or early 1586, that it was time to go. He may well have been in his mid-sixties. Antonio, his son, had just completed his studies at the university, and was returning to Koper; probably Gasparo went with him. It is to Antonio Bruni, the closest of all Gasparo's surviving relatives, that we must now turn.[26]

16

Antonio Bruni and the Jesuits

Antonio Bruni first emerges in the records in May 1572, when he joined a famous Jesuit school in Rome. The usual age of entry was fourteen, though arrival at thirteen or even twelve was possible; so he was born most probably in 1557–8, or perhaps one or two years later. Nothing can be known about his mother, except – given the absolute prohibition on married men joining the Knights of Malta – that she was not Gasparo Bruni's wife. And since there is no definite information about Gasparo's activities in the period before he became a Knight in 1567, it is difficult to speculate about Antonio's early upbringing, beyond the assumption that he probably spent some of his childhood in Ulcinj. Gasparo may have been a distant father, away on commercial or other business before 1567 and in the Pope's employ thereafter; but he must surely have become a more caring one after 1571, when Antonio would have been, for him, the most precious remnant of his otherwise devastated family.[1]

Gasparo Bruni had received at least a basic education. His letters, though peppered with unconventional spellings, are fluently written, managing a good command of courtly deference. Evidently he had the schooling that was sufficient for a man of action such as himself. For his son, however, he aimed much higher, sending him to an institution which offered certainly the best education in Rome, and possibly the best in Italy. Not only was it academically excellent; it also had an international intake including many youths of high social rank, a fact which gave extra prestige to its alumni. Gasparo seems to have been particularly touchy about his own status and reputation; as a member of the 'nobility' of a small, rather backwaterish society (which had itself been swept away), he may have been particularly keen that his son should be able to hold his own with the nobles of Italy and elsewhere. But perhaps the choice of this school depended more, in practical terms, on the nature of Gasparo's employment in the early 1570s. Antonio's path into it may have been smoothed by a letter of recommendation from the Pope, and it may also be significant that, as we shall see, there was a special connection between the Jesuits' educational activities in Rome and Marcantonio Colonna.

At all events, there is a satisfying complementarity about this man of the sword sending his son to an élite Jesuit school. For the Counter-Reformation, in its broadest sense, looked both outwards and inwards, using both physical force and mental persuasion. Outside Western Europe, it involved the fight against infidels (as practised by Gasparo in 1570–2), the projection of a new would-be Catholic geopolitical order beyond the existing Catholic realms, and the sending of missionaries to distant parts of the world. Inside Western Europe, it comprised the fight against Protestantism, both by the sword (as conducted by Gasparo after 1573) and also by the pen, in the form of 'controversial theology' – i.e. theology controverting the heretics. And within the Catholic realms, it also included – most fundamentally of all – a major programme of internal evangelization, deepening and strengthening the practice of the Catholic faith among the believers, and infusing Catholic values, and a positively Catholic agenda, into society and politics. For this last purpose, the active involvement of the Church in education was essential. What was needed was not just the traditional practice of teaching literacy to the general population and giving a basic training to the clergy, but rather a new kind of pedagogy, which attracted pupils because it represented the highest standards of humanist culture, and, having attracted them, instilled the right religious values into their hearts and minds. That was what the Society of Jesus (generally known as the Jesuits) achieved. Together with the fact that it also supplied many of the most active missionaries and controversial theologians, this helps to explain why the Jesuits more than any other order came to represent the spirit of the Counter-Reformation.

From the moment of their official foundation in 1540, the Jesuits had included education among their leading aims. In 1548 they set up a college in Messina, which rapidly acquired a high reputation; 1551 saw the foundation of the Collegio Romano, and in the following year the Collegio Germanico opened, also in Rome. A Jesuit 'college' could operate either as a school or as a school combined with a university. Most, like the one in Messina, gave an enhanced secondary education, but the Collegio Romano did include university-level teaching, with higher courses in theology (where much 'controversial theology' would be hammered out, by prominent thinkers such as Roberto Bellarmino, before the end of the century), and its reputation as a centre of learning quickly outstripped that of the University of Rome. Altogether, the success of these colleges was phenomenal – as was that of the order itself. When Ignatius Loyola, the founder of the Jesuits, died in 1556, there were eighteen colleges in Italy; by 1600 there were 49. Elsewhere 187 such colleges had been created, and the number of Jesuits overall had risen from 938 to 8,272. There were many features of the Jesuit system of education that set it apart from traditional pedagogy in Italy; some had in fact been borrowed from the University of Paris (where Loyola and other founding fathers of the order had studied), but they were skilfully adapted and extended in Jesuit hands. They included careful division of the pupils into classes, subdivided by level of ability; seating according to merit; promotion only through written and oral exams; firm discipline; a detailed prescriptive curriculum, which filled each day of study with a variety of work; an emphasis on fluency in spoken Latin; frequent exercises, declamations, and public displays of literary performances, such as Latin verse compositions and plays; encouraging emulation between individuals or groups of pupils; frequent prize-giving; and, as time went by, an increasing emphasis on teaching manners, civility and courtly behaviour.[2]

Generally, these colleges offered an education to youths who would go on to have lay careers. But they were also particularly involved in the preparation of students for the priesthood – that is, priesthood in general, not limited to membership of the Society of Jesus. The Collegio Germanico in Rome was created to train boys from the territories of the Holy Roman Empire who intended to become priests; typically, six or seven would enter each year. In the summer of 1563 the Council of Trent decreed that every diocese should set up a 'seminary' – a word borrowed from gardening, meaning a nursery for seedlings – to prepare boys aged twelve or above for divine ministry. In direct response to this decree, and with the encouragement of Carlo Borromeo and the Pope (who promised to take care of its finances), the Jesuits now set up a Seminario Romano, which opened in 1565. The students here were divided into two categories: scholarship boys, who received free education, and fee-paying boarders. The former were committed to entering the priesthood; the latter were, in the early years, also expected to follow that path, although in practice there was nothing to stop them leaving and pursuing a lay career thereafter. At the Collegio Germanico a similar division operated, but it developed in a different way. Diego Laynez,

who took over the leadership of the Jesuits after Loyola's death, encouraged rich and prominent families to send their sons as fee-paying pupils
there: he saw this as a way of raising the funds needed to subsidize the
education of the scholarship boys, and realized that it would also enable
the Jesuits to form long-term connections with influential nobles. These
fee-payers were not expected to have any priestly vocation, and they
could be drawn from any part of Europe, not just the Holy Roman
Empire. Many cardinals sent their nephews there, and the roll-call of
names includes some of the most famous families in Italy: Orsini, Doria,
Gonzaga, Carafa and others. The Collegio Germanico was transformed
by this social success; while it continued with its annual intake of six
or seven mostly poor German-speaking scholarship boys (who were
looked upon with great condescension by the noble pupils), fee-payers
entered at the rate of 80 or 100 every year. Marcantonio Colonna,
Rome's leading nobleman, took a special interest in this college, and in
late 1570 it moved into part of the Palazzo Colonna. When he was
given his 'triumph' in Rome after Lepanto, the pupils covered the walls
with celebratory emblems, poems and mottoes.[3]

However, in the early 1570s it was decided that the noble pupils at
the Collegio Germanico should be transferred to the Seminario Romano
instead. There were two reasons for this. One was that, in the words of
an early account, 'it had been very well observed and experienced for a
long time that uniting the German nation with the Italian one, by making them live together, did not produce a good alloy': the German
scholarship boys were, it was said, corrupted by the Italians (who dominated the fee-paying intake), and became much less easy to govern.
Accordingly, a large number of the noble students at the college were
moved in late 1571 and during 1572 – against the protests of their
parents – to the seminary, and new fee-paying applicants to the former
were automatically diverted to the latter. The other reason was a growing concern about the strength of Protestantism in the German lands. In
1573 it was decided that a much more intensive programme of priestly
training was needed at the Collegio Germanico, involving at least 100
German-speaking scholarship boys. (This was part of a broader papal
strategy of producing priests for particular countries or areas: between
1577 and 1584 Rome would acquire a Greek college, an English, a
Hungarian, and one for Christian Arabs.) Special funding was pledged,
so the fee-payers were no longer needed to balance the books; and a
new building was also found for the college. On 17 October 1573, the
last day of the Collegio Germanico in Colonna's palazzo, a grand

ceremony took place. The students of the Seminario processed to it, and joined those of the Collegio for Mass and a banquet; there were songs and literary performances all afternoon and evening, including a setting of Psalm 136, 'By the rivers of Babylon', by the choirmaster of the college, the great Spanish composer Tomás Luis de Victoria; evening prayers were said, and then the exodus of the final contingent of noble fee-payers began. The presence in the Seminario Romano of so many boys and young men from influential families would transform that institution, from a small theological seminary which had got off to a somewhat shaky start, into a near-replica of the highly successful German college.[4]

It seems very likely that Antonio Bruni was accepted at the Collegio Germanico, but then diverted – before he could actually take up a place at that institution – to the Seminario Romano. This would explain two things: the fact that his father described him, quite wrongly, as a student at the college, and the fact that he evaded the otherwise strict rule of the seminary that its pupils must be of legitimate birth (a rule which did not exist at the college). He entered the Seminario on 12 May 1572. Others who joined that year included two members of the Carafa family, and a Scot, William Chisholm, a grandson of King James IV, who would later succeed his uncle as Bishop of Vaison in the Avignon enclave. The following year's intake would contain three members of the Cenci family (Roman nobles, whose kinswoman Beatrice would be at the centre of a lurid murder trial in the 1590s), and one Piccolomini (a Sienese dynasty famous for its military commanders). And among those who had been moved from the college to the seminary before Antonio's arrival was Alexander Seton, who would later become Lord Chancellor of Scotland and first Earl of Dunfermline. Other pupils in this period came from Spain, France, Germany, Poland, Dubrovnik, Cyprus and Crete, but the great majority were from mainland Italy. By the time all the Collegio Germanico fee-payers had transferred to the seminary in 1573, there were roughly 120 fee-paying boarders, and half that number of scholarship boys committed to the priesthood. The fee-payers were divided into 'chambers' ('camerate'), with between ten and fifteen boys to a chamber; these were not just dormitories, but rooms where they also washed, had breakfast, studied, played (at least, when the weather was bad) and prayed. Each chamber also had a prefect, usually a young priest in his twenties, who would lead prayers on waking and going to bed, and enforce discipline; no student was allowed to enter another chamber without its prefect's permission. The chambers were named after saints, and each celebrated its own saint's day with special festivities, for which its members composed odes and orations.[5]

A document of the late sixteenth century lists the things that boys needed to bring with them to the seminary. It will have a familiar ring to those who have attended boarding schools in more recent years: shirts, towels, shoes, handkerchiefs, two sheets (but also a mattress), ink, pens, paper (and a wax tablet, on which it was possible to write, erase and rewrite repeatedly) – plus a chest to contain all these things, which was placed at the foot of the pupil's bed. The uniform, clerical in style, was supplied by the seminary, which employed its own full-time tailor: while the scholarship boys wore purple, the colour of the papal household, the fee-payers were dressed in black cloth – which, however, was of better quality than the purple variety, and could be discreetly enhanced with ruffs and lace. The diet, though perhaps repetitive, was that of the upper classes. Each boy had one pound of meat per day, preceded by soup and followed by fruit or cheese; the bread was of the finest kind, as supplied to cardinals and prelates, and good-quality wine was also served. During lunch and dinner there were readings from the Bible, sermons and lives of saints; after each of these meals there was an hour's rest, during which the students were required to talk among themselves 'about those things that conduce to virtuous recreation'. One report complained that on rainy days, or very hot days in summer, they would sit inside either listening to 'seditious discourses' or having 'excessive and ear-splitting fun' – or, even worse, gambling for large sums of money. It seems that in this seminary there was some inevitable tension between the quasi-monastic form and the aristocratic content. But while ordinary discipline was strictly enforced, there was another, more important way of modifying behaviour: the intense religiosity with which life in the seminary was infused. Students attended Mass each day, and confessed and took communion once a month. They recited the Hours of the Virgin every day, and the seven penitential psalms every Friday and Sunday. Most influential of all were the two Marian 'congregations', bodies similar to lay confraternities, to which all students belonged: they inspired the boys to extra feats of praying and piety, with huge efforts devoted to preparing for the four great Marian feasts (Annunciation, Visitation, Nativity and Circumcision). This was a phenomenon which had begun at the Collegio Romano in 1563; by 1576 these congregations had spread through almost all Jesuit schools, acquiring at least 30,000 members.[6]

Antonio Bruni stayed at the Seminario for just over five years, so it seems likely that he underwent the basic school curriculum, which began with grammar and went on to 'humanities', i.e. the study of classical literature, and rhetoric. The higher, university-level courses were in philosophy and theology, and those were mostly taken by students preparing for the priesthood. All the lessons took place in the Collegio Romano, but the seminary had its own 'study prefects', who supervised the boys' work, and 'repetitori', who made them repeat what they had learned. During the standard five-year course the main emphasis was on acquiring skill in writing persuasive and elegant Latin: as an official visitation summed up in 1576, 'they are exercised in composing Latin orations, and Latin and Greek verses.' The ability to present oneself to, and move, an audience was also enhanced by taking part in theatrical performances. At Jesuit schools this was something of a speciality, into which the staff would enter with enthusiasm. (Too much enthusiasm, in some people's eyes: critical comments in a visitation report on the Seminario in 1578 led to an internal decree that in future 'priests shall not take part in comedies or tragedies, at least, not dressed as soldiers or women, or other characters unbecoming to their status.') In 1574 the seminary put on a religious tragedy by Father Stefano Tucci, 'Christus iudex' ('Christ the Judge'); it had first been presented in Messina five years earlier, and would go on to have an international success, being translated into Italian and Polish. The performance at the Seminario Romano was treated as an important social occasion, with cardinals and prelates, and Marcantonio Colonna, among the audience; but whether Colonna took any special notice of the son of his former galley captain is, unfortunately, not known. Music was also studied seriously at the Seminario: there were four cantors and a 'maestro di capella' or precentor, who, until shortly before Antonio Bruni's arrival, had been the composer Giovanni Pierluigi da Palestrina. However, the musical training was very much focused on the needs of those preparing for the priesthood, and may have had little impact on the studies of the fee-paying pupils.[7]

This was a very closed community. The boys were forbidden to go out into the streets of Rome, or to take any meals outside the seminary, except, 'extremely rarely', with relatives. Antonio, who did not have a parental home to go to, may have lived in the Seminario full-time – unless his cousin Matteo Bruni, if he was working at the papal court during this period, had a room where he could stay during the vacations. Each fee-paying boarder had a 'procurator' in Rome, a sort of guardian who took legal responsibility for him and was meant to visit him once a week. It is not known who performed this task; but if it was not Matteo, it might possibly have been Aurelio Ingegneri, the papal secretary to whom Gasparo would write in 1583, as we shall see, about the Pope's funding of Antonio's university education. Possibly Antonio was also receiving some kind of papal scholarship while he was at the Seminario. If so, it seems that the authorities were not efficient at processing it, since in December 1575 a list of students whose payments were in arrears included 'Antonio Bruno', owing 18 scudi (15 ducats), or three months' fees. He was in good company, though, as the other late payers included an Orsini, a Cenci and a Carafa. As one official memorandum noted during that period – a time of severe financial strain for the seminary – it was extremely hard to get the fee-payers to hand over the money they owed. The visitation report of 1576 also observed that a difficulty arose with the foreign fee-payers when they fell ill: often they would get the seminary to buy expensive medicines, for which they never paid. In the eyes of some Jesuits, the problems involved in having these fee-paying boys outweighed the benefits. In 1580 one member of the seminary's staff wrote to the General of the order, saying that the practice made enemies among those families whose boys were not accepted, and that it also damaged the order's reputation because many people accused the Jesuits of being motivated primarily by money-making. Worse than that, the practice had gradually introduced 'a certain secular, political spirit, of liberty and licentiousness, which is in the end contrary to religious discipline and observance'. But there were also memorandums arguing the opposite case. One of them listed nine-teen reasons in favour of maintaining the practice, including 'the opportunity to unite such a great variety of nations in one discipline'. And that was not a small point, in the eyes of Jesuits – an international order devoted to re-energizing the faith and practice of the entire Catholic world.[8]

Antonio Bruni left the Seminario Romano on 28 August 1577. It was at the beginning of that month that Gasparo wrote to Cardinal Como asking for permission to visit Rome in order to put his family affairs in order; but, as we have seen, he did not make the journey until several months later, arriving in the second half of December.* Whether Antonio was still in Rome is not known. The next mention of him comes in January 1581, when Gasparo wrote to Como: 'I have been informed that my son Antonio has withdrawn to Venice because of some fight

* Above, pp. 291–3.

that happened in Perugia; and because I wish to avoid all the troubles that might follow from it, I would like him to continue with his learning, and would like him to study at Padua. But I cannot do so without the assistance which our lord [the Pope] so kindly agreed to give him.' So he asked that the Pope be requested to continue the subsidy at the University of Padua, 'so that what he has learned up until now will not be lost'. The Cardinal's reply mentioned that the payments, which were of 10 scudi (8.3 ducats) per month, had begun in January 1580, so probably that was the date of Antonio's arrival at the University of Perugia.[9]

Given the fact that he acquired a doctorate in law just five years later, it seems most likely that Antonio's studies in Perugia were in that subject, probably after the speedy acquisition of a basic arts degree; the high quality of his Jesuit education would have put him well ahead of most arts undergraduates. Law was certainly one of the strengths of that university. The law faculty in Perugia had a special method of teaching: each lecture would end with a summary of the next lecture and a reading-list for it, so that students were already fully engaged with the topic when they heard it discussed. There were four distinguished law professors there, the most famous of whom, Rinaldo Ridolfi, was a humanist scholar steeped in literary studies; the poet Torquato Tasso wrote a sonnet in his honour, and Ridolfi's most eminent pupil, the jurist Alberico Gentili (later Professor of Civil Law in Oxford), would praise both 'his wonderful method of teaching' and 'the purity of his [Latin] speech, which almost all Italians lack'. As for the reason for Antonio's departure from Perugia: having written that it was because of 'some fight' in 1581, Gasparo would later refer in the plural to 'some incidents' and 'some fights'. It is possible that Antonio, having some of the same touchiness about his honour and status as his father (and perhaps with even greater sensitivity, given that he was an illegitimate son), had got involved in the relatively new practice of duelling, which was sweeping through Italian society in the sixteenth century. In December 1563 his uncle Giovanni had been present when the Council of Trent issued a stern decree against 'the detestable practice of duels', excommunicating all duellists, their seconds and their witnesses.[10]

Whether Antonio did transfer to the University of Padua – the home university for Venice, and another institution famous for its legal school – is not known; detailed matriculation records do not survive for this period. In July 1583 Gasparo Bruni was still asking the papal secretary Ingegneri for the renewal of the payments for Antonio's education, and requesting that the money be sent to the care of a merchant draper in Venice, Nicolò de' Michieli. The next mention of Antonio came in April 1584, when, as we saw at the end of the last chapter, Gasparo thanked Cardinal Como for securing the continuation of the payments, and explained that his son had now come to Avignon to study. He referred to Antonio again in November of that year (saying that he was 'at his studies' in Avignon), when writing a letter to Ascanio Colonna, whose father, Marcantonio, had recently died. While this was phrased as a letter of condolence, it was at the same time an open request for patronage: 'since I have not been able to fulfil my desire to serve him [Marcantonio] again, as loyally as I served him for three years in the anti-Ottoman fleet as captain of his galley, I present that same desire to your most illustrious lordship, begging you to accept both me and my son Antonio as your perpetual servants.' The request would have very positive consequences where Gasparo's own career was concerned, but not, so far as is known, for the future of his son.[11]

Once again Antonio was studying at a university best known for its law faculty. The University of Avignon was a papal foundation, dating from the early fourteenth century, and for its first 200 years or so the municipal authorities had taken little interest in it; in 1477, for instance, they positively refused to contribute to the professors' salaries. But in the early sixteenth century they had a change of mind, realizing that an eminent law faculty would add to the prestige of the city and bring in many more international students. The university had never had a very active arts faculty, and such limited teaching as it gave in that area was made redundant in 1565, when the Jesuits set up a college in Avignon under a dynamic young Rector, Antonio Possevino (the author of the treatise on the Christian soldier, with its pious but impractical advice that military men spend their time reading the works of Bede and Orosius).* But the Jesuit college, with roughly 500 pupils, did create a well-educated intake for the university, which now tried to strengthen its credentials in the fields of law and medicine. Briefly, in 1570, it appointed to a lectureship one of the most brilliant French legal scholars of the century, Jacques Cujas, who had married a woman from Avignon; but his wife died, and he went elsewhere. In 1581 the city petitioned the Pope for an annual grant of 1,000 scudi (833 ducats) to pay for 'an extremely famous teacher' to come to the law faculty from Italy; unfortunately the papal finances, already stretched by the security

---

* On the treatise see above, pp. 116–17.

needs of the enclave, could not extend to this. So the university appointed instead the best of its local talent, Louis Beau (or Belli), who had recently gained his own doctorate there; he would serve as Professor of Canon Law from 1581 until his death roughly 50 years later, and a volume of his legal opinions would be published posthumously in 1635.[12]

Antonio may not have had the most distinguished teachers, but he did complete his studies quite rapidly, proceeding to the degree of Doctor of Civil and Canon Law in 1585. The records of the university state that on 30 October of that year 'Antonio Bruni of the diocese of Ulcinj' was awarded his doctorate in the presence of Louis Beau and three other professors. This was an elaborate business. The candidate would invite the legate or co-legate, the archbishop and all the resident doctors of law to the ceremony, which took place in the Franciscan church. There, in front of the Vice-Chancellor of the university, Antonio had to give a lecture on a particular law, and defend his argument against two bachelors of law who disputed it; then the Vice-Chancellor made a speech in praise of him, and the assembled doctors agreed to award the doctorate. After that, Antonio made a second speech, larded with citations of legal texts, before being given the various symbolic 'insignia doctoralia': a book, a chair, a biretta (clerical-style square cap), a kiss and a blessing. The whole affair was very expensive; he had to give ceremonial bonnets to all participants, and pay one ducat for each doctor, fifteen ducats to the Vice-Chancellor and 25 to the person who gave him the insignia, in addition to providing a banquet with musicians and entertainers. The total cost might well have exceeded the annual subsidy he had received from the Pope. Probably his proud father, who was surely present, dug deep into his own pockets.[13]

At some point during the next two years Antonio Bruni went to live in Koper. Whether he found legal work to do there, or in Venice, is not known. The evidence of his stay in the Istrian city comes from a volume of compositions produced by members of the 'Accademia Palladia', Koper's literary society and dining club. One of its leading figures was Girolamo Vida, who published a little volume of his own work in 1590, when he was 27 years old; at the end of that book he printed a list of the 'conclusioni amorose' or 'arguments about love' which he had propounded. He died in the following year, but more than 30 years later a volume appeared containing the texts of some of these arguments, which had served as literary exercises in the Accademia. First Girolamo Vida had set out a question at some length – for example: which kind of beauty exercises the greatest power in love: beauty of mind, of voice, or

of body? – and then he had appointed an individual member of the
academy to defend each option. (For the question about the three kinds
of beauty, the person assigned to speak in favour of beauty of the body
was Rizzardo Verzi, the husband of Antonio's cousin Caterina Bruti.)
Turning out an elegant declamation on any given theme was something
for which Antonio Bruni was supremely well prepared by his Jesuit education, so it is not surprising to find a contribution by him to this
volume.[14]

The question posed was: which colour of dress adds most to a
woman's beauty: purple, green, blue, yellow, black, mixed colours, or
white? Antonio was allotted yellow. His oration, in suitably flowery
Italian, runs deftly through a range of arguments, including reasons for
eliminating each of the other colours from the competition; it appeals to
heraldry and to Latin poetry, citing Virgil and Propertius; it adduces the
yellow veils worn by Roman women at their weddings, and the golden
cloaks of the Roman emperors and empresses; and it concludes with a
delicate nine-line Italian poem, in the style of a madrigal. (At the end of
this debate, the president of the Accademia, the physician Santorio Santorio, allowed Vida to speak on all the colours; that dates the occasion
to 1587 at the latest, as Santorio left Koper in that year.) One other
published work by Antonio Bruni may also derive from his membership
of this group: a six-line poem in Latin, in which the city of Koper speaks,
proudly declaring that she was founded by both a goddess, Pallas
Athene (hence the 'Accademia Palladia'), and an emperor, Justinian.
Antonio was not only in the company of friends, such as the husband of
his cousin Caterina; he was also among young men of a similar cultural
and literary formation, several of whom, such as Marc'Antonio Valdera, Ottonello del Bello and Cesare Barbabianca, went on to become
published authors. And this so-called 'academy' was very much a young
man's club: in 1587 Antonio Bruni was in his late twenties, Santorio
was 25, Vida was 23 and Barbabianca was only 17.[15]

One other episode in Antonio's life probably belongs to this period.
In 1603 an Albanian bishop, Niccolò Mechaisci (Nikollë Mekajshi),
would write an angry letter to Rome denouncing his colleague, the
Bishop of Lezhë, who was a Ragusan Benedictine called Innocentius
Stoicinus. The charges were many and various: he seldom performed
Masses, failed to keep fasts, sold property belonging to convents, denied
the power of the Pope or of bishops over friars, and was notoriously
unchaste, being, according to rumour, 'born in the cities of Sodom and

Gomorrah'. Mechaisci noted also 'the scandals he caused in the province of Venice when he was found in lay dress among the prostitutes and theatres in that city. He was arrested by the constables and put in gaol, where he stayed imprisoned for several days, but then he broke out of gaol and fled, an apostate, to Rome; by the favour of signor Antonio Bruni, an Albanian from Ulcinj, he was freed from the punishment of being put in the galleys.' The date of this episode is entirely unknown, but presumably it took place in Stoicinus's youth, quite a long time before he was appointed Bishop of Lezhë in 1596. Perhaps Antonio knew him through a circle of friends in Venice, some of whom may also have been frequenters of the theatre, and of other unclerical attractions in that city. Or there may have been a family link; but so little is known about Stoicinus that it is not possible to make a definite connection.* Also unclear is whether Antonio's help consisted simply of string-pulling among his Roman contacts, or of a more formal intervention in a judicial process – though there are otherwise no signs of him putting his legal training to practical use at this time. However, a doctorate in law was not regarded simply as a qualification to join the legal profession; the doctoral certificate issued by the University of Avignon explicitly said that those who held it could work 'with princes and the most prudent governors and administrators of states, helping them to govern and rule their states well'. The next stage in Antonio's career would involve working for his cousin Bartolomeo, helping him to govern and rule the state of Moldavia.[16]

Gasparo Bruni, meanwhile, was seeking new employment. He eventually found it thanks to his cultivation of Marcantonio Colonna's son Ascanio. After studying philosophy, theology and law in Spain, Ascanio Colonna was made a cardinal by Pope Sixtus V in 1586; in late March 1589 the Pope also appointed him Prior of Venice in the Order of the Knights of Malta. Just seven weeks later, on 13 May, Gasparo Bruni wrote an effusive letter from Venice to Ascanio (who lived in Rome), thanking him for deigning to remember Gasparo's previous service to his father, declaring himself 'infinitely obliged' to his generosity, and promising that 'I shall never fail to procure with all my heart everything

---

* We do know that he was from Dubrovnik, where Gasparo had once been stationed on papal service. 'Stoicinus' might be either Stojičić or Stojković, and the latter was itself a slavicized version of Stay; the Stays had come originally from Bar, and one member of that family is known to have traded in Vlorë.

which I think can be of benefit to this, your most illustrious lordship's Priory.' Ascanio had just given him the position of 'ricevitore', the receiver of all the incomes of the Priory of Venice.[17]

This was in principle an important post, and Gasparo seems to have held it for at least three years. At some stage he apparently shared it with a co-receiver: an account of the official visitation of the Priory's buildings in Venice in 1591 refers both to Giovanni Contarini, the lieutenant-general and receiver of the Priory, and to 'Fra Gasparo Bruni, Knight, receiver of the same Priory'. Gasparo's work brought him into contact with members of some of the leading Venetian families: not only a Contarini, but also two Giustinianis and a Morosini. But relations between the Order and the Venetian government were not at all good; they had deteriorated severely in the early 1580s, and had remained bad thereafter. In 1583 a prominent Spanish Knight, the Grand Prior of Castile, had captured three Ottoman trading vessels, one of which was taking a large consignment of grain to the Venetian territory of Crete; his own ship (a refitted English galleon) was then attacked by the Venetian fleet, and he and his crew were taken off in chains. In another episode that year, two of the Order's galleys were seized by Venice's Cretan squadron and taken first to Crete and then to Corfu, where they were held captive, with crew members dying of hunger and disease, for four months; this episode also caused extreme anger among the Knights. The following year, in retaliation, a Venetian merchant ship was detained at Malta: its sailors were put in irons, its cargo was taken, and the ship was sunk. Venice reacted by sequestrating all property of the Order in its territory, dismissing all Knights who were in Venetian government service, and banning all trade and correspondence with Malta, declaring that the Knights were henceforth to be treated as enemy corsairs – whereupon Malta responded by saying that it would seize any Venetian ships it found. Heads were banged together, to some extent, by Pope Sixtus V, who in 1586 ordered the Knights to refrain from molesting all legitimate trade between Christian ports and Ottoman ones; in the following year he forbade them to seize the goods or persons of Levantine (i.e. Ottoman) Jews, who were active both in Venice and at the Pope's own port of Ancona. With some protests, the Grand Master and his Council did accept these orders. But the sequestration of the incomes of commende in Venetian territory continued, and Cardinal Ascanio Colonna was still asking for it to be lifted, if only partially, in 1593. In these circumstances, the 'receiver's' main task may have been only to gather the incomes and hand them over to the Venetian state.[18]

In the spring of 1592 Gasparo Bruni was summoned to Rome, where Ascanio gave him instructions, and letters to take with him to Malta. After a long wait in Messina for the Order's galleys, he reached the island in early June. One of his tasks was to find out whether Ascanio Colonna, as Prior, had the right to take one of the major commende of his Priory for himself; Ascanio seems to have been keen to milk the system for any advantage, and in the following years he would campaign hard to be allowed – against all the conventions of the Order – to trade in his Priory for another, more lucrative one. Gasparo was apparently in Malta in November 1592, when the Grand Master awarded him an annual pension of 100 scudi (83 ducats), part of the income of a Grand Magisterial commenda. Whether he then went back to Venice is not known. But it seems that at some stage after his arrival in Malta his duties on behalf of Ascanio Colonna came to an end; a new 'ricevitore', Fra Leonida Loschi, was sent from Malta in late 1594 and confirmed by a papal bull in the following year. Gasparo would spend most or all of five years in the new city of Valletta, where the Order had now established its headquarters.[19]

Having seen Valletta briefly in 1567, when it was little more than a rudimentary but ambitious building site, Gasparo must have been astonished by the progress that had been made. The writer Giovanni Battista Leoni, who visited Malta in 1583, was impressed by the massive fortifications that had already been constructed on the landward side of the city, defending the neck of the peninsula on which it stood; part of the plan was to dig a deep channel below them out of the solid rock, which would eventually fill with water. (It was decreed that houses in the city had to be made of rock from this excavation; thousands of tons were dug out, but the channel never became deep enough to form a sea-moat.) Leoni observed that roughly 2,000 houses had been built, and that many Knights had paid for them out of their own money, on the basis that these properties would be exempted from the normal rule by which the Order took four fifths of every Knight's estate on his death. He noted that the streets and squares had all been laid out, and that the buildings included a splendid infirmary (where, recalling their Hospitaller origins, the Knights tended the sick and served them food on silver platters), two arms stores with weapons for 6,000 fighters, and the church of St John the Baptist – for which, 25 years later, a 'cavaliere di grazia', the artist Caravaggio, would produce a startling portrayal of that saint's beheading. When the German adventurer Michael Heberer visited Valletta in 1588 – having joined a disastrous Maltese corsairing expedition in 1585 and spent the next three years as an Ottoman slave – he too was struck by the 'many beautiful buildings', including the infirmary and the Grand Master's palazzo, which had a pleasure-garden filled with flowers and fruit-trees. He also noted that a French Knight had imported glass for his windows, and that this novel fashion, replacing the translucent linen that had previously been used, was quickly catching on. Among the new buildings were the 'auberges' or hostels of the different langues, where meals were served for their members; Leoni called them 'extremely beautiful palazzi'. At any time there were roughly 600 Knights in Malta; in the mid-1590s more than 200 of these were from the langue of Italy. Only a minority of the members of each langue stayed in the auberge; those who had built houses naturally preferred to live surrounded by their own comforts. But we may guess that Gasparo Bruni, who in comparison with many of these well-funded aristocrats was a pauper, became a resident in the auberge of the langue of Italy and a frequent diner at its table.[20]

Gasparo's main activity during this period seems to have been climbing the greasy pole of preferment within the Order – the longed-for prize being a commenda that would give him a good income in his old age. One of the basic requirements was 'antianitas' or seniority, traditionally calculated in terms of the number of years a Knight had spent in Malta. Under the statutes of the Order, a minimum of five years' continuous residence was required before any Knight could be considered for a commenda. Luckily for Gasparo, however, time spent as a 'ricevitore' at any Priory was also counted as residence. A bull of antianitas was issued to him in May 1594 (despite the objections of a rival Knight), exactly five years after his appointment as ricevitore in Venice. The Grand Master, Hugues Loubenx de Verdalle, who was from the south of France, showed him some favour; in April 1595 he exchanged Gasparo's 100-scudi pension for one worth 200 scudi. A year later, the next Grand Master, Martín de Garzez, from Aragon, granted him another pension of 50 ducats. Gasparo had clearly made a good impression. So it was reasonable that, in December 1595, he should throw his hat into the ring: he was one of three Knights who applied to be given the commenda of Cosenza, a relatively small estate based on the city of that name in a part of Calabria which, perhaps coincidentally, contained a number of Albanian villages.[21]

What followed was a wearisome sequence of claims, counter-claims and challenges – wearying, certainly, to the historian who tries to untangle it, and no doubt deeply frustrating to Gasparo Bruni, who had to

live through it for well over a year. The general problem was the practice of Knights jockeying for higher incomes by swapping, or being told
to swap, one commenda for another; the specific problem was a quarrel
between two Knights, Michele Cadamosto and Bernardo Capece, over
an arrangement of that kind. Cadamosto had been asked by the Grand
Master to give up one commenda, La Motta, in order to take another,
Racconisi; he had then been stymied by the Pope, who gave Racconisi
to someone else, but not before La Motta had been granted to Bernardo
Capece; so Cadamosto claimed Cosenza as a substitute for Racconisi,
while still contesting Capece's claim to La Motta. Other Knights were
also putting in claims to each of these. The disputes were conducted
both by legal representations to the Grand Master and Council, and
by more underhand means; in 1596, for example, Capece wrote to an
influential cardinal at Rome, pointing out that the non-noble Cadamosto had been made a Knight by special dispensation because his
father was one of the Order's physicians – so that, as he sneeringly put
it, he had 'entered by the window, not by the door'. On 21 June 1596
the Grand Master and Council issued a judgment: Capece kept La
Motta, Cadamosto would receive a different commenda, Cerri, and
Cosenza was offered to another Knight, Ferrante Averoldo, with the
proviso that Gasparo Bruni would have it if Averoldo turned it down.
Cadamosto promptly lodged an appeal; the Knight who currently held
the commenda of Cerri also objected; and so too did Gasparo Bruni,
who appeared in person before the Council on 28 June to argue his
case. More investigations and arguments followed. In January 1597 the
authorities upheld their previous decision; but two months later Ferrante Averoldo did announce that he was giving up his claim to Cosenza.
So at long last, on 27 March 1597, a formal bull was issued assigning
that commenda to Bruni. (The other three Knights, meanwhile, kept up
their complaints; after eight months of further wrangling, a special tribunal would hammer out a compromise solution for them.) Gasparo
Bruni was a 'commendatore' at last.[22]

This was a position which brought honour as well as income – and
in this case, much more of the former than of the latter. The commenda
consisted of a scattering of many small land-holdings around the city of
Cosenza, where the Order maintained a little church of St John the Baptist. The total income was between 300 and 360 ducats a year, but
roughly half of that was consumed by dues paid to the Order and local
taxes. While commendatori with large estates to manage (and incomes
from them of thousands of ducats) might go to live on them, there was

little reason for Gasparo Bruni to settle in Cosenza. Had he done so, he might have found that he had more problems to contend with, as various Knights who belonged to local families lived nearby, and they seem to have been a particularly troublesome lot of people. (One, Maurizio Barracco, was imprisoned by the local authorities in 1594; another, Pietro Antonio Parisio, was charged with the murder of a Knight in 1595.) Most probably Gasparo now retired to Koper, to live with his son Antonio. As he had complained of having a salary of less than 35 ducats a month while serving in Avignon, his income now, even with the two other pensions – assuming that he was allowed to retain them – would not have enabled him to live in the style to which, perhaps, he felt entitled. In any case, it seems that he did not have long to live. A study of the commenda of Cosenza records that in 1598 it passed to Fra Pier Luigi Parisio, another member of a local Calabrian family. If that is correct, it surely implies that Gasparo Bruni had died, as there is absolutely no sign of him, at this stage, jockeying in Malta for further commende. One thing at least we may assume: this man of the sword, a veteran of a notorious siege and a distinguished participant in the most famous naval battle of the century, had in the end died peacefully in his bed.[23]

17

Moldavia, Tatars and Cossacks

When Bartolomeo Bruti travelled from Istanbul to Moldavia in the spring of 1580 he was not moving outside the Ottoman Empire, but he was entering a territory very different in kind from that empire's directly governed heartland. Many histories of the Ottomans concentrate heavily on the heartland, because it was the central territories of Anatolia and the Balkans that were ruled in accordance with the classic 'Ottoman system', with the military-feudal estates of the spahis, the local *kadi*s administering justice, the *sancakbeyi*s governing their large districts, and the *beylerbeyi*s governing groups of *sancak*s. Yet at the same time the Ottoman system of imperial rule, in its broadest sense, involved incorporating many other kinds of polity without directly administering them at all. The case of Dubrovnik has already been discussed; the three Romanian principalities of Transylvania, Wallachia and Moldavia were also self-governed; the Khanate of the Crimean Tatars, while in some ways acknowledging Ottoman suzerainty, was ruled by its own Khans; the corsair states of North Africa were essentially self-administering territories with rulers appointed from Istanbul; a dynasty of sharifs of Mecca continued to govern the Hijaz; in the Yemen the application of Ottoman rule was often little more than nominal; in parts of eastern Anatolia populated by Türkmen and Kurdish tribes there were hereditary *sancak*s held by traditional ruling families; and when the Ottomans acquired much of Georgia in the sixteenth century they mostly left local princes in place as tribute-paying vassals. Altogether, the Ottoman Empire was not a monolithic structure at all; the secret of its huge and rapid expansion, indeed, is to be found not only in its military strength but also in its adaptability to local conditions and traditions in the territories where it took power. As one modern historian has emphasized, some of the commonest normative phrases in the Ottoman official documents of the centuries of conquest

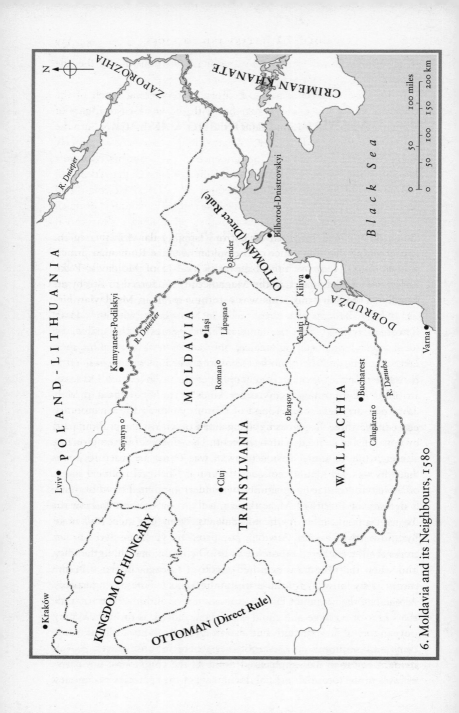

6. Moldavia and its Neighbours, 1580

are 'customary practice' and 'the way things were done during the rule of the kings'.[1]

In the case of Moldavia – a territory encompassing much of the modern country of Moldova, together with the north-eastern part of Romania that bears the same name – the process of absorption into the Ottoman Empire had been a very lengthy one. Its 'voivods' or princely rulers had paid tribute to the Sultan since 1455–6, and its two most valuable ports on the Black Sea coast, Kiliya (Rom.: Chilia; Trk.: Kili) and Bilhorod-Dnistrovskyi (Rom.: Cetatea Alba; Trk.: Akkerman) had been seized by the Ottomans in 1484. The Ottoman conquest of much of Hungary, after the crushing defeat of the Hungarian army in 1526 at the Battle of Mohács, shifted the entire strategic balance in the region, strengthening the dominance of the Sultan over the Romanian principalities. In 1538 an ambitious maverick voivod of Moldavia, Petru Rareş, who defied Süleyman the Magnificent, was forced to flee by an invading Ottoman army. This was a turning-point in Moldavian history: a new voivod was brought in by the Sultan and installed with an Ottoman ceremony, and in the same campaign Süleyman seized the town of Bender (Rom.: Tighina; an important customs post on the river Dniester) and turned the entire coastal strip of Moldavia, including the two previously captured ports, into a directly ruled *sancak*. Ottoman attitudes had hardened since Mohács: whereas the tribute paid by Moldavia had originally been a kind of ransom payment for a temporary peace, it was now viewed as implying submission, like the poll-tax paid by non-Muslim subjects within the central territories of the empire. But although the military invasion of 1538 was sometimes used to imply that this was just another conquered territory, the legal-political status of Moldavia remained ambiguous for quite a long time. The whole issue is necessarily a murky one, as there is a three-way mismatch between the concepts available to the Moldavians themselves (who talked in Byzantine style about 'bowing', or 'prostrating' themselves, to an emperor), the Islamic legal theory of the Ottomans (which, in the tradition they followed, distinguished starkly between countries in the enemy 'house of war' and those within the 'house of Islam' – a territory such as Moldavia being rather obviously in neither), and Western European concepts, whether feudal ('vassalage') or modern (acknowledging 'sovereignty'). What can be said is that from the mid-1560s onwards there was a definite shift in Istanbul towards seeing Moldavia and Wallachia as integral parts of the empire, within what were officially called its 'well-protected domains'. Significantly, in 1572 Sultan Selim ordered the voivods of Moldavia to mint Ottoman coins for internal circulation. In 1574 there was a further tightening of the screw, after an anti-Ottoman revolt by the Voivod, Ioan cel Cumplit ('John the Terrible'), was punitively suppressed by Ottoman forces. Uncertainty about the future of Poland, after its newly crowned French king absconded in that year, also made Istanbul anxious to strengthen its hold over Moldavia, Poland's neighbour. Up until this time, the voivods had been drawn from those who belonged to, or at least claimed descent from, Moldavia's own noble and princely families. Now the Ottomans imposed a member of the Wallachian ruling dynasty, Petru Şchiopul ('Peter the Lame'), who had spent much of his time in Istanbul; he experienced instant unpopularity in Moldavia because he had no essential connection with that country at all.[2]

By this stage, the degree of autonomy enjoyed by Moldavia and Wallachia was as follows. They had their own administration, their own Church and their own army. The voivod was appointed by the Sultan and could be dismissed by him, but would normally be chosen on the basis that he was of suitable lineage. He dispensed justice, and governed with his own *divan* or governing council – in Moldavia, an eight-member group which included leading noblemen and the Metropolitan, who was the head of the Orthodox Church in that country. There were no mosques in Moldavia, and no significant Muslim presence, beyond a few 'scribes' or officials seconded from Istanbul, a small guard of janissaries sent very exceptionally to assist Petru Şchiopul during his first, unpopular, period of rule, and at any given time a small number of Muslim merchants. (A sultanic decree in 1577 said that Muslims should not settle in Moldavia or Wallachia; they were forbidden to marry infidels there, and should leave when they had finished their business.) Moldavian merchants, on the other hand, were permitted to trade freely within the Ottoman Empire. Among the major duties of the voivod of Moldavia, the first was to pay the annual tribute: by the 1570s this was the equivalent of 35,000 ducats, but it underwent some fluctuations thereafter, with higher payments being promised by, or extorted from, incoming voivods, and unintended reductions following from debasements of the Ottoman coinage. Another duty was to supply troops when called upon to do so – reports in this period refer to 10,000 cavalry – though only for campaigns in the region; and at all times the voivod was naturally expected to repel any hostile forces entering his territory. He was also required to provide Istanbul with intelligence, both political and military. (A sultanic order to the Voivod in January

1566 said: 'We have received a letter from you concerning what the spies in Germany have communicated about the gathering of the German army; in this situation do not cease to be vigilant, and make the necessary preparations against the enemy's attack.') The voivod was forbidden to conduct his own foreign policy – though most did keep up direct relations with their important non-Ottoman neighbours – and was not allowed to marry a foreigner without permission.[3]

The duty to supply Istanbul with goods and provisions was less clearly defined, but it grew in importance during the sixteenth century. In wartime, Moldavia and Wallachia could simply be ordered to provide foodstuffs for the Ottoman army; for the Hungarian campaign in 1552, for instance, the Moldavian voivod was told to send 30,000 sheep, and the Wallachian one 3,000 oxen. But as the population of Istanbul grew during this century, rising from half a million in the 1550s to perhaps 700,000 by 1580, the demand for food from these fertile territories constantly increased. In 1566 the Sultan decreed that the Voivod of Moldavia must send 1,000 sheep and 1,000 head of cattle every month to the imperial capital. Official orders also went out for large quantities of grain, and for timber. Generally these products were paid for; the Ottoman system of *celep*s, state-appointed contractors who bought sheep locally and sent them to Istanbul, extended as far as Moldavia, where in 1591 they bought 24,500 from just one part of the country. (In the late 1580s an observer estimated that 100,000 Moldavian sheep went to Istanbul every year.) An attempt by the Sultan to impose the normal Ottoman tariff of fixed maximum prices was made, but then quickly abandoned, in the late 1570s. But the Ottomans did, in a sense, try to rig the market, by prohibiting the export of sheep, cattle and various other commodities – on the sometimes spurious basis that they were of military value – to non-Ottoman lands. No sooner had the newly appointed Voivod, Iancu Sasul (Bartolomeo Bruti's candidate), arrived in the Moldavian capital of Iaşi, than he received a stiff decree from the Sultan complaining that the Moldavians were still engaging in the forbidden practice of selling sheep and cattle to Hungary and Poland – and, for good measure, that Iancu himself had just sent to Austria 24,000 head of cattle that he owed to creditors in Istanbul. Huge numbers of cattle were in fact sold via Poland; they were taken, on the hoof, as far as Venice, where their meat was prized more than any other. All the 'boyars' (nobles) of Moldavia traded livestock from their own estates, and the voivod was both the greatest landowner and the greatest trader of them all.[4]

The wealth of these principalities came, in the first place, from their own tremendous fertility. Stefan Gerlach recorded a comment made by his ambassador in Istanbul in 1575: 'today my gracious lord said that nowadays Moldavia and Wallachia are nothing other than the dairies of the sultans and pashas; and their princes, as they call themselves, are their dairy-farmers.' Moldavia exported not only the 'dairy' products of meat, cheese and tallow, but also grain, honey, wax, fur, wine, beer, and huge quantities of fish: a Jesuit traveller in the 1580s was amazed to discover that you could buy a quantity of dried fish as big as a man, and the equivalent of a barrel of caviar, for just one scudo. The other source of Moldavia's prosperity was the fact that it lay on an important trade route from Anatolia and Istanbul to Poland. Goods passed from Istanbul either overland to Galaţi or by boat to Kiliya, and were then taken via Iaşi to the important Polish border town of Kamyanets-Podilskyi (Pol.: Kamieniec Podolski). From there they went to Lviv (Pol.: Lwów; now in the Ukraine, like Kamyanets-Podilskyi, but then a Polish-Lithuanian city), and on either to Kraków, for further transit to southern Poland, Austria and the Czech lands, or to Poznań, for Germany, or to Gdańsk (Germ.: Danzig), for the Baltic region, or northwards to Brest, and thence either to Vilnius or even to Moscow. Spices formed an important part of this trade for much of the sixteenth century, coming from southeast Asia via Persia.* Other high-value commodities from the east included pearls and jewels, and luxury textiles such as silk, mohair and camlet.[5]

Muslim merchants brought many of these goods to Poland. They would then travel as far as Muscovy to spend the proceeds on furs, which were greatly prized by the Ottomans. Poland was the only Christian country to be quite thoroughly penetrated by Muslim traders; mostly their presence was accepted, though sometimes they were suspected of espionage. But there were other nationalities and religions taking part in this east–west trade: Armenians, Jews, Ragusans and Greeks. In Iaşi, the Moldavian capital, there was a significant Armenian colony. Jews and Armenians were prominent traders in Lviv, where, from the second half of the sixteenth century, there were resident Spanish Jews with close

---

* The development of a sea route round Africa by Portuguese traders at the end of the previous century, which at first caused great alarm to those Venetian merchants who also purchased south-east Asian spices in the Levant, took a long time to undermine the overland trade. For decades, spices brought via Moldavia to Kraków remained much cheaper than those that came by sea all the way from Goa via Lisbon to Gdańsk, and thence overland through Poland.

links to Jewish merchant families in Istanbul. In the 1580s the Polish Chancellor arranged for a number of Spanish and Portuguese Jews to move from Istanbul to the town of Zamość, which he had recently founded, to boost its trade. The omnipresent Ragusans were involved in this commerce, especially in Iaşi and on the Black Sea coast. And Greeks, not only from Galata, Chios (Ottoman territory from 1566) and Cyprus (Ottoman from 1570–1), but also from Venetian Crete, dominated the trade in strong and sweet red wines from the Mediterranean; these commodities, much valued during the cold Central European winters, came mostly via Moldavia. There were also a few Albanian traders; and some of the 'Greeks', from Pogon, may have been from the territory of present-day Albania, with Vlach – a language usefully similar to Romanian – as their mother tongue.[6]

Much has been written about the so-called 'closing' of the Black Sea during this period. The phrase refers only to the discouragement or prohibition of non-Ottoman traders – who, in an earlier period when important Crimean ports had been run by the Genoese, had been frequent visitors. This process seems to have been a gradual one, beginning in the 1550s or 1560s and becoming formalized only at the end of the century. Istanbul's growing hunger for the products of the Romanian lands – and of the Tatar Khanate – was the main cause; that meant that there was less and less for foreign traders to buy. And while the Moldavians were formally forbidden to sell various commodities to non-Ottomans on their north-western borders, it would have been illogical to allow non-Ottoman merchants to come and buy them on their eastern ones. Nevertheless, some foreign traders were active. Cretans who brought wine took back cargoes of hides and caviar; in the latter part of the century French ships sometimes penetrated the Black Sea; some Venetian merchants traded there using Ottoman ships or business partners; and the Ragusans, who had an important outpost on the Bulgarian Black Sea coast, were often taking the goods they acquired to Ancona and other Italian ports. If foreign traders shied away from the area in the 1590s, that was as much to do with security concerns (thanks to a new Ottoman–Habsburg war, from 1593, and the growth of piracy by Ukrainian Cossacks) as with any prohibition. What must be emphasized, at all events, is that the 'closing' of the Black Sea did not mean stagnation. On the contrary, the decades up to the 1590s seem to have witnessed a positive boom in the trade that passed through Moldavia.[7]

Thanks to taxes, customs dues and his own revenues as both

producer and trader, the voivod had a large income, estimated in the
1580s at between half a million and a million thalers (333,000 to
666,000 ducats). Military and other state expenditure had to come out
of this, in addition to the tribute to Istanbul, but the rulers of both Moldavia and Wallachia were still rich men; it is not surprising that Venetian
jewel-sellers gathered around them like wasps round a jam-jar. The high
revenues, together with the increasing appetite for cash at the Ottoman
court, also explain the development of the practice – in which Bartolomeo Bruti took part so successfully – of merchants and other investors
paying for the deposition of one voivod and the installation of another:
so long as the new one remained in power for a few years, the investors
could be confident of recouping their money handsomely. But this does
raise the question of why these territories, which were of such economic
and strategic importance to the Sultan, were not taken over and ruled
directly. The threat of turning them into *beylerbeylik*s was deployed
from time to time, and at a moment of crisis in wartime, in 1595, it was
briefly carried out; but general Ottoman policy was firmly in favour of
indirect rule. One important reason must have been the cost of garri-
soning such a territory with janissaries; in Ottoman-ruled Hungary in
the mid-century, for example, there were at least 20,000 occupation
troops, who all had to be paid for. An interesting comment was made by
the Imperial Ambassador in Istanbul, David Ungnad, in January 1578:
noting a rumour that the former pasha of Timişoara would be declared
beylerbeyi of Moldavia, he wrote that 'in that case Poland would be
well on the way to becoming an Ottoman possession; but it seems to me
virtually unbelievable, because Moldavia is the main supplier to this
city of meat, lard and other foodstuffs, and the population here would
be partly or mostly deprived of them, if Moldavia were possessed by
Ottomans' – meaning that the Ottoman administration would consume
more of the local production, and perhaps also that agricultural effi-
ciency would go down. His remark about the implications for the Poles
is perhaps even more important. Poland's objections to the full Otto-
manization of that principality were very strong: militarily, it required
Moldavia to act as a buffer state, and in political terms the Poles wanted
a neighbour that they could continue to influence and manipulate on its
own separate basis.[8]

Modern histories of the Ottoman Empire in this period, written
mostly by West Europeans, tend to pay very little attention to Poland.
There are various reasons for this: the dominance of West European
sources and secondary literature is one, and the fact that Poland was at

peace with the Ottomans from 1533 onwards is another. But Poland mattered very greatly to the Ottoman Sultans; that they maintained peaceful relations with it is itself testimony to that fact. After the Union of Lublin in 1569, which united the Kingdom of Poland and the Grand Duchy of Lithuania into a single 'commonwealth', the Polish state covered a huge stretch of Europe from the Baltic coast to the borders of the Crimean Khanate, embracing most of present-day Poland, all of modern Latvia, Lithuania and Belarus, and the western half of what is now the Ukraine. Thanks to its constitution, with an elective monarchy and a fractious, veto-ridden parliament of nobles, it could not and did not undergo all the processes of centralization of power that were beginning to take place in several West European states; but with the help of its powerful regional lords it could raise large military forces, which in this period were mostly directed against its eastern rival, Russia. Poland mattered to Ottoman geopolitical strategy not only because of its size, but also because it was situated between two potentially or actually anti-Ottoman powers, Russia and the Holy Roman Empire. If it conquered Russia, or was taken over by the Habsburgs, or underwent any other kind of merging or close alliance with either of those, it would pose a huge threat to the security of the Ottoman Empire. As Giovanni Barelli commented in his intelligence report from Istanbul in 1575, the Ottomans thought that Poland, being 'rather divided', could be defeated by them in war. But they feared that this would force the Poles to choose the Russian Tsar as their king, which would 'give excessive power to one of their [sc. the Ottomans'] chief foes'.[9]

Hence the concern felt in Istanbul each time an election to the Polish crown was impending. The Sultan was happy to support Henri de Valois in 1573, in view of the long-standing Franco-Ottoman alliance and French hostility to the Habsburgs. However, when Henri decamped so abruptly soon after entering his kingdom in the following year, there were real fears that the Holy Roman Emperor, Maximilian II, might obtain the Polish crown. The upper house of the Polish parliament did vote for him, but the lower one chose Stephen Báthory, the Catholic Hungarian Voivod of Transylvania, who cemented the deal by promising to marry the late king's 52-year-old sister. Stephen became King of Poland in early 1576; one of the reasons why many nobles had voted for him was that they wished to avoid a war with the Ottoman Empire (a strategy which, so long as Russia remained the primary enemy, was logically required). The Sultan was very content with this election. Stephen had been a reliable vassal ruler in Transylvania; he was a known quantity, and the fact that his accession to the Polish crown created a personal union between Transylvania and Poland – even though he passed the administration of the former to his brother Christopher – gave Istanbul a pretext for demanding more influence over Poland. His election also had negative consequences for the onward march of the Counter-Reformation in Central Europe; although he was a sincere Catholic, Stephen Báthory did promise at his coronation to respect the Warsaw Confederation, a recent pledge of mutual toleration by all the major Christian confessions, Catholic, Protestant and Orthodox, in the Polish–Lithuanian commonwealth. The Papacy was seriously wrong-footed by Stephen's accession to the throne, not least because it had openly backed his Habsburg rival. With some grinding of gears, it now began to concentrate on promoting peace between Poland and Russia, in order to create the conditions for an anti-Ottoman alliance. Gradually, too, it began to insinuate the idea that if Poland did join a war against the Sultan, it could take Moldavia as its prize.[10]

What nearly brought Poland and the Ottoman Empire into armed conflict in this period was not the deliberate policy of the King, the Sultan or the Pope, but the unpredictable actions of two mutually hostile powers: the Tatars and the Cossacks. The Crimean Tatars were at least nominally subject to the Sultan. Although the Tatar Khans collected their own taxes and minted their own coins, they did acknowledge a higher power in Istanbul; a new Khan would be elected in the Crimea from the ruling Giray dynasty, but the election would then be submitted to the Sultan for approval, and the Ottomans did sometimes depose an uncooperative Khan in order to put a more compliant one in his place. Because of their military and marauding activities, the Tatars acquired a grim reputation in Russia and Central Europe as savage Asiatic nomads. The English Ambassador in Istanbul in the 1580s solemnly reported that 'theie are borne blynde, openinge theire eyes the thirde day after; a thing peculiar to them onlye, a brutishe people, open vnder the ayer lyvinge in cartes covered wth oxe hides'; all the adult men, he said, were 'theeves and Robbers'. While it is true that Tatar herdsmen did travel in carts with their flocks during the summer months, at the core of the Tatars' territory was a settled society, with agricultural estates (worked mostly by slaves they had captured). Their ruling family and nobility contained educated men: Gazi Giray II, who was installed by the Sultan in 1588, was a poet with a good knowledge of Arabic and Persian, and the Khans' palace contained a well-stocked library. But Tatar light cavalry (typically, a force of 20–30,000 men when led by the Khan) was a much feared auxiliary element in the Ottomans' European campaigns, and at other times large bands of Tatars would go raiding in Polish and Russian territory for slaves and other booty.[11]*

Opposing them in the south-eastern part of the Polish state was an official defence force of roughly 3,000 men, stretched out over an area more than 600 miles across. Its efforts, very inadequate in themselves, were supplemented by those of a much more informal fighting population, the Zaporozhian Cossacks, who were based in the marshy territory of the lower Dnieper river, south-east of Kiev ('Zaporozhian' is from a word meaning 'below the rapids'). Like their equivalents on the southern Russian steppes, the Don Cossacks, these people developed enough of a socio-political system to form at least a loose military organization, but not enough to become a state-like entity. They enjoyed the protection and sponsorship of some powerful landowners in the region, and in normal circumstances were willing to cooperate in a broad defensive strategy with the official forces of the Crown. But their 'pursuits' of Tatar raiders could often turn into raiding expeditions of their own, openly supported by local lords and administrators who took their share of the booty. Twentieth-century attempts to portray them as fighting either against feudalism or for national liberation are unconvincing; raiding was primarily an economic activity, and all classes could have an interest in it. The Tatar bands not only paid a tax on their booty to the Khan, but also, in some cases, had merchant investors who would give them horses on credit in return for half of the spoils. On the Polish side, Crown soldiers would sometimes provoke raids by the Tatars and then take care to intercept them only on their way home, when they were laden with goods (which could then be appropriated, or returned to the original owners for a fee). But the larger Cossack expeditions could also have a political dimension, whether by design, as their local protectors flexed their muscles vis-à-vis the Polish government, or by unintended consequence.[12]

To the modern eye, such raiding, even on a large scale, seems like a regrettable and peripheral phenomenon, something to be understood as a transgression of the normal system, not a component of it. Yet if one

---

* Captain John Smith (famous for his work in Virginia in 1607–9, and for his alleged relationship with Pocahontas) was held as a slave in Tatar territory in 1603. The account he later wrote of the Tatars' way of life is the most detailed eye-witness description by any Englishman in the early modern period. Understandably enough it is a very negative account; he found them 'generally nasty, and idle, naturally miserable, and in their warres, better theeves than souldiers'.

looks at all the frontier zones between Christendom and the Ottoman world in this period, from the Dnieper marshes in the north to the maritime quasi-frontier of the Mediterranean in the south, one begins to see that it was very much part of the system. On both sides of the lengthy Ottoman–Habsburg border, local auxiliary forces grew up for which raiding was a constant feature of military and economic life. In the north-eastern corner of the Adriatic a small but highly active population of 'Uskoks', Slavic refugees and adventurers who theoretically acted as frontier troops for the Habsburgs, caused real harm to Ottoman trading interests – and much damage to Venetian–Ottoman relations – by their corsairing and piracy. The corsairs of the Albanian coast, based first in Vlorë and Durrës and later also in Ulcinj, preyed on much Christian shipping. And in the Mediterranean, the corsairs of North Africa were pitted against another group for which raiding was a central activity, the Knights of Malta. In all these cases, booty was either essential to the economy or (in the case of Malta) a vital motive for offensive action; this in itself implied that these societies were enmeshed in a larger pattern of economic interests, as they often depended on merchants coming from elsewhere to buy the goods they had seized.* Of course, organized predation of this kind was not just a border phenomenon. Communities based at least partly on raiding, or on raiding combined with a sort of protection racket, could operate against domestic targets as well as foreign ones; in the northern Albanian mountains, a group of clans led by the warlike Kelmendi developed such a practice, and other bellicose populations such as the Himariots and the Maniots may at times have been fairly indiscriminate in their choice of prey. But the advantage of a frontier was that it provided a ready-made legitimation for all activities of this kind, so long as they were conducted against the other side; and even more legitimation was available when that frontier lay between two religions.[13]

A whole range of these raiding societies thus existed, from states and state-like entities (Algiers, Tunis, Tripoli, Malta, the Crimean Tatar Khanate) to broad regional forces (the Cossacks, the 'Grenzer' communities of the Habsburg borders and their Ottoman counterparts) and

---

* How this happened is curiously under-studied. We know that Dubrovnik was sometimes accused of acting as a clearing-house for the booty of Ottoman corsairs, and that when Livorno was developed as a 'free port' towards the end of the century, West European merchants would buy goods from the North African corsairs and sell them there. But for every hundred pages published about pirates and corsairs, barely a paragraph gets written about this aspect, even though selling the goods was essential to the entire operation.

small corsairing groups such as the Uskoks of Senj and their Albanian rough equivalents. Contemporaries sensed some of the similarities between them; for instance, the German writer on Ottoman affairs Johannes Leunclavius remarked that the Cossacks resembled both the Uskoks and the Morlachs (the Vlach and Slav fighters used on both sides of the Habsburg–Ottoman frontier), and Ottomans described the Tatars and the North African corsairs as the Sultan's two 'wings'. Modern historians seldom consider all these raiding entities together, perhaps because they do not fit the standard model of international history, based on the direct interactions of unit states, which the present naturally projects onto the past. Nevertheless, they should be regarded as an important element in the picture; one might think of them as the 'irregular powers', conjoined in a complex system of inter-power relations with the regular ones. Often they caused serious trouble not only to their enemies but also to their sponsors. Why did the latter tolerate them? Some parts of the answer are clear: they provided a relatively cheap form of permanent frontier defence; they became valuable auxiliaries in wartime; in peacetime their raiding activities honed the martial skills of large numbers of men; their constant probing of the enemy (or potential enemy) revealed points of weakness, while being covered by a degree of 'deniability'; and up to a certain point, the harm they caused by their offensive actions could be useful, as the other side might offer concessions of various kinds in order to have them called off. All these points are valid, but to list them like this risks giving the impression that the irregular powers functioned as mere instruments, the tools of their sponsors' regular power-politics. And that would be to ignore the fact that they often had interests and policies of their own, to which their protector-powers were sometimes forced, with great reluctance, to adapt.[14]

The activities of the Tatars and Cossacks bedevilled relations between Poland and the Ottoman Empire, and sometimes carried war and rebellion into the heart of the Moldavian state. In 1575 and again in 1577, Polish territory underwent large Tatar raids, in retaliation for Cossack attacks. The Voivod of Moldavia at this time was Petru Şchiopul, the Wallachian prince who had been imposed by the Sultan in 1574 in place of the rebellious Ioan cel Cumplit. A man claiming to be Ioan's brother, known as Ioan Potcoavă ('John Horseshoe' – he broke them with his bare hands), raised a Cossack army and invaded Moldavia, seizing the capital, Iaşi, in late 1577; he then withdrew to Polish territory, where the authorities arrested and executed him, but in the following year two more Cossack invasions took place under other leaders. During 1578 the Sultan warned Stephen Báthory that if the Cossacks were not restrained, he would invade Poland. Stephen's attempt to meet this challenge by setting up a small official Cossack army and giving it strict instructions not to attack Moldavia or any Ottoman territory was largely symbolic; it staved off the threatened invasion, but it did not give him real control of these warriors. In late 1579 a local Polish grandee organized a Cossack attack on the Ottoman fortress of Akkerman (Bilhorod-Dnistrovskyi). This formed the immediate context of the Sultan's decision to replace Petru Şchiopul; for Petru was regarded as pro-Polish, and therefore not the right person to develop a more hard-line policy against the Poles. Also, because he was a foreigner from Wallachia, Moldavian boyars had petitioned at Istanbul for him to be replaced by Iancu Sasul; those boyars represented, in effect, an anti-Polish party, and granting their wishes would strengthen their position. So it was that political circumstances, as well as the large payments organized by Bartolomeo Bruti, brought Iancu to the throne.[15]

Iancu was generally believed to be an illegitimate son of Petru Rareş, the voivod who had been driven out by Süleyman the Magnificent in 1538 (but later reinstated); and he was called 'Sasul', 'the German', because his mother was the wife of a German leather-worker in the city of Braşov. Since the administrative records of the Moldavian government have not survived from this period, it is impossible to give any detailed and objective account of his rule. Instead, the picture is dominated by the later narrative of the Moldavian chronicler Grigore Ureche, who, writing in the 1640s, had nothing good to say about Iancu Sasul. According to Ureche, he introduced an unheard-of tithe of all cattle in the country, and this provoked a major revolt in the eastern province of Lăpuşna, which was crushed by the Moldavian army. Iancu was an evil man who 'did not love the Christian religion'; he raped the wives of boyars, and several leading nobles consequently fled into exile. This account seems rather simplistic. We know that Iancu performed some routine acts of religious piety, donating numbers of Gypsy labourers, for example, to Orthodox monasteries – though the fact (if it is one) that he converted to Catholicism before his death may have tainted him in Moldavian eyes. It is indeed true that some leading nobles and ecclesiastics fled to Poland, but their reasons may have been primarily political, as they represented a pro-Polish lobby to which Iancu was opposed. He had a different policy which would, however, have pleased the Ottomans even less, had they known about it: from the start he was secretly

in touch with the Habsburgs through their military commander in
Upper Hungary. Towards the end of his rather brief rule in Moldavia he
was apparently trying to acquire an estate in Habsburg territory, seeing
it as a bolthole in which to evade another round of internal exile in the
Ottoman Empire; but there may have been a larger strategic aspect to
his cultivating these connections. When the Poles found out about them,
in 1582, they were quick to inform Istanbul.[16]

Stephen Báthory lobbied hard to get Iancu deposed; in the summer of
1582, when he despatched an envoy to a grand festivity in Istanbul celebrating the circumcision of the Sultan's son, he sent with him, as a
present to the Sultan, two captive Tatar princes. This magnanimous gesture, plus a large under-the-counter payment to Sinan Pasha, had the
desired effect. Later that summer, when news reached Iancu that he was
about to be recalled, the Voivod gathered all the cash reserves of the
Moldavian treasury and headed for his Habsburg refuge. Unfortunately
his route had to pass first through Poland. He was arrested there, and,
after a brief detention, executed on the King's orders in late September,
before the Ottoman çavuş could arrive to take him back to Istanbul.
Stephen Báthory offered various justifications for this: Iancu had opened
his letters to the Sultan when Polish couriers had passed through Moldavia, and had added spurious passages to them; he had burnt down
villages in Polish territory; and Poles who had sought justice from him
had been beaten and imprisoned. (The papal nuncio in Poland also
wrote, perhaps just repeating a standard line, that Iancu had made himself 'utterly hateful' to his people by violating their women.) Stephen did
not mention the huge quantity of cash – between 400,000 and a million
ducats, as rumour had it – which he expropriated. Nor did the Sultan
make much fuss about that; a resetting of Ottoman–Polish relations had
just taken place, and it was a sign of the Ottoman willingness to be con-
ciliatory that the new Voivod of Moldavia was, once again, Petru
Şchiopul.[17]

Not much is known about Bartolomeo Bruti's life in Moldavia during these years. As we have seen, a French ambassadorial despatch
stated in 1580 that he was granted a boyar's estate and an income of
3,000 ducats from the customs dues of a port – which was presumably
Galaţi, the only significant port left to Moldavia, on the northern bank
of the Danube.* That despatch's statement that he was also made general of the army might seem implausible, in view of Bartolomeo's total

* Above, p. 277.

lack of military experience; yet in January 1582 he was indeed joint commander of the Moldavian army, with the boyar Condrea Bucium, when it fought a major battle to crush the rebels of Lăpușna. Bartolomeo had the official position of 'postelnic', meaning seneschal or court chamberlain, while Bucium was the grand 'vornic' or count palatine of Lower Moldavia; neither was 'hatman' (general of the armed forces), but it seems that Bartolomeo was in effect the senior minister for external affairs, and Bucium for internal ones. As the Postelnic, Bartolomeo also held the prefecture of Iași, the capital city, and judged its citizens. These honours – which depended above all on the fact that he was Iancu's personal link to Sinan Pasha – represented an extraordinary transformation in his fortunes, from the ill-paid trainee dragoman and neglected underground agent of the previous years.[18]

Bartolomeo must have found his new conditions strange as well as exhilarating. He was now in an overwhelmingly Eastern Orthodox country, and its language, Romanian, would have taken some time to learn, even though his knowledge of Italian gave him a good head-start. This was a very traditional society, a far cry from the Venetianized city communities of the Adriatic that were familiar to him, with their statutes and municipal rights; the Moldavian towns and their surrounding villages were regarded as the personal property of the voivod, and the laws were customary and unwritten. Whilst the dress of the voivod and his courtiers was partly Ottoman in style, with richly decorated cloaks like caftans, the hierarchy and ceremonies derived from the Byzantine tradition. In 1574 a French traveller, commenting on court life in Iași, wrote that 'they honour their voivods like God, and drink excessively' – though a few years later Stefan Gerlach assured a friend that the Moldavians were at least more civilized than the Wallachians. In the late 1580s a Jesuit would write about Moldavia that 'literary writing is not held in esteem there, nor is it taught'; but he added that 'the people are excellent and talented, and shrewd rather than simple.' The population was quite mixed, especially in the towns; the merchant community included, as we have seen, both Armenians and Greeks (some of whom, especially those from Chios, were Roman Catholic), and Ragusans were active as tax- and customs-farmers. There were Protestant Germans, Hungarians and Hussites; and although the Jews had been expelled in 1579 at the insistence of Christian merchants, some seem to have returned under Iancu Sasul. There were also Albanians – villagers, traders and others. In 1584 the Jesuit Antonio Possevino would report from Poland that 'the Voivod of Moldavia's guard consists of 400 Trabants [a

Central European word for bodyguard], who are Hungarian, and 50 Albanian and Greek halbardiers, who live like Muslims.' So Bartolomeo Bruti would have found some people to talk to in his native tongue. But in any case he was not leading a solitary life. In these early years, at least, his wife Maria was with him. They had a son, probably within less than a year of their arrival in Moldavia, and had him baptized in Kamyanets-Podilskyi, the nearest town with a Catholic bishop. The boy was christened Antonio Stanislao – the first name honouring Bartolomeo's father, and the second presumably paying respect to an influential Polish godfather.[19]

In 1582 Bartolomeo Bruti went to Istanbul as the Voivod's envoy to attend the festivities for the circumcision of the future Mehmed III. Public celebrations of such events, and of the accessions of new sultans, were not uncommon, but this was the most elaborate and extravagant that had ever been seen, lasting more than 50 days from early June to late July; half a million *akçe*s (more than 8,000 ducats) had been set aside for staging it, invitations were sent to rulers in such distant places as Morocco and Uzbekistan, and the preparations took several months. It is not hard to guess the underlying reason for a jamboree which entertained much of the population of Istanbul. The Persian war, begun in 1578, was proving intractable, costly and increasingly unpopular; a large and distracting boost to morale, including displays of deference by foreign powers, was greatly to be desired. Certainly, nothing larger or more distracting could have been imagined. In the early stages of the festivities, senior pashas and the ambassadors of Muslim and Christian rulers presented lavish gifts. For the viziers and *beylerbeyi*s, this was the most demanding instance of the whole Ottoman cult of gift-giving. Sinan Pasha presented the Sultan with fine horses, large quantities of luxury cloth, a gold-illuminated Koran and a golden bowl encrusted with rubies and turquoises, while giving the Sultan's son a bejewelled golden sword, six male slaves, three horses and four illuminated books. The gifts of some foreign states were barely as lavish as that. The King of Poland sent quantities of highly prized Russian sable fur; the Venetian envoy, Giacomo Soranzo, brought 8,000 ducats' worth of gold, silver and silk; and Iancu Sasul's presents consisted of a silver fountain and other pieces of silverwork, to the value of 3,000 ducats.[20]

The celebrations were held in the Hippodrome, which had been specially fitted up for the occasion, with a three-storey wooden stand for distinguished guests. Christians, such as the Ragusan envoys and Bartolomeo, were placed in the bottom storey. For the first few weeks the formal present-givings were interspersed with entertainments, involving athletes, fighting animals (the fight between a boar and three lions was almost won by the boar), rope-dancers, musicians and others; one jaded French observer, Jean Palerne, found the music 'tuneful enough to make donkeys dance'. Sugar animals were paraded, including life-sized elephants and camels, and in the evenings the crowds were given free food and lavish firework displays. Then there were military performances (put on, Palerne noted, by Sinan, who wanted 'to be recognized as a great warlord'), with realistic-seeming battles involving mock-castles; the Christian castles, which were triumphantly overrun, had squealing pigs inside them. In the second week of June the processions of the Istanbul guilds began, with elaborate displays, sometimes on large carriages or floats, demonstrating or symbolizing their work. More than 200 guilds took part, including nailsmiths, bucket-sellers, javelin-makers, pickle-sellers, caftan-makers, silk-spinners, tart-bakers and snake-charmers. On the helva-makers' carriage a man made helva in a huge cauldron; on the barbers', a barber shaved customers while standing on his head; the Jewish gunpowder-makers' float had a powder-mill, and a man constantly igniting little explosions of powder against his bare skin. (The helva-makers also amused the crowd by trying to blow up a live rabbit with fireworks.) The mirror-makers dressed in clothes made out of pieces of mirror, while the manufacturers of coloured paper had 130 apprentices dressed in coloured paper. When they reached the Sultan the guildsmen gave him their own presents, both symbolic (giant shoes, paper tulips as tall as trees) and real: the guild of bird-catching pedlars solemnly presented two vultures, ten partridges and 100 sparrows. In return the Sultan conferred significant cash presents on the major guilds, and threw handfuls of coins at their apprentices. After that there were more military entertainments, with Albanian horsemen jousting at each other with lances; this was not mere play-acting, as several horses were killed in the process. Morale was boosted both by processions of genuine Christian captives from the Habsburg frontier, and by mass episodes of Christian Ottoman subjects, especially Greeks and Albanians, volunteering – to the dismay of Western observers – to convert to Islam. Everything went well from the Ottoman point of view, until the very last days of the festival, when serious fighting broke out between some of the Sultan's soldiers. It started with some young spahis (cavalrymen) who were found in a brothel by a janissary patrol led by the *subaşı* of Istanbul. Violence began when they resisted the round-up of prostitutes, and quickly turned into public fighting between much larger numbers of spahis and janissaries. Two of the spahis were killed. Sinan Pasha blamed the *ağa* (commander) of the janissaries, Ferhad Pasha, and dismissed him; Ferhad would become a redoubtable rival to Sinan thereafter.[21]

Bartolomeo presumably enjoyed the festivities, and the experience of rubbing shoulders with West European dignitaries who would have paid scant regard to him a few years earlier. But the most important element in this visit would have been his meetings with his relative Sinan Pasha, at which the future of the Voivod of Moldavia must have been discussed. Seven years later the papal nuncio in Poland would write, on the basis of what Bartolomeo had told him, that 'because Iancu did not observe the conditions he had promised, and did not pay the tribute he had promised to Sinan Pasha, by whose means he had been appointed voivod, Bruti in Istanbul arranged for Iancu to be deposed, and for this prince Petru, the current ruler, to be appointed.' That a failure to make the special personal payments to Sinan was a factor is easily imagined, but the claim that Bartolomeo 'arranged' the deposition sounds like self-aggrandizement; and it is difficult to believe that Bartolomeo, of all people, would have promoted the reinstatement of Petru Şchiopul, who could reasonably have been expected to bear a deep grudge against him for his previous dismissal. The decision was surely taken by Sinan, who obliged Petru to retain Bartolomeo's services. Petru Şchiopul's investiture took place in Istanbul on 28 August 1582, and he travelled to Moldavia with Bartolomeo a couple of weeks later. The Venetian bailo reported that Petru made a grand exit from Istanbul with an escort of more than 1,000 cavalry. He also wrote – again, surely on the basis of what Bartolomeo had said – that Petru was reinstated thanks to Bartolomeo's intercession; he added, significantly, that Bartolomeo went with him 'and will have the most important and most valuable position, having been warmly recommended by the Grand Vizier, who told him that whether he stays a long time in office will depend on the good treatment he gives to Bruti'.[22]

18

Bartolomeo Bruti in Power

The chronicler Grigore Ureche paints a very attractive portrait of the Voivod Petru Şchiopul, 'Peter the Lame'. 'He was a defender of his country, and compassionate to the poor; he was held by all in high regard and affection.' Petru showed notable piety and generosity towards the Orthodox Church: he set up an endowment (witnessed by Bartolomeo) for the monastery of St John on the island of Patmos, gave a Moldavian village to the monastery of St Sava in Jerusalem, made various gifts to the ecumenical patriarchate in Istanbul, and acted as protector of the Orthodox Church in Lviv. An account of him in a Greek Orthodox chronicle emphasizes not only his patronage of priests and monasteries, but also that he was 'compassionate in the highest degree towards slaves and the poor'. It notes that he was fluent in Romanian, Greek and Turkish, and adds that he was 'very just in the judgments he gave, and very learned in every art, and in literature', with a special interest in astronomy. The point about slaves is confirmed by a Polish diplomat who later testified that Petru had redeemed many Christians from Ottoman slavery. Other sources leave one wondering, however, whether this rather gentle spirit was well suited to the rough geopolitical environment in which he lived. In 1582 Stephen Báthory commented on his 'pleasant and easy-going tendency to give way to any violence', and in the following year the Polish king was reported to have said, a little complacently, that Petru was 'not a man of courage, but nevertheless a good-natured person, and rather dependent on him'.[1]

No sooner had Polish–Ottoman relations been mended by the reappointment of Petru Şchiopul than they were broken again, in 1583, by the Cossacks. After a failed attempt to enter Moldavia with yet another pretender to its throne, they turned towards the Ottoman-ruled territory around Bender, attacking a recently built fort to the north of that town and then the suburbs and citadel of Bender itself. Because the fort was on territory claimed by the King of Poland, it was widely assumed that this was an officially sponsored attack. On 7 July Bartolomeo wrote to his brother Cristoforo in Istanbul, saying that he and the Voivod had just left Iaşi with an army of 15,000 men to help the *sancakbeyi* in Bender; he described the enemy forces as 10,000 'Cossacks, and other soldiers of the King of Poland', and concluded that 'here, on this frontier, peace between the Poles and the Sultan has gone to pot.' The Ottoman authorities were enraged by this attack; soon afterwards, they arrested one Polish envoy and murdered another. But Stephen Báthory had not in fact ordered the campaign, and he now made strenuous efforts to avoid war with the Ottomans, hunting down the Cossack leaders and having 30 of them beheaded in front of a *çavuş* in Lviv. So when Bartolomeo went with his soldiers to Bender, he was not actually fighting for the Ottoman Empire against a Christian state. Nevertheless, he was fighting, as minister of an Ottoman vassal state, for the interests of the Ottoman Empire.[2]

Again there is a lack of detailed evidence about the internal working of the Moldavian state in this period, and thus also about Bartolomeo's activities. Clearly he was flourishing: in the summer of 1584 the Jesuit Antonio Possevino reported from Poland that 'in the city of Iaşi there is the Venetian Bartolomeo Bruto, who is a Catholic, and the favourite of the Voivod; he is his counsellor, and military commander, and not long ago he sent his family in Venice 6,000 Hungarian ducats.' Bartolomeo and his wife Maria had had a second son, Alessandro, probably in 1583; from Possevino's comment it seems that she had now gone to 'Venice' – in fact, to Koper, where she lived thereafter – to bring up the children and bank the large earnings that Bartolomeo was now making. (Later his income would rise, reportedly, to the colossal sum of 12,000 ducats a year.) The Jesuit Giulio Mancinelli, who visited Iaşi in 1585, described Bartolomeo as 'highly honoured, and very dear to the Voivod'. A similar impression was gained by a French traveller, François de Pavie, sieur de Fourquevaux, who came early in the following year: he kissed Petru Şchiopul's hands 'by the favour of, and escorted by, the lord Bruti, an Albanian gentleman, who is the Voivod's great favourite'. (Fourquevaux also witnessed the dispensing of justice by Petru, in a square in front of his residence: flanked by his chief ministers and several hundred Hungarian soldiers armed with scimitars and axes, he listened to each subject who knelt before him and uttered a grievance, and then issued his instant judgment.) These comments about the Voivod showing special favour to Bartolomeo cannot be discounted simply as signs that

Petru was bending his will to Sinan Pasha's instructions. For Sinan had been dismissed from the post of Grand Vizier in December 1582; while he remained an influential figure, he no longer had the whip-hand in Istanbul, until his return to power near the end of the decade. So it seems that Bartolomeo really had impressed Petru with his personal qualities and abilities, and had become his indispensable right-hand man. That relations between the two men were good is confirmed by a document of 1587, in which Petru mentioned that he had given Bartolomeo a village, Childeşti, in gratitude 'for his true and faithful service to us'.[3]

Thanks to the favour he enjoyed, Bartolomeo – who also continued to hold the high office of 'postelnic' – was able to obtain positions or estates for several members of his own family. His brother Benedetto became 'cup-bearer', an honorific position at the voivod's court, and acquired property in Moldavia; in 1589 Petru sold him a village for 20,000 *akçe*s (roughly 166 ducats). Their brother Cristoforo spent some time in Moldavia in 1588–9 and would himself be made cup-bearer, and a member of Petru's governing council, in 1590. Another brother, Bernardo, also acquired property there, and took part in a Moldavian diplomatic mission in 1589. Their nephew Bernardo or Bernardino Borisi, son of Pietro Borisi and Jacoma Bruti, was also well established in Iaşi by 1587, when he was working as an interpreter at Petru Şchiopul's court; this was the 'Barnadyno Barrysco' who translated for the adventurous English traveller Henry Cavendish (son of Bess of Hardwick and brother of the first Earl of Devonshire) when he passed through Iaşi two years later. And, as we shall see, another nephew would also spend some time at Petru's court in the late 1580s: Antonio Bruni.[4]

Bartolomeo was certainly keen to promote his family; after the wreck of their fortunes at the fall of Ulcinj this was a chance, not to be missed, to make the Brutis prosperous and influential again. But his desire to extend his patronage and assistance went much further than that, as he made it his special mission to support and promote Roman Catholicism in Moldavia. The first clear sign of this comes in a letter he wrote in the summer of 1584 to an old friend who had contacted him, Tommaso Nadali or Natali (a Ragusan physician who had worked for several years in Istanbul, treating Sultan Murad for his asthma, before moving to Poland and becoming a canon of Kraków cathedral). 'I have never failed,' Bartolomeo wrote rather grandly, 'both in Turkey [i.e. directly ruled Ottoman territory] and in this country, to assist in every way the introduction of people of exemplary life and good doctrine, and to root out the curse of heresy – which, if I could, I would root out of the world, not just out of these regions.' As proof of this he mentioned that when he had found a heretical 'false bishop' in Moldavia, he had made him recant in church and then sent him to do the same in front of the Bishop of Kamyanets-Podilskyi. He also referred to 'my long service to the holy Church, both in freeing slaves and in other matters'; and he asked that a priest be sent to visit him and minister to the Catholics in Iaşi.[5]

The letter from Nadali to which Bartolomeo was replying was not a merely casual note from a friend; this Ragusan had been enlisted in an initiative which was part of a much larger strategy to push forward the work of the Counter-Reformation in Central and Eastern Europe. The underlying aim was nothing less than the conversion to Rome of the Orthodox Churches. To some observers that might have seemed utopian; it certainly was, where the Russian Church was concerned, as the papal envoy Antonio Possevino (former Rector of the Jesuit College in Avignon) discovered when he visited Moscow in 1581. But there were other potential breakthroughs in the Orthodox world that seemed quite feasible. The Ruthenian Church, to which the large Orthodox population in the Ukrainian and other territories of the Grand Duchy of Lithuania belonged, became more of a target after that state was united with Poland; the Rector of the Jesuit College in Vilnius campaigned energetically for the conversion of the Orthodox in the 1570s, and the Jesuits helped to set up several more seminaries in Lithuanian territory.[6]

The Greek Church was another potential prize to be won. Rome was convinced – despite some evidence to the contrary, from places such as Cyprus – that Orthodox Greeks would much prefer Western European rule to being governed by Muslims. In any case, at the Council of Florence in 1439 the Patriarch of Constantinople had actually signed up to a reunion of the Orthodox and Roman Churches; this was viewed as more than just a precedent, being in some ways enforced, as we have seen, in Venetian territory.* (The Orthodox Albanians and Greeks who settled in southern Italy and Sicily were also expected to abide by it, being allowed their own priesthood and liturgies but required to acknowledge the primacy of Rome.) Pope Gregory XIII had a strong interest in winning over the Orthodox world: he set up a 'congregation' or department for 'Greek' (i.e. Orthodox) affairs in 1573, sent a mission to the Patriarch of Constantinople in 1575, and founded the Greek College in Rome in 1577. When Giacomo Soranzo went to Istanbul as Venetian representative at the circumcision festivities in 1582, he took

---

* Above, pp. 19–20.

with him a papal agent, Livio Cellini, who had several discussions with the Patriarch; but although some of the Patriarch's senior advisers were pro-reunion, the recent reform of the calendar imposed – without consulting the Eastern Churches – by Gregory XIII caused great offence, so the negotiations made no real progress. Nevertheless, Rome did have some reason to hope for a positive response from the Patriarch, Jeremias II. A few years earlier, when West European Protestants had contacted Jeremias in the hope of obtaining an anti-papal statement from him, he had written a document firmly rejecting Protestant views. That document had been obtained from Istanbul, through the good offices of Bartolomeo's friend Tommaso Nadali, by a Polish Catholic priest in Kraków, who published it in 1582 to great acclaim in the Catholic world. Further papal missions to Jeremias took place in 1583 and 1584, but before the second of those could reach him he was deposed by the Sultan and exiled to Rhodes. Among the accusations against him was the charge that he was secretly plotting with the Pope.[7]

It was in these circumstances that Gregory XIII and Cardinal Como, his secretary of state, decided in 1583 on a new initiative, aiming to win over two Orthodox countries of obvious strategic importance to any long-term anti-Ottoman plans: Wallachia and Moldavia. In the belief that Petru Şchiopul was well-inclined towards Catholics, and with the knowledge that the young Voivod of Wallachia, Mihnea (Petru's nephew), had partly Catholic ancestry, the Pope wrote letters to the two voivods and four of their ministers, including Bartolomeo Bruti. The original plan was that Possevino, who was now based in Vienna, would take the letters to them; but there were various delays and problems (the Jesuit was worried that his role as a papal envoy was known to the Ottomans, who had had a çavuş in Moscow when he was there), plus the fact that in the summer of 1583 Mihnea was deposed and replaced by a rival claimant, Petru Cercel ('Peter the Earring' – so called because he had adopted this strange Western fashion after a stay at the French court). In the end it was Nadali who went to Wallachia with the letters – he seems not to have got as far as Moldavia in person – and brought back, in late 1584, Bartolomeo's encouraging reply.[8]

Over the next few years there were some more contacts. In 1585 the Jesuit Giulio Mancinelli passed through Iaşi on his way from Istanbul to Poland, and was looked after by Bartolomeo. (Mancinelli had been a 'study prefect', and director of one of the Marian congregations, at the Seminario Romano in 1575; one wonders whether, on learning that Bartolomeo was an Albanian from Ulcinj and Koper, he made the

connection with his former pupil Antonio Bruni.) He was shocked to
find that many of the Roman Catholics there had gone over to the
Orthodox Church because of the lack of Catholic priests, and that their
church in Iaşi was 'profaned by Lutheran ministers', who often come
here to serve the artisans, who are almost all Lutheran Germans or
Hungarians'. Bartolomeo urged him to stay, saying that Petru would
make him Bishop of Moldavia; but he felt unable to accept such an offer
without the authorization of his superiors. In the following year, Aleksandar Komulović ('Alessandro Comuleo'), the Pope's special Apostolic
Visitor to the Balkans, arrived with a Ragusan Jesuit and held further
discussions; at his request, and with Bartolomeo's encouragement, Petru
banned all Lutheran ministers from the country. But two issues remained.
There was the practical problem of how to supply the small Roman
Catholic population of Moldavia with priests. And, more fundamentally, there was the question of how the entire Orthodox Church of
Moldavia might be persuaded to accept the primacy of Rome. Bartolomeo Bruti was to play an active role in both of these matters.[9]

Two senior Catholic figures had important parts in this story. One
was Jan Dymitr Solikowski, a Polish humanist scholar and former royal
secretary who became Archbishop of Lviv in 1583. The other was the
aristocratic Archbishop of Naples, Annibale di Capua, son of the Duke
of Termoli, who was sent to Poland as papal nuncio in 1586 to improve
the clergy's compliance with the decrees of the Council of Trent, and
was mostly based in Warsaw or Kraków. In May 1587 Solikowski wrote
to di Capua, giving a glowing report of the work that was being done
for Catholicism by Petru Şchiopul and Bartolomeo Bruti; he had
received letters from both of them, and the one from Bartolomeo
included a request – to be repeated in many subsequent letters – that the
Pope reward him by granting a benefice to his young son Antonio. The
nuncio forwarded this information to Rome, and at the same time sent
an encouraging letter to Bartolomeo in Iaşi. In his reply Bartolomeo
thanked him on behalf of all the Catholics in Moldavia (he estimated
the total at 15,000), proudly declaring that since the expulsion of the
Protestant preachers, they all now lived 'in conformity with the most
holy decrees of the most holy Council of Trent'. What they needed,
he said, was a number of Jesuits who knew German and Hungarian,
the main languages of the Catholic and ex-Protestant population:
the Voivod would grant them the town of Cotnar, which was mostly
German and Hungarian, with its three old Catholic churches, and
Bartolomeo would provide 'everything that is needed', in the hope that

they would set up a seminary there. Thus did Bartolomeo declare his support for the full Counter-Reformation programme.[10]

Meanwhile Pope Sixtus V had written a grateful letter to Petru; and at the same time his nephew and secretary of state, Cardinal Montalto, sent one to Bartolomeo, giving him personal credit for expelling Protestant ministers and 'bringing back a large number of people to the Catholic religion'. He also said that the request for 'ecclesiastical revenues' for his son would be granted. These letters seem to have taken a long time to reach Moldavia; but in early January 1588 Bartolomeo wrote to the Pope, saying that when the letter to Petru had arrived, he had read it, translating it into Romanian for the Voivod, who had kissed it and placed it reverentially on his head. (This was an Ottoman custom: a Moroccan ambassador who went to Istanbul in 1581 observed that if one gave somebody a present he would 'kneel, receive it with both hands, and place it on his head, to show his esteem for it, and his respect for the giver'.) In this letter Bartolomeo repeated the request on behalf of his son in Koper, and added one for his own benefit: he wanted to be given the honorific title 'Defender and Protector of the Roman Church against the Heretics'. In an accompanying letter to Cardinal Montalto, he described some of the measures that had already been taken at his urging: the Voivod had told the Franciscans in Moldavia that they had the authority to arrest and imprison heretics, and had restored the original revenues of all Catholic churches. At the same time Bartolomeo wrote to the nuncio, asking him to send four Jesuits and six Observant Franciscans who could speak German and Hungarian. Annibale passed on all of this to Rome, begging the authorities there to favour Bartolomeo's two personal requests, 'as I see with what ardour he labours in the service of holy God'. He had already reported the news, given to him by Solikowski, that the Voivod was promising 'to send his ambassadors to give his submission to His Holiness [the Pope], when the affairs of his kingdom were pacified'. Thus, by the spring of 1588, all the key themes had appeared that would recur again and again in the dealings between Iaşi, Lviv, Warsaw and Rome: the need for Jesuits and/or other priests in Moldavia; the promise by Petru Şchiopul to make, via an official embassy, a formal pledge of submission to Rome; and Bartolomeo Bruti's oft-repeated two personal demands.[11]

That near-obsessive interest in the benefice and the title naturally raises, in modern minds, the question of Bartolomeo's motives – as it did in the minds of the Catholic authorities at the time. Bartolomeo was aware that some might think ill of his wish for such a fine-sounding title; in one letter (giving the title even more grandiosely as 'Protector-General of the Catholics in Moldavia and the Ottoman Empire') he declared that he wanted it not out of 'ambition', but because if he held it he would have greater authority in opposing all kinds of heretics, even in the Ottoman-ruled lands. With a similar rhetorical flourish he said in another letter that he hoped the benefice for his son would be 'not trivial', so that everyone, including the heretics, would see how his work was valued, and many would be inspired to serve the Church with greater ardour. Such rhetoric is easy to discount; motives, after all, can be mixed, and self-interest often forms part of the mixture. But while it can naturally be supposed that some self-centred motives were present, it is hard to believe that they formed the dominant reason for Bartolomeo's intense involvement in this cause – especially since, as he emphasized, he spent his own money in pursuit of it. (He actually gave two of his own villages to the Jesuits when they arrived in Moldavia.) Solikowski, who met him in January 1589, testified a few months later that Bartolomeo was sincere, and that 'I honestly say that I cannot detect any fraud in these matters.' Had he been motivated only by self-interest, Bartolomeo Bruti would have converted to Islam when his cousin was Grand Vizier, after which he would have been fast-tracked to the governorship of a *sancak* and then a *beylerbeylik*; so his attachment to his own religion can definitely be taken as genuine. Possibly the fact that he was now working at one remove for the Ottoman Empire actually strengthened, in a compensatory way, his desire to serve the cause of Christianity. So perhaps when he wrote to the Pope in 1591 that he wanted to 'sacrifice myself in the service of the holy Church, as did my father and my uncle, the most Reverend Archbishop of Bar, who were killed by the infidels', he was not just cynically using those bereavements to boost his credentials. When Solikowski met him in late 1588 he was struck not only by Bartolomeo's 'exceptional piety, ardent eagerness and incredible zeal', but also by the fact that he seemed to be aiming at a larger goal, 'to plant the holy Catholic religion not only in the soil of Moldavia, but also in many other provinces that are under the power of the Ottomans, and forthwith to set them free, and enlarge them'.[12]

What of Petru Şchiopul's own motives? The surprising thing is not his willingness to force German and Hungarian Protestants to revert to Catholicism (rulers are easily persuaded that any kind of rejection of authority is to be suppressed), but his interest in the idea of putting his own Orthodox Church under the Papacy. Naturally there were suspicions about him in Rome. In early 1589 Cardinal Montalto wrote to the

nuncio in Poland: 'since we have been informed that this prince is adapting to circumstances, and shows himself willing to become a Catholic
more from fear of being driven out of his position by the Sultan, perhaps, than from innate inclination, be aware of this and take careful
note of everything that happens.' But in order to assess the Voivod's
intentions, it is necessary also to understand the nature of the Moldavian Church in this period. Since the fall of Constantinople it had been
more or less autocephalous (self-governing), under a Metropolitan who
was neither appointed nor dismissed by the Patriarch. For a period in
the sixteenth century it was formally placed under the Archbishopric of
Ohrid, an ancient seat of the Orthodox Church in Macedonia; this
seems to have been satisfying to the Moldavians, who continued long
thereafter to assert a connection with Ohrid as a way of establishing
their freedom from Patriarchal control. The senior Jesuit who visited
Iaşi in 1588 reported that they could easily be brought to acknowledge
the primacy of Rome, as 'they do not recognize the Patriarch of Constantinople.' He also described a discussion he had witnessed between
the Voivod and 'a certain Orthodox monk'. Petru asked the monk two
questions: to whom did Christ give the keys of the Church (answer: St
Peter); and where did St Peter place his head when he died (answer:
Rome). It followed, said the Voivod – sounding as if he had been well
coached by Bartolomeo – that Rome was where St Peter intended the
future heads of the Church to be. In April 1589 Solikowski wrote, summarizing what that Jesuit mission had told him, that Petru was willing
to accept both the primacy of the Pope and the Roman Catholic articles
of faith (on such contentious matters as whether the Holy Ghost proceeded from the Father and the Son – the famous 'filioque' clause), but
that he wished to retain the Orthodox liturgy. He was thus feeling his
way towards a Church union resembling the one that would be agreed
between Rome and the Ruthenian Orthodox Church in 1596, which
created the first of a series of 'Uniate' Churches that kept their own
rites. The Uniate Churches have remained an important part of the political and ecclesiastical landscape of several East European countries
down to the present day.[13]

    It has sometimes been suggested that Petru's pro-union policy was
little more than a political ploy, arising from the fact that after the death
of Stephen Báthory in December 1586 he was keen to be elected King
of Poland – for which papal support would be extremely valuable. But
that does not explain the continuation of that policy long after the
Swedish prince Sigismund Vasa was chosen as King of Poland in August

1587 and crowned in December of that year. If there was a political background to Petru's Uniate tendencies, it is to be sought much more in the long-standing pro-Polish attitudes of a section of the Moldavian nobility that supported him – especially the powerful Movilă family. Its two most prominent members, Ieremie and Gheorghe, had both gone into exile in Poland during the reign of Iancu Sasul. When Gheorghe became Metropolitan of the Moldavian Church in December 1587, conditions became much more favourable for a rapprochement with Rome. (It was in fact unusual for a boyar to hold high rank in the Church; normally the Orthodox hierarchy consisted of men with low social status and – despite the Metropolitan's formal place on the voivod's council – little political influence.) Both the Metropolitan and his brother Ieremie played active roles in the pro-papal policy; when Cardinal Montalto wrote to Solikowski in January 1589 that the desire to join Rome was to be found in 'the Voivod and the Metropolitans themselves [sic – there was only one] and also the nobles and indeed the whole people', he may have been exaggerating, but his exaggerated notions were acquired from letters he had just received from Petru Şchiopul, Bartolomeo Bruti, and both Ieremie and Gheorghe Movilă.[14]

Of the two key policies promoted by Bartolomeo, the introduction of more Catholic priests to Moldavia and the formal submission of the Moldavian Church to Rome, only the former was carried out successfully, at least for a while. In late August 1588 a group of three Jesuits and a lay assistant, headed by Stanisław Warszewicki, the Rector of the Jesuit College in Lublin, set off for Moldavia. They arrived in Iaşi on 1 September, 'where a brother of signor Bruti met us and took us to his home'; as soon as they got there, 'a nephew of signor Bruti arrived in a carriage, to take us the next day to the camp' – plague was raging, and Petru had set up his court in a military encampment in the open fields. The next evening they reached the camp and were taken to see Bartolomeo, 'who, having given us dinner, offered us his tent to stay in; it had carpets on the ground, in the Ottoman manner.' It was in this encampment, surrounded by more than 1,000 soldiers who played 'Ottoman and Hungarian drums and trumpets' deafeningly three times a day, that Warszewicki had his discussions with Petru Şchiopul, and with his Metropolitan and senior clergy. The plan to set up a seminary was one of the things they talked about, though it became clear that Petru's finances were so strained by the many payments he had to make to Istanbul that he could not fund it himself. Meanwhile the two junior Jesuits were settled in the town of Roman, which had a significant German population; it was to help provide them with an income that Bartolomeo gave them two Hungarian-inhabited villages that he owned.[15]

A few months later, in December 1588, the authorities in Transylvania announced that the Jesuits (who had set up a college in the central Transylvanian town of Cluj nine years earlier) must leave that country; some of them then travelled to Moldavia. They were welcomed by the Voivod, who issued decrees enjoining obedience to the Jesuits on all his Catholic subjects. In late February Bartolomeo felt able to write to the head of the order in Poland: 'if we have lost Transylvania, God has given us the new possession of Moldavia, and using this province we shall perhaps go into Transylvania.' A year later, writing either to him or possibly to the General of the Jesuits in Rome, Bartolomeo said that the Jesuits in Moldavia had done great things, converting many and baptizing many. He now wanted the Pope to pay for a grand church for them in Iaşi which, to impress the non-Catholics, should be built out of stone, unlike all the existing churches there. (When Henry Cavendish and his servant visited Iaşi they observed that it was 'but a poor wodden toune and the prynce's pallas ys but of wood and covred with boordes'.) He promised to donate another village, and to obtain two more from the Voivod, plus 400 labourers to build the church. He also urgently requested a bishop, because many of the Hungarian pupils from the Jesuit college in Cluj had come to Moldavia, and the opportunity to ordain them as priests was being lost. And finally, in a gesture both deferential and lordly, he explained that he was enclosing as a gift a caftan 'of Turkish brocade, of the kind worn by grandees in the Ottoman Empire'; please accept it, he wrote, 'because Ottoman lords have given me not only this one, but many like it, in order to flatter me'.[16]

As for the plan that the Moldavian Orthodox Church would make a formal submission to Rome: this seems to have fallen victim to a series of misadventures. The original promise, quoted above, was that Petru Şchiopul would send ambassadors to Rome to do it 'when the affairs of his kingdom were pacified'; but in October 1588, after Warszewicki had returned from Moldavia, Petru wrote to Annibale di Capua saying that it had not proved possible to carry this out because of 'disturbances by the Ottomans and the Tatars'. So he was now ordering Bartolomeo Bruti and Ieremie Movilă, who were going on a diplomatic mission to the King of Poland, to visit the papal legate in that country and make the act of submission to the Roman Catholic Church in Petru's name. When they reached Kraków, however, they found that the King had travelled northwards to Brest, so they had to follow him there; and on the other hand the legate, Ippolito Aldobrandini, had left for Prague. Bartolomeo thus narrowly missed the opportunity to meet Aldobrandini, the Florentine lawyer who would become Pope Clement VIII just over three years later; instead he sent him a letter from Brest in early December, begging him to think favourably of 'the risks I run and the great efforts I make for the glory of God, not to mention the great expenses'. The letters he had brought from the Voivod and the Metropolitan were forwarded to Rome, but the formal act of submission was not made. Almost a year later, Bartolomeo wrote to Annibale di Capua, promising again that ambassadors would be sent to Rome, and explaining that recent serious tensions between Poland and the Ottoman Empire (which had indeed made Moldavia's position quite perilous) had prevented this. In August of the following year he wrote to Cardinal Montalto to explain that his time had been taken up by 'constant troubles' and 'long journeys', and that just at the moment 'when I thought I could set off for Rome in order to kiss the most holy feet of our lord [the Pope] in the name of the most illustrious Prince of Moldavia', the simmering Polish–Ottoman conflict had required him to stay. All of this was true, and Polish–Ottoman affairs would keep him busy until well into 1591 – the year when Petru Şchiopul ceased to be Voivod. But of course Bartolomeo was not the only person who could have performed the Rome mission; so the possibility remains that, eventually, Petru had changed his mind, or had entered a state of permanent hesitation on this issue. Even if the formal submission had been made, its practical effects – such as they might have been – would have lasted no longer than Petru Şchiopul's own rule.[17]

At an early stage, in May 1588, Cardinal Montalto had promised that Bartolomeo would receive the honour he craved, and the benefice for his son, when the Moldavian ambassadors arrived in Rome. Early in the following year he repeated this promise where the son was concerned, but said that the Pope was dubious about the title Bartolomeo had requested, since 'such a thing is normally given only to great princes, or to powerful peoples and nations.' Solikowski and di Capua lobbied hard on Bartolomeo's behalf, and in early 1590 Montalto wrote to both of them, agreeing in principle to grant the title – though this promise was never fulfilled. Meanwhile, more information was required about Bartolomeo's son, starting with his precise age, as anyone receiving a benefice had to be at least ten years old. By June 1590 di Capua had established – correctly – that the boy was under the age of ten, and therefore eligible only for a simple monetary 'pension'. Rather brazenly, in September of that year Bartolomeo raised his estimate of his son's age to 'roughly twelve'. It seems that in the end no benefice was granted, and no pension was paid.[18]

As some of these details will already have suggested, this final period of Petru Şchiopul's rule was troubled by many problems, including plague, Ottoman pressures and Tatar actions. His greatest underlying problem, though, was money. On his reinstatement in 1582 the official tribute had been raised, and at the last minute he had been forced to come up with an extra 200,000 ducats (which he borrowed at 60 per cent interest), with another 200,000 promised for two years later. He had also been required to pay off debts of 60,000 ducats left behind by Iancu Sasul. By 1587 he was complaining that he had to pay a 'secret tribute' of 100,000 a year, and that the Porte frequently sent him çavuşes with no real business to conduct, merely to oblige him to hand over more honorific presents. He was always borrowing money, either directly from merchants in Moldavia or through his agent in Istanbul (who raised substantial loans from, among others, rich janissaries). Constantly, the voivods of Moldavia and Wallachia were threatened by the prospect of potential rivals outbidding them in Istanbul; the secretary at the French embassy commented in 1585 that 'they have to set aside more than a third of their revenues every year for the chief ministers here, because of continual new predatory demands based on the annual bids of their competitors.' The Ottoman authorities showed tremendous ingenuity in thinking up ways of extorting money from these cash-cows. At the end of 1589 Petru was theoretically deposed, and replaced by his six-year-old son, who underwent a grand coronation service in Moldavia in the following February; Petru's rule continued uninterruptedly, but the nominal accession of a new voivod meant another payment of 100,000 ducats to Istanbul. This particular money-making method, commented the Venetian bailo, was 'a ridiculous invention'.[19]

On top of his financial problems, Petru Şchiopul was also troubled by the effects of serious Polish–Ottoman tensions in the latter part of the 1580s. Following the death of Stephen Báthory in December 1586, there was a long interregnum in Poland as rival candidates sparred for the succession. Archduke Maximilian, son of the Emperor Maximilian II, worked hard to get himself elected, but the Grand Chancellor who ran the country during the interregnum, Jan Zamoyski, was stoutly anti-Habsburg, and in the end his strategy prevailed: the Poles chose the Catholic Swedish prince Sigismund Vasa, whose mother had belonged to the Polish Jagiellonian dynasty. Maximilian contested the election, bringing an armed force to Poland and besieging Kraków in late 1587, before he and his supporters (who included a significant faction of the Polish nobility) were defeated in battle in January 1588. Maximilian was captured; hence the mission of the papal legate Ippolito Aldobrandini, which was to obtain his release, and negotiate a lasting settlement between King Sigismund and the Habsburgs. Meanwhile, these events had two damaging consequences for Polish–Ottoman relations: they gave the Cossacks the opportunity to do more raiding, and they made Istanbul more nervous about the long-term future of the Polish state. There were some serious Cossack attacks on Moldavia in 1587–8, possibly stimulated by the Habsburgs, and in February 1589 the Sultan issued a strong complaint to Poland about Cossack raids on his fortresses at Akkerman (Bilhorod-Dnistrovskyi) and Bender. The Poles had in fact tried hard to reassure Istanbul of their intentions, sending an envoy in May 1588 to confirm what they called their 'ancient treaty' with the Ottomans. However, when Aldobrandini's diplomacy finally paid off in March 1589 with a Polish–Habsburg agreement and the release of Maximilian, the Ottomans became more suspicious of Sigismund's intentions. And although he was not seeking war against the Sultan, there were some good reasons for suspecting him: he was imbued with the spirit of the Counter-Reformation, having been educated by Jesuits, and in 1589 he did in fact negotiate secretly with the Habsburgs to transfer the Polish crown to another archduke, Ernest, so that he himself would be free to seek the crown of Sweden. Feeling that their protests about the Cossacks had no effect, the Ottoman authorities ordered the Tatar Khan to attack Polish territory in July 1589, and sent an army under the *beylerbeyi* of Rumeli (the Ottoman province of the central and southern Balkans, encompassing Bulgaria, Macedonia, Albania and parts of Greece) to northern Moldavia, to begin raiding across the border. One of its first actions was to devastate the Polish town of Snyatyn – where, with insouciance verging on madness, traders had just congregated for the annual fair.[20]

These events put Moldavia in a very difficult position. On the one hand Petru Şchiopul had his duties as an Ottoman vassal to perform; they included supplying intelligence (in 1587, for example, he had transmitted to Istanbul the detailed political news sent by his representative in Poland), and could easily involve providing armed forces too. On the other hand he had always been pro-Polish, and he enjoyed good relations with Zamoyski. So too did Bartolomeo Bruti. (In September 1588 Zamoyski sent a personal letter to Bartolomeo thanking him for 50 bullocks he had sent, and requesting his help in arranging the delivery of 400 cattle, for Zamoyski's personal needs, from the Voivod; he ended with the words 'I commend myself to your gracious friendship.') In April 1588, when the Tatars first began threatening Poland, Petru tried to mediate between the Poles and the authorities in Istanbul. And in October of that year he sent Bartolomeo and Ieremie Movilă on a mission to King Sigismund; this was when they had to follow him northwards to Brest. The official reason for their mission was simply to congratulate him on his accession to power, and, as Bartolomeo put it in a letter to Cardinal Montalto, 'confirm the alliances that exist between this kingdom of Poland and Moldavia'; but the security problems of the region must have loomed large in their discussions with both the King and his Grand Chancellor. The Voivod of Moldavia was pig-in-the-middle in a growing Polish–Ottoman crisis, and had every reason to try to promote peace.[21]

Luckily for him, an important change happened in April 1589: Bartolomeo's relative Sinan Pasha was re-appointed Grand Vizier. This meant that Bartolomeo himself could become much more closely involved in negotiations in Istanbul. He went there in May to congratulate Sinan, and to make the necessary financial promises to secure the continuation of Petru Şchiopul's rule. (While he was there, he visited the bailo every day, telling him his news; the bailo was impressed, and described him as 'a person who is no less devoted to this most serene Republic [Venice] than he is discreet and prudent'.) An Italian who witnessed Bartolomeo's triumphant return to Iaşi told Annibale di Capua: 'Bruti enjoys great authority, as this Sinan Pasha who has now been made Grand Vizier is his cousin. And when he came back just now from Istanbul on 20 June, all the nobility of that province came out to meet him, and the Voivod himself had sent all his court and gave him many presents, fearing that Bruti, with the favour of this Grand Vizier, might wish to be voivod of Moldavia himself.'[22]

The notion of placing a non-Romanian – or at least a non-Romanian who did not even claim, however spuriously, some Romanian dynastic credentials – such as Bartolomeo Bruti on the throne was an idea ahead of its time; one generation later, a very similar figure, Gaspare Graziani, a Dalmatian who worked as a dragoman, slave-ransomer and jewel trader in Istanbul, would get to rule Moldavia for nearly two years. But Bartolomeo remained loyal to Petru Şchiopul, and indeed to Petru's family. Six days later he went back to Istanbul and used his influence – plus the promise of a large payment – to block an attempt by 'Peter the Earring', who had been ejected from Wallachia in 1585 in favour of Petru

Şchiopul's nephew Mihnea, to return to power. On this visit he also freed two Christian slaves, one Italian and the other Spanish, whom he took to Iaşi and then sent on to the papal nuncio in Poland. Bartolomeo's personal and political credit was riding high; in August he was even able to persuade Sinan to rescind an order requiring Moldavia to contribute forces against the Poles. So it is not surprising that when, in early November 1589, Sinan decided to open negotiations with Poland, the method he chose was to tell Petru Şchiopul to send Bartolomeo, as if on a personal mission from the Voivod himself. The purpose of Bartolomeo's trip to Poland was, as the Imperial Ambassador in Istanbul noted during the following month, to transmit to the Poles a request that they send an envoy to the Ottoman government.[23]

One reason for Sinan's willingness to negotiate was that Poland had put up unexpectedly strong resistance. While King Sigismund was absent in Sweden, Jan Zamoyski had devoted great energy to raising an army. At first he sent letters (via Petru Şchiopul) to the *beylerbeyi* of Rumeli, suggesting diplomatic negotiations; but by October, with 25–30,000 men at his disposal, Zamoyski was feeling more belligerent, advising the Polish senators that if the *beylerbeyi* did not immediately reaffirm the Polish–Ottoman peace treaty they should plan an offensive war for 1590, involving the full occupation of Moldavia and an invasion of Tatar territory. A Tatar attack, meanwhile, had been routed by Cossacks, and the Khan himself had been wounded. During the winter, while the Ottoman force was stationed on the Black Sea coast, Zamoyski did send an ambassador, first to the *beylerbeyi* and then on to Istanbul, but he broke his leg on the way from Poland and began to suffer from serious complications. Apparently he stayed for some time en route in Iaşi, and was given advice and help there by Bartolomeo Bruti. Tantalizingly, there is an entry in a nineteenth-century inventory in the Polish state archives summarizing a letter, now missing, from Bartolomeo to Jan Zamoyski, written in Iaşi on 10 January 1590. In it, according to this summary, Bartolomeo 'reports about the services which he has performed for the Polish envoy, both with the *beylerbeyi paşa* and also with important and essential people in Istanbul; he asks that the royal Chancellor grant him his good favour and continuing desire for services, both in war and in peace; and finally he warns the Chancellor against putting his full trust in the Ottomans.' A few days later, in mid-January, the Polish Ambassador reached the Ottoman capital. The authorities there placed him under virtual house arrest, and within eight days he had died of his illness. Before he did so, the basic Ottoman demands had become clear: Poland must restrain its Cossacks, and pay the Sultan a tribute. In February two of his entourage were sent back to Poland with an ultimatum along those lines, threatening war if the Poles did not undertake to meet the requirements within 60 days.[24]

The Grand Chancellor decided to temporize a little, by sending a more junior envoy, a cousin of his, also called Jan Zamoyski; and since Bartolomeo Bruti had just come to Poland to consult with him, he asked Bartolomeo to accompany this other Jan Zamoyski to Istanbul in order to smooth his path. They passed through Iaşi together on 14 March. They seem to have made a rapid and rather secret visit to Istanbul, and to have returned to Poland by 5 April; for on that date, the Polish authorities demonstrated their gratitude to Bartolomeo – and, no doubt, sought to strengthen his loyalty to Poland – by making him a member of the Polish nobility. In the grandiloquent document granting him this status (and describing him as 'born of most noble parents in the most noble kingdom of Albania' – was he the first Albanian to become a Polish nobleman?), the King specified that he had 'always performed the most valuable services to us, our kingdom and our subjects', especially by 'introducing' the envoy to Istanbul, and giving him 'advice in the most important matters'. It also specifically entitled him to include the Polish crowned white eagle in his coat of arms; he did so, and it can be seen in a carved version of the Bruti arms in Koper to this day.[25]

Bartolomeo seems to have been engaged in 'shuttle diplomacy'; there is some evidence that he was back in Istanbul in the first half of May, from where the English Ambassador reported on the 16th that a *çavuş* was being sent off with the Moldavian Voivod's 'cheife gouerno'', a phrase he used elsewhere to describe Bartolomeo, 'to establishe the Peace'. Meanwhile the younger Zamoyski was travelling again towards Istanbul, meeting the *beylerbeyi* on 19 May. He took with him an ill-judged letter from the Grand Chancellor, which warned that if the Ottomans invaded, the rulers of France, Germany and many other countries would rush to Poland's aid. In a memorable put-down, the *beylerbeyi* replied: 'We know well who are our friends and who are our enemies. The ambassadors of those kings are constantly present at the most sublime and splendid Porte, and bring their normal tributes and gifts without any delay; doubtless their ambassadors would let us know if there were any perturbations of that kind.' At the same time the senior Zamoyski was corresponding indirectly with Sinan Pasha, via Petru Şchiopul, and doubtless with Bartolomeo's help. While the Grand Chancellor refused on principle to pay tribute, Sinan was willing to reformulate the demand in terms of a war indemnity and a lavish gift. Proper nego-tiations were at last beginning. The junior Zamoyski entered Istanbul on 29 May 1590, and Bartolomeo Bruti either came with him or joined him shortly afterwards.[26]

Soon after his arrival in Istanbul, this Zamoyski went to see the Eng-lish acting ambassador, Edward Barton. He gave him a letter in which the Polish Grand Chancellor begged him to help, as Barton later put it, 'to the vttermost of my power'. This was not an issue for which Barton's general instructions had prepared him, but he quickly decided that averting a Polish–Ottoman war would harm Habsburg interests, help France (Queen Elizabeth's policies at the time were pro-French) and, if he were able to play a role both prominent and successful, redound to the honour of his country. Another reason might also have occurred to him: given that England obtained some of its own military supplies from Poland, the Queen would not have wanted the Poles to become engulfed in a major war against the Ottomans. Edward Barton now threw himself into the task of negotiating peace.[27]

The English were a relatively new international presence in Istanbul. A small group of enterprising merchants, led by William Harborne, had acted as pathbreakers; Harborne gained ambassadorial status in 1583, and Edward Barton, a young but already experienced trader who had served as his secretary, took over in 1588. Like France, only more so, England was pro-Ottoman because it was anti-Habsburg, and Elizabeth made great efforts to direct Ottoman military power against Spain. In the early 1580s it was even suspected that she was planning to use Eng-lish sailors to seize Malta and give it to the Ottomans as a forward base for new offensive campaigns. William Harborne devoted much effort to disrupting Spanish attempts to renew the naval truce after 1585; he suc-ceeded in reducing Spain to paying a large subsidy for a more provisional arrangement, and even in getting one Spanish envoy turned away. As Protestants, the English could in some ways be more openly pro-Ottoman than the French. For example, they could ignore the papal prohibition on selling war matériel to infidels: shipments of English tin for the Ottoman cannon-foundries were particularly welcomed at Istan-bul, and the English brought other kinds of weapons too. Harborne was not averse to exploiting some of the apparent resemblances between Protestantism and Islam, making speeches to the Sultan in which he denounced the Pope and the King of Spain as 'idolaters'. But what clinched the emerging special relationship between the Queen and the Sultan was the defeat of the Spanish Armada in 1588. As the Venetian

bailo wrote in 1590: 'whereas previously they did not have a high opinion of the Queen of England, as she was a woman and the ruler of just
half an island, nevertheless they think highly of her now, as they see that
she had the boldness to make offensive war on the King of Spain, and
they hear from all sides about her many naval forces.' Edward Barton,
who had good contacts in the Ottoman government and – very unusually
for a Western diplomat – spoke fluent Turkish, kept up the active promotion of this new-found English importance. So the Grand Chancellor
of Poland had chosen well when he enlisted his help.[28]

By the middle of June a deal had been hammered out. The Sultan
would call off his army, and, in return, King Sigismund would undertake to restrain the Cossacks. The demand for tribute had been reduced
to an agreement that Poland would give the Sultan 100 bundles of sable
furs; inevitably, there were also large cash payments to the Grand Vizier.
What exactly the division of labour was between Barton, Bruti and
Zamoyski is hard to judge, but we may presume that Bartolomeo played
an essential role in the direct dealings with Sinan Pasha. On 14 June
Edward Barton wrote to London about these negotiations, and included
an account of Bartolomeo, the 'assistant' to the Polish envoy, 'who', he
wrote, 'in the sayed seruice behaued him selfe verie wisly; both in deed
and worde manteyning the Hon.ʳ and credit of his Majesty [sc. the King
of Poland]'. He continued: 'this Bruto is both cheife gouernor vnder the
Prince of Moldauia, and latly for his good seruice made Nobilis Polonus,
who hauing longe scince desyered too see hir highnes [sc. Queen Elizabeth's] courte, maye perhaps by fauour of the King of Poland be sent
with his l[ette]res of thankfulnes to her Majesty for the fauour heere
shewed by me.' So he requested that, if Bartolomeo came to England, he
be treated with 'honᵇˡᵉ courtesie'.[29]

As it happens, there is other evidence that confirms that Bartolomeo
had 'longe scince' desired to go to England. In June 1587 he sent a
rather flowery letter to Elizabeth from Iaşi, pledging her the 'most loyal
and perpetual friendship' of the Voivod and his own 'most loyal service'; the letter ended with an openly anti-Spanish flourish, praying to
God 'for your greatness and the confusion of your enemies'. Bartolomeo certainly would have met some of the English merchants who
travelled to and from Istanbul via Moldavia, and he was probably
involved in the drawing up of a trading 'privilege' for them in August
1588, which gave the English a Moldavian customs rate of only 3 per
cent. But the nature of his special interest in visiting England – the idea

of doing so, as described by Barton, clearly came from Bartolomeo Bruti, not from the Polish King – is rather mysterious. Two months later, when Bartolomeo was in Warsaw, he sent another letter to the Queen, praising her in lavish terms, offering his service and describing the peace agreement in Istanbul as a 'triumph' brought about by 'the authority of your lord Ambassador, and my diligence'. Elizabeth's reply, sent from Windsor on 2 October, thanked him no less effusively, and concluded that 'we very greatly wish that the opportunity may arise to show our good affection towards your lordship, and your Prince.' Bartolomeo was certainly happy to keep, and/or acquire, a variety of political patrons in this period. He had renewed friendly relations with Venice in 1589, by giving regular briefings to the bailo. But his desire for a relationship with England may have been a less straightforward matter. Surprisingly, there is evidence that he was still being paid a retainer by the Spanish government, via their embassy in Venice, at least until mid-1586. And despite his close links to the Grand Chancellor of Poland, he was soon putting out feelers (as we shall see) to the Imperial authorities, with an evident desire to move to Habsburg service. Within a few months he would also be offering to give the Habsburgs sensitive information about Anglo-Ottoman affairs. The most likely explanation of his eagerness to visit the court of Queen Elizabeth is that he intended to act there as a spy for one or more of the major Catholic powers of Europe.[30]

There is one other case of Bartolomeo's possible involvement in international affairs at this time, which raises a different puzzle. The summer of 1590 also witnessed a sudden strain in relations between Dubrovnik and the Ottoman government, and the Ragusans suspected Bartolomeo of orchestrating hostility towards them. This was the so-called 'Ine Han crisis', which had begun in 1588 when senior Ottoman officials claimed to have discovered that a large part of Dubrovnik's coastal strip of territory had in fact been made over to the Ottomans in the fifteenth century. The *nazır* (superintendent) of Belgrade, an ambitious official called Ine Han (Srb.: Ejnehan; Ital.: Enecano) took up the argument; in early 1590, with Sinan Pasha's help, he obtained not only a sultanic decree declaring that Ine Han was the *sancakbeyi* of this newly discovered *sancak*, but also a demand that Dubrovnik pay a notional backlog of tribute for it, calculated at 150,000 ducats. Ragusan diplomacy, both formal and informal, went into overdrive. Large gifts were dispensed in Istanbul, many favours were called in, and agents of influence such as Rabbi Abeatar, the personal physician of the Sultan's chief treasurer, were put to work. Before long Dubrovnik had three viziers, two important *beylerbeyi*s and several eminent *kadi*s on its side. But still Ine Han persisted, with Sinan's support, and in mid-June he turned up at the borders of Ragusan territory with 2–300 armed men; two representatives of Dubrovnik who went to speak with him were taken prisoner and beaten. While his further advance onto Ragusan soil was blocked by a small opposing force, Dubrovnik sent two special envoys post-haste to Istanbul. On 12 July the Ragusan government wrote to them: 'It has come to our notice that Bruti, who was in Moldavia with its prince, has been the originator of the troubles that Ine Han has made for us, or at least has been his patron, and that Ine Han has had the benefit of his favour with Sinan Pasha.' It asked them to investigate whether this were true or not. If it was, they should approach Bartolomeo in person: 'speak to him, and beg him not to perform these kinds of ill services against us, but rather against Ine Han, because the Bruti family has always behaved towards us with great friendship, and his father received many good services from us on many occasions.'[31]

The fact that there is no further mention of Bartolomeo in this connection, during the weeks and months that followed before the resolution of the affair, suggests that the claim about him was not found to be true. Given the long gestation of the crisis, the lack of corroboration from any other sources, and the fact that Bartolomeo's energies had been intensively concentrated on the Polish peace negotiation, that seems the most likely conclusion. Of course it is possible that he might have been heard to make some anti-Ragusan remarks; he is unlikely to have forgotten – as the Ragusans pretended to have done – the way in which Dubrovnik had hunted him down and had him imprisoned in Lezhë, eleven years earlier. But there are other plausible explanations for Sinan's attitude. The most obvious is money, since any crisis of this kind generated large propitiatory payments. Another, more intriguing reason was stated in Dubrovnik's instructions to its envoys in October: it was important to give Sinan lavish gifts because he was known to be offended at not being treated as generously as previous grand viziers, 'who were of our language'. Once again the theme emerges of a certain kind of ethnic-linguistic solidarity – or, in this case, *ressentiment*. Dubrovnik had done well from a series of Serbo-Croat-speaking viziers, most notably Mehmed Sokollu; if Sinan had anti-Ragusan tendencies, they may have been partly because of his general feeling that he had been looked down on, as an Albanian, by a privileged circle of South Slavs, both Christian and Muslim, in Istanbul.[32]

In early July 1590 Bartolomeo left for Poland with the documents setting out the peace agreement between the Polish King and the Sultan. Travelling with him was Thomas Wilcocks, an English merchant who was conveying Barton's despatches, and letters to the Queen from the Sultan and Sinan Pasha, to London. Towards the end of the month they met the Grand Chancellor Jan Zamoyski in Lviv. He too wrote a letter to Elizabeth, thanking her for her ambassador's help, and delicately harping on an anti-Habsburg (or even anti-Counter-Reformation) tune: their efforts had succeeded, he said, despite the opposition of 'some of our neighbours', who had a desire to oppress common liberty and to make war for the Catholic religion. By early August the travellers had reached Warsaw, where the King and nobles began to discuss the terms of the deal. Wilcocks went on his way at the end of the month (taking Bartolomeo's letter to the Queen), but Bartolomeo was obliged to stay in Warsaw, awaiting further developments; during this period he had several very positive meetings with the papal nuncio, Annibale di Capua. By November Thomas Wilcocks had come back to Warsaw, bringing the Queen's gracious letter to Bartolomeo; but nothing had yet been decided about the peace terms, as the Polish parliament was just about to meet. It debated the matter from late November to early January, finally agreeing to settle, though (in Wilcocks's words) 'with much difficultie', because of 'great numbers toe much addicted to the house of Austria, spaine and rome'. Wilcocks then went on to Istanbul with an Ottoman çavuş, but Bartolomeo was asked to take part in the formal Polish embassy which was now being prepared. In mid-February, di Capua was able to report: 'on the 10th of this month signor Bartolomeo Bruti left Warsaw for Lviv, where he was to await the Polish ambassador who is to go to Istanbul with the sable furs to confirm the peace settlement.' But in mid-March Bartolomeo was still in Lviv, from where he wrote a letter to the Grand Chancellor, summarizing the latest news, which included the disturbing information that Mihnea, the Voivod of Wallachia for whom he had intervened with Sinan Pasha just two years previously, had been deposed.[33]

It was during these many months of residence in Poland – the first extended period he had spent outside the Ottoman Empire since his time in Italy and Spain in 1576–7 – that Bartolomeo began to explore the possibility of a change in his career. Talking to one of the two Habsburg envoys in Poland in January 1591, he offered to perform services

for the Emperor in Istanbul.* The diplomat concluded: 'He has property in Venetian Istria, and his sons are there; he would like to move to
Archducal Istria, and to leave Moldavia quite soon.' The second Habsburg envoy recorded that Bartolomeo was so keen to serve the Holy
Roman Emperor that he would happily do so without pay. He urged the
Emperor to take up this offer, emphasizing what a catch this would be
by saying that he had seen an original letter to Bartolomeo from the
Queen of England; Bartolomeo, as we have seen, never lacked skill in
impressing people with his own importance. Two months later Annibale
di Capua wrote to an unnamed correspondent:

> This Bartolomeo Bruti, who was readily offering his services in Istanbul
> whenever needed, both to His Imperial Majesty [the Emperor] and to the
> King our lord [meaning probably the King of Spain – di Capua was Arch-
> bishop of Naples], has very close relations with Sinan Pasha the Grand
> Vizier, and for that reason the English Ambassador in Istanbul attaches
> himself very closely to him, seeking to make use of him. Bartolomeo Bruti
> was offering in particular to give, to anyone nominated by the ministers of
> our King, information about everything that the pretended Queen of Eng-
> land [a standard Catholic phrase, used since the papal bull of 1570 which
> said that Elizabeth's subjects were under no duty to obey her] was negoti-
> ating with the Sultan; and I believe that he would have performed the task
> fully, showing himself to be a good Catholic and a person eager to serve
> those most serene princes.[34]

In response to such information, the Habsburg authorities sent an
agent to Koper in June 1591 to speak to Bartolomeo's family. Jacomo
Bruti told him that Bartolomeo 'is extremely eager to do some service to
the Emperor, and wants to free himself from Ottoman servitude'; he
suggested dealing with him via his brother-in-law Demostene Carerio,
who had been with Bartolomeo and was now returning to Koper via
Istanbul. The following month, another Habsburg agent was in Poland,
trying to build up support among the Polish nobility and clergy for
Archduke Maximilian. He reported that the pro-Habsburg Archbishop
of Gniezno suggested making use of Bartolomeo Bruti, 'who knows a
great deal about the [Grand] Chancellor's secret business, and has in his

---

* Also during this conversation, when the diplomat said it was doubted whether the
Ottomans had ever seriously intended an invasion of Poland, Bartolomeo insisted that they
had; he had stayed several days in the Ottoman camp, sleeping in the *beylerbeyi*'s tent, and
the army had been just about to cross the Dniester when he persuaded the *beylerbeyi* not to
proceed unless he got explicit orders from Istanbul.

possession several original documents written in his own hand', to undermine Zamoyski's reputation and thus remove the main obstacle to Habsburg interests in Poland. In late August this agent went to stay with the Archbishop, who said that Bartolomeo had 'revealed amazing things' to him. And he advised: 'The Emperor can bring this Bruti over to him all the more easily, because in any case he wants to free himself from his lord, entrusting himself to that place [sc. Moldavia] only until he can get his maintenance and protection elsewhere.'[35]

Bartolomeo was not the only person to be thinking of leaving. Petru Şchiopul was unnerved not only by the deposing of his nephew Mihnea in Wallachia, but also by the fact that when Mihnea was subsequently threatened with punishment in Istanbul, he secured his release by converting to Islam. (He is thus known in Romanian history as 'Mihnea cel Turcit', 'Mihnea the Renegade'.) In the summer of 1591 there were renewed Cossack attacks on Ottoman territory, with the threat of another Cossack invasion of Moldavia, headed by yet another claimant to the Moldavian throne. Besides all this, Petru had never stopped struggling with ever-increasing financial burdens. And, to cap it all, on 1 August 1591 Sinan Pasha – who, thanks to Bartolomeo, was Petru Şchiopul's ultimate protector – was dismissed as Grand Vizier, to be replaced by his bitter rival Ferhad Pasha. Petru Şchiopul drew up his accounts, paid off his servants and settled his debts; and on 15 August he left in the night-time, with his young son and a large retinue of faithful boyars and retainers, for Poland. The Venetian bailo reported two weeks later that he had sent back the ceremonial Ottoman banner and voivod's hat (with its heron feather) in a box to the Sultan, together with a letter saying that he could no longer bear the financial demands imposed on him. His real motive, according to the bailo, was concern for his son, Ştefan, who he feared might be forced to become a Muslim; it was said that he had taken with him 'a huge quantity of gold', with which he planned to buy some suitable estate or position for Ştefan in western Christendom.[36]

Suddenly, Bartolomeo found himself in a very exposed position: he too was bereft of his powerful protector in Istanbul, and he would now face a new voivod in whose appointment he had played no part. Petru's successor, who left Istanbul in mid-November and was installed in Moldavia in late December, was called Aron, and was the son of a previous voivod. He had had to promise an increase in the tribute, and a colossal amount of extra money – said to be 400,000 ducats, with half of it paid up front. To help raise this money, he also had backers in Istanbul.

Prominent among them were Edward Barton and his associate Paolo Mariani, a Venetian merchant who had served as French consul in Egypt and had fingers in many pies; as Thomas Wilcocks explained in a report to London, Barton put together a consortium of 'grekish marchants' and 'other marchants both christians turks and Jewes, m^r Barton his friends'. Possibly Barton's involvement provided some guarantee of Bartolomeo's position; at any rate, he was not ejected from Iaşi. But on the other hand this new exertion of English power over Moldavian affairs meant the rapid undoing of Bartolomeo's whole pro-Catholic policy: a note written in the English embassy in Istanbul in 1592 recorded that 'Tho. Wilcockes went into Bugdania ['Bogdania', a name for Moldavia] wth Rich[ard] babyngton. In bugdania, a sect of Hussites ar restored to ther churches, from which certain Jesuitts had expelled them. wch Auron prince of bugdania hath commanded to be doone.'[37]

The first reports of Aron's conduct as voivod were not encouraging: he had one of Petru Şchiopul's officials executed merely 'on suspicion', and ordered the castration of someone accused of ravishing another man's wife. Looking back on his career, the chronicler Ureche would have nothing good to say about Aron. His main passions, allegedly, were 'pillage, debauchery, gambling and bagpipe-players'. According to Ureche, he hired Hungarian mercenaries, executed prominent boyars (including Bartolomeo's old comrade in arms, Bucium), sent out tax-collectors accompanied by Ottoman officials and, in desperation, ordered the seizing of one cow from every Moldavian. By June 1592, tax revolts were breaking out in various parts of the country. Months before that, Bartolomeo Bruti had already decided that it was time to leave Moldavia. Following in the footsteps of Petru Şchiopul, he travelled with a small group (including the state treasurer) to the Polish border in late March or early April. Aron sent guards after him, and he was arrested just before he could cross the river. Bartolomeo was held in prison for as long as seven weeks; he was able to send a message to Istanbul, and a çavuş was despatched to demand that he be handed over. But at some point in May 1592, shortly before the arrival of the çavuş, Bartolomeo was made to die 'with ignomiry': his nose was cut off and he was strangled. One contemporary Polish chronicler stated that Aron had him 'drowned in the river Dniester'; but it seems that his body was merely thrown into the river after his death. This was both a miserable ending to his life, and a very premature one. He was only 34 or 35. Bartolomeo Bruti had been extraordinarily unlucky; not only was his relative Sinan Pasha out of power – he would return as Grand

Vizier in January of the following year – but Aron was on the point of being dismissed himself. Following a change of Grand Viziers in April 1592, orders were issued in late April or early May for Aron's recall, so that he could be replaced by his nephew. (In the event, Aron's dismissal caused uproar in Istanbul, because both janissaries and Muslim pious foundations had lent him large sums which, they complained, would simply turn out to have been swallowed by the Sultan's treasury if he were not given time to repay them; he was eventually reinstated.)[38]

No official reason seems to have been given for the execution of Bartolomeo, but a report circulating in Istanbul in the summer said that his enemies had forged a letter from him to the King of Poland in which he appeared to be plotting for the return of Petru Şchiopul. Some modern historians have accepted that that was his real aim, or that he was involved in one of the Moldavian revolts against Aron. But knowing, as we do, that he had been intending to cut his ties with the country for more than a year, we can discount these theories. It is also known that by 2 March 1592 his family in Koper was expecting his arrival there 'within days', and that in the following month, while he languished in gaol, Pope Clement VIII, who was unaware of his plight, wrote a letter to him, saying that he looked forward to welcoming him in Rome; clearly, a long-term exit from Moldavia had been planned. The simplest explanation for Aron's actions is the one that was current at the time: as the Imperial Ambassador reported when he first heard the news of Bartolomeo's detention on 16 April, Aron owed Bartolomeo 30,000 scudi (25,000 ducats). The bailo would later write that Aron took from Bartolomeo cash and IOUs worth more than 30,000 ducats. The King of Poland's secretary, Reinhold Heidenstein, who had worked for Jan Zamoyski and probably knew Bruti personally, wrote that he was executed 'for no other reason than for the sake of not paying the debts which he created when he loaned money to that voivod'. The desire for wealth had been one of the driving forces in Bartolomeo's life, and it was, in a sense, money that killed him. Another great motive was his devotion to his religion – not just to Catholicism as such, but to the Counter-Reformation programme of Catholic reassertion and *reconquista*; he had poured his energies into this project, but everything he had achieved was already unravelling by the time he died. The third driving force – connected, naturally, with the first – was his devotion to his family. Here, at least, the story did not end. Brutis and Brunis lived on after his death, and their lives were still shaped, in some ways, by Bartolomeo's own career.[39]

19

Cristoforo Bruti and the Dragoman Dynasty

Bartolomeo Bruti had spent one year (1573–4) training to be a dragoman – an interpreter, principally of the Turkish language – before deciding that it was not the life for him. But he had set a precedent for his family. In 1579 his younger brother Cristoforo came to Istanbul to embark on the same course of study, and he would follow the career of a dragoman, on and off, for the rest of his life. He was approximately sixteen years old when he arrived. The first year of his training underwent some interruptions, with the imprisonment of his elder brother and his own expedition with a *çavuş* to rescue him from Lezhë, but he seems to have made good progress. Cristoforo lodged in the house of the bailo's secretary, and received the standard rate of pay, which was 50 ducats a year; in 1580 the bailo, Paolo Contarini, observed that 'this is a studious young man who will profit from his studies, and will do so quickly.'[1]

By the spring of the following year the bailo was sounding even more enthusiastic, setting out – in a part of his despatch that was sent in cipher – a special reason for valuing this young man's presence. 'By means of Cristoforo Bruti, who lives here learning the Turkish language, I get many important pieces of information about Persian affairs, as he has very familiar dealings with the nephew of Sinan Pasha, and with other important people of his household. I hope also that when Sinan comes to the Porte he will be of even more use to me, as he and his brother have tremendous access to the pasha's household.' (Sinan was currently in charge of the war against Persia, and his nephew was probably the pro-Venetian Mehmed Bey with whom, as we have seen, Alessandro Giubizza had enjoyed such good relations in 1575. In the light of this statement by the bailo, we may suspect that Mehmed Sokollu's claim that Bartolomeo Bruti was sending information about the Persian campaign to Naples in 1579 may have had some real basis to it.)* In his final report, Contarini lavished more praise on Cristoforo. He wrote that he was fluent in Albanian (his mother tongue) and Slav, and also in Italian, Greek and Turkish; once more he emphasized the value of 'the friendships he has with great people in Istanbul', and the important information he had obtained. This was no ordinary giovane di lingua, and it must have been in recognition of these special services that the Doge ordered his salary to be raised to 200 ducats a year.[2]

Commenting on the departure of Petru Şchiopul and Bartolomeo Bruti for Moldavia in September 1582, Paolo Contarini wrote that the Voivod had also been keen to take Cristoforo with him. But Cristoforo, 'finding that he still had the same favour and access to His Excellency the Grand Vizier', had decided to continue working for the good of Venice in Istanbul. Soon afterwards Cristoforo made a brief trip to Venice and/or Koper, travelling presumably with Contarini, who left Istanbul in November. In December the next bailo, Giovanni Francesco Morosini, wrote a letter to the government urging that Cristoforo be sent back as soon as possible; very unusually, he enclosed with it a letter from an official in Sinan Pasha's household, who also praised Cristoforo and asked for his return. The bailo wrote that the Venetian authorities should treat him very generously, 'because, apart from the fact that he is already well advanced in the Turkish language, he is also of such good judgement, and so devoted in his service, that you can be sure of all possible loyalty, sincerity and diligence from him; and besides, if His Excellency Sinan were to come back to his previous position [he had just been dismissed as Grand Vizier], this young man would be a very suitable instrument for performing productive and distinguished services for Your Serenity.'

Cristoforo was in Istanbul again by early February 1583, when Morosini paid a courtesy call on Sinan Pasha and, knowing the way to his heart, presented him with a gift of 3,000 ducats. Cristoforo sat at Sinan's feet and counted out the money, which came in six bags of 500 coins each. Recounting this episode, the bailo extolled his young giovane di lingua once again: 'this Bruti works to my great satisfaction, and to the good of our state, in all the business which I have to negotiate with these favourites of the pasha, since he is much loved by them, and has a fairly good command of the Turkish language, so that we can

* On Mehmed Bey and Giubizza see above, pp. 263–4; on Mehmed Sokollu's claim see above, pp. 269–70.

hope that he will shortly become perfect in speaking and writing it.'
Conscious of the family history, he added: 'however, as he is poor, and
has lost his father and all his goods and property in the service of this
most serene state, I am conscience-bound to recommend him, as I do,
with great affection to Your Serenity.'[3]

Even without the benefit of such special connections with a powerful
pasha, to have a trainee dragoman who was displaying all the right
skills and aptitudes – linguistic and otherwise – for the job was a cause
for some celebration. For the dragomans performed an essential role in
the working of the bailate, and Venice had been struggling for some
time to develop a reliable system for their training and employment.
Until the middle of the sixteenth century the Venetian bailo had mostly
relied on local translators, usually Catholics from the Perot community
who were fluent in Italian, Greek and Turkish. Some of these did much-
valued service over many years; but there were always doubts about
the wisdom of using such people. Dragomans were intermediaries for
confidential discussions and had access to sensitive documents, so one
constant concern was that they might at the same time be dealing behind
the scenes with rival Christian powers in Istanbul. (We have already
seen an example of this, albeit to the benefit of Venice: Bartolomeo's
friend Ambrosio Grillo, who acted as dragoman for a Tuscan envoy,
sent copies of secret Tuscan documents to the Venetians.)* The other
main worry was that they would not defend the interests of Venice with
sufficient vigour, or even provide accurate translations of strongly
worded Venetian protests, for fear of the wrath of the Sultan, whose
subjects they were. As the bailo Paolo Contarini put it, 'it is always more
advantageous to be served by your own citizens', because 'they speak
with boldness, while Ottomans are afraid to do so.' So in 1551 Venice
decreed that two young notaries from its chancery, or, failing that, two
sons of Venetian citizens, should be sent to live in the bailo's house and
learn Turkish. The idea was that they would study there for five years
under a 'cozza' or 'coza' (Trk.: hoca, 'teacher'; the 'zz' or 'z' was pronounced with the soft 'zh' of the Venetian dialect). The cozza, normally
a native Turkish-speaker, could also act as a scribe for the bailo, producing documents in Turkish; his official duties were confined to teaching
and writing, and he would be used as a face-to-face interpreter only
when proper dragomans were lacking. Once they had attained the
necessary level of competence, the giovani could be used as dragomans

* Above, p. 269.

either in Istanbul or in other ports of the Levant where Venetian consuls operated. At any one time there would be at least two, but sometimes four or more, students of Turkish at the bailate.[4]

Thus was the system of 'giovani di lingua' born. The idea seemed in principle a good one; it was quickly imitated by Dubrovnik, which in 1558 decided to pay for one of its youths to be taught in Istanbul, and by Poland, which sent several young men to study Turkish there at the expense of the royal chancery. In 1568 the Imperial Ambassador in Istanbul similarly urged the authorities in Vienna to send out one German and one Croatian student, emphasizing the dangers of depending on Ottoman subjects. (That suggestion fell on stony ground. Arriving in Istanbul five years later, Stefan Gerlach recorded that the Imperial embassy had four dragomans: two Perots – one of them being Matteo del Faro, whose niece Bartolomeo Bruti would marry – and two converts to Islam, of whom one was from Bavaria and the other was a Transylvanian Hungarian. He was of course unaware that del Faro was a salaried agent of the King of Spain.) France would take up the practice of sending out its own youths to learn Turkish a century later, and it in turn would be imitated, belatedly, by England.[5]

But in practice the Venetian system was not without its problems. Linguistic talent was a variable commodity, and, as one bailo observed, for some students five years was just not long enough. In 1558 the bailo Marin Cavalli argued that the whole scheme was a waste of money, since these trainees would not want to devote their newly acquired skills to minor tasks, and where the major task of negotiating with the Ottoman government was concerned, 'I am sure that the pashas would not be happy to have them, and perhaps they would not allow them.' There were potentially worse problems than that: the case of Girolamo Colombina, who in 1562 had a fight with a long-serving Venetian dragoman and then, to escape punishment, converted to Islam and entered Ottoman service, became a cautionary tale. Thirty years later the former bailo Lorenzo Bernardo would complain that instead of sending young chancery officials, as was originally intended, Venice just sent the children of poor citizens, 'as if this were a seminary or college for educating poor boys at public expense'; parents sent their problem children, thinking that Istanbul would supply strict discipline, but the opposite was the case. 'The freedom of Ottoman life and the luxury of these Ottoman women, together with the corrupt customs of the renegades, would suffice to turn a saint into a devil.' It was not only the Ottoman women from whom Venetian youths had to be guarded. That was one reason why the age of the giovani di lingua was kept fairly high (though the only clear case of such sexual impropriety in this period involved one of them having an intimate relationship with the Venetian barber who resided at the bailate). In 1575, and again in 1577, the bailo suggested sending a cozza to Venice to teach boys there; one of the advantages would be that the pupils could be younger, when they were better able to absorb a difficult language. As it was, there was some conflict between the desire to retain moral control over these youths and the wish to improve their Turkish as quickly as possible: in 1575 the bailo also proposed that the giovani di lingua should be boarded out with 'some Ottoman dragomans', so that they could be fully immersed in the language.[6]

Marino Cavalli's fear that the Ottomans would not accept these young Venetians as interpreters turned out to be unfounded. But there were never enough of them to fulfil all the bailate's needs. In 1568 one died, and another returned to Venice because of illness; a third was killed during the Cyprus war. For quite a long period after that war, during 1574–5, the bailo was chiefly dependent on the Lucchese renegade Hürrem Bey, who was one of the Sultan's own dragomans. Venice never stopped using Perot families; in 1592 Lorenzo Bernardo would complain that it was the sons of these people, who were subjects of the Sultan, that were now being accepted as giovani di lingua. At times of need, outsiders who were more unknown quantities could be put to work: in 1558 the bailate employed Michele Cernovicchio (Černović), a man of partly Slav origin who may have been brought up in Istanbul. He helped to teach the giovani, and was rapidly promoted to 'grand dragoman', conducting the bailo's most important business at the Sultan's court. One Venetian report in 1562 described him as 'utterly loyal'; but he was in fact sending detailed information about Venice's dealings with the Ottomans, in cipher, to the Imperial government in Vienna. When he was exposed as a spy in 1563 the Venetian government told the bailo to have him arrested by the subaşı and sent to Venice – or, if that failed, to have him killed. Yet he remained a resident of Istanbul for another eight years, sending news reports to the Imperial government and earning a living as a slave-ransomer.[7]

The Cernovicchio case naturally strengthened Venetian security concerns. In 1591 the bailo wrote that it was essential to have at least one competent dragoman who was a Venetian; if that person left, 'I would be deprived of the safe and loyal intermediary which it is necessary to have, very often, in the bailate.' A year later, his successor remarked on how odd it was that the government imposed strict secrecy in its dealings with the bailo, sending him instructions in cipher, when the business they instructed him to undertake might then be passed to a dragoman who was an Ottoman subject. Concerns of this kind applied, in the end acutely, to one of the longest-serving dragomans, Matteca Salvego (or Salvago), who was from a Perot family of Genoese origin; in June 1592 the bailo was ordered to find a way of bundling him off to Crete, or otherwise just to poison him in the bailate, and in November of the following year the authorities instructed the next bailo to murder him en route from Dubrovnik to Istanbul, helpfully adding that this should be easy on a winter journey 'in cold and icy conditions'. The precise nature of his offence is not clear, but an enciphered passage in a report from the outgoing bailo that month did refer to 'his very close involvement in dealings at the Ottoman court, from which he cannot be turned aside, and his careless and malicious talk'. And yet, when one reads such comments, it is necessary to bear in mind that the practice of the baili themselves fell far short of what would be required of a modern security-conscious diplomat. In 1580 Solomon Ashkenazi wrote directly to the Venetian government, saying that whereas he spoke every day on a confidential basis with the bailo, the bailo would then have lunch and, 'being at the table with dragomans and renegades, would recount everything I had recounted to him' – to Solomon's own serious detriment.[8]

Security concerns applied above all to the sensitive issues on which the bailo negotiated with the Ottoman government. But such negotiations formed only one part of the range of work done by the dragomans. From the 1540s onwards, there were three at the Venetian bailate who had particular job descriptions. The 'grand dragoman' did the official business at the Porte; the 'little dragoman' or 'port dragoman' worked mostly for Venetian merchants, helping them with the customs authorities and in any disputes that came before the *kadi*; and the 'road dragoman' ('dragomanno da strada') accompanied the bailo on any excursions he made, including the journeys to and from Venice by outgoing and incoming baili, while otherwise attending mostly to the business of freeing slaves. There was also much low-grade practical translating to be done at the bailate itself. At the English embassy in the 1580s there were three dragomans, of whom the senior one – 'Mustafa the Chiefe Drogueman', an Ottoman *çavuş* – would accompany the ambassador to the Sultan's court, while the other two, who were Christian Perots, had a variety of tasks. Interestingly, while the Venetians complained that Perots would be afraid, as Ottoman subjects, to translate direct complaints to the Ottoman authorities, the English gave that task to them rather than to their Muslim chief dragoman, who was significantly more inhibited: 'the second drogueman is to relate Verbatim to the Vicereye [sc. Grand Vizier], what we may inferr or obiect vnto him in cause of anie difference, wch the chaouse [sc. çavuş] will not, fearinge to lose his tymare [sc. *timar*, military-feudal estate] or anuitie of the towne.' But otherwise the second dragoman's duties included procuring 'the receipte of our provicion in haie wood and Barley at the courte', and accompanying the Ambassador when he went out, while the third dragoman 'goeth wth the stuarde at tymes to make provicion for the howse' and 'goeth [on] our afaires to inferior p[er]sons & to accompanie gentlemen Servants and others of our howse'.[9]

For the Venetians and for the English, much of the daily work was concerned with the affairs of their merchants – who, respectively, contributed half the costs of the Venetian dragomans, and paid all the costs of the English embassy. In the Venetian case, the port dragoman also received a commission from each merchant whose business he helped. Dragomans were themselves allowed to engage in trading activities, and this is a major reason why the ones of Venetian origin did not form a separate administrative caste isolated behind the walls of the bailate; on the contrary, they rapidly became enmeshed in the commercial world of Galata. That, together with their close working relationships with Perot dragomans, and the endogamous and hereditary tendencies of professions in this period, helps to explain why it was that, instead of seeing the traditional flow of Perots replaced by a separate stream of Venetian dragomans, the baili found that the two quite quickly fused, creating a new, mixed and increasingly interrelated population of dynastic dragoman families.[10]

It is not known how long Cristoforo remained a giovane di lingua; but it is clear that, given the flexible world of work at the bailate, he was not merely studying but acting as an interpreter – in some cases, probably, of Albanian or Slav rather than Turkish – from an early stage. Contarini, who left in late 1582, said that he had used his services 'especially in listening to those who gave me information about daily occurrences, and who were helpful concerning the business which I had to conduct at the Porte'. He was also used for commercial affairs: in 1584 he represented the interests in Istanbul of a merchant draper in

Venice, Nicolò de' Michieli.* At some point in 1585, when the bailo Lorenzo Bernardo dismissed the Perot Ambrosio Grillo from the post of grand dragoman, he used Cristoforo as his temporary replacement, until Venice appointed someone who had much more experience of negotiating at the Porte. And in 1586 Cristoforo performed one of the major symbolic tasks of the bailo in Istanbul, presenting the annual tribute payment for the island of Zakynthos to the Ottoman treasury.[11]

During that year he also became caught up in an affair which showed how blurred the boundary might be between public and private status where a dragoman's work was concerned. An Ottoman subject called Marino Scarvoli, a Greek whose father was the chief tax-farmer of the *sancakbeyi* of the Peloponnese, had had a very valuable cargo of valonia (a type of acorn used in wool-dyeing and leather-tanning) seized in 1580 by a group of merchants in Venice. The merchants were led by Giacomo Ragazzoni, the person who had been sent to open negotiations with the Ottomans during the 1570–3 war; their aim was to obtain compensation for the unpaid debts of Scarvoli's father. Marino Scarvoli challenged this seizure in a Venetian court, but the sentence went against him; in 1583 he sent two representatives, Ömer and Ibrahim, to organize an appeal, but that too failed. Further litigation followed in an Ottoman court in 1586, treating the bailo as legally responsible for the actions of Venetian merchants. Here Scarvoli had more success: first he got a Venetian ship impounded, and then he obtained a promise from the bailo to pay back the value of his valonia in return for the freeing of the ship. That promise was made to the Ottoman judge by Cristoforo Bruti, who was described in the court documents as 'dragoman and agent of the bailo'. For some reason the promised payment was delayed, whereupon Scarvoli obtained an order to have Cristoforo imprisoned. After the bailo had pledged to pay the sum in full, and had lobbied both the Sultan and Siyavuş Pasha, the Grand Vizier (whom he approached via his confidential adviser, an Italian-trained Jewish physician called Dr Benveniste), Cristoforo was released; how long he spent in an Ottoman gaol is not known. But his imprisonment depended on his being regarded as a mere commercial agent, not a public officer of the bailate. The

---

* When Gasparo Bruni asked in July 1583 for the money for his son's university education to be transferred to a Venetian merchant, this was the man whose name he gave: see above, pp. 307–8. We catch here a tiny glimpse of what must have been a larger web of connections between Brunis and Brutis and their various friends and associates in Venice.

Venetian government sent an official complaint to Istanbul, and the bailo obtained a sultanic decree stating that Cristoforo, having been gaoled against the terms of the peace with Venice, must not be 'molested' in future. In May 1587 the Sultan even sent a formal letter about this to the Doge of Venice, regretting that Cristoforo had been wrongly treated, and assuring the Doge that Scarvoli had now been incarcerated himself.[12]

During the period when Sinan Pasha was out of power (from late 1582 to the spring of 1589), Cristoforo's *entrée* to the world of viziers and pashas may have waned a little in importance. But he still had some valuable contacts at a high level. One of these was Hasan Pasha 'Veneziano', a Venetian sailor who, captured as a young man, had converted to Islam and enjoyed a rapid rise to power as a protégé of Kılıç Ali Pasha. He served two terms (1577–80, 1582–7) as governor of Algiers; Miguel de Cervantes, who was a captive there from 1575 to 1580, owed his life to Hasan's clemency towards his various doomed attempts to escape, and would refer to him several times in his writings. In 1587 Hasan was spending some time in Istanbul before leaving to become governor of Tripoli. Although he had fallen out personally with Kılıç Ali Pasha (who died in the summer of 1587), he very much shared his strategic views, being against a land war in Persia and in favour of a naval war against Spain.[13]

This made Hasan Pasha a natural ally of the English, who, as Philip II's plans to launch a full-scale invasion of England became clearer, were constantly urging the Ottomans to commit their navy against the Spanish. A key part of Elizabeth's strategy at this time involved using a claimant to the throne of Portugal, Don Antonio, to make trouble for Spain in that country. After the death in battle of the impetuous – and childless – King Sebastian, the throne had passed to Sebastian's great-uncle, an elderly cardinal who was himself without any direct heirs.* On his death in 1580, Philip II had moved quickly to establish his own claim. Don Antonio stood in a more direct line of succession, being a nephew of the Cardinal and a grandson, in the male line, of the previous king but one; he had had a noble upbringing, entering the Order of the Knights of Malta and receiving that order's most senior Portuguese position, the Priory of Crato. But he suffered from two big disadvantages: he was an illegitimate son, and he could not compete with the huge wealth of the Spanish crown, which quickly suborned key members of the Portuguese nobility. No sooner was he publicly acclaimed as King in

---

* On the death of Sebastian see above, p. 258.

Lisbon in June 1580 than Philip threatened all his supporters with death, infamy and the confiscation of all their property. Don Antonio fled first to France and later to England, where he became caught up in Elizabeth's anti-Spanish plans. One of his supporters was a rich Portuguese Jewish merchant, Álvaro Mendes, who moved from France to Ottoman territory in 1585 and reverted publicly to the Jewish faith, becoming Solomon Abenaes (Ibn Ya'ish); conveniently, he was also the brother-in-law of Queen Elizabeth's personal physician. He established good relations with William Harborne, who reported that Solomon Abenaes had successfully cultivated the Sultan by giving him 'sondrie ritche jewels' and was pressing him for a more anti-Spanish policy.[14]

In despatches written on 11 November 1587, the two baili (outgoing and incoming) noted that Hasan Pasha and Harborne frequently went to look at the galleys in the Istanbul Arsenal, together with Solomon Abenaes. They wrote that an English agent had come secretly to discuss a plan for Don Antonio to seize control of Portugal with Ottoman and English help, on the understanding that he would then hold it, like Transylvania, as a tributary state of the Ottoman Empire. (This idea remains, like the earlier plan to turn Algiers into a French protectorate, one of the more curious counter-factual possibilities in the history of the period.)* And they also described a long private conversation Cristoforo Bruti had had with Hasan Pasha about these matters, in which Hasan discussed both the idea – which he favoured – of sending out the Ottoman navy for a joint Ottoman–English campaign against Spain, and an alternative plan, which was for Don Antonio to seize control of the Portuguese possessions in Asia. Hasan saw the acquisition of Portugal by Philip as a long-term threat, because of the extra wealth it gave him; unfortunately, he said, the viziers had no understanding of matters of state, being ignorant fools and liars whose only aim was 'to get money, with which to gain the favour of the Sultan'. Bruti was with him as a trusted individual, not as a translator (the conversation, naturally, would have been in Italian); that Hasan spoke so freely to him gives some indication of the way in which this young but well-connected dragoman could gain the confidence of senior Ottoman pashas and officials.[15]

A month later, Cristoforo travelled with the outgoing bailo to Venice, from where, presumably, he was able to visit his family in Koper. His next task shows how various the work of a dragoman could be. In

---

* See above, p. 187.

mid-March 1588 he was asked to go down the coast to Kotor to help put an end to acts of piracy against Venetian shipping which were being committed by 'many Ottoman subjects' and sponsored by a prominent spahi of Bar, 'Cassain' (Hasan). In one recent episode, a Venetian vessel taking refuge from a storm off Herceg Novi had been seized, its goods stolen and all its crew killed, except for the two ship's boys, who were enslaved. The governor of Kotor obtained petitions to the Sultan from both the janissary captain of Herceg Novi and an official of the *sancakbeyi* of Dukagjin, asking for the miscreants to be punished. In response, the Ottoman government sent a *çavuş* with instructions to meet Cristoforo Bruti in Kotor and go with him to the *sancakbeyi* of Hercegovina, who was then obliged to travel to Herceg Novi and arrest the offenders. Cristoforo was thus attending an internal Ottoman disciplinary action, not as an interpreter but as a kind of diplomatic representative. By mid-May he was able to confirm that ten of the guilty men, including two ringleaders, had been seized in Herceg Novi; but soon after his departure from that place another report said that they had been released, so Venice's efforts to have them brought to justice had to begin all over again.[16]

The formal instruction which Cristoforo Bruti received from the Doge and Senate in mid-March 1588 said that the bailo was requesting his return to Istanbul; nevertheless it authorized him, once he had completed the business in Herceg Novi, to travel first of all 'to Moldavia, to be with your brother'. From there, it said, he could go to Istanbul quite quickly if the bailo wished, and if there was no further risk of being molested by Scarvoli. (It also granted him the generous sum of 100 ducats to cover the cost of his journey.) Apparently Cristoforo had requested some leave for the purpose of making this fraternal visit. Whether he was already planning to abandon Venetian service, or whether he succumbed to his elder brother's blandishments when he reached Iaşi, is not known; but there now followed first an Ottoman interlude, and then a Moldavian one, in his career.[17]

To begin with, when Cristoforo Bruti returned from Iaşi to Istanbul, he entered the service of the *beylerbeyi* of Rumeli, Doğancı Mehmed Pasha. This man was an Armenian who had become a personal favourite of Sultan Murad, having been his hunting companion in his youth; after Murad's accession he had rapidly progressed from chief hawker (*doğancı*) to chief falconer, then head of the janissaries, and then *beylerbeyi*. He seems to have been politically aligned with Sinan Pasha; he had been part of the anti-Sokollu faction towards the end of Sokollu's life, and when Doğancı Mehmed's own life had to be sacrificed in 1589 to quell a riot of spahis complaining about being paid in debased coinage, the Sultan, upset at having to order the death of his old friend, dismissed the Grand Vizier, whom he suspected of instigating the riot, and put Sinan in his place. (Commenting on Doğancı Mehmed, the historian Mustafa Ali, who admired Sokollu and loathed Sinan, sniffed: 'He was an ignorant and unqualified person . . . a post as one of the palace hunts-men would have been too high an honour for that bungler.') So possibly there was a personal connection between the *beylerbeyi* and Sinan, which had given rise to Cristoforo's employment by him. There are only two pieces of evidence attesting to that employment; but they are clear enough to leave no doubt that, at least for a short time, one or two members of the Bruti family worked not just for an Ottoman vassal ruler, but directly for a high official of the Ottoman government – or even, as one of the documents suggests, for the Sultan himself.[18]

One is a report by the bailo saying that in June 1588 a Venetian mer-chant in Istanbul, Pasqualino Leoni or Lion, had been beaten up in the bazaar by a janissary and some janissary cadets, and had demanded the arrest of his assailants. An investigation showed that the janissary had been hired by a certain Francesco da Feltre; he was an employee of Cris-toforo Bruti, who was now in the service of the *beylerbeyi* of Rumeli. The janissary also confessed that one year earlier Cristoforo had hired him directly to perform such a beating, and that da Feltre had recently promised him a cloak of crimson cloth if he would do it again. When da Feltre was put in the Galata prison, Cristoforo went to the *beylerbeyi* and asked him to demand his freedom, which he did; but the *kadi* of Galata refused to release him. Da Feltre was then taken to the bailate for questioning, and while he was there a janissary helped him to escape, after which he took refuge in the *beylerbeyi*'s house. This was a serious affair, as Leoni was a prominent merchant, described in a sultanic decree of 1592 as having traded in Egypt, Aleppo and Istanbul for 20 years; he would later develop close links with the Sultan's household. While the origins of Cristoforo's hostility are completely unknown, the *modus operandi* he chose was quite a common one; eight years later, when John Sanderson deputized for Edward Barton at the English embassy in 1596, his preferred way of dealing with an obstreperous English mer-chant in Istanbul was 'to have tamed him by janesaries, yf any could at that time have bine had for mony'. The other piece of evidence is a Turkish document addressed to the Venetian government in which the *beylerbeyi* recommends the bearer, Cristoforo Bruti, and his brother

'Bado' (probably Benedetto), describing them as former employees of Venice who were now in the service of the Sultan. It bears no precise date, but the likely sequence of events is that the two brothers travelled on the *beylerbeyi*'s business – or the Sultan's – to Venice some time after the Leoni affair, in the late summer or early autumn of 1588.[19]

From Venice or Koper, Cristoforo and his brother returned to the Ottoman Empire. Very possibly their cousin Antonio Bruni travelled with them, to begin the Moldavian episode in his own life. Perhaps they stayed in Istanbul for a while; if so, the violent end of the *beylerbeyi* in April 1589 would have terminated Cristoforo's employment, and given him a reason for moving to Moldavia. Among other activities in that country, he became a joint collector of the tribute with Bartolomeo; and he may have performed some other services to merit the award of the honorific position of 'cup-bearer' to Petru Şchiopul by January 1590. Possibly he was involved in the education of Petru's young son: a document survives, dated 5 May 1590, in which Petru authorizes payment to Cristoforo on account of little Prince Ştefan.[20]

By late November of that year, however, Cristoforo Bruti was back in Istanbul, performing services for the bailo, Girolamo Lippomano. He testified in an Ottoman court on the bailo's behalf about an Ottoman ship which had been seized by Maltese galleys and then freed by the Venetians. A few days later he translated a Turkish document which had come into Lippomano's hands, a sultanic decree addressed to the Emperor Rudolf II, agreeing to renew the peace treaty between them so long as the Emperor fulfilled certain conditions. Yet it seems that Cristoforo was acting as a freelance here, not having formally re-entered Venetian service. Six months later, in mid-June 1591, the former bailo Lorenzo Bernardo – who had previously written high praise of Cristoforo's work as a *giovane di lingua* – suddenly reappeared in Istanbul; he had been sent to arrest Girolamo Lippomano on suspicion of transmitting state secrets to Spain, and on 25 June he put him on a Venetian ship and sailed for home. (As the ship came in sight of the Lido at Venice, Lippomano jumped, or was pushed, into the sea and drowned.) In 1592 Lorenzo Bernardo produced a report on the situation in Istanbul, reflecting his brief experience of it in June 1591. While listing the various dragomans at the bailate, he commented on Cristoforo Bruti: 'he is a young man, 28 or 30 years old; now he has no particular job, which is why he has applied himself to some business affairs involving jewels, wheat and other things. But when, as it suits him, he leaves that business aside, and applies himself fully to public service, he can be very useful, and will give great satisfaction to the baili, since he has excellent Turkish, Greek, Italian, Slav, Romanian and Albanian.' By the time Bernardo wrote those words, however, Cristoforo Bruti may already have been dead; the precise date of death is not known, nor is the cause (though we do know that Istanbul suffered an outbreak of plague in 1592), but the aftermath of his death was discussed in a report by the bailo written in mid-August. The bailo was making an inventory of Cristoforo's property, to be given to Cristoforo's brother-in-law Demostene Carerio, who had just come to Istanbul from Moldavia. The heirs were Cristoforo's brothers Benedetto and Jacomo; he had outlived his brother Bartolomeo by three months at the most.[21]

The death of Cristoforo Bruti did not end the connection between the Bruti family and the bailate in Istanbul. Writing about his period as bailo (1585-7), Lorenzo Bernardo had added a postscript to his praise of Cristoforo: 'He has a nephew who has come to accompany me in this city; he knows Turkish, Albanian, Slav and Italian like his mother tongue, has the rudiments of Greek, and is learning to read and write Turkish. Your Serenity can place great hopes in the service of this subject.' This was Marcantonio Borisi, one of the sons of Jacoma Bruti and Pietro Borisi. Clearly he did make good progress; by 1590 he was acting for the bailo in front of the *kadi* in an Ottoman court. In his report on his brief visit in 1591 Lorenzo Bernardo referred to him again, this time by name, and praised his excellent comportment, his modesty and his skill in negotiating; he said that although he was aged between 20 and 22, he had the prudence of a 40-year-old. He also commented that Marcantonio had no property and had to live on the giovane di lingua's stipend of 50 ducats a year, which was hardly enough for buying hats and shoes; in response to this, the Doge doubled the young man's salary in 1592. Marcantonio would go on to have a long career in Venetian service. He was praised by the bailo in 1600 as knowing Romanian, Albanian, Greek, Persian and some Arabic, and as speaking Turkish with such elegance that pashas took pleasure in listening to him (though one modern scholar has found his written translations rather mediocre), and in 1603 he was promoted to grand dragoman. Marcantonio married first of all into one of the most prominent Catholic Perot families, the Pirons; thereafter several Pirons would become giovani di lingua. His second marriage was to a cousin of his first wife, Caterina Olivieri, the daughter of a Perot dragoman at the French embassy. Marcantonio's career was distinguished, though not untroubled by suspicions in Venice that he was giving information to Spain; but in the end it was the

Ottoman government that executed him, by impalement, in 1620, for having spoken disrespectfully. Towards the end of his life he had a connection with the Dalmatian adventurer Gaspare Graziani, who became Voivod of Moldavia in 1619. Graziani negotiated for some time to marry one of Marcantonio's daughters, and it was said that his revolt against the Ottomans in 1620 was prompted by the news of Marcantonio's death.[22]

Marcantonio Borisi was not the only Bruti nephew working in Ottoman territory towards the end of Cristoforo's life. His brother Bernardo Borisi, who acted as an interpreter for Petru Şchiopul in Iaşi in 1587–9, has already been mentioned.* He would spend some time in Koper in the 1590s, serving as captain of 500 members of the local militia, but in 1602 he was given permission to go to Istanbul on family business, and much of the rest of his life was spent in the Romanian lands. He held high offices in Wallachia and Moldavia between 1613 and 1618; Graziani made him 'hatman' (commander of armed forces) in 1619, and it was this connection that led to Graziani's wooing of Bernardo's niece. The link between the Borisi family and Wallachia had been established as early as 1588 by another brother, Marino, who travelled there on behalf of a Venetian merchant in Istanbul to sell valuable jewels to the Voivod, Mihnea. He went there again in 1590, asking his uncle Bartolomeo Bruti for help in obtaining payment, and early in the following year Bernardo Borisi accompanied Marino on another such trip, to Transylvania.[23]

The fact that these Borisi brothers were involved in selling jewellery might suggest a connection with Cristoforo Bruti, given Lorenzo Bernardo's comment that Cristoforo was occupied with 'some business affairs involving jewels, wheat and other things'. Yet the common factor may be merely that dragomans had a specialized form of social capital that could be put to commercial use: they had frequent contact with very important people, understood how to speak to them and knew how to gain their favour. Jewellery was much desired by the rich and powerful in the Ottoman Empire, for two reasons: its portability, which mattered for those who might fall from power at very short notice, and its giveability – such prestige gifts being needed by grandees to cultivate or assuage those even grander than themselves. All visitors to Istanbul commented on the dazzling array of gold, jewels and items set with precious stones in its *bezistan* or covered bazaar. The rabbi Moses

* Above, p. 338.

Almosnino, who wrote a description of life in Istanbul in the 1560s, remarked that their main purchasers were 'very great lords' seeking to regain favour at the Sultan's court; for this reason, he said, prices could fluctuate wildly, depending on the urgency of the demand, and the jewel traders could oscillate likewise between riches and poverty. The removal of Mihnea from power caused some panic among those who had supplied such goods to him, as significant payments were still outstanding; but the flow of debts and investments was a two-way one, and in 1592 yet another brother, Francesco Borisi, was recorded as owing Mihnea (now known, after his conversion, as Mehmed Bey) 4,500 ducats. There was, in any case, a special bond between Mihnea and the Bruti–Borisi family. When he was removed from power in early 1591 and converted to Islam, he entrusted his five-year-old son to either Bartolomeo or Cristoforo Bruti, who sent him for safe-keeping to Jacomo Bruti in Koper; presumably the main motive was to prevent the boy, Radu, from being brought up as a Muslim and thereby disqualified from ever becoming Voivod of Wallachia. In early 1592 the Venetian government intervened, decreeing that he should be moved to Venice; he was placed in the household of a 'Misser Bernardo' (perhaps Lorenzo Bernardo, the former bailo and envoy), from where Mihnea reclaimed him in the following year. Radu would rule Wallachia at various times between 1601 and 1623, and several members of the Bruti–Borisi family would benefit from his patronage.[24]

Gradually, from the children of Jacoma Borisi, and those of her brother Jacomo Bruti, a web of dragoman careers and dragoman-dynasty-fortifying marriages extended down the generations. One of Jacomo's sons, Bernardo Bruti (known also, in the Venetian style, as 'Barnaba'), became a giovane di lingua in 1602 and served at the bailate for more than 20 years; in 1619 he was rewarded, like his grandfather Antonio before him, with the title 'Cavaliere di San Marco'. Three years after his arrival in Istanbul, his cousin Cristoforo Bruti, son of Benedetto, started as a giovane di lingua there; and seven years later Bernardo's brother Bartolomeo arrived, in the same capacity. So in 1612 the bailo had Marcantonio Borisi as grand dragoman, Bernardo Bruti as another working dragoman, and two younger Brutis studying Turkish. At the same time there were two Navons, members of a long-established Perot dragoman family in Venetian service; one of Marcantonio Borisi's daughters married a Navon, and their son would also become a Venetian dragoman.[25]

Angela Bruti, a daughter of Jacomo, married a member of one of the old noble families of Istria, the Tarsias; her son Cristoforo Tarsia would start work as a giovane di lingua in 1618 and go on to have a successful career as grand dragoman, while her daughter Bradamante would marry into another Capodistrian noble family, the Carlis, who began to produce dragomans thereafter. Clearly these locally prestigious but rather poor nobles, whose incomes came mostly from low-grade Istrian agricultural estates, could only benefit from entry into the world of government service and Venetian–Ottoman commerce. The Tarsias took to this profession particularly well, becoming the dominant family in the Venetian dragomanate in the second half of the seventeenth century. So successful were they, and so proud of the social status their work conferred on them, that they commissioned a superb series of portraits of themselves in Ottoman dress – the first known paintings of individual dragomans – which today can be seen flanking the grand staircase of the Belgramoni-Tacco Palace, the Regional Museum of Koper. Familial links with Perot dragoman families were renewed from time to time, but these interlinked dynasties always retained an Istrian base. Altogether, the sons, nephews, cousins and grandchildren of these Brutis, Borisis and Tarsias would exercise this profession for well over a century, making Koper, that little Venetian possession on the edge of the Slav and Ottoman worlds, the home of a huge succession of people who developed the skills to mediate between Venice and Istanbul. All of this was the legacy of Bartolomeo Bruti's brief venture, in 1573–4, into the world of the dragoman, and of his brother Cristoforo's later persistence in it.[26]

20

The Exiled Voivod and
his Counsellor

On 24 September 1591, after more than a month in exile, Petru Şchiopul
was in Satu Mare, an Imperial Free City close to the Polish–Hungarian
border. From there he wrote a letter to Archduke Ernest, brother of the
reclusive Emperor Rudolf II, asking for permission to settle either in
Hungary or elsewhere, in the Empire. He assured the Habsburgs that
his presence would not be troublesome, but said that if they thought
otherwise, he would like to receive a passport to visit the Pope in
Rome. Unfortunately for him, relations between the Habsburgs and the
Ottomans had reached a very delicate stage, with an on-going renegotiation of the peace treaty between them; the Ottomans had various
grievances – above all, raiding and piracy by the Uskoks, who were
Habsburg subjects – and it was thought that giving asylum to Petru
might be taken as a provocation. (A few months later, the Grand Vizier
did accuse the Empire of having organized Petru's flight from Moldavia.) So at first Rudolf refused to let Petru settle in his domains, giving
him only a safe-conduct to pass through them. During the winter
months Petru stayed for some time at Tulln, near Vienna, from where he
showered the Emperor with gifts: a sabre encrusted with diamonds,
emeralds and rubies; ten camels; two fine horses, and so on. Eventually,
by late April 1592, the ex-Voivod managed to persuade Archduke
Ernest to let him stay in the Südtirol; Ernest's uncle the Archduke Ferdinand, whose territory it was, reluctantly agreed to this. After spending
some time in Bavaria in the summer, Petru moved to Hall, near Innsbruck (where his presence caused some perplexity: one local chronicler,
misled by his quasi-oriental dress, recorded the arrival of 'an Ottoman
pasha with some 100 Ottomans'), and then, in late September, to
Bolzano. This was a small and rather unprepossessing place; when
Michel de Montaigne passed through it eleven years earlier, he found it
ugly in comparison with the German and Austrian towns he had seen,

'with narrower streets and no fine public square' – though he did comment on the good quality of its bread, and the abundance of its wine. Petru was given the town hall to live in, together with a group of four private houses for his entourage. One of the houses had been the residence of Ferdinand von Kühbach, the local administrative officer; he was given the public task of seeing to Petru's needs, and the less openly acknowledged one of keeping a close eye on his activities and contacts.[1]

When Petru Şchiopul had been planning to proceed to Rome, before the Habsburgs' change of mind, he had written to the new Pope, Clement VIII – the former papal legate in Poland, Ippolito Aldobrandini, who was elected in January 1592. Clement's reply, dated 20 April 1592, survives. It begins: 'From your letter, and from a conversation with my beloved son Antonio Bruni, to whom you gave your letter for me and your instructions, I learned how eager you are to visit me, and why you wish to do so, all of which greatly pleased me.' The Pope then went on, in general terms, to encourage Petru to make the visit. A few months later the attitude in Rome towards the ex-Voivod seems to have cooled. In July the new papal secretary of state, Minuccio Minucci, wrote to the papal nuncio in Graz to say: 'As for the request made by the prince who was expelled from Moldavia, it is not clear what answer can be given; if he wants to come to Rome he does not need any passport for Italy.' Minucci doubted, however, whether the Pope could or should get involved in Petru's affairs, 'since he is a schismatic, and not in union with this holy Church'. But two months later Petru felt able to write, in a letter to Archduke Ferdinand: 'I used to have good friendly relations with the Holy Pope; I had a certain man, called Bruti, whom I sent quite often from my court to the Pope. Recently, in these autumn days, I received a letter from the Pope, which I have now. When there is time, he asks that by Your Majesty's favour I may be allowed to come to Rome and go back again.' In that text, although the name is clearly spelt 'Bruti', there are good reasons to think that Antonio Bruni was the man he referred to; no doubt Petru thought of him as one of a number of relatives of Bartolomeo Bruti who had been in his service. Not only had Antonio Bruni taken his letter to Clement VIII, but he was also, of all the members of Bartolomeo's family involved in Moldavian affairs, the one most likely to have had good contacts in Rome.[2]

From the fact that he would soon be acting as an interpreter for Petru in his Tyrolean exile, it is clear that Antonio Bruni had spent enough time in Moldavia to become fluent in the Romanian language. As we have seen, he had been living in Koper after 1585, perhaps until 1587 or a little later. In August 1591, however (just at the time when Petru was abandoning his throne), Antonio was elected – together with his cousin Matteo Bruni – one of the overseers of the municipal grain store in Koper. So his residence in Moldavia probably took place at some time between 1587 and 1591. He may have travelled with his cousin Cristoforo and Cristoforo's brother (Benedetto or Bernardo) when they went from Venice or Koper to Istanbul, and thence to Iaşi, in 1588–9.* In the little treatise on the *beylerbeylik* (province) of Rumeli which he later wrote, Antonio displayed some special knowledge of the Albanian port of Vlorë, and of conditions on the Bulgarian Black Sea coast; these places are likely to have been on his itinerary – perhaps more than once, if he did indeed go 'rather often' from Iaşi to Rome. And in that same text he also showed a detailed acquaintance with Moldavian affairs, commenting, for example, on 'those Tatars who normally live in the corner of Moldavia which, lying between the river Dniester and the Danube up to the Black Sea, constitutes the *sancak*s of Bender and Akkerman', and giving the alternative names of Bender and Akkerman in both Romanian and Polish. How Antonio spent his time in Iaşi is not known, but it is possible that his cousin gave him work within the administration, perhaps in the treasury. The Venetian writer Lazaro Soranzo would have close relations with Antonio, not only reading his manuscript treatise but also very probably getting information from him in person; so it may be significant that when he discussed the finances of the Romanian principalities in his own book on the Ottoman Empire, Soranzo gave detailed figures for the tribute they paid, adding: 'Such is the information which I have obtained from people who have seen the accounts of Moldavia and Wallachia.'[3]

At some point in early 1592, then, Petru Şchiopul had probably contacted Antonio in Koper, sending him a letter to the Pope and asking him to deliver it in person. Once the Pope's reply was sent off in April, Antonio seems to have had no further involvement in Petru's affairs for roughly a year. But in May 1593 he travelled to Bolzano, where Petru issued a formal document, in Romanian (written rather erratically in the Cyrillic alphabet), stating: 'I have authorized Mr Antonio Bruni to speak, write, make arrangements and act as he thinks best in this lawsuit with Dživa the Ragusan, wherever it may be necessary, both before the Pope and before the honoured Holy Roman Emperor and before the

honoured Archduke Ferdinand and before any other Christian lord.'
Antonio Bruni was now to play an essential role in the ex-Voivod's
affairs, as his counsellor, occasional interpreter, and chief legal adviser.[4]

'Dživa the Ragusan' was a Ragusan merchant, Giovanni de Marini
Poli ('Dživa' being a Croatian abbreviation of 'Giovanni'), who had
pursued a career in the Romanian lands from 1583 onwards. Witnesses
assembled by Petru Şchiopul said that he had fled from Sofia to Wallachia to escape his creditors, inveigled himself into the Voivod's court
there, and then played the same trick in Moldavia; but these were the
most hostile witnesses that Petru could find. Giovanni must certainly
have made a good impression at the time. While in Wallachia he married a first cousin of the Voivod, Mihnea, converting to the Orthodox
Church in the process, and when he moved to Iaşi he was quickly
befriended by Bartolomeo Bruti. Thanks to Bartolomeo he obtained the
lucrative Moldavian tax-farm on cattle and sheep. The financial year
ran from mid-August to mid-August; he and two partners had just finished the first year's contract, and – crucially – had paid Petru a large fee
for the next, when Petru went into exile. The departing Voivod did send
an instruction to his successor to honour the arrangement, but Aron did
not feel bound by that, and gave the tax-farm to other applicants. Giovanni de Marini Poli was, with his partners, seriously out of pocket, and
he began to pursue Petru in exile for a total of just under 17,000 thalers
(11,333 ducats), of which he personally claimed one third. In early
1593 both sides were gathering documents and witness statements for a
confrontation in court. Much of this work had been done on Petru's
behalf by the time Antonio Bruni was put in charge of the case in May.
The hearings began in late June, and in August the high court of Upper
Austria issued a ruling against de Marini Poli; he appealed, but the final
judgment went against him in November 1593. He and his brother
Pasquale would make repeated attempts thereafter to reopen the case.
Giovanni de Marini Poli complained that the witnesses who appeared
for Petru were mostly the ex-Voivod's former servants, and that one of
them, who pretended to be travelling through Austria by chance, had in
fact been summoned by Petru's team to pay back a large favour: his
brother had once been saved by the intervention of Bartolomeo Bruti
from a death sentence for murder in Poland. Antonio Bruni did not himself appear in court as a lawyer (he hired two practitioners, one Austrian
and one Italian), but he seems to have organized, by fair means or foul,
a very successful operation.[5]

As a confidential adviser to Petru, Antonio Bruni was naturally drawn into the management of his other affairs. The most important change that affected them was the re-appointment of Sinan Pasha as Grand Vizier in January 1593: stimulated by this, and tiring already of his life in exile, Petru Şchiopul began to think of returning to the Moldavian throne once again. It was probably in the early months of 1593 that a friend or agent sent Petru a letter from Istanbul, saying that he and his associates there had been lobbying Sinan and the Sultan to restore Petru to his domains. The letter, written in Greek, uses ecclesiastical terminology in a charmingly simple code, referring to the Grand Vizier as a churchwarden, Moldavia as a monastic estate, and so on. In response, Petru sent a letter written in similar terms to Sinan, apologizing for his retreat into exile (he said it had become necessary when Sinan was dismissed from office, as Petru's enemies had then grown too strong), and begging him to seek forgiveness from the Sultan so that Petru could take possession again of his monastic land. A reply from Sinan Pasha, in June 1593, said that his errors were forgiven, and that he should travel as soon as possible to Chios, to wait there while the details of his reinstatement were worked out.[6]

These manoeuvrings did not escape the notice of the Habsburgs, who, as they slid unwillingly in the summer of 1593 towards war against the Ottoman Empire, were increasingly suspicious of anyone connected with Istanbul.* The Imperial Ambassador there, Friedrich von Kreckwitz, had close relations with Benedetto Bruti, who spoke to him quite freely about the campaign – which Benedetto himself was helping to organize, thanks to his connection with Sinan – to restore Petru to his throne. By 1 June von Kreckwitz was able to report that Benedetto had promised 30,000 ducats to the Sultan, 20,000 to Sinan, and 8,300 to Sinan's son, the *beylerbeyi* of Rumeli; that very evening, for a payment of 6,000 ducats, he was getting the safe-conduct that would enable Petru to return to Ottoman soil. A few weeks later the Ambassador noted a rumour that Petru Şchiopul was going to take a galley to Dubrovnik. On 3 July Archduke Ferdinand wrote to the Emperor saying that he had learned from von Kreckwitz's reports that Petru was 'negotiating hard at the Porte through someone called Bruti', and added: 'Also, someone called Antonio Bruti [sc. Antonio Bruni] recently came here to the Voivod; he is, I think, a hard-bitten, crafty and cunning fellow, whom the Voivod uses in his secret and confidential affairs as an assistant and translator. He is said to be the cousin and close kin of the

* On the drift to war see below, pp. 393–8.

Bruti in Istanbul.' (At this stage Ferdinand had not encountered either
Petru or Antonio; his comments on the latter must have reflected only
hearsay and suspicion.) One month later Petru met the Archduke for
the first time when he visited him at his residence, the castle of Ambras
in the mountains above Innsbruck. Ferdinand questioned Petru about
his interest in returning to power in Moldavia, reporting the next day to
the Emperor that he had replied, 'through his interpreter, Bruti [sc.
Bruni]', that 'indeed he could not deny that he is not disinclined to do
so, but he does not completely trust the Sultan.' (This was not the only
topic they talked about. In his manuscript treatise Antonio Bruni would
mention that they had discussed how to defeat the Ottomans in battle,
and that Petru had insisted that small Christian forces could beat large
Ottoman ones 'first, by the help of God, and secondly, by advantage of
arms and discipline'.) Less than two weeks later, Ferdinand received a
letter from his agent in Venice, Bernardino Rossi, saying that two men,
a Greek and a Spaniard, were preparing to conduct Petru Şchiopul to
Istanbul.[7]

   All such plans, whether real or imagined, were quickly overtaken by
events. By mid-August 1593 the Holy Roman Empire was formally at
war with the Ottoman state. Sinan had more important things to think
about than shuffling voivods; and over the next few months Petru's successor, Aron, began to hedge his bets by making positive overtures to the
Habsburgs, which made them even more wary of any possible return to
power by Petru himself. (Early in the following year, the Imperial government would decide to send a secret envoy to Aron, and would choose
none other than Giovanni de Marini Poli for the task.) Soon after the
outbreak of the war, a group of boyars fled from Moldavia to Poland,
and encouraged King Sigismund to invite Petru there. In December
1593 Petru wrote to Archduke Ferdinand, saying that he would like
eventually to settle in Poland, but asking for permission to travel first to
see the Pope in Rome. It was Antonio Bruni who had transmitted to
Rome his renewed request to visit. The contact Antonio made use of
there was Lazaro Soranzo, who served in the papal household; Soranzo
would later write that Petru wished to kiss the Pope's feet, 'as I arranged
with His Holiness at his [sc. Petru's] request, and through the efforts of
Antonio Bruni, an Albanian gentleman'. Clement VIII was keen on this
idea, and in February 1594 he wrote to both the Emperor Rudolf and
Archduke Ferdinand requesting that Petru be allowed to travel: he
explained that he was hoping to extract information from him that
might contribute in some way to defeating the Ottomans. But still the

Habsburg authorities remained obdurate. Petru would never leave the Tyrol.[8]

Antonio Bruni enjoyed more freedom, and after the completion of the court case in November 1593 he returned to Venetian territory. (The evidence for this is a letter he sent to Ferdinand on the 17th of that month, asking for an attestation that his seven months' stay in Austria had been the sake of Petru's legal business; most likely he feared the suspicions of the Venetian authorities when he returned, since Venice was maintaining strict neutrality in the war, and would be on the look-out for Habsburg agents.) In March 1594 he was in Koper, and in the following month Ferdinand permitted Petru to send gifts – some armour and a clock – 'to Antonio Bruni in Italy'. Perhaps these were long-delayed payments, or gratuities, for Antonio's services. If so, they were the last he received; he would not see Petru Şchiopul again.[9]

In May 1594 Petru drew up a will, in Greek, which left all his property to his son Ştefan. The bulk of the document consisted of a denunciation of Petru's daughter and her husband, and also of his nephew Gheorghe (who had enjoyed the title of 'hatman' or military commander), for having previously abandoned him without his leave; he revoked an earlier document in which he had made his nephew the guardian of Ştefan and all his property after his death. At the same time he repeated his request to Ferdinand that he be allowed to go to Rome; so it seems that he was not seriously infirm. According to a later account by Ferdinand von Kühbach, the official who had been appointed to monitor his activities and had become a real personal friend, it was the excessive heat in June that caused a sudden deterioration in Petru's health. Von Kühbach took him to a house he owned two miles away, which was in a cooler position on a mountainside. As he continued to weaken, Petru entrusted the care of his son to von Kühbach and Archduke Ferdinand, saying that Ştefan was 'the only reason for his present exile and tribulations, by means of which he had snatched him from Ottoman tyranny'. Towards the end, he called for Gheorghe Movilă, the Metropolitan (who had gone into exile with him); von Kühbach rode for hours to fetch him, but on his return found that Petru could no longer speak. Petru Şchiopul received the sacrament from Movilă, 'according to the Orthodox rite'. The next day Petru recovered a little, and was able to tell von Kühbach how grateful he was to him for all his help; and then he died. He was buried in Bolzano on 3 July.[10]

Two problems now arose. The first concerned the future of Petru's son, who was aged ten. Archduke Ferdinand decided that he should be

brought up in the Tyrol, and appointed von Kühbach and two others to
act as his guardians. A request later came from King Sigismund of Poland
that he be sent to the Polish court, but it was declined. If this young prince
were ever to be used on the chessboard of Romanian dynastic politics, he
must be fully attuned to Habsburg values and interests – and he must
also be a Roman Catholic. This last point was not in fact at variance
with his father's wishes: in 1592, shortly before he settled in Bolzano,
Petru had written to Ferdinand that whilst he wanted to build a little
Orthodox church for himself, he was willing for his son to become a
Catholic. So Ştefan would be sent to the Jesuit college in Innsbruck,
where in due course he became a prefect of the Marian congregation.
He fell ill and died while still a student there, in 1602, leaving legacies
to the poor of the city, and was buried in the parish church.[11]

The other problem arose within hours of Petru's death. Von Kühbach
had travelled immediately to Petru's residence in Bolzano and given
orders to forbid access to his effects; but then he had to come back to
his mountainside home, and as soon as his back was turned, what he
called 'the barbarous rabble' who belonged to Petru's household began
hunting for valuables. Chief among these unscrupulous scavengers was
Petru's son-in-law, Zotu Ţigara, but there were several others involved,
including Petru's mistress, who was a Circassian slave called Rada,
Gheorghe the Hatman, Costea the Postelnic (chamberlain) and even the
Metropolitan himself, Gheorghe Movilă. Large quantities of gold coins,
jewels and other portable objects were smuggled out of the house, and
the thieves then set off for Venice to divide the spoils. There they quickly
fell out among themselves. It was Antonio Bruni who, hearing about
this, contacted Archduke Ferdinand's agent in Venice to warn the Austrian authorities. On 29 August the agent, Bernardino Rossi, reported
that Antonio had forced the culprits to make a formal deposit of the
goods they had taken, and to promise that they would return them to
Ştefan; but their word was not to be trusted. On 2 September, and again
eight days later, Rossi wrote that most of the loot was in Zotu Ţigara's
house in Venice, and that since Zotu was now going back to Bolzano to
collect his wife, he should be seized on arrival and held there until the
valuables were returned. All of this information, he wrote, had come
from Antonio Bruni; but at the same time he added a note of caution
about him, saying that 'while the Voivod was alive he did not reveal to
me that he was his agent, or that he had on previous occasions been in
Istanbul; he is an Albanian, originally from Ulcinj, and so far as I now
understand he is related to Sinan.' However, he added, 'I do not mean to

judge him rashly, or to make him seem suspect, as I see that he is extremely eager to seek and procure the good of the Voivod's son.' By the beginning of October Rossi was more sure of Antonio's bona fides in the affair, saying that he was 'rather well-intentioned' and that he was motivated by a desire to see the goods restored; but he did mention also that there was bad feeling between Antonio and Zotu Țigara, who disputed Antonio's claim that Petru had left him 500 ducats. And another complication had also emerged: apparently 'the wife of Bartolomeo Bruti is owed 7,000 ducats, which her husband lent to the Voivod.'[12]

Petru's thieving relatives took refuge in the fact that he had once given them a document which put his nephew, Gheorghe the Hatman, in charge of Ștefan and his estate after his death. That was the document revoked in Petru's will, copies of which were available; the Austrian authorities merely needed to get reliable translations of the will and some associated papers, from both Greek and Romanian. One possible translator was, of course, Antonio Bruni; but von Kühbach advised against using his services, writing to Ferdinand that 'I am worried that writings may exist in which the late old Voivod appointed him, Bruni, to be a full guardian of his son, over both his person and his property: that is what he is fishing for.' No such ulterior motive emerges, however, from Antonio's own comments on these matters. On 20 October he wrote from Koper to Rossi, suggesting a complex procedure in which the Romanian Cyrillic texts would be transliterated by Ștefan, then translated into Greek independently by two of the parties, and those two Greek versions translated by others into Italian, so that any attempts to alter the substance of the text would be clearly visible. He also suggested holding a criminal trial in Innsbruck, at which Pasquale de Marini Poli could translate from both Turkish and Romanian. At no point did he recommend his own services – though two weeks later Rossi did decide to visit him in Koper to obtain a translation of the Romanian documents into Italian.[13]

Eventually, much of the stolen property was recovered; one modern study puts the value of the coins, jewels and other elements of Petru Șchiopul's estate at more than 20,000 ducats. Two years after Petru's death, however, the estate was still entangled in legal disputes, and Rossi wrote to von Kühbach that there were 'other creditors, among whom there is Bruti's widow'. (The claim by Maria Bruti would finally be settled in 1600, when her legal representative agreed to accept a mere 300 ducats from von Kühbach.) Antonio Bruni did not lose interest in the young prince's affairs. In 1596, as the Habsburg–Ottoman war still

raged, he submitted a memorandum to the Austrian authorities suggesting some sort of geopolitical stratagem in which, 'merely using his [sc.
Ştefan's] name, and with the secrecy that is necessary in such affairs, His
Imperial Majesty might make use of him in the most exceptional way,
both in Moldavia and elsewhere.' Referring to this advice again in a letter of May 1597, Antonio said – with a flourish of Counter-Reformation
fervour – that 'it is the duty of a good Christian to desire the extension
of the Catholic faith, and the extermination of its enemies.' Towards the
end of that year Antonio wrote again, asking for permission for Costea
the Postelnic to visit Ştefan in Innsbruck; the authorities consulted von
Kühbach, who said that he could come if he promised not to engage in
any 'secret dealings', and recommended that Antonio travel with him.[14]

It seems that von Kühbach's lingering suspicions towards Antonio
Bruni had at last been dispelled. There is – or was – some evidence that
von Kühbach now began to employ him (probably in connection with
his own guardianship of Ştefan), as an entry relating to Antonio occurs
in a notebook of accounts in which von Kühbach summarized the payments he made. The historian Nicolae Iorga studied this notebook in
the late 1890s; he reproduced some of the original entries in German,
but this particular passage, relating to the summer of 1598, was
presented by him only in the form of a minimal description in Romanian: 'the journeys of Bruni, who died at the end of July in Trieste'.
Unfortunately the Innsbruck archive, where Iorga read this, later
changed its classification of the documents, keeping no record by which
to convert old references into new ones, and it has not been possible to
locate this notebook, even after an intensive search. Burial records from
Trieste in this period do not survive, so there is no other information
about the date of Antonio's death or its cause. On 4 October 1598 the
municipal government of Koper resolved to take preventive measures
against the plague, 'understanding that both in the country of Friuli and
in the city of Graz, places that are too close to us, that evil is making
lamentable progress'. So perhaps it was that disease that had claimed
Antonio Bruni's life.[15]

Antonio's death thus took place in what was probably the same year
as that of his father, Gasparo. Of his immediate Bruni family there was
now only one member left alive: his cousin Matteo, whose civic career
in Koper, progressing from the late 1580s through a series of public
offices, has already been noticed.* Matteo's first wife, Camilla Verzi,

* Above, p. 202.

made her will in 1602; it mentioned two nieces and a nephew, but no children of her own. After her death Matteo married Zanetta (Giannetta), sister of Alessandro Pola; the Polas were another well-established Capodistrian family, who had been inscribed in the city's register of nobility in 1431. Matteo's will survives in the archive in Koper – or rather, tantalizingly, part of it does: the pages have been cut in half horizontally, and only the bottom half of each remains, giving a series of substantial fragments. Its date does not appear there, but since we know that Matteo was living as 'a very learned and venerable old man' in Koper in 1623, the will can probably be assigned to the early 1620s. Here too no living children are mentioned. As his heir Matteo nominated 'the very distinguished Cavaliere Barnaba Bruti, his nephew, the son of the very distinguished Captain Jacomo Bruti, his first cousin'. This was the dragoman Bernardo, *alias* Barnaba, who had been made a Cavaliere di San Marco in 1619.* Matteo asked that the Republic of Venice defend Bernardo against any who might challenge the will, adding that Venice was under an obligation to do so because 'his [sc. Matteo's] ancestors were always in its service, and because of the service his ancestors gave it when they brought the city of Ulcinj, his native land, into its hands' – a reference, perhaps, to the family of Matteo's grandmother, the de Nichos, who had helped negotiate the submission of Ulcinj to Venice in the early decades of the fifteenth century. But aside from such elevated historical claims, the will also contained some more domestic touches: it demanded, for instance, that his heirs 'take back as soon as possible the olive oil press which is in the possession of the Borisis, and that, having taken it back, they may never let it out to them again for any reason, since the house and the oil press go so much together'.[16]

Perhaps the most important instruction in Matteo's will was his request that a tomb be made in the church of San Domenico in Koper, with the coat of arms of the Brunis carved on it. In it would be placed his own remains, and 'those of his uncle, the most distinguished cavaliere and commendatore Gasparo Bruni; those of his cousin, the most excellent Antonio Bruni, and of his son, signor Giovanni Stefano, which are in Trieste, and those of signor Gasparo Bruni'; above it a plaque in gold letters would commemorate his uncles Gasparo, the commendatore, and Giovanni, the Archbishop of Bar and Primate of Serbia. The wording suggests that Giovanni Stefano was a son of Matteo, and

* Above, p. 377.

perhaps also that he had been travelling with Antonio when both were struck down by the same cause of death in Trieste; whether the second Gasparo Bruni was another son is less clear. At all events the church of San Domenico (the Dominican friary), which had been one of the finest in the city, does not exist today, so the tomb is no longer to be seen. Gasparo and Antonio Bruni, who in their lifetimes had roamed so widely, have no final resting-place.[17]

21

Habsburg–Ottoman War and Balkan Rebellion

The fighting between Habsburg and Ottoman forces which broke out, formally, in 1593 became known in German as 'Der Lange Türkenkrieg', 'The Long Ottoman War', and with good reason: it lasted for thirteen years. It might be expected that such a major war would have had deep-rooted causes, leading the parties inexorably towards all-out conflict. And yet, if one looks at the situation just two or three years earlier, it can be said only that some conditions were satisfied that made this war possible – not that any long-term causes applied that made it necessary. The most important condition was the ending of the Ottoman war against Persia in 1590. According to Western observers, the Sultan had been losing 80–100,000 men each year in that conflict; for some states that would have been a large disincentive against engaging in warfare again, but on the other hand an empire that could sustain such losses year after year could contemplate a new war in Europe with some equanimity. The other main background condition was the constantly simmering irritation caused by border raiding. The Uskoks of Senj, that little port on the coast of Habsburg-ruled Croatia, were very active in the Adriatic, attacking Ottoman merchants and sailing down the Dalmatian coast to launch raids into Ottoman territory. A half-hearted attempt by the Habsburg authorities to suppress the Uskoks in 1589 had failed, and Venice, which feared that their piracy would lead to a permanent Ottoman naval presence in the Adriatic, was unable to crush them without Habsburg help. When Sultan Murad wrote to the Emperor Rudolf in December 1590 offering an eight-year renewal of the peace treaty between them, to begin in 1592, he imposed three conditions: the Empire must stop its hostile activities on the border, pay a recompense for damage caused to Ottoman territory, and remove the Uskoks permanently from Senj. These were real concerns – just as, on the other hand, cross-border raiding by Ottoman forces was a constant headache for the Habsburgs.[1]

Even when such conditions were not met, it was far from obvious why a major war should follow. The Polish–Ottoman peace treaty, co-negotiated by Bartolomeo Bruti in 1590, formally agreed by Poland in early 1591 and eventually signed by both sides in 1592, meant that Poland's traditional role – from an Ottoman point of view – as a security buffer protecting the vulnerable territories of Moldavia and Transylvania was fully restored. Of course, if the Sultan had been planning an offensive war against the Holy Roman Empire, squaring Poland would have been a precaution well worth taking; but there is no evidence of such intentions. On the contrary, in 1590–1 Ottoman strategic planning seemed to be concentrated on a new war against Spain. Encouraged by the admiral Hasan Pasha Veneziano, the Sultan and the Grand Vizier (Sinan Pasha) decided to rebuild the Ottoman fleet on a huge scale, having hit upon a new method of funding it by extracting money from the personal wealth of *beylerbeyi*s and *sancakbeyi*s throughout the empire. Letters sent by Sultan Murad to King Henri IV of France and Queen Elizabeth in December 1590 (at the same time as he sent his conditional message to Rudolf II) promised military collaboration with them against Spain in the following year. Henri was desperately in need of help; having succeeded to the French throne in 1589, this Protestant ruler had been forced out of the northern part of his new kingdom by the hard-line Catholic League, which was openly supported by Spain. It was in the Ottoman Empire's most fundamental geopolitical interests that Spain should not be allowed to dominate or take over France. As for Elizabeth: she had spent several years importuning the Sultan, through her ambassadors in Istanbul, for naval action against the Spanish. Her scheme to make use of the Portuguese claimant Don Antonio had run into trouble when, in a miscalculated attempt to secure Moroccan help for it, she had allowed Don Antonio's son to become a hostage in Morocco; the Sultan of Fez refused to give him back, despite demands from Istanbul that he do so. The arrival of a large Ottoman fleet in the western Mediterranean might concentrate Moroccan minds.[2]

These plans all foundered on a simple inability to raise the money, and gather the materials, needed for a new and much larger navy. The Ottomans were not facing or thinking that they faced an existential threat, in the way that they had in 1571–2; the astonishing feat of logistical prestidigitation that took place after Lepanto could not be repeated.

In any case, Henri IV's military position was stabilized by a number of victories, and he was strengthened politically when the man nominated as king by the Catholic League died in 1590, with no obvious replacement. This did not mean that the Sultan automatically turned towards planning an offensive war against the Holy Roman Empire; there was no special reason for him to do so. As late as the final months of 1592, rather, his main concern seems to have been planning a defensive war against what he thought was a new Holy League. In November or December of that year he sent a message to the *beylerbeyi* of Bosnia, Hasan Pasha, saying that he had been told that Spain, the Holy Roman Empire and the Papacy were forming an 'unholy alliance' to attack Ottoman territory. The message concluded, referring to Hasan Pasha in the third person: 'If all this is true, why has he up till now failed to report it?' Where the Sultan had got the idea from is not clear (it was probably based on an exaggerated account of some efforts in that direction by Pope Clement VIII), but this *beylerbeyi* was hardly the person most likely to dispel it, for he had his own interest in stirring up conflict in the region. Three months later he sent his own personal envoy to Venice, to complain that the Venetians were entering into a league against the Ottoman Empire. Nothing could have been further from the truth.[3]

The single most important cause of the outbreak of war in 1593 was, in fact, this *beylerbeyi* of Bosnia, a Serb or Vlach from Hercegovina whose original name was Nikola Predojević. Taken in the *devşirme* and renamed Hasan, he had become a bellicose anti-Christian; as the governor of the frontier territory of Bosnia he adopted the mentality – and the interests – of the raiders and irregular soldiers who lived along its north-western border, turning a province of the Ottoman Empire, in effect, into an 'irregular power' in its own right. This was doubtless also a strategy for Hasan's own personal advancement. From soon after his arrival in Bosnia in 1591 he conducted, in disregard of his official orders, large attacks on Habsburg territory. (So large, indeed, that Hungarian historians date the beginning of the war to 1591, though it was not declared until two years later.) The border had stabilized over time thanks to the development of a complex system of fortresses and palisaded forts. In the areas between these, casual raiding was endemic in both directions, in a kind of terrestrial corsairing known to the Austrians as 'Kleinkrieg' ('little war'). But this had its own conventions: major forts were not to be attacked; enemy territory was not to be seized on a permanent basis; and artillery was not to be used, as that would be a sign of full-scale warfare. Hasan Pasha Predojević – known also as 'Deli

Hasan', 'Mad Hasan' – broke all of these rules, crossing the border with large forces, repeatedly threatening the fortress of Sisak, and conquering the stronghold of Bihać (with, as the Habsburgs complained, the use of artillery) in 1592. He was evidently not as mad as his nickname suggested: in late 1592 he cannily manipulated opinion in Istanbul by sending prisoners and large quantities of captured artillery, which raised his profile and his popularity in ruling circles there. Earlier that year, the Grand Vizier Ferhad Pasha had summoned him to the capital for a dressing-down; but Ferhad's tactic had badly misfired when Hasan impressed the Sultan as a doughty defender of the Ottoman Empire.[4]

Some modern accounts of these events present Hasan as a protégé of Sinan Pasha, and portray Sinan's return to power as Grand Vizier in January 1593 as the tipping-point in the move towards all-out war. Yet the Ottoman chronicler Peçevi recorded that Sinan was a personal enemy of Hasan, whose hatred had arisen from Hasan's refusal, years earlier, to sell him the fine house he owned in Istanbul. Certainly Sinan's son Mehmed, who as *beylerbeyi* of Buda had frequent contacts with the Habsburgs, was no supporter of Hasan; after the fall of Bihać he encouraged Archduke Ernest to protest to the Sultan over the lies Hasan had told about that event, and even promised that he would send a letter in support. What made war more likely was, rather, the fact that the Habsburgs played into Hasan's hands by seeking to retaliate in two ways: they encouraged more raiding by their own local commanders, in Hungary as well as Bosnia, and they tried to put pressure on the Sultan by withholding the annual tribute which they paid to him. This tribute of 30,000 ducats, a condition of the Habsburg–Ottoman peace treaty of 1568, was euphemistically described by the Habsburgs as a 'gift'; in practical terms it may have been no more than a bribe to secure continuing peace, but symbolically it mattered greatly to the Sultan, who saw it as implying a degree of submission. The Habsburgs sometimes tried to gain leverage by delaying its payment, usually causing more irritation than compliance thereby; by early 1593 the 'gift' was more than six months overdue, which meant that a double payment would be required that summer. In March 1593 Sinan Pasha wrote complainingly to Rudolf II, saying that his son the *beylerbeyi* of Buda had promised, on the basis of the assurances he had received from Vienna, that the delayed gift would be sent, whilst Hasan Pasha of Bosnia had told Istanbul that the Habsburgs were lying; the promise had not been fulfilled, so Hasan had risen in favour with the Sultan and Sinan's son had been dismissed from his post. Meanwhile, he said, the Habsburgs' own raiding expeditions did not cease. Sinan warned him that if he did not send the two years' gifts in the next 60 days, and also return two prominent Ottoman *beys* who had been captured, war would follow. At almost the same time, Rudolf was writing to his ambassador in Istanbul, Friedrich von Kreckwitz, saying that although war seemed to be looming, the Habsburg forces were not ready for it; so he must play for time, promising at least one 'gift' to arrive that summer.[5]

Such was the very tense situation in the spring and early summer of 1593. Sinan's son Mehmed, restored to favour with the Sultan, was appointed *beylerbeyi* of Rumeli, and his first task was to put the forces of that large province in readiness. This did not mean that war was already decided on; it was a precautionary measure, and a way of stepping up the psychological pressure. Other forms of pressure were also applied: restrictions were put on von Kreckwitz's residence in Istanbul, and his dragoman Matteo del Faro was imprisoned. Fortunately for von Kreckwitz, he had recently made the acquaintance of someone who was able to act for him not only as a dragoman but also as an essential adviser. This was Benedetto Bruti, who, having acquired land in Moldavia and served as 'cup-bearer' to Petru Şchiopul, had presumably left that country in a hurry after the killing of his brother Bartolomeo. At the beginning of June von Kreckwitz wrote a formal letter to Sinan Pasha, beginning with the words, 'In accordance with what I have told Your Excellency on previous occasions via this signor Benedetto Bruti . . .'. In it, he promised that the Emperor would restrain his forces, and deliver the two years' worth of 'gifts' within three months, so long as the Sultan commanded his soldiers to keep the peace; and he asked for his residence to be restored to its previous state, and his dragoman to be released. On the evening of 3 June, as he later reported, Benedetto gave this letter to Sinan, who had his son Mehmed with him: Sinan 'proved to be quite moderate on the subject, and definitively said that he had entrusted this matter entirely to his son; he would be content with whatever his son might negotiate and agree about it.' After that, when Mehmed went back to his own house, 'he took Bruti with him, and after a long discussion, at about midnight, he sent him to me at my house, having ordered him to tell me that everything would be perfectly fine. The next morning, the dragoman would be released from prison and brought to my house, and then I would be taken straight to an audience with the Grand Vizier, after which I would immediately send the courier to His Imperial Majesty.'[6]

On the following day this agreement encountered some opposition.

The dragoman was taken first of all to Mehmed's house, where he witnessed an argument between Mehmed and two senior military judges (who, von Kreckwitz felt sure, had been rustled up by the Istanbul agent of Hasan Pasha). They demanded to know why Mehmed was opposing his father's will and trying to stop the advent of war. 'The *beylerbeyi* replied', von Kreckwitz wrote, 'that in this matter he was doing nothing against his father's will; everything he did was with his father's knowledge and permission. The Sultan did not want war, he wanted the two presents, and since I had given a certain and definite promise about them I must be treated with respect.' The judges said that von Kreckwitz's promises were merely a feint, and that they had news from Hasan Pasha that the Habsburgs had assembled an army of 40,000 men in Croatia; the gift would not be sent this year, any more than it had been the previous one. Mehmed's reply was that 'it was impossible to send the gift one year ago, because the Pasha of Bosnia was doing such great damage to His Imperial Majesty's territory' – a remarkable defence of the Habsburgs' own position. After this, Benedetto Bruti was sent to von Kreckwitz with the task of suggesting that he make a large personal payment to Mehmed to show his gratitude; von Kreckwitz sent him back with 2,000 thalers, but then he returned with the news that Mehmed would like 6,000, and von Kreckwitz had to explain that there were only 4,000 in the embassy. To modern eyes this might make it seem that Mehmed's policy-making was merely venal; but it was the normal way of doing things, and the policy itself had already been more than implicit in his correspondence with the Habsburgs from Buda.[7]

These dealings between von Kreckwitz and Mehmed continued over the next few weeks. In his despatch of 14 June the Ambassador wrote:

> Benedetto Bruti really has served me in the most constant and useful way; for when I was in extreme peril, abandoned by everybody, and with my dragoman in prison, this man – whom I had previously never seen in my life, still less known personally, knowing only that he was acquainted with the dragoman – not only offered himself for these dangerous services, but immediately engaged in the business, and went everywhere making enquiries, gaining information, taking soundings and making proposals.

He had played an essential role in dealing with both Sinan Pasha, 'who for a long time has permitted him access to his house', and his son, who gave him similar access, 'on several occasions at night'. Von Kreckwitz advised that Benedetto should be not only rewarded for this, but also given a regular pension of 300 or 400 thalers, 'for so long as he is here (for he has indicated that he wants to move to Christendom)'. He continued:

> Whilst he is in fact not perfect in the Turkish language, nevertheless as an Albanian he has acquaintance and dealings with, and access to, the most prominent people at this Porte (as almost all of them are from that place), and many other significant people in these territories; he is, for a Christian, in considerable credit with them, and in any important matter he can very quickly obtain information, negotiate and get things done, better than anyone else. He is not under an obligation of service to anyone in this place, and is here only in order to obtain vengeance for the murder of his brother.

(That last comment also suggests the reason why Benedetto was so willing to help von Kreckwitz stave off a Habsburg–Ottoman war: his strategy involved, as we have already seen, getting Petru Şchiopul re-instated in Moldavia, and the outbreak of such a conflict would throw any such plans into doubt.) The Ambassador concluded that if things took a turn to the worse and he, von Kreckwitz, were put in prison – as Sinan Pasha had previously threatened – there would be no one better placed than Benedetto to send messages and news secretly to the Emperor.[8]

So, by mid-June, thanks to Benedetto Bruti's assistance, Mehmed Pasha's sympathetic attitude and Sinan Pasha's forbearance, the threat of war seemed to have been averted. For all his support at the Ottoman court, Hasan Pasha Predojević was just a provincial governor, whereas Mehmed was the most senior of the *beylerbeyi*s, and Sinan the most powerful of the viziers. Only one thing could overturn this state of affairs – and it did. On 22 June 1593, when Hasan was on the Habsburg side of the river Kupa, besieging the important fortress of Sisak (35 miles to the south-east of Zagreb), a Croatian and Slovenian relief army surprised his force and drove it back across the river with heavy losses. Hasan fell from the bridge and was drowned; also killed were several prominent *bey*s, and a total of perhaps 8,000 Ottoman soldiers. Naïvely, the Habsburgs assumed that this lucky elimination of the main trouble-maker would help restore normal relations. On 4 July Arch-duke Matthias sent a letter to the Pasha of Buda, proposing a prisoner exchange (modelled explicitly on the one Bartolomeo Bruti had been involved with in Dubrovnik in 1575), and adding dismissively that

Hasan Pasha had been punished with drowning by God for having disobeyed his own sovereign. Six days later Rudolf II wrote to von Kreckwitz, saying that the presents were now on their way; a list survives of the payments that had been prepared, which begins with 90,000 thalers (60,000 ducats) to the Sultan, but also includes 18,000 for the Grand Vizier, 1,000 to each of the other most important pashas, an extra 1,000 to Ferhad Pasha just in case he might soon be restored as Grand Vizier, and so on, and so on, to a total of 144,040 thalers. But while the Habsburg authorities were blithely sending off these messages, everything had changed in Istanbul. In the words of one report, when the news of the defeat at Sisak reached that city on 3 July, 'the Sultan and his wife were in tears; the Grand Vizier offered himself as commander to seek revenge, and he has put on a red robe to symbolize that.' Mehmed Pasha left immediately for Croatia, and scribes were put to work writing summonses to order fighters to assemble. Von Kreckwitz was, as he had feared, arrested and thrown into prison, together with his entire household. Formal declarations of hostilities were issued by the Ottomans in July, and by the Habsburgs in August. The Long Ottoman War had begun.[9]

Once the die had been cast for him in this way, Sinan Pasha reverted to his more accustomed role as a war-leader. His offer to command the troops was accepted, and so he set off, aged 73 or 74, for the front. By the time he had marched his army to Belgrade it was early September. Actions in the field, against Habsburg territory in Hungary, began towards the end of the month, when there were barely four weeks left of the normal campaigning season. The Ottomans made some small gains; then, unusually, instead of following the traditional practice of taking the army back to Edirne and Istanbul, Sinan stationed much of it in Buda and Belgrade for the winter. Habsburg forces made inroads at several points on the border in the spring, and in May they began a siege of the northern Hungarian city of Esztergom (Germ.: Gran), which had been conquered by Süleyman the Magnificent in 1543. (Hungary's greatest Renaissance poet, Bálint Balassi, was killed by a cannon-ball at this siege.) But Sinan Pasha received reinforcements from Istanbul, led by the commander of the janissaries, and drove off the besiegers; he then moved to attack the strategic fortress of Győr (Germ.: Raab; Ital.: Giavarina), in the strip of northern Hungarian territory that was held by the Habsburgs. The historian Mustafa Ali noted that at this point Sinan dismissed the janissary commander and replaced him with Yemişçi

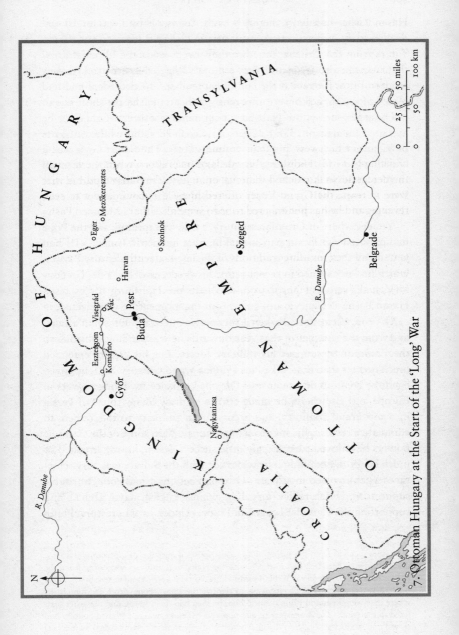

7. Ottoman Hungary at the Start of the 'Long' War

KINGDOM OF HUNGARY

TRANSYLVANIA

OTTOMAN EMPIRE

CROATIA

o Eger
o Mezőkeresztes
o Szolnok
• Szeged
Belgrade
o Harvan
Visegrád
Vác
• Pest
• Buda
Esztergom o
o Komárno
Győr
o Nagykanizsa

R. Danube
R. Danube
R. Danube

N

0   25   50 miles
0   50   100 km

Hasan Pasha – allegedly, merely because Yemişçi Hasan was an Albanian.* In early August Sinan's army was joined by a force of 30–40,000
Tatars from the Crimea; together they swept aside the Imperial army
that stood before Győr, and after a month's siege they received the surrender of that fortress at the end of September. The defenders had had
plenty of supplies, but were apparently disheartened by the sheer size of
the besieging army; the Habsburg commanding officer would later be
executed for treason. Tatar raiders now roamed as far as the outskirts
of Vienna, which was less than 70 miles away. The fall of Győr was a
crushing blow for Habsburg morale, and its effects would be felt much
further afield: in late October the Venetian envoy in Rome reported that
Pope Clement VIII was deeply depressed by the news, and was even
thinking of urging the Emperor to sue for peace.[10]

Yet, elsewhere in Ottoman territory, a tide was turning, and the Pope
had played a significant part in making that happen. Clement VIII had
kept up all the crusading traditions of the late-sixteenth-century Papacy,
which had not waned in recent years; his predecessor but one, Gregory
XIV, had even sent papal troops to help the Habsburg forces resist
Hasan Pasha Predojević in 1591. From the moment he was elected, in
early 1592, Clement had taken a very active interest in Ottoman affairs,
and from the summer of that year onwards he was sending subsidies to
the Emperor to support his military forces. But his efforts extended
much further than that. Like Pius IV, Pius V and Gregory XIII, he envisaged the creation of a huge anti-Ottoman alliance involving powers in
Europe and elsewhere; he made efforts to draw Shah Abbas of Persia
into this grand coalition, and even sent an emissary to the Yemen, to
stimulate a revolt against Ottoman authority. With some of the Catholic
powers he enjoyed frustratingly little success. Spain, having invested so
much effort in obtaining its naval truce with the Sultan, was very reluctant to get involved in any anti-Ottoman action; it had enough trouble
suppressing Dutch rebels, guarding against English naval attacks and
supporting the Catholic League in France. Under papal pressure, Philip

* Another incident from the spring of 1594 also raises a question of motivation. Hearing
that the Serbian Patriarch was in touch with the Habsburgs and was suggesting using the
cult of St Sava, the medieval Serbian saintly king, to rally anti-Ottoman resistance, Sinan
ordered the *sancakbeyi* of Hercegovina to remove the saint's bones from the monastery
where they were kept and bring them to him; he then had them burnt, and the ashes scattered to the winds. The monastery in question was Mileševa, where Mehmed Sokollu had
served and studied as a boy, so the unavowed motive may have been personal as much as
ethnic in this case.

agreed to send some large cash subsidies to his cousin Rudolf II; but that was almost all that he was willing to do.[11]

Venice resisted the Pope's entreaties even more doggedly, insisting that its Dalmatian territories were an outpost of Christendom that would swiftly be overrun in a new war, and that the Ottomans might even send an army of 150,000 men into Friuli, the area just to the north-east of Venice. No doubt commercial interests also played their part, but these security concerns formed the terms in which the public argument was conducted. The Venetian Ambassador in Rome, Paolo Paruta, told the Pope in late 1593 that Venice would not join a Holy League, as such leagues usually turned out to be divided and weak; the Emperor was suspected of seeking peace already with the Sultan, he said, and would become even more likely to do so if the Ottomans turned their forces, instead, against Venice. When the Pope asked Paruta for his advice, he said that the most important thing to do was to mend the damaging division within Christendom between Spain and France. What he meant – and this was a basic goal of Venetian policy anyway, regardless of the Ottoman war – was that the Pope should accept the legitimacy of Henri IV. Brought up as a Protestant, but originally baptized as a Roman Catholic, Henri had just returned to Catholicism, allegedly with the remark that Paris was worth a Mass. Clement VIII was sticking to the principles of canon law, which said that someone who had become a heretic and waged war against the Church could never be reconciled with it. But on the other hand he could see the practical advantage of settling the conflict between France and Spain: not only would this free Spanish resources for the anti-Ottoman campaign, but he might even be able to extract from Henri, as a price for his forgiveness, a promise to join that campaign too. The Pope would wrestle with this problem for many months, before he finally allowed canon law to be trumped by political necessity in September 1595. Even then, however, the trad-itional pro-Ottoman policy of the French remained unaltered. In 1595–6 Henri would try to persuade the Sultan to take part in a joint Ottoman–French attack on the Kingdom of Naples, with the prospect of sharing out that territory between them.[12]

Where Clement VIII's energizing activities did have some real and fairly rapid effect was in the Romanian territories of the Ottoman Empire. In November 1593 he sent the Dalmatian cleric Aleksandar Komulović as a confidential envoy to those countries. Komulović was not only knowledgeable about south-eastern Europe (he was the man who, as Apostolic Visitor of the Balkans, had previously passed through

Moldavia, meeting Bartolomeo Bruti); he was also filled with the spirit
of the Counter-Reformation, having applied to join the Jesuits earlier in
the year. His mission was to draw the ruler of Transylvania into the
anti-Ottoman alliance, and to find out whether Wallachia, Moldavia,
Poland and the Cossacks might be brought into it too; three months
later he received further instructions adding Russia to the list. His key
target was the 22-year-old Catholic ruler of Transylvania, Sigismund
Báthory, nephew of Stephen Báthory, who was a promising subject for
papal influence, having a Spanish Jesuit as his father confessor.[13]

Reaching the Transylvanian court in February 1594, Komulović
received a cautiously positive response from Sigismund, who was also
in contact with his Wallachian and Moldavian counterparts. He then
passed briefly through Iaşi in March, having a secret meeting with Aron;
he found the Voivod 'between hope and fear', but when he gave him the
formal breve from the Pope inviting him to join a league of Christian
princes, Aron immediately agreed to do so. Komulović had been warned
by the papal secretary of state Minuccio Minucci that 'it is not safe to
trust schismatics [sc. Orthodox people] before they have fully revealed
the interests and passions that drive them'; nevertheless, Minucci
thought there was a real possibility of turning the voivods of Moldavia
and Wallachia, as their fragility of tenure under the Sultan must make
them yearn for fundamental change. Aleksandar Komulović then spent
some time in Poland, trying both to influence the policy of the government and to stir up the Cossacks; but the Grand Chancellor Jan
Zamoyski was positively hostile to him, allegedly putting about the
rumour that Komulović was an Ottoman spy or *agent provocateur*, and
it did not help that the Cossack leader contacted and then subsidized by
Komulović was a sworn enemy of Zamoyski. The Voivod of Moldavia,
after some backsliding, did agree to fight against the Tatars, but did not
want to do so with the Cossacks, so Komulović persuaded the latter to
attack the port of Kiliya, which was under direct Ottoman rule. Then
the Cossacks turned to attack Aron, either because they regarded him as
still pro-Ottoman, or because they wanted to seize his cash reserves
before his deposition by the Sultan, which was expected shortly. He was
driven out of Iaşi, and had to take refuge in Transylvania.[14]

Despite the messiness of some of these developments, the Pope's central strategy was a success. Prince Sigismund of Transylvania did commit
himself to the Imperial side in June 1594, in the teeth of serious opposition from some of his Hungarian nobles. Aron did so, in theory at least,
in August; his experiences over the next few months with the Cossacks,

and his dependence on Sigismund, turned that theory willy-nilly into practice. More important than either of these, as it turned out, was the role of Mihai, Voivod of Wallachia, who made his own agreement with Sigismund on 5 November 1594. This man, known in Romanian history as Mihai cel Viteaz (Michael the Brave), had only just been made voivod in September; he had been through the usual process of raising huge sums to bid for the appointment, and one of his first acts of rebellion was to kill all the Muslims in Bucharest, many of whom were merchants from whom he had borrowed money. When news of this reached Istanbul on 18 November, the Sultan declared war – or, at least, a punitive campaign – against Wallachia. One of the leading cardinals in Rome commented a month later that it was important that the Emperor should take control of either Transylvania or Moldavia and Wallachia during that winter, 'not because those people can be of much use as fighters, but on account of the provisions'; without the food they produced, the Ottoman army would starve. He was right about the economic importance of those countries, but he did an injustice to their fighters. Voivod Mihai proved to be a skilled and energetic military leader, and over the next few months he harried the Ottomans in several places, including some of their strongholds on the Black Sea coast.[15]

In January 1595 Murad III died, and was succeeded by his son Mehmed III. The new Sultan replaced Sinan Pasha with his rival Ferhad, declared that he was deposing Mihai in favour of a son of Iancu Sasul, and ordered Ferhad to assemble an army for the invasion of Wallachia. Mihai took his own forces across the Danube, defeated the Ottoman army and killed its commander; Iancu's son fled, reportedly avoiding ignominy by converting to Islam. The Sultan now declared that Moldavia and Wallachia would become beylerbeyliks, Ottoman provinces, and appointed an Albanian, Satırcı Mehmed Pasha, to be beylerbeyi of Wallachia. He also restored Sinan Pasha to the Grand Vizierate, and sent him with an army of more than 40,000 men to attack Mihai's forces. The Wallachian commander, who had only 16,000, waited until Sinan's troops had crossed the Danube and reached marshy land near the village of Călugăreni; in a major battle there, on 23 August 1595, he inflicted heavy losses on the Ottomans, killing several prominent beys and wounding Satırcı Mehmed. Sinan Pasha himself was nearly killed, owing his life to an ordinary soldier who rescued him from the mêlée. (While both Satırcı Mehmed and Sinan Pasha were Albanian, it is worth noting that Albanians also fought under Mihai cel Viteaz: one of his senior commanders was an Albanian called Leka, and volunteers from an Albanian village in Bulgaria would come to serve in the Wallachian army.)[16]

The Battle of Călugăreni was widely acclaimed as a great victory, and it certainly had a huge psychological and symbolic importance: here was an army of Christian subjects of the Sultan killing large numbers of the Sultan's troops and capturing their battle-standards. But the military reality was that the Ottoman army was still too powerful to be stopped in its tracks. Mihai had to retreat to the Transylvanian border, leaving Wallachia to become, for a couple of months, an Ottoman province. In October, fortified with new troops from Transylvania and the Empire, plus 100 Italian soldiers (the remnants of a force of more than 3,000 sent by the Grand Duke of Tuscany to Hungary, most of whom had died at Győr), Mihai and Sigismund pushed the Ottomans back towards the Danube. During the last days of that month Sinan's entire army was forced into the narrow bottleneck of the crossing over the river, and the congested traffic was further slowed, to begin with, by the efforts of Ottoman bureaucrats, who stood on the bridge collecting the Sultan's one-fifth share of all booty. The Romanian forces, with the help of their Tuscan allies, concentrated withering fire on the bridgehead, and the Ottoman retreat turned into a rout and a massacre. Sinan's reputation was badly damaged, and on his return to Istanbul in November he was dismissed. The man chosen to replace him was Lala Mehmed Pasha, a former tutor or adviser to Mehmed III; but Lala Mehmed died only nine days later, and Sinan was then restored, *faute de mieux*, as Grand Vizier. In January 1596 he sent another expedition to Wallachia, but it was driven back; that was his last military intervention. During the second half of March Sinan took to his bed, and on 3 April, after an illness lasting sixteen days, he died. Unprecedentedly, he had served five times as Grand Vizier of the Ottoman Empire. The historian Mustafa Ali, an embittered critic of Sinan Pasha, wrote that poets rejoiced at Sinan's death, a claim that is hard to verify. (Václav Vratislav, who was in prison in Istanbul at the time, recalled that 'great lamentation was made by the people for his death; they ... composed mournful songs about his heroic deeds, and sang that the light of valour and heroism was extinguished.') But there may have been some rejoicing shortly afterwards on the part of the Sultan: on 16 April Edward Barton reported that 'The grand signior hath found in Sinan Bassa his treasury to the value of seauen millions of Gold, in coyne and Jewells, wch hee hath taken to himselfe.'[17]

While the Romanian revolts of 1595 had caused a dramatic shift in the war in favour of the Habsburgs (symbolized also by the fact that during that year Prince Sigismund of Transylvania married a Habsburg archduchess), not everything had gone smoothly. Aron of Moldavia, suspected of making secret overtures to Istanbul, was deposed by his hatman in April and delivered to Sigismund, who put him in prison; he would die there two years later. During the summer, however, the Poles decided to realize one of their own long-term policy goals, by taking control of Moldavia; they invaded the country, drove out the hatman, and placed Ieremie Movilă, the pro-Polish boyar and former colleague of Bartolomeo Bruti, on the throne. Grand Chancellor Zamoyski presented this to the outside world as a strategy to block the Tatars; but the truth was that he made an amicable arrangement with the Tatar Khan (on the basis of yet another promise to restrain the Cossacks), setting up what has been called a joint tributary protectorate over Moldavia, with the blessing of Istanbul. Although King Sigismund of Poland was not comfortable with this policy, especially when he received a fiercely critical letter about it from his cousin Prince Sigismund of Transylvania, the basic rules of Central European geopolitics took priority. Poland could live with the Romanian principalities as an Ottoman-ruled buffer zone; but it could not accept the idea of their becoming clients and creatures of the Habsburgs, and would take any measures that seemed necessary to avoid such an outcome.[18]

The other main development of 1595 was the revival of Habsburg military fortunes in Hungary. After a fierce siege lasting from July to early September, which relief forces under Sinan's son Mehmed Pasha failed to dislodge, the Imperial army took the important stronghold of Esztergom; it then captured the nearby castle of Visegrád. Pope Clement VIII had good reason to celebrate these victories, since he had supplied a significant part of the army. Recruitment had begun in Papal territory in the spring, with a target of 14,000 infantry (though that total was missed by roughly 2,000); the Venetian Ambassador in Rome wrote rather cynically that they were rough and inexperienced men, 'more inclined to sack the places held by their friends than to fight those held by their enemies'. The most professional element in this force was its Albanian light cavalrymen, some armed with lances and some with arquebuses. These were experienced stradiots, who were normally used to hunt down brigands in the Papal States. They were poorly paid; one group of them had absconded to Milan in the previous year, and had to be tracked down and brought back to Rome. Nevertheless, a total of 596 were raised for this expedition. The papal army travelled via

Bolzano to Vienna, and reached Esztergom on 22 August, just in time
for the final stage of the siege. (Once again, Albanians would have found
themselves fighting against Albanians. The Ottoman army in Hungary
included a large contingent under the *sancakbeyi* of Shkodër, for
example, while the *sancakbeyi* of Vlorë had taken part in Sinan's Wallachian campaign.) It acquitted itself well at Esztergom and again at
Visegrád, where the papal general was put in charge of the entire operation; but its ranks were then badly thinned by disease in the autumn.[19]

With his financial support, diplomatic intervention and military help,
Pope Clement was playing an even more active role in this conflict than
his predecessor Pius V had done during the campaigns of 1570–2. He
was convinced that a major reversal of Ottoman power in Europe was
possible, and was keen to explore every way in which that might be
brought about. Naturally, therefore, his thoughts also turned to the Balkan lands south of the Danube. Since the early 1570s, people in papal
circles had never ceased to plan or dream about scenarios for the
destruction of Ottoman rule that would involve uprisings by Balkan
Christians. In 1586, for example, the political theorist Girolamo Frachetta, who worked for a cardinal in Rome, wrote a little treatise
advocating a new war; he said that if Western forces landed in the Peloponnese the Greeks would rise *en masse*, and many janissaries would
refuse to fight against their Christian fathers and brothers. At some
point after his Balkan visitation of 1584–6, Aleksandar Komulović prepared a text for the Pope, saying that the Catholic Albanians could raise
40,000 fighting men and the Orthodox people of Albania and Macedonia 100,000; his plan was to get the Tsar of Russia to attack through
Moldavia, whereupon 3–400,000 Balkan Christians would rise and
join the assault on Istanbul. That was extremely wishful thinking, but it
was not at all untypical. When Girolamo Frachetta returned to this
theme in another proposal, written probably in late 1594, he advocated
an attack by two armies – one Habsburg, one Transylvanian and
Wallachian – and insisted that this would animate those subjects of the
Sultan who were unhappy with his rule, 'who are surely most of them,
since the majority are Christian', to 'rise up and take arms against him'.
In the following year the well-known political writer Scipione Ammirato
(who, as a protégé of the Medici in Florence, was especially keen on the
prosecution of this war) wrote an 'oration' addressed to the Venetian
government, arguing that if Venice joined with the Empire, Transylvania
and Poland, their combined forces could march to the heart of the Ottoman Empire. Do you not think, he asked, that if that happened, 'the

Greeks, Albanians, Macedonians and so many others would try to use such a wonderful opportunity to revolt, if only with stones and their bare hands?'[20]

Another leading intellectual who adopted this cause was Francesco Patrizi, one of the most prominent philosophers in late-sixteenth-century Italy. He had a particular interest in the Balkans, since he was himself from the Dalmatian island of Cres (Ital.: Cherso), and traced his family – whose name was probably Petrisević – back to the medieval kings of Bosnia. He even had direct experience of anti-Ottoman war-fare; as a boy he had been on his uncle's galley at the Battle of Preveza in 1538, and had witnessed the taking of Herceg Novi shortly there-after. Invited to Rome by Clement VIII in 1592 to teach Platonic philosophy, he lodged with Clement's nephew, the influential cardinal Cinzio Aldobrandini. (That was the name commonly used for him, although strictly speaking he was Cinzio Personeni, being the son of Clement's sister.) Patrizi took part in Cinzio's salon of intellectuals, known as his 'Accademia', which also included important figures at the papal Curia. In 1595, for example, the Pope's secretary of state Minuc-cio Minucci gave a 'discourse' on neutrality, strongly criticizing those Christian rulers who thought they could simply stand aside from the present war; he referred in it to a discourse given to the same group by Patrizi, in which the philosopher had listed 21 rulers who had lost their realms by failing to join a common fight against the Ottomans. During 1595 Patrizi published the second part of his great treatise on military affairs, *Paralleli militari*, recommending an invasion of the Balkans by an Italian force of 30,000 men. He put forward three options, Dalmatia, Albania and Greece, saying that in each case the local people would immediately rebel against the Ottomans. 'If we landed in Albania', he declared, 'all the Albanians would come to our side; they are a courage-ous people, so much feared by the Ottomans, both because of the ancient memory of their glory under Skanderbeg, and because of the very fierce hatred they feel at present.' Fortified by these rebels, the Christian army would then march straight to Istanbul. As always with such proposals, there was a large element of wishful thinking here about the speed and simplicity of the operation. But Patrizi was not a head-in-clouds intellec-tual; he was close to policy-makers, and, as we shall see, had access to detailed information about Albania.[21]

Some real efforts to organize revolts were being made during these years by people in the Balkans. In the summer of 1593, just before the formal outbreak of the war, a group of leaders of the northern

Albanians had sent a message to the Pope, saying that they were willing to rise if a Christian army came to their region. In response to this, the instructions to Komulović when he left Rome in November of that year said that when he reached Venice he should 'find out what is happening about the business which was started by the Albanians', and try to get a message to them that they should send a reliable representative to Rome. Unfortunately, when Komulović left Venice he forgot that he had hidden some papers about a possible Albanian revolt under the mattress of the bed in his lodging-house. They were found and taken to the Venetian authorities, who, keen to stop their own subjects from being involved in any such anti-Ottoman initiatives, wrote immediately to Kotor and Budva, putting the governors there on the alert. Venetian intelligence was already aware of a link between Komulović and an Albanian stradiot captain, Tommaso Pelessa (Toma Plezhë), who had long been in the service of Venice and had been made a Cavaliere di San Marco in 1572. From now on it would try to monitor Pelessa's movements closely – and with good reason.[22]

During the latter part of 1594 two separate initiatives took place in the Albanian lands. In September two representatives of Himarë arrived in Rome, asking for arms and ammunition; the Pope gave them a general message of encouragement to take back with them (and eventually, it seems, sent a small quantity of weapons). And in November a gathering took place at a Franciscan friary in Mat, in north-central Albania, involving leaders from the Mat area itself, the Rodon peninsula, the Dukagjin highlands, and the districts of Krujë and Elbasan, as well as two Catholic bishops. They appointed Tommaso Pelessa their 'ambassador' to the Pope, and in late March he came to Rome with a document setting out their proposals. The northern Albanian lands could raise 40,000 fighting men, they said, but there was a great need for weapons and munitions of all kinds – plus a force of 15,000 trained arquebusiers. If they received these, they would seize Bar, Ulcinj and Krujë; the great fortress of Shkodër would then be surrounded and cut off, and it would shortly surrender. These would-be rebels were making large plans; they said that 'men have been sent to Vlorë, to Himarë and as far as the Peloponnese to discover what their thoughts are, since in the previous war [of 1570–3] they all decided to take up arms against the Ottomans.' They were also aiming at some large-scale strategic consequences. The first goal, they said, was to force the Sultan either to abandon the war in Hungary, or to divide his forces in two; and the second was to change the policy of Venice, which, if it saw 'the army of the King of Spain, and of some other Christian ruler' taking possession of this Balkan coast-line, would fear losing its own control over both Dalmatia and the Adriatic, and would feel obliged to join the war against the Sultan.[23]

The authorities in Rome were a little sceptical about the feasibility of all this (especially since the Pope was now digging deep into his reserves, as he planned the recruitment of his army for Hungary – he could not possibly raise another 15,000 men for the Balkans). But they did not want to be discouraging; so Cardinal Cinzio wrote to the Bishop of Korčula, Agostino Quinzio, asking him to find out more. In September and October that bishop spoke with Pelessa and other leaders, meeting them secretly in Budva, and he himself made two undercover trips into Ottoman Albania; on the second of these he met the governor of the castle of Shkodër, who offered to betray it to Christian forces. Also recruited to this project was Marco Gini (Mark Gjini), Pelessa's brother-in-law, who was from Ulcinj; a stradiot captain, he had served in Avignon, and more recently had been the commander of a Venetian anti-Uskok force of six boats with 300 Albanian fighters. He went to Rome in October 1595 with letters from Quinzio, confirming the truth of Pelessa's previous report. There were some doubts about his reliability (he had only just left Venetian service), but these were strongly opposed by Francesco Patrizi, who vouched for his integrity. Patrizi was also asked to comment on two documents that came in at roughly this time, one arguing that the fortress of Shkodër could easily be seized, and the other saying the opposite; having assembled much information about conditions in northern Albania, he concluded that the first was correct and the second was the work of a trouble-maker or an Ottoman agent.[24]

Patrizi's sources also gave him some more unwelcome information: Bishop Quinzio had talked carelessly and openly about his plans in Zadar, Korčula, Dubrovnik (where Patrizi's regular correspondent had heard about them) and Budva. The Venetian authorities became well informed about his group's activities, not least because one of the people recruited by Pelessa in Budva, and sworn to secrecy by him, revealed every detail to the governor of that city. One comment in that person's statement to the governor deserves special mention: he said, in October 1595, that 'when we heard recently that there were galleys, i.e. Spanish ones, in the Adriatic, we thought that they had with them the cavaliere Bruni, who lives in Malta, since he is an Albanian; we thought he was coming to his homeland to free it from the hands of the infidels.' Even during his quasi-retirement in Malta, it seems, Gasparo Bruni still had a considerable *réclame* among the people of the former Venetian Albania. But he was not part of this story, which, in any case, would soon be brought to an end. Hearing that Marco Gini had gone to Naples, the Venetian authorities told their agent there to organize his assassination. (He failed.) They also issued orders in May 1596 to seize Pelessa, and to deal with the troublesome Bishop of Korčula either by expelling him from Venetian territory or by putting him under quasi-arrest and bringing him to Venice. Within three months they had Pelessa in prison, and the Bishop had fled to Rome with no possibility of return. Fierce protests from Cardinal Cinzio had no effect. In Venice's eyes, the risk of being dragged into an unwanted war against the Ottomans outweighed all other concerns.[25]

While Pelessa and Bishop Quinzio had been putting together their plans in the autumn of 1595, another would-be organizer of rebellion had become involved: Francesco Antonio Bertucci. This man was a Dalmatian, originally from the island of Hvar (Ital.: Lesina); his family name was Brtučević. He had become a Knight of Malta, and had impressed the Pope when he was employed to hunt down a troublesome bandit leader in the Papal States. Impressing important people was something to which he devoted great efforts, and for which he had some talent; being endowed with more charisma than judgement, he felt destined to play a historic role in the conflict between Christendom and the Ottoman Empire. During 1594–5 Bertucci bombarded the Emperor with messages and memorandums, proposing a range of initiatives, including the formation of a new league of Christian powers and the liberation of Albania, Bosnia and Dalmatia. He visited Albania in the early summer of 1595, contacting potential rebel leaders there, and making large promises to them; he then travelled overland through Montenegro, before meeting Pelessa and Bishop Quinzio in Dubrovnik in September. A month later he was at the Imperial court in Prague, where he persuaded Rudolf II to support another of his schemes, the seizure of the Ottoman fortress of Klis. This castle, perched dramatically on a hillside five miles to the north-east of the Venetian-ruled city of Split, controlled one of the major land routes from the Dalmatian coast to the Bosnian hinterland, and was of real strategic importance. Bertucci had been agitating about it, with both the Emperor and the Pope, for two years, and he was not bluffing when he said that he had made plans with a group of Uskoks and a number of anti-Ottoman activists in Split to seize it. In early April 1596, while he was still making arrangements in Austria for a force to undertake the operation, his small group of conspirators went ahead and took the castle anyway. They immediately came under siege from a large Ottoman force; Bertucci and the Austrians, plus a number of Uskoks, marched quickly to their relief, but were defeated when they got there, and Klis fell to the Ottomans again. While it lasted, the seizure of Klis caused much jubilation in Prague and Rome; so the Papacy was shocked when it learned that the Venetian authorities were obstructing the advent of any more Imperial troops, and assisting the supply of the Ottoman forces. One year later, the Pope would have been even more scandalized if he had known that the local Venetian commander tipped off the Ottomans about another plan to seize the castle. Venice was simply determined not to be manoeuvred into a Balkan war.[26]

It was, therefore, poor judgement on the part of the next major anti-Ottoman activist, Athanasios Riseas, to travel to Corfu in January 1596 and ask the Venetian governor there to support a Balkan revolt. Athanasios was Archbishop of Ohrid, the historic centre of Orthodoxy in western Macedonia which governed the Church in a large part of the central Balkans and enjoyed, as we have seen, some special links with the Romanian lands. As he explained, it was the victory of Mihai cel Viteaz at Călugăreni that had inspired him to plan a general rising. But he had also become aware of some agents from the Spanish Viceroy in Naples operating in his territory; whether for ecclesiastical reasons or because of more general political concerns, he preferred the relatively light rule of the Venetians over their Orthodox subjects to that which he thought the Spanish would impose, and so he came to make his proposition to the Venetians first of all. (Being originally from the Greek community in Messina, he did have real knowledge of conditions under Spanish rule.) The Venetians, placed in a rather awkward situation, tried to fob him off with fair but non-committal words. Soon afterwards they began to investigate some small shipments of arms from Naples which were going, seemingly on the Pope's account, to Himarë. Although reluctant to get directly involved in the Emperor's war effort in Central Europe, the Spanish authorities were apparently willing to contribute on a moderate scale to trouble-making in the Sultan's Balkan domains. (The Venetian agent in Naples reported that Petros Lantzas, the former Venetian officer from Corfu, had been getting the authorities to send arms, via him, to the Himariots, who then sold them to the Ottomans and gave him a cut of the proceeds; it is impossible to know

how accurate this claim was.)* Evidently tiring of Venetian procrastina-
tion, Athanasios travelled in late March to Naples, where he received
some encouragement, and then to Rome, where more help was promised. After his return to Himarë the rising began in the second half of
July. News reached Venice at the end of that month that Athanasios had
made an attempt to seize Vlorë, marching dressed in red at the head of
a makeshift army of 10,000 men. Vlorë did not fall, and the report was
clearly exaggerated; the Archbishop himself would later say that he had
had only 500 troops. On 10 August his force attacked a recently built
Ottoman fortress on the coast; this time he was said to have 1,300 men,
of whom 200 had firearms. The fortress was briefly overrun, but when
the Ottomans counter-attacked most of the Himariots fled to the hills,
with their archiepiscopal leader. Athanasios tried to keep up the struggle, but his requests for further assistance from the Kingdom of Naples
were unsuccessful, and the people who had joined his force began to
blame both him and the Spanish for having deceived them. In 1597 he
set off on a long sequence of journeys in search of foreign sponsors,
which would take him as far as Prague, Tübingen and Flanders, but
would ultimately prove fruitless.[27]

In the summer of 1596 Minuccio Minucci, who had just been
appointed Archbishop of Zadar, made a speech to the Venetian Senate
urging them to join the war. He placed great stress on the traditional
loyalty to Venice of the Albanians, as well as the people of former Venetian possessions in Greece, declaring that 'as soon as the revolt began
in Albania, the Peloponnese would immediately follow its example, and
also Euboea, the islands and the mainland'; the fizzling out of Athanasios's venture would put an end to that argument. He also raised the
fear that the Spanish would seize Vlorë, 'which would have the effect of
narrowly confining the operations of Venetian shipping': this shows
how these Balkan events could be instrumentalized for larger purposes,
but it too was an argument that lost force when Spain very visibly
stayed its hand. Minucci's most basic argument was that the Ottomans
would attack Venice next, regardless of whether they defeated Austria
or were defeated by it; some good reasons were given for this claim, but
it did highlight, perhaps unintentionally, Minucci's inability to judge
whether the Sultan was likely to win or lose.[28]

The papal nuncio in Venice took a very different tack when trying to
entice the Venetian government into the war during that same year. He

* On Lantzas see above, p. 238.

told them that the Sultan was 'immersed in an extremely deep slothful slumber; the government is riven with disagreement; in the war they lack commanders of any courage, or at least of any reputation. Among their soldiers discipline has decayed and has even been completely destroyed, with the introduction of disobedience and sedition. The people are in a state of commotion, and yearn of their own volition to rebel.' Some of these claims, at least, could be supported with evidence. There were cases of poor morale among Ottoman troops: in 1595, for example, one cavalry unit murdered its officers and refused to mount an attack, and the fall of Visegrád was said to have been caused by a janissary who betrayed it (and later became a Christian priest). Twice during that year there was politically motivated unrest among the cavalry regiments in Istanbul; on the first occasion it was orchestrated by Sinan Pasha, who was resisting his dismissal by the new Sultan, Mehmed III. Since the great uprising of the janissaries of 1589, when they invaded the Sultan's palace and threatened to depose him, there had been many janissary revolts both in Istanbul and elsewhere (in Buda in 1591, angered by delays in the payment of their salaries, they had killed the *beylerbeyi* and plundered the treasury); whilst, on the other hand, the use of janissaries to quell the cavalry regiments' unrest in Istanbul had not improved the atmosphere in the Ottoman armed forces. It was reported that when Ferhad Pasha tried to gather an army in northern Bulgaria for the Wallachian campaign of early 1595, only 4–5,000 out of the 40–50,000 men called up actually reported for duty.[29]

These problems raise the much larger question of so-called Ottoman 'decline' in this period. The traditional historical literature, drawing mostly on Venetian *relazioni* and other accounts by Western writers, has put much emphasis on such things as corruption and luxury among the ruling élite, the growing political influence of women in the Sultan's harem and the increasing remoteness of the Sultan from his subjects and even his administration. These points were not invented out of thin air by the contemporary observers; but caution is needed in handling them, as they did accord so neatly with Western paradigms of corruption and despotism derived from classical writers such as Suetonius. For instance, the apparent 'withdrawal' of a sultan such as Murad III did not mean that he was abandoning government for the pleasures of harem life; on the contrary, he was becoming a more hands-on ruler, rendering decision-making more inaccessible to the Grand Vizierate which had previously been encroaching on it. This in itself was not so much a 'decline' as an emergent struggle between a new variety of absolutism and a new political class of vizieral dynasty-families. More generally, historians have tended to be fixated on a golden age of the Ottoman 'classical system', from Mehmed the Conqueror to Süleyman the Magnificent; any deviation from it is liable to be described as a decline, although no one would think of applying such an approach to, say, the England of 1450–1550 or the France of the same period. To give just one example: it should not surprise us that a military system based on feudal cavalrymen coming to war with their retainers might need to change in some ways in response to new developments in warfare (above all, the use of firearms).[30]

And yet, when all due cautions and provisos have been made, the inescapable fact remains that the Ottoman system was in trouble from the 1580s onwards, and some things were getting distinctly worse. The fundamental change was financial: in 1581 the budget developed a deficit of one million ducats, and by the latter part of that decade the deficit had become permanent. The huge cost of the Persian war was the main reason for this, and hence also for the disastrous devaluation of the coinage during the years 1584–9; the growing influx of Spanish silver from the New World, on which historians used to place so much emphasis, is now thought not to have been decisive. From the deterioration in finances and currency, other problems quickly flowed. The military-feudal and fiscal system began to break down in several ways: the *timar*s or fiefs deteriorated as tax-gathering units, and the government turned increasingly to tax-farming and the raising of extraordinary taxes on the rural population. Many of the spahis, the holders of the fiefs, began to ignore the call-up or even abandoned their estates. The sale of high offices accelerated, and the meritocratic principle, which had seemed so striking to Westerners brought up in societies obsessed with hereditary status, was eroded. Many Ottomans interpreted these changes primarily in moral terms, and a whole literature grew up in the late sixteenth century deploring the decay of justice and equity. According to the historian Mustafa Ali, during the 1580s the nature of the heartland of the Ottoman Empire 'changed from . . . justice and fairness into a land of tyranny and oppression'. To some extent the Western observers – especially those who, like the baili, stayed in place for a long time and conversed with many subjects of the Sultan – do seem to have been echoing the concerns of the Ottoman thinkers themselves. But the kind of criticism that was moralizing and hand-wringing on the Ottoman side became, on the Christian side, wishful thinking about the impending collapse of the entire Ottoman Empire. That wish was not to be fulfilled.[31]

22

Pasquale 'Bruti' and his
Peace Mission

Despite its many tribulations and growing structural problems, the Ottoman Empire remained a colossally powerful entity, and still had the ability to organize war on a very large scale. The Hungarian campaign of 1596 would demonstrate that. It also showed that the Sultan, far from having retreated into a private world of mutes, dwarves and eunuchs in his palace, was determined to take executive power into his own hands: he announced that he himself would lead the army on its campaign. This was the first time that a sultan had done such a thing since Süleyman the Magnificent's Hungarian expedition of 1566. Mehmed III also asked Edward Barton – somewhat to his surprise – to come with him. The idea of taking a foreign envoy as an observer was not a novelty for the Ottomans: in 1548, for example, the French Ambassador had accompanied Süleyman the Magnificent as he made war against Persia, giving him advice on how to deploy his artillery, and in 1569 the Polish envoy had been asked to join the Ottoman–Tatar campaign against Muscovy. Alongside Barton, the French Ambassador, François Savary de Brèves, was also invited, though he declined, pleading financial difficulties, whilst the Venetian bailo was disappointed not to be asked. The Sultan left Istanbul with the army on 20 June. Barton waited until the orders for his daily provision had been confirmed (the document survives, requiring Ottoman officials at every halting-place on the journey to supply his party with bread, five sheep, 20 chickens, quantities of honey and sugar, and barley and hay for his horses); then he set off on 12 July 1596. In a despatch to London at the end of June he justified his participation as follows:

> my personall presence in this formidable warre, may be most beneficiall to all Christendome, and alike honorable [to] the queen of England and Country, in as much as by my knowledge in the Turkishe and Latine

tongue, of wch two languages noe one man in this Empire is practicke but my selfe, I shalbe secretary to both partes their designes, yea and perhaps sole meanes of reconciliacon when I should see matters tend to the detriment of Christendome.[1]

Barton's reference to 'reconciliacon' was testimony to a significant shift in English policy. In his first years as acting ambassador he had vigorously continued Harborne's policy of trying to set the Sultan against Spain; and although Philip II was the prime target, the prospect of an Ottoman war against his Austrian cousins was also to be welcomed, as Philip might well be drawn into such a conflict in their support. Barton personally felt that any belligerence against either of these two major Catholic powers would be a good thing; as late as January 1596 he wrote that 'in my small Judgement [I] thinke it nothing offensiue to God to set one of his enemies against the other, the Infidell against the Idolater, to the end that whilst they were by the eares, Gods people might respire and take strength.' However, in 1593 Queen Elizabeth had a change of heart where the Holy Roman Empire was concerned. This was prompted by growing anti-English feeling among the important 'Hanse' trading towns of northern Germany; fearing that the Hanse would persuade the Empire to adopt measures against English commerce, she began a charm offensive with Rudolf II. The Emperor's main request was that Elizabeth cease agitating at Istanbul for an attack on his lands, and she immediately complied, sending instructions to Barton that he should stop the war – which reached him, awkwardly, just at the moment when Sinan set off for his first campaign in the summer of that year.[2]

One Italian observer commented in 1594 that Barton had 'lost reputation to a large extent' with the Ottomans, and that they merely 'make use of him as a spy to get information about the affairs of Christendom'. But in fact his peace-making efforts were of value to them, partly because so much of his energy was devoted to persuading the rebellious Romanian principalities to accept a reconciliation with the Sultan. In 1595 he sent a letter to Sigismund Báthory in Transylvania, asking him to return to the fold; and in 1597 he would write to him again urging a ceasefire, and to Mihai cel Viteaz commending Ottoman peace proposals. (In 1596 the Venetian bailo complained that whereas Barton was instructed by his Queen merely to promote the maintenance of peace between Poland and the Sultan, he was going further and encouraging the Poles to unite with the Ottomans and the Tatars against the

Romanian rebels.) The other reason why Barton's efforts were valued in Istanbul was that there was a significant element in the governing circles there that favoured a speedy conclusion to the war. This included Sinan Pasha himself – contrary to the view of those contemporary Western observers, and modern historians, who accepted his bloodthirsty 'spiel' at face value. When Barton spoke to him in July 1595, just before the Grand Vizier left for his Wallachian campaign, and told him of 'the queen of Englands desire for the effectuatinge a peace with the german Emperour', Sinan reacted very favourably; he said that he thought the capture of Győr had satisfied the Sultan's honour, and that if the Queen desired peace he would be happy to arrange it 'wᵗʰ more honorable and easie condicons then the german Emperour himselfe could devise, requiringe . . . nothing more then the ordinary tribute and that the german Emperour should not hinder him in the chastisement of his rebellious subiects the princes of Bugdania [sc. Moldavia], Walachia and Transilvania'. After Sinan's death Barton noted that there were still important figures, including the Sultan's mother (the Albanian Safiye, who had been close to Sinan Pasha), who wanted peace. But he was now somewhat inhibited by the fact that he had received, in January 1596, a letter from Elizabeth telling him to stop trying to influence Ottoman policy. (Not that English policy had turned against the Sultan; in the same month an English ship arrived in Istanbul with a cargo of armaments and metals, including 'Tyn and [iron] Wyer', without which the Ottomans 'could not cast certeyne field artillery wᶜʰ the grand Signiour had ordeyened'.) So it was with some trepidation that Edward Barton agreed to set off, alone among the Western diplomatic corps, to accompany the Sultan to the Hungarian front.[3]

Before leaving Istanbul, Barton negotiated the release from imprisonment of the household of Friedrich von Kreckwitz, the Imperial Ambassador. It was agreed that he could take these people with him to the front and send them on, under safe-conduct, to Vienna. This gave a humanitarian colouring to his role in the campaign; and at the same time the sending of prisoners to the other side would create a fresh opportunity for a tentative peace negotiation. Sinan Pasha had taken von Kreckwitz himself, together with five members of his household, to Belgrade and then to Buda at an early stage in the war, and had tried to use them to open negotiations; in February 1595 Sinan's son Mehmed, who was based in Buda, sent one of them with a set of peace conditions to the Emperor, demanding that he give up various fortresses, cease helping the Romanian rebels, and promise to send the tribute every year.

(The reply from Prague was not just uncompromising but positively insulting: it required the Sultan to allow all of Moldavia, Wallachia and Transylvania to be united under the crown of Hungary, and to recognize that that crown belonged to the Emperor.) The 23 members of von Kreckwitz's household who remained in Istanbul had spent most of their time imprisoned in appalling conditions in the Rumeli Hisarı fortress's notorious 'Black Tower' – so called because no daylight entered it – suffering from lice, malnutrition, dysentery and other ills. Two had died, so there were 21 to be freed. They were brought before the new Grand Vizier, Damad İbrahim Pasha, who questioned them via Edward Barton's dragoman. İbrahim informed them, as the young Bohemian nobleman Václav Vratislav later recalled, 'that the mighty Sultan, out of his natural goodness, released us all from so grievous an imprisonment, and counselled us to show gratitude in return, and never to wage war against him'. Eventually they were taken to Barton's house; he arranged baths – their first in two years – and put up tents in the garden for them to sleep in. For Barton's expedition to the front the Sultan sent not only 36 camels, laden with 'tents, carpets, mattresses, cooking equipment and all kinds of provisions', but also coaches for the ex-prisoners to ride in. As Friedrich Seidel, the former apothecary at the Imperial embassy, later wrote, they set off in grand style with a trumpeter at the front, then Barton followed by his twelve retainers dressed in the Polish style, then the ex-captives, 'every four of us in a carriage with red cloth hangings, drawn by two horses, just like the ones used to take Ottoman ladies', and then the camels. Also with them was Matteo del Faro, the long-serving dragoman of the Imperial embassy (and uncle of Bartolomeo Bruti's wife). And among Barton's retainers was his own dragoman, who would have two special tasks to perform: conducting these men across the front line to the Habsburg side, and then negotiating secretly with the Emperor Rudolf for a possible peace settlement.[4]

Barton's dragoman was commonly referred to as Pasquale Bruti. He was in fact Pasquale Dabri, the son of Marco Dabri and of Lucietta Bruti, who was a sister of Bartolomeo, Jacomo, Cristoforo and the rest. In some documents he was called Dabri, but it seems that in the small world of Istanbul and its dragomans this young man was assimilated to the much better-known surname of his uncles – rather in the way that Cardinal Cinzio was accorded the family name of his uncle the Pope. The Dabris had been an old noble family of Ulcinj, recorded there from the fourteenth century onwards; from the 1480s to the early 1500s a Pasquale Dabri was one of the leading men in the city (he gave his

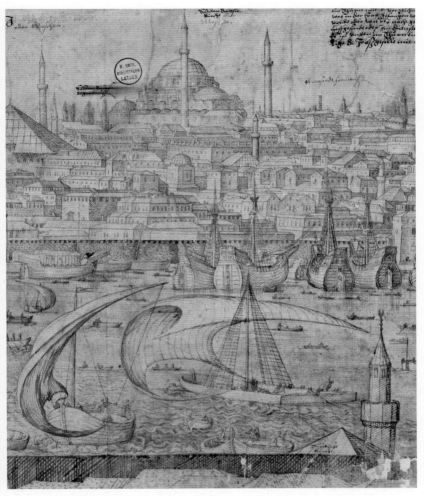

17. Istanbul: part of a panoramic view, seen from Galata, by Melchior Lorck (based on drawings he made there in the period 1555–9).

18. The Venetian bailo's house, Istanbul (the sole surviving image, from a seventeenth-century Ottoman picture-book). The giovani di lingua (trainee dragomans) lived on the upper floor; the two figures on the balcony (*right*) are probably a giovane di lingua and his cozza (teacher).

19. The initial audience of the Imperial Ambassador, David Ungnad, with the Sultan (1573), from a copy (1580) of an Ottoman picture-book commissioned by Ungnad. A procession brings the Ambassador's gifts (*bottom left*); the Ambassador is escorted by two guards (*right*); he will be taken past the members of the Sultan's *divan* (who stand in line), towards the Sultan, who sits in the upper corner of the audience chamber.

20. A finely dressed young Greek Orthodox woman from Pera (Galata): a woodcut of 1576, adapted from an image first published in 1567.

21. Sinan Pasha: a portrait published in 1595, the year before his death.

22. A spahi (cavalryman), from a costume-book made in Istanbul (1590).

23. A janissary (member of the salaried infantry corps), from a costume-book made in Istanbul (1590).

24. Koper: the main square, with the cathedral (*left*) and the 'Praetor's Palace', which housed the Venetian governor, his civil and military administration, and the town council.

25. Ménerbes: the remains of the castle (*centre and left*), on the steep ridge that rises from the surrounding land.

26. The circumcision festival in Istanbul, 1582 (from an Ottoman illustrated manuscript, 1588). The entertainments (here including two buffoons) took place in the Hippodrome, with its Obelisk of Theodosius. The three-tiered wooden stand for dignitaries, erected for the occasion, included a separate viewing-chamber for the Sultan (*top left*, with shutters closed). Non-Muslim dignitaries, including Bartolomeo Bruti, were in the lowest tier, and are depicted here with Western head-gear.

27. Voivod Petru Şchiopul, with his son, Ştefan (a contemporary engraving).

29. The Venetian bailo, with his dragoman, also in Western head-gear, standing behind him, at an audience with the Grand Vizier (an image from a seventeenth-century Ottoman picture-book).

28. King Stephen Báthory of Poland, by Martin Kober (c. 1580).

30. Valletta: a plan of the city (by Ignazio Danti, 1580), as projected and partly built. Note the projected sea-moat on the neck of the peninsula, which was never completed.

31. Coat of arms of the Bruti family, surviving on a street corner in Koper. Top left and bottom right quarters: an arm holding a sword, with a scroll across the sword bearing the word 'Libertas' ('freedom'); top right and bottom left quarters: a phoenix rising from a fire towards the sun; central oval: the Polish crowned eagle, which Bartolomeo Bruti incorporated in his arms after he was made a nobleman of Poland in 1590.

32. A luxurious Ottoman silk caftan (mid-sixteenth century), of the kind referred to by Bartolomeo Bruti in 1589: 'Ottoman lords have given me ... many ... in order to flatter me' (p. 346).

daughter in marriage to the famous Albanian humanist scholar Marin Beçikemi, who went on to become Professor of Rhetoric at Padua), and a Niccolò Dabri, a canon of Ulcinj, was Bishop of Lezhë in the 1510s. So, like his cousins the Borisis, but unlike those other cousins who had Capodistrian fathers or mothers, Pasquale would have been brought up with Albanian and Slav as languages spoken by both his parents.[5]

The first mention of Pasquale Dabri comes in a letter written by Marioara Adorno, an aunt of Voivod Mihnea of Wallachia. Marioara, a Catholic woman from Pera, had married a Genoese merchant and moved to Venice, settling on the island of Murano; after the death of her husband in the 1570s she lived as a lay resident in a nunnery there, but kept closely in touch with her Romanian relatives. In 1590 she wrote to Bucharest, recommending Pasquale and asking Voivod Mihnea to take him into his service. Evidently the connections already established between Mihnea and Bartolomeo Bruti, and his Borisi nephews, had drawn the young Pasquale to Marioara's attention. It is not known whether he spent some time at Mihnea's court, before the Voivod was deposed in early 1591; but if he did, he seems to have moved thereafter to Istanbul, where he came under the quasi-guardianship of his uncle Cristoforo Bruti. A report from Iaşi in January 1592 said that Pasquale Dabri had just been sent to the Moldavian capital by his uncle Cristoforo to get married to a young woman from the household of Benedetto (or possibly Bartolomeo) Bruti. Later that year Pasquale was in Istanbul again, where he seems to have worked as a dragoman, taking over some of the work of his uncle Cristoforo after the latter's death. At some stage his brother Marin Dabri settled in Pera, probably as a merchant; Pasquale may have been involved in his business ventures. When Marin died in 1600 he was described – by Matteo del Faro – as much loved by the Venetian bailo. But Pasquale himself had had some kind of falling-out with the Venetians: as Edward Barton left Istanbul for the Hungarian front in July 1596, the bailo reported cryptically to Venice that 'of our people there went in his suite Pasqual Dabri, whom I had to dismiss for reasons which really merited severer punishment.' The nature of his offence is not known.[6]

Edward Barton's caravan of horses, carriages and camels set off from Istanbul in a July heatwave. They travelled in short daily stages; Friedrich Seidel would recall that Barton took care to choose river-banks for their overnight halts, where they could relax with music, ball-games and fishing. But the heat was intense, particularly in Bulgaria, and the road from Sofia to the Serbian town of Niš was littered with stinking

dead cattle, horses and camels. The travellers also passed the bodies of
two Christian men impaled ('hauing each of them a stake thrust in at his
Fundament, through his bodie, and so out by his necke; the stake being
set vp right on end') for killing a janissary, two Transylvanians who had
suffered the same punishment for espionage, and the heads, stuffed with
straw, of 300 Bosnian rebels whose revolt had been suppressed by
Sinan's son in March.[7]

Eventually they reached the Ottoman encampment outside Belgrade,
and on 17 August they had a meeting with the Grand Vizier, Damad
İbrahim Pasha. This was a friendly encounter, with Barton talking directly to İbrahim in Turkish. The Grand Vizier announced that he was
going to send all the members of the Imperial Ambassador's household
to the Emperor, and they went one by one to show their gratitude by
kissing İbrahim's feet. After that they were given a tour of the camp, so
that they could give a suitably intimidating report of the size of the
Ottoman army when they reached Vienna and Prague; Václav Vratislav
estimated that there were 300,000 men, though this total included 'the
rabble and the worthless mob, the muleteers, and the drivers of asses
and camels'. In early September, when they had travelled with the army
to the southern Hungarian town of Szeged, their position was endangered when Habsburg forces seized the Ottoman stronghold of Hatvan
and 'did most cruelly, without compassion, put all the Inhabitants to the
sword', including pregnant women and infants; suddenly there was a
hunger for revenge in the Ottoman camp. But İbrahim kept his word,
and the Imperial prisoners were sent on to the Ottoman Hungarian
town of Szolnok (to the south-east of Buda and Pest) with an order that
the governor of that town should give them an armed escort to Buda.[8]

It was at this point that they parted company with the English
Ambassador, who was required to stay with the Ottoman army as it
marched northwards towards its main target, the Habsburg fortress of
Eger (Germ.: Erlau; Trk.: Eğri; Ital.: Agria), to the north-east of Buda
and Pest. Barton hired four peasant carts for the ex-prisoners to sit in,
and sent them on their way with 100 ducats, one of his personal janissaries, and Pasquale Dabri. Those two rode on horseback in front, to
protect them from any challenges by marauding troops from either side;
several times they encountered Tatars, but the janissary produced their
letter of safe-conduct from the Grand Vizier, which he kept in his hat,
and solemnly warned the Tatars not to molest them. He and Dabri managed to catch several stray horses, so that other members of the party
could also ride. They spent their first night in a large Hungarian village

which had been occupied by a Tatar squadron; they slipped surreptitiously into the church, where the priest gave them bread and cheese, but soon the Tatars discovered their presence and threatened to kill or enslave them. Providentially, a violent thunderstorm broke out, during which the Tatars went to look after their horses, and in the confusion the party was able to escape, taking local guides who soon became lost in the pitch darkness and pelting rain. After another day of travelling, and further encounters with a large force of Ottoman cavalry that was moving towards Eger, they finally reached Pest, where they lodged with the judge of the Christian community. The next morning they met the Ottoman governor of Buda, who read the Grand Vizier's letter and immediately released the other five members of von Kreckwitz's household who had been in that city since the early part of the war. (Von Kreckwitz himself had fallen ill and died.) He arranged for a boat to take all of them, the next day, up the Danube to Vác, the nearest fortress held by the Habsburgs, with *martoloses* (local Christian auxiliary soldiers) to haul the boat by rope against the stream. Only one member of the party now decided not to go with them: Matteo del Faro, the elderly dragoman, 'who beinge marryed in Pera wold nott depart'. Somehow he would find his own way back to Istanbul.[9]

And so the final part of the journey began on 23 September 1596, with Dabri and the janissary riding on horseback along the river-bank. As they approached the fortress, Dabri released the janissary from his task, giving him ten ducats for his return journey. They all assumed that the peasant guides who had come with them from the Hungarian village, whom they had sent ahead by land, would have notified the authorities in the fortress of their coming; but in fact those guides had been captured and killed by Tatars. So they were greeted instead with a cannon shot, which narrowly missed their boat. Frantically they waved their hats (Western head-gear, not turbans) and shouted in German and Hungarian that they were Christians; the artillery officer stayed his hand, and two armed boats came from the fort to inspect them. They were allowed into the fortress – where, rejoicing at the end of more than three years of captivity, they knelt and wept – and, at their request, Dabri was also brought in. The next day they were taken up the river to Esztergom, where the former captives met Archduke Maximilian. He questioned them about the Sultan's army, asking whether he was heading in the direction of Eger; as Vratislav later wrote, 'About this the archduke knew nothing whatever, and we were very much surprised that the Christians possessed such poor intelligence.' Maximilian was

shocked by the news they gave him, and immediately issued orders that
Eger be reinforced – though in fact the siege of it had already begun.
Finally, having spent three days in Esztergom, Pasquale Dabri and the
ex-captives travelled from there to Vienna.[10]

As early as 2 October Francesco Vendramin, the Venetian Ambassador at Rudolf II's court in Prague, was able to report the news of the
safe arrival of these former prisoners in Habsburg territory. He said that
their release had been arranged by Barton, whose sole aim was to make
peace between the Sultan and the Emperor so that the Ottoman navy
could be sent to attack Spain instead. The political nature of the operation was thus never in doubt; and it was understood that there was a
definitely pro-Ottoman and anti-Catholic colouring to the English policy, which cannot have commended it to Rudolf's advisers. One week
later Vendramin wrote that the members of von Kreckwitz's household
had just arrived in Prague, but that Dabri and two others had been held
back in Vienna, as the Emperor suspected them of being Ottoman spies.
Eventually, by 13 November, Pasquale was permitted to come to Prague
and present Edward Barton's proposals. But by this time the mood
among the Emperor's counsellors had darkened considerably. After a
short siege, the castle of Eger had surrendered on 12 October. All those
within it were put to the sword, as an act of revenge for the massacre at
Hatvan. Twelve days later Archduke Maximilian's army approached;
the Ottomans went out to meet it, and the two armies engaged on the
plain of Mezőkeresztes, fifteen miles south-east of Eger. The battle lasted
two days, and until a late stage on the second day the Habsburg forces
seemed to be winning; they had penetrated to the heart of the Ottoman
camp, and had seized the chests of gold coins and other rich parapher-
nalia of the Sultan's court that were stored there. But that was their
undoing. In the words of Edward Barton, who was an eye-witness, 'the
cavalry dismounted, and the infantry threw away their pikes and arquebuses in order to plunder more effectively' – whereupon they were
subjected to two sweeping counter-attacks, one by Tatar light cavalry,
and the other by the Ottoman commander Cığalazade Yusuf Sinan
Pasha (Scipione Cigala, the son of a Genoese nobleman, who had been
captured as a teenager at the Battle of Djerba in 1560 and had risen
rapidly in Ottoman service). The Habsburg soldiers fell back, and this
turned into a general rout.[11]

Reporting on the long conversation he had with 'Pasqual Bruti' on
13 November, Vendramin noted Pasquale's insistence that the Sultan
had been ready to negotiate peace, not least because he had encountered

great difficulties in assembling his army that summer; avoidance of the call-up was still a serious problem. Pasquale also said that the 'honest conditions' proposed by Barton would have satisfied both sides. But now, after Eger and Mezőkeresztes, 'as the state of affairs had been changed by these very important victories, it was no longer possible to negotiate on the same basis as before.' At another meeting one week later, Pasquale discussed the strength of the Ottoman army, putting the total number of personnel of all kinds at over 200,000, and emphasizing that they had 800 pieces of artillery. He also said that the campaign had at first been intended for Transylvania, being diverted to the northern Hungarian front only in response to the atrocities at Hatvan. As for his peace negotiation: after many delays he had at last been allowed to discuss the matter with members of the Imperial council, who had blithely told him that the Emperor would be willing to accept a settlement if the Sultan gave back Eger or Győr. He had said that the Sultan would never agree to that, and that on the contrary the Habsburgs would need to yield Esztergom or Vác; if they did so, and paid a large sum of money, the Ottomans would make peace. On 18 November he had met the Emperor himself, and had said all this to him. But, Vendramin wrote, 'whilst all decision-making here is so slow, he [sc. Pasquale] felt sure that the business would not be brought to any conclusion.' So he was just waiting to be given the two generous gifts – one for him, and one for Barton – that had been promised, before leaving Prague in a few days' time. His plan was to travel to Buda, and then, 'changing into Ottoman clothes', to go on to Belgrade, where he hoped to find Barton waiting for him.[12]

On 27 November Pasquale came to say his farewell to Vendramin. He had received the gifts: a jewel worth 2,500 ducats for Barton, and a gold chain worth 200 thalers (133 ducats) plus 800 florins (a little under 800 ducats) in cash for himself. He took with him letters to the Grand Vizier, and a letter of thanks to Barton written in Rudolf's own hand. But the terms of his attempted negotiation had been rejected, as he had feared; at most, the Habsburgs were willing to hand over Esztergom and Vác, but only if Eger and Győr were also given back, thus restoring the status quo ante. One of the ministers in Prague had told Pasquale that there was a good prospect of bringing Poland into the war as an ally, on the grounds that the Ottoman advance in northern Hungary was a threat to Polish security; Pasquale said that this was a false hope, since the Grand Chancellor Zamoyski was 'completely on the Sultan's side'. Overall, Pasquale made a very good impression on Vendramin, who clearly thought that he had mature judgement (although he was 'very young'). He described him as devoted to Venice, and eager to end his employment with Barton in order to return to Venetian service.[13]

But that was not to be. On his return journey Pasquale got as far as Belgrade, which he reached by late December. He did not find Edward Barton there, as the bulk of the Ottoman army had returned to Istanbul, taking the English Ambassador with it. On 21 February 1597 Barton reported from the Ottoman capital that 'My Interpretor ... is two monethes scince returned, so far as Bellograd bringinge l[ette]res to me fro[m] the Emperor acknowleginge the receipt of his sayed subiectts and rende[r]inge princeley grattfulnes therfor.' He had received only a very brief message to that effect from Pasquale, so he did not know what response, if any, Rudolf had given to the proposed terms. What he did know was that 'Hassan Bassa Generall of the confines, resident in Bellograd, hath reteyned him, and will not suffer him to come hether.' This was Hasan Pasha, the new *beylerbeyi* of Rumeli, who had been left in charge of the frontier zone. On 4 April Barton reported that the Grand Vizier had said he suspected that Hasan had put Pasquale to death, 'butt bad me haue patience whilst some certen newes came from Bellograd'. By 17 April he still had no news, other than a long-delayed letter from Pasquale, written in January, which had just reached Istanbul. It merely stated that the freeing of the captives had been greatly appreciated by the Emperor, who was sending not only a personal letter of thanks but also 'something else, which I hope you will like, but I respectfully remain silent about it; as soon as possible I shall come to kiss Your Illustrious Lordship's hands, and give you an account of what I have done in your service on this journey of mine.' Those were Pasquale's last recorded words. The delicate way in which they refer to Rudolf's gift to Barton may serve to remind us of one likely motive for Hasan's actions, even if he pretended that he was detaining the young dragoman because of security concerns; there is no further mention in the records of either the jewel or the gold chain and cash. By early June Barton was writing to Bartholomäus Pezzen (a senior counsellor in Prague, and former Imperial ambassador in Istanbul): 'we remain in despair about the dragoman Pasquale, in view of the many accounts given to us that Hasan Pasha has had him killed.' Later that month an Italian 'avviso' from Istanbul stated this as a matter of fact. In October Edward Barton made a formal petition to the Sultan, demanding the punishment of Hasan Pasha for Pasquale's murder; but a month later it was reported that Hasan was ridiculing the accusation, and suggesting that Barton had sent Pasquale into hiding in Galata. So the deed was never avowed, and certainly never punished. Edward Barton fell ill with dysentery, and died on 28 January 1598. He was only 35 years old.[14]

On two occasions, members of the Bruti family had done their best to help stifle this major Habsburg–Ottoman conflict: Benedetto in the summer of 1593, and his nephew Pasquale in the winter of 1596. The former attempt had come very close to success; the latter, with prospects that were in any case much more dubious, had been overtaken by military events. The role played by the Brutis in these momentous affairs now came to an end (though their relative Matteo del Faro continued for several years to send news and intelligence to his masters in Vienna and Prague). The war itself dragged on inexorably. Habsburg forces retook Győr in 1598, but the Ottomans under Damad İbrahim Pasha seized Nagykanizsa, a stronghold of equivalent importance in the south-west of Hungary, two years later. When İbrahim died in the following year he was succeeded by Yemişçi Hasan Pasha, the Albanian who may have been Sinan's nephew. By this stage the leading general on the Habsburg side was also an Albanian, Giorgio Basta, son of Demetrio, a stradiot officer in southern Italy; Giorgio had had a dazzling career as an innovative cavalry strategist, serving the Spanish in Flanders and France, and would prove the most effective of all Rudolf's commanders.[15]

Much of the fighting around the turn of the century was concentrated on Transylvania, where Sigismund Báthory relinquished power in 1598 and then tried more than once to regain it. Mihai cel Viteaz reacted by seizing Transylvania, with Rudolf's approval, and then made peace with the Sultan in order to consolidate his rule both there and in Wallachia. In 1600 he took Moldavia too, thus earning his special place in Romanian history by uniting – very briefly – the three principalities under one Romanian ruler. In 1601 Mihai and Giorgio Basta jointly defeated an attempt by Sigismund to retake his territory; but Basta mistrusted Mihai because of his dealings with Istanbul, and had him murdered shortly afterwards. After one further campaign by Sigismund, Giorgio Basta was left fully in control of Transylvania from 1602 onwards. With great severity he implemented Rudolf's stringent Counter-Reformation policy of re-imposing Catholicism on the whole territory of Transylvania – a place where, famously, Catholics, Lutherans, Calvinists and even Unitarians had enjoyed a *modus vivendi* of mutual acceptance. (The Orthodoxy of the Romanian peasants had also been tolerated, though without formal recognition.) This new hard-line policy – a short-lived but fateful divergence from Rudolf's usual religious moderation – led to a large revolt under the Calvinist nobleman István Bocskai, which convulsed the area until 1606. Meanwhile a significant Ottoman counter-offensive in 1605 recaptured Esztergom, Visegrád and several other fortresses. So when the two sides finally entered peace negotiations in 1606, the Sultan did so from a position of strength – though he was keen to end this war, since from 1603 a new Persian offensive had been threatening the eastern flank of his empire. The final agreement, the Treaty of Zsitvatorok, left most things as they had been before the start of the conflict; Győr remained in the hands of the Emperor, Esztergom in those of the Sultan, and the only significant gains were the latter's retention of Eger and of Nagykanizsa. No sane person could have claimed that those two fortresses were worth thirteen years of bitter warfare. But there was, perhaps, one positive outcome. The fact that the two sides had achieved so little, fighting each other to a virtual standstill, may be one reason why they would remain at peace – 'Kleinkrieg' raiding excepted – for the next 57 years.[16]

Many accounts of the Ottoman Empire in this period give the impression not only that it was a spontaneously and unceasingly belligerent power, but also that its actions were driven by an ideology that demanded constant warfare against the Christians, since Islamic legal theory viewed everything outside the House of Islam as belonging to the House of War. It had certainly been an expansionary power in Europe until the end of the reign of Süleyman the Magnificent, and the possibility of an invasion of southern Italy still had to be taken seriously. Yet neither of the two major wars discussed in this book, that of 1570–3 and that of 1593–1606, really fits such a picture. The war against Venice and the Holy League may have been, in the first instance, a war of aggression against Cyprus, but it was undertaken for reasons of long-term security in the eastern Mediterranean, not out of sheer belligerence or religious zeal. The 'Long War' was a war that the Ottomans stumbled into by accident rather than design. Within the first three years they were willing to end it on reasonable terms, but those were rejected by the Emperor. Thereafter, it was the Habsburg involvement in Transylvania that made the Ottomans unwilling to settle; the Romanian principalities mattered so much to the Sultan, both strategically and economically, that he could not contemplate going to the negotiating table while his position in those places remained weak.

Overall, then, it was the normal power-calculations of geopolitics that drove Ottoman policy in this period, not the claims of its religious or legal theory, useful though those sometimes were for justificatory purposes. And the same is true, obviously enough, of most of the Western powers with which it had dealings. Venice, Poland, France and England all had their own calculations to perform, and they made them quite unsentimentally. As has already been pointed out, an interlocking mechanism of power-politics operated across Europe, pitting the anti-Habsburg powers against the Habsburg ones, and thus requiring the former to be, in varying ways, pro-Ottoman; and that mechanism extended further eastwards, embracing Persia too. If there was one overriding determinant of Ottoman policy in this period, it was the struggle for dominance against its eastern neighbour. Mehmed Sokollu's geopolitical thinking was, as we have seen, deeply concerned with Asia; such concerns may have been the underlying reason for the decision to take Cyprus. It was his desire to engage in a large-scale war of territorial conquest against Persia that made him the initiating partner in the move towards an Ottoman–Spanish naval truce in the 1570s. Probably the exhaustion of resources caused by the twelve-year-long Persian war which ended in 1590 was a major reason why even the belligerent-sounding Sinan Pasha was reluctant to start a new European war in 1593. Ottoman relations with Persia – a Muslim foe, not a Christian one – mattered indirectly, but profoundly, to the whole pattern of European geopolitics in this period.

As a primary motive for political action, religion did play a part in this story – but only on the Christian side. Of course, in the case of some actors who habitually invoked it, the religious motive can be discounted to a large extent. The Knights of Malta had a strong enough economic motivation for their corsairing activities, which in any case did not spare the Christian subjects of the Sultan. An ideology of religiously inspired combat became almost a necessity for the Order's survival, for two main reasons: in order to overcome internal tensions between national groups (for example, French Knights and Spanish ones) whose own countries were often at war, it was necessary to focus on a common enemy; and the only way to justify the large incomes that poured into Malta from commende all over Catholic Europe was to be visibly engaged in a higher cause. But when we turn to the crusading Papacy of this period, the role of directly religious motivation becomes undeniable. Naturally other motives were present too; these popes had institutional and political reasons for wanting to strengthen their leadership role, especially at a time when national rulers were gathering more and more power into their own hands. And, like any politicians,

428   AGENTS OF EMPIRE

the popes could make compromises when it suited their interests to do
so: the fact that Muslim merchants were warmly welcomed at the Papal
port of Ancona is an example of that. Nevertheless, the extraordinary
efforts made by Pius V to put together the Holy League in the early
1570s, and by Clement VIII to support the Imperial side in the 1590s
(not only sending his own troops, but pressing Spain to contribute
money and, eventually, some soldiers too), cannot be understood unless
we recognize that these men really did believe what they preached.
Theirs was a project of holy war. One might almost call it Christian
jihad, were it not for one basic difference: their aim was not simply to
fight infidels because they were infidels, but to fight them because they
ruled over populations of Christians. And that difference also had an
effect on their plans, making them fixated with fantasy-scenarios in
which mass risings in the Balkans would be seamlessly coordinated with
invasions by Western armies. Just how unrealistic those plans were was
something that many actual rebels in the Balkans would learn, at great
cost to themselves.

The Counter-Reformation, taken in its broadest sense, was possibly
the most important development in this period of European history.
Thanks to the patient work of the Jesuits and others, the culture and
religious life of Catholic Europe were gradually but profoundly transformed. Through the radicalizing of rulers and élites, the groundwork
was laid for the recovery – often by brute force – of large parts of Europe
by Catholicism in the following century. The role of the Counter-
Reformation Papacy in strengthening policy against the Ottomans,
during the half-century covered by this book, should not be underestimated; without the work of Pius V, the Battle of Lepanto would never
have taken place. And yet, at the end of the century, it was Counter-
Reformation fervour that sabotaged what might otherwise have been a
significant Christian victory. If the Habsburg régime in Transylvania
had respected local religious arrangements, and the social and political
balance of forces which they embodied, that country might have become
a new bulwark of Western power, blocking the Tatars' main access route
and seriously weakening the Sultan's grip on his Hungarian possessions.
The great historical irony is that it was Catholic triumphalism that nul-
lified the prospect of such a genuine triumph.

But there were many varieties of Counter-Reformation experience, as
the story of the Brutis and Brunis helps to show. Religion was, for them,
the strongest determinant of loyalty – stronger even than their sense of
belonging to Venice (which Bartolomeo abandoned politically soon

after the outset of his career, and was planning to abandon physically at the time of his death). Their contributions included helping to make the Counter-Reformation happen at Trent, fighting for Christendom at Lepanto, and plotting for the transfer of Algiers to the King of Spain. Yet at the same time they knew full well that the Ottoman Empire was not an alien, purely hostile or in any way monolithic entity. It was a complex world, intertwined in many ways with their own. To work for the interests of their own Christian world, however they conceived of it, could involve working with the Ottomans as well as against them – as in the grain trading and local diplomacy of Antonio Bruti, or the political and diplomatic activity of Bartolomeo Bruti as minister of an Ottoman vassal state. Religion mattered at a deep level, which must help to explain why none of these people went over to Islam; but in most cases it did not direct their lives, nor did it prevent some of them from cultivating their connection with a powerful relative who was a Muslim convert. Whilst the fact that they were Catholics from one of Christendom's frontier zones may have given them an enhanced sense of their Catholicism, the fact that they were Albanians, connected by language, blood and history to Ottoman subjects and Ottoman territory, gave them an ability to see things also from something more like an Ottoman perspective. As popes and kings made ever more unrealistic plans for the defeat of the Sultan and the triumph of Christendom, the day-to-day business of interacting with the Ottoman world depended, in reality, on people such as these.

Epilogue
The Legacy: Antonio Bruni's Treatise

The story of the Brunis and Brutis told in this book draws to an end in the late 1590s. After the first wave of deaths which happened around the time of Lepanto, a second took place: Bartolomeo and Cristoforo Bruti in 1592, Pasquale Dabri in 1597, and both Gasparo and Antonio Bruni in 1598. As we have seen, there were children and nephews who went on to have active careers as dragomans and generated dynasties of their own; but theirs is a different story. Of the people who have played a role in this book, a few lived on for many years: Benedetto Bruti was listed as a dignitary at the court of Mihnea's son Radu, Voivod of Wallachia, in 1618; Jacomo Bruti died in that year, aged 76; and Matteo Bruni was still alive, probably an octogenarian, in 1623. It is not known by how many years Bartolomeo's widow, Maria, survived her husband; the last trace of her existence is the legal document of 1600, signed in her house in Koper, by which she accepted a small payment from the estate of Petru Şchiopul. She was described there as the mother of Antonio and of Alessandro, who was aged sixteen. No details of Antonio's career have been preserved, so perhaps he did not live long. Alessandro seems to have remained in Koper; he wrote a Latin epigram which was published in a book by a Capodistrian author in 1611, and in that year the Venetian authorities granted him the income of 200 salt-pans at Koper, in recognition of the faithful services of the Bruti family. The Brutis – at least, those descended from Alessandro's uncle Jacomo – would have a long and flourishing existence in that Istrian city, and their eighteenth-century family palazzo with its elegant façade of white limestone, located just behind the cathedral, serves as the municipal library of Koper today.[1]

But there is one other legacy that deserves special notice: the little treatise on the Ottoman Empire in Europe – or, to be precise, on the province of Rumeli, which covered much of that territory, excluding

Bosnia, Hungary and the Romanian lands – written by Antonio Bruni in 1596. This work has been completely unknown in modern times, but it had a significant influence in its day. It survives in two early scribal copies, one in the Vatican Library and the other in the library of the Museo Correr in Venice. (However, since the text underwent some circulation in manuscript, it is very possible that other copies remain to be discovered.) This treatise is an unusually interesting piece of work, differing in character from the usual run of Western relazioni with their formulaic listings of government officials, military forces and so on. And it attests both to Antonio's own previous experiences within the Ottoman Empire, and to the particular circumstances, in the early phase of the Long War, in which it was written.[2]

At one point in this text Bruni refers to the Ottoman conquest of Bar '25 years ago', which shows that it was written in 1596. Another passage dates it more specifically to the second half of 1596, when the revolt of the Himariots, led by Athanasios Riseas, was under way and had not yet ended in evident failure. 'The Himariot highlanders have now risen up,' Bruni writes, 'persuaded by some people, and especially by the efforts of Archbishop Athanasios of Ohrid, who, on the pretext of a visitation (Ohrid being roughly four days' journey from Himarë), has made them think that he had an agreement with the Emperor, and that men would very soon come from the King of Spain. But this revolt of theirs cannot last long if it is not supported by outside help.'[3]

A more precise dating is provided by a letter from Antonio to Angelo Ingegneri, which also gives a clearer sense of the origins of the text. We have briefly encountered Angelo Ingegneri already: he was the nephew of the Bishop of Koper who had planned to travel to the Istrian city in order to write a commentary on Tasso with his uncle's help.* That link with Koper in itself might suffice to explain his acquaintance with Antonio Bruni. There is another possibility too, which is that Angelo was a son or nephew of the papal secretary Aurelio Ingegneri, to whom Gasparo had written in 1583 about the arrangements for subsidizing Antonio's education; possibly the Ingegneri family had played some sort of guardianship role towards Antonio during his schoolboy years in Rome.† In 1592 Angelo had been taken on as a literary assistant by Cinzio Aldobrandini. Cinzio chose him especially because of Angelo's friendship with Tasso, as he wanted him to prepare the poet's

* Above, p. 204.
† Above, pp. 307–8.

Gerusalemme conquistata – a thoroughly rewritten version, dedicated to Cinzio, of his *Gerusalemme liberata* – for publication; it duly appeared in 1593. But Angelo also did more general secretarial work, and in 1594 he published a little guide to the duties and requirements of a good secretary, also dedicated to Cardinal Cinzio. One of its chapters, entitled 'On news reports about the world', says that the secretary needs to know 'the daily information contained in the ordinary news reports about the world, since these constitute a history which is present and live'; so he should gather 'full information about the interests and intentions of all living princes, and about the forces they have, the nature of countries, the customs of nations', and so on. 'For a study of this kind, it will be very useful to read writings that can be seen in manuscript, such as the relazioni of ambassadors, the instructions to nuncios, and innumerable things of that sort.' This gives a sense of the background to the commissioning of Antonio's treatise (in its final form, at least), in which Angelo Ingegneri seems to have played a vital role.[4]

After Tasso's death in April 1595, Angelo Ingegneri left Cardinal Cinzio's service. He appears to have had a falling-out with him soon afterwards, when his attempt to print a posthumous work by the poet was summarily halted by Cinzio, who wanted to retain the exclusive rights to the manuscript. Nevertheless, in 1596 Angelo went to his native city of Venice at Cinzio's request, and the evidence of Antonio Bruni's letter to him shows that he was still acting to some extent in the service of the Cardinal. Writing from Venice on 17 October, Antonio thanked Angelo for a letter he had sent, and said he was sorry to have just missed him during his visit. He continued:

> Now, since you write that you have been notified from Rome that information written up in that way would not be unwelcome to your most distinguished patron, I begin to think that it has been represented by you as something much greater than it really is. So I do not know how to satisfy that expectation – and the fault will be yours, rather than mine. If it pleases your lord, I shall think you have done me a great favour. Nor do I think that his most distinguished lordship will disdain to honour me with a reply. So in the end I am resolved to embrace your most prudent and kind advice, so that the lord Cardinal may know that the text will be sent by me to him, by means of you, my most especial patron.

What emerges from this, if one strips away the elaborately deferential language, is that Angelo had heard that Antonio had just written, or was writing, or was capable of writing, a text, and had requested a version of it for his master. And since members of Cardinal Cinzio's immediate circle, including the philosopher Francesco Patrizi, were actively exploring the possibilities of raising anti-Ottoman revolts in Albania and elsewhere, it must seem very likely that the text in question was Antonio's treatise on the province of Rumeli.[5]

This short work – of just over 4,000 words, filling thirteen pages in one manuscript and 27 in the other – is entitled 'On the *beylerbeylik* of Rumeli' ('Del Bellerbegato della Romania'). It begins with a brief geographical account of the territories involved, but then quickly turns its attention to the peoples who live in them; the unspoken question, to which Bruni constantly attends, is whether the Christian population of the province is willing or able to rise up. From the outset a note of caution is struck: 'just as there are different religions, so too you find different languages, which cause a certain disunity among the peoples, and that increases the disagreement that normally obtains as a result of religious difference.' The account he gives is detailed and nuanced. He writes, for example, that most Greek-speakers are Orthodox, but not some Perots or some of the inhabitants of the Greek islands, who are Catholic; similarly, most Serbs and Bulgars are Orthodox, but there are Catholic Slav villages near Skopje, and occasional Catholic households all the way up to the Danube; and he also notes the existence of Paulician villages in Bulgaria – the Paulicians being the remnants of an early sect, compared by him with good reason to Manichaeans, that would be gradually assimilated to the Roman Church by Catholic missionaries. By the standards of the day, this is an unusually well-informed piece of work. Bruni comments also on the tensions that exist between some of these Christian populations. 'The Greeks retain the pride of their ancestors, and their hatred of Catholics', he observes. Discussing the mixed Albanian–Slav population of the highlands of northern Albania and neighbouring Montenegro, he says that 'the Slavs, who live in accordance with Orthodoxy, are more schismatic than the others of their nation; they abhor the Catholic denomination, which is usually persecuted by the Archbishop of Pejë [sc. the Serbian Orthodox Patriarch], who oppresses the Catholic prelates in order to get the recognition of his authority that he demands from them.'[6]

The Muslim population is also described. The Turks, Bruni writes, are all of one religion and one language, 'except for the Yürüks, manufacturers of very fine felt, who were once nomadic shepherds but have now been settled; they are descended from those people from Asia who followed the party and sect of "Zecchelle" the Persian, whoever he was, and it may be that in their hearts believed more in Ali than in Muhammad. And they live, under their own leader, more in Dobrudža than in the rest of Bulgaria.' This passage is also remarkable for its time. It is hard to find any reference in West European writings of this period to the little-known Yürüks, a semi-nomadic population of mixed Asiatic origin that was settled by the Ottomans in some parts of the Balkans. Many had come in the fifteenth century, and there was indeed a significant concentration of them on the Black Sea coast of Bulgaria, where they were sedentarized and became famous for their manufacture of felt. The reference to followers of 'Zecchelle' is also striking. This was a charismatic rebel called Şahkulu who led a major revolt in the Teke region of southern Anatolia in 1511. (Bruni's 'Zecchelle', if pronounced with the Venetian soft 'Zh', might perhaps be a version of 'Şahkulu'; more likely it derives from 'Tekeli', the adjective from Teke.) The followers of Şahkulu were Shiites, known as *kızılbaş* ('red-heads', from their head-gear), who had strong pro-Persian sympathies. Many had been deported to the Balkans less than a decade earlier, and many more followed after the crushing of the revolt, bringing with them, as Bruni correctly noted, a radical Shiite devotion to Ali. Their veneration of Şahkulu continued unabated; a 1543 register of the district of Varna, on the Bulgarian Black Sea coast, lists Yürüks who were named 'Şahkulu' – striking confirmation of the accuracy of Antonio Bruni's account, which was surely based on personal experience as he travelled through that region on his journeys between Iaşi and Istanbul.[7]

Antonio's main concern in this text, however, was not ethnographic description but an assessment of relative strength and military potential. He noted that in the Balkans the 'Turks' had lost their original military ethos and had turned to agriculture, trade and business, especially money-lending. (At this point he seems to refer to ethnic Turks, or at least Turkish-speakers, describing them as the original conquerors; but he goes on to use the term more generally for Muslims.) In Bulgaria, Serbia and Albania the ordinary Muslims 'are afraid of any revolt; they are armed in the old-fashioned way, with bows and scimitars, though the ones on the coast have some arquebuses.' As for the feudal spahis who responded to the call-up with their horses and their military retainers: this system, he wrote, was greatly decayed. The spahis mostly held their estates because they had bought them, not because they had been granted them for good service; they were poorly armed, and both they and their men were unused to the rigours of military life. 'They do not wish to risk their lives in war, so many either sell their estates again, or send their servants in their place.'* Many spahis were in serious financial difficulties because they had bought their estates with money borrowed at interest, and the war had absorbed all their income; others had lent money at interest to soldiers who had themselves gone bankrupt. And the total number of spahis was smaller than fame had it; here Bruni made a quick survey of all the *sancak*s of Rumeli, estimating the numbers of spahis they could supply. He then turned to the auxiliary forces, giving details of the *akıncı* irregular cavalry and the Crimean Tatars. The latter, he pointed out, were costly allies for the Ottomans: 'the members of that greedy nation usually will not leave home unless they are first given provisions for the family which they leave behind, as well as weapons for themselves, and clothing – even down to their boots.'[8]

The final section of the text begins: 'It remains for me to add something about Albania.' This was evidently the special task which Antonio Bruni had been asked to perform, as the strategic thinkers in Cardinal Cinzio's circle were particularly interested in the possibilities of an Albanian revolt. And for the modern reader the comments on Albania – both in this section, and in several previous passages – are of exceptional interest, as this is the first known text, by an identifiable Albanian, to offer a general description of the Albanian lands and their inhabitants. There are earlier texts by known Albanians, such as the document brought to Rome by Tommaso Pelessa, that comment on some specific conditions inside the country; and there is, as we have seen, an important general survey of Albania written in 1570, whose anonymous author was almost certainly from Ulcinj, and may very likely have been Antonio Bruti.† But this is the first piece of writing of which it can definitely be said that an Albanian author is giving a general account of Albania.[9]

When introducing the Albanians in the early part of his text, Antonio Bruni observed that those close to Dalmatia were Roman Catholic, while those from Durrës southwards were Greek Orthodox. Their language was 'very different from Slav and Greek'; drawing on his knowledge of late Roman history, he speculated that it might be derived from Alan or Gothic, brought into the region by Alaric, but then added that it was more likely

---

* It was at this point in his account that he quoted what Petru Şchiopul had said to Archduke Ferdinand about disciplined Christian soldiers being able to defeat much larger numbers of Ottoman troops: see above, p. 384.

† Above, pp. 129–30 (anonymous), 408 (Pelessa).

to be 'the ancient language of the Macedonians'. He also noted that 'the Albanian nation extends quite a lot further than its territory: Albania begins in the west at Ulcinj and the lake of Shkodër, ending in the east at Bastia opposite Corfu, but the Albanians live beyond that in many places in the Peloponnese and Greece, having taken refuge there from wars, or having been transported there by the Byzantine emperors, who dealt in that way with their rebellions.' In his main discussion of the country he wrote that the Orthodox part of the country was divided into three *sancak*s, Delvinë, Vlorë and Elbasan. 'In the *sancak* of Delvinë almost all of them know the Greek language; in that of Vlorë, the majority. There are also many villages of Bulgarians there, who extract pitch. Vlorë is the only place in all the territories of Albania to be inhabited by foreign Turks of Asian origin, coming from those who followed Zecchelle.'* Bruni also commented on the Himariots, expressing his fear, as we have seen, that they would be forced to submit to the Ottomans again. He added that such a fate had recently befallen their neighbours just to the north, the people of Dukat, whose revolt had been crushed; their numbers had been reduced to a couple of hundred, and they had been forcibly transplanted from their mountain village to a lowland site close to the coast. As for the Catholics of northern Albania: these were 'the best armed and also the most faithful Christians of the Ottoman Empire'. The authorities there feared them because of their frequent revolts, 'as they rise up for the slightest reason, those of the plains no less than those of the mountains'. Often, though, the *sancakbeyi*s would deliberately provoke a rebellion, 'either in order to pillage them, or to take revenge on them, or to have an excuse for not going to a distant war; for that reason the *sancakbeyi* of Dukagjin never leaves, just like the one of Angelokastro [Karlıeli, a *sancak* in north-western Greece that included Preveza] who, on the pretext of defending his territory against armed Christians, always stays at home.'[10]

Much of this information would have encouraged those optimistic armchair strategists in Rome who were thinking about stimulating a new revolt in the Albanian lands. But Bruni now added a serious note of caution:

* That the original Muslim population of Vlorë consisted of deported *kızılbaş* is a fact not recorded in any other source. Yet it helps to explain an otherwise puzzling comment in the travelogue of Evliya Çelebi, who visited the city in 1670 and observed that the young men of Vlorë habitually invoked Ali, and were 'devoted to the Prophet's family' – a code-phrase for strong Shiite tendencies.

On the side facing the Adriatic, Albania is ringed by very high mountains; as a plain it is watered by frequent and large rivers, which prevent those moving on foot from gathering together. And the Christians have no cavalry, nor do they have the means to make bridges. The strongholds are held by the Ottomans, even if not all of them are garrisoned or guarded. The main ones, at least, are secure enough, so that they cannot be surreptitiously seized by the Christians. I wished to point this out because of the opinion which some have about these people, that they can achieve a lot by themselves, without foreigners, and that the mere rumour of help from Italy and Spain, with the raising of a flag, will be enough to make them rise up. I hope to God that these unfortunate people do not fall into danger, and that these dealings with them, which are so public, do not completely destroy the opportunity to achieve something in the future.[11]

Conscious that his words would be read by an influential cardinal, Bruni made a plea for the better support of the Catholic Church inside Ottoman Albania. He pointed out that there were only two bishops actually resident in the territory. Unlike them, the Bishop of Lezhë lived in his home town of Dubrovnik, pleading illness; 'and because of his absence, and because he does not speak the language [sc. Albanian], he can achieve little.' This was a reference to Antonio's old friend Innocentius Stoicinus, whom he had allegedly once saved from punishment for immorality; and the point about ignorance of Albanian was in fact one of the criticisms made about him by his nemesis, Niccolò Mechaisci, who wrote that bishops 'of other nations, not knowing the language and customs, are good for nothing except making confusion'.* As for Mechaisci himself, Bruni wrote, 'because he entered into a plan to take Krujë by surprise, by the means of a Muslim highway robber called Nidar Manasi (which may or may not succeed), he has gone into hiding, as the Ottomans have already found out about the plan, and I think they are treating it with ridicule.' The other resident bishop, Niccolò Bianchi, did what he could, but he had a huge area to minister to; that winter he had performed a visitation of the Catholics of Serbia (a geographical term which was used to include Kosovo). It was essential that the bishops should live in their dioceses, but in order to do so they must have incomes sufficient to employ servants, as otherwise they would be despised by Muslims and Christians alike. 'Thus episcopal dignity is

---

* On Stoicinus and Mechaisci see above, pp. 310–11.

degraded, and the churches go to ruin, not so much because of the tyranny of the Ottomans, as because of the poverty of the clergy.' Finally,
returning to the strategic situation, Bruni wrote that he would not try to
describe the various access routes into the province of Rumeli, partly
because he had not seen all of them, and partly because there were
others who, having analysed the long-term military history of the region,
could write better about that. He ended on a note that both affirmed
the validity of what he had written, and expressed a due sense of deference. 'I am content to have set out simply and in real terms the present
state of the Muslims and Christians. As it is permitted to anyone to nar-
rate what he has seen and heard, so it is not permitted to everyone to try
to persuade rulers of that which they should or can do.'[12]

This remarkable text gives an idea not only of Antonio Bruni's previous experiences of travel within the Ottoman Empire, but also of the
close interest he was taking in current developments, especially in the
Albanian lands. Venice was of course a good vantage-point from which
to gather reports about that region; the news about Athanasios Riseas's
rising, for example, might have been generally available there. But it
seems that Antonio had more particular sources of information. The
detail he gave about the recently suppressed rising of Dukat does not
appear in standard accounts of this period. And his knowledge of Bishop
Mechaisci's involvement in the plot to seize Krujë suggests that he may
have been in direct contact with at least one Catholic informant in
northern Albania. Other members of the extended Bruti family in Koper
perhaps had their own sources of news about the region, from which he
could also benefit. So Antonio was certainly someone worth seeking out
for his expert knowledge in this area.

One person who did seek him out was Lazaro Soranzo, who was in
the process of writing a major work of his own on the Ottoman Empire.
As we have seen, the two men were already well acquainted; it was
through Soranzo that Antonio Bruni had transmitted Petru Şchiopul's
request to visit the Pope in 1594.* How and when they had first met
is not known. The connection may well have been made through Lazaro's uncle Giacomo, the Venetian who, among other diplomatic tasks,
had travelled to Istanbul to attend the circumcision festival in 1582,
taking with him the papal agent Livio Cellini to negotiate with the
Orthodox Patriarch Jeremias.† In July 1584 Giacomo Soranzo had

* Above, p. 384.
† Above, pp. 339–40.

been found guilty by the Venetian authorities of revealing state secrets to Cellini, who was described by them as a writer of avvisi; the real fear may have been that Cellini was working (as before) for the Pope, and it was also rumoured that Soranzo was angling for a cardinal's hat. He was condemned to banishment in Koper, living there for just over two years before the authorities had mercy on him. The Brunis and Brutis in Koper – who, for some time, included Antonio Bruni, after the completion of his studies at Avignon in late 1585 – would have had plenty of opportunities to make his acquaintance; indeed, Giacomo Soranzo must already have known Antonio's father, since he had been one of the Venetian commanders in the joint fleet which sparred with Kılıç Ali's ships off the Peloponnese in 1572. Lazaro may well have visited his uncle during his Istrian exile (in a laudatory memoir of him, written after Giacomo's death, he would describe Koper as 'that small but delightful city'), also making the acquaintance of Antonio Bruni.[13]

It would have been a meeting of like minds. Both were the sons of naval commanders; Lazaro's father, Benedetto, was the heroic Venetian captain at Lepanto who blew up his ship, or at least was blown up with it, just as victorious Ottoman forces were crowding aboard.* Both were illegitimate sons – a greater handicap in Lazaro's case, as it excluded him from the whole range of public offices and honours that members of the noble Soranzo family might otherwise expect to enjoy. Both had received a thorough humanist education: in 1578 Lazaro had displayed his skills by publishing a five-page poem in Latin hexameters in honour of another uncle, Giovanni Soranzo (who, as Venetian envoy to Rome, had helped negotiate the Holy League in 1570–1), and the classical scholar Giulio Salinerio would thank Lazaro for his comments on emendations of Tacitus. Both would pursue careers involving the role of secretary or counsellor. While Antonio advised Petru Şchiopul, Lazaro was a 'cameriere d'onore' to Clement VIII. The official duties of such an honorary chamberlain were mostly ceremonial, but Lazaro's special task seems to have been to function as a publicist, defending papal policy. In that capacity he wrote first a 'Discorso' in defence of Clement's refusal to accept the return of Henri IV to the Catholic Church, and then, shortly after Clement's change of mind, an 'Oratione' celebrating that decision. The latter work, addressed to Henri and transmitted to France, where it circulated widely in translation, was written at Clement's request. Significantly, it ended with an appeal to the French king to imitate his

* Above, p. 163.

pious medieval predecessors who had sent armies to Palestine to recover
the Holy Sepulchre: 'where better can you use your arms and your valour than in such a sacred and praiseworthy enterprise?'[14]

For Lazaro Soranzo was, like his master, an enthusiast for war against
the Ottomans. And it was his special interest in the Ottoman Empire,
finally, that drew him together with Antonio Bruni in 1596, when
Lazaro was drafting the book that would make his name. Lazaro had
himself spent time in Ottoman territory, perhaps in the service of his
uncle. Some baili did take members of their family in their entourage,
and Giacomo Soranzo was not only bailo in 1566–8 (when Lazaro
might have been a teenager) but also a special envoy in both 1575–6,
when he dealt with the post-war border settlement, and 1582. In the
preface to his book Lazaro wrote that he had sought out information
about the present conditions of the Ottoman Empire, 'above all by
conversing with people of much experience and judgement who have
recently come from those parts, not putting my trust even in those things
which I myself have seen, and considered very carefully, on previous
occasions'; but some of the information in it surely does derive from his
earlier personal experience. He also read widely: defending his work
soon after its publication, he would declare that 'I have not said new
things, invented by me, but things drawn from printed and approved
writers, and from writings [sc. manuscript ones] that are read by the
public in Venice and Rome.' The result was one of the best-informed
studies of the Ottoman Empire to be published in Renaissance Europe.
And among Lazaro's sources, Antonio Bruni was possibly the most
important – both in writing and in conversation.[15]

Lazaro Soranzo began to draft his book while taking the waters on
the island of Ischia in 1596. He then moved to Venice, 'for family
affairs', where he was able to make use of many sources of information
about the Ottoman Empire. A possible scenario is that after some conversations with his friend Antonio Bruni, he asked Antonio to set down
some of the things he had said, and that it was Soranzo who told Angelo
Ingegneri (whom he probably knew from the latter's work for Cardinal
Cinzio) about Bruni's writings, whether actual or in prospect. The form
which Antonio's text finally took, however, seems very much tailored to
Cardinal Cinzio's requirements; and it was, in the end, that version of
the text that was used by Soranzo when writing his book. The first draft
of his L'Ottomanno was written in the final months of 1596. By the end
of January 1597 a manuscript version of it was sent by Soranzo to
Vincenzo Gonzaga, the Duke of Mantua, who was planning a military

expedition in support of the Imperial forces in Hungary. Other manuscript copies quickly began to circulate. (Defending the work in July 1598, Soranzo would say that 'it has been read in manuscript in Venice and throughout Italy for two years' – meaning, it seems, roughly eighteen months.) One surviving copy, in the Ambrosian Library in Milan, is dated June 1597. Finally, in May 1598, Soranzo decided to have the book printed; it came out two months later in the city of Ferrara, which had just become part of the Papal States after a triumphal ceremony of annexation.[16]

Despite his wide reading, Soranzo did not give many references to sources in his book. Of the few that he did acknowledge, several were works that circulated in manuscript – by the geographer Girolamo Bardi, for example, or the military man, traveller and political writer Filippo Pigafetta (who had composed an account of the fall of Győr). In this category he also referred to Bruni's text, which seems to have been more valuable to him than any other. When he first mentioned 'Antonio Bruni, in his treatise on the beylerbeylik of Rumeli', it was to make a general policy point: he warned that it was wrong to provoke revolts unless one was able to bring sufficient forces to guarantee success, as otherwise this would merely have the effect of alerting and arming the enemy. Later he referred to him specifically as a writer on Albania: 'Of the Catholic Albanians, that same Bruni, who is their compatriot, writes in the aforementioned treatise that just as they are the best armed, so also they are the most faithful Christians in the Ottoman Empire . . .' What followed was a very long extract, almost verbatim, from Antonio's text. And this was not the only borrowing. Substantial passages elsewhere were taken directly from the same source – on the poor state of Ottoman forces, on the devşirme, on auxiliaries, on spahis not accepting the discomforts of war, on Petru Şchiopul's advice to Ferdinand, on the clans of the Albanian–Montenegrin highlands, and on Athanasios, the Himariots and Dukat.[17]

These were probably not the only details that Lazaro Soranzo obtained from his Albanian–Venetian friend. His statement that he had spoken to 'people who have seen the accounts of Moldavia and Wallachia', who gave him details of the tribute paid to the Sultan, has already been noticed.* There is other information about Moldavia in the book which may well have come from conversations with Antonio Bruni: Soranzo discussed the tribute given by the voivod to the Tatars, the

---

* Above, p. 381.

lucrative taxes on cattle, the relations between the voivods and Poland, and the different geographical terms used for Moldavia and Wallachia. He also noted many details about Albania and the Albanians, some of which could have been derived from Bruni: about the timber of the Dukagjin highlands which was floated down the river Drin to Lezhë, the manufacture of biscotto in Vlorë, the ports of the Albanian coast from Durrës to Sarandë, the presence of Albanians among the soldiers of Mihai cel Viteaz, and the feasibility of seizing Ulcinj, Shkodër or Durrës. And it was surely from Antonio that he learned both about the origins of Sinan Pasha, whom he correctly described as from the village of Topojan, and about the summoning of Gasparo Bruni to papal service before the Lepanto campaign. Overall, there is much more information in Soranzo's book derived certainly or probably from Antonio Bruni than from any other known source.[18]

When he referred to Antonio's treatise, Lazaro Soranzo seems to have assumed that it would be available to his readers – if they took the trouble to look for it – as a manuscript. Some copies did circulate, but the story of how this happened is obscure. Of the two manuscripts known today, one is dated February 1598 or 1599, and the other, which is undated, must have been copied in 1598 or later; both of them reproduce a scribal error describing the death of Petru Şchiopul as having happened in 1597 (instead of 1594). There are other errors in both of them, from which it becomes clear that they were copied from differing versions, neither of which was the original. In the late 1590s Filippo Pigafetta, who had been a member of the Tuscan force that inflicted such damage on Sinan's retreating army in 1595, was living in Venetian territory and sending a steady stream of 'relazioni' to a friend at the Medici court who passed them on to the Grand Duke. Writing from Padua in mid-January 1599, he said that he was commissioning copies of three manuscript texts he had recently come across: an account of the 1597 campaign by Giorgio Basta, a relazione about the state of Ferrara, and 'a discourse about the beylerbeylik of Rumeli and the people who live under it, about the territories, and the mountain passes from it to Hungary, and other fascinating information'. And at the end of the month he wrote: 'I am sending a relazione of the state of the Ottoman Empire in Europe, written by an experienced man who, being of the Albanian nation, lived for a long time in those parts.' There can be little doubt that this was Antonio Bruni's text (even though, in reality, it referred to the passes into Rumeli only to say that it was not going to describe them – when he wrote that comment, Pigafetta was probably dependent on the sales patter of his source). So some copies were available, and were read with interest. This distribution of Bruni's text pales into insignificance, however, when compared with the print publication of Soranzo's book.[19]

L'Ottomanno had many readers. Unfortunately for its author, they included members of the Venetian government, who reacted ferociously against it as soon as it was published. On 21 July 1598 they wrote to their ambassador in Rome, asking him to arrange the abduction of Lazaro Soranzo (for which they authorized payment of 2,000 ducats to the person who kidnapped him) so that he could be brought to justice. The offence, as they explained, was caused by some passages in which Soranzo gave reasons why the Ottomans might want to attack Venetian territory. One of these was a general section arguing that if the Sultan made peace with the Emperor, he would most likely turn his armed forces not against Persia, Morocco, Malta, Spain, Poland, the Tatars or Muscovy, but against Venice, or possibly against the whole of Italy. The underlying argument was not new; it resembled that used by Minuccio Minucci (another Venetian in papal service) when he told the Venetian Senate in 1596 that if the Sultan won the war, he would attack Venice next. Most readers would surely not have found this section of Soranzo's book inflammatory or indeed anti-Venetian, as it referred benignly to Venice's 'just and long-standing neutrality', gave a glowing account of Venetian military strength, and insisted that it would be in the interests of all other Christian powers to go to its assistance. Much more troubling, though, was a discussion of arguments allegedly put forward by Cığalazade Yusuf Sinan Pasha and other pashas for seizing one or more of several Venetian possessions, including Zadar, the port of Pula (Ital.: Pola) in Istria, and, most temptingly of all, the entire island of Crete. As the Venetian authorities wrote to their ambassador, these were 'very important matters of state, which should be kept in profound silence, especially in the heart of a Christian and a Venetian'.[20]

Within five days, Lazaro Soranzo had heard something about this hostile reaction; he wrote to the Venetian authorities from Rome, begging forgiveness, disclaiming any malice, offering to make changes in the next edition, and saying that he was willing to defend himself at their tribunal. But a report in mid-August from the papal nuncio in Venice may have given him a better idea of the gravity of the situation. The nuncio said that the government there had forbidden the sale or even the possession of the book, and that if its author went to Venice he might find himself condemned to perpetual imprisonment; if he did not, his property would be confiscated and he would be banned from Venetian territory. At the end of that month the Council of Ten in Venice duly declared Soranzo's banishment, with a price on his head, to be paid to anyone who found him on Venetian soil and brought him in, dead or alive. The only qualification was that if he surrendered within the next two weeks, he would be sent to live in internal exile in Koper for 20 years. The nuncio wrote that this sentence was 'rather milder than had been feared'. Soranzo did not take up the option of Capodistrian exile; but three years later, after intense lobbying by the Pope, Venice agreed to give him a safe-conduct entitling him to enter Venetian territory for a period of three years. So perhaps he was able to revisit some of his friends and relations in Venice, before his death in April 1602.[21]

L'Ottomanno, meanwhile, was a tremendous publishing success. Its notoriety in Venice may well have contributed to this, and it seems that it took some time for the prohibition to have an effect within Venetian territory: in October 1598 the authorities wrote to the governors of Verona, ordering them to confiscate the copies which booksellers there were still offering for sale. The book's original printer, Vittorio Baldini, who was producing a great series of works about and against the Ottomans, issued another edition of it in papal Ferrara in 1599, and during that year a rival printer brought it out in Milan; a fourth edition appeared in 1600 in Naples, and Baldini would re-issue the work in 1607. Two years after the initial publication, much of the text appeared in a French translation, incorporated into a history of the Ottoman Empire. The translator/author was Jacques Esprinchard, a Huguenot from a merchant family of La Rochelle who had studied law at Leiden University before going on an adventurous tour of Europe in 1597–8; his travels had taken him as far as the Hungarian frontier, where he watched Ottoman prisoners working on the rebuilding of Esztergom while they waited to be ransomed. His book enjoyed some success, and was reprinted in Paris in 1609. Meanwhile, a German translation had been published in 1601, and in 1603 an English version of Soranzo's book had appeared, translated by Abraham Hartwell. This Cambridge graduate, who had previously translated a popular Italian history of the recent Ottoman–Persian war, worked as the secretary of John Whitgift, the Archbishop of Canterbury, and also served twice in the 1590s as a Member of Parliament. In his dedicatory epistle to the Archbishop he said that his translation had lain unpublished for two years, until he was prompted by a question put to him by Whitgift about how Grand Viziers were chosen at the Ottoman court. While he was forced to admit that Soranzo was 'greatly addicted to the popish religion', he assured his patron that the book contained 'a very deepe and subtle consideration of al the designments & purposes' of the Ottomans.[22]

French was quite widely read in continental Europe; Italian even more so; English hardly at all. The universal language of the educated was Latin, and only when a book became available in that language could it gain a truly Europe-wide readership. The Latin translation of *L'Ottomanno* appeared in 1600, and was re-issued in 1601, together with a Latin version of an upbeat anti-Ottoman work by Achille Tarducci, *Il Turco vincibile* ('The Sultan can be defeated'), which Baldini had first published in 1597. The translator was Jakob Geuder von Heroltzberg, a citizen of Nuremberg who had studied law at Strasbourg and would later serve as a counsellor at Amberg, in the Upper Palatinate (not far from Nuremberg); Jacques Esprinchard had got to know Geuder during his European travels, so it seems likely that it was the Huguenot who first stimulated his interest in Soranzo's work. Following the Ottoman invasion of Austria in 1663, these Latin translations by Geuder were rather opportunistically reissued, with some other classic works of the same kind, in a volume edited by the well-known German academic Hermann Conring. One might imagine that Soranzo's text, by this stage, was looking quite out of date; yet when the oriental scholar Hiob Ludolf produced a book of his own on warring against the Ottomans in 1686, during the next great Habsburg–Ottoman conflict, he went out of his way to praise *L'Ottomanno* as a work 'which contains many things worth knowing'. The modern scholar can whole-heartedly agree.[23]

So it was that while the original text written by Antonio Bruni disappeared completely from sight, much of what it contained, together with some other information derived from him, found its way into one of the most widely read works of its period on the Ottoman Empire. Europe learned – though without knowing that it did so – about the Ottomans, and about the Albanians, from Antonio Bruni. And it was from Soranzo's work, eventually, that the writer of this book learned of Antonio Bruni's existence, began to search for the text he had composed, and, having found it, discovered that it led him into the complex and almost entirely forgotten story of an Albanian family in the sixteenth-century Mediterranean world.

Glossary

This glossary lists terms that have recurred in this book. Ottoman terms are given in italics.

ağa   title given to senior officers and some palace officials; the janissary *ağa* was the commander of the entire janissary corps.

akçe   Ottoman silver coin and unit of currency. Before the mid-1580s there were 60 to a ducat; thereafter, 120 (until further debasements).

arquebus   long muzzle-loaded gun (a predecessor of the rifle), firing a half-ounce bullet which could penetrate armour at close range.

auberge   'hostel', building belonging to a langue on Malta, where members of the langue could live and have meals.

avviso   news-letter.

bailate   house and office of the bailo.

bailo   permanent representative of Venice in Istanbul, also with responsibilities for, and powers over, the Venetian merchant community there.

bey   'commander' or 'lord', in this period used mostly for *sancakbeyi*s.

beylerbeyi   governor of a *beylerbeylik*.

beylerbeylik   large military-administrative province of the Ottoman Empire, normally containing two or more *sancak*s.

biscotto   'biscuit', made from bread baked a second time: the long-lasting ship's tack that was the principal foodstuff of galley-crews.

boyar   Moldavian nobleman and land-owner.

brigantine   small galley-style vessel, smaller than a foist, larger than a frigate.

camlet   luxury fabric, made from silk and cashmere.

Capodistrian   pertaining to Koper.

çavuş   official messenger of the Sultan.

commenda   income-yielding estate awarded to a Knight of Malta.

corsair   individual acting under some political authority (local or national) to attack and rob shipping on a non-indiscriminate basis.

cozza, coza   (Trk.: *hoca*) teacher of Turkish to the giovani di lingua.

defterdar   state treasurer, senior financial official in the Ottoman government.

devşirme   periodic 'collection' of boys (aged *c*.12–18), mostly from Christian Balkan families (and Bosnian Muslim ones), for enslavement and training as janissaries or palace servants and officials.

divan   council, especially the Imperial Council of the sultan; the term was also used for the council of the voivod of Moldavia.

dragoman   interpreter (primarily, in Istanbul, from and to Turkish).

ducat   Venetian gold coin and unit of currency; in this period an unskilled labourer in Italy might earn between 10 and 20 ducats per annum.

emin   superintendent (e.g. of customs collection at a port), a salaried official.

foist   (Ital.: 'fusta'): small galley-style vessel, smaller than a galiot, larger than a brigantine.

frigate   smallest galley-style vessel, smaller than a brigantine.

galiot   small galley-style vessel, smaller than a galley, larger than a foist.

galleass   large galley-style vessel, larger than a galley, with three masts, and a deck above the rowers.

giovane di lingua   literally, 'language youth': trainee dragoman, adolescent sent and paid for by Venice to study Turkish in Istanbul.

Grand Vizier   the most senior of the viziers.

haraç   tribute paid by territories such as Dubrovnik and Moldavia; more generally, tax paid by non-Muslim subjects of the Ottoman Empire.

hatman   commander of the armed forces of the voivod of Moldavia.

hüküm   (Ital.: 'cochiumo') document giving the Sultan's authorization (typically, to buy grain for export).

Imperial   pertaining to the Holy Roman Empire.

janissary   infantryman, member of the salaried infantry corps (recruited primarily by the *devşirme*).

kadi   (or *kadı*) judge.

Kapudan Paşa   admiral, the commander of the Ottoman navy.

kızılbaş   literally, 'red-head': militant Shiite of Anatolia (and Kurdistan).

langue   literally, 'tongue' or 'language': one of the eight quasi-national sections, divided on geographical/linguistic lines, of the Knights of Malta.

levend   corsair or pirate (also a brigand on land); qualified as *harami levend* to mean pirate more specifically.

martolos   local Balkan Christian employed as auxiliary fighter; an Ottoman term (from the Greek 'armatōlos', armed man), used sometimes by Christian powers for their own equivalent fighters.

Metropolitan   primate of the Orthodox Church, ranking above an archbishop but below a patriarch.

narh   maximum permitted market price of goods.

nazır   superintendent (e.g. of customs collection at a port), a salaried official.

pasha   'lord', an honorific title for viziers, *beylerbeyi*s and the commander of the navy.

Porte   esp. 'the Sublime Porte': traditional term for the Ottoman government, from Turkish *kapı* (gate), referring originally to the administration of government and justice in front of the Sultan's gate.

postelnic   seneschal or court chamberlain, a senior position at the court of the voivod of Moldavia.

presidio   fortress with garrison: a term used especially for the Spanish fortified outposts on the North African coast.

Priory   administrative-geographical subdivision of a langue of the Knights of Malta.

Ragusan   pertaining to Dubrovnik.

relazione   written report: in general, a description of current conditions and recent events in a foreign country; in particular, the formal report submitted to the Venetian government by a bailo or ambassador on his return (a type of document that was officially confidential, but in fact widely copied and circulated).

ricevitore   'receiver' (of revenues).

Rumeli   the *beylerbeylik* of Rumeli (sometimes called 'of Greece') was the largest province of the Ottoman Empire in Europe, including most of its European territory other than Bosnia, Hungary and the Romanian principalities.

sancak   large military-administrative district of the Ottoman Empire.

sancakbeyi   governor of a *sancak*.

scudo   Italian unit of currency, worth ⅚ of a ducat; the French écu was slightly more valuable than the Italian scudo.

Serenissima   'the most serene': traditional honorific term for the Republic of Venice.

spahi   cavalryman, either a holder of a military-feudal estate, or a salaried cavalryman from the central cavalry corps.

staro   a measure of volume: for wheat, the Venetian staro contained 62 kg.; the Ragusan staro contained 74 kg.

Stato da Mar   collective term for the overseas territories ruled by Venice (including Istria).

stradiot   member of light cavalry, recruited mostly from the Greek and Albanian lands.

subaşı   military officer who acted as police chief for a district.

Terraferma   collective term for the territories ruled by Venice on the Italian mainland.

thaler   Austrian, German and Dutch coin and unit of currency, worth ⅔ of a ducat.

Uskoks   fighters of mostly Slavic origin, based in Senj (on the northern Croatian coast) and used as a frontier force by the Habsburgs, active both as raiders of Ottoman territory and as pirates in the Adriatic.

Venetian Albania   up to 1571, the Venetian-ruled coastal territory from the Gulf of Kotor in the north to the Ottoman border just below Ulcinj in the south.

vizier   high minister of the sultan, belonging to his *divan*; until 1577 there were six, thereafter seven, ranked in strict order of seniority.

voivod   ruler of Moldavia, Wallachia or Transylvania.

voyvoda   local official, normally a tax-collector, though the term was used also for the managers of large Ottoman estates in their capacity as revenue-gatherers.

Notes

1. ULCINJ, ALBANIA AND TWO EMPIRES

[1] Scholem, *Sabbatai*, 882–3, 917; Zirojević, *Ulcinj*, 1–44 (early history); Bošković, Mijović and Kovačević, *Ulcinj 1*, 6–11 (early history); Ushaku, *Ulqini në gjurmët*, 9–21 (early history); Malović-Djukić, 'Privredne veze', 58–65 (trade, Dubrovnik); Pertusi, 'Per la storia', 213–19 (mint). The origins of the Balšić or Balsha family may have been Albanian or Vlach; but by this stage they seem to have had a predominantly Slav (and Orthodox) culture. [2] Ljubić, ed., *Commissiones*, ii, 225–31 (226: 'i nobili e cittadini cavano il nervo delle loro intrade'; 227: customs, taxes), iii, 5 (territory, grain etc.), 116 (sailors; defence spending; soldier's salary). The first 1553 report has been misdated to 1571 (Sirdani, 'Per historín', 227; Zamputi, ed., *Dokumente*, i, 303); the 1558 report has been misdated to 1500 (Iorga, *Notes*, v, 272). [3] Ljubić, ed., *Commissiones*, ii, 228 (forces; 'uomini ferocissimi'), iii, 4 ('non fortificata'); BL, MS Add. 8262, fo. 379r ('muraglie alte, et uecchie', 'parte della muraglia minaccia rouina' (Ljubić, ed., *Commissiones*, iii, 115)); Čoralić and Karbić, *Pisma*, 99 (complaint), 102 ('algune artellarie et schioppi totalmente inutili'). [4] Ljubić, ed., *Commissiones*, ii, 227 ('Hanno questi Albanesi costumi barbari; parlano lingua albanese tutta differente dalla Dalmatina, ma sono degni di comendazione in questo, che sono fedelissimi al suo prencipe. Fra loro non vivono estreme persecuzioni et odii intestini, ma sono però prestissimi di colera, et gariscono volentieri nella piazza con parole, ma anco presto si risolve questa lor natural grinta'); Bošković, Mijović and Kovačević, *Ulcinj 1*, 37 (carving); Ushaku, *Ulqini në përmasa*, 30 (carving). [5] Čoralić, 'Iz prošlosti istočnoga', 51–2 (Slav minority); Bošković, Mijović and Kovačević, *Ulcinj 1*, 10 (other churches), 65–71 (city hall), 109–24 (cathedral); von Šufflay, 'Die Kirchenzustände', 235–6 (Orthodox); Pertusi, *Martino Segono* (Segono; 16(n.): Orthodox); Čoralić, 'Iz prošlosti istočnoga', and 'Od Ulcinja' (émigrés). [6] Ljubić, ed., *Commissiones*, ii, 231 (both languages), 234 (2,500), 237 (exports); Čoralić, 'Izbjeglištvo', 119 (emigrants in Venice), 137–8 (Albanian minority). [7] Ljubić, ed., *Commissiones*, ii, 231 (end-point); Sferra *et al.*, *L'Albania* (Venetian); Katib Çelebi, *History*, 5–6 (Ottoman); Ljubić, 'Marijana Bolice', 193 (Ulcinj); Rosaccio, *Viaggio*, fo. 25v (Drin). [8] Ljubić, ed., *Commissiones*, ii, 231 (stradiots), 234 ('sono grintosi et naturalmente nemici dei forestieri, et appena amano se stessi, maledici e fastidiosissimi', 'guerra', 'cani

pieni di rabbia'), 235 (Ratac), iii, 6 (farms), 7 (origin of hostility, intermarriage), 118 (denounced men); Lala, 'Violence', 49–50 (priests); Marković, 'Benediktin-ska', 210–11 (Ratac); Schmitt, *Das venezianische*, 470–1 (Mrkojevići coopted); Milošević, *Boka Kotorska*, 124–5 (Mrkojevići). **[9]** Ljubić, ed., *Commissiones*, ii, 238–9 (800, 200, conversion, 'di costumi barbari, et vivono sordidamente a guisa di cingani, stando in una stanza medesima con suoi animali, come fanno quasi tutti gli Albanesi, il che procede dall'estrema povertà, ch'è in quella provincia'), 239 (related, 'fedelissimi'), iii, 119 (vineyards, 1,200, 'quasi come fanno li Svizzeri'); Milošević, *Boka Kotorska*, 129–31 (advantages); Pederin, *Mletačka uprava*, 135 (advantages). See also Šerović, 'Paštrovići'. **[10]** Stanojević, *Jugoslovenske zemlje*, 72 (population); Ljubić, ed., *Commissiones*, ii, 246–7 (trade (300,000), territory, 'Vicinano tutti questi Cattarini et suoi sudditi con Turchi benissimo'), iii, 114 (appeals); Milošević, *Boka Kotorska*, 166–9 (trade); BLY, MS 381, fo. 4r–v (appeals). **[11]** On the general conditions see İnalcık, *Ottoman Empire*, 70–118; on migrations to Ottoman territory see Mutafčieva, *Agrarian Relations*, 140. **[12]** On Skanderbeg and his campaigns see Gegaj, *L'Albanie*, and Schmitt, *Skanderbeg*. **[13]** Armao, *Vende*, and Cantelli, *Albania* (maps: Lezhë, Drin). **[14]** Schmitt, *Das venezianische*, 230–8 (1390s transfers); Barleti, *Siege* (siege of Shkodër). **[15]** Duka, 'Coast', 265–6 (Shkodër population, using ×5 household multiplier); Bartl, 'Religion', 312 (Muslim majority, giving statistics); Ljubić, ed., *Commissiones*, ii, 230 (goods on Bunë, grain at Lezhë); Karaiskaj, *Die spätantiken*, 211 (Lezhë); Simon, 'Les Dépêches', i, 325 (Persian silk). **[16]** Duka, 'Coast', 264–5 (Durrës garrison); Yerasimos, *Les Voyageurs*, 26 (in ruins); Tenenti, *Cristoforo*, 164, 185(n.) (Durrës corsairs); Simon, 'Contribution', 110 (1559 bombardment). Note, however, that 15th-century visitors to Durrës had also described it as a ruined place (e.g. da Sanseverino, *Viaggio*, 46); it seems that the physical effects of the massive earthquake of 1267 (on which see Elsie, *Early Albania*, 12–13) remained permanently visible. **[17]** Ducellier, *La Façade* (pre-Ottoman period); Veinstein, 'Une communauté', and 'Avlonya' (Jews) (cf. Duka, 'Coast', 262–3); Botero, *Relationi*, i, fo. 50r (wine, salt); Vinaver, 'Dubrovačko-albanski', 208 (pitch); DAD, LCL, 33, fos. 73r, 106r (Ragusan purchases of pitch, wine, 1577); cf. Evliya Çelebi, *Evliya*, 129, 143 (pitch, salt). **[18]** Veinstein, 'Une communauté', 795 (Abraham, Sinan); Luetić, 'Lundruesit', 118 (Mustafa, Ioannis); Ljubić, ed., *Commissiones*, ii, 231 (Rodon); Ducellier, *La Façade*, 481–2 (14th century); Pedani, *Dalla frontiera*, 32 (1479 orders). **[19]** von Šufflay, *Qytetet*, 117–35 (municipal rights); Thëngjilli, *Shqiptarët*, 36 (Berat, Elbasan figures); cf. Prifti *et al.*, eds., *Historia*, i, 548–9 (early Ottoman towns; but note that the urban network in Kosovo was more dense). The mass exodus from Shkodër was orderly, however, under a Venetian–Ottoman agreement: see Schmitt, *Südosteuropa*, 397–8. **[20]** Moretti, 'Gli albanesi', 9 (Shkodër refugees in Venice); Schmitt, *Das venezianische*, 560–2 (waves of emigration); Fine, *Late Medieval*, 602 (later waves); Petta, *Despoti*, 16–17 (sceptical of popular tradition; cf. Mazziotti, *Immigrazioni*, 77–80); Petta, *Stradioti*, 17–18 (Avetrana), 132 (Flanders); Tallett, *War*, 90 (Boulogne, French Wars); Poullet, ed., *Correspondance*, iv, 607 (Brussels). **[21]** Kiel, *Ottoman*

Architecture, 21–2 (peace, population growth, towns). **[22]** Morris, *Venetian Empire*, 54 (donkey). For good summaries see Arbel, 'Colonie', 947–51, and O'Connell, *Men of Empire*, 17–38; for a vivid general account see Crowley, *City*. **[23]** Capponi, *Lepanto*, 189 (replenishment: water every 2–3 days); Hanlon, *Twilight*, 9–10 (1 metre); Pederin, *Mletačka uprava*, 224 (navigational argument). **[24]** Crowley, *City*, 124 (Koroni–Methoni requirement); Ljubić, ed., *Commissiones*, ii, 226 (information), 231 (Rodon signals); Gertwagen, 'Venetian Colonies', 354–67 (information). **[25]** BCP, MS C.M. 139/1, fos. 83v–84r (1562 fusta); Molino, *Barzeletta*; *I fatti*; *Manoli Blessi*; *Il vero successo* (stradiot poems). **[26]** Arbel, 'Greek Magnates' (Cyprus mixed élite); McKee, *Uncommon Dominion*, 5 (Crete); O'Connell, *Men of Empire*, 77–81 (Koroni–Methoni, civil law, qualifying the claim (e.g. McKee, *Uncommon Dominion*, 28) that Venetian civil law ruled in Crete); Arbel, 'Colonie', 975 (Orthodox); Šimunković, 'La politica' (no Italianization). **[27]** Doumerc, *Venise*, 73–6 (salt); Raukar, 'La Dalmazia', 74–5, 86 (salt); Vrandečić, 'La Dalmazia', 153 (ship-building rule); Hocquet, *Le Sel*, ii, 594(n.) (Ulcinj); Schmitt, *Südosteuropa*, 33, 52–4 (Adriatic requirement ignored); Greene, 'Trading Identities', 130, 134 (rule abandoned). **[28]** Arbel, 'Colonie', 954 (constitution); Ventura, *Nobiltà*, 40–3 (dedition); Karapidakis, *Civis*, 48–52 (dedition); Raukar, 'La Dalmazia', 67 (change of workings); O'Connell, *Men of Empire*, 115 (Ulcinj villages); Yotopoulou Sicilianou, 'Alcune considerazioni' (embassies, adulatory). **[29]** da Mosto, *L'Archivio*, ii, 4, 18 (officials); Pederin, *Mletačka uprava*, 24–5 (officials); Setton, *Papacy*, iv, 927 (criticism); Queller, *Venetian Patriciate*, 172–211 (corruption); O'Connell, *Men of Empire*, 119–39 (corruption, Syndics). **[30]** BLY, MS 381, fos. 2v–6r.

2. THREE FAMILIES

[1] Ljubić, ed., *Commissiones*, ii, 227 ('Oltra le tre sorti d'abitanti sono ridotte in questa città alcune reliquie d'onorate famiglie delle città vicine, ora signoreggiate da Turchi, come da Scutari, d'Allessio, di Durazzo et d'altri luoghi, fra i quali è principalmente quella dei Bruni, Pamaltotti, et Brutti, della quale è solo misser Marc'Antonio gentiluomo virtuosissimo e fedelissimo alla republica, il quale discende dall'ilustre famiglia dei Brutti Romani ... Quelli delle famiglie forestiere attendono per la maggior parte ai trafichi, et praticando le scale della Turchia vivono assai comodamente'). **[2]** Barbarano, *Historia*, iv, 103–4, 150 (genealogy; 150: 'e d'altri castelli'), 152 ('un Vecchio molto dotto, e venerando'); von Šufflay, *Qytetet*, 48–9 (Medun); Armao, *Vende*, 125 (Tuscena; another source (Venturini, 'La famiglia', 351) says the Brunis were lords of 'Trassano' and 'Giubano': 'Trassano' might be another distortion of 'Tuscena'; Giubano might be Zhupan, a village near Velipojë: see Cordignano, ed., *Catasto*, ii, 159). **[3]** Farlati, *Illyrici*, 102 (1551), 105 (Nicolò 29; in the 'Mediterranean Marriage Pattern', the average age of marriage might be in the range 28–33 for grooms, and 18–19 for brides: see Rheubottom, *Age*, 87–8, 107). That Giovanni was the eldest son is suggested by the fact that he was given his grandfather's name; the same argument applies to Matteo. [4] Barbarano, *Historia*, iv, 150 ('Lucia del Nico, nobilissima Dama'); Schmitt, *Das venezianische*, 468 (de Nicho negotiations). [5] Xhufi, 'La Population', 153–5 (names); cf. Zamputi, ed., *Dokumente*, i, 304 (noting 'Keqi', 'bad', as a nickname). [6] Venturini, 'La famiglia', 350–1 (account of family, 'signor di Durazzo'), and family tree (marriages) (cf. Fine, *Late Medieval*, 239, 248–9 on actual rulers of Durrës); Schmitt, *Das venezianische*, (index, s.v. Dukagjin, Span, Kastriota); Valentini, ed., *Acta*, xiii, 206, xiv, 190, xvi, 57–61 (58: 'fidelissimus et praticus ad similia'). Venturini, 'La famiglia', 350, writes that Bartolomeo, son of Giacomo, married Laura Dukagjin and became vice-governor, but gives his date of birth as 1413, which must be wrong. Valentini notes also (*Acta*, xvii, 86) a Bartolomeo Bruti whose father, Antonio, was a notary and citizen of Durrës in 1427; the different father's name and lower status suggest this was a different man. [7] Venturini, 'La famiglia', 351–2 (move to Ulcinj, Maria, 'un'ingente fortuna'), family tree (Lucia, 'Stefano', other sisters). [8] Cordignano, *Onomasticon*, 47 (Greek: 'Pamaliotēs'); Zamputi, ed., *Dokumente*, i, 304 ('Pal Maloku, Maleta, Mileta'); Valentini, ed., *Acta*, ix, 78 (Albanian origin: 'Pa-Maloki'), xi, 211, 261 (help 1423), xii, 17–19 (grants), 94 (complaints 1424; cf. Pertusi, 'Per la storia', 240–1), xviii, 19, 159–60 (recruited 1443–4), xix, 77 (confiscation), 124 (reward 1445); von Šufflay, 'Povijest', 200 (mistakenly identifying them with the Mrkojevići; his evidence does not support this, as it locates them 'in Saboiana', i.e. along the Bunë); Schmitt, *Das venezianische*, 206, 209–10 (Vlachs in Shkodër region); Fine, *Late Medieval*, 517 (role against Serbs); Valentini, 'L'elemento', 271, 274, identifies the Pamaliotis as Vlach. [9] Ljubić, ed., *Commissiones*, ii, 228 ('che da Scutari et circumvicini luoghi sono venuti, et per benemeriti loro possedano case e possessioni dategli dalla serenissima signoria, della quale sono stati anco esentati dai datii, et hanno altri particolari privileggi'); Valentini, ed., *Acta*, xii, 7–8 (Nika leader), 17–19 (1424); Čoralić and Karbić, *Pisma*, 95 (1505), 111 (1545). Valentini suggests that the name came from 'Roman', and notes a Vlach village near Shkodër called 'Rëmani' ('L'elemento', 271, 274). An even closer derivation would be from the Vlach word for 'Vlach': 'Aromân'. [10] O'Connell, *Men of Empire*, 132 (Medono); Polić Bobić, *Medju križom*, 205 ('capitan de vnos Albaneses que se rebelaron contra el Turco y se vinieron a la deuocion de Ven.os'). [11] Polić Bobić, *Medju križom*, 205 ('Con quien trato esto es clerigo noble de Albania que era como Vn obispo, y tenia diez o doze cassares y su hermano era señor de todos aquellos Albaneses que al tiempo de la liga la S.a de Venecia hizo que se rebelassen contra el Turco y quando Vino la Armada en este Golfo se metio en dulcigno este hermano del clerigo con 400 hombres donde fue muerto, con todos los suyos llamaua se don Andrea Aramani el que Viue se llama Jorge Aramani y sus Villas estauan baxo de scutari'). [12] Ibid., 205 ('son personas de Importancia'); Luetić, 'Lundruesit', 124 ('Arman Albanac', 1580), 135 (1584); Farlati, *Illyrici*, vii, 324 (Duca); Rački, 'Izvještaj', 74 (Thoma). Cf. the 'Duche Armenia' of 1424 (above, 28). [13] Schmitt, 'Storie', 92 (Korčula); Pederin, 'Die venezianische', 107 (pro-Hungarian); Vrandečić, 'La Dalmazia', 157 (pro-Hungarian); Ventura, *Nobiltà*, 151 (rich non-nobles); Krekić, 'Developed

Autonomy', 193–4 (poor nobles); Raukar *et al.*, *Zadar*, 264 (1528). **[14]** Praga, *Storia*, 163–4, Ventura, *Nobiltà*, 151–62, and O'Connell, *Men of Empire*, 142–9 (Hvar etc., 1510–12). **[15]** Milošević, *Boka Kotorska*, 122 (Bar, 1507), 123–4 (Bar, 1512); Sanuto, *I diarii*, xv, cols. 419 (20 Dec.), 469–73 (desperate letter; col. 470: 'cum ischiopeti, saete et arme diverse'); Ventura, *Nobiltà*, 163 (Bar, 1512); Ljubić, ed., *Commissiones*, ii, 233 (Bar: two councils), 235 ('antico et inestinguabile'), 245 (Kotor), iii, 117 (ciborium). On the tensions in Bar see also Čoralić, 'Staleški raskol'. **[16]** Ljubić, ed., *Commissiones*, ii, 226–7 (Ulcinj), 238 (Budva); Čoralić, 'Iz prošlosti ulcinjske', 67(n.) (1505, Dabre), 70 (1544); Venturini, 'La famiglia', 358 (1562 decree). On the Dabre (Dabri) connection see below, 418. **[17]** Krekić, 'Latino-Slavic' (Old Ragusan, Slav influx, Italian); Schmitt, *Das venezianische*, 125–6 ('Latini', 'Sclavi', Black Death); Ljubić, ed., *Commissiones*, ii, 215 (Split); Dursteler, 'Speaking', 70 (Dubrovnik). On the Bruti marriages in the Istrian town of Koper see below, 198–9. Some of the men the Brutis married may have had some knowledge of the Slav language spoken in the nearby Istrian villages, and the Bruti women probably knew some Serbo-Croatian; but social life among the élite families of Koper was conducted in Italian. **[18]** e.g. Apostolescu, 'Un aventurier', 567 ('un albanez italienizat'); Stoicescu, *Dicţionar*, 295 ('albanez italienizat').

3. ANTONIO BRUTI IN THE SERVICE OF VENICE

[1] ASVen, CCD, Suppliche, filza 1 (1478–1594) (file); Venturini, 'La famiglia', 351–7. **[2]** Baiocchi, 'Contarini' (incident); Shaw and Shaw, *History*, i, 98–9 (shift to Corfu); Ljubić, ed., *Commissiones*, ii, 121 (Bar, Ulcinj); Mallet and Hale, *Military Organization*, 227–33 (war, Preveza); Pujeau, 'La Préveza'; Poumarède, *Pour en finir*, 223–6 (League, Preveza). **[3]** Venturini, 'La famiglia', 352–3. **[4]** On the importance of news see Sardella, *Nouvelles*. **[5]** Tenenti, *Cristoforo*, 9–10 (da Canal's tenure as Provveditore, 1555–62); Venturini, 'La famiglia', 354 ('nova Sorte di Zifra'); ASVen, Senato, Deliberazioni, Secreti, registri, no. 71 (1558–9), fo. 16r ('per esser auisato delli progressi de ditta armata', 'possate esser auisati de ogni successo'). **[6]** Venturini, 'La famiglia', 356 (Corfu–Venice), 359 ('più facil modo di trattenersi in Amicitia con li Ministri del Sereniss.mo Sig.r Turco a quei Confini, et acquistarne de novi per valersene nelli servitij del Stato nostro'). **[7]** Ibid., 353–4 (Vendramin's ship, Durrës, Vlorë), 362 (June, 1563); BCP, MS C.M. 139/1, fo. 87r ('gionto à Dolcigno leuai sopra la mia galera il K.ʳ Bruti persona pratica nelle marine dell'Albania, et nelli maneggi con Turchi, et . . . me ne andai à Durazzo, et alla Valona per ricuperare le doi marciliane di Mauro-cini prese dalle fuste sopra Ostuni cariche di ogli', 'à diuersi del paese', 'hauendo egli le man in pasta (come si suol dire) con li Corsari mi dolsi grandem.ᵗᵉ della sua ingiust.ᵃ et mi parti da lui'). **[8]** Vratislav, *Adventures*, 43 (traveller's complaint); Davis, *Gift*, 143 (France: quotation); Čoralić and Karbić, *Pisma*, 93–4 ('ben conuicinar cum sanzachi et uayuodi'); Ljubić, ed., *Commissiones*, ii, 237 ('sotto nome di negoziatori publici', Shkodër, 'tacito tributo'), iii, 3 (30,000 ducats, inflated prices), 40 (horses). **[9]** DAD, Acta Consilii Rogatorum, 58, fos. 68r, 211v, 262r, and 59, fos. 74v, 75r. Cf. Šundrica, *Tajna kutija*, i, 133–44, emphasizing the two-way nature of Ragusan gift-giving. **[10]** Pedani, *Dalla frontiera*, 72 (1550); Stefani, ed., 'Viaggio', 22 (1591); ASM, Archivio Gonzaga, busta 1259, fos. 126r–127v, 605r–606v (605v: 'Hoggi ... è uenuto un mio parente Turco homo d'autorità, et in humanis ueram.^te homo da bene'). **[11]** Venturini, 'La famiglia', 356–7 (Antonio's contacts, friends); Polić Bobić, *Medju križom*, 138 ('un hombre honorade pratico para que fuese a negociar con el sanjaque con nombre de embax.or', 'en cierto lugar deshonesto'). **[12]** Ljubić, ed., *Commissiones*, ii, 229 (Giustinian); Venturini, 'La famiglia', 353 ('il Territorio di Dolcigno, con la Villa del Gierano'), 363–5 (Doge's instructions, successful negotiations); Farlati, *Illyrici*, vii, 103, 259 (1553 lease). Gerami/Gerano later ceased to exist, so no modern Albanian or Slav name for it can be given; it is 'Gerana' in Marin Bolizza's account of 1614 (Ljubić, 'Marijana Bolice', 173), and 'Gerama' in the map by Coronelli (1687–8) reproduced in Armao, *Vende*. **[13]** Ljubić, ed., *Commissiones*, ii, 227, 231 (Giustinian, horses), iii, 5 (horses, grain); Venturini, 'La famiglia', 355 (nephew); Luetić, 'Lundruesit', 120 (1577); Popović, ed., *Pisma*, 204–5 (Rizvan). **[14]** Borghesi, *Il Mediterraneo*, 17 (calories); Aymard, *Venise*, 17 (staro, consumption); Braudel, *Mediterranean*, i, 576–8 (cities), 596 (arguing that Venetian imports exceeded Terraferma production until the 1580s); Sardella, *Nouvelles*, 10 (158,000); Lane, *Venetian Ships*, 257, and Simon, 'Contribution', 978–80 (1558–60 list); Ljubić, ed., *Commissiones*, iii, 31 (Giustinian); Greene, 'Ruling', 197–8 (Crete); Veinstein, 'Un achat', 16 (500,000). Murphey, 'Provisioning Istanbul', suggests 205 tons, on the basis of a record for 1717 when the population was 310,000 (which confirms the per capita rate); but his estimates of the population in the 16th century seem low, based on a multiplier of only 3 per household. Cf. the higher estimates in Mavroeidē, *O Ellēnismos*, 27–8. **[15]** Murphey, 'Provisioning Istanbul', 229–31 (Istanbul); d'Atri, '"Adi 2"', 574–6 (Rupe); Martinat, 'L'Annone' (Rome); Judde de Larivière, *Naviguer*, 248 (non-noble, foreign); ASVen, Provveditori alle biave, busta 4, vol. 1, fos. 39r ('quei m[er]cada[n]ti Turchi, che han[n]o uenduti li loro fro.^ti all Illmo D[o]mi[n] io'), 86v, 87r (Faruk); Mavroeidē, *Aspetti*, 49, 51, 60–2 (Greeks). **[16]** Krivošić, *Stanovništvo*, 51 (Dubrovnik population 6,000 or less); Anselmi, 'Motivazioni', 35 (Dubrovnik population 6–7,000); Parker, *Global Crisis*, 19–20 (gearing effect); Hrabak, *Izvoz*, 258 (1548–50, Apulia 1555 and Ottoman ban, Sicily 1560 and Ottoman ban, crisis 1568–9); Raukar *et al.*, *Zadar*, 248 (Zadar 1551); Cassar, *Society*, 46 (Palermo, Malta, crises 1568–9, 1573–5, 1588–90); McGowan, *Economic Life*, 35 (Ottoman ban); d'Atri, 'Per conservare', 80–2 (Dubrovnik, special measures), 84–5 (interception 1560); Braudel, *Mediterranean*, i, 575 (interception 1560); Aymard, *Venise*, 137 (crisis 1568–9). On the broader background to the grain problems of the period 1550–1600 see also Tabak, *Waning*, 125–32. **[17]** Brummett, *Ottoman Seapower*, 103 (1505; and cf. 135); Braudel, *Mediterranean*, i, 583 (1528); Hrabak, *Izvoz*, 259 (Varna early 1550s); Simon, 'Contribution', 979 (Egypt, Syria late 1550s). **[18]** Miović, *Dubrovačka republika*, 106 (condition, sometimes broken); Veinstein, 'Un achat', 17–24 (*narh*, noting that, officially, outside buyers paid a supplement); White, *Climate*, 23–4 (*narh*), 96–7 (1563 report); Vrandečić, 'Islam', 300–1 (differential, devaluation); Hrabak, *Izvoz*, 264 (1560–90). On the *narh* system see also Kütükoğlu, 'Narkh'. **[19]** BCP, MS C.M. 139/1, fos. 83v (Barletta), 94r (Budva); Hrabak, *Izvoz*, 265 (1565–6); BAR, MS 1479, fo. 25r (Knights of Malta); DAD, LCP, 1, fos. 150r–154v (Ragusan seizure; 150v: 'uniuersale carestia per tutto il mondo, et spetialmente per la Dalmatia'), 2, fos. 20v ('scostandoui totalmente da tutti li altri luoghi della S.ᵣⁱᵃ di Venetia, et da i legni armati di quella'), 32r ('ui potesse fare qualche fauore contra le Galere Venetiane'), 39v (Venetian seizure Sept.), 52r–v (Venetian seizure Nov.), 58r–60v (Ragusan seizure); Ljubić, 'Poslanice', 3–4 (Venetian seizure Aug.). On Venice's grain blockade of Dubrovnik, 1569–70, see Popović, *Turska*, 254–5. **[20]** d'Atri, '*Per conservare*', 86 (Ragusan purchases from early 1560s); Hrabak, *Izvoz*, 314–17 (Ragusan purchases 1560s, '70s); DAD, Acta Consilii Rogatorum, 59, fo. 170v (*Kapudan Paşa*); DAD, LCP, 2, fos. 31r–33v (fo. 32v: 'ancor che non haueuamo tanto bisogno'); Binark, ed., *5 Numaralı*, ii, 21, no. 106 (sultanic order 1565); DAD, LCL, 33, fos. 43r–v, 46v, 190r–191r, 217r–218v (letters to Coduto about corsairs 1576–9). **[21]** Schmitt, *Das venezianische*, 477–8 (Jonima family); DAD, LCP, 2, fos. 28v–29r ('col nome di Dio et della Vergine maria, uene anderete nelle dette parti di Albania, in quei lochi che a uoi pareranno piu à proposito, et quiui attenderete con la uostra solita diligentia di comprar per conto nostro tanti formenti quanto qual si uoglia altra sorte di Biaue che parera a uoi et a quel minor preggio che si potra'), 38v (Gionima's purchases; the tonnage given here is calculated for the Ragusan staro, which was roughly 1.2 Venetian stari), 48r (to Gionima in Lezhë), 67r (E. Suina: oil, couriers); DAD, Acta Consilii Minoris, 48, fo. 276r (L. Suina: forwarding to Vlorë); Venturini, 'La famiglia', family tree ('Lavio' Suina, an error for Lauro). **[22]** DAD, LCL, 34, fos. 218v–220r (fo. 219r: 'un gran numero di Turchi di Durazzo'), 35, fos. 1r–2r, 6v (death of Gionima), 7r ('insolenti', Vlorë); DAD, Acta Sanctae Mariae Maioris, 16th cent., item 451, no. 4 ('el comesso di Vri Sig:ⁿʳⁱ Ill:ᵐⁱ é statto in gran parte caggione, che le biaue in queste parti siano molto accresciutte di prezzo, p[er] il che questo populo . . . è redeutto a estrema misseria'). **[23]** Ljubić, ed., *Commissiones*, ii, 231 (150,000), iii, 116 ('Appresso si trarria gran quantità di formento dall'Albania, a la qual opera non mancheriano m. Antonio Brutti et compagni'); Venturini, 'La famiglia', 354 (Corfu), 355 (2 years, 'grandissimi pericoli e fatiche', Ragusan ships at Lezhë); Simon, 'Contribution', 1016 (despatch); ASVen, Provveditori alle biave, busta 4, vol. 1, fos. 50r (3,000), 68r, 73r (6,000). **[24]** Pazzi, *I cavalieri*, 14–18 (anomalous, three kinds); ASVen, Senato, Deliberazioni, Secreti, registri, no. 71, fo. 103r ('Si ha ueduto in diuerse occasioni . . . qua[n]to seruitio et beneficio alle cose n[ost]re . . . ha fatto il fidel.ᵐᵒ nro Dns Antonio Bruti da Dulcigno, appresso li agenti Turcheschi a quei confini, hauendo con alcuni di loro pratica, et familiarita grande, et apresso tutto molta reputatione, et credito . . . nelle cose che di giorno in giorno occorreno non solam:ᵗᵉ p[er] liberatione de Nauilij, sudditi n[ost]ri, et robbe loro, et tratte di biaue, ma p[er] altri maneggi anchora importanti'). **[25]** Pazzi, *I cavalieri*, 19–20 (ceremony, costs), 27 (600 g), 408 (totals); ASVen, Senato,

Deliberazioni, Secreti, registri, no. 71, fo. 103r (100 scudi); Venturini, 'La famiglia', 358(n.) ('nullum unquam Onus decretaverit, nulli Labori, aut expensae peperit, nullum non Vitae periculum obierit'). The Order is strangely neglected by historians; Pazzi's unique study is excellent, but hard to find, being published by a monastery in Montenegro.   [26] Venturini, 'La famiglia', 357 (1569 request).   [27] Aymard, *Venise*, 145 (continued buying, for up to 10,000 ducats p.a.); Venturini, 'La famiglia', 361 (instruction to bribe), 366–7 (offer for navy, official letter, sons); Zamputi, ed., *Dokumente*, i, 262 ('estremissima necessitta', 'in questi tempi di guerra, Pestilentie et fame' (Čoralić and Karbić, *Pisma*, misdate the letter he enclosed (133–4) from the commune of Budva); ASVen, Provveditori alle biave, busta 4, vol. 1, fos. 156v–157r (the explicit order, threatening immediate deprivation of the governorship); ASVen, Annali, 3, fo. 323r (Antonio, letter to Venice, 1 Nov. 1570, saying he returned at the infantry commander's request, leaving 10 archers on flagship); BMC, MS Provenienze diverse, 581. c. misc., fo. 22r (Antonio, letter to Girolamo Zane, 13 Dec. 1570, saying he left Corfu on 28 July for Ulcinj). Venturini, 'La famiglia', 381, cites a much later document by Jacomo, saying that he and Marco were volunteers on Zane's flagship, but at the same time saying that they fought heroically at Lepanto, when the flagship was under a different commander, Venier.

4. GIOVANNI BRUNI IN THE SERVICE OF GOD

[1] Merkle *et al.*, ed., *Concilium*, ix, 802 (Trent, citing Aquinas, *Quaestiones de quodlibet*, 9, art. 15); Farlati, *Illyrici*, vii, 102 (canon), 259 (Dalmas virtuous); Čoralić, 'Izbjeglištvo', 98–9 (Dalmas family), and 'Iz prošlosti ulcinjske', 67(n.) (Dalmas dates, noting he was administrator of the see from 1532), 70 ('confussione et scisma'); ASVen, Savi all'eresia (Santo Ufficio) busta 8, fasc. 4, fo. [1r] ('heretici lutherani', 'grande scandalo et co[n]fusio[n]ne').   [2] Barbarano, *Historia*, iv, 99–100 (Chieregatto); Čoralić, 'Iz prošlosti ulcinjske', 68(n.) (Chieregatto); Merkle *et al.*, eds., *Concilium*, x, 835–6(n.) (resignation, letter to Pope), 886 (subsidy); Farlati, *Illyrici*, vii, 102 (appointment of Bruni). Chieregatto is commonly referred to as 'Chieregati'; I adopt the spelling by which he signed his name in his letter to the Inquisition.   [3] ASVat, Congr. Concilii, Relat. Dioec. 56, fasc. 1 (Marin Bizzi visitation, 1618), fos. [2r] (pre-1571 churches in Bar diocese), [4r] (purple, 70 sees); Čoralić, 'Duhovne' (Bar priests in Venice); Barbarano, *Historia*, iv, 150 (9 suffragans); Ritig, 'Primacijalni', 93–4 (title, Split–Bar).   [4] Ljubić, ed., *Commissiones*, ii, 231 ('incontrati dal reverendissimo arcivescovo e dal magnifico podestà, et salutati con gran suoni di campane e con grandissimo sbarar di artilerie'); Farlati, *Illyrici*, vii, 259 (papal letter about land); Cordignano and Valentini, *Saggio*, 71 (Laç); Pllumi, 'Pak histori' (Laç, destruction); Merkle *et al.*, eds., *Concilium*, ii, 655 ('por el disimulado, porque no podia andar de otra manera por estar en poder de Turcos', story).   [5] Draganović, 'Massenübertritte', 197(n.) ('per causa che non hanno delli buoni pastori'); de Gubernatis and de Turre, *Orbis*, 444 ('propter mysteriorum Fidei ignorantiam, et

defectum eorum qui eadem edisserent'). Cf. Malcolm, *Kosovo*, 125–31, and the series of Propaganda Fide reports edited by Bartl, *Albania sacra*. **[6]** Giannelli, 'Documenti', 54 (Kosovo letter); Cordignano, 'Geografia', 234 ('li popoli di Seruia et Macedonia', 'tutti li Christiani, che sono nel paese Turchesco, quali sono della fede, et riti di S. Chiesa Romana, non solo quelli del Regno di Seruia, ma etiam tutti quelli di Macedonia, et li Vescoui stessi nelle loro occorrenze ricorreuano da lui, et lui ancora in persona li uisitaua, et alli Popoli lontani mandaua Vescoui prouedendogli di Predicatori, et Confessori') (cited also by Farlati, *Illyrici*, vii, 105); ASVat, Congr. Concilii, Relat. Dioec. 56, fasc. 1, fo. [4r] ('presertim Joannis Bruni'). **[7]** Setton, *Papacy*, iii–iv, and Housley, *Later Crusades*, are exceptions, fully accepting the term. But cf. more recently Housley, *Crusading*, 1, 15, which seems to imply that crusading ended in 1504–5. **[8]** Zlatar, *Our Kingdom*, 198–9 (envoys to Moscow; on Leo's crusade plans see also Setton, *Papacy*, iii, 150, 172–93); Fischer-Galați, *Ottoman Imperialism* (Diets), Ursu, *La Politique*, and Isom-Verhaaren, *Allies* (Franco-Ottoman alliance). **[9]** Merkle *et al.*, eds., *Concilium*, iv, 3 (Paul's 3 aims), 226 ('tutam atque munitam ab infidelium armis atque insidiis rempublicam optaremus', 'a plurimis impendentibus periculis', 'conceptum et meditatum contra Italiam contraque Austriam et Illyricum terra marique bellum, cum impius et immitis hostis noster Turca nullo tempore requiesceret, nostrorumque inter se odia et dissensiones suam bene gerendae rei occasionem duceret'), 227 ('saevus et perpetuus hostis noster Turca'); Setton, *Papacy*, iii, 413–15 (Paul's plan for Mantua). **[10]** On the Council see Jedin, *Geschichte* (the classic modern history), Bäumer, ed., *Concilium*, and O'Malley, *Trent*. **[11]** Masiá, ed., *Cartas*, 39–41, 118–24. **[12]** Setton, *Papacy*, iv, 769 ('depressionem Christiani nominis hostis Turcae'); Šusta, ed., *Die römische*, i, 281–2 (Shah, Prester John, Ivan, 'accommodandosi le cose di christianità contra i Turchi piacendo a Dio per la ricuperatione di Constantinopoli et del santissimo sepolchro et per estirpar la setta Mahomettana', 'mettere ogni suo studio et ogni suo potere et non perdonare a spesa alcuna'); Weczerka, *Das mittelalterliche*, 192 (Moldavia). **[13]** Šusta, ed., *Die römische*, ii, 133 ('il Turco non può viver molto, essendo hydropico et molto travagliato di mente et di corpo … cerchiamo, Monsignori, di finir presto et fruttuosamente questo concilio et unir bene tutta la christianità et voltar li armi contra infideli, heretici et schismatici, chè questo è il fine al quale dovemo star intenti'), iv, 17 (Bova; the Pope's reply was that he should be given permission to leave if he were likely to vote on anti-papal lines); Merkle *et al.*, eds., *Concilium*, ii, 867 (Oran), viii, 338 (Castellana), 351 (Pécs), 395–6 (Esztergom); Rangoni Machiavelli, 'L'Ordine', 375 (Malta: 'illud haud dubie gravissimum toti reipublicae Christianae, ac forsitan insanabile vulnus accideret'). **[14]** Merkle *et al.*, eds., *Concilium*, viii, 300 (roll-call), 320 (10 Feb.); Šusta, ed., *Die römische*, i, 162 ('cominciando dal dì che arriverà costà'); Farlati, *Illyrici*, vii, 103 ('Carolo Borromaeo maxime acceptus'; but misdating this meeting to 1551); Trisco, 'Carlo Borromeo'; Fois, 'Carlo Borromeo'; Wojtyska, 'Carlo Borromeo'. **[15]** Merkle *et al.*, eds., *Concilium*, iii(1), 172 (subsidies), iii(2), pp. xxv (20–25 scudi), 223 (Zadar etc.), 274–95 (grain purchases); Languet, *Epistolae*, ii, 253 ('vix sufficient alendo asino & famulo');

Ehses, 'Bericht', 62 (list of 6, 'nihil habent'); Gorfer, *Trento*, 27 (8,000); Jedin, *Kirche*, ii, 336 (numbers in March), 337–41 (entourages), 345 (secretary, cook, stablehand); Barbarano, *Historia*, iv, 152 (Koper); Cucchetti, *Storia*, 151 (merchants, cattle); Šusta, ed., *Die römische*, i, 155 (instructions, 'sumptuosa convivia'). **[16]** Šusta, ed., *Die römische*, i, 125 (Borromeo letter, 'conventicule secrete'); O'Malley, *Trent*, 6 (list of nations); Merkle *et al.*, eds., *Concilium*, ii, 358 (Ciurleia), iii(1), 216 (Ciurleia spoke with his usual 'hilarità'; cf. also 640), vii, 364 ('Graecus'), ix, 634 ('Graecus'). **[17]** Merkle *et al.*, eds., *Concilium*, viii, 320, 330, 349 (Index), 378 ('nonnisi iustis, honestis, necessariis et ecclesiae catholicae utilibus de causis'), 402(n.) (Easter recess); Jedin, *Geschichte*, iv(1), 113–14 (80 in Rome, reformists' fears); O'Malley, *Trent*, 179–80 (residence and divine law). **[18]** Merkle *et al.*, eds., *Concilium*, viii, 403 ('neque nunc declarandum est, quo iure residere tenemur, sed ineunda est ratio, quomodo episcopi residere debeant'; eliminating problems), 464 (20 Apr.); 466 (reforms), 678, 692 (supervisory authority), ix, 247 ('Ipseque, cum diocesim in dominio Turcarum habeat et expositus sit continuo periculo mortis, et pensione gravissima oneratus sit, tamen residere non recusat'). Chieregatto would die in 1573, aged 91, having outlived Bruni. **[19]** Ibid., viii, 652 (canons), 656 (Patriarch: 'ne Graeci comprehenduntur', 'dummodo privilegia Graecorum non tollantur'), 657 (Bruni agrees), 826 (Bruni on Bohemians). **[20]** Ibid., ix, 686 (ambassadors), 690 (Bruni agrees); Bressan, *Il canone*, 138–40 (legal not theological). **[21]** Merkle *et al.*, eds., *Concilium*, ix, 644 (clandestine marriage), 696 (dispensation), 781 (4th degree); Durham, *Some Tribal*, 15–16 (taboo), and *High Albania*, 21–2 (12th degree). **[22]** Merkle *et al.*, eds., *Concilium*, ii, 832, 867 (committee on ordination), iv(2), 33 (committee on ordination), ix, 801 (visitations); cf. 750–1 for text of canon), 990 ('bonis et antiquis archiepiscoporum iuribus', 'paene tota hierarchia ista ecclesiastica destruatur'). **[23]** O'Malley, *Trent*, 218–19 (residence compromise), 247 (quotation). **[24]** BAM, MS F 104 inf., fos. 539r (chapter and clergy of Bar to Borromeo: Fra Silvestro aged 70, travelled with Bruni, preached in Serbo-Croat ['lingua illirica']), 540r (Commissary General Luigi dal Pozzo to Fra Silvestro: 'qui tum in Antiberina ciuitate, tum etiam in quocu[n]-q[ue] loco suae diocesis sicut ipsi R.^{mo} Archiep[isco]po uidebitur oportunem praedicationibus, ac lectionibus subditas eius oues Instruere possit'). **[25]** Farlati, *Illyrici*, vii, 103 (Ratac dispute, secretary's letter) (also in Poggiani, *Epistolae*, i, 351–2); Marković, 'Benediktinska', 211–12 (Ratac dispute, Pisani). **[26]** Farlati, *Illyrici*, vii, 103 (administrator of Ulcinj, Budva), 259–60 (Giubizza, dispute). **[27]** BAM, MSS F 94 inf., fos. 214r (Bruni to Borromeo: 'sempre mi son forciato conseruar questi pouer popoli . . . nela fede catholica . . . tutto cio che questa pouer prouincia sia oppressa da scismatici et mahometani'), 215r (Franciscan authorities to Marco Pasquali), F 104 inf., fo. 539r (chapter and clergy of Bar to Borromeo: 'ha tranquilissimam.^{te} retto et gouernato il suo grege, Il qual no[n] solo ha dato saggio da buon pastore, ma di padre et fratello uniuersale'). On the Pasquali family see Čoralić, 'Staleški raskol', 64, 66, 80, 82. **[28]** ASVat, Sec. Brev. Reg. 11, fo. 132v ('diligentiam et pietatem', 'Infidelium faucibus', 'ex populis illis quaecunque superstitionum semina penitus euellantur, horrendumque et immani illud feritatis exemplum, quod ante in defunctorum corporibus factitare consueuerant, prorsus ab illis tollatur, et omnino aboleatur'). **[29]** BAM, MS F 94 inf., fo. 48r (Bruni to Borromeo: 'li ho caricati sop.ᵃ un nauilio p[er] condurli in Ancona con Mathio mio nepote qual co[n] questa occassione [*sic*] mando in vece mia p[er] basciarli s.ᵐⁱ Piedi di sua Beat.ⁿᵉ et le sacratiss.ᵐᵉ mani di v.s. Illᵐᵃ', 'insieme col sudetto mio Fr[at]ello, et parenti'); Caracciolo, *La gloria*, 309 ('gagli-ardi'); Binark, ed., *5 Numaralı*, ii, 181, no. 1106 ('düşman kalelerinde kafirlere'); Barbarano, *Historia*, iv, 152 ('servito lungamente nella Corte di Roma, nella quale havrà havuto carichi honorevoli, conforme alli suoi degni meriti'). For a 1560s Ottoman list of forbidden exports see İnalcık, 'Question', 77–8(n.); on the ban on horses see also Pedani, *Dalla frontiera*, 112.

5. GASPARO BRUNI AND THE KNIGHTS OF MALTA

[1] For Antonio's date of birth see 299.   **[2]** Sire, *Knights*, 3–24 (early history); Vatin, *L'Ordre* (Rhodes period).   **[3]** Cassar, *Society*, 30 (grain from Sic-ily).   **[4]** Hess, *Forgotten Frontier*, 36–84; on Hayreddin see Fisher, *Barbary Legend*, 41–80.   **[5]** Brogini, *Malte*, 111–16 (Tripoli), 121 ('la professione nostra sia principalmente contra infideli e cacciare li corsari da limiti e mari de cristiani'), 123–4 (analysis).   **[6]** Mafrici, *Mezzogiorno*, 21–2 ('pirate' mostly later); Laiou, 'Levends', 232–6 ('levend' from 'levantino', 'korsan', 'harami lev-end'); Villain-Gandossi, 'Notes' ('levend' from Persian, 'korsan'); Brookes, ed. and tr., *Ottoman Gentleman*, 33–7 (Ottoman on pirates); cf. the entry 'corsaro' in Kahane *et al.*, *Lingua franca*, 193–6. Only in French was 'pirate' more com-mon; the traveller Pierre Belon explained the meaning of 'corsaire' to his readers, but did so only by assimilating it to 'pirate', describing raiders of the indiscrimin-ate kind: *Voyage*, 249–51.   **[7]** García Martínez, *Bandolers*, 83 (Valencian corsairs); López Nadal, 'El corsarismo', 267–8 (authorization, legal controls); Earle, *Corsairs*, 123–9 (private Maltese corsairs' tithe and distribution); Fisher, *Barbary Legend* (Barbary corsairs' codes of conduct); Manca, *Il modello*, 59–64 (Barbary corsairs' tithe and distribution). For the old view see, e.g., Bradford, *Shield*, 133 ('basically concerned with stabilising the trade routes in the central Mediterranean, and with imposing some form of law and order upon a sea that had become utterly lawless'). Fontenay, 'Corsaires', 363–4, criticizes the old view but underestimates the 'predatory' element in this period.   **[8]** NLM, AOM, MS 447, fos. 279v–280r ('Sion figlio di samuele di saffet huomo di piccola stat-ura et barba negra di circa trenta anni d'età hebreo n[ost]ro schiauo'); Wettinger, *Slavery*, 40–1, 200–2 (Jewish slaves); Greene, *Catholic Pirates*, 66 (Greek Ortho-dox, Dubrovnik); de Leva, ed., *La legazione*, i, 169(n.) (torture allegation; 'cavalieri ladri'); Mallia-Malines, *Venice*, 18–19 (sequestro), 28–9 (attitude to Rhodes siege), and *passim* (confrontations).   **[9]** Testa, *Romegas*, 69–70 (Romegas's seizures); Cassola, ed., *1565*, 97 (quotation).   **[10]** Guilmartin, *Gunpowder*, 191–2 (mili-tary historian); Granucci, *L'eremita*, fo. 102r (313 dead; the figure may come from an early pamphlet (reproduced in Cassola, ed., *1565*, 111), but note that

Granucci's main informant, Pardini, was a soldier at the siege); Mori Ubaldini, *La marina*, 243 (210 dead, 79 missing); BAR, MS 1479, fo. 11v (total 1,000 Knights, early 1580s); de Vertot, *Histoire*, v, 119–20 (founding of Valletta); de Giorgio, *A City* (building of Valletta).   **[11]** BAR, MS 1479, fos. 30v–31r (figures for income); on the structure see the valuable summary by Freller, *German Langue*, 69–73.   **[12]** van Beresteyn, *Geschiedenis*, 9 (quarters); Waldstein-Wartenberg, *Rechtsgeschichte*, 149–50 (exclusion of Jews, Muslims, illegitimate, bourgeois); Bosio, *Gli statuti*, 11 (exclusion of trade).   **[13]** Waldstein-Wartenberg, *Rechtsgeschichte*, 153–4 (servienti, chaplains); BAR, MS 1479, fo. 34v (commende only for Knights of Justice); BL, MS Add. 8277, fo. 81r–v ('uinto dalla importunità de Cardinali, et altri concede le Commende à chi gli piace ... in gran pregiudicio delli poueri Caualieri', 'fà anche di questi Caualieri ... senza proue alcune de nobiltà, et senza altra ceremonia. Ma questa accade solo nella pouera lingua d'Italia').   **[14]** Waldstein-Wartenberg, *Rechtsgeschichte*, 149–51 (applying to Priory, exclusions, two Knights); BL, MS Add. 8277, fo. 79r (three primary witnesses, three secondary, entry-fee, langue).   **[15]** NLM, AOM, MS 92, fo. 38v ('In causa receptionis in Ven.[da] Lingua Italiae sub gradu D[omi]nor[um] Fr[atr]um Militum D[omi]ni Gasparis Bruni', 'contradicentes', 'super ipsa c[aus]a pr[in]cipali receptionis et non in praetensa gratia partes audiant, scripturas uisitent, Testes si opus fuit examinent').   **[16]** dal Pozzo and Solaro, *Ruolo*, 86–7, 92–3 (Avogadro, Cataneo), 110–11 (Morizzo); NLM, AOM, MS 2125, fo. 13r ('fu fatta gratia spetiale co[n] scrutino di ballotte nemine discrepa[n]te al s:[r] Gasparo bruno p[er] qua[n]to era fuori de limiti Tantum e s'intende cosi co[n]tentandosi lui accettato dal giorno d'oggi'); Bosio, *Gli statuti*, 14 (statute on borders), 16 (probationary year (statute of de Verdalle)), 210–11 (Italian borders).   **[17]** NLM, AOM, MS 2125, fo. 13r ('furono passate p[er] bone le p[ro]ue di Nobiltà del s:[r] gasparro bruno nemine discrepa[n]te et accettato p[er] fra cauaglier conforme ut supra'), 92, fo. 43r (1 Nov. plea), 431, fos. 129r–v (Ferretti enquiry), 134r (Lucarini enquiry); dal Pozzo and Solaro, *Ruolo*, 114–15 (Lucarini excluded).   **[18]** NLM, AOM, MS 431, fo. 268v (31 Oct.); Bosio, *Gli statuti*, 6–8, and *Li privilegii*, sigs. N1v–N4r (ceremony); BL, MS Add. 8277, fos. 82r–86v (ceremony).   **[19]** Chetta-Schirò, *I Castriota*, 55(n.) (admission 1561); Bosio, *Dell'istoria*, iii, 551–2 (Sant'Elmo). Chetta-Schirò, who mistakenly claims direct descent for Costantino from Skanderbeg's son, has a few pages (89–93) on Gasparo Bruni, derived almost entirely from Bosio; he is the only modern author to have written about him.   **[20]** Padiglione, *Di Giorgio Castriota*, 17–23 (Granai family); Petta, *Despoti*, 61–83 (Granai, Branai family; father, uncle, grandmother, stradiots, spy network); Floristán Imízcoz, 'Los contactos', vols. 11–12, 133 ('capitanio de la Cimarra et de l'Albania'); Masiá, ed., *Cartas*, 140 ('Dimitro Massi, fiollo di Andrea Massi, fo parente de la bona memoria di signor marchese da Tripalda'; I take 'Veduni' to be a mistranscription of 'Redoni').   **[21]** Petta, *Despoti*, 87–90 (Arianiti, literary work, claim of non-awareness), 180–1 (Arianiti); Chetta-Schirò, *I Castriota*, 58–9, 65 (Musacchi consulted); Bosio, *Dell'istoria*, iii, 777 (fined, 'capriccioso'); NLM, AOM, MS 2125, fo. 102v (1569); dal Pozzo, *Historia*, i, 211 (1581). On his literary works see Pastore,

'Castriota'; see also his treatise 'De Republica', BPCG, MS M256. On Arianiti see also Babinger, *Das Ende*, 85–6. **[22]** Testa, *Romegas*, 103–4 (decrees); de Vertot, *Histoire*, v, 122–3 (Spanish Knights); Hanlon, *Twilight*, 87 (Venetian discouragement). **[23]** Soranzo, *L'Ottomanno*, 122 ('Pio V. che chiamò da Dulcigno Frà Gasparo Bruni Commendator Gierosolimitano per seruirsi di lui, e nell'armata contra il Turco, & in altre cose di momento appartenenti a quella guerra'). Soranzo need not be taken to imply that Gasparo was already a Knight when he was summoned from Ulcinj; he merely uses his full later title, including the much later 'commendatore'. **[24]** Bosio, *Dell'istoria*, iii, 803–4 ('amici', biscotto, recruiters, ambassadors); Setton, *Papacy*, iv, 925 (Venetian intelligence); NLM, AOM, MS 431, fos. 132v ('ex l[ite]ris multorum, et nuntijs, exploratoribus n[ost]ris'), 207r ('l[iter]ae quotidie afferuntur Selinum ... classem multo validiorem, et exercitum numerosiorem ad hanc Insulam inuadendam ... comparare'); Paoli, *Codice*, 233–4 (papal letters to Spanish, French kings). **[25]** Bosio, *Dell'istoria*, iii, 804 ('mandato fù anco dal G. Maestro à far residenza nella Città di Ragugia il Caualier Fra Gaspare Bruni Albanese, per riceuere le lettere de gli Amici di Costantinopoli; i quali scriuendo ordinariamente al Gran Maestro in cifra'). **[26]** ASVat, Sec. Brev. Reg. 7, fo. 411r ('Dilecti filij salutemus. Mittimus ad istas partes dilectum filium Gasparem Brunum, qui has nostras literas ad vos afferet pro nonnullis nostris, et apostolicae Sedis negotijs, eique mandauimus, ut si opus fuerit vostrum auxilium, et fauorem nostro nomine à vobis petat. Quare etsi non dubitamus vos pro singulari, solitaque erga nos, et eamdem apostolicam Sedem reuerentia, ac deuotione ipsi Gaspari promptè, ac benigne praesto futuros tamen vobis certum exploratumque esse uolumus, quidquid studij, et adiumenti in eum consuluentis nobis sane fore gratissimum; vestrumque ... obsequium, si quando se se dederit occasio, libenter compensabimus'). **[27]** e.g. DAD, Secreta Rogatorum, 2, fos. 159r–160r, gives the text of a breve of 5 Aug. **[28]** Bojović, *Raguse*, 190–4 (1442 decree); Harris, *Dubrovnik*, 80–7, 92–6 (rise of *haraç*); Biegman, *Turco-Ragusan*, 29–43 (status in Ottoman eyes); Kunčević, 'Janus-Faced' and 'Discourses' (status in Ottoman eyes and self-presentation). **[29]** BNM, MS It. VII. 213 (8836), fo. 368v ('non è ogni cosa del S.ʳᵉ?'); Miović, *Dubrovačka republika*, 47–51 (supplying intelligence), 51–5 (prisoner exchanges), 55–9 (transportation, grain, pitch), 169 (order to celebrate victory). **[30]** Biegman, 'Ragusan Spying', 242–4 (Süleyman quotations), 246–7 (news of fleet, 1570, 1571); DAD, Secreta Rogatorum, 2, fos. 168r (Huguenots, referring to the Peace of Longjumeau of 23 Mar. 1568), 178r ('in seruiano'); Gürkan, 'Espionage', 403 (Habsburg agent quotation, adapted); BNM, MS It. VII. 213 (8836), fo. 403r (Sept. 1568); Lesure, *Lépante*, 239–40 (Don John); DAD, LCL, 37, fos. 90v–91r ('paghiamo dua [*sic*] Tributi, et non vno solo p[er] le grandi, e Continue spese che facciamo nel tenere huomini in ogni parte del Mondo, p[er] sapere quello, che si fà, et si tratta, e poi p[er] notificarlo alla fel: porta', 'il Gran Sig.ʳᵉ non hà bisognio del u[ost]ro Tributo, perche sete poueri, ma hà bisognio d'esser da voi giornalmente auisato delle Cose del Mondo, dunque attendete di s[er]-uirlo'). On the intelligence sent in 1570–2 see also Žontar, *Obveščevalna služba*, 28–9, and Kumrular, 'Ragusa', 153–4. **[31]** Harris, *Dubrovnik*, 111 (1530s),

114 (news to Rome); Žontar, *Obveščevalna služba*, 24 (military intelligence to Naples); Tadić, *Španja*, 145–6 (news to Naples); Preto, 'La diplomazia', 160 (Venetian network), and *I servizi*, 236 (excluding Venetians).   [32] Tadić, *Španja*, 145–7 (news to Naples, 1566 crisis, decree, exile, protest); DAD, Secreta Rogatorum, 2, fos. 157v–158r ('hauesse ardire, et presumesse qui nella Città et D[omi]nio n[ost]ro significar le dette nuoue ad alcun principe, ò uero alli suoi ministri, ò ad altri priuati, ò che riceuesse ò dasse recapito alle dette lettere', 'senza saputa et espressa licenza del Mag.ᶜᵒ S.ʳ R. et del suo Cons.ᵒ').   [33] BNM, MS It. VII. 213 (8836), fo. 368v (fears of Ottoman fleet); ASVat, Sec. Brev. Reg. 11, fo. 33r (papal offer); Bosio, *Dell'istoria*, iii, 804 ('Belforte', 'Hebbe carico il detto Caualier Bruni, di spedir Fregate à posta, quando era necessario, e di dar ricapito alle Spie, & all'intelligenze, che da Costantinopoli veniuano, & andauano, senza sparagnar in ciò nè spesa, nè fatica alcuna'); Canosa and Colonnello, *Spionaggio*, 165(n.), and Gürkan, 'Espionage', 236–7 (Malaga brothers).   [34] Carr, *Blood*, 150 (decree), 155–8 (rebel preparations, intercepted letter); Hess, 'Moriscos', 12(n.) (Uluç Ali appointment); Williams, *Empire*, 162–5 (fear of Ottoman expedition); Caro Baroja, *Los moriscos*, 169 (genuine fear).   [35] Bosio, *Dell'istoria*, iii, 804 (Philip's thanks to Grand Master), 817 ('secretamente auisato con lettere in cifra dalle sue Spie, ch'ordinariamente stipendiate teneua in Costantinopoli, le quali penetrarono, e seppero le negotiationi, che'l Rè d'Algeri, & altri Capi de' Mori di Barbaria faceuano alla Porta, sollecitando, e facendo instanza al Turco, che mandasse l'Armata sua nelle Marine di Spagna, che verso l'Africa riguardano, per fare spalla, e dar aiuto, e calore a' Granatini'); Chasiōtēs, *Oi Ellēnes*, 49–54 (Barelli and family); Mavroeidē, *Aspetti*, 29, 59, 66 (Varelēs family); Karapidakis, *Civis*, 281 (Varelēs family); dal Pozzo and Solaro, *Ruolo*, 110–11 ('di Costantinop.'); Arce, 'Espionaje', 265 ('con dos turcos prinçipales (a cuyo cargo está el gouierno y mando de todo lo del Ataraçanal) de quemar toda la armada del Turco').

6. GALLEYS AND GEOPOLITICS

[1] Setton, *Papacy*, iv, 953–4 (Kubad's arrival (correcting the date given in other accounts), Zane); Pedani, *In nome*, 29 (Membré) and *Venezia*, 27, 146 (Kubad's visits); Pedani and Bombaci, *I 'documenti'*, 201–2 (ultimatum); Barbero, *La Bataille*, 76–81 (Barbaro, with much valuable detail); Yriarte, *La vie*, 152 (Senate vote); ASVen, CCD, Dispacci (Lettere) di Ambasciatori, busta 4, item 16 (irritation).   [2] Pedani and Bombaci, *I 'documenti'*, 201–2, and Pedani, 'Some Remarks', 23 (grievances); Barbero, *La Bataille*, 43–5 (Nasi), 77 (mosques argument); Grunebaum-Ballin, *Joseph Naci*, esp. 134–5 (theories about Nasi), 156 (wine imports). The mosques argument was also discussed in Venice: see Charrière, ed., *Négociations*, iv, 759(n.). The reference was probably to a brief period of Arab domination in the mid-7th century, though more recently, in 1424–6, Cyprus had been subjugated by the forces of the Mamluk sultan of Egypt. [3] Murphey, *Ottoman Warfare*, 50 (Egypt, finances).   [4] Casale, *Ottoman*

Age, 14–131 (Indian Ocean), 135–7 (canals), 137–8 (Sokollu's reluctance); Kortepeter, *Ottoman Imperialism*, 28 (Astrakhan, Don–Volga canal); Davies, *Warfare*, 12–13 (Astrakhan campaign); Allen, *Problems*, 22–8 (Don–Volga canal, Hajj); Ágoston, 'Where Environmental', 60 (Don–Volga canal not even begun). Pedani, 'Some Remarks', 25–6, and Capponi, *Lepanto*, 116–17, integrate the Cyprus campaign into the geopolitical strategy. [5] Capponi, *Lepanto*, 96–8 (Chios (with harm), Naxos, Andros, Kea, Siphnos); Setton, *Papacy*, iv, 936 (Knights' liquidation), 943–5 (Arsenal fire, harm to Chios). [6] Kafadar, 'Death', 198 (trade boom); Albèri, ed., *Relazioni*, ser. 3, i, 283–4 (trade, boycott argument), 286 ('bisogna procedere con gran destrezza e prudenza fra quelle due vie di fargli e non fargli la guerra. Bisogna certissimamente non farla, ma non però perchè credano che non si possa fare'). Some merchants were anti-war for commercial reasons in Mar. 1570, but only a minority: see Stella, 'Lepanto', 217. [7] Setton, *Papacy*, iv, 933 (information about Spanish fleet), 946, 954 (policy towards Spain, Jan., Mar.), 955 (fears of North African involvement); Vatin, 'L'Empire', 376–7 (Ponentini in Ottoman waters, *c*.1559); Pagkratēs, *Oi ektheseis*, 177–9 (Ponentini causing trouble for Venice, 1570s); Braudel, *Mediterranean*, ii, 879 (Sicilian corsairs). [8] Serrano, ed., *Correspondencia*, iii, 304–5 ('vi è assai poca amarevolezza verso li SS.ri Venetiani per non haversi voluto mai movere in aiuto d'altri, et molto manco confidanza che ogni volta che potessero uscire de la guerra non lo faccino volentieri, lassando l'impresa sopra altri et mirando solo all'interesse proprio'); Hess, *Forgotten Frontier*, 76–8 (Tripoli, Bougie, Oran); Anderson, *Naval Wars*, 8–13 (Djerba); Braudel, *Mediterranean*, ii, 973–85 (Djerba); Setton, *Papacy*, iv, 758–65 (Djerba; 763: Venetian policy). [9] Mafrici, *Mezzogiorno*, 190–200, and Fenicia, *Il regno*, 173–5 (Naples fleet); Braudel, *Mediterranean*, ii, 1008–12 (ship-building, taxes); Parker and Thompson, 'Battle', 15–16 (ecclesiastical taxes, tensions); Setton, *Papacy*, iv, 887 (Pius V, subsidio). [10] del Moral, *El virrey*, 63–73 (Atripalda reports, Albanians, Mustafa (but misidentifying Atripalda as a Lomellini)); Sola, 'La frontera', 299–303 (Atripalda reports, successor); Coniglio, *Il viceregno*, ii, 346–53 (347: 'credo che in essa se includa la Velona'; 351: 'tutto il regno e provincia di Albania'); Charles I of Naples was indeed proclaimed King of Albania in 1272, 6 years after his defeat of a previous ruler of Albania, Manfred of Sicily. [11] Setton, *Papacy*, iv, 956–8 (papal envoy), 959–60 (taxes), 961 (key condition); Braudel, *Mediterranean*, ii, 1081 (report of Ottoman fleet against Spain, from Istanbul, 22 Jan. (Braudel suspects Venetian misinformation, but Sokollu's misdirection was still operating then), taxes); Barbero, *La Bataille*, 125 (confidential assurance). [12] Fichtner, *Emperor*, 173–6, 189 (Maximilian); Halecki, *From Florence*, 174–9 (Ivan); Charrière, ed., *Négociations*, iv, 760(n.) (de Foix, letter to Catherine, Mar. 1570). [13] BAP, MS 4769, fo. 46r ('Discours' of Dax to Charles IX, Apr. 1572: 'pour contrepeser l[']excessiue grandeur de la maison d'Autriche'); BIC, MS 1777, fo. 7v ('Mesmes durant que nous auons este en guerre auec luy et qu'il a fomenté auec ses forces et moyens noz diuisions ciuilles estant certain qu'il eut faict tout auttre progres sur nous sans le soign et les despenses qu'il a esté obligé d'employer pour la conseruation de ses Costes maritimes tant du costé d'Italie que d'espagne', 'luy sont tellement necessaires et Importans que par le moyen d'Iceulx Il pourroit en toute seurete et plaine Liberté passer d'espagne en Italye ... et par consequent auroit beaucoup plus de moyen de se rendre M.ᵉ de toute l'Italye'). De Brèves was ambassador in Istanbul from 1591 to 1605.   [14] Capponi, *Lepanto*, 108–11, 143–4 (Siena, Cosimo, title); Guarnieri, *Cavalieri* (Santo Stefano); Aglietti, 'La partecipazione', 60–96 (Cosimo's relations with Philip and Pope); Levin, *Agents*, 89–93 (title, Philip); Fichtner, *Emperor*, 173–4 (title, Maximilian).   [15] Barbero, *La Bataille*, 184–6 (24–12 galleys, cardinals, distinct fleet); Lane, *Venice*, 362 (1560s fleet and reserve); Pezzolo, *L'oro*, 135 (1560s fleet).   [16] Bazzano, *Marco Antonio*, 47–125 (Colonna family, early life, Spanish connection); Capponi, *Lepanto*, 124 (Venetian worries); Barbero, *La Bataille*, 186–7 (Venetian worries); BSS, AC, II CF 3, fos. 3v–6r (payments for galley-crew, 1565), 176r–177v (sale), and AC, II CF 5 (Borromeo galleys); Hanlon, *Twilight*, 30 (7 galleys).   [17] Barbero, *La Bataille*, 187 (ceremony), 572 (quinquereme); Setton, *Papacy*, iv, 964 (ceremony, Colonna's commission); BSS, AC, II CF 1, fos. 6r (list of captains), 8v (Capizucchi commission); Petrucci, 'Pompeo Colonna' (career); Brunelli, *Soldati*, 75 (Capizucchi pro-Colonna); Guglielmotti, *Storia*, vi, 17–21 (commissions of captains), 24–7 (Ancona, Venice, flagship); Stella, 'Lepanto', 220–1 (in Venice; 220(n.): 'grandissima sollecitudine'); Lane, *Venetian Ships*, 65–8 (quinquereme, architect).   [18] BSS, AC, Corrispondenza Marcantonio il Grande, busta 44, nos. 4490 ('Questa matina ariuai qui Co[n] una fregata armata Co[n] 36 huomenj et 3. officiali', 'hò uoluto Co[n] la p[rese]nte reueren.ᵗᵉ darle noticia, dicendole et[iamdi]o questo che io di gia hò dato ordine in venetia ad un mio Nepote figliuolo del Sᵒʳ Caual[ier] Bruti che douesse procurar di trouarmi li officiali, et però le scriuo che debba ancor lui far saper V. E. che sorte di officiali hauera trouato'), 4450 ('di officiali non hauendo fatto mio Nepote prouisione').   [19] BSS, AC, Corrispondenza Marcantonio il Grande, busta 44, nos. 4490 ('Gouernator di Galera di N. S.'), 4450 ('Gouernator di galera di Sua San.ᵗᵃ'). An alternative account of Gasparo's career might posit that he had been a captain of one of the Borromeo galleys (following a recommendation from his brother Giovanni) and had come to Colonna's attention in that way. But the timing is tight (given Giovanni's first meeting with Borromeo in 1562); the existing documentation of those galleys does not mention him; and Soranzo's account gives the key role to the Pope (see above, 90).   [20] BSS, AC, II CF 1, fos. 49r ('Il Caualiere Fra Gaspar Bruno vi dirà in nome n[ost]ro l'ordine che hauete da tener p[er] el Caricamento di alcune vettouaglie necessarie no[n] mancate cosi esseguirlo'), 50v ('Perche conuiene al seruitio di S. S.ᵗᵃ et à l'honor et sodisfattion n[ost]ra di hauer p[er]sona di esperienza et ualore al gouerno della n[ost]ra Galera Cap.ᵃ et sapendo esser queste parte nel magnifico et molto honorato Sig.ʳᵉ Fra Gaspar Bruno Caualiere Hierosolimitano per la relatione che tenemo degno di fede della vertù et meriti suoi lo hauemo eletto come per la p[rese]nte lo eleggemo et deputamo Gouer:ʳᵉ et Cap.ⁿᵒ di detta n[ost]ra Galera con tutta l'auttorità facultà honori pesi prerogatiue et emolumentj solitj: Comandamo però espressamente che da tuttj gli huominj del seruicio di detta Galera, sia ubedito rispettato et riuerito come la p[er]sona mia').   [21] Monga, ed. and tr.,

Journal, 10–12 (galley details, 41 × 5.5 m); Cerezo Martínez, *Años cruciales*, 34 (galley details, 43 × 6 m; speed); Guilmartin, 'Tactics', 46–8 (galley details, 41.5 × 5.2–5.8 m; on lantern galleys, distinguishing from 'capitana' (flagship) galleys; but cf. Pantera, *L'armata*, 148, saying a capitana was larger than a normal galley). **[22]** Lutrell, 'Late-Medieval Oarsmen', 93 (Venetian shift to forzati); Tucci, 'Marinai', 683 (Venetian shift to forzati); Williams, *Empire*, 111 (Naples, 60%); Fenicia, *Il regno*, 175 (Naples, 11%–21%); Crescentio, *Nautica*, 95 ('i Mori pigliati sù le loro Fuste sono megliori, che quei che in terra si pigliano ... Bonauoglie sono gente vagabonda, a chi la fame, ò gioco forzò a vendersi, ò giocarsi in Galea'); BSS, AC, II CF 5, fos. 22v, 31v, 32r ('Ussain embram de Durazzo', 'Ussain de Mastafa de Velona', 'Peruena de Casson da durazzo', 'Assan de alli de bossona'; the list also includes two men with Spanish Christian names, who were probably Moriscos); Languet, *Epistolae*, i, 159 (Maltese galleys captured). **[23]** Imber, 'Navy', 265–7 (Ottoman rowers); Vratislav, *Adventures*, 138–9 (description of agony); Lubenau, *Beschreibung*, i, 219 ('So viel ich ... gesehen und erfahren, haben die Gefangenen auf den turkischen Galleen viel besser als auf der Christen oder hispanischen Galleen; den da ich von Neapolis in Siciliam auf der Galleen gefahren, bin ich selber erschrocken, wie tirannisch und greulich man da mit den Gefangenen umgingk'). **[24]** BSS, AC, II CF 1, fos. 14r (listing of galley complement), 61r ('Francesco da Corsola'). For a detailed and slightly fuller list of galley officers and sailors, see Crescentio, *Nautica*, 88–95; cf. also Pantera, *L'armata*, 115–29. **[25]** Pantera, *L'armata*, 115–16 ('nobili in poppa'); ASVat, Misc., Arm. II, 110, fos. 393r ('in galera par che sia dismenticato il modo che si suole bestemmiare in terra, ma tengano un modo nuouo, che l'inferno si stupisce'), 394v ('si mettano la maschera, che si fa per essercitarlj: et a[n]co che sono lor parenti: et è uero che s'essercitano al modo di satanasso et che sono loro moglie, non che parenti'); Barbero, *La Bataille*, 188 (distribution of Possevino); Possevino, *Il soldato*, 20–1 (blasphemy, duels), 26 ('le detrattioni, la menzogna, la Lussuria, la Gola, il giuoco, & le pompe'); BSS, AC, Corrispondenza Marcantonio il Grande, busta 67, no. 3900, fo. 1v (accounts in Ancona). **[26]** Capponi, *Lepanto*, 125 (agreement on overall command, Philip's order to Doria), 135 (Philip's letter to Colonna); Barbero, *La Bataille*, 220–4 (Philip's order to Doria, Doria's attitude, council of war, Souda). **[27]** Barbero, *La Bataille*, 156–7 (Zadar), 167–72 (Corfu); Mallett and Hale, *Military Organzation*, 235 (over 20,000). **[28]** Barbero, *La Bataille*, 226–9, 253–7 (discussions, review); Setton, *Papacy*, iv, 978–84 (discussions, review); ASVen, Senato, Deliberazioni, Secreti, registri, no. 76, fo. 141r ('qualche loco d'importa[n]tia'); BL, MS Add. 8314, fo. 298r ('dato ordine à un suo Cau.^re Bruno', 'mandò il Cau.^re Bruno à notificare à ciascuno il suo luogo nel marciare'). Colonna's retrospective account is DHI, MS Minuccio Minucci, 7, fos. 324r–329v; Doria's is BL, MS Add. 8279, fos. 188r–195v. **[29]** Setton, *Papacy*, iv, 982 (final total); BL, MS Add. 8279, fos. 202v–203r (Euboea, Vlorë, etc.); BNF, MS Italien 723, fos. 110r–111v (descriptions of Colonna–Doria quarrel by Sforza Pallavicino and Giacomo Celsi); Barbero, *La Bataille*, 261 (return to Crete, galleys lost), 271 (de' Massimi's galley). **[30]** Setton, *Papacy*, iv, 985–7 (allies on Crete); BSS, AC, Corrispondenza

Marcantonio il Grande, busta 44, no. 4451 ('feci reuerentia a nome di V. E. al S.ᵒʳ generale il qual à mal dormito questa notte et sente ancora di dolor Colici'). **[31]** Crescentio, *Nautica*, 287 ('dà 24 di Settembre per fino à 22. di Nouembre, il Nauigare non è in tutto sicuro, ne in tutto pericoloso; & in questo tempo i prudenti Prencipi . . . retirano le sue armate in porto'); 288 ('pericolosissima'); Bosio, *Dell'istoria*, iii, 869 (disease, Cephalonia), 870 ('essendosi nondimeno saluate tutte le Genti, gli Stendardi, e tutte le cose di valore, per opera, e diligenza di Fra Gaspare Bruni . . . il quale nondimeno corse in quell'occasione pericolo grandissimo di rimaner nel fuoco, o nell'acqua estinto. Percioche mentre si trateneua egli nella Galera, per saluar, e dar ordine alle più importanti cose, fù dalle fiamme sforzato à gettarsi in Mare'); Barbero, *La Bataille*, 272 (decommissioned); Guglielmotti, *Storia*, vi, 102–6 (Kassiopi, Kotor, Dubrovnik); Setton, *Papacy*, iv, 988 (Kassiopi, Kotor, Dubrovnik, Ancona); BSS, AC, II CF 2, fo. 384v (laudatory narrative). **[32]** BSS, AC, II CF 2, fo. 288r (wreck, mill-house, Dubrovnik); de Torres, *Chronica*, fo. 26v ('negaron que no sabian dellos teniendolos escondidos'); Voinovich, 'Depeschen', 551–2, 556, 558 (Gondola); DAD, LCP, 1, fo. 234r (Sept.), 3, fos. 7v (equipment), 108v (1,011 scudi, reminder in 1578); Serrano, ed., *Correspondencia*, iv, 98 (Nov.); BSS, AC, II CF 4, fo. 1r (money spent); Guglielmotti, *Storia*, vi, 106 (Ancona, Rome). **[33]** Bazzano, *Marco Antonio*, 134 (9 galleys lost; Granvelle), 377 ('no [es] mucha cosa dezir que el Rey puede confiar de Marco Antonio, pues tambien mejor puede confiar Su Mag.ᵈ en su hermana y por esto no le daria cargo de guerra').

7. REBELLION AND OTTOMAN CONQUEST

[1] Barbero, *La Bataille*, 84 (raids, Dalmatia, esp. Zadar), 107 (1,000 men); Setton, *Papacy*, iv, 953 (raids, Dalmatia, Albania). **[2]** On Cypriots welcoming Ottoman rule see Barbero, *La Bataille*, 239–40, 247–8; this interpretation is contested by Costantini, *Il sultano*, 62–4, but cf. Barbero's listing of contemporary sources (593, n. 16). On pro-Ottoman revolts in Crete in 1571 see Barbero, 355–6. **[3]** On the development of the clans in the north see Kaser, *Hirten*, 107–11; Pulaha, 'Formation'; Thëngjilli, *Renta*, 43–5; on Himarë see Floristán Imízcoz, 'Los contactos' (quasi-clans, revolts); Duka, 'Aspekte' (population growth). **[4]** Masiá, ed., *Cartas*, 140 ('fina el paese de Duchagini', bishop; I take 'Fiomara' here as a mistranscription of 'Himara' or 'Chimara'). **[5]** Floristán Imízcoz, 'Los contactos', vol.13, 53–4 (taxation, revolt, gunpowder; the further request was brought by 'Gioni Alexi Zaccani', identified by Floristán Imízcoz as 'Zaccaria', but surely 'Zahne', a leading Himariot); Setton, *Papacy*, iv, 903 (Piyale force, 8,000 men); Marmora, *Della historia*, 338 (Piyale force, 10,000 men); Chasiōtēs, *Oi Ellēnes*, 153–4 (Tsountsaros, 'arvanitovlachos'); Charrière, ed., *Négociations*, iv, 762 ('escorte': Apr. 1570). For Ciucciaro's frequent attempts to stimulate Western support for Albania see Magdaleno, ed., *Papeles*, 86, 107, 115, 116, 122, 215. **[6]** Floristán Imízcoz, 'Los contactos', vol. 13, 53–4 (Sopot), 74 (2 palms thick); Karaiskaj, *Die spätantiken*, 247–50 (Sopot); Hysi, *Southern Albanian*,

152–4 (Sopot); Zamputi, 'Disa fletë', 22 (Mormori, noting that he was described as very experienced in this territory; he was from Nafplio in the Peloponnese, so perhaps from the Albanian population there (on which see Raça, *Shtegtimet*, 163–4)); Chasiōtēs, *Oi Ellēnes*, 150–1 (Margariti). **[7]** BNM, MS It. VII. 213, fo. 334r (200 enslaved); Barbero, *La Bataille*, 162–3 (29–30 June); Manoussacas, 'Lepanto', 227–8, 235–6 (Mani revolt); Lesure, *Lépante*, 67 (Malaxas); Chasiōtēs, *Oi Ellēnes*, 59–65 (Barelli), 129–33 (agent from Chios); Canosa and Colonnello, *Spionaggio*, 84–90 (Barelli). On Albanians in the Peloponnese see Raça, *Shtegtimet*. **[8]** Pulaha, *Qëndresa*, 60–75 (Dukagjin revolts); Gürkan, 'Espionage', 226 (1571 collaboration); Barbero, *La Bataille*, 160 (Ulcinj, Bar attack); Zamputi, ed., *Dokumente*, i, 266 (Ulcinj attack, reported in Venice 14 June: 700 men, stradiots; I take 'Devino' to be a mistranscription of 'Ducaino'); Ljubić, 'Marijana Bolice', 199–200 (larger incursion, grain exhausted). **[9]** Ljubić, 'Marijana Bolice', 193–200 ('Relazione dell'Albania e sue città, fiumi, monti, laghi, piani, confini etc.'), 196–8 (grain, pitch, 'io ho veduto vendersi tre o quattro libre grosse al soldo' (the libra grossa was 12 oz; the author also gives the price of mineral pitch at Vlorë), Elbasan, Berat), 200 (written in harvest-time, 'li Dulcignani potranno andar alli Reddoni, dove sono aspettati da quei Albanesi con grand'amorevollezza non ostante la guerra Turchesca, perchè essi non danno piena obbedienza alli Turchi, e questi potranno estrazer dalli Reddoni ogni sorte di biave in gran copia a beneficio non solamente dei Dulcignani ma per sostentamento della città d'Antivari, la qual è come assediata, per non esser a marina, e per sostentamento di Budua, Cattaro e Dalmatia, conciosiacosachè al tempo di pace si cavava dal golfo del Drino fino a 50.000 stara d'ogni sorte di biave per la città di Venezia'). The text is reprinted in Zamputi, ed., *Dokumente*, i, 273–88, and translated in Elsie, *Early Albania*, 59–66. **[10]** Ljubić, 'Marijana Bolice', 194–5 (Durrës, Shkodër), 196–7 ('della Medoa', 'Sacca'), 198–9 ('per il mio gusto', *sancakbeyis*, 'pericolosissimo', 'inespugnabile', previous war); BMC, MS Provenienze diverse, 581. c. misc., fo. 22r–v (Antonio, letters to Girolamo Zane and Sforza Pallavicino, 13 Dec. 1570; Pallavicino, letter to Antonio, 19 Dec. 1570). The surviving MS of the anonymous text is a copy made in the early 18th century by Antonio Bisanti, a scholar from Kotor who spent much time in Venice and gathered materials there. **[11]** Čoralić and Kardić, *Pisma*, 85–6 ('l'altre, che sono molte: le quali per essere la sicurezza della Fortezza di Scutari sono di grandissima importanza', 'Con le solleuationi, et ribellioni di questi huomini bellicosi … et con la noua in questi giorni venuta della Vittoria (la Iddio gratia) dell'armata della Vostra Serenità contra il suo nemico tutta questa Prouincia è talmente alterata, che non desiderano, che vedere una mezza ombra di stendardo di misser San Marco per prender l'armi in seruitio di lei', 'Et io … quando hauessi hauuto li soldati, che tante uolte le ho ricercato hauerei fatto tal dimostratione del desiderio che io ho di seruire alla Patria mia, che la Vostra Serenità non mi riputerebbe indegno cittadino suo'); Conti, *Delle historie*, ii, 128–9 (other tactics). **[12]** Conti, *Delle historie*, ii, 129 (Bunë to Shkodër); ASVen, Annali, 3, fos. 269v (Donato, 4 Oct.: baptism, instruction); 302r–v (Venier, 14 Oct.: 'i primarij de i villagi dell'Albania di quà del Drino', 28 villages), 321r (Venier, 30 Oct.: list of 37 villages). **[13]** ASVen, Annali, 3, fos. 269v–270r (Donato report, 6 Oct.: letter from Briska, 'alcuni uechij', visit, message, diamond), 270r–v (letter from Briska in Italian), 270v (Bruni report on Briska visit: Shkodër situation, Mustafa Bey willing to surrender; Bruni letter to Mustafa: 'A uoi Mustaffa beg parente mio car.^mo salute nel S.^re', 'Cristo S.^or n[ost]ro ui illumini à riconoscer la uera, et piu secura strada'), 340r (Donato report, 10 Nov.: return of *sancakbeyi*), 366v–367r (Bruni, report on river-port meeting); Barbero, *La Bataille*, 159 (Venier's doubts); Zamputi, ed., *Dokumente*, i, 307 (nocturnal visit); Novak, ed., *Commissiones*, 95–6 (Contarini). Mustafa's precise relation to Bruni is not known; nor is the rest of his career. He was evidently not the Mustafa Bey who was *sancakbeyi* of Dukagjin at this time (see Pulaha, *Qëndresa*, 51). **[14]** BMC, MS Provenienze diverse, 581. c. misc., fos. 22r (returned 14 Aug., 'ben disponere, et confermar gl'Animi di questi nostri Albanesi nella fede uerso il Ser.^mo Dominio'), 22v ('un Cap.^o Valoroso, et esperto ad espugnar lochi così con artelaria, come con scale, et con mine di fuochi', 'la conquista d'Albania'); ASVen, Annali, 3, fo. 323r ('ho talmente disposto gl'animi di e nostri Albanesi, che niente altro manca ad effettuar il negocio et che l'Albania retorni sotto il stendardo della Sta v. eccetto le galee, et un cap.^o con qualche n.^o de soldati', 'perche ... l'Albania è mia patria, et molto credono alle promesse mie, le qual sono che V. Sta non è per abbandonarli mai, ma li conseruara per sudditi, et grati seruitori, pero talmente sono infiamati contra li Turchi, che magior difficoltà è di retenerli che non faciano auanti tempo furioso impeto, che di eccitarli à prender l'armi contra di loro ... alla Sta v. prometto gl'animi dagl'Albanesi resoluti di uenir sotto l'obedienza sua, et gli offerisco la mia uita, con li mei figlioli, et robba in seruitio et honor suo'). The reply from Sforza Pallavicino, the infantry commander, sent from Budva on 19 Dec., politely promised to pass on the request to the authorities in Venice when he got there: BMC, MS Provenienze diverse, 581. c. misc., fo. 22v. **[15]** ASVen, Annali, 3, fos. 410v–411r (Bruti report, 15 Dec.: urging by Dukagjin, Bruti's advice, 'oue li n[ost]ri subito si impatronirono d[e]l borgo, et li Turchi fugirono, et si serorno nel castello, et alli 9, il Sanzacco de Ducagin ue[n]ne co[n] 200 lanze per soccorrerli, ma fu da noi rotto, et fugato, Et perche queste n[ostr]e genti non sono esperti, et il tempo si fece cattiuo, h[aue]ndo i n[ost]ri sachegiato, et abbrugiato il borgo, se ne tornassero à casa', 'mandar soldati, arme, et galee, accio ch[e] possiamo prender non solo il castello di Alessio, ma anco la fortezza di Scutari, et l'altre Terre nemiche'), 424v–425r (Venier report, 4 Jan.: Mat revolt); Barbero, *La Bataille*, 159 (Lezhë); Zamputi, ed., *Dokumente*, i, 306 (other account, referring mistakenly to Shkodër); Marmora, *Della historia*, 342 (Margariti). **[16]** Pulaha, *Qëndresa*, 51 (Dec. 1570); Binark, ed., *12 Numaralı*, ii, 51–2 (Shkodër, mid-Feb.), 132–3 (13 Mar.: 'Bar ve Ülgün nâm harbî kal'alar keferesi Arnavud âsîlerin ıdlâl idüp'), 154–5 (eyes and ears), 165–6 (4 Mar.). **[17]** Chasiōtēs, *Oi Ellēnes*, 157–9 (Dukagjin request); Morosini, *Historia*, 396 (Margariti), 397 (Barbarigo, captain); ASVen, Annali, 4, fo. 30v (Donato report, 21 Mar. 1571: 'impatronirsi di tutta l'Albania, Seruia, Chercegouina, et molti altri, non essendosi altra fortezza fino à Const.^li'). **[18]** BNM, MS It. VII. 11, fos. 251r–v (Margariti), 252r (Nivica, 'grosso num^o de Albanesi'); Molmenti, *Sebastiano*, 289 (Kardhiq plan, hostages, corsair, wind), 290 (Durrës, failure at Kardhiq); Karaiskaj, *Die spätantiken*, 201–2 (Kardhiq described); Morosini, *Historia*, 396 (Durrës, artillery). **[19]** Vargas-Hidalgo, *La batalla*, 214–15 (30,000, 4 Apr. report); BSS, AC, Corrispondenza Marcantonio il Grande, busta 67, no. 3890 (early Mar. report); BSS, AC, II CF 2, fo. 443r (mid-Apr.); ASVen, CCD, Dispacci (Lettere) di Ambasciatori, busta 4, item 16 ('par che la più ferma opinione sia ch'egli uada per Dalmatia'); Lesure, *Lépante*, 66 (Transylvania). **[20]** Setton, *Papacy*, iv, 1002(n.) (9 Apr.); Novak, ed., *Commissiones*, 99 (2,500); Passerini, 'Malatesta' (biography); Mallett and Hale, *Military Organization*, 314–23 (condottieri, sources of troops, Priuli). On the date of arrival in Kotor: Barbero says after 15 Apr. (*La Bataille*, 326); Morosini says the end of May (*Historia*, 397), but the report of Malatesta's capture is from 31 May (see below, n. 22). **[21]** Novak, ed., *Commissiones*, 99–100 (meetings, 'quei principali della Bogiana'); Morosini, *Historia*, 397 (Lezhë–Shkodër plan); Gentilezza, 'L'Albania', 67 ('per confermar in fede gli Albanesi, fatti non [*sic*, for 'nuovi'] sudditi di Venetiani', 'Drugnini' [*sic*, for 'Ducagini'], Lezhë–Shkodër plan). **[22]** Novak, ed., *Commissiones*, 100 (2,000 more); Gentilezza, 'L'Albania', 67 (Lezhë–Shkodër plan, hostages), 68–9 (expedition of 200 + 500, capture); BAV, MS Urb. Lat. 1042, fo. 70v (expedition of 200, 100 casualties); ASVen, Annali, 4, fo. 119v (Donato report, 4 June 1571: 'disperatione grandiss.ᵃ'). Morosini's account (*Historia*, 398) suggests the more elaborate expedition; the governor of Kotor's (Novak, ed., 100) suggests the simpler one, attacking Orahovac, just north of Kotor. **[23]** Guerrini, *Una celebre famiglia*, 416–19, 430–2 (Martinengo biography); Barbero, *La Bataille*, 290 (ban lifted); Mallett and Hale, *Military Organization*, 347 (Brescia forbidden); BAV, MS Urb. Lat. 1042, fo. 81r (Chioggia fight, noting they killed some of their own men too); Charrière, ed., *Négociations*, iii, 262–3(n.) (Chioggia fight, dating it to before Easter, i.e. 15 Apr.); Novak, ed., *Commissiones*, 104 (like plague). **[24]** Novak, ed., *Commissiones*, 100 (spies, request for Sveti Srdj); ASVen, Annali, 4, fos. 146v–147v (Suriano report, from Budva, 9 July); 146v: 'in compagnia d'Albanesi'). The river-port was named after the nearby abbey of SS. Sergius and Bacchus. 'Shirgj'/'Sergio' was often mistaken by Italians for 'Giorgio'; the place is called Sveti Djordje (St George) today. **[25]** Barbero, *La Bataille*, 320 (Zadar plan), 353–61 (raids, Crete to Corfu), 365 (Sopot); Doglioni, *Historia*, 849–50 (account of Sopot). Contarini, *Della veneta*, ii, 133–4, gives a heroically defiant speech to Mormori, and describes a large nocturnal attack; one early report says that after resisting the initial attack, most defenders fled in the night (Gentilezza, 'L'Albania', 70); Doglioni's account partly reconciles the two; but Fedele Fedeli describes a prolonged assault, from which only a few defenders escaped with the Himariots' help: BNM, MS It. VII. 11, fos. 265v–266r. **[26]** Morosini, *Historia*, 405 (15,000); Doglioni, *Historia*, 850 (70,000); Contarini, *Della veneta*, ii, 134 (70,000); Gentilezza, 'L'Albania', 70 (80,000), 71 (artillery); ASVen, Annali, 4, fos. 147v (Suriano: 30,000), 154v–155r (Venier report, 18 July), 155r (Venier report, 20 July: 'prendono i fagoti, et s'ascondono'), 155r (reply by Contarini, governor of Kotor), 168v (Martinengo: 80,000); Ljubić, ed., *Commissiones*, iii, 260 (Feb. report). **[27]** ASVen, Annali, 4, fo. 167v (Suriano report, 1 Aug.:

bombardment 29 July, Martinengo went to Ulcinj that day, injured same day); Gentilezza, 'L'Albania', 71 (artillery bastion, masonry); Novak, ed., *Commissiones*, 101 (contemplated flight, Martinengo went to Ulcinj); BAV, MS Urb. Lat. 1042, fo. 358r (food and water, bell, 'portato uia come morto', deputy); Ljubić, 'Marijana Bolice', 199 ('pericolosissimo'). [28] ASVen, Annali, 4, fos. 168v (Venier report, 14 Aug.; Martinengo report: 'impauriti'), 169r ('essendo la citta debole con mancamento di vettaglie, et munitioni, et di materia da far repari'); Gentilezza, 'L'Albania', 71-2 (Ragusan report, claims about ammunition); BAV, MS Urb. Lat. 1042, fo. 358r (lack of water); BNM, MS It. VII. 11, fo. 266r-v (Fedeli). [29] Albèri, ed., *Relazioni*, ser. 3, iii, 188 (Pertev Albanian); von Saurau, *Orttenliche Beschreybung*, 109 (Pertev Albanian, aged *c*.60 in 1567); Radonić, ed., *Dubrovačka akta*, ii(2), 330 (Ahmed a Slav from Hercegovina); Gentilezza, 'L'Albania', 70 (Ahmed an Orthodox Serb from Herceg Novi); Morosini, *Historia*, 405 ('Orembeius' from Lucca, 'Antonius Brutus Olchiniensis eques, qui egregiam Reipublicae operam in Epyro nauauerat, deditionem impugnauerat, Acmatisque conatibus obstiterat, summam aduersus se gentis inuidiam veritus, Liburnica conscensa, cùm in Apuliam transiturus in altum se eiecisset, à Turcica triremi interceptus, captiuus ad Halim Bassam est perductus'); BAV, MS Urb. Lat. 1042, fo. 358v (3 assaults). [30] Venturini, 'La famiglia', 367 (family tradition). Cf. also the statement by his son Bartolomeo that he was executed by the Ottomans: below, 264. [31] BAV, MS Urb. Lat. 1042, fo. 358v (entrato q[ue]l da Terra fece tagliar à pezzi tutti q[ue]lli, che erano restati, et dare il fuoco ad alquante case che erano piene de donne & putti'); Anon., *Gli avisi ultimi*, [fo. 4r] (resentment); Sereno, *Commentari*, 129 (resentment); Gentilezza, 'L'Albania', 73 ('loro ritiratisi in alcune case si difesero con gran valore, alle quali fu dato fuoco, onde una parte di essi fu abrugiata et l'altra fu ammazzata non senza grande uccisione di Turchi'; the version of this report in the Ragusan archive has a slightly different wording, adding that they fought for six hours: Radonić, ed., *Dubrovačka akta*, ii(2), 278). [32] Morosini, *Historia*, 404 (Mrkojevići); Novak, ed., *Commissiones*, 101 ('Antiueri poi fornido di vituaglie, Di Munitionij, di soldati, et altra gente valorosa da combatere, senza chel campo li fosse uenuto sotto senza che l'armata hauesse fatto segno di sbarcare uilisiuamente [*sic*, for uilisimamente] si rese o fu reso a turchi'); BAV, MS Urb. Lat. 1042, fo. 358v ('Il Podesta di quel luogo senza uoler aspettare pur una botta d'archebuso si rese, al ca.° di mare. Non ostante, che i soldati, per quanto si dice, uolessero combattere & aspettare al manco uno o doi assalti'). [33] BAV, MS Urb. Lat. 1042, fo. 142v (Donato punishment); Conti, *Delle historie*, 128 ('vna parte de i cittadini incominciò à tumultuare, dicendo, non volere in si estremo disagio di tutte le cose necessarie sperimentare la fortuna della guerra'); Morosini, *Historia*, 405 ('Ioannes Brunus Antibaris Antistes Antonij Bruti affinis summa in religionem pietate, magna in Venetos fide ad hostium impetum fortiter sustinendum, nèque per metum, atque ignauiam hosti se deditionem facerent, vehementi dicendi ardore incitauerat', Hürrem Bey); Kesterčanek, 'Pad grada', 569-72 (Vidaccioni; 571: 'debbole'). [34] BAV, MS Urb. Lat. 1042, fo. 358v ('Quelli del paese restornò tutti nelle sue case'); Kesterčanek, 'Pad grada', 570-2 (affidavits);

Gentilezza, 'L'Albania', 73 ('subito molte famiglie della seconda Classe rinegorno Christo, per potersi con si scelerata occasione vendicare delle Antiche inimicitie, che havevano con li nobili'). Milošević, 'Boka Kotorska', 22, says that quarrels between nobles and townsmen played a role in the fall of Ulcinj, but I have seen no evidence of this. I discount, as obviously fictitious, the story that Donato and the entire garrison left secretly, and that Bruni was celebrating Mass in the cathedral when Ottoman soldiers unexpectedly entered and killed him (Kesterčanek, 'Pad grada', 567).   **[35]** Gentilezza, 'L'Albania', 72 (hostility to Gascons), 73 (Budvans and Kotor); Novak, ed., *Commissiones*, 102 (reoccupied); Barbero, *La Bataille*, 368 (lost again), 502 (women freed); ASVen, Annali, 4, fos. 168r (11 Aug. report), 169r (dozen); BSS, AC, II CF 3, fo. 60r (list of Christian women and children freed at Lepanto); BAV, MS Urb. Lat. 1042, fo. 359r (naked).   **[36]** İnalcık, 'Lepanto', 187 (20 corsair galleys), 188 (jubilation); Gentilezza, 'L'Albania', 73 (garrisons); Bartl, 'Die Dulcignoten', 19 (corsair claim); Zirojević, *Ulcinj*, 55 (corsair claim); Villain-Gandossi, 'Contribution', vol. 28, 36 (1592); Ljubić, 'Marijana Bolice', 173, 191 (local inhabitants' piracy 1614); Miović, *Dubrovačka republika*, 124 (sporadic till 1630s); Pedani, *Dalla frontiera*, 34 (sporadic till 1670s).   **[37]** İnalcık, 'Lepanto', 188 (deserted); BNF, MS Français 16,142, fo. 113v ('si contagieuse et chaulde, quil ny demeure presque rien, de sorte que les Villes de Dulcine Antiuary et Boudoua ... Castelnouo durazzo et Infinies autres sont presque habandonnees tant des habitans dicelles que des soldatz'); Biegman, *Turco-Ragusan*, 114 (olive-groves 1582); DAD, LCL, 34, fos. 201v–202r, 211r (Ragusan oil purchases from Bar 1583); Rački, 'Izvještaj', 65 (Bar 1610: Muslim minority, cathedral, residence); ASVat, Congr. Concilii, Relat. Dioec. 56, fasc. 1, fos. 1v–2v (Bar 1618: Muslim majority, churches).

8. THE LEPANTO CAMPAIGN

[1] Barbero, *La Bataille*, 294–5 (Zane); Mallett and Hale, *Military Organization*, 306 (Zane, Pallavicino); Bazzano, *Marco Antonio*, 136 (cardinal's lobbying); Aglietti, 'La partecipazione', 93 (son of Cosimo).   **[2]** Capponi, *Lepanto*, 142 (Spanish difficulties); Serrano, ed., *Correspondencia*, iv, 175–82, 185–7 (Philip's instructions); Levin, *Agents*, 98–9 (envoys' policy).   **[3]** Capponi, *Lepanto*, 147–9 (Ragazzoni mission); Stella, 'Lepanto', 230 (admitted later); Bosio, *Dell'istoria*, iii, 871 (Maltese intelligence); ASVen, CCD, Dispacci (Lettere) di Ambasciatori, busta 4, item 16 ('per ciò era p[er] fargli gran guerra, et che le piglierebbe et candia, et corfú', 'il suo s:ʳᵉ haueua forze da resister à tutti, et da guerreggiar in molti luochi in un tempo medesmo, oltra che'l sapeua benissimo quanto pocho si potesse fidare la ser. v. delli Principi christ.i').   **[4]** Yriarte, *La vie*, 159–60 (early May message (dated '4', but actually 7, May)); BNF, MS Italien 723, fos. 101r–102v (14 Apr. speech), 103r–105r (requests, demands, replies to them); Stella, 'Lepanto', 231 (6 May, 'giovane desideroso di gloria'); Rivero Rodríguez, *La batalla*, 128–9 (mutual distrust overcome). As a result of the new Venetian optimism Ragazzoni and Barbaro became over-confident, at one point even demanding that the Sultan give Venice Vlorë, Durrës and Herceg Novi in exchange for Famagusta (see Barbero, *La Bataille*, 313). **[5]** Jačov, *L'Europa*, 166–84 (articles of League). Guglielmotti, *Storia*, vi, 125–6, gives a slightly different version of the text. **[6]** Anon., *Il bellissimo*, sigs. [2r]–[3r] ('non vi dico poi il rumore, le allegrezze che si fece di campane, di arteglierie, e gridi del popolo; subito che fu letta la Lega, e publicata, quasi tutti piangeuano, e rideuano tutt'a vn tempo di allegrezza'). **[7]** Aglietti, 'La partecipazione', 88 (investigating possibility, Spanish opposition), 90 (Genoa alternative), 106(n.) (Colonna dissuading), 107 (sticking-point, reduction). Some accounts ascribe all 12 galleys to the Order of Santo Stefano, but only 5 were in fact drawn from it (see Aglietti, 130, 133(n.)). **[8]** Ibid., 112–13 (contract; 112: 'concerto di trombetti et ogni altra cosa solita portarsi da l'altre galere Capitane'); Capponi, *Lepanto*, 174 (figures for 1570); Salimei, *Gli italiani*, 73–4 (appointments), 75 (correctly giving Bruni as captain), 76(n.) (historians' suppositions). The contract is also given in Theiner, ed., *Annales*, i, 464–5. **[9]** Guglielmotti, *Storia*, vi, 153–7 (Civitavecchia, Serbelloni); Barbero, *La Bataille*, 347 (Pope's order); Zapperi, 'Bonelli' (biography, scheming); Salimei, 'La nobiltà', 14–15 (Ghislieri, Capizucchis, Orsini); Foglietta, *Istoria*, 359 (Carafa); Promis, 'Biografie', 208–22 (Serbelloni); dal Pozzo, *Historia*, i, 13 (Romegas, Bruni). **[10]** Guglielmotti, *Storia*, vi, 157–8 (Naples, Messina); Barbero, *La Bataille*, 373–6 (Naples, strategic uncertainties, Granvelle), 377 (Venier); de Torres, *Chronica*, fo. 36r–v (fight); Capponi, *Lepanto*, 191 (viceregal palace), 199 (Korčula, Hvar); Molmenti, *Sebastiano*, 84(n.) (Hvar), 296 (Venier); Foretić, 'Korčula' (Korčula). **[11]** Guglielmotti, *Storia*, vi, 166–72 (Don John, discussions), 177 (Cretan squadron), 179 (review), 181–3 (council, departure); Serrano, *La liga*, i, 116–17 (Spanish report); Barbero, *La Bataille*, 429–31 (Doria, Santa Cruz); Civale, *Guerrieri*, 78 (fasts, Masses, procession, 'infiniti cavalieri'), 114 (quayside); Brunelli, *Soldati*, 16 (chaplains). **[12]** Guglielmotti, *Storia*, vi, 186–7 (arrival, news of enemy fleet), 197–8 (spies into mainland); Barbero, *La Bataille*, 438–9 (renewed attack), 477 (landing party members); Monga, ed. and tr., *Journal*, 133 (Albanian spy). **[13]** Barbero, *La Bataille*, 456 (Karaca Ali), 476–7 (Kara Hoca, Ottoman underestimate of Christian fleet), 652 (Germans); BSS, AC, II CF 2, fo. 132r ('malissimo ad ordine di gente cosi da combatter; come da remo; p[er]che quest'anno hanno hauuto malissimo modo di armar, per mancamento di gente'); Carinci, ed., *Lettere*, 58–9 (early Aug. report); BAV, MS Urb. Lat. 1042, fo. 327r (later Aug. slave report); Fernández Navarrete *et al.*, eds., *Correspondencia*, 192 (other informant); BL, MS Add. 8314, fo. 301r–v ('e gli Tedeschi sono poco utili in mare, et hanno pocco archibugiara', 'io non credo che li nemici possano hauer gente molto buona, ne miglior della n[ost]ra', 'Quanto poi al numero, e qualità de legni dell'Armata Turchesca, son tanto differenti gli auuisi, che io non sò molto ben giudicare s'ella è inferiore, ò superiore alla n[ost]ra'). I follow here the analysis of the Ottoman fleet in Barbero, 484–5; Bicheno, *Crescent*, 300, and Capponi, *Lepanto*, 274–5, give larger estimates. **[14]** Capponi, *Lepanto*, 210 (4 Oct.); Setton, *Papacy*, iv, 1037–42 (fall of Famagusta); Barbero, *La Bataille* , 413–22 (fall of Famagusta); BL, MS Add. 8279, fos. 238v–239r (treatment of Bragadin). **[15]** de Cervantes, *Don*

Quixote, 344 (part 1, ch. 38). This brief summary draws on: Guilmartin, *Gunpowder*, 149–63 (firearms, artillery); Capponi, *Lepanto*, 165–9 (artillery); Cerezo Martínez, *Años cruciales*, 38–43 (artillery); Bicheno, *Crescent*, 77–85 (firearms, artillery); Rodgers, *Naval Warfare*, 187 (fire-balls). More generally, one military handbook said crossbows were better than arquebuses because they worked in the rain and did not give away the user's position at night (Palazzuolo, *Il soldato*, 64). **[16]** My account draws on the three best modern works, Barbero, *La Bataille*, Capponi, *Lepanto*, and Bicheno, *Crescent*, as well as Cerezo Martínez, *Años cruciales*, Rivero Rodríguez, *La batalla*, and Muscat, 'Lepanto'; I give references here only for specific points not generally treated there. Rodgers, *Naval Warfare*, 178 (four miles); Bicheno, *Crescent*, 247 (map of islands, modern coastline). **[17]** Groto, ed., *Trofeo*, sigs. †7v–†8r (second shock); dal Pozzo, *Historia*, i, 24 (engaged by sons of Ali); Sereno, *Commentari*, 208 (great-nephew, majordomo). **[18]** Manoussacas, 'Lepanto', 228–9 (Greek crews); Conti, *Delle historie*, ii, 150–1 (4, 5 galleys, scrivano); Sereno, *Commentari*, 201 (Soranzo); Caracciolo, *I commentarii*, 39 (death of Ali). **[19]** Caracciolo, *I commentarii*, 45 ('la credenza c'hebbero i nimici del terreno'); Cerezo Martínez, *Años cruciales*, 182–4; Guilmartin, *Gunpowder*, 246–50; Barbero, *La Bataille*, 513–24 (523: 'inévitable'), 650 (half new recruits). On Ottoman desertions see also Lesure, *Lépante*, 93, and Williams, *Empire*, 70–1. Williams also stresses the depletion of the Ottoman rowing crews; but their strength was not a critical factor once the galleys were engaged in close combat. **[20]** Peçevi, *Historija*, i, 405 (argument); Barbero, *La Bataille*, 477–8 (argument: Western sources); BNF, MS Supplément turc 926 (translation of Zirek's text by the student dragoman Antoine Fonton in 1743). On the later Ottoman historiography see Yıldırım, 'Battle'. On Zirek (not mentioned by Yıldırım) see Babinger, *Geschichtsschreiber*, 113–14; Schmidt, *Catalogue*, iii, 74–5; on the translation see Berthier, 'Turquerie', esp. 314. **[21]** BNF, MS Supplément turc 926, 4 ('les soldats non contents de se saisir du bien des habitants, enlevoient les femmes, et les filles, les jeunes, et les vieillards'), 8–10 (25,000, Kara Hoca), 19 (blames Ali), 20 (40–50), 24 ('de tous cotéz des coups de canons semblables a un tonnerre, la noble flotte etoit entourrée d'une fumée epaise qui couvroit le Ciel'), 25 ('les hommes succomboient sous la grêle des bales de fusil'), 26 (inaccurate), 36–8 ('A cette nouvelle l'armée Ottomane devint comme un potager ruiné par la Grêle, ou une ville assiezgée; les forces manquerent aux soldats, on abandonna les vaissaux qu'on avoit pris sur l'ennemi, et chacun chercha dans la fuite son salut ... Les Infidels qui s'étoient dispersés comme des chiens enragéz ... reprirent courage, et devinrent plus furieux qu'un dragon a sept testes'); Yıldırım, 'Battle', 534 (Katib). **[22]** Caracciolo, *I commentarii*, 42 ('il mare era pieno d'huomini morti, di tauole, di vesti[,] d'alcuni Turchi, che fuggiuano à nuoto, d'altri che affogauano, di molti fracassi di vascelli, che ardeuano, & altri che andauano à fondo'); Sereno, *Commentari*, 210–11 ('piena di giubbe, di turbanti, di carcassi, di frecce, di archi, di tamburri', 'colpi di archibugiate e di zagagliate'); Foglietta, *Istoria*, 369 (hands). Sereno was an eyewitness, but this description seems to have adapted de Torres, *Chronica*, fo. 74r; cf. also the 'anonymous' text edited by Pagès (in fact a version of de Torres), *La*

Bataille, 153. **[23]** Caracciolo, *I commentarii*, 44 (12,000); Capponi, *Lepanto*, 244 (12–15,000); de Torres, *Chronica*, fo. 73v ('como oyeron dezir victoria, victoria, rompiendo las cadenas, con las armas de los Turcos que hauia derramadas hizieron grande estrago y mortandad, vengandose de las muchas injurias y crueldades que dellos hauian rescibido'); Barbero, *La Bataille*, 510 (flag); Caracciolo, *I commentarii*, 44. **[24]** Giacomo Foscari, cited in Barbarano, *Historia*, iv, 151 ('ammazzati per mano de Turchi'); Farlati, *Illyrici*, vii, 105 (Jesuit account); Jačov, *Spisi*, 133 ('nel primo assalto'); Viscovich, *Storia*, 256 ('al momento in cui la galera fu presa'). See also Milošević, 'Boka Kotorska', 23(n.). **[25]** ASVat, Misc., Arm. II, 110, fo. 384r–v ('molti soldati spagnolj ... uestiti di tutt'arme, ammazzorno molti pouerj schiaui Christiani per spogliarlj et toglier loro quella poca preda, che Dio haueua loro concessa, et tra gl'altrj uccisero il pouero Arciuescouo d'Antiuarj, fatto cattiuo dall'armata Turchesca, l'Agosto passato, quando fu presa detta Città, il quale con tutto che gridasse son Vescouo, son Christiano, non li uolsero credere, ma l'ammazzorno, et dagagliorno [*sic* – for 'zagagliorno'], et manco male se fusse stato nel combattere, ma fu molto doppo'). **[26]** Barbarano, *Historia*, iv, 151 ('prigioni del Bassà', 'schiavi del Bassà'); Barbero, *La Bataille*, 504–5 (battle), 650 (*tercio*); Capponi, *Lepanto*, 232–3 (Pertev's galley); Bicheno, *Crescent*, 250 (Cardona). **[27]** Barbarano, *Historia*, iv, 151 ('è stato di grandissimo servizio, e ajuto nostro in cose d'importanza per farli quella vittoriosa giornata, nella quale anco è stato malamente ferito', 'degno di compassione'). **[28]** Barbero, *La Bataille*, 527–8 (8,000); BIC, MS 587, fo. 409r ('molti in Constantinopoli si misero in punto per fuggirsene in Natolia et molti si raccommandauano à Christiani, et à Rinegati aspettando di giorno in giorno l'armate Christiane'); Mantran, 'L'Écho', 248–9 (chronicler's account, Uluç Ali); Lesure, *Lépante*, 180–6 (orders); İnalcık, 'Lepanto', 192 (orders); Panzac, *La Marine*, (28 Oct. order). **[29]** Patrizi, *Paralleli*, ii, 87; Carinci, ed., *Lettere*, 82 ('credo ci troveremo tanti feriti che non andremo avanti verso Costantinopoli, come si pensava di fare, non avendo vittuaglia, se non per un mese, nè potendo svernar fuori. Credo che ne torneremo in Golfo a pigliar la Velona, Durazzo e Castelnovo'); Lesure, *Lépante*, 165–6 (Margariti, Sopot); Molmenti, 'Sebastiano', 13–14 (Lefkas), 15, 59, 68–9 (Margariti, Sopot); Caracciolo, *I commentarii*, 49–50 (Lefkas). **[30]** BSS, AC, II CF 3, fos. 51r–60v ('Merinde de dulcigno Xriano reneg^to A 40' (cf. fo. 55r: 'Marin di dulcigno'), 'Martino calabrese reneg^to A 30', 'Ossain albanese reneg^to soldato 30', 'Ciafer rinegato Todesco', 'Jusuf ... Arnaut: Buonauoglia', 'Zingaro mutolo di costantinopoli', 'Giorgio di Manoli Cipriotto rinneg.^to Ragazzo'); Fernández Navarrete *et al.*, eds., *Correspondencia*, 232 (gift of slaves); March, *La batalla*, 55–6 (tenth); Barbero, *La Bataille*, 533, 536–7 (Venier, division, 100 ducats); Carinci, ed., *Lettere*, 93–4 (Messina, Naples). **[31]** Borino *et al.*, *Il trionfo*, 11–12 (triumph, Spaniards offended). **[32]** Fenlon, *Ceremonial City*, 177–83 (Venice festivities); Voltaire, *Collection*, xiii, 280 (commenting on Venice's total lack of territorial gains, and the subsequent Spanish defeat at Tunis); Braudel, *Mediterranean*, ii, 1088 ('spell'). Braudel also argues that the Christians received 'a tremendous crop of prisoners to man the oars, enough to bolster their strength for many years to come'. The official total was 3,486 (Fernández Navarrete *et al.*, eds., *Correspondencia*, 229), which, if they were all still able-bodied, would man roughly 16 galleys. The real total was probably higher; but the strategic advantage would still seem relatively slight.   **[33]** Iorga, *Byzance*, 138 (letter to Wallachia); Pippidi, 'Les Pays', 314 (letter to Wallachia); Fleet, 'Ottoman Expansion', 146 (Otranto 1480-1), 162-3 (1550s); Marmora, *Della historia*, 338 (1566); Charrière, ed., *Négociations*, iii, 59 (1569); Lesure, *Lépante*, 223 ('ont été construits précédemment dans ces régions pour le siège de Corfou'); Floristán Imízcoz, 'Los prolegómenos', 41 (1573); AGS, Estado, leg. 488, item [112] (Spanish agents); ASVen, CCD, Dispacci (Lettere) di Ambasciatori, busta 5, item 7 (bailo report, 27 May 1576); Niederkorn, *Die europäischen Mächte*, 147 (Henri IV).   **[34]** Languet, *Epistolae*, i, 184 ('Si forte Turcae occupauerint oppidum aliquod maritimum Apuliae, vel veteris Calabriae, & validas copias eo inuexerint, quod ipsis non erit difficile, ob breuem traiectum ex Macedonia & Epiro, ego non dubito, quin plerique incolae Regni Neapolitani pertaesi [*sic*] Tyrannidis Hispanicae, quae est acerbissima, ad ipsos deficiant'); Malcolm, 'Crescent' (Campanella); Masiá, ed., *Cartas*, 156 (Salerno plot, 15-20,000, 1553); Hernando Sánchez, *Castilla*, 330-4 (Salerno plot, 1551-2, Trani); Maffei, *Degli annali*, i, 99 (Ancona conspiracy). On the circumstances of the Prince of Salerno's exile and anti-Habsburg activities see Coniglio, *Il regno*, 256-61.

9: WAR, PEACE AND OTTOMAN RESURGENCE

[1] Panzac, *La Marine*, 20-4 (galleass-maker, 200 ships, 22 sites, orders, janissaries); Ágoston, *Guns*, 44-5 (Christian workers); Dursteler, *Venetians*, 84 (Cretans).   **[2]** Peçevi, *Historija*, i, 406-7 ('Ova država je takva da ako želi sva sidra može napraviti od srebra, debelu užad od svile, a jedra od atlasa, i to bez ikakvih problema'); White, *Climate*, 16(n.) (estimate of acres), 28-31 (timber supplies); Imber, 'Navy', 231-5 (cloth, pitch, tallow); BNF, MS Français 16,142, fo. 113v ('l'extreme faulte . . . de bronze p[ou]r faire de lartilherie pour les gallees et de fer pour les ancres'); Panzac, *La Marine*, 28-30 (metallurgy centres, problems); Capponi, *Lepanto*, 77, 98 (Chios). See also Lesure, *Lépante*, 229, and Imber, 'Reconstruction'.   **[3]** Charrière, ed., *Négociations*, iii, 271-2 (Malatesta detained); Stella, 'Lepanto', 243 (244 galleys); Panzac, *La Marine*, 50 (225 and 5). **[4]** Stella, 'Lepanto', 241 (green timber, artillery shortage); Albèri, ed., *Relazioni*, ser. 3, iii, 152 (1558 report); Polić Bobić, *Medju križom*, 138 (request to Dubrovnik), 149 (report from Dubrovnik); Pedani, ed., *Relazioni*, 184 (bombardiers), 187 ('lavorati da rinegati, hebrei et da Turchi'); Panzac, *La Marine*, 33-45 (mariners, rowers, soldiers, more arquebusiers); Imber, 'Reconstruction', 96 (janissaries, spahis, volunteers); BNF, MS Français 16,142, fo. 113v ('presque despeuples et deshabites'); Lesure, *Lépante*, 230 (mariners); Charrière, ed., *Négociations*, iii, 362(n.) ('une armée composée de vaisseaux neufs, bastis de bois vert, vogués de chiourmes qui n'avoient jamais tenu rame en main, garniz d'artillerie dont la fonte avoit esté hastée, et en plusieurs pièces meslée de matière aigre et corrompue, guides et mariniers apprentifs, et armez d'hommes encore estonnez du dernier combat, et qui faisoient ce voyage à coups de baston'). [5] Lesure, *Lépante*, 88–90 (1571: Patras etc., Ahmed). [6] Ibid., 89 (Elbasan, Ohrid), 194 (Salonica, Wallachia), 197–200 (Greek mainland, archipelago), 203 (Mani); Matkovski, 'Kryengritje', 56, 180 (Ottoman concern, Jan. 1572); García Hernán, 'Price', 243 (Mani); Yıldırım, 'Battle', 538 (Wallachia, Poland, Russia); Kolias, 'Epistolē' (triple strategy). [7] Molmenti, 'Sebastiano', 102 (Venier report: 'richissimi', 'solevano esser delli primarii apresso il Signor della Valacchia'); Stoicescu, *Dicţionar*, 60, 77, 312 (personal links); Beduli, *Kishë*, 64, 68, 107 (cultural links); Molmenti, *Sebastiano*, 327 ('Pano Stolico'); Pippidi, 'Les Pays', 304 (the Stolnic); BSS, AC, II CF 3, fo. 76r ('se non uorranno dar niente aiuto a noi Xriani tutti saremo presi schiaui'). [8] García Hernán, 'Price', 233 (network), 236 (30,000 scudi; but cf. Manca, *Il modello*, 83(n.), giving up to 9,000 as the normal monthly figure), 245 (king of Greece proposal); Chasiōtēs, *Makarios*, 34–5 (de Stay mission); BSB, MS Cod. Ital. 6, fo. 433v ('inuitando l'A. V. à uenir à liberarli, et promettendo di prendere l'armi, scacciar i Turchi, e darsi à V. A.'). De Stay is commonly described as from the island of Kythera (Ital.: Cerigo), perhaps on the basis of documents which merely say that he travelled to the Mani from that island; the name suggests that he belonged to the di Stai family of Dubrovnik (also called Stoiković), which was originally from Bar (see Appendini, *Notizie*, ii, 75). [9] Jačov, *L'Europa*, 212–16 (text of agreement); Brunetti and Vitale, eds., *La corrispondenza*, ii, 767–8 ('centro', 'circonferentia', 'vanamente s'espetteriano li movimenti et le sollevationi de popoli greci et albanesi et de altri christiani quando, in luoco di essere assicurati con le forze della lega, vedessero li nostri capitani impiegati in Barberia'); Levin, *Agents*, 101 (Spanish diplomats in Rome); Lesure, *Lépante*, 161 (Philip on Preveza etc.); Serrano, ed., *Correspondencia*, iv, 620 (Requesens point). [10] Braudel, *Mediterranean*, ii, 1115–16 (Don John shuttling, Philip's message 20 May); Manfroni, 'La lega', 367 (papal flagship); Aglietti, 'La partecipazione', 141(n.) (Tuscan agreement); Levin, *Agents*, 102 (instructing ministers). [11] Manfroni, 'La lega', 366 (appointment confirmed), 376–7 (Naples, Messina, Mani representatives), 380–2 (papal troops, targets, proclamation), 410–12 (ultimatum, numbers); BSS, AC, II CF 1, fos. 223r ('V.S. farà pagare al sig:ᵒʳ Caualier Bruno Capitano della nostra galera Capitana la sua prouisione conforme à come li è stata pagata l'anno passato, cioè quel che deue hauere del' decorso dal p:ᵒ di Decembre pross:ᵒ passato per tutto Maggio, et farseli continuar di pagarseli per l'auuenire nel medesimo modo, facendone pigliar riceuuta da lui'), 283r (Capizucchi); Braudel, *Mediterranean*, ii, 1116–17 (Philip, pretext). [12] Guerrini, *Una celebre famiglia*, 434–6 (Herceg Novi plan, failure); Molmenti, 'Sebastiano', 22–4, 102–20 (Herceg Novi, overconfidence); Polić Bobić, *Medju križom*, 145 (Ottoman intelligence); Theiner, ed., *Annales*, i, 473–5 (Igoumenitsa, fleet numbers); Caracciolo, *I commentarii*, 72 (soldiers captured, slave: 'maggior commodità à nimici di hauer certo auuiso di Christiani'). [13] Manfroni, 'La lega', 422–3 (Philip's decision), 429 (Cretan squadron), 431 (chronology); Braudel, *Mediterranean*, ii, 1118–19 (Philip's decision, Don John's instruction); Grimaldi, *Copia*, sigs. A2r–v (battle array, Kythera,

150 galleys, 'mal a ordine di Ciurma però piene di huomini a combattere fra le quali vi sono gran Malatie', 10 Aug.), A3v (numbers); Theiner, ed., *Annales*, i, 476 (12 miles, 140 galleys). Braudel's account of the chronology and his estimate of the superior quality of the Ottoman fleet (1120–1) are hard to reconcile with the available evidence. **[14]** Theiner, ed., *Annales*, i, 476 ('quasi tutta la Morea, perchè i Christiani stanno in arme et aspettano il fine di questo negotio'), 482–3 (hesitations, error, 'al General del Papa parse stranio col stendardo di Santa Chiesa andar solo'); Manfroni, 'La lega', 437–45 (Don John and Colonna); Caracciolo, *I commentarii*, 83 ('auuisò per lo Caualier Bruno à Don Gio: che i nimici erano partiti quella notte'). **[15]** Manfroni, 'La lega', 37–42 (aborted attempts), 52–3 (Corfu, loss); Caracciolo, *I commentarii*, 90–5 (skirmishes, aborted attempts); Theiner, ed., *Annales*, i, 485 ('molti Spagnoli et Dalmatini se ne sono passati all'inimico, et fattosi, se forsi non eran prima, Turchi'), 487 (Corfu, loss). **[16]** Manfroni, 'La lega', 53 (Lefkas); Molmenti, 'Sebastiano', 129 (Bar plan); ASVat, Fondo Borghese III 128, fasc. 1, fos. [9v] (fraudster, alchemist), [10r] ('non viue di altro che di astutie, e di ribalderie'); Šopova, ed. and tr., *Makedonija*, 34–5 (Ohrid revolt). **[17]** Stella, 'Lepanto', 232 (250,000), 246 (nuncio's report); Capponi, *Lepanto*, 124–5 (10 m.); *CSPVen.*, vii, 521 (14 m.); Pezzolo, *L'oro*, 121 (total income); du Fresne-Canaye, *Le Voyage*, 16 (Ragusan boom); Freidenberg, *Dubrovnik*, 131–2 (Ragusan boom); Lesure, *Lépante*, 244–5 (ambassador and nuncio's reports); Charrière, ed., *Négociations*, iii, 278–80 (Sokollu's suggestion), 291–2(n.) (Algiers), 310–11(n.) (Venetian envoy to France). **[18]** Charrière, ed., *Négociations*, iii, 312, 348(n.), 355 (Dax movements), 368 ('les villes prinses par ceulx-cy en l'Albanye', 50,000 ducats, comment); Gattoni, 'La spada', 619–20 (1540 terms); Predelli *et al.*, eds., *I libri*, vii, 6 (formal text, Italian); Theunissen, 'Ottoman–Venetian', 471–6 (formal text, Turkish; 475: 'Arnavudlukda ve Bosna vilayetinde'); Caracciolo, *I commentarii*, 104 (Mani, publication); Pedani, *In nome*, 165 (secret); Zamputi, ed., *Dokumente*, i, 319–20 (bailo's son, secret). **[19]** Stella, 'Lepanto', 249–50 (Pope's reaction, 'tutta accensa'); Levin, *Agents*, 104–5 (Nov.–Feb.); BAV, MS Vat. Lat. 12,199, fos. 92r–94v, '1573 Per l'Impresa contro Il Turco, dil S. P. C.' (92v: 'per quanto me uien detto'; 93r–v: Rodon, Krujë, etc., 'quelli Populi delle montagne de Ducaghini'); Bartl, *Der Westbalkan*, 221 (Samuele text). **[20]** Braudel, *Mediterranean*, ii, 1128–9 (Ottoman fleet movements), 1132–3 (Don John's fleet (107), Tunis, Bizerte); Hess, *Forgotten Frontier*, 89 (Ottoman conquest of Tunis); Anderson, *Naval Wars*, 56 (Don John's fleet (104), Bizerte); Poullet, ed., *Correspondance*, iv, 585 (Granvelle). **[21]** Villani, ed., *Nunziature*, i, 278 ('gagliarde provisioni', 'benissimo munite'); Braudel, *Mediterranean*, ii, 1134–6 (starved of resources), 1137 (40,000); Coniglio, *Il vicereggno*, ii, 372 (late-May assurance); Poullet, ed., *Correspondance*, v, 152 ('le bruict commun'); Šopova, ed. and tr., *Makedonija*, 40–1 (orders to *sancakbeyi*s); Hess, *Forgotten Frontier*, 94–5 (agents to Dutch). **[22]** Promis, 'Biografie', 231 (moat incomplete), 232 (Margliani), 233–6 (fall of La Goletta and Tunis fort), 242 (Giovanpaolo); Braudel, *Mediterranean*, ii, 1138–9 (Don John efforts); BNF, MS Supplément turc 926, 79–110 (110: 'il ny eut que cent personnes qui eschapperent, le reste ayant eté la Victoire

des Sabres des Musulmans'). On the siege see also the original reports in de la Primaudaie, 'Documents'.   [23] Guilmartin, *Gunpowder*, 18–19; Brummett, 'Ottomans', 15 (regular tasks). For examples of phrases about lordship of the sea, etc., see Barbero, *La Bataille*, 238, O'Connell, *Men of Empire*, 38, and Williams, *Empire*, 205; cf. also Tamaro, *Storia*, ii, 81–2, on the Venetian–Imperial debate of 1563 about Venice's rights over the Adriatic. As Williams notes (*Empire*, 233–7), both Spain and the Ottoman Empire did maintain quite substantial fleets in the decades after Lepanto; but the uses to which they were put had little or no geopolitical impact.   [24] Murphey, *Ottoman Warfare*, 17–18 (high cost of Ottoman navy).

10. THE BRUTIS AND BRUNIS IN ISTRIA

[1] ASVat, Segr. Stato, Malta, 1, fo. 5r ('li fr[ate]lli, parenti, et quanto haueua'); Barbarano, *Historia*, iv, 151 ('essendo morti molti honorati suoi parenti nella Città di Dulcigno per mano de Turchi'); above, 53 (nine sons; cf. the family tree in Venturini, 'La famiglia', where I discount the erroneous inclusion of an Antonio Bruti, Archbishop of Ulcinj).   [2] Venturini, 'La famiglia', 369 ('eletta da loro dopo la perdita della Patria per ferma loro habitazione'), family tree (Jacomo b. 1542; Benedetto, son of Ilarieta Bruti and Demostene Carerio, 1572).   [3] Žitko, *Koper*, 21–5 (early history); O'Connell, *Men of Empire*, 32 (own statutes); Quarantotti Gambini, 'I nobili', vol. 82, 75–6 ('più veneto che istriano, più burocratico che aristocratico'). Istria was sometimes treated as part of the Terraferma in the 15th century, but thereafter it was normally seen as part of the Stato da Mar: see Arbel, 'Colonie', 954–5.   [4] Manzuoli, *Nova descrittione*, i, 70 (court from 1584); Ljubić, ed., *Commissiones*, ii, 191 ('devotissimo', 'Tutti gli abitanti così nobili come popolari sono ornati di bellissimi costumi; gli abiti loro sono all'italiana, e vi sono molti dottori e letterati, ma il territorio tutto abitato e coltivato da gente slava'); Luciani, 'Relazioni', vol. 6, 70–2 (3,600 (applying a multiplier of 4 to the 900 fighting men, as implied by the figures given for the territory)), 75 (2,300; 'in maggior calamità per le continue carestie, tempeste et farsi pochi sali'), 384 (1583: 4,800), 439 ('poco habitata, ha molte case rovinate', 'per la povertà loro parte attendono all'agricoltura, altri al pescar, altri al navegar. In questa Nobeltà vi è quasi in tutti povertà grandissima per non si applicar a mercantia, nè ad essercicio alcuno'); Manzuoli, ed., *Rime*, 126 ('crassissime, & puzzolentissime palude'); Anon., 'Senato Mare', vol. 11, 68–9, 72 (drainage).   [5] Luciani, 'Relazioni', vol. 6, 70 (1560: 6,000), 77 ('molto più belle et comode sono le stale di terraferma, dove stan li animali bruti, che in questo territorio dove habitan li huomini con piccoli tugurij quasi tutti di paglia'), vol. 7, 97 (1596: 5,000), 106 (1598 report); Ljubić, ed., *Commissiones*, ii, 191 (Giustinian); ASVen, Collegio (Secreta), Relazioni, busta 54, item 3, fos. 77v (1591 report: 'Alemagna'), 78v–79r (salt sold for grain); Bonin, *Solne poti*, 97 (destinations of salt); Anon., 'Regesti', 76–8 (news of salt-works, order to destroy); Tamaro, *Storia*, ii, 83 (salt-works outside jurisdiction). Cf. also Manzuoli, *Nova descrittione*,

i, 9 (wine, oil, salt sold via Venice to 'Alemagna').   [6] Darovec, *Breve storia*, 86 (state property), 97 (50–70,000), 113 (Greeks, Albanians adapting); Lane, *Venetian Ships*, 224–5 (timber); Cella, 'Documenti', 229 (timber, also for firewood); ASVen, Collegio (Secreta), Relazioni, busta 54, item 2, fo. 21v ('non è ne habitato ne coltivato, come si conuerrebbe parte per lo pocho numero delle persone, parte per una negligentia naturale che uiue in loro, donde auuiene che non raccolgono quasi la metà di quello che si potria raccorre'); Vrandečić, 'Islam', 291 (1540); Ivetić, *La popolazione*, 89 (total 53,000), 89–91 (15%); Bertoša, *Mletačka Istra*, i, 67 (Cyprus refugees), 88–128 (Bologna programme); Puşcariu, *Studii*, ii, 32 (Vlachs etc.); Anon., 'Senato Mare', vol. 11, 52–8 (Cyprus and other Greek refugees). On the immigration see also Stanojević, 'Naseljavanje', 429–34.
[7] Cherini and Grio, *Le famiglie*, 39 (Albanese), 81 (Brati), 223 (Verzi from Giorgi); AST, AMC, MS 549, fos. 59v–60r (reel 687, frame 201) (Giacomo, Paolo and Pomponio Ducain); Manzuoli, *Nova descrittione*, i, 80 (Ducain family noble, but extinct by 1609); Radossi and Žitko, *Monumenta*, 420 (Verzi most powerful); Stancovich, *Biografia*, 403 (Verzo Verzi holder of many feoffs, 1254); Venturini, 'La famiglia', family tree (marriages of Jacomo, Caterina, Ilarieta, Laura, Jacoma; unlike Venturini I give the name as 'Jacoma', by analogy with her brother, who signed his name as 'Jacomo'); Schutte, *Pier Paolo*, 156 (noting a Francesco Carerio, son of Demetrio, in 1541 (perhaps uncle of this Demostene), who was a nephew of Alvise Verzi); Valentini, ed., *Acta*, xx, 174 ('fuisset causa dandi castrum Antibarj in manus nostri dominij'; cf. also xix, 75–6); Luciani, 'Notizie', 1304 ('li trasse parimenti ad habitar questa Città per la perdita ch'essi ancora fecero d'Antivari patria loro'); Marković, 'Barski patricijski rod', 81 (Bernardo Borisi, 1590). On Rizzardo Verzi's career see Anon., 'Senato Mare', vol. 12, 94. Marković's article is the fullest study of the Borisi family. Venturini writes (368) that Pietro Borisi was already resident in Koper when Jacoma married him; but the 1575 decree specified that two sisters had married there, which must refer to Caterina and Ilarieta.   [8] Venturini, 'La famiglia', 369 ('Si è dimostrata in tutti i tempi così fedele, et affezionata al Stato Nostro la Famiglia de Bruti, et particolarmente il fedelissimo et honorato Kavalier D.no Antonio Bruti di buona memoria hà prestato in tutto il corso de sua vita così diligente, e fruttuoso Servizio . . .'); AST, AMC, MS 548, fos. 82v–83r (reel 687, frame 33) ('per questo hauendo parso à m.r Iacomo Brutti da Dolcigno, et fratelli di per altra uia tentar di esser fattj di questo conseglio').   [9] Venturini, 'La famiglia', 381 (poverty); AST, AMC, MSS 549, fo. 89 bis, recto (reel 687, frame 236) ('egreggius D.nus Iacobus Bruti'), 550, fos. 6r, 8r (reel 688, frames 96, 98) (Fonteca: Demostene, Jacomo (and fo. 11r (frame 101), a statement signed in this capacity by 'Jacomo Bruti')), 32r, 33v (frames 122, 124) (appointed judge, selected by 'Collegio delle Biaue'); Manzuoli, ed., *Rime*, 128 ('solo, & vnico sostegno delli poueri').
[10] AST, AMC, MS 550, fos. 34r (reel 688, frame 124) ('il miserimo stato nel qual si ritroua questo pouero popolo, et terretorio intiero, rispetto à quelli dui banchi d' hebrei, i quali già 70 anni si ritrouano in quella Città, et con il fenero à 12[½]. per cento, hanno reduto in estrema miseria ogni stato, et condittion di persona', Monte di Pietà proposal), 34v (frame 125) ('il commercio, e traffico de'

sali, che ha questa Città di Capod:ᵃ con sudditi Arciducali, è il solo sustentam:ᵗᵒ de tutti i poueri Cittadini, et il mantenimento insieme de' datij dà sua Ser.ᵗᵃ poiche in questo modo uengono espediti i nostri sali, et in luoco loro uien à noi portato formenti, lane, formazi, biaue d'ogni sorte'), 40r (frame 130) ('stante questi calamitosi tempi la pouertà di questo fideliss.o popolo, et l'estrema inopia nella quale al pre.nte si ritroua in modo tale, che non habbi pane per otto giorni con pericolo manifestiss.o di solleuatione di popolo et di total ruina di questa Città'); Manzuoli, ed., *Rime*, 128 (1579–80 bail-out); Majer, 'Gli ebrei', 173–6 (Jews resisted); Vatova, *La colonna*, 126 (Venice's response). In fact 12½% was the maximum formally permitted by the city: see Anon., 'Senato Mare', vol. 11, 94.   **[11]** AST, AMC, MSS 550, fo. 102v (reel 688, frame 194) (grain store 1593), 551, fo. 32r (reel 689, frame 39) (giustizieri); Venturini, 'La famiglia', 379 (Captain, Sept. 1593); Anon., 'Senato Mare', vol. 12, 68–9 (Captain, Sept. 1593), 443 (death of Jacomo, 1618); Bonin, ed., *Vodnik*, 47–8 (role of Captain); ASVen, Collegio (Secreta), Relazioni, busta 54, item 2, fo. 22r ('una sorte di gente mescolata d'Istriani e Morlacchi'); Luciani, 'Relazioni', vol. 6, 403, 410 (400 to 500), vol. 7, 107 ('sono tutti questi chiamati sotto nome di schiavi, et hanno un capitano gentiluomo della città per privilegio de' cittadini, il quale in occasione di Vacantia viene elletto da rapresentanti suoi ... Ha questo carico di protegerli diffenderli, et procurar che non li venghi fatto qualche estorsione, et ha di provisione dalla camera fiscal ducᵗⁱ 156, all'anno, et al presente si ritrova capitano il Sig.ʳ Giacomo Bruti, qual essercita il carico suo con universal sodisfatione'). On the origins and meaning of 'Morlach' see Malcolm, *Bosnia*, 74–5, 79. **[12]** AST, AMC, MSS 77, fo. 180r–v (reel 115, frames 81–2) (Camilla's will), 549, fo. 184v (reel 688, frame 86) (health inspector), 550, fos. 27r (reel 688, frame 117) (overseer, 1589), 58v (frame 149) (overseer, 1591), 69v, 70r (frame 160) (cathedral overseer and judge, 1592), 102v (frame 194) (advocate, 1593); Lavrić, *Vizitacijsko poročilo*, 31 (endowment); Majer, 'Gli ebrei', 179 (Tiepolo case); Manzuoli, *Nova descrittione*, i, 79 (Brunis noble); Cherini and Grio, *Le famiglie*, 83 (Brunis noble).   **[13]** Schutte, *Pier Paolo* (Vergerio); Muzio, *Selva* (polemics); Luglio, *L'antico vescovado*, 145–6 (vindictive); Tacchella and Tacchella, *Il Cardinale Agostino Valier*, 54–5 (12 tried); Lavrić, *Vizitacijsko poročilo*, 31–3 (revenues, canons, not preaching), 34 (no printers, 'Nescit certo quod in hac urbe sint haeretici, sed de nonnullis suspicatur'), 37 (seminary), 52–3 (request for Jesuit college); above, 69 (500 ducats minimum).   **[14]** Ziliotto, *Capodistria*, 53 (procession, 'bellissimo mottetto', paintings); Ludwig and Molmenti, *Vittore Carpaccio*, 42–5 (family connection, arguing against birth there); Naldini, *Corografia*, 174–5 (Titians; I am very grateful to Prof. Charles Hope for his comments on this); Manzuoli, *Nova descrittione*, i, 72–3 (monasteries, churches, 'bellissima'), 89 (Cristoforo Verzi); Luglio, *L'antico vescovado*, 148 (Ingegneri); Ingegneri, *Fisionomia*; Tasso, *Gerusalemme*, sig. †5v ('vniuersal eruditione'); Grmek, *Santorio*; Santorio, *La medicina*, 5–16; Ziliotto, *Accademie*, 16–33 (academy; 23, 33: Valdera); Valdera, *Epistole*. For Antonio's work see 310.   **[15]** Cella, 'Documenti', 238 (Durazzo), 250 (secretary (Carlo Berengo); he was later allowed to stay in Padua, because of illness).

11. BARTOLOMEO BRUTI AND
THE PRISONER EXCHANGE

[1] Venturini, 'La famiglia', 376 (petition; 'Persona tanto benemerita del Stato Nostro', 'per la prontezza, et facilità d'ingegno, che dimostra[,] potrà in breve tempo farsi molto atto à servire la Signoria Nostra, quando possederà la Lingua, et Idioma Turchesco'), family tree (Bartolomeo b. 1557). On the 'giovani di lingua' and dragomans, see below, 364–8.   [2] Luca, *Dacoromano-Italica*, 107 (dismissal, payment); ASVen, Dispacci, Costantinopoli, filza 7, fo. 430r (Serbelloni moved to Grand Vizier); AsVen, CCD, Dispacci (Lettere) di Ambasciatori, busta 4, items 159 ('questo è quello che non mi seppe dire il Bruti quando me lo mandò a dire p[er] lui'), 271 (resumption Jan. 1576), busta 5, item 11 ('che fuori d'attender à Imparare questa lingua, secondo che fu designato, che non le è Inclinato mente, nel resto l'ho conosciuto sempre di buo[n] uolere, et pieno di desiderio di s[er]uire a q[ue]sto Illmo Dominio').   [3] Bono, *Schiavi*, 35 (Italy); Stella, *Histoires*, 78–9 (Spain); Davis, *Christian Slaves*, 14–15 (35,000); Martínez Torres, 'Corso', 84 (38,500); Davies, *Warfare*, 14 (Tatar trade); Vatin, 'Une Affaire', 162 (17,500); Pedani, ed., *Relazioni*, 280 (Soranzo); Seng, 'Liminal State', 28 (roughly 40%). On Western slaves in the Ottoman Empire see also Müller, *Franken*, 368–94.
[4] Martínez Torres, *Prisioneros*, 63 (better treated); Mafrici, *Mezzogiorno*, 105 (typical ransom price); Wild, *Reysbeschreibung*, 49 (30 ducats); Dursteler, *Renegade Women*, 8 (unskilled earnings: 16 to 20 ducats). Prices varied according to individual circumstances, age, etc.; one bombardier captured at Famagusta was redeemed in 1580 for only 63½ ducats (ASVen, CCD, Dispacci (Lettere) di Ambasciatori, busta 5, items 179–80).   [5] Tenenti, *Piracy*, 23 (white flag); Vratislav, *Adventures*, 126 (punishment); Brogini, 'Intermédiaires', 48 (Malta 1544–80); Rudt de Collenberg, *Esclavage*, 23 (hostage); Sugar, 'Ottoman "Professional Prisoner"', 84–6.   [6] Bono, *Schiavi*, 438–9 (Sicilian woman); ASVen, Dispacci, Costantinopoli, filza 12, fos. 305v–310r (306r: 'dopò passato vn mese credendo hauer detto suo figliuolo per cambio da detto Pietro gli fù detto da quei sig:^ri, che se'l uolea suo figliuolo egli douesse dar un' altro christiano ancora'). 'Son of Abdullah' was a formula commonly used for converts to Islam.   [7] Dursteler, *Venetians*, 75 (Jews); Wettinger, *Slavery*, 208–24 (Malta); Manca, *Il modello*, 101 (Barbary merchants); Bono, *Schiavi*, 395 (speculative practice); DAD, Acta Consilii Rogatorum, 58, fo. 213v (payment to janissary); DAD, Acta Consilii Minoris, 48, fo. 234r (payment to janissary, specifying that the father must pay one third); DAD, LCL, 33, fo. 235r (*emin*s: they had in fact been captured by the *emin*s' own men).   [8] Kaiser, 'Négocier', 504–7 (Marseille, Provence); DAD, Acta Consilii Rogatorum, 59, fo. 33v (Dubrovnik); Villani and Veneruso, eds., *Nunziature*, ii, 238 (Naples: 'riscatto generale'), 245–6; Manca, *Il modello*, 96 (horses etc.); Martínez Torres, *Prisioneros*, 80–2 (confraternities, orders), 99–112 (ceremonial progresses); ASVen, CCD, Dispacci (Lettere) di Ambasciatori, busta 5, item 174 (Pérez); Sola, *Uchalí*, 318–20 (Pérez).   [9] Bono, *Schiavi*, 457 (freeing Ottomans); Predelli *et al.*, eds., *I libri*, vii, 52 (freeing

39 Muslims from a Spanish ship); Seneca, *Il Doge*, 223 (legalistic); ASVen, CCD, Dispacci (Lettere) di Ambasciatori, busta 4, item 17 (1,000 ducats); Dursteler, *Venetians*, 74 (1586 system); ASVen, Dispacci, Costantinopoli, filza 26, fo. 317r ('Qui si troua gran numero di Schiaui, parte presi in seruitio della Ser:ᵗᵃ Vra in diuersi luochi in tempo di guerra, et molti in tempo di pace'). **[10]** Charrière, ed., *Négociations*, iii, 266(n.) (Dax); ASVen, Dispacci, Costantinopoli, filza 7, fos. 49r–v (1574 demand), 497v, 540r–v (Jan.–Feb. 1575), CCD, Dispacci (Lettere) di Ambasciatori, busta 4, item 168 (1575 bribe, petition); Albèri, ed., *Relazioni*, ser. 3, ii, 156 (Ahmed's help). **[11]** Džaja *et al.*, eds., *Austro-turcica*, 427 (1550); Polić Bobić, *Medju križom*, 141 (1572); Sola, *Uchalí*, 310–11 (1581); Gerlach, *Tage-Buch*, 153 (1576 group caught), 382 (description of agents' methods: 'Spionen'), 412 (by sea every year); ASVen, CCD, Dispacci (Lettere) di Ambasciatori, busta 4, items 258–9 (Albanian couriers). Presumably they dressed as Albanians or Bulgarians because those were humble manual workers who came and went without attracting attention. On the flight of slaves see also Müller, *Franken*, 397–405. **[12]** Sola, *Uchalí*, 215 (betrayal, 1574). **[13]** BSB, MS Cod. Ital. 6, fos. 430r–434r (Barelli report); Floristán Imízcoz, 'Felipe II', 186 ('io ho acquistato gran fama apreso i turchi per rispecto di haver nome che faccio loro servizio in fare riscatare turchi schiavi'); Gürkan, 'Espionage', 173–4 (Franchis); Floristán Imízcoz, ed., *Fuentes*, ii, 600 (Renzo); García Hernán and García Hernán, *Lepanto*, 151 (Tripoli, 1572); Lamansky, *Secrets*, 90, 95–6 (Mustafa); Preto, *I servizi*, 105 (Mustafa, poison); Pedani, *In nome*, 194 (Mustafa, Koper). Barelli's 1575 report is not signed, but the description of its author as a Knight of Malta sent to Istanbul by Don John makes him the only obvious candidate. Other copies are in BAM, MS Q 116 sup, fos. 136r–146v, and ASVen, Miscellanea di atti diversi manoscritti, filza 34, item 11. **[14]** Miović, *Dubrovačka republika*, 52 (returned slaves); DAD, LCP, 1, fo. 68r (letter to Kara Hoca), Secreta rogatorum, 2, fo. 174v (4 at 50 ducats); Popović, *Turska*, 288–9 (merchants, military captives, prominent Ottomans); DAD, Acta Sanctae Mariae Maioris, 16th cent., item 354 (Grand Master); DAD, LCL, 33, fo. 111r ('Siamo stati ricercati da persona, alla quale desideriamo far seruitio'). **[15]** Floristán Imízcoz, 'Felipe II', 173(n.) (Vhelmi and other Albanians, Mormori, Costanzo); Conti, *Delle historie*, ii, 127 (Costanzo captured); BAV, MS Vat. Lat. 12,199, fos. 177–8 (Costanzo); Barbero, *La Bataille*, 540 (Venier); Molmenti, 'Sebastiano', 33 (order to Venier); Stella, 'Lepanto', 237 (Doge); Theiner, ed., *Annales*, i, 462–4 (son of Ali, Bregante, 40 sent to Rome; 462: 'mediocris staturae, barbae castaneae rarae, oculorum nonnihil straborum'); Predelli et al., eds., *I libri*, vi, 328–30 (40 sent to Rome); Floristán Imízcoz, ed., *Fuentes*, ii, 587–9, 602–4, 613 (Bregante); Rudt de Collenberg, *Esclavage*, 39 (20,000 scudi). **[16]** Lamansky, *Secrets*, 88–9 (Venetian requests); Floristán Imízcoz, 'Felipe II', 163 (Barelli), 169–70 (Spanish pressure); Anon., ed., *Correspondencia*, 46–7, 179 (Barelli, Peloponnese); Villani, ed., *Nunziature*, i, 268, 276 (Barelli, Salonica, ransom). **[17]** Charrière, ed., *Négociations*, iii, 267 (demand for Zadar etc.); DAD, Acta Sanctae Mariae Maioris, 16th cent., item 341 (Urbino to Dubrovnik), 17th cent., item 2014 (Urbino to Dubrovnik); Brunetti and Vitale, eds., *La corrispondenza*, ii, 471 (Urbino to Philip); BNF, MSS Dupuy 937,

fos. 150r–151v (King's letters to Sultan and Grand Vizier about Malatesta), Français 16,142, fos. 89r (freed at King's request), 196r (arrived Venice 26 Aug.); BL,
MS Add. 8279, fo. 240v (Ercole at Famagusta); BAV, MS Vat. Lat. 12,199, fo.
149r–v (memorandum for Pope); Rosi, 'Alcuni documenti', 159–61 (Pope agreed),
166 (Philip).   [18] ASVen, CCD, Dispacci (Lettere) di Ambasciatori, busta 4,
item 168 (bailo report on negotiation); Floristán Imízcoz, 'Felipe II', 172 (ambassador's surmise); Rosi, 'Alcuni documenti', 167–8 ('Bartolomeo Bruti, latore della
lettera imperiale, condurrà da Roma i prigionieri turchi'); Apostolescu, 'Un aventurier', 567 (employee claim); ASVen, Dispacci, Costantinopoli, filza 7, fos. 524v
('Et disidera il S. Gabrio il midesmo Bruti passi à Roma con le mie lettere'), 529r
('fù figliuolo del Cauallier Brutti da Dulcigno'); Pedani and Bombaci, Inventory,
58 (Serbelloni letter); HD, xi, 91 (4 Feb. departure); Polić Bobić, Medju križom,
222 (della Marra report: 'El hijo del cauallerio Bruto', 'da a Mehmet quanto gana
por lo qual es muy fauorido'); Venturini, 'La famiglia', 375–6 (in Venice).   [19]
AGS, Estado, leg. 488, item [20] ('trouandosi in Constan:[li] l'anno del 1574, per
affari della Sig.[ria] di Venetia, cioe, a instruire, et in caminare gli loro Bayli, et
Ambasciatori, della manera [sic], et proceder, che si costuma, in quella Corte, a
trattar gli negocij appartenenti a detta Republica', 'un giorno fra gli altri fui da lui
ricercato con boni terminj, et con efficace raggioni, perche mi risoluesse di seruire
a V.M.', 'il statto honesto, in che mi trouauo appresso dittj Sig.[ri] Venetianj', 'della
setta Maumettana', 'vendicar in parte le offese che tutta la casa mia hanno riceuuto, da detta maledetta setta', 'mi lassai facilmente vincere dalle raggionj dette da
esso Gio: Marigliani, et cosi sotto bon colore, et per seruicio di VM procuramo,
che fossi inuiato a Roma per solicitar, con sua Sta Il cambio delli priggioni'); Rosi,
'Nuovi documenti', 40–2 (other captives: Margliani, priests, women).   [20] On
the relationship with Sinan see below, 263–4.   [21] Rosi, 'Nuovi documenti', 44
(12 Mar., 'Di Vostra Serenità Devotiss.[o] vassallo et servitor'), 44–5 (Mehmed's
letter); Rosi, 'Alcuni documenti', 195 ('con molte parole destrissimamente aquie-
tai gl'animi loro', Mehmed Subaşı problem), 204 ('il sig.[r] Bartolomeo Bruti non
ha mai mancato dapoi che arrivammo a Fermo farli instansia per detta fede; ma
è homo di dura cervice, et difficile da contentare et negotiar con esso lui'), 209–15
(murder, affidavits).   [22] Rosi, 'Nuovi documenti', 45–6 (petition); Biegman,
Turco-Ragusan, 145–6 (Sultan's order); Predelli et al., eds., I libri, vii, 9 (Venetian
galleys, 6 men); Razzi, La storia, 118 (exchange); Pedani and Bombaci, Inventory,
58 (22 July), 62 (Mehmed to Doge); DAD, LCL, 33, fo. 25r–v (letter to ambassadors); HHStA, Türkei I, Karton 81, 1st foliation, fos. 3v–4r (Matthias).

12: ESPIONAGE AND SABOTAGE IN ISTANBUL

[1] Isom-Verhaaren, 'Ottoman Report' (Dhuka); Zamputi, ed., Dokumente, i,
233 (Bucchia); Echevarría Bacigalupe, 'El espionaje', 148–9 (Spanish merchants'
privileges); ASVen, CCD, Dispacci (Lettere) di Ambasciatori, busta 4, item 248
('per l'anno futuro si faria grandissima armata'). The rumoured naval expedition
did not take place.   [2] van der Does, De itinere, 35. On the devşirme see

Papoulia, *Ursprung*, Imber, *Ottoman Empire*, 121–30, and Ménage, 'Devshirme' (noting some intake from Anatolia too); on foreign-born Ottoman dragomans see Matuz, 'Die Pfortendolmetscher', Ács, 'Tarjumans', and Müller, *Franken*, 262–72. **[3]** Predelli *et al.*, eds., *I libri*, vii, 69 (1594 list); Albèri, ed., *Relazioni*, ser. 3, i, 406–7 ('La casa del bailo ordinariamente è frequentata da molti Turchi, li quali aspirano a donativi, e sono appunto come le api attorno il miele', 'altrimente la sua casa havria più avviamento di una bottega sopra il ponte di Rialto'). **[4]** Preto, *I servizi*, 100 (Passi warned of Cyprus); Levin, *Agents*, 172 (volunteered for Spain); Burdelez, 'Role', 193 (Passi peace negotiations, family); Özgen, 'Connected World', [10], at n. 38 (Passi family); Bodl., MS Tanner 78, fo. 40v (English Ambassador); Popović, *Turska*, 356 (Abeatar); ASVen, Dispacci, Costantinopoli, filza 7, fo. 183v (signature); Gerlach, *Tage-Buch*, 59 (Solomon's brother in Vienna), 155 ('bey dem Bassa in solchen Gnaden: als sein geheimer Rath in Französischen, Venedischen, Polnischen und Ungerischen Sachen'), 323 (Solomon helped Empire, Spain, France); ASVen, CCD, Suppliche, filza 1, item of 14 Jan. 1574[/5] (Solomon request to Venice for sons), CCD, Dispacci (Lettere) di Ambasciatori, busta 6, item 55 (further request for sons, 1582); Pedani and Bombaci, *Inventory*, 74 (Venetian pension); BNF, MS Français 16,143, fo. 45r ('fidelissimo seruitor', 'massime in la electione che V. M.ᵗᵃ fò electo per Rè De polonia che io fu causa De tutto quelo se operò qui si be' credo che mo[n]sior De acx auerà tirato il tuto a ssè'). On Solomon see Arbel, *Trading Nations*, 77–86, and Lucchetta, 'Il medico', 13–16; see also above, 187. **[5]** Soranzo, *L'Ottommano*, 66–7 ('tengono fin dentro Constantinopoli molte spie pagate, stipendiando etiandio Hebrei, e Turchi de' più confidenti, & intimi de' primieri Bassà'); Pedani, ed., *Relazioni*, 388–9 ('accarezzato e gratificato molti capi et altri huomini da mare'); ASVen, CCD, Dispacci (Lettere) di Ambasciatori, busta 5, item 103 (1579); ASVen, Dispacci, Costantinopoli, filza 28, fos. 186r–187v (1588, Tripoli), 202r–v (1588, Persia); *HD*, iv(2), 212 (1596, Poland). **[6]** Gerlach, *Tage-Buch*, 137 ('Venedischen, Polnischen, Sibenbürgischen, Frantzösischen, Spanischen, Ungarischen Sachen, durch lauter Türcken', Pest agent, janissary, spahi), 158 ('d[er] führet auch unwissend, meines Herrn Brieff, dann der Agent hat ihn in den seinen eingeschlossen, und seinen Freunden zu Ofen zugeschrieben, dass sie das inliegende Schreiben gleich dem Herrn Kielman nach Gomorren überschicken sollen'); Vratislav, *Adventures*, 102 (1593, quotation). **[7]** Poliakov, *Jewish Bankers*, 185 (Sixtus, Lopez, doctors); Soranzo, *L'Ottommano*, 66 ('Di Giouanni Lopes . . . si sà certo, che communicò ad Amorato molti secreti di Papa Sisto V. i quali egli spiò, mentre dimorò in Roma'); Arbel, *Trading Nations*, 59 (Nasi myth); Preto, *I servizi*, 101 (Nasi myth); Albèri, ed., *Relazioni*, ser. 3, iii, 316 (1585: 'minutissimi avvisi di quanto passa', 'falso'). **[8]** García Hernán, 'Price', 235 (1572 Spanish warning); ASVen, CCD, Dispacci (Lettere) di Ambasciatori, busta 4, items 156 ('di 40. anni in circa di conueniente statura, di carne piu bianca, che bruna, di barba tonda et negra . . . non mi contentano questi segni p[er]che molti si troueranno di questa sorte'), 165 (Benkner mission); HHStA, Türkei I, Karton 38, 2nd foliation, fo. 373v ('Mahmut Abdallah Frenck'); Müller, *Franken*, 273–9 (spies; 277: Mehmed Abdullah Frenk, *né* Ferdinand Bollus, from

Antwerp); Barbero, *La Bataille*, 163 (30 in 1570); Gürkan, 'Espionage', 134 (1559 suggestion), 376–7 (1574 engineers); Ciorănescu, ed., *Documente*, 69 (Benkner mission, translator for Spain); AGS, Estado, leg. 488, item [109] (Benkner mission, cipher); Graf, '"I am Still Yours"', 212–17 (Benkner mission, terminated). Benkner is best known as the companion of Adam Neuser, a German anti-Trinitarian convert to Islam.　　**[9]** Hess, 'Moriscos', 17–18 (Moriscos), 19 (Netherlands); Sola, *Uchalí*, 229 (Netherlands); Chasiōtēs, *Oi Ellēnes*, 53–4, 59–65 (Barelli plan); Canosa and Colonnello, *Spionaggio*, 84–7 (assassination plan 1569); Lamansky, *Secrets*, 90 (reactivated 1571); Floristán Imízcoz, 'Felipe II', 174 (palace arson); Pedani, *Venezia*, 208 (Doge's Palace, offer, fire).　　**[10]** García Hernán, 'Price', 228 (1540s); Levin, *Agents*, 170–3 (1540s, 1550s, and later, but overstating Venice's later role); Floristán Imízcoz, ed., *Fuentes*, ii, 586–605 (Renzo network), 623(n.) (Santa Croce biography); Canosa and Colonnello, *Spionaggio*, 165(n.) (Murad Ağa, *né* Simon Barca; a letter from him to the Doge of Genoa in 1563 is in Pittioni, *Korrespondenz*, 200–3, but misidentified and mistranscribed); Sola and de la Peña, *Cervantes*, 84–5 (Santa Croce reports, role); Sola, *Los que van*, 225–6 ('Capo').　　**[11]** Floristán Imízcoz, ed., *Fuentes*, ii, 613 ('palabrero y mentiroso'), 614 (Granvelle, 1571); Canosa and Colonnello, *Spionaggio*, 115 (Granvelle, 1571); Coniglio, *Il viceregno*, ii, 380 ('me traygan ... cosas viejas y generales y que por dezir que han acertado lo dizen todo y cosas contrarias por donde no puede ser que algo no succeda'); Villani, ed., *Nunziature*, i, 268 (Barelli's warning), 276 ('poco o nullo credito').　　**[12]** AGS, Estado, leg. 488, item [20], fo. [1r–v] ('fui introdutto a bassiar le mani al Ser.ᵐᵒ Sig.ʳ D Gio., Dal qual fui racolto benignam.ᵗᵉ, et con il qual trattai molte cose appartenenti al seruicio di V.M.', 'cosi pocodoppoi mi fu ordinato douesse rittornar in Constantinopoli, et mi fu datto da esso Gio Marigliani, il modo di tornar honoratam.ᵗᵉ con una instrucione fermata da Gio: di Sotto nella qual mi cometeua gli particolari, in che hauea di seruire V.M.').　　**[13]** Gerlach, *Tage-Buch*, 32 (del Faro Orthodox, Galata resident), 155 (wedding, Santa Croce father-in-law, 'Hr. Bruli'), 156 ('Herr Bruli', 'Pronubus', ring); Lesure, 'Michel Černović', 145(n.) (del Faro from 1559); Carrasco, 'L'Espionnage', 216–17 (payroll 1571–5). Further details about del Faro are in Müller, *Prosopographie*, ii, 354–6, where, however, he is mistakenly described as Spanish.　　**[14]** Braudel, *Mediterranean*, ii, 1144–50 (citing Dax).　　**[15]** Sola and de la Peña, *Cervantes*, 86–9 (missions of early 1570s), 90 (Curenzi, explosion); BAP, MS 4769, fo. 46r (Dax report); Polić Bobić, *Medju križom*, 195 (40 captives); Gerlach, *Tage-Buch*, 37 (horses, gold, clothes, Ottomans astonished), 152 (slave of Piyale); Floristán Imízcoz, 'Los prolegómenos', 44 (Avellán recruited by Renzo); de Torres, *Chronica*, fo. 93v (Avellán slave, spoke Turkish); ASVen, CCD, Dispacci (Lettere) di Ambasciatori, busta 4, item 107 (Dax complaint); AGS, Estado, leg. 488, item [95] (Curenzi).　　**[16]** Sola, *Uchalí*, 219 (Losada and Uluç Ali), 220–31 (report; 222: 'la Puerta del Gran Señor era abierta, y que quien venía a ella no se iría descontento'); ASVen, CCD, Dispacci (Lettere) di Ambasciatori, busta 4, item 269 ('una piccola recognitione'); Floristán Imízcoz, 'Felipe II', 186 (Barelli report). Cf. also the report of May 1573, by a Spanish agent in Dubrovnik, that the Sultan had been persuaded by

Sokollu and Kılıç Ali to seek peace with Spain: Polić Bobić, *Medju križom*, 188. The only evidence of a Spanish peace initiative is a mention by Gerlach in 1577 of a 'Johann Peter Gusin', a Spaniard, who had approached Sokollu in 1575 (*Tage-Buch*, 322); but I have not found an equivalent name in any Spanish document.   **[17]** Sola and de la Peña, *Cervantes*, 94 (volunteer, assassination); Floristán Imízcoz, 'Los prolegómenos', 43–4 (Avellán plan); Polić Bobić, *Medju križom*, 229 (Ragusan attempts); ASVen, CCD, Dispacci (Lettere) di Ambasciatori, busta 4, item 269 (ostensible mission, interview); AGS, Estado, leg. 488, item [27] (denunciation, Sokollu's threat).   **[18]** AGS, Estado, leg. 488, item [20], fos. [1v] ('non hauerci altro rimedio, che il trattarne con me Bartolomeo Brutj, et uedere si poteano disponermi a incaricarmi di cosi grande, et difficil impresa', 'cognoscendolo ancora molto piu atto, ad alcunj seruicij, cosi per esser molto instrutto delle cose della christianità, come per la pocca sadosfacione, che tiene di suoi seruicij dal Gran Turco'), [2r] ('hora minaciandomi, hora consentendo'); ASVen, CCD, Dispacci (Lettere) di Ambasciatori, busta 5, item 11 (departure, release). The royal letter to Murad Ağa of June 1575, asking him to bring over Kılıç Ali too, is AGS, Estado, leg. 488, item [30].   **[19]** Floristán Imízcoz, 'Los prolegómenos', 47 (Avellán claim); AGS, Estado, leg. 488, items [21] ('di p[rese]nte ridutto alli suoj seruicij Bartol⁰ Brutj Caual[ie]r Alban. che mantiene tutta uia il Credito di suoi antecessorj nella sua patria, et hà parenti d'importanza, in Constant^li), [110] ('hauendo considerato molto bene, che era cosa giusta, et che potea seruire VM. cosi de soldato, come in cose oculte in la negociacione di leuante, per molta pratica, et amicitia, che ha in quelle parte, et per molti parentj persone di autorita che ha, et anco perche hauea gia datto ferma intentione a sua Al.^za per mezzo di Gio. Mariglianj di seruir VM. con la p:[rossi]^ma honorata occ.^ne che si presentera, si ha messo al seruicio di VM').   **[20]** Sola, *Los que van*, 228 (arrival, Oct.); AGS, Estado, leg. 488, item [20], fo. [2r] (Sesa, Aurelio's letter); Carnicer and Marcos, *Espías*, 332–3 (Dulis, Bastia, Lantzas), 344 (Lantzas frigate); Floristán Imízcoz, ed., *Fuentes*, ii, 619 (*sancakbeyi*s), 682–8 (letter); AGS, Estado, leg. 1073, item 21 (Renzo recruited Dulis); Laskaris, 'Petros Lantzas' (biography), and 'Sumplērōmatika', 237–40 (Sopot).   **[21]** AGS, Estado, leg. 488, item [110] (Bruti paper; fo. [1v]: 'di nacione schiauonj', 'di uiaggio in uiaggio'). On the Venetian courier system, used by merchants as well as officials, see De Zanche, *Tra Costantinopoli*.   **[22]** AGS, Estado, leg. 488, item [20], fos. [2r] ('molto gli piaque'), [2v] ('Non saj ch'io sono el Re in questo regno'); Sola, *Uchalí*, 247 (Acuña slave of Murad Ağa); AGS, Estado, leg. 1073, item 22, fos. [1r] ('consignate alli capitani particolari'), [1v] ('gli schiauj del Gran Signore per dinari non si possono liberare, se non per cambj, et bisogna stare mesi à trattare la loro libertà con suppliche auanti del Gran Bassa', 'balle artificiose', 'Soliman Venetiano, quale io conosco, è giouane di pochi annj, et di poca esperientia'), [1v–2r] ('ro[m]pendo il disegno di molti huominj importantj, che han[n]o Incaminato, et stabilito molte cose per seruitio di Dio, et di Sua Mag^tà, et riputatione di Vra Ecc^tia').   **[23]** AGS, Estado, leg. 488, items [20], fo. [3r] (advice, letters, guide, 'o, che tu mi dirai, che negocio e questo, o, che ti faro mettere infondi d'una torre, onde starai tanto che ti pessera [*sic*] la uitta', 'parole, et offerte amoreuoli'), [25] (auditor-general's letter: 'yo le conozco por muy de bien y verdadero, y q[ue] [e]s persona noble y q[ue] puede en su patria hazer mucho seruicio a la Xriandad ... y en const^na, de donde ha venido, tiene grandes y verdaderas inteligencias, con q[ue] ha seruido y siruira a su M^d'). **[24]** Ibid., item [87] (Mehmed Bey's plan, condition); Rodríguez Salgado, *Felipe II*, 49-50 (Council's consultations, approval). On the son of the former ruler of Tunis (Muley Hamida) see Alonso Acero, *Sultanes*, 144. **[25]** Floristán Imízcoz, 'Los prolegómenos', 56-7 (Acuña mission); Sola and de la Peña, *Cervantes*, 98-9 (Acuña mission); Sola, *Los que van*, 237 (Acuña mission, del Faro); Rodríguez Salgado, *Felipe II*, 51-3 (Acuña mission, Nasi letter); Gerlach, *Tage-Buch*, 319 ('der *Spanische Gesante* bey dem Bassen gewesen, und ihm die Credentz-Schreiben seines Königs überreichet'); HHStA, Türkei I, Karton 36, 1st foliation, fo. 256v (release of Albanian). **[26]** Parker, *Grand Strategy*, 144-5 (bankruptcy, need for savings); Floristán Imízcoz, 'Los prolegómenos', 52 (Margliani warning), 60-1 (Pérez paper, King's decision, choice of Margliani, Bruti); Rodríguez Salgado, *Felipe II*, 71-6 (debate; 72: Mondéjar warnings, 'reputaçion'); Sola, *Los que van*, 238 (Mondéjar warnings), 239 ('un pequeño monumento literario de expresividad, desequilibrio y frescura').

13. SECRET DIPLOMACY AND THE GRAND VIZIER

[1] AGS, Estado, leg. 1337, item 15, fo. [1r] ('in Corte di V.M. haueua preditto Al secretario Antonio Perez; che quello, che D. Martin Diceua di tregua secreta ... non poteua esser vero, et affermai, che D. martin haueua alterato le translation delle littere, che Mehemet Bassa scriueua à V.M., et che al'ora non mi fù prestat' orecchie', 'gli Turchi non sanno, ne uogliano trattar Cosa alcuna secreta Con alcun Principe, et massimam.^te con V.M.'), Estado, leg. 1074, item 190 ('pòrque por la buena relaçion q[ue] tenemos de su p[er]sona y de la platica & Intelligencia q[ue] tienne de las cosas de Leuante, le auemos mandado q[ue] vaya a residar a Costantinopla. Y que ste ally con la dissimulaçion q[ue] hasta a qui lo ha hecho para que tenga Cuydado de embiar los auisos y aduertimy[ent]^os q[ue] le paresçiere Convenir, de los andamy[ent]^os del Turco'; cf. the similar document printed in Coniglio, *Il viceregno*, ii, 542). **[2]** AGS, Estado, leg. 1073, item 157, fos. [1v] ('Il bruti fa sapere al detto aurelio come e venutto et egli Viene a vederlo et andorno a cenare Insieme'), [2r] ('Il quale erano molti ani che non haueua Visto', 'scoperto Il tutto'), [2v] (Mehmed Bey project). **[3]** Ibid., item 157, fos. [2r] ('mal hombre'), [3r] (safe-conduct), [3v] ('li contrasegni secreti'). **[4]** Ibid., item 157, fos. [4r] (revealed mission), [4v] ('non volere andare a la morte per alcuno'), [6r] (Aurelio's advice), Estado, leg. 1337, item 15, fo. [1r-v] (Aurelio's revelation, 'hor uedete, che quello io predissi in Corte, è reuscito il uero', Bartolomeo urges Margliani). **[5]** Rodríguez Salgado, *Felipe II*, 58-60 (Sokollu's mistrust, Aurelio's falsification, Philip's awareness); Gerlach, *Tage-Buch*, 370 ('dann sein Herr, der König, wolle gegen die Moren auff Fessa und Marocko gehen'); AGS, Estado, leg. 488, item [3] (Aurelio's forged letter to Hürrem). **[6]** HHStA, Türkei I, Karton 36, 1st foliation, fos. 75r ('spero con gran vittoria ritornar à Constantinopoli con la conclusione del negocio ... che penso me [*sic*] sara raccommandato à me, per non li essere altri prattichi in Hispania per trattar tal negocio'), 82r ('dar maggior honor et reputatione alla Ambasceria'); AGS, Estado, leg. 488, item [2] (Sokollu letter to Philip of 2 Rabi' al-awal (= 2 June)); Floristán Imízcoz, 'Los prolegó-menos', 65 (Aurelio to Spain by late Dec.); Sola, *Los que van*, 244–5 (Aurelio imprisoned).   [7] Skilliter, 'Hispano-Ottoman', 508 (Stefano family); AGS, Estado, leg. 489, items 13, fo. [1r–v] (voyage from Brindisi), 47, fo. [16v] (Stefano alfiere in Tunis); Breuning, *Orientalische Reyss*, 12–13 (merchants pursued, 50 ducats); Carlier, *Voyage*, 36–8 (merchants pursued, 60 ducats), 38 ('estoient prins et faicts esclaves, ou bien mis a mort, s'ils estoient soubçonnez d'estre espions'), 39 (merchant vessel, 'y voit on amener journellement du butin').   [8] AGS, Estado, leg. 489, item 13, fos. [1v–2r] (arrival; fo. [2r]: 'smonto subito il S.ʳ Bartlᵒ et mio alfere, et Insieme Andorno col salvo condutto Hauuto dal S.ʳ Aurelio al Cadi'), [2v] ('a in ogni luogo Compadri da uisitare'), Estado, leg. 1337, item 15, fo. [1v] ('paricolouamo [*sic*], se non trouaua il Vice Re di quella prouintia parente mio, qual ci raccolse con molta cortesia, et ci libero dalla furia de leuenti, quali s'haueuano soleuati Contra di noi, per esser la Valona Nido de Corsari'); DAD, LCL, 33, fo. 76v (document of 11 Mar. 1577, referring to 'Mustaffa celebia Nasir in Valona').   [9] AGS, Estado, leg. 488, items [5] (letter to Hürrem: Berat, *san-cakbeyi*, 'per risoluere la pratica pochi mesi auanti promosa col S.ʳ Don Mar.ᵒ de Acuna'), [31], fo. [1r] (arrival in Istanbul), Estado, leg. 489, item 13, fo. [2r] (expecting Spanish ambassador, Tuscan fiction).   [10] AGS, Estado, leg. 488, item [31], fos. [1r] ('Se fosse cristiano mi farei il segno della croce, doue ha sog-nato Don Mart.ᵒ tanta falsità; Il Basa aspetta embasatore, p[er]che cosi si è scritto p[er] Don Mart.ᵒ ... Il Basa sentira gra[n]demente questa nouita, et uoglia Dio non se segua qualche danno inremediabile nelle persone loro'), [1r–2r] (Hürrem, Spinelli, Solomon); ASVen, CCD, Dispacci (Lettere) di Ambasciatori, busta 4, items 159, 228 (reports on Spinelli as giovane di lingua).   [11] Samardžić, *Mehmed*, 14–15 (Sokollu origins); Radojčić, *Mileševa*, 47 (Mileševa); Albèri, ed., *Relazioni*, ser. 3, i, 319–20 ('solo provvede ed ordina tutte le cose, e massimam-ente le più importanti, ed in somma passano per mano sua tutte le cose civili, criminali e di stato, nelle quali altro consiglio non vi è che la sua sola testa ... È religioso, sobrio, amico della pace, non vendicativo, nè rapace ... È sano, di buona complessione, grave di presenza, grande, ben formato di corpo, e d'ottima memoria'), 364 (ambassador Badoero calling Sokollu good-willed towards Chris-tianity), ii, 157 (taken at 18, 'Pare destrissimo, perchè ascoltando quietamente risponde poi senza alterarsi', 'potria stimarsi negoziare piuttosto con principe Cristiano, che con Turco'), 179 ('Quell'estremo desiderio poi che è in lui di accu-mular tesoro'); HHStA, Türkei I, Karton 38, 2nd foliation, fo. 160r ('wass man heut mit Ime tractiert, Er categoricè verspricht, zuesagt vnd abhandlet, das laugnet, widerspricht oder vndert Er das anderen, od[er] wol desselben tags wider'); Gerlach, *Tage-Buch*, 414 (bribe); Peçevi, *Historija*, ii, 20, 39 (viziers, *beylerbeyis*; cf. Fleischer, *Bureaucrat*, 46; Tezcan, *Second Ottoman Empire*, 94); Freidenberg, *Dubrovnik*, 119–20 (Ragusan relations).   [12] AGS, Estado, leg. 488, item [31], fos. [2v] ('mareuigliato, et affrontato'), [2v–7v] (reply, boast, meetings of 23, 28 Dec.);

HHStA, Türkei I, Karton 36, 2nd foliation, fo. 1r (list of states, 'Domanda ancora sua M.^ta che da tal suspensione non segua comunicatione ò comertio alcuno, se non con Licenza ò saluacondotto de tutte due le parti'), Türkei I, Karton 37, 1st foliation, fo. 81r (black patch, complaint).   [13] AGS, Estado, leg. 488, items [31], fos. [10v–11r] (consulting Solomon), [86] (Sokollu letter, last day of 'ziliade' (30 Dhu al-qa'da, = 8 Feb.)), Estado, leg. 489, item 40 (4 Feb. document); HHStA, Türkei I, Karton 36, 2nd foliation, fo. 60v (Orange proposal); Charrière, ed., *Négociations*, iii, 713–14 (departure 12 Feb., Orange proposal); Skilliter, 'Hispano-Ottoman', 498–9 (text of agreement; cf. Rodríguez Salgado, *Felipe II*, 89–90, and Floristán Imízcoz, 'Los prolegómenos', 65).   [14] AGS, Estado, leg. 488, item [31], fo. [11r] ('non hauendo commodita di far fuoco, et anco non potendo far essercitio'), Estado, leg. 489, item 16 ('essendo statti sempre in una cameretta, doue ne conueniua, in un istesso loco parechiar il uitto, et dormire, cosa d'hauerne compasione, poiche per causa del fummo non poteamo lumar il fuoco et senza fuoco moriuamo di fredo'); HHStA, Türkei I, Karton 36, 1st foliation, fos. 256r–258r (Imperial report); Sola, *Uchalí*, 260–1 (bailo's report, anonymous report); Polić Bobić, *Medju križom*, 203 (1573 accusation); Charrière, ed., *Négociations*, iii, 705 (French report, 28 Dec.), 710 (French report, 22 Jan.), iv, 435(n.) (Aurelio working for Venice, 1585). Gilles de Noailles had replaced his brother in 1575.   [15] AGS, Estado, leg. 489, item 47, fos. [16v] ('Il bruti e Il magior traditore, Il magiore vegliaco Il piu Insolente et da poco Corpo che viua ... Non è q[ue]sta una delle maggior calamità dil mondo, hauer, à uiuere un Cauaglier di bona intencione gli anni interi, con uno huomo de cosi rea et mala condicione, et per non offendere al seruicio, nel qual si troua, hauere à cedere sempre, et hauer pacienza'), [16v–17r] ('Douendo mandare questo despacho, fu cosi insolente che mi disse in faccia, che tocaua a lui a portarlo, et che haueua tanta parte in q[ue]sto negocio como me, et che parleria di tal manera al Basa, che la porteria'); BL, MS Add. 28,415, fo. 1r (secret message, conspiracy); HHStA, Türkei I, Karton 36, 2nd foliation, fos. 58v (lemon juice), 59r ('nur auf betrug', 'allain die Zeit den Turkhen abgewinnen, vnd heurig Armada disturbieren wolle', 'Ainer genant Bartholomeo Brutj, so mit Im komen, solle gleichesfals dahin Practicieren, damit Er Brutj zu Ir Ku:[niglichen] W:[ürde] gefertigt werde, vnd Marigliano hie bleibe, daruber sey fast vnd also entzwait seien, das man maint, Bruti Participier auch mit dem Aurelio vnd dem Hurem Beg; daher dan Marigliano seine tractationes vor dem Bruti sehr gehaimb halten, vnd weil Bruti der Venediger Vnd[er]than ist, durchauss nit willigen solle, Ine Brutj zu Ir Ku:[niglichen] W:[ürde] abzufertigen').   [16] AGS, Estado, leg. 489, items 16, fo. [1v] ('patisco la persecucion delli sigg.^ri venetianj, gli qualli non puono lassar di perseguitarmi dispiacendo loro, che habbia abandonato il loro seruicio'), 53, fo. [3v] (reform, finances); Charrière, ed., *Négociations*, iii, 862–3 (French request, Venetian answer).   [17] AGS, Estado, leg. 1337, item 15, fos. [1v] ('palesato à molti', protest over galleys), [2r] ('poi ogni giorno Cresceuano gli suspetti dal canto suo, forse dubitando egli non scriuesse lo secretame[n]te V.M. quello si fa et faceua in queste parti; et uedend'io questa suspition sua, presi per espediente di partirmi dalla sua Compagnia', 'non hò zifra, et il Mariglianni mi hà negato

quella che d'ordine di V.M. ci fù data commune').   **[18]** Sola, *Uchalí*, 262–6
(lobbying); Murphey, *Ottoman Warfare*, 138 (planning Persian war); Kortepeter,
Ottoman Imperialism, 44–61 (Persian war).   **[19]** de Queiroz Velloso, *D.
Sebastião*, 309 (landing), 342–3(n.) (8,000 Portuguese, 1,600 Spaniards, 600
'Italians'), 337–420 (battle); Bovill, *Battle*, 83 (10,000 Portuguese, 2,000 Spaniards, 600 'Italians'), 92 (landing), 127–40 (battle); Holmes, 'Stucley' (700 English
etc.); BL, MS Add. 28,415, fo. 2r ('stetti circa xv me[si] in due camere, ne hauendo altro transtullo, che uenire à una fin[estra.] quando il Re di portugalle passo
in Africa, essendo comparso [io in] q[ue]lla finestra, mi fu lapidata la casa ...
Tutte le uolte che V M[ta] ha fatto armata, mi sono trouato in periculo, perche
l'Amb[re] di Fran[a] persuadeua che si pensaua all'Impresa de Algeri'); AGS, Estado,
leg. 489, item 53, fo. [3v] ('come escusara Giouanni questa andata dil Re di Por-
tugale in barberia con Mehemet Bassa').   **[20]** AGS, Estado, leg. 489, items 25,
fos. [2v] ('che gli era stato mandato giontamente con me da sua M.[ta] per tratare
questa pace, che io lo haueua escluso dal negoçio per potere destruere questa
platica, perche hauendo hauuto carico sopra l'armata desideraua che la pace non
seguisse perche seguendo la pace sua M[ta] non teneria armata, et non tenedola
veneria a restare priuo del mio carico'), [3r–v] (marriage to niece, avoiding Solomon), [4r] ('larga Informatione de la sua persona, et poco bona'), 53, fo. [4r]
(planning to flee).   **[21]** Rodríguez Salgado, *Felipe II*, 108–9 (choice of Rocafull,
instructions); Cascales, *Discursos*, 465 (Lepanto); AGS, Estado, leg. 489, item 1
(Rocafull instructions), Estado, leg. 1337, item 15, fo. [2r] (Bartolomeo's later
complaint); Charrière, ed., *Négociations*, iii, 777 (arrival of de Ferrari, 2 months);
HHStA, Türkei I, Karton 38, 2nd foliation, fo. 80r (arrival of de Ferrari, *çavuş*);
Türkei I, Karton 39, 3rd foliation, fo. 82r–v (Margliani asking Solomon); ASVen,
Dispacci, Costantinopoli, filza 13, fos. 42v (Mar. news), 168v (May news), 184r
('un pocco indisposto'), 223r, 280v (rumours), 307v–308r (rumours dispelled,
promise).   **[22]** Glücklich, ed., *Václava Budovce*, 9 (4 Oct.); Rodríguez Salgado,
Felipe II, 110 (Echevarría), 116–17 (papal reaction), 124–5 (credentials and
instructions for Margliani); ASVen, Dispacci, Costantinopoli, filza 13, fo. 365r
(Margliani accepted as ambassador, mid-Oct.), CCD, Dispacci (Lettere) di
Ambasciatori, busta 5, item 93 (Echevarría); Parker, *Grand Strategy*, 27–45
(drowning in paperwork); Karttunen, *Grégoire XIII*, 33–4 (papal reaction);
Fernández Collado, *Gregorio XIII*, 112–20 (papal reaction).

14. SINAN PASHA AND THE MOLDAVIAN VENTURE

[1] AGS, Estado, leg. 489, item 25, fo. [3r] ('presto'), Estado, leg. 490, item 36, fo.
[1r] (Margliani accounts, loans); Venturini, 'La famiglia', family tree; Palerne,
D'Alexandrie, 270 (fine dress, girls' hair, dye, 'certaines petites façons languis-
santes, avec un regard si doux, & attrayant, qu'il est bien difficile d'évader leurs
pièges'); Cleray, 'Le Voyage', 42 (Lescalopier: 'Les femmes y paroissent plus
qu'elles ne sont belles, pource qu'elles se fardent au possible et employent tout
leur avoir à se vestir et parer avec forces anneaux aux doigtz et pierreries sur la

teste, la plus part desquelles sont fauces'); Heberer, *Aegyptiaca servitus*, 370 (fine dress).   **[2]** du Fresne-Canaye, *Le Voyage*, 261 (wedding description, 'Il splendore delle sue perle rubini et gioie m'abbagliava'); Palerne, *D'Alexandrie*, 269 ('suivant chascun sa Religion, comme icy une Huguenote avec un Catholique'; cf. de Nicolay, *Dans l'Empire*, 144); Gerlach, *Tage-Buch*, 156 ('Sie sah, als wann sie ein lebloses Bild wär, und kein Wort reden könte', ceremony, dinner), 157 (music, dumb-show), 357 (mixed marriages anathematized).   **[3]** AGS, Estado, leg. 489, item 25, fo. [3r] ('per potere viuere piu quietam^{te}').   **[4]** Theiner, ed., *Vetera monumenta*, iii, 143 (nuncio: 'cugino'; cf. a similar comment by a writer in 1588: Shmurlo, *Rossiia*, ii, 471); ASVen, CCD, Dispacci (Lettere) di Ambasciatori, busta 4, item 270 ('in corte di Sinan bassà, il quale è germano di mia madre p[er] esser di nation albanese', 'cosi tratenendomi in quella citta, et spesso essendo col nepote d[el] Sinan Mehemet bey, et col suo checaia al partir mio hauendo pressa con loro strettissima amicizia restassemo d'accordo, che douessero sempre che si haueua cosa al.[cun]^{a} contra questi SS:^{ri}, et spezialmte della città di catharo et quei confini, loro p[er] buono à posta à spese mie mi dessero auiso d[e]l tutto'); ASVat, Fondo Borghese III 128, 1st fasc., fo. 8v (Alessandro Giubizza, Pope, Spain); Čoralić and Karbić, *Pisma*, 112–13 (Marco Gliubizza); AGS, Estado, leg. 488, item [20], fo. [1r] (autobiographical memorandum: 'a mio padre et a dui [*sic*] mei tij carnali l'uno Arciuescouo d'Antiuari, et l'altro uescouo di Dolcigno hanno tagliato le teste tiranigiando la pouera patria mia'). The name 'Giubizza' or 'Gliubizza' may go back to the 'Lubici' or 'Lubisi' family recorded near Shkodër in 1417: Valentini, ed., *Acta*, viii, 199, 276.   **[5]** Soranzo, *L'Ottomanno*, 56 ('Albanese da Topoiano villa del Sangiaccato di Preseremo'); Kaleshi, 'Veliki vezir', 111–12 (citing and dismissing Serb claims), 114 (father 'Ali *bey*'); Pulaha, 'Krahinat', 38–9 (Slav predominance, Topojan Albanian); Gentilezza, 'L'Albania', 70(n.) (Ragusan list: 'Albanese cattolico'); Stefani, ed., 'Viaggio', 41 (born 1519); Sahillioğlu, ed., *Koca Sinan*, xviii (born *c*.1520; but cf. Faroqhi, *Die Vorlagen*, 133); Hoxha, *Shqiptari*, 13(n.), 15 (legends); Dokle, *Sinan*, 24–6(n.) (legends); Albèri, ed., *Relazioni*, ser. 3, ii, 239 (Venetian writer's story, though with some inaccuracies); Bodl., MS Rawl. D 618, fo. 102v ('altri uengono posti in detti seragli per fauori, come tt^i i grandi di questa Porta che hanno parenti Christ.^{ni} li fanno fare Musulmanni, e gli mettono in questi seragli'); Michel, 'Les *waqf*-s', 270 (4 brothers); Vratislav, *Adventures*, 55 (kitchen); von Saurau, *Orttenliche Beschreybung*, 117 (*çaşnigir*s); Brookes, ed. and tr., *Ottoman Gentleman*, 20–1 (*çaşnigir*s, uniforms); Michel, 'Chronologie', 261 (governorships). Topojan seems to have been an Albanian Catholic village in a mostly Slav area: see Dokle, *Sinan*, 28, 32, 105. Some places in and around Topojan are popularly associated with Sinan today, though the authenticity of such traditions is difficult to assess.   **[6]** Fleischer, *Bureaucrat*, 46(n.) (distant relative), 48–50 (rivalry, Sokollu's role); BNM, MS It. VII. 213, fo. 351r ('tutto fu fatto per opera di Mehemet per mostrar quanto sia il suo potere'); Smith, *Lightning*, 2–6 (rivalry, campaign), 188–90 (Hajj, Mecca); Panzac, *La Marine*, 17 (Mecca).   **[7]** BSB, MS Cod. Ital. 6, fo. 431v (Gabrio story); Rosi, 'Alcuni documenti', 163 (Gabrio story); Charrière, ed., *Négociations*, iii, 473 ('homme fort austère, cruel et ennemy des chrestiens'); Albèri, ed., *Relazioni*, ser. 3, ii, 153–4 ('di natura rozza, arrogante e superba', 'minaccia senza rispetto la serenità vostra, l'imperatore, e tutto il mondo', 'inimicissimo a tutti li Cristiani'), iii, 421 ('nel governo ordinario della Porta dicono che valga molto, perchè nell'operare è indefesso e così nell'ascoltare, rimettendo le cause ai suoi giudici competenti, ed è acuratissimo in procurare l'abbondanza della città'); Gerlach, *Tage-Buch*, 109 ('Was bringst du mir an deme? du weist wol, dass ich keinen Wein trincke. Wann du mir etwas verehren wilt, so bringe mir Büchsen, Harnisch, Pantzer und andere Waffen, dass ich die eurigen damit bekriegen möge'; cf. Schweigger, *Reyssbeschreibung*, 66; Lubenau, *Beschreibung*, i, 199–200); Vratislav, *Adventures*, 44 (shepherd); Fleischer, *Bureaucrat*, 51(n.) (Peçevi dependent), 135, 164–5 (criticisms of Sinan, poets); Peçevi, *Historija*, ii, 56 (criticism of Sinan); Brookes, ed. and tr., *Ottoman Gentleman*, 41 (long words); Fetvacı, *Picturing History*, 218–20 (patronage, manuscripts, tomb library); Michel, 'Les *waqf*-s' (foundations); Meier, 'Charities' (foundations). On a fine illustrated manuscript given by Sinan to Sultan Mehmed III, see Uluç, 'Vezir-i Azam'. **[8]** Kortepeter, *Ottoman Imperialism*, 51 (rivalry, dismissal); Murphey, *Ottoman Warfare*, 138 (rivalry, dismissal); Albèri, ed., *Relazioni*, ser. 3, ii, 160 (Tiepolo), 240 (later report), 359 (Safiye Albanian, influential), iii, 293 (1585: 'grandemente amato'); Pedani, 'Safiye's Household', 11 (Safiye Albanian); Fleischer, *Bureaucrat*, 164–5 and n. (Mustafa Ali); Kunt, 'Ethnic-Regional Solidarity'. Fine, *When Ethnicity Did not Matter*, is a valuable corrective to anachronistic 'national' interpretations; but the evidence here suggests that ethnicity could matter in some ways. **[9]** Ciorănescu, ed., *Documente*, 74 ('se conosceva Bruti, se viveva in casa mia, et perchè non viveva in casa mia, essendo venuto meco'), 75 ('per haver la lingua albanese et per haver pratica di questa Porta', threat of arrest, execution by impalement, 'mala vita', Margliani's response). **[10]** Ibid., 76 ('di verdad dubitando che come questo huomo si trovasse in prigione, si facesse Turco', 'si veneva medemamente [*sic*] a destruere la pratica della inteligentia', 'certi Greci'), 77 ('alcuni Albanesi suoi compatrioti renegati'); AGS, Estado, leg. 490, item 36, fo. [1r] (loan of 44 scudi, 29 June), Estado, leg. 1337, item 15, fo. [2r] ('Con il fauor del sig.ʳ sinan Bassa; et della Moglie del Gran Turcho, qual è di mia Nation et terra', 'con hauer io offerto al Gran Turcho per nome di detto Principe 80 m. cechini, oltra molt'altri p[rese]nti di Gran Valuta alla Moglie, et hauendo il tutto Concluso; peruenne a l'orecchie di Mehemet Bassa; qual ... subito mi fece prendere'); above, 259 (immunity); Luca, *Dacoromano-Italica*, 119 (Grillo); ASVen, CCD, Dispacci (Lettere) di Ambasciatori, busta 5, item 163 (copies of Tuscan documents). The deal involved gifts of 80,000 ducats to the Sultan and 20,000 each to the Sultan's mother and Sinan, plus 150 horses for Sinan: Ciurea, 'Relaţii', 35. **[11]** HHStA, Türkei I, Karton 39, 3rd foliation, fo. 187r (imprisonment, Persian intelligence, 'Meh: Bassa dem Sinan Vesier starckh zu gesprochen, weil diser Bruti als ain Albaneser sich gleichsamb bej dem Sinan Vesier anfreundten wöllen, was Er Sinan fur ainen freundt, der seines herrn und Kaisers Ertzverräter wäre'), 187v (Margliani suggests expulsion); AGS, Estado, leg. 490, items 34 (dates of imprisonment, Margliani efforts, instruction to Ragusan ambassadors), 36, fo. [1v] (money, cloth), 49

(24 Aug.: 'tanto sfazato et tristo'), Estado, leg. 1337, item 15, fo. 2r–v (imprison-ment, Istanbul intelligence, Sinan's intercession); *HD*, xi, 638(n.) (sent to Dubrovnik, Sokollu's message); DAD, LCL, 33, fo. 234v (instructions to Ragusan ambassadors). **[12]** AGS, Estado, leg. 490, item 16 (Novi Pazar), Estado, leg. 1337, item 15, fos. [2v] (Dubrovnik, Echevarría, letter to Margliani, request refused), [3r] (Mljet, Korčula); DAD, LCL, 33, fo. 235r (boat to Barletta). **[13]** AGS, Estado, leg. 1337, item 15 (letter to Philip). **[14]** Ibid., item 15, fo. 3r ('alcuni gentil'huomeni, miei Amici', 'hauendo Inteso la sorella del sig.ʳ Sinan Bassa la mia retention in Alessio espedite un suo figliolo Con una squadra di Vinti Cinq[ue] huomeni, tutti ben armati à Cauallo, mi leuorno d'Alessio per forza, et mi posero in mia libertà dandomi homeni et Commodità per accompagnarmi in Constan-tinopoli', Sinan's action, arrest of Ragusans, return to Istanbul); DAD, LCL, 33, fos. 234v (couriers' report), 235r ('habbiamo con molta diligenza mandato huomini aposta in Alesso per farlo prendere, et ritenerlo in forze'), 237v ('c[he] in modo alcuno no[n] comunichiate seco questo negotio ne che ue ne fidiate di lui in cosa alt.ᵃ ma che ue ne guardiate come dal fuoco'); Dokle, *Sinan*, 13 (sister); Hoxha, *Shqiptari*, 57 (sister). Both Dokle and Hoxha suggest that the sister was the mother of the future Yemişçi Hasan Pasha; so perhaps he was the son who rescued Bartolomeo. **[15]** Samardžić, *Mehmed*, 549–50 (assassination); Glück-lich, ed., *Václava Budovce*, 9 (2 hours, incapable of speech); Charrière, ed., *Négociations*, iii, 834(n.) (fanatic, galley-slave); Schweigger, *Reyssbeschreibung*, 80 (*in flagrante*); Maxim, *L'Empire*, 120 (fanatic paid by rivals); Gentilezza, 'L'Albania', 70(n.) (Herceg Novi origin); Pedani, ed., *Relazioni*, 255 (mother-in-law). For a memorandum drawn up by Hürrem for Ahmed soon after the death of Sokollu, summarizing the state of play over the truce, see de La Veronne, 'Gio-vanni Margliani', 72–3. **[16]** AGS, Estado, leg. 490, items 4, fos. [1r] (news of 17 Nov.), [2r] ('un gran pezo', 'Se è cosi, che si faccia la uolunta del mio fratello, et che si mandi in puglia', official order), [2v] ('Che ha fatto costui, Ha ammazato alcuno, Che è il suo contrario, Chi l'accusa, Io ho da far Justicia, et non mirare alle passioni di alcuno'), 24, fo. [1v] (news of 5 Nov.). **[17]** Ibid., items 4, fo. [2v] (Christians, 'Viueuano l[']uno et l[']altro come christiani'), 23, fos. [1r] ('Sinam Bassa gli haueua dimandato se sapeua che l[']arnaut intendendo del Brutti era fugito che haueua resposto che non lo sapeua che egli haueua detto e fugito et dalui si sapera la verita di quello si sara tratato con Mehemet Bassa sog-giongendo non potremo piu essere inganati, per che egli dira a me la Verita de ogni cosa'), [3r] (alteration, fear of exposure by Bruti), 27 (alteration after Rocafull instructions), 31, fos. [2v–3r] ('respose Sinan che dal Bruti il qual le diceua la Verita, haueua Inteso questo il contrario et a questo proposito mi dize il Chauz che disse tante cose le quali diceua di hauere intese da esso Brutti che restay espantatto'). **[18]** Charrière, ed., *Négociations*, iii, 886–8 (Mar. 1580); Rodríguez Salgado, *Felipe II*, 139 (Mar. 1580), 157–60 (Feb. 1581); Fernández Collado, *Gregorio XIII*, 130 (foot-dragging, impalement); Skilliter, 'Hispano-Ottoman', 492–6 (Feb. 1581), 504 (renewal 1584); Anon., ed., *Cartas*, 55–6 (Feb. 1581, permission to leave); Sola and de la Peña, *Cervantes*, 169–72 (Pérez, Naples); de Foix, *Les Lettres*, 36–7 (Rome, 'fort habile negociateur'); BL,

MS Add. 28,415, fos. 228r, 239r, 307v (de Ferrari activities, 1583–5); Zinkeisen, *Geschichte*, iii, 510–11 (renewals 1584, 1587); Bodl., MS Tanner 77, fo. 2r (expensive compromise); von Hammer, *Geschichte*, iv, 159 (renewal 1587); Niederkorn, *Die europäischen Mächte*, 189–92 (de Ferrari and Ruggiero). Skilliter expresses surprise (500–1) at the nature and format of the 1581 agreement; for an explanation see Kołodziejczyk, *Ottoman–Polish*, 47–8. **[19]** AGS, Estado, leg. 490, item 4, fo. [6r] ('Hanno data la bugdania à q[ue]llo, per il quale trataua il Brutti per una certa quantita de danari'); Mureşan, 'L'Émergence', 67–70, 121 (system, investiture, anointment); Pedani, 'Sultans', 198–200 (insignia, heron, *hüma*); Maxim, *Noi documente*, 214 (heron feather), 219 (21 Nov.); BNF, MS Français 16,143, fo. 8r (26 Nov., 8 Dec.). **[20]** AGS, Estado, leg. 1337, items 15, fos. [3r] (visited Margliani), [3v] ('il mio servir a V.M. non è fondato sopra il mio particolar interesse; ma mi glorio chiamarmi servitor del più Gran Re del mondo', 'Io sono chiamato dal Principe di Moldauia, et solicitato da Sinan Bassa, andarui, Con titolo di Generale di tutta la sua gente, qual grado io non hò riffiutato; ma non hò uoluto andarui, se prima non pigliaua licenza da V.M. hauendogli giurato fideltà, perche douunq[ue] ch'io sarò sempre mi chiamarò seruitor del Catolico Re'), 21 ('Certo ch'io tengo, che la pace non sarà, et tutto quello fin'hora il Mariglianni hà trattato con spese, per la reputation di V.M. sarà Annulato, perch'a me in Corte non hanno prestato orecchie'); de La Veronne, 'Giovanni Margliani', 74 ('no se ha pasado cosa ninguna de la pensión de Bruti, ni [*sic*] se pagará si no fuesse advirtiendo V. m., que era esto necessario para evitar las cosas que este traydor ha y querra intentar . . . Sólo se ha de contemporizar con el hasta que la persona de V. m. esté en salvo'). **[21]** BNF, MS Français 16,143, fo. 94r ('Le Brutti . . . ayant négotié en ceste Porte la restitution du Vayuode de la Bogdauie [*sic*] regnant a p[rése]nt, et l'estant allé trouuer puis peu de jours a esté largement recongneu [*sic*] de ses seruices par led[it] Vayuode, faict general de sa Cauallerie & fanterie, heu vne eschelle ou dace d'un port vallant trois mil ducats par an, & l'vsuffruict de la succession & hoirie d'un seigneur signalé executé par Justice').

15. GASPARO BRUNI AND THE HUGUENOT WAR

[1] ASVat, Segr. Stato, Malta, 1, fos. 5r ('Il Cau.^ro f: Gasparo Bruni Albanese . . . ha seruito continuamente in questi tre anni di guerra contra il Turco p[er] cap.^no de la galera g[e]n[er]ale di SS.^ta nel qual tempo ha perso la patria, le faculta, li fr[ate]lli, parenti, et quanto haueua che tutto l'anno passato andò in preda de Turchi; et S B^ne uolendo proueder in qualche modo al bisogno, et à la necessita del d^to Cau.^ro benemerito di questa s.^ta sede, ricerca p[er] suo breue che VS Illma lo proueda de la p.^a Commenda di gratie che uacara'), 33r (Romegas from Malta, describing arrival in early Feb. and acceptance of Priory); Testa, *Romegas*, 134–6 (Turcopilier), 144 (Prior); NLM, AOM, MS 93, fos. 39v (resisting, Turcopilier), 105v–108r (accepting, Prior). **[2]** Galea, *Grand Master*, 66 (disputes); ASVat, Segr. Stato, Malta, 1, fo. 32r (breve, reply); Manfroni, 'La lega', 406–8 (Colonna,

Nuncio's threat, papal correspondence); NLM, AOM, MS 93, fo. 91v ('murmuratione et imprudenti loquatione aliquoru[m] Fratrum palam dicentium nolle proficisci ad expeditionem contra immanes Turcas unà et sub Ill.ᵐ D. Marcantonio Columna'). [3] ASVat, Segr. Stato, Malta, 1, fos. 3r ('perche conosce il merito, et la bonta del Cau.ʳᵒ et il stato in che si troua spogliato da Turchi di quanto haueua al Mondo, non la pregaro à usar diligenza et amoreuolezza in questo negocio, poiche son certiss.ᵒ che da se è per farlo'), 34r ('e di piu abbocca li Narrai li seruizij che questo S:ʳ brul hauea fatti alla SS:ᵗᵃ'), 35r ('non posso in alcuno modo obedire in cio à S. B.ⁿᵉ come cosa à me dal tutto impossibile'), Segr. Stato, Legaz. Avignone, 3, fo. 165r (Oct. 1573: reappears); below, 287 ('continuously'). [4] Perrin, États, 5–7, 31 (history of territories, 100,000), 33 (not covering costs); ASR, Soldatesche e galere, busta 646, unfoliated (town populations); Moulierac-Lamoureux, 'Le Comtat', 118–19 (Bourbon, d'Armagnac), 141–6 (legal rights); Achard and Duhamel, Inventaire, 102–4 (freedom from taxes, legal rights). [5] Perrin, États, 68–73 (Serbelloni, Mérindol, Orange); Chossat, Les Jésuites, 42 (confiscations). [6] Brunelli, Soldati, 12 (papal forces, Jesuits), 15 (battle standards); Jouanna, La Saint-Barthélemy, 99–200. Roughly 3,000 died in Paris; reliable figures for the rest of the country are not available. [7] Fornery, Histoire, ii, 159 (order to retire), 161 (Martinengo and Colonna), 167–8 (Ménerbes); Guerrini, Una celebre famiglia, 490–1 (Martinengo biography, Lepanto); Duhamel, Inventaire-sommaire, 106 (Martinengo plea to Rome); ASVat, Segr. Stato, Legaz. Avignone, 2, fos. 269r–270v (Martinengo plea to Rome); BMA, MS 2398, fo. 281v (de Valavoire, brother); Hurtubise, ed., Correspondance, i, 648 (5 Oct.), 656 (19 Oct.: 'et 600 fanti s'incamineranno di qui fra tre giorni'), 665 (in return for properties). Provence had joined the kingdom of France in 1486. [8] ASVat, Segr. Stato, Legaz. Avignone, 3, fos. 165r ('ogni giorno cresce il bisogno di cotesto presidio nel stato d'Auignone'), 172r (4 Nov.), 183r (reply to letter of 16 Nov.); Parrott, Business, 43 (condotta system); da Mosto, 'Ordinamenti', 82–5 (shift to new system); Brunelli, 'Poteri' (militia). [9] ASVat, Segr. Stato, Legaz. Avignone, 2, fos. 515r (arrival, refusal, drawing lots), 536r (governor and dignitaries, refusals), 610r ('questa notte hauemo fornito di sbarcharli tuttj, prego Dio che li conduchi saluam.ᵗᵉ'), 620r–621v (Monterentio; 620v: 'è vna pieta vederli poueri et senza arme'); Hurtubise, ed., Correspondance, i, 684–7 (nuncio, promise, refusal). [10] ASVat, Segr. Stato, Legaz. Avignone, 3, fo. 224r (Bruni assigned to Carpentras), 4, fos. 123–4 (numbers, distribution of soldiers), 171r (Sérignan, Orange, 'con maliss.ᵃ satisfacione de tuti li soldati p[er] hauer perso cosi bella occasione contra li ribelj'), 255r (Beaumes), 404r ('e massimamente del sig.ʳ Cauagliero Bruno Il quale per q[ues]to cognosco, è molto di buono animo, e di gran' ualore'; on Sacrati see Reinhard, Die Reform, 40–6). Historians of Carpentras have not apparently noticed that the city once had an Albanian governor. [11] ASVat, Segr. Stato, Legaz. Avignone, 3, fos. 405r (Como reply about Monterentio), 510r (Como reply about Pompeo), 4, fos. 95r ('Duol mi bene che hauendo perso p[er] mia disauentura le faculta con la patria, che hora non possa con questa misera paga mantener il grado, et condicion mia in questo Gouerno. et però supp.ᶜᵒ V. S. Ill.ᵐᵃ che si degni agiutarmj appresso N. S.re uenendo qualche occasione di comenda'), 640r (Bruni complaint about Monterentio), 5, fos. 274r–v (14 Apr.: 'la totale oscuratione della reputation mia', 'cinq[ue] anni continui'), 325r (28 Apr.: 'reputacion'), 404r (3 June), 637r (18 Aug.), 6, fo. 399v (50 and 70). On Catilina, who was from Rieti and had been in Venetian service, see Brunelli, Soldati, 77.   [12] Fornery, Histoire, ii, 176–7 (royal visit); Theiner, ed., Annales, ii, 505 (cavalry, arquebusiers); Hurtubise, ed., Correspondance, ii, 154–6 (council of war proposals).   [13] Theiner, ed., Annales, ii, 506–7 (fear of 'recatolezati', guard); AMA, MS BB19, 15, fo. 19r (request for 200); Hurtubise, ed., Correspondance, i, 116 (agreed 300, fear of French conspiracy).   [14] Hurtubise, ed., Correspondance, i, 117–18 (bull of restitution, peace agreement); ASVat, Segr. Stato, Legaz. Avignone, 5, fo. 453r (Venasque, 'cosi fù rotto il disegno con gran dispiacer di tuti noi. I superiori possono fare quel che le pare, et io conuengo contentarmi di quel che piace a loro'), 6, fo. 469r (anonymous informant), 8, fos. 182r (Bruni report of betrayal of Entrechaux), 225r ('in molte occasioni che si sono apresentate conosco che non si à possuto far cosa che sia in seruicio di N. S.re ne beneficio di questo pouero paese, manco d'aquistar honor nessuno, ma ben di perder al' in grosso', 'se son buono seruirla in qualche altro locco che li piacia leuarmi de qui'); Fornery, Histoire, ii, 184 (fighting continued), 191 (commanders refused, Saint-Léger, 400 men), 193–4 (Entrechaux).   [15] Fornery, Histoire, ii, 193–4 (decision, Matteucci, Grimaldi), 195–7 (army, 1 Sept., forces, de Valois, assumption); Anon., La vita (life of Matteucci); Valentianus, Panegyricus (life of Grimaldi); Guglielmotti, Storia, vi, 238 (Grimaldi at Lepanto). Some early accounts do refer to the defenders' use of artillery: e.g. BMA, MS 2562, fo. 304v.   [16] Fornery, Histoire, ii, 194 (vacating of Entrechaux), 195 (Pilles); ASVat, Segr. Stato, Legaz. Avignone, 8, fo. 428r (1 Aug. 1577: 'sapendo ella beniss.o che essendo io cacciato dalla patria mia da Turchi nemici della uera fede di Cristo, p[er] la qual molti di mei maggiori in diuersi tempi hano sparso il sangue, et essendo rimasti alcuni mei Nepoti et altre misere reliquie di Casa mia tute disperse, che iuuono col medesimo animo, tra le quali ui è un mio unico fiolo che ormai sono sei anni che sta nel Collegio Germanico et desiderando di redurle insieme, et dar qualche ordine alle cose mie che hano grandiss.o bisogno, Vengo humilm.te suplicar V. S. Ill.ma ... impetrarmi gratia da N. S.re che fatto il racolto del Vino, come si è fatto quel del Grano, possa p[er] dua mesi solam.te tra il uenir, star, et rettornar, Lassar la mia Comp.a al mio Alfiero persona ualorosa, diligente, et fedele, et uenirmene à Roma, p[er] dar ordine alle cose mie che patiscono molto', 'un ualoroso giouane mio parente'), 18, fo. 30r (Paolo Emilio, 1588); Manzuoli, Nova descrittione, i, 87 (death of Paolo Emilio). Grimaldi noted in 1586 that Paolo Emilio was the nephew of Giacomo Verzi of Koper: BMA, MS 6431, fo. 107r.   [17] ASVat, Segr. Stato, Legaz. Avignone, 5, fo. 404r (3 June 1575: 'uenir à dar ordine ad alcune mie cossete [sic] in Roma'), 7, fo. 326r ('horache l'operatione è forse piu utile et piu necessaria che mai'), 8, fo. 532r ('se ben il bisogno mi stimola di venirmi uia, essendosi cominciata già questa impresa di Minerba desidero uederli al fine', 'dil modo tenuto e di progressi fatti fin qui nella espugnatione non uoglio dir altro, senon prega dio che il fine sia buono').   [18] ASVat, Segr. Stato, Legaz. Avignone, 8, fos. 504v

(967 volleys in a day), 505r (Catilina wounded); Fantoni Castrucci, *Istoria*, i, 419 ('alle prime aperture si diedero assalti con perdita de' più forti soldati, massime delle compagnie d'Italia; difendendosi que' di dentro si arditamente, che al cader dell'vno suppliua l'altro ... & i feriti dalle scheggie della muraglia, rimandauano i sassi tinti del proprio sangue'); Fornery, *Histoire*, ii, 197–203 (events of siege). Some early accounts regarded Ferrier's agreement to surrender as a ruse: BMA, MSS 2398, fo. 294v, and 2562, fo. 305r. [19] Fornery, *Histoire*, ii, 204–10 (peace treaty, withdrawal, forts, trench); ASVat, Segr. Stato, Legaz. Avignone, 9, fo. 252r (Grimaldi shot); Cottier, *Notes*, 215 (Grimaldi shot through cheeks). [20] ASVat, Segr. Stato, Legaz. Avignone, 7, fos. 385r, 386r (Bruni in Rome in late Dec., with letters dated 24, 25 Nov., met Como, Pope), 463r (Como to Bruni, Apr., referring to previous plan in Feb. to visit), 506r (Como to Matteucci, promoting Bruni to colonel), 9, fos. 370r (Monterentio to Como, 45 scudi, refusal), 404r (Bruni to Como, 31 July, 'disgratia'), 441r (death of Matteucci). [21] Fornery, *Histoire*, ii, 212 (Montacuti), 214–18 (peace agreement, forts rased, Malvezzi, gold chain, Grimaldi co-legate); Cloulas, ed., *Correspondance*, 259, 284 (surrender of Ménerbes); Theiner, ed., *Annales*, ii, 626 (d'Armagnac to Pope). [22] Fornery, *Histoire*, ii, 219–20 (raids, harvest), 222 (Grimaldi attacked), 227–8 (plague); ASVat, Segr. Stato, Legaz. Avignone, 11, fos. 58r (captains' protest), 694r (100 per day), 12, fo. 393r (half dead, 1,500 destitute); BMA, MS 2562, fos. 309r–315r (plague journal; fo. 310r: woman and child); Cottier, *Notes*, 219 (Grimaldi attacked); Theiner, ed., *Annales*, iii, 689 (Grimaldi attacked); Adami, *Elogii*, 95, 118 (Biagio); Salimei, 'La nobiltà', 14 (Capizucchis at Lepanto); Chossat, *Les Jésuites*, 62–4 (plague). [23] ASVat, Segr. Stato, Legaz. Avignone, 13, fos. 26r ('Hò inteso con mio dispiacere il miserabil caso de Monterentio, et prego Dio che habbia pieta del'anima sua'), 37r–v (suicide of Monterentio), 71r–72v (Monterentio note to Como); Fornery, *Histoire*, ii, 231 (embezzlements). [24] ASVat, Segr. Stato, Legaz. Avignone, 10, fos. 386r ('doue mi sono morti molti soldati parte in facione, et altri di maletia', 'affronto'), 623v, 624v (105 men), 11, fo. 273v (152 men), 12, fo. 47r ('questo quartiero circondato da nemici'), 13, fos. 253r ('piena di cattiuissimi humori'), 253v (killings, retreat to friary), 254r ('alla q.^{a}le concorse con grand.^{mo} furore tutti gli huomini di quella uilla chi con armi, et chi senza, con i q.^{a}li fu necessario che il cau.^{re} Bruni usasse buone parole, et operò tanto che li fece retirare sendo egli molto amato in quel luogo, che altrimenti era facil cosa che tagliassero a pezzi la maggior parte di quel presidio, et forse tutto', 'con grandissima difficultà con la patienza, et prudenza del Cau.^{re} Bruni'), 733r (191 men); Pagnol, *Valréas*, 165–7 (Valréas). [25] ASVat, Segr. Stato, Legaz. Avignone, 14, fos. 193v (move to Ménerbes), 520r (rumours, sentries), 579r (tensions, 'uoglio sperar ... che sono destinato di andare sempre doue nascono disordeni, come fu à Vorias ... et vltimame.^{te} à Minerba'), 15, fos. 191r ('il quale essendo uenuto qua p[er] uedermi, et desiderando io, che non ritorni p[er] adesso in Ittalia, [*sic*] ma che si fermi in questa città apresso di me p[er] la comodita che auera di studiare et nelle occasioni poter seruir la Sta Sede App.^{ca}'), 307v (July 1584), 425r (Sept. 1584: 'senon un anno, al meno questo inverno in Avignone, accio che non entri nelli animi

degli huomeni oppinione che p[er] qualche mio mancamento, io sia stato cacciato da questa città'); ADV, Archives communales MS AA 44, item 35 (Como to Avignon, 20 Nov., nomination of Grimaldi). Boschetti had replaced Vitelli in 1582. **[26]** Brunelli, 'Gallio' (Como left); BMA, MS 6431, fos. 5r ('buoni s[ervi]t[o]r^i del Papa'), 26v–27r (news of Odoardo, unsettling), 34v, 37v, 39v, 44r, 50r, 55r–v (urging to retain), 61r (Odoardo arrived, Nov.), 74v (letter, 1 May), 100v (Paolo Emilio captain, Sept.), 109v ('non mi son mai sentito più sollagiato in questo gouerno quanto nel tempo che ui erano tre cap.^{nij} vecchi, et di sperienza che furno il Caualier Bruno, il Coll.^{o} ludouico Manari, et il Coll.^{o} Pompeo Catalina'); ASVat, Segr. Stato, Legaz. Avignone, 18, fo. 30r (4 companies in 1588, of which one had been brought by Odoardo and the other 3 were under Catilina, Manari and Carerio); on Carerio see above, 291. Manzuoli, who knew the Bruni family in Koper, wrote that Gasparo spent 13 years in Avignon (i.e. 1573–86): *Nova descrittione*, i, 87.

16. ANTONIO BRUNI AND THE JESUITS

[1] ACGH, MS Hist. 145, fo. 39r (entry for Antonio, 12 May 1572); Testa, *Fondazione*, 339, 341, 348 (14 normal, some 13, one 12). **[2]** Giard, 'Le Devoir', xiii (numbers of colleges, Jesuits), lix (classes, exercises, discipline, etc.); Lukács, 'Introductio generalis', 30*–33* (plays, subdivision, seating, etc.); Murphy, 'Jesuit Rome', 73 (number of colleges); Villoslada, *Storia*, 39–40 (outstripped Rome University); Codina, '"Modus"' (Parisian model); Farrell, *Jesuit Code*, 240–3 (declamations, prizes, promotion, etc.); Botteri, '"Buona vita"' (manners, civility). **[3]** Steinhuber, *Geschichte*, i, 45 (6 or 7), 46–7 (development under Laynez), 49–50 (cardinals, noble families), 61 (Palazzo Colonna), 62 (80 or 100, triumph), 94–5 (17 Oct.); Testa, 'Dalla fondazione', 16–24 (decree, origins of Seminario), 27 (boarders). **[4]** ACGH, MS Hist. 145, fos. 200v ('s'era molto ben osseruato e p[er] lungo tempo esperimentato che l'Vnione tra la Natione Alemanna, et Italiana con uiuere insieme non faceua buona lega'), 224v–225r (17 Oct.); Steinhuber, *Geschichte*, i, 88–9 (new German plan), 94–5 (17 Oct.); Testa, 'Dalla fondazione', 30–3 (shaky start, transformed); Schmidt, *Das Collegium*, 2 (other new colleges), 16 (new German plan). **[5]** Above, 291 (Gasparo's description); Lukács, ed., *Monumenta paedagogica*, ii, 347 (entry rules for Collegio), 388 (entry rules for Seminario); ACGH, MS Hist. 145, fos. 33v, 39r (Seton), 39r (Bruni), 39v–40r (Carafa, Chisholm, Cenci, Piccolomini), 252r–v (chambers, saints, festivities); Dilworth, 'Chisholm'; Lee, 'Seton'; Testa, *Fondazione*, 330 (numbers), 382–4 (chambers); ARSI, MS Rom. 51/1, fo. 13r–v (prefects). **[6]** ARSI, MSS Rom. 51/1, fo. 16r (confession, communion), Rom. 155/1, fos. 73r (dress), 133r (food, wine), 135r ('discorsi seditiosi', 'allegrie spropositate et fragorose'), 138r (list of clothes etc.); Testa, *Fondazione*, 362, 368–9 (dress), 415–22 (Marian congregations); Lukács, ed., *Monumenta paedagogica*, ii, 390 (Mass, Hours, psalms), 395 ('de his que [*sic*] ad honestam recreationem faciant'); Murphy, 'Jesuit Rome', 76 (30,000). **[7]** Testa, *Fondazione*, 93–8 (study prefects), 436–9 (lessons in

Collegio Romano), 539–52 (music, Palestrina), 555 (Tucci performance); ARSI, MS Rom. 51/1, fos. 16v ('si esercitano di co[m]poner or[atio]ni latine et comporre uersi greci et latini'), 17r (study prefects, repetitori), 73r ('I preti non entraranno nelle comedie o tragedie almeno uestitj de soldati o donne, o altri personaggi indecenti al stato loro'). **[8]** ARSI, MSS Rom. 51/1, fo. 21v (medicines), Rom. 155/1, fos. 82r (difficult to get payment), 87r (owing 18 scudi, Orsini etc.), 104r (enmity, fees accusation), 104v ('certo spirito secolare, politico, di libertà, licentioso, et finalmte contrario alla disciplina et osseruanza religiosa'), 110r ('l'occasione di unir tanta uarietà di nationi in una disciplina'), 137r (procurator), 137v ('rarissime uolte'). **[9]** ACGH, MS Hist. 145, fo. 39r (28 Aug.); ASVat, Segr. Stato, Legaz. Avignone, 12, fo. 47r ('son auisato che mio figliolo Ant.° p[er] qualche Costione che gli è occorsa à Perosa si è retirato in Venetia, et p[er] che desidero schiuar tuti li desordini che puono nascer, et uorei che continuase le litere et che studiase à Padoa, ma non posso farlo senza l'agiuto che N. Sʳᵉ p[er] sua benignita li è piaciuto concedermi', 'che sara causa di non perder quello che fin hora hà imparato'), 14, fo. 431r (began Jan. 1580). **[10]** Gentili, *Laudes*, 11–12 (special method), 24 ('admirabilis docendi methodus'), 24–5 ('sermonis puritas, qua Itali penè omnes destituuntur'); Ermeni, *Storia*, 425–9 (4 professors: Lancellotti, Eugeni, Ridolfi, Alfani); ASVat, Segr. Stato, Legaz. Avignone, 14, fos. 430r ('alcuni accidenti'), 740r ('alcune costioni'); Setton, *Papacy*, iv, 822 (decree: 'detestabilis duellorum usus'). **[11]** ASVat, Segr. Stato, Legaz. Avignone, 14, fo. 430r (July 1583, de' Michieli); BSS, AC, Corrispondenza Ascanio Colonna, unnumbered, Bruni to Ascanio, 2 Nov. 1584 ('poi ch'io no[n] hò potuto adimpir il desiderio ch[e] haueua di seruirla unaltra uolta, cosi fedelmen.ʳᵉ come lhò seruita tre anni nel'Armata contra Turchi p[er] Capitanio della sua galera, Quel medesimo desiderio offerisco à V. S. Ill.ᵐᵃ pregandola ch[e] uoglia accettare, a [me?], et Antonio mio figliolo p[er] seruitori perpetuj', 'al studio'). On the law school at Padua in this period see Woolfson, *Padua*, 41–5. **[12]** Venard, 'L'Université' (early history, 1477 refusal, change of mind, 1581 petition, 'un famosissimo dottore'); Marchand, *L'Université*, 5 (arts faculty inactive), 281 (effect of Jesuit college); Brémond *et al.*, *Le Collège*, 8–11 (Jesuit college, Possevino, 500 pupils); Cadecombe, *Speculum* [= ADV, D 41], 17 (Cujas); de Barjavel, *Dictionnaire*, 152–3 (Beau); Beau, *Consilia*. **[13]** ADV, MS D 36, fo. 105r ('Antonius Brunus dioces. Olciniensis'); de Teule, *Chronologie*, 42 (doctorate, showing that he was one of 9 in 1585, the others all being from Avignon and the south of France); Fournier, *Histoire*, iii, 682–4 (ceremony). **[14]** Vida, *Il Sileno*, 115–24 ('conclusioni amorose' list); Vida, *De' cento dubbi*, fo. 19r–v (kinds of beauty, Verzi). **[15]** Vida, *De' cento dubbi*, fos. 66v–68r (Antonio on yellow); Ziliotto, *Accademie*, 25, 30(n.) (Santorio, ages); Manzuoli, *Nova descrittione*, i, 97 (Latin poem; printed also in Stancovich, *Biografia*, 240). **[16]** ASVat, Fondo Borghese III 60h, fos. 69r–70v ('nato nelle Città di Sodoma, e Gomorra', 'li scandoli che ha fato nella prouincia di Venetia quando fu trouato vestito da secolare nelle Putane et Comedie in detta Città et preso dalli sbirri et messo in prigione doue è stato parechi giorni carcerato ma poi ha rotto la prigione et fugi apostata a roma et per fauor del sigʳ Antonio Bruni albanese da Dolcigno fu liberato del castigo delle galere'); Bartl, ed., *Albania* *sacra*, i, 18 (1596, Ragusan); Vekarić, *Pelješki rodovi*, ii, 255 (Stojičić); Popović, *Turska*, 252 (Stojković); Appendini, *Notizie*, ii, 75 (Stojković, Bar, Stay); DAD, LCP, 1, fo. 136; 2, fos. 25r, 41r–42v (Stay in Vlorë); ADV, MS D 155, fo. 1r ('apud Principes, prudentissimosque rerumpublicarum gubernatores & moderatores pro eorum assistentia, ad gubernandas beneq[ue] regendas respublicas'). **[17]** de Leva, ed., *La legazione*, i, 148(n.) (Ascanio appointments); BSS, AC, Corrispondenza Ascanio Colonna, 1 II CF 2059 ('infinitamente ... obligatiss.°', 'Ne mancaró mai di procurare con ogni affetto di cuore tutto quelle, che pensaró, che possa resultare in beneficio di questo Priorato di V. S. Illma'). **[18]** GPLV, MS 578, 2nd item, 1st document ('frater Gaspar Brunus miles et in eodem Prioratu Receptor', Giustinianis, Morosini); Mallia-Milanes, *Venice*, 77–80 (Spanish Knight), 81–3 (2 galleys), 85–6 (retaliation, reaction, response), 90–7 (Sixtus V); Tenenti, *Piracy*, 37 (retaliation); de Leva, ed., *La legazione*, i, 148 (Colonna's request; cf. also i, 193(n.), 197, 237, 267). **[19]** BSS, AC, Corrispondenza Ascanio Colonna, 1 II CF 2149 (Bruni to Colonna from Malta, describing travel and task); NLM, AOM, MSS 98, fos. 153v, 155v (attempt to change Priory), 446, fo. 246v (pension of 100 scudi), 448, fo. 195v (Loschi confirmed); de Leva, ed., *La legazione*, ii, 299–300, 312–17, 347, 395 (attempt to change Priory), 508 (Loschi sent); dal Pozzo, *Historia*, i, 349–50 (attempt to change Priory). **[20]** BAR, MS 1479, fos. 6v–10r (Leoni description; 9r: 'bellissimi palazzi'), 31v (600 Knights); Heberer, *Aegyptiaca servitus*, 421–2 ('viel schöner Gebew [*sic*]', infirmary, palazzo), 434–5 (glass); ASVat, Segr. Stato, Malta, 6, fo. 86r (200 of langue of Italy). On the building of Valletta see de Giorgio, *A City* (esp. 152–6 on the auberge of Italy). **[21]** Bosio, *Gli statuti*, 202–4 (statutes); NLM, AOM, MSS 98, fos. 161v, 166v (bull of antianitas), 99, fo. 55r (applied for Cosenza), 449, fos. 111v–112r (pension, Apr. 1595), 128v (50 ducats). **[22]** NLM, AOM, MSS 99, fos. 57r (Cadamosto versus Capece), 89v (Pope granted Racconisi), 90v (21 June 1596 decision), 91r–92r (appeals), 143v (bull for Bruni), 100, fos. 38v–39v (special tribunal), 446, fo. 58v (Cadamosto to resign La Motta), 447, fo. 148r (Cadamosto to get Racconisi); ASVat, Segr. Stato, Malta, 6, fo. 109r–v ('entrato per la finestra non per la porta'). **[23]** Gattini, *I priorati*, 83–4 (income, dues); Borretti, *Il S. M. Ordine* (income, dues; p. [2]: Pier Luigi Parisio); Valente, *Il Sovrano Ordine*, 55 (imprisonment, murder charge). For the earlier history of the commenda, and its estates in the 16th century, see Salerno, *L'Ordine*.

17. MOLDAVIA, TATARS AND COSSACKS

[1] Murphey, 'Ottoman Imperial Identity', 86 ('ola-gelmiş', 'kırallar zamanında olduğu gibi'). On these issues see also Faroqhi, *Ottoman Empire*, 75–97, Ágoston, 'Flexible Empire', and Kármán and Kunčević, eds., *European Tributary States*. **[2]** Panaite, 'From Allegiance', vol. 48, 200 (tribute from 1455–6), 213 (prostration), vol. 49, 206 (viewed as conquered after 1538); Iorga, *Studiĭ*, 155–64 (ports seized), 185–7 (Bender, *sancak*); Gemil, *Românii*, 186–7 (1538 turning-point, Ottoman ceremony); Panaite, 'Voivodes', 65–6 (changing view of tribute); Panaite, 'Legal and Political Status', 21–5 (changing view of tribute); Hunt, 'Romanian Lands' (dichotomous legal tradition; 407: shift from 1565, Ottoman coins); Maxim, *L'Empire*, 13, 19 (shift from 1568), 113–16 (1574 tightening); Gorovei, 'Moldova' (1574 tightening); Ciobanu, *La cumpănă*, 30–1 (1574 tightening, Polish factor); David, *Petru Şchiopul*, 12–17 (Petru's origins), 78 (unpopularity); Andreescu, *Restitutio*, 164–6 (unpopularity). **[3]** Alzati, *Terra romena*, 192 (*divan*); ASVat, Segr. Stato, Germania, 95, fo. 165v ('scrivanj'); Gerlach, *Tage-Buch*, 310 (janissaries); Cantemir, *Descrierea*, 296 (Muslim merchants); Maxim, *L'Empire*, 12 (1577 decree), 18 (marrying foreigners); Panaite, 'The re'ayas', 98–104 (Moldavian merchants); Bodl., MS Rawl. D 618, fo. 107r (10,000, 1574); Albèri, ed., *Relazioni*, ser. 3, ii, 144 (10,000, 1576); Pedani, ed., *Relazioni*, 206 (10,000, 1576); Cristea, 'Friend', 261 (campaigns in region); Maxim, 'Haraciul' (tribute); Panaite, 'Voivodes', 76–8 (intelligence); Binark, ed., *5 Numaralı*, ii, 131 ('Nemçe'deki casusları, Nemçe askerlerinin toplanmakta olduğunu bildirdiklerine dair kendisinden gelen mektubun alındığı; bu durumda kendisinin de gaflette bulunmaması ve düşman saldırısına karşı gerekli hazırlıkları yapması'); Panaite, 'Legal and Political Status', 21–2 (foreign policy). **[4]** Veinstein, 'Some Views', 179 (1552 campaign); Mavroeidē, *O Ellēnismos*, 27 (population); Maxim, 'Les Pays', 99–100 (prohibiting exports, 1566 decree), 101 (stiff decree to Iancu); White, *Climate*, 30, 32 (timber, grain); Nistor, *Handel*, 44–7 (boyars, voivod trading), 159 (24,500 sheep); Filitti, *Din arhivele*, ii, 44 (100,000 sheep); Maxim, *L'Empire*, 24–5, 124 (fixed prices); Carter, *Trade*, 242–4 (cattle to Poland); Holban *et al.*, eds., *Călători*, ii, 381 (meat in Venice; cf. 641 on exports). On the *celep* system see Kiel, *Art*, 77–86. **[5]** Gerlach, *Tage-Buch*, 135 ('Heut sagt mein Gnädiger Herr: dass die Moldau und Walachey nunmehr nichts anders seyen, als dess Türckischen Käysers und der Bassen Meyerhöfe, und ihre Fürsten, wie sie sich nennen, ihre Meyer'); Nistor, *Handel*, 157–64 (grain, honey etc.); BNC, MS Gesuiti 7, fo. 89r (fish, caviar); Dziubiński, 'Drogi handlowe', 237–40 (routes to Polish border); Małecki, 'Die Wandlungen' 145–7 (routes from Polish border); Dziubiński, *Na szlakach*, 89 (routes to Vilnius, Moscow); Carter, *Trade*, 196 (overland spices cheaper); Veinstein, 'Marchands ottomans', 729 (pearls, silk etc.); Rybarski, *Handel*, i, 179–80 (textiles). **[6]** Dziubiński, *Na szlakach*, 89–93 (Muslim merchants, furs); Veinstein, 'Marchands ottomans' (Muslim merchants, furs); Dudek and Kowalewicz, 'Przyczynek' (suspected of espionage); Giurescu, *Tîrguri*, 246 (Armenians in Iaşi); Małecki, 'Die Wandlungen', 146–8 (Armenians, Jews in Lviv); Israel, *European Jewry*, 29 (Zamość); BNC, MS Gesuiti 7, fo. 89r (Ragusans); Mollat, 'Istanbul', 157 (Ragusans, Albanians); Barbulescu, 'Relations', 119–20 (Ragusans); Mavroeidē, *O Ellēnismos*, 118, 124, 133, 138 (Greeks); Iorga, *Relaţiile*, 49–53, 57, 73, 90 (Greeks); 63, 105 (Pogon); Hoszowski, *Les Prix*, 40 (wines); Shmurlo, *Rossiia*, ii, 443 (Albanians). On Pogon see above, 179. **[7]** İnalcık, 'Question', 108–9 (gradual process); Beldiceanu, 'La Moldavie', 158 (Istanbul); Luca, *Dacoromano-Italica*, 22, 73 (Cretan merchants), 22–4 (Venetians using Ottomans); Heberer, *Aegyptiaca servitus*, 371–2 (French ship, 1588); Cvetkova, 'Vie économique', 336–7 (Ragusans on Black Sea coast); Spissarevska, 'Alcuni problemi', 721–2

(Ragusans to Ancona); Luca, 'Associazionismo', 158 (war, Cossacks); Ostapchuk, 'Human Landscape', 39–40 (Cossacks). For a good summary of the 'closing' debate, see Popescu, 'La Mer Noire'. **[8]** Filitti, *Din arhivele*, ii, 45 (500,000); Iorga, *Acte*, i, 37 (million); Luca, 'Veneziani', 245–6 (jewels); Luca, *Ţările*, 278 (jewels); Decei, *Relaţii*, 225 (briefly made *beylerbeyliks*); Murphey, *Ottoman Warfare* (20,000 in Hungary); HHStA, Türkei I, Karton 36, 2nd foliation, fo. 48r ('Damit wär Poln schon guetes thails des Turken, aber es will vns fast vnglaublich furkhomen, weil Moldaw dise statt mit fleisch, schmalz vnd andere victualien zum maisten versicht, dessen hieige resident ganzlich od[er] maistns thails beraubt wurde, wo die Moldaw durch Turkhen solte geeignet'); Maxim, 'Les Pays', 94 (Polish attitude). Cf. the King of Poland's comment in 1582: the Sultan would not replace voivods with pashas, as the latter would consume most of the territories' revenues (Bolognetti, *Epistolae*, i [= v], 498). **[9]** BSB, MS Cod. Ital. 6, fo. 431v ('disuniti assai', 'agrandire eccesiua.^{te} un suo capital nemico'). **[10]** Fichtner, *Emperor*, 204–5 (rival candidates for throne); Ciobanu, *La cumpănă*, 42 (pretext for more influence), 43 (insinuated idea); Kuntze, 'Les Rapports', 141–6 (Papacy wrong-footed, Warsaw Confederation), 160 (nobles wishing to avoid war). **[11]** Królikowska, 'Sovereignty' (status of Khans); Podhorodecki, *Chanat Krymski*, 160 (deposition of Khan, Gazi Giray II); Bodl., MS Tanner 79, fo. 219r (quotation); Ivanics, 'Military Co-operation', 281–4 (size of Tatar force), 294–5 (Gazi Giray II, library); Smith, *Generall Historie*, ii, 147–58 (153: quotation). **[12]** Davies, *Warfare*, 33–5 (official defence force); Golobutskii, *Zaporozhskoe kazachestvo*, 88–90, 97 (anti-feudal, for national liberation); Hrushevsky, *History*, vii, 45–8 (nature of raids, economic interests). **[13]** Rothenberg, *Austrian Military Border*; Bracewell, *Uskoks* (with, exceptionally, a good account of the economics: 110–17) ; Ljubić, 'Poslanice', 6–7 (Dubrovnik accused); Manca, *Il modello*, 76 (Livorno); Greene, *Catholic Pirates*, 92 (Livorno); Malcolm, 'Kelmendi', 156–7. **[14]** Leunclavius, ed., *Neuwe Chronica*, 110; Manca, *Il modello*, 14 ('ali'). **[15]** Hrushevsky, *History*, vii, 115–17 (Ioan Potcoavă, Cossack invasions, Tatar attacks), 118–20 (official Cossack army); Pippidi, 'Cazacii', 267–8 (Cossack invasions); Sękowski, ed., *Collectanea*, ii, 302–8 (Sultan's warning, Mar. 1578); HHStA, Türkei I, Karton 38, 2nd foliation, fos. 134r–135v (Sultan's warning, Nov. 1578); Ciobanu, *La cumpănă*, 35–7 (Şchiopul pro-Polish, granting wishes of boyars), 48 (Akkerman attack, response); Iorga, *Histoire*, v, 206 (boyars' petition); above, 269 (payments). **[16]** Papiu Ilarian, *Tesauru*, iii, 48 (German); Tudoran, *Domnii trecătoare*, 177 (German); Ureche, *Letopiseţul*, 199–200 (tithe, revolt, rapes, exile, 'legea creştinească nu o iubiia'); Anon., ed., *Documente, veacul XVI*, iii, 159–61 (donating Gypsies), 181–2 (nobles fled to Poland); Ciurea, 'Relaţii', 36 (converted); *HD*, xi, p. xlviii (secretly in touch); Apostolescu, 'Un aventurier', 568 (Poles informed Istanbul); Dopierała, *Stosunki*, 122 (Poles informed Istanbul). **[17]** Dopierała, *Stosunki*, 122 (gift of Tatar princes, payment to Sinan); Ciurea, 'Relaţii', 36 (arrest and execution); Iorga, *Relaţiile*, 54–5 (opened letters, burnt villages, beaten and imprisoned Poles); Bolognetti, *Epistolae*, i [= v], 488 (opened letters, 'odiosissimo'); Ciurea, 'Relaţii', 36 (rumoured cash). **[18]** Ureche, *Letopiseţul*, 199 (joint commander); Pippidi,

Tradiţia, 253 (postelnic); Stoicescu, *Dicţionar*, 296 (Bucium); *HD*, xi, l (external, internal); Cantemir, *Descrierea*, 200 (prefecture of Iaşi). **[19]** Goldenberg, 'Le Pouvoir', 41–2 (towns); Nicolescu, *Istoria*, 121–35 (caftans); Nistor, *Handel*, 59–60 (Jews), 95 (unwritten law); Cleray, 'Le Voyage', 48 ('Ilz ... honorent comme Dieu leurs vaïvodatz, et ... Ilz boivent excessivement'); Crusius, *Turcograeciae*, 248 (Gerlach's assurance); Benda, ed., *Moldvai Csángó-Magyar*, 94 ('Litterae ibi nullae vigent, neque docentur. Gens est egregia et ingeniosa, et magis callida quam simplex'), 853–4 (Hungarians, Hussites); Pippidi, *Tradiţia*, 253 (Chiots, Ragusans); Weczerka, *Das mittelalterliche*, 82–5 (Germans, Hungarians), 173 (Hussites); Shmurlo, *Rossiia*, ii, 443 (Albanian traders); ASVat, Segr. Stato, Germania, 95, fo. 165v ('La guardia del Moldauo è di 400 Drapanti che sono vngheri, et di 50 alabardieri Albanesi, et Greci che uiuono alla Turca'), Segr. Stato, Polonia, 26, fo. 419r (Antonio Stanislao, baptized by bishop (who was Marcin Białobrzeski); on the approximate date cf. below, 347). A differing account exists of the voivod's guard in 1587: 400 Hungarian arquebusiers and 150 Hungarian, Albanian, Greek and Slav cavalry (Filitti, *Din arhivele*, ii, 46). **[20]** Gürkan, 'Efficacy', 29(n.) (voivod's envoy); von Hammer, *Geschichte*, iv, 118 (budget, preparations, Morocco, Uzbekistan); Reindl-Kiel, 'Power', 43–4 (Sinan's gifts), 53 (Polish gift); Leunclavius, ed., *Neuwe Chronica*, 513–14 (Venetian and Moldavian gifts). **[21]** von Hammer, *Geschichte*, iv, 119 (wooden stand); Reusner, *Operis*, 29 (boar, lions, dismay at conversions, spahi–janissary fight); Palerne, *D'Alexandrie*, 280 ('assés mélodieuse pour faire danser les asnes'), 282 (sugar animals), 287 ('pour estre recognu quelque grand guerrier'), 289 (Christian captives); Peçevi, *Historija*, ii, 64 (prostitutes, spahi–janissary fight, Ferhad Pasha). All other details are from the eye-witness account in Leunclavius, ed., *Neuwe Chronica*, 468–514, and the poem by Intizami cited in Procházka-Eisl, 'Guild Parades'. **[22]** Theiner, ed., *Vetera monumenta*, iii, 142 ('quale non osservando le conditioni promesse esso Giacula, et non pagando il tributo promesso à Sinan Bassa, per mezzo del quale era stato promosso, l'istesso Bruto in Constantinopoli procurò che fusse deposto il Giacula, et promosse questo Principe Pietro che hora governa'); Maxim, *Noi documente*, 220 (investiture); Veress, ed., *Documente*, ii, 230 ('et haverà luogo principalissimo et di molto utile, essendo stato caldamente raccomandato dal Bassà con dirli che' l suo star longamente in quel stato dipenderà dalla bona compagnia che farà al Bruti').

18. BARTOLOMEO BRUTI IN POWER

[1] Ureche, *Letopiseţul*, 204 ('Ţărîi era apărătoriu, spre săraci milostivu ... de avea de la toţi nume bun şi dragoste'; cf. a similar account by the chronicler Azarie: Andreescu, *Restitutio*, 166); Năsturel, 'Petru Vodă' (Patmos; 122–3: St Sava); Anon., ed., *Documente, veacul XVI*, iii, 262 (Bartolomeo witness), iv, 75 (testimony on slaves); Alzati, *Terra romena*, 202–5 (St Sava, Istanbul); *HD*, Supplement, ii(1), 315–17 (Lviv); Crăciun, *Protestantism*, 183–4 (Lviv, protector); [pseudo-]Dorotheos, *Vivlion*, sig. 4F3v ('eleēmōn eis to akros, eis sklavous, eis ptōchous', 'dikaiotatos eis tas kriseis tou, kai . . . dokimōtatos eis pasin technēn, eis grammata'); Bolognetti, *Epistolae*, i [= v], 587 ('piacevole et facil natura sua in cedere ad ogni violenza'), ii [= vi], 412 ('non era huom' di valore . . . ma però persona da bene et dipendente assai da S. Mtà'). **[2]** Hrushevsky, *History*, vii, 128 (failed attempt, beheadings); Kuntze, 'Les Rapports', 186 (recent fort at Iagorlik, murder of envoy); *HD*, iv(2), 118 ('cosacchi, et altri soldati del Re di Polonia', 'qui a queste frontiere la pace tra Poloni et il Turcho è andata a monte'); Heidenstein, *Rerum polonicarum*, 213 (Ottoman rage, arrest). **[3]** ASVat, Segr. Stato, Germania, 95, fo. 156v ('nella detta città di Giasso è Bartolomeo Bruto Vinitiano, il quale è catolico, et fauorito del Principe, et è consigliere, et commanda . . . et non ha molto che ha mandato a suoi in Vinetia sei mila Ducati Vngheri'); AST, AMC, MS 84 (reel 124, frame 62) (Maria Bruti, document of Mar. 1600 in Koper, describing Alessandro as aged 16); *HD*, xi, p. lxii (12,000); BNC, MS Gesuiti 7, fo. 89v ('honoratissimo, et carissimo al Sig.^re Principe'); Iorga, *Acte*, i, 37 ('avec la faveur et conduite du sieur Brutti, gentilhomme albanois, fort favori du Prince'), 37–8 (justice); Anon., ed., *Documente, veacul XVI*, iii, 360–1 ('pentru slujba sa dreaptă şi credincioasă, ce ne-a slujit'). **[4]** Anon., ed., *Documente, veacul XVI*, iii, 199 (postelnic), 441–2 (Benedetto 'ceaşnic' [= cup-bearer], 20,000 akçes); Anon., ed., *Documente, veacul XVII*, ii, 201–2 ('ceaşnic'); Venturini, 'La famiglia', 374 (Cristoforo in Moldavia from 1588); Pippidi, *Hommes*, 145 (Cristoforo member of council); Pippidi, *Tradiţia*, 253 (Cristoforo 'paharnic' [= ceaşnic], Bernardo Borisi interpreter 1587); Luca, *Dacoromano-Italica*, 110 (Bernardo, property); *HD*, xi, p. lxv (Bernardo, mission); Wood, ed., 'Mr. Harrie Cavendish', 19 ('Barrysco'). The suggestion (*HD*, xi, p. xlvii, and Caproşu, 'Creditul', 114–15) that Bernardo Bruti was the 'Bernat' who was governor of Neamţ under Iancu Sasul in 1580–1 (see Anon., ed., *Documente, veacul XVI*, iii, 133, 169) seems very doubtful, on grounds of age and chronology. **[5]** Tadić, *Dubrovački portreti*, 349–68 (Nadali); ASVat, Segr. Stato, Germania, 95, fo. 198r ('ch'io non hò mai mancato sì in Turchia come in questo paese di far ogni sorte di buon officio per introdur' persone di essemplar' uita et buona dottrina, et estirpar questa maledittione di heretici se per me se potesse dal mondo non che da queste parti', 'falso ep[iscop]o'), 198v ('la longa seruitù mia fatta à S. Chiesa si in liberar schiaui come in altre cose'). In 1578 Nadali had written to the Grand Duke of Tuscany from Istanbul, offering intelligence: Sola, *Uchalí*, 275. **[6]** Madonia, *La Compagnia*, 179–8 (Possevino, seminaries); Halecki, *From Florence*, 197–200 (Vilnius), 210–11 (Possevino in Moscow). **[7]** Hofmann, 'Griechische Patriarchen', 228–40 (Cellini's mission); Sokołowski, ed. and tr., *Censura* (Jeremias's document); Cichowski, *Ks. Stanisław*, 137–9, 140(n.) (Sokołowski–Nadali link); Halecki, *From Florence*, 196 (Gregory XIII), 215 (further missions to Jeremias, deposed). **[8]** Bolognetti, *Epistolae*, ii [= vi], 291–2 (initiative, Petru pro-Catholic, Mihnea's mother's family), 350 (letters, known in Moscow); Karalevskij, 'Relaţiunile' (1913), 184–6, 187–8 (texts of letters to voivods). **[9]** ACGH, MS Hist. 145, fos. 239v, 240v (Mancinelli at Seminario); BNC, MS Gesuiti 7, fos. 89v ('profanata da Ministri luterani, che spesso ueniuano in quel luoco per seruitio dell'artigiani, che sono quasi tutti Tedeschi, ouero Vngari luterani'), 90r (Lutheran ministers banned); Alzati, *Terra romena*, 273–4 (Komulović mission). On the growth of Protestantism in Moldavia see Weczerka, *Das mittelalterliche*, 176–91, Szakály, 'Grenzverletzer', 286–9, and Crăciun, *Protestantism*.   **[10]** Kotarski and Kumor, 'Solikowski'; Woś, *Annibale*, 10 (family), 18 (mission as nuncio), 110–11 (details of Solikowski news of May 1587); Theiner, ed., *Vetera monumenta*, iii, 5 ('conforme gli santissimi decreti del santissimo Concilio Tridentino', 'tutte le cose necessarie').   **[11]** Shmurlo, *Rossiia*, ii, 428 (Pope to Petru); Veress, ed., *Documente*, iii, 108 ('ridotto molto numero di persone al culto de la fede cattolica', 'intrate ecclesiastiche'), 126 ('mandare suoi ambasciatori a dare obedienza a Sua S^{tà} come le cose di questo regno fossero state quiete'); ASVat, Segr. Stato, Polonia, 26, fo. 52r ('uedendo io con quanto ardore s'adopra nel seruitio del s:^{ro} Dio'); Theiner, ed., *Vetera monumenta*, iii, 14 (request for son, 'deffensor et protetor della Chiesa Romana contra gli Eretici'), 15 (request to nuncio); et-Tamgrouti, *En-nafhat*, 65 ('se met à genoux, le reçoit des deux mains et le place sur sa tête, afin de montrer le cas qu'il fait du présent, ainsi que son respect pour le donateur'); Benda, ed., *Moldvai Csángó-Magyar*, 82 (Bruti to Montalto, Jan. 1588).   **[12]** Theiner, ed., *Vetera monumenta*, iii, 50 ('eximia pietas, ardens studium et zelus ... incredibilis', 'ut Sacrosanctam Catholicam Religionem non solum in terris Moldaviae, sed etiam in plerisque aliis Provinciis Turcarum potestati subiectis plantet, ac e vestigio in libertatem asserat et dilatet'), 94 ('protettore general delli Catolici in questi paesi et Turchia', 'ambicione'), 192 (spent own money, 'servir et sacrificarmi nel servitio della santa Chiesa, come hanno fatto mio padre et il R[everendissi]mo Arcivescovo d'Antivari mio zio, quali sono morti per mano d'infideli'); Shmurlo, *Rossiia*, ii, 462, 468 (2 villages), 479 ('Ingenue dico, me nullam hisce in rebus posse subolfacere fraudem'), 492 ('non ... volgare').   **[13]** Shmurlo, *Rossiia*, ii, 471 ('Et perche veniamo informati, che quel principe si accomoda a i tempi, et mostra di volere essere catholico forse più per timore, che ha di essere cacciato di stato dal Turco, che per naturale inclinatione, V.S. ci vada avvertita, et osservi minutamente tutto quello che passa'); Völkl, *Das rumänische Fürstentum*, 30 (quasi-autocephalous); Maxim, *L'Empire*, 83–90 (period under Ohrid); Benda, ed., *Moldvai Csángó-Magyar*, 94 ('non agnoscunt patriarcham Constantinopolitanum'); Shmurlo, *Rossiia*, ii, 462–3 ('quodam monacho graeco'); Theiner, ed., *Vetera monumenta*, iii, 91 (Solikowski, Apr. 1589); Halecki, *From Florence*, 287–310 (Ruthenian Uniate agreement).   **[14]** Weczerka, *Das mittelalterliche*, 192 (political ploy); Mesrobeanu, 'Rolul', 187–8 (Movilă family); Anon., ed., *Documente, veacul XVI*, iii, 181–2 (exile in Poland); Bulboacă, *Bartolomeo Brutti*, 40–1 (role of Gheorghe as Metropolitan); Zach, 'Bemerkungen', 42–5 (low status, influence); Karalevskij, 'Relaţiunile' (1913), 201 ('Palatinum et Metropolitas ipsos tum proceres atque adeo populum universum'). On Petru's Uniate tendency see also Bârlea, *De confessione*, 43–5, and Alzati, *Terra romena*, 209–10.   **[15]** Benda, ed., *Moldvai Csángó-Magyar*, 92 ('Inventus est in ea frater D^{ni} Bruti, qui nos ad domum ejus deduxit', 'supervenit nepos D^{ni} Bruti cum curru, ut sequenti die in castra veniremus', 'qui nobis, postquam cibo refecti sumus, tentorium suum pro hospitio concessit, cum tapetibus in terra, more turcico', 'tympanis et tubis turcicis ac hungaricis'); Shmurlo,

Rossiia, ii, 442–3 (settled in Roman), 448, 462 (seminary), 468 (gave villages). The brother was probably Bernardo, and the nephew Bernardo Borisi. **[16]** György, 'A kolozsvári római katolikus', [ch. 1] (expulsion from Cluj); Lukács, ed., *Monumenta antiquae*, iii, 313 (Transylvanian Jesuits welcomed); Shmurlo, *Rossiia*, ii, 472–3 (Şchiopul decrees), 476 ('se habbiamo perso Transilvania Iddio ha dato l'acquisto di Moldavia, et con questa provincia forsi metteremo li piedi in Transilvania'), 488–91 (Bruti letter on Jesuit activities; 491: 'broccato turchesco de quelli che portano li grandi dell' imperio Ottomano', 'poichè a me dalli signori Ottomani non solo questo ma molti come questo mi hanno dato per [lisciarmi]'); Wood, ed., 'Mr. Harrie Cavendish', 19. **[17]** Theiner, ed., *Vetera monumenta*, iii, 13 ('molestias a Turcis et Tartaris'), 93–4 (Bruti to di Capua, 31 Oct. 1589), 176 ('disturbi continui', 'longhi viaggi', 'quando credevo metermi in camino per venir à Roma à basiar li santissimi piedi di N.S. per nome dell' Ill[ustrissi]mo Principe di Moldavia'); ASVat, Fondo Borghese III 72a, fo. 308v ('gli mei pericoli le mie gran fatiche per non nominare le gran spese fatte per gloria di Dio'). There is one report of Petru sending an Orthodox bishop to Rome at the end of 1588 to perform the submission, but nothing else is known of this: Czubek, ed., *Stanislai Rescii diarium*, 247. **[18]** Shmurlo, *Rossiia*, ii, 433 (Montalto promise, May 1588), 475 ('il quale non è solito di darsi, se non a principi grandi, o a popoli et nationi potenti'), 488 (Montalto to di Capua, agreeing); Karalevskij, 'Relaţiunile' (1913), 206 (Montalto to Solikowski, agreeing); ASVat, Segr. Stato, Polonia, 26, fo. 399v (established under 10); Theiner, ed., *Vetera monumenta*, iii, 177 ('di anni 12 in circa'). **[19]** Maxim, 'Haraciul' (increase); Filitti, *Din arhivele*, ii, 47 (extra payments, Iancu's debts, 'tributo secreto', çavuşes); Caproşu, 'Creditul', 108–10 (borrowing, janissaries; cf. Luca, *Dacoromano-Italica*, 20); BNF, MS Français 16,144, fo. 38v ('auoir a faire part ch[ac]un an a ces principaulx ministres de plus du tiers de leur reuenu & estat po[ur] les co[n]tinuelles nouuelles mangeryes sur les annuelz enchérissements de leurs competiteurs'); Mureşan, 'L'Émergence', 123 (coronation); *HD*, iv(2), 147 ('inventione ridicole'). **[20]** Macůrek, *Zápas*, p. iv (contested, defeated, Aldobrandini mission); Ciobanu, *La cumpănă*, 64 (Cossack raids, Habsburg role); Ureche, *Letopiseţul*, 204 (Cossack attack, Nov. 1587); Ciurea, 'Relaţii', 37–8 (Cossack raids, Sultan's complaint); Bodl., MS Tanner 79, fo. 76r ('vetustum . . . foedus'); Niederkorn, *Die europäischen Mächte*, 471 (Ottomans suspicious); Madonia, *La Compagnia*, 255–6 (Jesuit education), 257–8 (secret negotiation); *HD*, Supplement, ii(1), 296–7 (Snyatyn). **[21]** ASF, Miscellanea medicea, 101, 31 (intelligence from Poland: I am very grateful to Andrei Pippidi for letting me see his transcription of this document); Lepszy, ed., *Archiwum*, iv, 227 ('sie łaskawej przyjaźni WM. zalecam'); *HD*, Supplement, ii(1), 294–5 (mediation); Veress, ed., *Documente*, iii, 141–3 (mission); Shmurlo, *Rossiia*, ii, 467 ('affirmar le confederationi qualli sono tra questo regno di Polonia et Moldavia'). **[22]** *HD*, iv(2), 139–40 ('persona altratanto divota di quella Serenissima Republica quanto discretta et prudente'); Theiner, ed., *Vetera monumenta*, iii, 143 ('il Bruti è in molta autorità essendo suo cugino questo Sinan Bassa, che al presente è fatto primo Visire. Et quando ultimamente alli 20 di Giugno era tornato da Constantinopoli tutta la nobilità di quella Provincia l'era uscita all'incontro, et il Principe istesso l'havea mandata tutta la sua Corte et fattoli molti presenti, temendo che il Bruti col favore di questo primo Visire voglia esser lui Principe di Moldavia'). [23] Stoy, 'Das Wirken' (Graziani); Păun, 'Enemies', 220–3 (Graziani); HD, iv(2), 141 (blocked Cercel), 143 (rescinded order), 146 (method to open negotiations), xi, 734 (Imperial ambassador, referring mistakenly to 'Christophoro Bruti', but describing him in a way that clearly implies Bartolomeo); Theiner, ed., Vetera monumenta, iii, 93–4 (blocked Cercel, freed slaves). [24] HD, Supplement, i, 295–8 (suggesting negotiations), 299–302 (more belligerent); Leunclavius, ed., Neuwe Chronica, 146 (25–30,000, Tatars routed); Hrushevsky, History, vii, 131 (Tatars routed); AGAD, AZ, MS 8, 113 ('donosi o usługach iakie czynił Posłoui Polskiemie tak u Baszy Beglerbeka iako żaluaiąc ... będącym w Konstantynopolu znacznym i potrzebnym osobom – prosi aby ... iego przychilność i dalszą chęć do usług tak w woynie iako i w pokoju, Kanclerz Krolowi żaluił – namienia wreszcie aby Kanclerz Turkom nie zapełnie zauierzał'); TNA, SP 97/2, fos. 3(a)r (arrival), 6r (broken leg, house arrest), 7r–v (death, 2 sent back (HD, iv(2), 148 gives a different dating)), 11r (60 days). [25] Shmurlo, Rossiia, ii, 491–2, 498–9 (Bruti movements, Iaşi); ASVat, Segr. Stato, Polonia, 26, fo. 399r (Bruti movements); Venturini, 'La famiglia', 379(n.) ('in Nobilissimo Aepiri [= Epiri, from 'Epirus', the preferred humanist term for Albania] Regno, Nobilissimis Parentibus Natus', 'Nobis, Regno, hominibusq[ue] Nostris omnia summa officia semper praestit', 'interponendo'), 380(n.) ('maximis in rebus consilio', eagle); Pippidi, 'Tre antiche casate', 64 (arms in Koper). [26] TNA, SP 97/2, fos. 19v (report of 16 May), 21v (arrival in Istanbul 29 May); HD, Supplement, i, 295–8 (suggesting negotiations), 299–302 (more belligerent), 309–15 (corresponding via Petru); AGAD, AZ, MS 649, no. 28, 70 (19 May, 'Nos amicos n[ost]ros et inimicos n[ost]ros benè scimus. Regum illorum Legati in excelsissima et splendissima Porta continui adsunt et tributa muneraq[ue] consueta sine deffectu aliquo in tempore adferunt, sine dubio, si aliqui huiusmodi tumultus essent illorum Legati significarent'). [27] TNA, SP 97/2, fos. 25r (Polish request, reasons for accepting); Coulter, 'Examination', 64 (English supplies from Poland). [28] Vella, Elizabethan–Ottoman (Malta); de Foix, Les Lettres, 320 (Malta); Bodl., MSS Tanner 77, fos. 2r, 4r (disrupting), Tanner 79, fo. 93r (disrupting); Ágoston, 'Merces', 183–6 (tin, weapons); Charrière, ed., Négociations, iv, 624–5 ('Idolatrae'); Pedani, ed., Relazioni, 371 ('se bene per avanti la regina d'Inghilterra era da loro poco stimata come donna e padrona di mezza un'isola solamente, niente di meno hora fanno molto conto d'essa, vedendo che ha havuto ardire di mover guerra offensiva al re Cattolico e perché da ogni parte intendono le sue molte forze per mare'). On Harborne see Rawlinson, 'Embassy', and Skilliter, William Harborne; on Barton see Podea, 'Contribution', and Skilliter, 'Turkish Documents'. [29] HD, iv(2), 152 (deal); Ciobanu, La cumpănă, 68 (deal); ASVat, Segr. Stato, Polonia, 26, fo. 409r (100 bundles); TNA, SP 97/2, fo. 25v (Barton report). [30] TNA, SP 97/2, fos. 39r (Bruti to Queen, 29 Aug.: 'l'auttorita del suo Sr Ambassador et mia diligentia', 'triompho'), 43r (Queen to Bruti: 'sommamente desideramo che si offerisca l'oportunita et occasione di mo[n]stra[r] buona affettione verso di V. S. & Vostro Principe'); Tappe, ed., *Documents*, 50 ('fidellissima et perpetua amicitia', 'fidellissime servitù', 'per la sua grandezza et confussion delli sui inimici'); Iorga, 'Les Premières Relations', 562–7 (merchants via Moldavia); Demény and Cernovodeanu, *Relaţiile*, 21–2 (privilege); Carnicer and Marcos, *Espías*, 183 (Spanish retainer). [31] Popović, *Turska*, 351–61 (Ine Han crisis); Biegman, *Turco-Ragusan*, 61–3 (Ine Han crisis); DAD, LCL, 37, fo. 75r ('Ci è venuto à notitia, che il bruti, il quale staua in bogdania appresso quel principe, è stato autore delli garbugli, che ci hà mosso l'enecano, ò almeno suo fautore, et che l'enecano si è aiutato del suo fauore appresso il Sʳ Sinan bassa', 'parlategli, e pregatelo, che non voglia vsar questi termini di cattiui offitij contra di noi, ma più presto contra l'enecano, p[er]che la casa di bruti sempre si è trattenuta con noi in molta amicitia, et il suo padre hà riceuuto da noi molti s[er]uitij in molte occasioni'). [32] Radonić, ed., *Dubrovačka akta*, ii(2), 569 ('li quali sono stati della lingua nostra'). [33] *HD*, iv(2), 152 (departure from Istanbul); Talbot, ed., *Elementa*, 95 ('quorundarum vicinorum nostrorum'), 151 (Wilcocks report); ASVat, Segr. Stato, Polonia, 26, fos. 409r–v, 414r (di Capua), 467r ('Il S.ʳᵉ Bartholomeo Bruti alli 10. di questo partiua da Varsouia per Leopoli, doue hauerebbe aspettato l'Ambasciador Polacco, che deue andare in Constantinopoli con li Zibellini per confermare la pace'); AGAD, AZ, MS 770 (Bruti to Zamoyski, 14 Mar. 1591). [34] *HD*, xi, 216 ('habet in Istria Venetorum bona, et ibi suos filios; cuperet se recipere in Istriam archiducalem et paulatim ex Moldavia subducere'), 217 (second envoy's report); ASVat, Segr. Stato, Polonia, 24, fo. 291v ('Quel Bartolomeo Bruti . . . che s'offeriua prontam.ᵗᵉ di ser.ʳᵉ in Constantinopoli in ogni occa.ⁿᵉ, et à S. M.ᵗᵃ Ces.ᵃ, et al Re n[ost]ro Sig.ʳᵉ tiene m.[ol]ᵗᵃ strettezza con Sinan Bassa p.º Uisier et per q.ᵗᵒ rispetto l'Amb.ʳᵉ d'Ingiltera, che resiede in Costantinopoli si stringe m.ᵗᵒ con esso Bruti cercando di ualerse di lui, et esso Bartolomeo Bruti s'offeriua in part.[icola]ʳᵉ di dare aduertimento a chi hauessero ordinato li ministri di Re n[ost]ro Sig.ʳᵉ di tutto quello, che trattaua la pretenza Regina d'Ingliterra appresso il Turco, et credo, che l'haurebbe fatto compitam.ᵗᵉ mostrandosi buon Catt.ᶜᵒ, et desideroso ser.ʳᵉ a q.ᵗⁱ Ser.ᵐⁱ P.ⁱ'). The first of the two envoys asked Bartolomeo if it was true that he was related to Sinan; 'he laughed and said, "so people say; each of us is an Albanian"' (*HD*, xi, 216: 'Risit: "Ita," inquit, "dicunt, uterque nostrum Epirotum esse"'). He was surely playing down his connection here, for fear that he might be suspected of being an Ottoman agent. [35] *HD*, xi, 231 ('è desiderosissimo di far qualche servitio a Sua Maestà Cesarea, et ch'hà desiderio di liberarsi dalla servitù turchesca'); Barwiński, ed., *Dyaryusze*, 5 ('der umb gar viel des Kanzlers geheime practicken wais und etzliche seiner aignen hand original documenta bey händen hat'); Macůrek, 'Diplomatické poslání', 100 ('wunderliche sachen offenbaret'), 101 ('Disen Brutus kan die Kay. Mᵗ sovil leichter an sich bringen, weyl er ohne das von seinem herrn sich losmachen begert und sich des orts nit lenger vertrawt, wan er nur anderwo unterhalt und schutz haben kan'). [36] *HD*, xi, pp. lxxiv–lxxv (Mihnea, Cossacks, accounts, departure); Danişmend, *Osmanlı devlet* (Sinan dismissed 1 Aug.); Veress, ed., *Documente*, iii, 330 (15 Aug.); *HD*, iv(2), 156–7 (bailo's report; 157: 'grossa quantità d'oro'). [37] David, *Petru Şchiopul*, 148 (400,000); Păun, 'Enemies', 228–30 (Aron's backers); Dursteler, *Venetians*,

139–41 (Mariani); TNA, SP 97/2, fos. 188r (1592 note), 277r (Wilcocks report). The Hussites were proto-Protestants from the Czech and neighbouring lands; many had fled into Moldavia in the 15th century (see Weczerka, *Das mittelalter-liche*, 173; Alzati, *Terra romena*, 249–51).   **[38]** Luca, 'Veneziani', 258 ('per suspicione', castration); Ureche, *Letopiseţul*, 205–6 ('prădarea ... sătura de curvie, de jocuri, de cimpoiaş', mercenaries, etc.); *HD*, iv(2), 161 (tax revolts), 162 ('con ignominia'); Apostolescu, 'Un aventurier', 573 (state treasurer); Bul-boacă, *Bartolomeo Brutti*, 64(n.) (7 weeks, nose, strangled); Bielski, *Dalszy ciąg kroniki* ('dał utopić na Niestrze'); Guboglu and Mehmet, eds., *Cronici*, 364–5 (uproar).   **[39]** Bulboacă, *Bartolomeo Brutti*, 86 (plotting for return), 87 (Pope's letter); *HD*, iv(2), 162 ('con ignominia', forged letter), 163 (30,000 ducats), xi, pp. lxxxi (involved in revolt), 253 (family expecting 'in dies'), 756 (30,000 scudi); Heidenstein, *Rerum polonicarum*, 296 ('non aliam ob causam tantum ob non exsolutionem debitorum, quae contraxit, dum Palatinum illum occuparet').

19. CRISTOFORO BRUTI AND THE DRAGOMAN DYNASTY

[1] Luca, *Dacoromano-Italica*, 108 (giovane di lingua 1579); Albèri, ed., *Relazi-oni*, ser. 3, ii, 416–17 (50 ducats); Lucchetta, 'La scuola', 20 (50 ducats); ASVen, CCD, Dispacci (Lettere) di Ambasciatori, busta 5, item 156 (lodged with secre-tary, standard rate, 'questo è giouene studioso, che farà proffitto, et presto').
[2] ASVen, CCD, Dispacci (Lettere) di Ambasciatori, busta 6, item 1 ('col mezo de missier Cristoforo bruti che sta qui in casa ad imparar la lingua turca ho molti et importanti avisi delle cose de Persia praticando egli assai familiarmente col nepote de Sinan bassa et con altri grandi de casa et spero che venendo a questa porta Sinan mi sara anco de magior comodo havendo grandissime intrature suo fratello et lui in casa del bassa'); Albèri, ed., *Relazioni*, ser. 3, iii, 248 (Albanian etc., 'dell'amicizie che egli ha in Costantinopoli di grandi'); Luca, *Dacoromano-Italica*, 19 (200 ducats). The family tree in Venturini, 'La famiglia', gives Cristoforo's date of birth as 1568, but it is unlikely that he would have been accepted as a giovane di lingua at 11; Lorenzo Bernardo's report of 1592 said he was aged 28–30 (Albèri, ed., *Relazioni*, ser. 3, ii, 415), so perhaps Venturini's '1568' was an error for '1563'.   **[3]** Veress, ed., *Documente*, ii, 230 ('ritrovan-dosi ancor lui nell'istessa gratia, et intratura col Mag.co primo Visir'; in this report Cristoforo is mistakenly called Bartolomeo's son); ASVen, CCD, Dispacci (Let-tere) di Ambasciatori, busta 6, items 51 ('perche oltre che è già molto innanzi nella lingua Turca, è anco di così buon giudicio, et tanto ardente nel suo seruitio, che si può prometter di lui ogni fedeltà, sincerità, et dilig.a oltre che se ritornasse il Mag.co Sinam nel suo primo luogo, saria questo giouane instrum.to attissimo di far nelle occasioni fruttuosi, et segnalati seruitij alla ser.tà v[ost]ra'), 63 ('q[uest]o bruti si adop[er]a co[n] molta satisfattione mia et b[e]n[e]ficio publico In tutti li negotij che mi occorreno trattar con questi fauoriti del bassa essendo da loro molto amato, et possedendo la lingua turchescha assai bene, onde si puo sp[er]ar

che In breue tempo habbia ad esser p[er]fetto In parlar et scriuer turcho però essendo egli pouero, et hauendo perso il padre, et tutta la robba, et facoltà in seruitio de quel Ser.ᵐᵒ D[omi]nio per conscienza son sforzato di raccommandarlo, come faccio, con molto affetto à V. Serᵗᵃ). **[4]** Albèri, ed., *Relazioni*, ser. 3, iii, 247 ('il servizio de' suoi proprii è più vantaggioso e con più dignità pubblica che quello de' sudditi turcheschi, perchè quelli non temendo li rispetti parlano con ardire, mentre li turchi temono farlo'); Lucchetta, 'La scuola', 19–20 (1551 decree, other ports); see also Palumbo Fossati Casa, 'L'École'. For examples of using the cozza as a dragoman see Albèri, ed., *Relazioni*, ser. 3, ii, 186 (1576); Seneca, *Il Doge*, 273 (1595). **[5]** Miović, *Dubrovačka diplomacija*, 109(n.) (Dubrovnik, 1558); Majda, 'L'École', 124 (Poland); von Hammer, *Geschichte*, iii, 776–7 (Imperial Ambassador, 1568); Gerlach, *Tage-Buch*, 32–3 (Imperial dragomans); Pippidi, 'Drogmans' (France); Séraphin-Vincent, 'Du drogman' (France); Wood, *History*, 226–7 (England). **[6]** Lucchetta, 'La scuola', 22 (1558 argument, 'credo cierto che li Bassà non li haveriano grati et forsi non li admetteriano'), 23 (5 years not enough), 24 (1577 suggestion to send cozza to Venice); Sola, *Uchalí*, 319 (Colombina); Albèri, ed., *Relazioni*, ser. 3, ii, 418 ('come se questo fusse un seminario o collegio per allevare poveri figliuoli a spese pubbliche', 'la libertà del vivere tuchesco, la lussuria di quelle donne turche, colli corrotti costumi delli rinegati, avriano forza di far di un santo un diavolo'); ASVen, CCD, Dispacci (Lettere) di Ambasciatori, busta 4, item 159 (1575 suggestion to send cozza to Venice, 'alcuni dragomani Turchi'), busta 6, items 99–104 (relationship with barber). **[7]** Lucchetta, 'La scuola', 22 (Cernovicchio), 23–4 (deaths, illness); ASVen, Dispacci, Costantinopoli, filza 7, fos. 111v, 513r–v (Hürrem Bey); Albèri, ed., *Relazioni*, ser. 3, ii, 419 (sons of Perots); Žontar, 'Michael Černović' (Cernovicchio biography); Lesure, 'Michel Černović' (Cernovicchio biography); Lamansky, *Secrets*, 70–3 (orders about Cernovicchio); Floristán Imízcoz, ed., *Fuentes*, ii, 596, 624 (Cernovicchio remained in Istanbul). On Cernovicchio (whom, in 1567–8, the Emperor planned to send as an envoy to Persia: von Palombini, *Bündniswerben*, 91–3), see also von Betzek, *Gesandtschaftsreise*, 29; Müller, *Prosopographie*, ii, 174–83. **[8]** ASVen, CCD, Dispacci (Lettere) di Ambasciatori, busta 6, items 127 ('resterei priuo di quel sicuro, et fedel incontro, ch'è necessario à hauer molte uolte in Casa'), 153 ('la sua stretta pratica In seraglio dalli qual non si può deuiarlo, et Il suo parlar Incauto, et maligioso'); Albèri, ed., *Relazioni*, ser. 3, ii, 420 (remark about secrecy); Lamansky, *Secrets*, 103–5 (orders about Salvego, 'in tempi di freddi et giacci'); ASVen, Dispacci, Costantinopoli, filza 13, fo. 468r ('estando a tauola con Dragumanni et renegati ragionaua tutto quelo io aueua ragionato secho'). The Salvego family had a particular hold on the baili, as the bailo's house in the leafy suburb of Pera belonged to them (Simon, 'Les Dépêches', i, 281). **[9]** Simon, 'Les Dépêches', i, 280–1 (3 dragomans); Albèri, ed., *Relazioni*, ser. 3, ii, 413, 415 (3 dragomans); Bodl., MS Tanner 79, fos. 150r (list of 3 English dragomans), 179r ('Mustafa a chaouce', quotations describing tasks of dragomans). **[10]** Simon, 'Les Dépêches', i, 281–2 (port dragoman's commission, tax on merchants paid half cost); Rothman, 'Interpreting',

779–80 (Venetian–Perot mixing).   **[11]** Albèri, ed., *Relazioni*, ser. 3, iii, 248 ('massime nell'ascoltar quelli che m'avvisano le cose che occorrevano per giornata, e che favorivano li negozj che mi bisognava trattar a quella Porta'); Luca, *Dacoromano-Italica*, 19 (Michieli); Pedani, ed., *Relazioni*, 391 (temporary replacement); Pedani and Bombaci, *I 'documenti'*, 243 (paid tribute).   **[12]** ASVen, Dispacci, Costantinopoli, filza 26, fos. 328v–329r, 362r, 369r–v, 370r (Scarvoli case; 328v: 'dragomano, et commesso del Bailo'; 370r: 'molestato'), Senato, Deliberazioni, Costantinopoli, registri, 7, fo. 76r–v (lobbying, Benveniste, official complaint); Pedani, *In nome*, 175 (Ömer, Ibrahim); Predelli *et al.*, eds., *I libri*, vii, 48–9 (Sultan's letter). On Scarvoli see also Pedani and Bombaci, *Inventory*, 95, 102–3, 113, 119, 125.   **[13]** de Leva, ed., *La legazione*, i, 181–3(n.) (Hasan's family background); Fabris, 'Hasan' (Hasan's career); Asín, 'La hija', 281–5 (Cervantes and Hasan).   **[14]** de Castro, *O Prior* (Don Antonio biography); de Queiroz Velloso, *O interregno*, 197–9 (acclamation, threat); Charrière, ed., *Négociations*, iv, 489(n.) (Mendes); Bodl., MS Tanner 78, fo. 40v (Harborne report).   **[15]** ASVen, Dispacci, Costantinopoli, filza 26, fos. 194r–195r (Bruti conversation, 'cauare danari co' li quali potessero acquestarsi la gratia del Gran sig.'', visits to Arsenal), 202r–v (English agent, plan).   **[16]** ASVen, Dispacci, Costantinopoli, filza 26, fos. 372r ('molti sudditi Turcheschi', Cassain, vessel seized), 402r (petitions), 402v, 403v (meeting in Kotor), 406r (*çavuş* and *sancakbeyi*), Senato, Deliberazioni, Costantinopoli, registri, 7, fos. 106r–107r (instruction to Cristoforo; 106r: vessel seized, 2 boys enslaved), 128r (Senate to bailo, 24 May: 10 arrested, released, need to apply to Sultan again).   **[17]** Venturini, 'La famiglia', 373–4 (instruction, as from Doge (misdated '1583'; the Doge, Pasquale Cicogna, was elected in 1585), 'in [Bogdania] appresso tuo Fratello'); ASVen, Senato, Deliberazioni, Costantinopoli, registri, 7, fos. 106r–107r (same text, as from Senate; fo. 107r: 100 ducats).   **[18]** Börekçi, 'Factions', 175–91 (Doğancı Mehmed's career), 193 (change of Grand Viziers); Boyar and Fleet, *Social History*, 91–2 (death of Doğancı Mehmed); Brookes, ed. and tr., *Ottoman Gentleman*, 26 (Mustafa Ali). For a dramatic description by an Albanian janissary of the killing of Doğancı Mehmed see Crescentio, *Nautica*, 478.   **[19]** Brown, *Studies*, ii, 29–32 (Leoni affair); Villain-Gandossi, 'Contribution', vol. 28, 30–31 (decree); Dursteler, *Renegade Women*, 25 (links with household); Foster, *Travels*, 14 (Sanderson); Pedani and Bombaci, *I 'documenti'*, 227 (Turkish document, misdated A.H. 989 but surely 996 (from Mehmed, who became *beylerbeyi* in Oct. 1584 (A.H. 992))). On Leoni see also ASVen, CCD, Dispacci (Lettere) di Ambasciatori, busta 6, item 128 (Leoni's 2 ships taking grain to Corfu and Venice, 1592); Dursteler, 'Commerce', 117 (trading with Hamza Çavuş, 1599–1600).   **[20]** *HD*, iv(2), 163 (tribute-collector); Pippidi, *Tradiţia*, 253 ('paharnic'); Iorga, *Ospiti*, plate facing 121 (5 May payment). A contemporary reference to Cristoforo going on a mission to invite the Poles to send an envoy to Istanbul in late 1589 is probably an error for Bartolomeo: see above, 509, n. 23.   **[21]** Predelli *et al.*, eds., *I libri*, vii, 56 (Nov. in court, Dec. translation); Stefani, ed., 'Viaggio', 7, 13–14 (Bernardo mission, charge against Lippomano); Coco and Manzonetto, *Baili*, 53 (25 June 1591 departure, drowning); Albèri, ed., *Relazioni*, ser. 3, ii, 415 ('è giovane di ventotto in trenta anni, entrante, pratico della Porta, pronto, ardito, vivo, istruito per drago-manno grande in tempo mio; hora non ha carico particolare, onde si è applicato a qualche negozio di gioie, formenti ed altro; ma quando, lasciati (come si con-viene) questi negozj, si applicherà tutto al servizio pubblico, potrà esser di molto beneficio, e darà molta satisfazione alli baili, perchè ha buonissima lingua turca, greca, italiana, schiava, bogdana e albanese'); Hrabak, 'Kuga', 33 (plague); *HD*, iv(2), 163 (bailo's report on death). **[22]** Pedani, ed., *Relazioni*, 392 ('Questo ha un suo nipote che è venuto ad accompagnarmi in questa città; sa la lingua turca, albanese, schiava e franca come sua naturale, ha principio della lingua greca et impara a legger e scriver turco et è soggetto del quale la Serenità Vostra può molto sperare in servitio suo'); Predelli *et al.*, eds., *I libri*, vii, 56 (acting in court); Albèri, ed., *Relazioni*, ser. 3, ii, 416 (Bernardo report on 1591 visit); Luca, *Dacoromano-Italica*, 114–15 (doubled salary, career); Pippidi, *Hommes*, 147–8 (1600 report, career); Villain-Gandossi, '*Giovani*', 37 (mediocre); Dursteler, *Vene-tians*, 147–8 (Pirons); Rothman, 'Between Venice', 256 (Olivieri); Luca, *Ţările*, 82 (suspicions, execution); Pedani, *Venezia*, 163 (suspicions, execution); Luca, 'Il patrizio', 87–9 (Graziani negotiation); Mesrobeanu, 'Nuovi contributi', 198 (revolt). **[23]** Luciani, 'Relazioni', vol. 7, 102 (captain); Anon., 'Senato Mare', 98 (permission 1602); Luca, *Ţările*, 84(n.) (Wallachian career); Stoicescu, *Dicţionar*, 352 (Wallachian career); Luca, 'Veneziani' (travels, commerce). **[24]** du Fresne-Canaye, *Le Voyage*, 252 (*bezistan*); Lubenau, *Beschreibung*, 177–9 (*bezistan*); Almosnino, *Extremos*, 18 ('grandissimos señores'), 19 (riches to poverty); Luca, 'Aspetti', 257, 264 (Francesco's debt); Iorga, 'Contribuţiuni', 100 (son entrusted to Brutis), 102(n.) (letter in Greek referring to 'Miser Pernardos'); *HD*, xi, 253 (moved to Venice). It is possible, but doubtful, that 'Pernardos' was Bernardo Bruti, brother of Bartolomeo; there is one reference to him coming from Venice in 1593 (*HD*, xi, 339), but that seems to be a confused reference to Antonio Bruni (see below, 515, n. 4). **[25]** Luca, *Dacoromano-Italica*, 110–12 (Bernardo, Bar-tolomeo, Cristoforo), 134 (Bernardo); Bertelè, *Il palazzo*, 415 (Bernardo/Barnaba); Pazzi, *I cavalieri*, 177 (Barnaba knighted); Luca, 'Venetian Merchants', 310–11 (Cristoforo); Barozzi and Berchet, eds., *Le relazioni*, 250–3 (Bartolomeo arrived 1612, list of dragomans, Navons); Rothman, 'Interpreting', 778 (Borisi–Navon marriage, son). **[26]** Pippidi, 'Tre antiche casate', 68–9 (Tarsia marriage, Cristo-foro); Cherini and Grio, *Le famiglie*, 203 (Tarsia family); Gürçağlar, 'Patterns' (first portraits); Venturini, 'La famiglia', 385–419 (later Bruti family, esp. descend-ants of Bernardo). There are family trees in Venturini; Pippidi, *Hommes* (at 160–1); Luca, *Dacoromano-Italica*. The fullest genealogy is in Rothman, 'Between Venice', 464; but Rothman has misunderstood the arrangement of Venturini's tree, with the result that she makes Antonio Bruti's children appear twice, as his children and his siblings.

20. THE EXILED VOIVOD AND HIS COUNSELLOR

[1] *HD*, xi, 237 (letter to Ernest), 238–9 (safe-conduct), 250–3 (Tulln, gifts), 255–62 (Südtirol, Ernest, Ferdinand); Loebl, *Zur Geschichte*, i, 93–6 (renegotiation, Uskoks, Grand Vizier); Hirn, 'Das Exil', 435–6 (Hall), 436(n.) ('ein türkischer Bassa mit etlich hundert Türken'), 437–9 (Bolzano, von Kühbach); de Montaigne, *Journal*, i, 183 ('les rues plus estroites, & point de belle place publicque'). [2] Theiner, ed., *Vetera monumenta*, iii, 209 ('Ex litteris tuis atque ex sermone dilecti filii Antonii [Bruni], cui eas litteras et mandata ad nos dederas, cognovimus, quam praestanti voluntate sis, quibusque de causis cupias ad nos venire. Fuerunt illa omnia nobis iucundissima'; Theiner mistranscribes 'Bruni' here as 'Bruti'; *HD*, iii(1), 163 does so as 'Bruti', while *HD*, iii(2), 387 does so as 'Shuni')); Rainer *et al.*, eds., *Nuntiatur*, 41 ('All'istanza fatta dal prencipe cacciato di Moldavia non si vede quasi che risposta si possa dare, se vuol venire a Roma non ha bisogno di passaporto alcuno per Italia', 'per essere egli schismatico et fuori dell'unione di questa chiesa santa'); TLA, MS O. Ö. Geheimer Rat, Selekt Ferdinandea, Pos. 86, fo. 85r ('Cum Sancto Papa habemus familiaritatem Bonam … Et D[ominu]m quenda[m] ex aula n[ost]ra habebam, nomine Brutus, sepius nam [*sic*: for 'eum'?] ad Papam mittebam, His Preteritis authunis diebus etiam habuj l[ette]ras à Papa, quas nunc etiam teneo sed quando tempus postulat ex fauore M V. concedat mihi uenire romam et iterum redibo'; the Latin here is defective, presumably the work of a member of Petru's entourage). For a comparable case of a Bruti relative being referred to as 'Bruti' although that was not his surname, see the comment on Pasquale Dabri, below, 418. [3] AST, AMC, MS 550, fo. 58v (reel 688, frame 149) (overseer); BAV, MS Barb. Lat. 5361, fo. 205r ('quei Tartari, che ordinariamente stanno in quell'angolo della Moldauia, che tra li fiumi [Niestro], et Danubio sino al mare maggiore constituisce li sangiaccati di Bendero, et Achermano'); Soranzo, *L'Ottomanno*, 42 ('Tale è l'informatione, ch'io hò hauuto da quelli, c'hanno veduti i libri della Moldauia, e della Valacchia'). [4] Chivu *et al.*, eds., *Documente*, 178 ('i-am dat teriia a lui jupuni Anton Burăni se ghirăiascu, se sicheri, se tocmesche, se fache cumu ştii ma bine panturu časta pera cu Ğiva a Ragozei … undu-i va tibui şi nainte sivintu pape şi nainte čistit parat cherăştinescu şi naintele čistit dom Herţec Ferdinaru şi nainte alt dom cherăştinescu'), 183 (copy of document, dated 28 May). That Antonio went in May is confirmed by his own letter to Ferdinand of Nov. 1593, saying he had been in the Tyrol for 7 months (*HD*, xi, 774; cf. ibid., 339, referring to Bernardo Bruti but surely meaning Antonio Bruni). [5] Anon., ed., *Documente, veacul XVI*, iv, 74–6 (Apr. 1593: hostile witness statements, converted; but cf. Holban *et al.*, eds., *Călători*, iii, 232–3, casting doubt on some claims); Ghinea, 'La Famille', 395 (cousin); David, *Petru Şchiopul*, 217–18 (tax-farm); Caproşu, 'Creditul', 113 (tax-farm); Veress, ed., *Documente*, iii, 331 (thalers), iv, 10–11 (late June, two practitioners), 18–25 (Aug., appeal; 23–4: complaints about witnesses), 37 (final judgment); Iorga, 'Contribuţiuni', 97 (further attempts). Giovanni had also lent 2,000 thalers to Bartolomeo Bruti, on Petru's orders, for buying sable furs for the Sultan; this debt was unpaid (Corfus, ed. and tr.,

Documente, 356). The 1593 litigation was an expensive business: see the listing of Petru's costs in Iorga, 'Documente', 441–2.   [6] Anon., ed., *Documente, veacul XVI*, iv, 66–7 (letter to Petru), 68 (letter from Petru), 88 (letter from Sinan).   [7] HHStA, Türkei I, Karton 80, 2nd foliation, fos. 118r–119r (report, 1 June), 227v (report of galley, 19 June); *HD*, xi, 346–7 ('durch ainen genant Bruti an denselben Porten starckh practicieren lasse', 'Sunsten, ist unlangst Ainer, seines Namens Anthonius Bruti, alher zu ermeltem Weyvoda khommen, der ist, mich beduncкht, ain abgefürter verschlagener listiger Khopff; denselben gebraucht er in seinen gehaimen und vertrawten Sachen fur ainen Beystand und Tolmetschen; der soll, wie man sagt, dess zu Constantinopl anwesenden Bruti Vetter und nachender Bluts Freünd sein'), 358 ('durch seinen Tolmetschen (den Brutum)', 'nun khönte ers zwar nit vernainen, dass er dartzue nit ungenaigt, aber doch trawet er den Turckhen nit allerdings'); BAV, MS Barb. Lat. 5361, fo. 204r ('per l' aiuto di Dio, secondariam.^te per l'auantaggio dell' arme, e della disciplina'); TLA, Hofrat, Journale, Einkommende Schriften (R), 22, fo. 107v (Rossi information).   [8] *HD*, xi, pp. lxxxiv–lxxxvii (boyars, Poland, Habsburg refusal), 376–7 (Petru's letter to Ferdinand), 418 (Habsburgs favouring Aron); BAM, MS S 102 sup., fo. 44v ('com' io trattai con sua S.^tà d'ordine suo, et per opera di Antonio Bruni gentilhuomo Albanese'); Filitti, *Din arhivele*, ii, 52–3 (Clement to Rudolf and Ferdinand).   [9] *HD*, xi, 433 ('Anthonio Bruno in Italien'); TLA, O. Ö. Kammer-Kopialbücher, 475, Gemeine Missiven (no. 103), fo. 425r–v (note of letter sent to Bruni in Koper, 19 Mar. 1594). On 3 Apr. 1594 Antonio was elected to another 'overseer' position in Koper: AST, AMC, MS 550, fo. 114r (reel 688, frame 206).   [10] *HD*, xi, 437–40 (will), 443–5 (request to go to Rome); Nilles, *Symbolae*, ii, 996–7 ('der allain Ursach seiner yetzigen Pilgerschafft und seines öllends sey, damit Er den Aus der Türggen Tyranney gerissen habe', 'nach dem Kriechischen ritum'; extracts from this document are in *HD*, xi, 524–7); Hirn, 'Das Exil', 440 (burial).   [11] Hirn, 'Das Exil', 440 (3 guardians, Sigismund's request), 441 (education, death); TLA, MS O. Ö. Geheimer Rat, Selekt Ferdinandea, Pos. 86, fo. 83r (Orthodox church, son to be Catholic); Nilles, *Symbolae*, ii, 1002–6 (education, death).   [12] Nilles, *Symbolae*, ii, 997 ('das Warbarisch gesindl'); Căzan, 'Urmaşii', 261–3 (the thieves); TLA, MS O. Ö. Geheimer Rat, Selekt Ferdinandea, Pos. 86, fos. 356r (Rossi, 29 Aug.), 358r–359r (Rossi, 2 Sept.), 360r–361v (Rossi, 10 Sept.; fo. 361r: 'mentre uiueua il Vaiuoda non si scoprisse á me per suo Agente, sia altre uolte stato in Cost.^li Albanese, deriuato da Dolcigno, et per quanto intendo al presente habbi parentela con Sinan', 'non intendo di farne giudicio temerario, ne renderlo suspetto, uedendolo ardentissimo nel desiderare, et procurare il beneficio del figliuolo del Vaiuoda'), 437r (Rossi, 1 Oct.: 'assai ben intentionato'), 440v (500 ducats), 443v ('la Moglie del Sig.^re Bortolomio Brutti ua Creditrice di 7. m. ducati, prestati da suo Marito al sig.^re Vaiuoda').   [13] TLA, MS O. Ö. Geheimer Rat, Selekt Ferdinandea, Pos. 86, fos. 483v ('Ich sorg ... Es werden, schrifften Vorhande sein d[a]s d[er] alt[er] herr Sellig Ime Brunj seinen Sun zu Einen Völligen Curatorj Uber Leib vnd gudt statuier dennen fischt Er nach'), 519r–520v (Bruni to Rossi, 20 Oct.), 515r–518v (Rossi, 4 Nov., planning to go to Koper).   [14] Căzan, 'Urmaşii', 263 (20,000 ducats), 265–6 (recovered); TLA, MSS O. Ö. Geheimer

Rat, Selekt Ferdinandea, Pos. 86, fo. 626v ('altri creditori, fra quali la Vedoua del Bruti'), O. Ö. Regierung-Kopialbücher, Parteibücher, 55, fo. 432r (von Kühbach, Dec. 1597: 'haimblichen Practicken'); AST, AMC, MS 84, reel 124, frame 62 (settlement for 300 ducats); HD, xi, 533 ('col nome suo solo et con la segretezza necessaria in tali maneggi, Sua Maestà Cesarea potria riceverne singularissimo servitio, et in Moldavia, et altrove', 'è obligo di buon' christiano di desiderare l'ampliatione dela fede cattolica, con l'esterminio degl'inimici d'essa'), 533(n.) (acting in prince's interests).   [15] HD, xi, 477 ('Călătorii ale lui Bruni, mort la sfârşitul lui Iulie, la Triest'); AST, AMC, MS 551, fo. 58v (reel 689, frame 93) ('intendendosi che cosi nella patria del Friuli, come nella Città di Graz luochi troppo uicini detto male fà progresi lacrimeuoli'). To my own searches were added the painstaking efforts of Michaela Fahlenbock, of the Tiroler Landesarchiv, to whom I am very grateful.   [16] Cherini and Grio, Le famiglie, 173 (Pola family); Barbarano, Historia, iv, 152 ('un Vecchio molto dotto, e venerando'); PAK, MS KP 6.1, item 91, item 4, 1st page, verso ('recuperino quanto p.ª il Torchio da oglio, che possedono li SS.ʳⁱ Borissi, et che recuperato, no[n] possino mai più p[er] qualsi-uoglia causa reconcederglilo, essendo tanto congionti insieme la casa, et esso Torchio', 'm.[ol]ᵗᵒ ill[ust]re S. Caualiere Barnabà Bruti suo nepote, et figl.ˡᵒ del m.[ol]ᵗᵒ Ill[ust]re Capitano Giac.º Bruti suo germano'), 2nd page, verso ('uechi sempre i[n] suo seruitio, et p[er] quelli seruitù, che essi suoi uechi gli p[re]starono, mentre gli fecero uenire i[n] mano la Città di Dulcegno sua Patria natiua'); above, 25 (de Nicho). The will is now divided into items 3 and 4; despite some variation in handwriting, these seem to be parts of a single will, not successive versions of it.   [17] PAK, MS KP 6.1, item 91, item 3, 1st page, recto ('quelle dell' Ill.ᵐᵒ S. Caul.ʳᵒ et Commendatore Gasp.º Bruni suo tio; quelle dell' Eccs:ᵐᵒ S. Ant.º Bruni suo cugino, et del S.ʳ Gio. Stef.º suo fig.ˡᵒ, che sono di Trieste . . . et q[ue]lle del S. Gasp.º Bruni', epitaphs); Naldini, Corografia, 173–5 (description of San Domenico).

21. HABSBURG–OTTOMAN WAR AND BALKAN REBELLION

[1] Fermendžin, ed., Acta, 338 (estimate of 100,000 p.a.); Albèri, ed., Relazioni, ser. 3, ii, 297 (estimate of 600,000 lost by 1586); Šmitran, Gli uscocchi, 62–3 (attempt in 1589, Venice unable); Predelli et al., eds., I libri, vii, 56 (Sultan's offer).   [2] Fodor, In Quest, 178–90 (plan for fleet, letters to Henri and Eliza-beth); Maclean and Matar, Britain, 53–6 (Don Antonio's son); Skilliter, 'Turkish Documents', 40–2, 51–2 (Don Antonio's son and Istanbul).   [3] Biegman, Turco-Ragusan, 143 (message); de Leva, ed., La legazione, i, 153–4(n.); Jaitner, ed., Die Hauptinstruktionen, i, 157 (Clement VIII's efforts); Niederkorn, Die europäischen Mächte, 193 (Clement's efforts).   [4] Loebl, Zur Geschichte, i, 64–81 (raids), 101 (impressed Sultan), ii, 49–53 (raids), 62–71 (Bihać); Bayerle, Ottoman Diplomacy, 153 (complaint about artillery); Peçevi, Historija, ii, 108 (prisoners, artillery); de Leva, ed., La legazione, i, 113(n.) (prisoners, artillery).

On Hasan's role see also Fodor, 'Prelude'.   [5] Peçevi, *Historija*, ii, 108 (Sinan's hatred); Bayerle, *Ottoman Diplomacy*, 153 (Mehmed to Ernest), 156 (Habsburg raids in Hungary); Reusner, *Operis*, 54–5 (Rudolf to von Kreckwitz), 55–6 (Sinan to Rudolf).   [6] Selaniki, *Tarih*, i, 314 (Mehmed *beylerbeyi*); HHStA, Türkei I, Karton 80, 2nd foliation, fos. 127r–v ('der hat sich zimblich moderato darauf erwisen, vnd conclusiue gesagt, Er habe seinen Sohn dise sachen gantz vnd gar haimbgestellt, was d[er] solle darinnen handlen vnnd beschliessen wordt, solle Ime auch gefallen', 'hat Er den Bruti mit sich genomben, vnd nach langem gespräch, vngeuahr vmb mitternacht, zu mir für das hauss geschückgt, vnnd anzuzaigen beuolhen, es seyen nunmehr alle sachen gantz vnnd gar richtig, volgenden morgen vor tags, solle d[er] Dragoman auss der gefangnis genomben, vnnd wid[er] inn diss hauss gebracht werden, alsdann Ich gleich ain audientz bey dem Obristen Vezir haben, vnnd hernach strackhs den Kurier zu der Khai: Ma[jestä]tt expedirn'), 139r–v (letter: 'in conformita di quanto gia altre uolte per mezo del presente Sig^r Benedetto Brutti ho auisato V. S. M.^{co}').   [7] HHStA, Türkei I, Karton 80, 2nd foliation, fos. 127v–128r ('Darauf d[er] Beglerbegh geandtwortet, Er thue disfalss nichts wid[er] sein Vattern, sond[er]n alles mit desselben vorwissen, vnnd erlaubnuss, begere auch Sulthanus khainen Khrieg, sond[er]n baide Presentten, weil Ich dann dieselben gwiss vnd aigentlich Versprich[en?], müesse man mich auch in acht habe'), 128r–v ('Es sei vnmüglich gewesen, die Presentt vor ainem Jaar hereinzuschücken, weil d[er] Bassa in Bossn in d[es] Khai. Matt s. Landt so grosse schaden gethan'), 133r (2,000 thalers), 134v (request for 6,000).   [8] Ibid., 2nd foliation, fos. 200v ('hatt mir … Benedetto Bruti wahrhafftig vill beständig vnd nuzlich gedient, dan alss ich in der aussersten Nottgefahr, vnd von aller Weltt verlassen gewesen, (et Dragomanno capto) … hat Er sich, den ich doch zuuor mein lebtag nie gesehen, weniger gekhant, allain d[a]s Er mit dem dragoman khundtschafft gehabt, nit allain ultro zu disen gefährlichen diensten anerbotten, sondern auch alsbaldt die sach angegriffen, aller ortten erkhündiget informiert, tentirt vnd fuergebautt'), 200v–201r ('inns Hauss, zugehen lengst vergunnet', 'etlichmall in d[er] nacht'), 201v ('so lang Er noch hie sein wirdt (dann Er begierd erzaigt, sich gar in die Christenhait … zu transferiren)'), 201v–202r ('Van ob Er zwar d[er] Turkische sprach nicht zum besten khundig, hat Er dannoch als ain Albaneser mit den fuernembsten Heubtenn bey diser Portten (so fast alle aus denselben ortten) vnnd vill anndern ansehenlichen Persohnen, inn disen Lannden, khuntschafft, Practica, zuetritt, vnnd ist fur ainen Christen in zimblichen credit bey Ihnen, vnd kan ain inde wichtige sach aller ortten wol so baldt Erkundigen, tracten vnd verrichten, als nimandts anderer, vnd ist nimandten alhier mit dienst[en] obligirt, sondern allein pro obtinenda uindicta necis fraternae'), 202r (conclusion).   [9] Selaniki, *Tarih*, i, 320–1 (death of Hasan, other *bey*s); Bayerle, *Ottoman Diplomacy*, 9–10 (8,000); HHStA, Türkei I, Karton 81, 1st foliation, fos. 3r–4v (Matthias letter), 29r–30v (Rudolf letter), 80r–v (list of payments), 107r (report: 'il Sultano et le Sultane habbino lacrimato, il Primo Vesir se fusse offerto Generale alla uendetta, in segno della quale se le hauesse posto una veste rossa indosso'); Isopescu,

'Alcuni documenti', 460 (Imperial declaration, Aug.). **[10]** Bayerle, *Ottoman Diplomacy*, 10 (arrival at Belgrade, actions); Woodhead, ed., *Ta'liki-zade's* şehname, 33 (season ended 26 Oct.), 35–6 (St Sava), 39(n.) (Yemişçi), 43 (Győr well supplied, commander executed), 44–6 (Tatars); Radojčić, *Mileševa*, 48 (St Sava); Finkel, 'Provisioning', 117–19 (stationed in winter); Kortepeter, *Ottoman Imperialism*, 136–7 (Habsburg inroads, Esztergom, Győr, 30–40,000 Tatars), 141–2 (Tatars, fall of Győr); Finkel, *Administration*, 102 (Tatar raids to Vienna); de Leva, ed., *La legazione*, ii, 465 (Pope depressed). It has been suggested that Yemişçi Hasan was Sinan's nephew: see Dokle, *Sinan*, 13, and Hoxha, *Shqiptari*, 57. **[11]** Loebl, *Zur Geschichte*, i, 67 (Gregory XIV); Niederkorn, *Die europäischen Mächte*, 71–2 (subsidies), 86–8 (Shah Abbas), 193–205 (Spanish policy, subsidies); von Palombini, *Bündniswerben*, 113–14 (Shah Abbas); Jaitner, ed., *Die Hauptinstruktionen*, i, 297(n.) (Yemen). On Clement's efforts see also Djuvara, *Cent projets*, 126–9; Bartl, '"Marciare"'. **[12]** Niederkorn, *Die europäischen Mächte*, 147 (plan for Ottoman–French campaign), 297–313 (Venetian refusal); de Leva, ed., *La legazione*, i, 215 (Friuli), 307 (canon law argument), 321 (Paruta's advice), ii, 103–4 (Paruta against league), 191 (outpost of Christendom). **[13]** Korade, 'Prijedlozi', 210 (applied to Jesuits); Jaitner, ed., *Die Hauptinstruktionen*, i, 186–204 (initial instructions); Theiner, ed., *Vetera monumenta*, iii, 210–11 (papal breves to rulers of Transylvania, Moldavia, etc.); Vanino, *Isusovci*, i, 67–8 (further instructions); Isopescu, 'Alcuni documenti', 461 (Spanish Jesuit). **[14]** Pierling and Rački, 'L. Komulovića izvještaj', 89 (Transylvania, Feb. 1594), 94 (Moldavia, 'inter spem et metum'), 100–1 (backsliding, Kiliya); Jaitner, ed., *Die Hauptinstruktionen*, i, 199 ('non è securo fidarsi di gente schismatica prima che si scoprino ben bene gl'interessi et le passioni che la predominano'); Pierling, 'Novi izvori', 232 (Zamoyski hostile); Halecki, *From Florence*, 265 (Cossack leader); Iorga, *Studiĭ*, 208 (Cossacks attack Aron); Niederkorn, *Die europäischen Mächte*, 478–9 (Cossacks against Aron as pro-Ottoman); Isopescu, 'Alcuni documenti', 461 (to seize his money). **[15]** Pernice, 'Un episodio', 258–9 (Sigismund, June 1594, opposition); Isopescu, 'Alcuni documenti', 461 (agreements, Aug., Nov. 1594); Decei, *Relaţii*, 224–5 (killed Muslims, declaration of war, harried Ottomans); Filitti, *Din arhivele*, ii, 59 ('non perchè possano con le loro armi apportare molto utilità, ma [per] conto delle vettovaglie'). **[16]** Decei, *Relaţii*, 225–7 (political and military developments, Călugăreni), 230 (Albanian volunteers); Iorga, *Geschichte*, iii, 311–12 (Călugăreni, Sinan); Randa, *Pro republica*, 110–14 (Călugăreni); Andreescu, 'Boierii', 78 (Leka). **[17]** Decei, *Relaţii*, 227 (Oct. campaign, Jan. expedition); Iorga, *Geschichte*, iii, 316–17 (bridgehead); Pernice, 'Un episodio', 265–72 (Oct. campaign, Tuscans, bridgehead); Hanlon, *Twilight*, 82 (Tuscans); Griswold, *Great Anatolian Rebellion*, 17 (bureaucrats); Danişmend, *Osmanlı devlet*, 25 (Lala Mehmed); Selaniki, *Tarih*, ii, 581–2 (illness, death); Fleischer, *Bureaucrat*, 164 (poets rejoiced); Vratislav, *Adventures*, 176 (quotation); BL, MS Cotton Nero B. xii, fo. 334v (Barton report). **[18]** Kortepeter, *Ottoman Imperialism*, 145–6 (Poles, Movilă, joint protectorate, King Sigismund). **[19]** Finkel, *Administration*,

55 (Esztergom, Mehmed); de Leva, ed., *La legazione*, iii, 153–4 ('più pronta al sacheggiare il luoghi degli amici che al combattere quelli de' nemici'), 169 (target 14,000); ASR, Soldatesche e galere, busta 90, unnumbered item (group absconded), busta 646, unfoliated (payments for 596 Albanian cavalry); da Mosto, 'Ordinamenti', 102 (via Bolzano); Bagi, 'Esztergom', 50 (22 Aug.); Selaniki, *Tarih*, i, 414 (Shkodër); Iorga, *Geschichte*, iii, 316 (Vlorë); Brunelli, *Soldati*, 106 (in charge at Visegrád); Hanlon, *Twilight*, 85 (disease).   **[20]** BAM, MS D 484 inf., fos. 15v–16r (Frachetta, 1586); Pierling and Rački, 'L. Komulovića izvještaj', 86–7 (Komulović); BAV, MS Urb. Lat. 1492, fos. 56r (two armies), 61v ('li quali senza dubbio sono la maggior parte, poiche la maggior parte sono Christiani', 'solleuarsi et prendere li armi contro di lui'); de Mattei, 'Una "Orazione"', 104 ('Greci, Albanesi, Macedoni et tanti altri, … se non altro co' sassi et con l'ignude lor braccia e mani non cercherebbono in si bella occasione di sollevarsi').   **[21]** Arcari, *Il pensiero*, 20–5 (Cres, Preveza); Patrizi, *Izabrani spisi*, 10(n.) (Petrisević); Patrizi, *Lettere*, 45–6 (kings, Preveza, Herceg Novi); Personeni, *Notizie*, 112–18 (members of Accademia); DHI, MS Minuccio Minucci, 9, fos. 263–78 (discourse; fos. 264r, 265r: Patrizi); Patrizi, *Paralleli*, ii, 87 ('se noi smontassimo in Albania, ci si accosteriano tutti gli Albanesi, gente valorosa, e da Turchi già tanto temuta, e per l'antica memoria della gloria loro sotto Scanderbego, e per l'odio fierissimo presente'), 92 (march on Istanbul).   **[22]** Zamputi, ed., *Dokumente*, ii, 11–12 (summer 1593 message), 16–18 (papers found, Venetian response); Jaitner, ed., *Die Hauptinstruktionen*, i, 188 ('intenderete ciò che passi intorno alla prattica cominciata dagli Albanesi'); Pazzi, *I cavalieri*, 139 (Pelessa).   **[23]** Krajcar, *Cardinal Giulio*, 117, 127 (Himarë request); Karalevskij, 'La missione', year 17, vol. 29, 193 (Pope's reply to Himarë); BAV, MS Chigi A VI 194, fos. 103r–104r (list of representatives), 106v–109r (Pelessa document; fos. 108v: 'Sono stati espediti huomini uerso la Valona la Cimara, et fino nella Morea per farli sapere li loro pensieri, perche la guerra passata haueano deliberato tutti di prender le arme contra Turchi'; 109r: 'l'esercito di sua M.ta Catt.ca et di qualche altro Prencipe Christiano'); Zamputi, ed., *Dokumente*, ii, 36–8, 40–1 (Pelessa in Rome).   **[24]** Bartl, *Der Westbalkan*, 84–7 (authorities sceptical, letter to Quinzio, meetings, undercover trips); ASVat, Fondo Borghese III 128, fos. [7v]–[8r] (Patrizi on Gini and his career), [9v]–[10v] (on the two documents).   **[25]** ASVat, Fondo Borghese III 128, fo. [8r] (Quinzio indiscreet); Zamputi, ed., *Dokumente*, ii, 52 ('quando li di passati intendessimo che vi erano galee in Golfo, cioè spagnuole, ne credevimo che vi fusse con esse il cavalier Bruni che stà in Malta, per esser lui di natione Albanese, et per venir … in patria et liberarla dalle mani de infideli'); Lamansky, 'L'Assassinat', 117 (order to Naples); Tomić, *Gradja*, 131–2 (order to seize Pelessa), 195–8 (Pelessa seized); Bartl, *Der Westbalkan*, 89 (Bishop, protests).   **[26]** Bartl, *Der Westbalkan*, 99 (Brtučević), 100–1 (travels in 1595); Springer, 'Kaiser Rudolf', 80–1 (Knight, hunted bandit), 88–90 (memorandums, agitating over Klis); Noflatscher and Springer, 'Studien', 61–71 (memorandums); Zamputi, ed., *Dokumente*, ii, 45, 47 (involvement with Pelessa), 52 (large promises); Jaitner, ed., *Die Hauptinstruktionen*, i, 257 (agitating with Pope over Klis); Niederkorn, *Die europäischen Mächte*, 285–90

(rejoicing, Venetian actions). **[27]** Zamputi, ed., *Dokumente*, ii, 98–100 (in Corfu, preferred Venice to Spain), 102–3, 110–13 (arms to Himarë), 114–15 (Athanasios in Naples), 115–16 (Lantzas accusation); Floristán Imízcoz, ed., *Fuentes*, i, 430–40 (Riseas), 458(n.) (from Messina); Pippidi, *Byzantins*, 128 (inspired by Călugăreni), 130–3 (Vlorë, fortress, journeys); Bartl, *Der Westbalkan*, 126–7 (10 Aug. and aftermath); Snǔgarov, *Istorija*, 98–9 (journeys). **[28]** BAV, MS Urb. Lat. 1028, part 2, fos. 301r–304v (basic argument), 308r ('la Morea subbito seguiria l'essempio, et cosi Negroponte, l'Isole, et il continente'), 315v ('il che uerrebbe à rinchiudere dentro angusti termini la nauigatione de Vinetiani'). **[29]** Valentini, 'Perpjekje', 251 ('immerso in un profondissimo sonno dell'otio ... Il gouerno discorde ... La guerra senza capi di alcun ualore, ò almeno di alcuna reputatione. Ne i soldati corrotta, et già del tutto destrutta la disciplina, et introdotta la disobbedienza, et le seditioni. I Popoli commossi, ... ardiscono per se stessi di ribellarsi'); Griswold, *Great Anatolian Rebellion*, 16–17 (cavalry unit, Visegrád); Tezcan, *Second Ottoman Empire*, 183 (cavalry regiments, Sinan); Crescentio, *Nautica*, 478 (1589 uprising); Petrosyan, 'Janissary Corps', 751 (janisssary revolts, Buda); Murphey, *Ottoman Warfare*, 140 (janissaries quelling cavalry, call-up in 1595). **[30]** Fodor, *In Quest*, 215–22 (Sultan versus Grand Vizier); Tezcan, *Second Ottoman Empire*, 94–100 (change in political system). **[31]** Maxim, *L'Empire*, 120 (deficit 1581); Fodor, *In Quest*, 173 (permanent deficit); Pamuk, 'Re-assessment' (Spanish silver not decisive, *timar*s deteriorated); Özel, 'Reign', 185 (meritocracy eroded); Sariyannis, 'Ottoman Critics' (Ottoman 'decline' literature); Howard, 'Ottoman Historiography' (Ottoman 'decline' literature, influenced Western account); Boyar, 'Ottoman Expansion', 138 (Mustafa Ali).

22. PASQUALE 'BRUTI' AND HIS PEACE MISSION

[1] de Nicolay, *Dans l'Empire*, 13 (1548, advice); Kołodziejczyk, 'Inner Lake', 134 (1569); Cernovodeanu, 'English Diplomat', 432 (de Brèves, bailo); Skilliter, 'Ambassador's *ta'yin*', 156–7 (document, departure); BL, MS Cotton Nero B. xii, fo. 356r (Barton despatch). **[2]** BL, MS Cotton Nero B. xii, fo. 301r (Barton, Jan. 1596); Niederkorn, *Die europäischen Mächte*, 112–17 (Elizabeth's change of policy). **[3]** Bodl., MS Ital. c. 7, fo. 160r ('molto caduto di reputatione'), 160v ('seruendosene li Turchi come spia da intendere le cose de christiani'); Kruppa, 'Okmányok', 57–8 (Barton to Sigismund, 1595; cf. *HD*, xii, 49(n.), 54–5), 63 (Barton to Sigismund, 1597); Filitti, *Din arhivele*, ii, 71 (Barton to Mihai, 1597); *HD*, iv(2), 212 (bailo); BL, MS Cotton Nero B. xii, fos. 215r–216r (interview with Sinan, July 1595), 300v–301r (letter from Elizabeth), 303r (tin and wire), 335v (Safiye and others). **[4]** Reusner, *Operis*, 101–5 (Feb. 1595 exchange); Vratislav, *Adventures*, 153–92 (Black Tower; 183: English dragoman, quotation), 193 (baths); Seidel, *Denckwürdige Gesandtschafft*, 76–7 (English dragoman), 80 (tents in garden), 81 ('Zeltern, Teppichten, Polstern, Küchen Geräth, und allerley Victualien'), 82 ('vier und vier in einem rothen verhengten Wagen mit zwey Rossen, gleicher Gestalt wie man das Türckische Frauenzimmer zu führen pflegt');

Foster, *Travels*, 58 (del Faro). Barton's own 'relazione' referred to just 4 carriages: BNC, MS Vittorio Emanuele 1034, fo. 453r.   **[5]** Venturini, 'La famiglia', family tree (parents); Jireček, 'Die Romanen' (ii), 18, (iii), 22 (Dabri family); Pertusi, *Martino Segono*, 21–2 (Pasquale's daughter and Beçikemi, 1480s); Čoralić and Karbić, *Pisma*, 94–5 (Pasquale, 1505–6); Bartl, ed., *Albania sacra*, i, 14 (Niccolò Dabri). Pasquale's date of birth is unknown; that given for his mother in Venturini, 'La famiglia', family tree (1564) must be an error, at least 10 years too late.   **[6]** Ghinea, 'La Famille', 390–5 (Marioara Adorno); Iorga, *Ospiti*, 99 (recommending to Mihnea); Luca, 'Veneziani', 246, 247(n.) (Jan. 1592, saying 'Benedetto', but calling him the Postelnic); Kruppa, 'Pasquale Bruti', 29 ('Pasquale took the place of Bartolomeo's brother in 1592' ('Helyébe Bartholomeo testvére, Pasquale lépett 1592-ben')); *HD*, xi, 530(n.) (Marin in Istanbul, 1597), xii, 337 (Marin in Pera, 1598), 676 (died 1600, much loved); *CSPVen.*, ix, 222 (bailo, July 1596). Puzzlingly, Kruppa also cites a Venetian report of Dec. 1591 describing Pasquale as the son of the late Cristoforo Bruti: 'Pasquale Bruti', 28–9.   **[7]** Seidel, *Denckwürdige Gesandtschafft*, 82–5 (journey); Purchas, *Pilgrimes*, ii, 1355 (impalement etc.: from the description by Barton's secretary, Thomas Glover).   **[8]** Seidel, *Denckwürdige Gesandtschafft*, 87–8 (meeting with İbrahim), 67–90 (endangered by Hatvan), 91 (Szolnok); Vratislav, *Adventures*, 195–6 (tour of camp, 300,000), 198 (Hatvan, women and infants); Purchas, *Pilgrimes*, ii, 1358 (Hatvan quotation: from a letter by Barton, 5 Oct.). I adopt the chronology given in a later report: Klarwill, ed., *Fugger-Zeitungen*, 193–5. This was probably derived from Vratislav: it used his phrase about drivers of asses and camels and estimated that only 100,000 of the men were fighters.   **[9]** Seidel, *Denckwürdige Gesandtschafft*, 91–2 (journey from Szolnok to Pest); Vratislav, *Adventures*, 200–6 (journey from Szolnok to Pest), 206–7 (governor of Buda, *martoloses*); TNA, SP 97/1, fo. 155v (quotation from Barton about del Faro).   **[10]** Klarwill, ed., *Fugger-Zeitungen*, 195 (23 Sept.); Seidel, *Denckwürdige Gesandtschafft*, 93–4 (Dabri and janissary, arrival at fort, Esztergom, Vienna); Vratislav, *Adventures*, 207–10 (guides killed, arrival at fort, Esztergom, Vienna; 209: quotation). Seidel and the Fugger report both name the fort as 'Waizen' (Vác); Vratislav calls it 'Towaschow' (apparently a confusion with Tovačov, in Moravia).   **[11]** *CSPVen.*, ix, 232–4 (Vendramin reports); Peçevi, *Historija*, ii, 163–5 (siege of Eger), 165–9 (Mezőkeresztes); BNC, MS Vittorio Emanuele 1034, fo. 460r ('i caullieri smontati da cauallo, et i fanti buttate le picche, et gli archibugi, per meglio rubbare'), 460v (counter-attacks). On the campaign see Schmidt, 'Egri Campaign'.   **[12]** Kruppa, 'Pasquale Bruti', 34 ('honeste conditioni', 'essendo alterata la conditione delle cose con questi importantissimi successi non si poteva trattar più di quella maniera, come si sarebbe trattato prima'), 36–7 (20 Nov. meeting; 37: 'mentre si fà qui tanto lentamente tutte le risoluzioni egli teneva per certo, che si ridurebbe il negozio a termini di nessuna conclusione', 'vestendosi in habito turchesco').   **[13]** Ibid., 37 (devoted to Venice, 'molto giovane'), 39 (gifts, letters), 40 (status quo idea, Poland, 'tutto del gran signore', eager to return).   **[14]** TNA, SP 97/3, fos. 163v–164r (quotation, 21

Feb.), 180r (4 Apr.), 180v (17 Apr.: 'e di piu manda una altra cossa, qual spero lei sara grata, ma per buon rispetto la taceo, et quanto sara possibile, presto veniro in la a basciare le mani di V. S. Ill.ᵐᵃ et renderli conto di quel ho effetuato p[er] suo seruitio in questo mio viagio'); Kruppa, 'Okmányok', 78 ('Del Pascale drago-mano restiamo desperati per le molte informationi che si vengono date, che Hassan bassa l'habbia fatto morire'); *HD*, xii, 1260 (avviso, 24 June); *CSPVen.*, ix, 291 (petition), 299 (ridicule); Woodhead, 'Barton' (death of Barton).   **[15]** *HD*, xii, 329–30 (del Faro), 497–9 (anonymous, but probably del Faro), 676 (del Faro); Randa, *Pro republica*, 153–4 (Basta biography); De Caro, 'Basta' (Basta biog-raphy).   **[16]** Kortepeter, *Ottoman Imperialism*, 192–4 (Transylvanian events); Evans, *Rudolf II*, 26, 68–70 (divergence); Lefaivre, *Les Magyars*, i, 266–76 (Bocs-kai revolt). For a good summary of the course of the war see Finkel, *Administration*, 12–20. On the fighting in the Romanian lands see Randa, *Pro republica*, 181–310; on Zsitvatorok see Bayerle, 'Compromise'.

EPILOGUE: THE LEGACY: ANTONIO BRUNI'S TREATISE

[1] Pippidi, 'Tre antiche casate', 64 (Benedetto); Anon., 'Senato Mare', vol. 12, 410 (salt-pans), 443 (Jacomo); Barbarano, *Historia*, iv, 152 (Matteo); AST, AMC, MS 84, reel 124, frame 62 (1600 document); Manzuoli, *Nova descrittione*, sig. A2r (Alessandro poem).   **[2]** BAV, MS Barb. Lat. 5361, fos. 200r–207r; BMC, MS Wcovich Lazzari 25, busta 9. Both are scribal, containing errors of transcrip-tion. I cite primarily from the BAV MS. I found the Museo Correr MS during my research on Antonio Bruti, under whose name it is mistakenly catalogued. The full text will be published in the 2015 volume of *Revue des études sud-est euro-péennes*.   **[3]** BAV, MS Barb. Lat. 5361, fos. 205v ('li Cimarioti montanari . . . sono adesso solleuati á persuatione d' alcuni, ma piú per opera di Atanasio Arciuesc.º d' Ocrida, che sotto spetie di uisita (che Ocrida é lontana dalla Cimerra intorno á quattro giornate) há fatto loro creder d'hauer intell.ᵃ con l'Im.ʳᵉ; et che tantosto sariano uenute genti del Ré di spagna . . . ma questo moto loro puo durar poco se non é mantenuto da aiuti forastieri'), 207r ('da uinticinque anni in qua').   **[4]** Serassi, *La vita*, ii, 231–2 (employment by Cinzio); Ingegneri, *Del buon segretario*, 22–3 ('Degli auisi del Mondo', 'la notitia cotidiana de gli ordi-nari auisi del Mondo . . . perche questi sono vn'historia presente, et uiua', 'piena informatione de gl'interessi, & delle voglie di tutti i Principi viuenti, & così delle forze loro, delle qualità de i paesi, de i costumi delle nationi . . . Per così fatto stu-dio tornerà molto à proposito la lettione di diuerse scritture, che si veggono alla penna, cioè Relationi d'Ambasciatori, Instruttioni di Nuntij, & di simile natura cose infinite').   **[5]** Serassi, *La vita*, ii, 258(n.) (left service, falling out); Person-eni, *Notizie*, 114 (Venice 1596); ASVat, Fondo Borghese IV 229, fo. 49r ('Hor poiche V. S. mi scriue, che da Roma li uiene acennato, che così fatta informatione al' Ill.ᵐᵒ suo Patrone non saria discara, uado entrando in openione [*sic*], che da lei sia stata rapresentata molto maggiore di qᵉllo, che è in effetti. nel che si come io riconosco la sua molta bontà, et amore uerso di me: così non sò come corrispondere all'espettatione. pur' la colpa sarà più sua, che mia. et se piacerà al suo Sig.^re me lo reputarò à gran gratia. ne credo, che S. S. Illma sdegnarà d'honorarmi con una sua resposta. Che io a la fine mi risoluo d'appigliarmi al suo prudentiss.^mo et amoreuoliss.^mo conseglio, acciò el Sor Card.^le sappia, che da me le sarà mandata la scrittura col mezo di V. S. mio singulariss.^mo patrone'). [6] BAV, MS Barb. Lat. 5361, fos. 201r ('si come ci sono diuerse religioni, cosi ui si trouano ancora differenti lingue, che causano ne popoli una certa disunione, che fa maggiore la discordia, che ordinariam.^te regna, per la diuersita della fede'), 201v (Greeks, Serbs, Bulgarians, Paulicians; on the Paulicians see Hupchick, *Bulgarians*, 77–82), 202v ('Conseruano li Greci la uanita de Maggiori, et l'odio uerso i cattolici'), 203r ('li Schiauoni, che fanno alla greca, piu scismatici de gl' altri della nation loro, abhoriscono il nome latino, perseguitato ordinariamente dall' Arciuescouo di Pegio, che ua opprimendo li Prelati cattolici, per la recognitione, che pretende da loro'). [7] BAV, MS Barb. Lat. 5361, fo. 203r ('ancorache le Iurucchi, maestri di finiss.^o feltre, gia pastori uagabondi, hora stabili, progenie di quei Asiatici, che seguirono la fattione, et setta di Zecchelle Persiano, ó chi che fusse, egli, potria essere, che nell' intrinseco credessero piu ad Hali, che á Maometo: et questi sotto capo part.[icola]^re habitano piu in Dobrutia, che nel resto di Bulgaria'); Truhelka, 'Balkan-Yürüken' (Yürüks); Werner, 'Yürüken', 472–3 (16th-century Yürük influx); İnbaşı, 'Rumeli Yörükleri', 159, 163 (Yürüks in Varna district); İnalcık, *Middle East*, 25 (felt), 97–136 (Yürüks; 116: felt); Kayapınar, 'Dobruca yöresinde', 93 (Yürüks in Dobrudža); Uluçay, 'Yavuz Sultan Selim', 61–74 (Şahkulu revolt); Sohrweide, 'Der Sieg', 145–56 (Şahkulu revolt); Yıldırım, 'Turkomans', 318, 321–2, 375–6 (earlier deportations), 384–412 (Şahkulu revolt); Mikov, *Izkustvoto*, 22–3 (Şahkulu rebels deported); Gökbilgin, *Rumeli'de Yürükler*, 214–16 (Yürüks named 'Şahkulu', 1543). The influential Italian historian Paolo Giovio had called Şahkulu 'Techellis' (*Historiarum*, fo. 95r–v), a name borrowed (as 'Techelles') by Christopher Marlowe for a character in *Tamburlaine*. [8] BAV, MS Barb. Lat. 5361, fos. 203r–v (business, 'pauentano d'ogni moto, armati all' antica, d' arco, e scimitara, ma li maritimi hanno anco qualche arcobugio', 'non uogliono arrischiar la uita nelle guerre; anzi che molti ó gli riuendono, ó mandano li seruitori in uece loro'), 204r (*sancak*s), 205r ('quella ingorda nation per il piu non parte da Casa se non é prima prouista di uettouaglia per la famiglia, che lascia, et per se d'armi, et uestimenti sino à stiuali'). [9] Ibid., fo. 205v ('Restami á soggiongere dell' Albania'). [10] Ibid., fos. 202r ('molto differente dalla Schiauona, et greca', 'l'antica lingua de Macedoni', 'é la natione Albanese assai maggiore della sua prouincia, l' Albania cominciando á Ponente da Dolcigno, et dal lago di Scutari, finisce in leuante alla Bastia incontra Corfu: ma gli Albanesi peró habitano piu in lá in diuersi luoghi della Morea, et Grecia, et ricoueratisi per le guerre, o trasportati da gl'Imperatori Constantinopolitani, che cosi rimediorno alle solleuationi di questa gente'), 205v ('Nel sangiaccato di Deluino quasi tutti sano [*sic*] la lingua greca: in quello della Vallona la maggior parte. Sonoui ancora molte ville di Bulgari, che cauano la pece. et la Vallona sola fra tutte le terre d'Albania é habitata da Turchi forastieri d'origine

Asiatica, di quei, che seguitarono Zechelle' ['Zechelle' in BMC MS, p. 20, 'Zecholle' in BAV MS]), 205v–206r (Himariots, Dukat), 206r ('li meglio armati, cosi anco sono li piú fedeli Christiani dell' Im.° Turchesco tumultuando essi per ogni minima cagione, non meno quei del piano, che li montanari', 'ó per depredargli, ó per uendicarsene, ó per hauer scusa di non andar á guerra lontana et per tale effetto quello di Ducagini non parte mai, si come anco il sangiaccho di Angelo Castro, che sotto pretesto di difender il paese dall' armate Christiane, sempre sta á casa'); Evliya Çelebi, *Evliya*, 145 (Vlorë; cf. similar comments on Gjirokastër: 81, 85; on devotion to the family of the Prophet see Moosa, *Extremist Shiites*, 78–87).   [11] BAV, MS Barb. Lat. 5361, fo. 206v ('L'Albania al mare Adriatico é circondata da altiss.ⁱ monti, piana, et irrigata da spessi, e grossi fiumi, che á pedoni prohibiscono la congiuntione tra di loro. et li Christiani non hanno cauallaria, ne modo di far ponti. li luochi serrati sono in poter de Turchi, ancorche ne presidiati, ne custoditi tutti. Li principali almeno sicuri, che da Christiani occultam.ᵗᵉ non possono esser rubati. Il che hó uoluto accennare per l'opinione, che s'há di questi popoli, che da se possano far cosa buona senza gente forastiera, et che la fame sola de gl' aiuti d' Italia, e spagna, col mostrar loro qualche bandiera, basti á solleuargli: Volesselo Iddio. pur che non pericolino gl'infelici, et che con questi trattati tanto palesi non si perda affatto l'opportunita di far bene per l'auenire').   [12] Ibid., fos. 206v ('et per l' assenza, et perche non há la lingua poco frutto puo fare', 'per esser entrato in uoglia di sorprender Croia co'l mezzo d'un Nidar Manasi stradaruolo Turco (che puó e non puó succedere) si ua ascondendo, che li Turchi hanno di gia scoperto il trattato, et credo se ne burlano'), 207r ('Cosi la dignita episcopale é inuilita, et le chiese ruinano non tanto per la tirannia de Turchi, quanto per la miseria di curati', 'contentandomi di hauer semplice, e realmente rappresentata la conditione presente de Turchi, e christiani: che si come il narrare quello, che s'há uisto, e sentito, á ciascuno é permesso, cosi il uoler persuader á Principi quello, che debbono, ó possono fare, non é lecito á tutti'); ASVat, MS Fondo Borghese III 60h, fo. 93v ('d'altra nacione, non hauendo la lingua, et i costumi, non sono buoni se non da meter confusione').   [13] Lazari, ed., *Diario*, 7–13 (Giacomo Soranzo biography); Cella, 'Documenti', 242 (sentence of banishment); Preto, *I servizi*, 59 (avvisi, noting also that Cellini was sentenced to perpetual imprisonment); Panciera, '"Tagliare"', 239 (cardinal); BNM, MS It. XI. 8 (6769), fo. 288v ('quella piccola ma delitiosa città'). Another possible Soranzo connection was Alvise Soranzo, governor of Koper in 1591–2, who later acted as procurator for Maria Bruti in her legal action against the estate of Petru Şchiopul (AST, AMC, MS 84, reel 124, frame 62); but he was not a close relative, being Giacomo's third cousin (see the genealogy in ASVen, Miscellanea Codici, serie 1a, storia veneta, reg. 23, 43–50.)   [14] Soranzo, *Carmen* (poem); Salinerio, *Annotationes*, 283–4 (Tacitus); Soranzo, *L'Ottommanno*, sig. 3†1r (cameriere d'onore); BNC, MS Vittorio Emanuele 1034, fos. 399r–410r ('Discorso'); Soranzo, *Oratione*, sig. π4r–v (circulated in France), fos. 30v ('doue meglio potete impiegar l'armi e'l valor vostro che in così sacrosanta e lodeuol impresa?'), 31r [misprinted '28'] (written at Clement's request).   [15] Albèri, ed., *Relazioni*, ser. 3, iii, 17 (baili taking relatives); Soranzo, *L'Ottomanno*, sig. A2v ('ragionando sopratutto con persone di molta sperienza, e giuditio, le quali son venute nuouamente da quelle parti: non mi fidando ne anco di quelle cose, ch'io stesso hò già vedute, e molto ben considerate altre volte'); Sforza, 'Un libro', 211 ('non haver detto cose nove, e machinate da me, ma cavate da scrittori stampati et approbati, e da scritture che si leggono publicamente in Venetia et in Roma'). Soranzo had perhaps spent time in Dalmatia, as he showed a good knowledge of Serbo-Croatian: *L'Ottomanno*, 35, 52, 70, 79. Iorga suggests, on the basis of a Greek letter by Marioara Adorno of 1583, that he was secretary to a bailo ('Contribuţiuni', 54, 56); but he has misread the Greek. For high (and justified) praise of Soranzo's book see Pippidi, *Visions*, 91–3.   [16] Soranzo, *L'Ottomanno*, sig. 3†1r (Ischia, 'per domestici affari'); Sforza, 'Un libro', 210 ('da due anni in qua si legge a penna in Venetia e per tutta Italia'); BAM, MS S 102 sup., fos. 410r–465r (Milan copy); Anon., *Lettera* (triumphal annexation). Soranzo sent the work to Mantua via Lelio Arrigoni, the Duke's ambassador in Rome (*L'Ottomanno*, sig. 3†1r); Arrigoni left Rome in Jan. 1597 (ASM, Archivio Gonzaga, busta 968, fos. 669–77).   [17] Soranzo, *L'Ottomanno*, 13 (poor state), 19 (*devşirme*), 20 (auxiliaries), 21 (discomforts), 96 (Pigafetta), 98 (Petru Şchiopul), 112 (clans), 113 ('Antonio Bruni . . . nel suo Trattato del Bellerbegato di Grecia'), 113–14 (Athanasios etc.), 117 ('De gli Albanesi Latini scriue lo stesso Bruni lor co[m]patriota nel Trattato allegato di sopra; che si come sono li meglio armati, così anco sono li più fedeli Christiani dell'Imperio Ottomanno'), 119 (Bardi).   [18] Ibid., 27 (tribute), 32 (taxes), 38 (timber), 40 (biscotto), 56 (Sinan), 58–9 (ports), 62 (Polish relations), 105 (terms), 120 (Ulcinj etc.), 122 (Gasparo).   [19] BMC, MS Wcovich Lazzari 25, busta 9, pp. 13 ('1597'), 27 ('1598. À ii. di febraro'); BAV, MS Barb. Lat. 5361, fo. 204r ('1597'); Pozzi, *Filippo Pigafetta*, ii, 203 ('discorso del Beglierbei della Grecia delle genti che ha sotto sé, de' paesi e passi de' monti per andar un Ungaria e d'altre notizie esquisite'), 205 ('Mando . . . una relazione dello stato d'Europa del Gran Turco, fatta da un valent'uomo che lungo tempo, essendo natio albanese, dimorò in quelle contrade').   [20] Tomić, *Gradja*, 310 ('considerationi tutte importantissime di stato et da esser tenute sotto profondo silentio et massime nel petto d' un Christiano et nativo Venetiano'); Soranzo, *L'Ottomanno*, 55–60 (pashas' arguments, Zadar etc.), 83–91 (general section; 89: 'giusta, & antica neutralità').   [21] Sforza, 'Un libro', 211 (Soranzo, 26 July), 212 (sentence, 31 Aug., 2 Sept.); ASVat, Segr. Stato, Venezia, 33, fos. 108r–v (nuncio, 12 Aug.), 123r ('sentenza assai mite à quello, che se ne temeua'); Tomić, *Gradja*, 322–4 (safe-conduct); de Thou, *Historiarum*, vi, 127 (death). [22] Lamansky, *Secrets*, 111 (Verona); Balsamo, '*Il Turco*' (Baldini; 213: editions); Balsamo, '"Une parfaite intelligence"' (Baldini series); Gorris, 'Naviguer' (Baldini series); Gorris, '*Prudentia*', 249–51 (Baldini series, calling *L'Ottomanno* one of his greatest successes); Esprinchard, *Histoire* (I have used the Paris, 1609, edn; it refers to a Geneva, 1600, edn which I have been unable to locate); Chatenay, *Vie*, 33 (La Rochelle), 38 (Leiden), 40 (tour), 162 (Esztergom); Soranzo, *Ottomannus: von Zustand*; DeCoursey, 'Society' (Hartwell biography); Minadoi, *History* (Ottoman–Persian war); Soranzo, *The Ottoman*, sigs. ¶2v (2 years),

¶3r–v (quotations).   **[23]** Soranzo, *Ottomannus, sive de rebus*; Soranzo *et al.*, *Turca nikētos*; Geuder, *Conclusiones* (Strasbourg); SAN, Rep. 2 Rst. Nürnberg, Losungsamt, Reverse, nos. 158 (Nuremberg), 187 (Amberg); Balsamo, '*Il Turco*', 213 (Esprinchard and Geuder); Conring, ed., *De bello* (1664); Ludolf, *De bello*, 52 ('qui multa scitu digna continet'). Achille Tarducci, of Corinaldo, had studied (as a scholarship boy) at the Seminario Romano from 1577 to 1581, overlapping there with Antonio Bruni by 5 months: ACGH, MS Hist. 145, fo. 5v. In his epistle to Whitgift, Hartwell wrote that he had also wanted to translate Tarducci's book: Soranzo, *The Ottoman*, sig. ¶4v.

List of Manuscripts

This list is confined to works cited in the text or notes of this book. Where appropriate, general descriptions are given; in other cases, the description concerns the specific item or items cited.

ACGH: Archivio del Collegium Germanicum et Hungaricum, Rome

Hist. 145: Girolamo Nappi, 'Annali del Seminario Romano'.

ADV: Archives départementales de Vaucluse, Avignon

Archives communales, AA 44: correspondence of consuls of Avignon, 1582–90.
D 36: University of Avignon, 'Livre concernant les noms ... des primiciers, docteurs ... et gradués', 1430–1651.
D 41: [P. de Cadecombe,] *Speculum illustriorum iuris interpretum qui publicè per quatuor saecula professi, vel interpretati sunt in celebri, ac famosa Universitate Avenionensi* (Avignon, 1712).
D 155: University of Avignon, formulary of letters of doctorate.

AGAD: Archiwum Główne Akt Dawnych, Warsaw

Archiwum Zamoyski [abbreviated: 'AZ'], 8: inventory of Jan Zamoyski correspondence by M. Stworzyński.
AZ, 649: letter from Hayder Pasha, *beylerbeyi* of Rumeli, to Jan Zamoyski, 1590.
AZ, 770: Bartolomeo Bruti to Jan Zamoyski, 1591.

AGS: Archivo General de Simancas, Simancas

Estado, legajo 488: documents relating to Bartolomeo Bruti and Giovanni Margliani, 1576–8.
Estado, legajo 489: documents relating to Bartolomeo Bruti and Giovanni Margliani, 1577–8.
Estado, legajo 490: documents relating to Bartolomeo Bruti and Giovanni Margliani, 1578–9.
Estado, legajo 1073: documents relating to Naples and the Levant, 1576–7.
Estado, legajo 1074: documents relating to Naples and the Levant, 1577.
Estado, legajo 1337: reports from Venice, 1580, including letters received there from Bartolomeo Bruti.

AMA: Archives municipales, Avignon

BB19, Délibérations du Conseil de la Ville, vol. 15 (1574–83).

ARSI: Archivum Romanum Societatis Iesu, Rome

Rom. 51/1: visitation reports, 1576–83.
Rom. 155/1: documents relating to the Seminario Romano.

ASF: Archivio di Stato, Florence

Miscellanea medicea, 101, 31: Moldavian report from Poland, 1587.

ASM: Archivio di Stato, Mantua

Archivio Gonzaga, busta 968: reports from Rome, 1597.
Archivio Gonzaga, busta 1259: reports from Venice, 1597.

ASR: Archivio di Stato, Rome

Soldatesche e galere, busta 90: 'Del S^{re} Guido Magalotti Per il Viaggio Di Milano à Ricuperar l'Albanesi 1594'.
Soldatesche e galere, busta 646: notes on garrison towns in enclave of Avignon; payments for Albanian cavalry, 1595.

AST: Archivio di Stato, Trieste

Archivio Municipale di Capodistria [abbreviated: 'AMC'], 77 (microfilm reel 115): Camilla Bruni, will, 1602.
AMC, 84 (microfilm reel 124): Maria Bruti, legal document, 1600.
AMC, 548 (microfilm reel 687): Libro del Consiglio Q.
AMC, 549 (microfilm reel 687): Libro del Consiglio R.
AMC, 550 (microfilm reel 688): Libro del Consiglio S.
AMC, 551 (microfilm reel 689): Libro del Consiglio T.

ASVat: Archivio Segreto Vaticano, Vatican City

Congr. Concilii, Relat. Dioec. 56, fasc. 1: Marin Bizzi visitation, 1618.
Fondo Borghese III 60h: Niccolò Mechaisci, letter about Stoicinus, 1603.
Fondo Borghese III 72a: Legazione di Polonia, Ippolito Aldobrandini, letters, 1588–9.
Fondo Borghese III 128: 'Manoscritti di Fran.^{co} Patricio sopra la Guerra di Albania'.
Fondo Borghese IV 229: Antonio Bruni, letter to Angelo Ingegneri, 1596.
Misc., Arm. II, vol. 110: papers on immorality of fleet; Bishop of Nardò on death of Giovanni Bruni.
Sec. Brev. Reg., vol. 7: breve of Pius V to Dubrovnik, 1567.
Sec. Brev. Reg., vol. 11: breves of Pius V to Giovanni Bruni, Dubrovnik, 1568.
Segr. Stato, Germania, vol. 95 (1584–5).
Segr. Stato, Legaz. Avignone, vol. 2 (letters from Avignon, 1573–4).

Segr. Stato, Legaz. Avignone, vol. 3 (letters to Avignon, 1572–5).
Segr. Stato, Legaz. Avignone, vol. 4 (letters from Avignon, 1574).
Segr. Stato, Legaz. Avignone, vol. 5 (letters from Avignon, 1575).
Segr. Stato, Legaz. Avignone, vol. 6 (letters from Avignon, 1576).
Segr. Stato, Legaz. Avignone, vol. 7 (letters to Avignon, 1576–8).
Segr. Stato, Legaz. Avignone, vol. 8 (letters from Avignon, 1577).
Segr. Stato, Legaz. Avignone, vol. 9 (letters from Avignon, 1578).
Segr. Stato, Legaz. Avignone, vol. 10 (letters from Avignon, 1579).
Segr. Stato, Legaz. Avignone, vol. 11 (letters from Avignon, 1580).
Segr. Stato, Legaz. Avignone, vol. 12 (letters from Avignon, 1581).
Segr. Stato, Legaz. Avignone, vol. 13 (letters from Avignon, 1582).
Segr. Stato, Legaz. Avignone, vol. 14 (letters from Avignon, 1583).
Segr. Stato, Legaz. Avignone, vol. 15 (letters from Avignon, 1584–5).
Segr. Stato, Legaz. Avignone, vol. 18 (letters from Avignon, 1587–).
Segr. Stato, Malta, vol. 1: correspondence between Rome and Malta, 1572–3.
Segr. Stato, Malta, vol. 6: letters of Knights to Rome, 1593–9.
Segr. Stato, Polonia, vol. 26 (1588–91).
Segr. Stato, Venezia, vol. 33 (1598–1603).

ASVen: Archivio di Stato, Venice

Annali, vol. 3 (1566–70).
Annali, vol. 4 (1571).
Capi del Consiglio dei Dieci [abbreviated: 'CCD'], Dispacci (Lettere) di Ambasciatori, busta 4 (Costantinopoli, 1571–5).
CCD, Dispacci (Lettere) di Ambasciatori, busta 5 (Costantinopoli, 1576–80).
CCD, Dispacci (Lettere) di Ambasciatori, busta 6 (Costantinopoli, 1581–99).
CCD, Suppliche, filza 1 (1478–1594).
Collegio (Secreta), Relazioni, busta 54: Syndics' reports on Istria, 1561, 1591.
Dispacci, Costantinopoli, filza 7 (1574–5).
Dispacci, Costantinopoli, filza 12 (1578).
Dispacci, Costantinopoli, filza 13 (1579).
Dispacci, Costantinopoli, filza 26 (1587–8).
Dispacci, Costantinopoli, filza 28 (1588–9).
Miscellanea Codici, serie 1a, storia veneta, reg. 23: Soranzo genealogy.
Miscellanea di atti diversi manoscritti, filza 34, item 11: [Giovanni Barelli,] 'Relazione', 1575.
Provveditori alle biave, busta 4 (registri 7–9).
Savi all'eresia (Santo Ufficio) busta 8, fasc. 4: Chieregatto, letter.
Senato, Deliberazioni, Costantinopoli, registri, no. 7 (1586–8).
Senato, Deliberazioni, Secreti, registri, no. 71 (1558–9).
Senato, Deliberazioni, Secreti, registri, no. 76 (1569–70).

BAM: Biblioteca Ambrosiana, Milan

D 484 inf.: Girolamo Frachetta, 'Discorso Alla S.ta di N. S. Papa Sisto Quinto essortandolo à procurar la guerra contra il Turco'.

F 94 inf.: Franciscan authorities to Marco Pasquali, 1561, Giovanni Bruni to Borromeo, 1564, Giovanni Bruni to Borromeo, 1565.

F 104 inf.: chapter and clergy of Bar to Borromeo, 1564; dal Pozzo to Fra Silvestro, 1564.

Q 116 sup.: [Giovanni Barelli,] 'Relazione', 1575.

S 102 sup.: Lazaro Soranzo, 'Relatione della potenza del Turco et in spetie delle cose d'Vngaria' (a version of *L'Ottomanno*).

BAP: Bibliothèque de l'Arsenal, Paris

4769: 'Traictez et ambassades de Turquie', vol. 3.

BAR: Biblioteca Angelica, Rome

1479: Giovanni Battista Leoni, 'Relatione dell'Isola di Malta, et de suoi Cauaglieri'.

BAV: Biblioteca Apostolica Vaticana, Vatican City

Barb. Lat. 5361: Antonio Bruni, 'Del Bellerbegato della Romania'.

Chigi A VI 194: 'Copia della patente del sig.^{re} cau.^{re} Thomaso Pelessa', 1594; 'Espositione fatta dal cau^{re} Thomaso Pelessa d'Alessio Amb.^{re} di Albania et Macedonia', 1595.

Urb. Lat. 1028, part 2: 'Parlamento di Monsr Minucci . . . in Senato Veneto per la lega, et guerra contra il Turco l'Anno 1596'.

Urb. Lat. 1042: news reports, 1571.

Urb. Lat. 1492: Girolamo Frachetta, 'Discorso de modi, che si possono tenere al presente per guerreggiare contra il Turco per terra'.

Vat. Lat. 12,199: '1573 Per l'Impresa contro Il Turco, dil S. P. C.'; memorandum on Giovanni Tommaso Costanzo; Giacomo Malatesta, memorandum.

BCP: Biblioteca Civica, Padua

C.M. 139/1: 'Relatione del Cl:^{mo} M. Filippo Bragadin Proueditore dell'armata'.

BIC: Bibliothèque Inguimbertine, Carpentras

587: 'Relationi di Constantinopoli'.

1777: Savary de Brèves, discourse.

BL: British Library, London

Add. 8262: Erizzo and Bon, 'Relazione di Dalmazia'.

Add. 8277: 'Informatione dell'Institutione, Priuilegij, et oblighj della Relig.^{e} de Cau.^{ri} de Rhodi hoggi di Malta'.

Add. 8279: Doria, 'Informatione del successo in queste armate'; 'Summario ragguaglio dell'assedio di Famagusta 1571'.

Add. 8314: Francesco Baglioni (papal commissary), 'Instruttione'; Ascanio della Corgna, paper for Don John.

Add. 28,415: Giovanni Margliani, letter to Philip II (undated); Giovanni Stefano de Ferrari, documents, 1583–5.

Cotton Nero B. xi: Edward Barton, reports, 1596.

BLY: Beinecke Library, Yale University, New Haven, CT

381: Instructions to governor of Ulcinj, 1513.

BMA: Bibliothèque municipale (Médiathèque Ceccano), Avignon

2398: Account of capture and siege of Ménerbes.
2562: J. Laurent Drapier, 'Journal historique et recherches pour servir à l'histoire d'Avignon'.
6431: Domenico Grimaldi, letters to Rome, 1585–9, 1592.

BMC: Biblioteca del Museo Correr, Venice

Provenienze diverse, 581. c. misc.: Antonio Bruti, letters to Girolamo Zane and Sforza Pallavicino, 1570; Pallavicino, letter to Antonio Bruti, 1570.
Wcovich Lazzari 25, busta 9: Antonio Bruni, 'Del Bellerbegato della Romania'.

BNC: Biblioteca Nazionale Centrale, Rome

Gesuiti 7: Giulio Mancinelli, 'Historia della Vocatione & Peregrinatione del N. P. della Compagnia di Giesù'.
Vittorio Emanuele 1034: Edward Barton, 'Relatione dell'Ambasciator d'Inghilterra delle cose più notabili successe nel Viaggio d'Vngheria col Gran Sultan Mehemet l'anno 1596'; Lazaro Soranzo, 'Discorso ... sopra la bend.^{ne} che desideraua il Re di Nauarra'.

BNF: Bibliothèque nationale de France, Paris

Dupuy 937 (microfilm MF 11993): Correspondence of Henri II, Charles IX and Henri III.
Français 16,142 (microfilm MF 8270): Letters of French ambassadors in Istanbul, 1569–77.
Français 16,143 (microfilm MF 8271): Letters of French ambassadors in Istanbul, 1579–84.
Français 16,144 (microfilm MF 8272): Letters of French ambassadors in Istanbul, 1585–1603.
Italien 723: Marcantonio Colonna, speech, 1571; Venetian requests to Rome and replies, 1571; Sforza Pallavicino and Giacomo Celsi, 'testificationi'.
Supplément turc 926 (microfilm R 194): Mohammed ibn 'Abd Allah Zirek el-Hoseini, 'Siège de Goulette et de Tunis', tr. A. Fonton.

BNM: Biblioteca Nazionale Marciana, Venice

It. VII. 11 (8378): Fedele Fedeli, 'Historia della guerra de Turchi contro i S^{ri} Venetiani per il Regno di Cipro'.
It. VII. 213 (8836): Giovanni Lippomano, 'Storia veneta dal 1551 al 1568'.
It. XI. 8 (6769): Lazaro Soranzo, 'Elogio del' Illmo Sig.^{re} il Sig.^{re} Giacomo Soranzo'.

Bodl.: Bodleian Library, Oxford

Ital. c. 7: 'Raguaglio dello stato nel quale si troua quest'anno MDXCIIIJ il gouerno dell' Imperio Turchesco'.

Rawl. D 618: 'Constantinopoli del 1584'.

Tanner 77: William Harborne, memorandum, 1588.

Tanner 78: William Harborne, reports, 1585.

Tanner 79: William Harborne, reports and related documents, 1582–8.

BPCG: Biblioteca Provinciale dei Cappuccini liguri, Genoa

M256: Costantino Castriota, 'De Republica'.

BSB: Bayerische Staatsbibliothek, Munich

Cod. Ital. 6: [Giovanni Barelli,] 'Relazione', 1575.

BSS: Biblioteca Santa Scolastica, Subiaco

Archivio Colonna [abbreviated: 'AC'], II CF 1: 'Scritture dell'armata navale', vol. 1.

AC, II CF 2: 'Scritture dell'armata navale', vol. 2.

AC, II CF 3: 'Scritture dell'armata navale', vol. 3.

AC, II CF 4: 'Scritture dell'armata navale', vol. 4.

AC, II CF 5: 'Libro delle galere'.

AC, Corrispondenza Ascanio Colonna, unnumbered: Gasparo Bruni, letter, 1584.

AC, Corrispondenza Ascanio Colonna, 1 II CF 2059: Gasparo Bruni, letter, 1589.

AC, Corrispondenza Ascanio Colonna, 1 II CF 2149: Gasparo Bruni, letter, 1592.

AC, Corrispondenza Marcantonio il Grande, busta 44, no. 4450: Gasparo Bruni, letter, 1570.

AC, Corrispondenza Marcantonio il Grande, busta 44, no. 4451: Gasparo Bruni, letter, 1570.

AC, Corrispondenza Marcantonio il Grande, busta 44, no. 4490: Gasparo Bruni, letter, 1570.

AC, Corrispondenza Marcantonio il Grande, busta 67, no. 3890: Ragusan newsletter, 1571.

AC, Corrispondenza Marcantonio il Grande, busta 67, no. 3900: Marcantonio Colonna, accounts.

DAD: Državni Arhiv, Dubrovnik

Acta Consilii Minoris, 48 (1567–8).

Acta Consilii Rogatorum, 58 (1566–8).

Acta Consilii Rogatorum, 59 (1568–70).

Acta Sanctae Mariae Maioris, 16th century, item 341: Duke of Urbino, letter (1571).

Acta Sanctae Mariae Maioris, 16th century, item 354: Grand Master, letter (1573).

Acta Sanctae Mariae Maioris, 16th century, item 451: Venier, letter (1570).

Acta Sanctae Mariae Maioris, 17th century [erroneously], item 2014: Duke of Urbino, letter (1572).

Lettere, e Commissioni di Levante [abbreviated: 'LCL'], 33 (1575–80).

LCL, 34 (1580–3).

LCL, 35 (1583–6).

LCL, 37 (1590–1).

Lettere, e Commissioni di Ponente [abbreviated: 'LCP'], 1 (1567–70).

LCP, 2 (1569–71).

LCP, 3 (1575–80).

Secreta Rogatorum, 2 (1567–9).

DHI: Deutsches Historisches Institut, Rome

Minuccio Minucci, 7: Marcantonio Colonna, 'Informatione … di quanto è successo in queste Armate'.

Minuccio Minucci, 9: Minuccio Minucci, discourse on neutrality, 1595.

GPLV: Gran Priorato di Lombardia e Venezia, Venice

578: 'Commende: Priorato di Venezia, Camere Priorali, Visite'.

HHStA: Haus-, Hof- und Staatsarchiv, Vienna

Türkei I, Karton 36 (1577–8).

Türkei I, Karton 37 (1578).

Türkei I, Karton 38 (1578–9).

Türkei I, Karton 39 (1579).

Türkei I, Karton 80 (1593)

Türkei I, Karton 81 (1593–8).

NLM: National Library of Malta, Valletta

Archive of the Order of Malta [abbreviated: 'AOM'], 92: Liber conciliorum (1567–70).

AOM, 93: Liber conciliorum (1570–3).

AOM, 98: Liber conciliorum (1589–94).

AOM, 99: Liber conciliorum (1595–7).

AOM, 100: Liber conciliorum (1597–1603).

AOM, 431: Liber bullarum (1565–7).

AOM, 446: Liber bullarum (1592).

AOM, 447: Liber bullarum (1592–4).

AOM, 448: Liber bullarum (1594).

AOM, 449: Liber bullarum (1595–6).

AOM, 2125: Deliberations of the langue of Italy (1564–94).

PAK: Pokrajinski Arhiv, Koper

KP 6.1, item 91, 'Deli testamentov, 1548–1689': Matteo Bruni, will.

SAN: Staatsarchiv, Nuremberg

Rep. 2 Rst. Nürnberg, Losungsamt, Reverse, no. 158: Jakob Geuder, document, 1609.

Rep. 2 Rst. Nürnberg, Losungsamt, Reverse, no. 187: Jakob Geuder, document, 1614.

TLA: Tiroler Landesarchiv, Innsbruck

Hofrat, Journale, Einkommende Schriften (R), vol. 22: entry for Bernardino Rossi, letter, 1593.

O. Ö. Geheimer Rat, Selekt Ferdinandea, Pos. 86: correspondence and documents relating to Petru Şchiopul.

O. Ö. Kammer-Kopialbücher, vol. 475, Gemeine Missiven (no. 103): note of letter to Antonio Bruni, 1594.

O. Ö. Regierung-Kopialbücher, Parteibücher, vol. 55: von Kühbach, document, 1597.

TNA: The National Archives, Kew (London)

SP 97/1: Edward Barton, account of the 1596 Hungarian campaign.

SP 97/2: despatches from Istanbul, 1589–93; Bartolomeo Bruti to Queen Elizabeth, 1590; Queen Elizabeth to Bartolomeo Bruti, 1590.

SP 97/3: Edward Barton, despatches from Istanbul, 1596–7.

Bibliography

This Bibliography is confined to works cited in the text or notes of this book. Anonymous works are listed under 'Anon.'. The alphabetical order is of the first element of the name that bears a capital letter. Diacritical marks on letters are disregarded for the purposes of the ordering here, which follows the English alphabet.

ABBREVIATIONS USED IN THE BIBLIOGRAPHY

AEMCS: *Aphierōma eis tēn Ēpeiron eis mnēmēn Christou Soulē (1892–1951)* (Athens, 1956).

AIIAX: *Anuarul Institutului de Istorie şi Arheologie 'A. D. Xenopol'*.

AMSIASP: *Atti e memorie della Società Istriana di Archeologia e Storia Patria*.

AO: *Archivum ottomanicum*.

ARSRSP: *Archivio della R. [Reale] Società Romana di Storia Patria*.

ASI: *Archivio storico italiano*.

BOAV: G. Ortalli and O. J. Schmitt, eds., *Balcani occidentali, Adriatico e Venezia fra XIII e XVIII secolo* (Venice, 2009).

CCP: *Croatica christiana periodica*.

CHT: S. N. Faroqhi and K. Fleet, eds., *The Cambridge History of Turkey*, ii: *The Ottoman Empire as a World Power, 1453–1603* (Cambridge, 2013).

CODOIN: *Colección de documentos inéditos para la historia de España*.

CSPVen.: *Calendar of State Papers Relating to English Affairs in the Archives of Venice*.

DBI: Istituto della Enciclopedia Italiana, *Dizionario biografico degli italiani* (Rome, 1960–).

DUSAL: P. Desan and G. Dotoli, eds., *D'un siècle à l'autre: littérature et société de 1590 à 1610* (Paris, 2001).

EI2: P. Bearman *et al.*, eds., *Encyclopaedia of Islam, Second Edition* (http:// referenceworks.brillonline.com).

EPEM: F. Bilici, I. Cândea and A. Popescu, eds., *Enjeux politiques, économiques et militaires en mer Noire (XIVᵉ–XXIᵉ siècles): études à la mémoire de Mihail Guboglu* (Brăila, 2007).

EREBN: *Erytheia: revista de estudios bizantinos y neogriegos*.

ETR: B. Guthmüller and W. Kühlmann, eds., *Europa und die Türken in der Renaissance* (Tübingen, 2000).

ETSOE: G. Kármán and L. Kunčević, eds., *The European Tributary States of the Ottoman Empire in the Sixteenth and Seventeenth Centuries* (Leiden, 2013).

GjA: Gjurmime albanologjike.

GOTC: K. Çiçek *et al.*, eds., *The Great Ottoman–Turkish Civilisation*, 4 vols. (Ankara, 2000).

HD: E. de Hurmuzaki, *et al.*, eds., *Documente privitóre la istoria Românilor*, 19 vols. (Bucharest, 1887–1938).

HOB: A. Tietze, ed., *Habsburgisch-osmanische Beziehungen*, Beihefte zur Wiener Zeitschrift für die Kunde des Morgenlandes, xiii (Vienna, 1985).

IJTS: International Journal of Turkish Studies.

ILO: F. Hitzel, ed., *Istanbul et les langues orientales* (Paris, 1997).

IZ: Istoriski zapisi.

LCC: W. Kaiser, ed., *Le Commerce des captifs: les intermédiaires dans l'échange et le rachat des prisonniers en Méditerranée, XVe–XVIIIe siècle* (Rome, 2008).

LGMM: R. Ragosta, ed., *Le genti del Mare Mediterraneo*, 2 vols. (Naples, 1981).

MÖS: Mitteilungen des Österreichischen Staatsarchivs.

MSHSM: Monumenta spectantia historiam slavorum meridionalium.

MSMCLL: G. Benzoni, ed., *Il Mediterraneo nella seconda metà del '500 alla luce di Lepanto* (Florence, 1974).

n.d.: no date of publication.

n.p.: no place of publication.

n.s.: new series.

OC: Orientalia christiana.

ODNB: Oxford Dictionary of National Biography (www.oxforddnb.com).

OM: Oriente moderno.

PP: Povijesni prilozi.

QCRV: Quaderni della Casa Romena di Venezia.

QSA: Quaderni di studi arabi.

REI: Revue des études islamiques.

RESEE: Revue des études sud-est européennes.

RRH: Revue roumaine d'histoire.

SB: Studia borromaica: saggi e documenti di storia religiosa e civile della prima età moderna.

SF: Südost-Forschungen.

SH: Studime historike.

SJAZU: Starine na sviet izdaje Jugoslavenska Akademija Znanosti i Umjetnosti.

SUH: P. Bartl and H. Glassl, eds., *Südosteuropa unter dem Halbmond: Untersuchungen über Geschichte und Kultur der südosteuropäischen Völker während der Türkenzeit* (Munich, 1975).

SV: Studi veneziani.

TDD: M. Polić Bobić, B. Baletić and L. Čoralić, eds., *Tajna diplomacija u Dubrovniku u XVI. stoljeću* (Zagreb, 2011).

VED: U. Israel and O. J. Schmitt, eds., *Venezia e Dalmazia* (Rome, 2013).

VLMV: F. Lucchetta, ed., *Veneziani in Levante, musulmani a Venezia*, supplement to *QSA*, 15 (1997).

ZOZPZ: *Zbornik Odsjeka za Povijesne Znanosti Zavoda za Povijesne i Društvene Znanosti Hrvatske Akademije Znanosti i Umjetnosti.*

BIBLIOGRAPHY

Achard, F., and L. Duhamel, *Inventaire sommaire des Archives Communales antérieures à 1790 de la ville d'Avignon* (Avignon, 1863–1953).

Ács, P., 'Tarjumans Mahmud and Murad: Austrian and Hungarian Renegades as Sultan's Interpreters', in *ETR*, 307–17.

Adami, A., *Elogii storici de' due marchesi Capizucchi fratelli Camillo e Biagio celebri guerrieri del secolo passato* (Rome, 1685).

Aglietti, M., 'La partecipazione delle galere toscane alla battaglia di Lepanto (1571)', in D. Marrara, ed., *Toscana e Spagna nell'età moderna e contemporanea* (Pisa, 1998), 55–145.

Ágoston, G., '*Merces prohibitae*: The Anglo-Ottoman Trade in War Materials and the Dependence Theory', *OM*, n.s., 20 (2001), 177–92.

— 'A Flexible Empire: Authority and its Limits on the Ottoman Frontiers', *IJTS*, 9, nos. 1–2 (2003), 15–31.

— *Guns for the Sultan: Military Power and the Weapons Industry in the Ottoman Empire* (Cambridge, 2005).

— 'Where Environmental and Frontier Studies Meet: Rivers, Forests, Marshes and Forts along the Ottoman–Habsburg Frontier in Hungary', in A. C. S. Peacock, ed., *The Frontiers of the Ottoman World* (Oxford, 2009), 57–79.

Albèri, E., ed., *Relazioni degli ambasciatori veneti al Senato durante il secolo decimosesto*, ser. 3, *Relazioni dagli Stati Ottomani*, 3 vols. (Florence, 1840–55).

Allen, W. E. D., *Problems of Turkish Power in the Sixteenth Century* (London, 1963).

Almosnino, M., *Extremos y grandezas de Constantinopla*, tr. I. Cansino (Madrid, 1638).

Alonso Acero, B., *Sultanes de Berbería en tierras de la cristiandad: exilio musulmán, conversión y asimilación en la Monarquía hispánica (siglos XVI y XVII)* (Barcelona, 2006).

Alzati, C., *Terra romena tra oriente e occidente: chiese ed etnie nel tardo '500* (Milan, 1981).

Anderson, R. C., *Naval Wars in the Levant, 1559–1853* (Liverpool, 1952).

Andreescu, Ş., *Restitutio Daciae (relaţiile politice dintre Ţara Românească, Moldova şi Transilvania în răstimpul 1526–1593)* (Bucharest, 1980).

— 'Boierii lui Mihai Viteazul', *Studii şi materiale de istorie medie*, 12 (1994), 47–93.

Anon., *Gli avisi ultimi circa la guerra che seguita il Turco contra la Illustriss. Signoria di Venetia, dichiarando molte cose notabili occorse nella Dalmatia, & in Arcipelago, & la Morea* (n.p. [Brescia?], 1571).

— *Il bellissimo et sontuoso trionfo fatto nella magnifica città di Venetia nella publicatione della Lega* (Brescia, 1571).

— *Lettera venuta da Ferrara, la quale raguaglia la solennissima entrata della Santità di N. S. Clemente Papa VIII. in detta città, li 9. di maggio. 1598.* (Rome, 1598).

— *La vita dell'insigne guerriere Saporoso Matteucci da Fermo generale delle armi della republica di Ragusi, e delle armi ecclesiastiche in Francia, contro gl'Ugonotti* (Fermo, 1699).

— ed., *Cartas y avisos dirigidos á Don Juan de Zúñiga, Virey de Nápoles en 1581* (Madrid, 1887).

— ed., *Correspondencia de Felipe II con los hermanos Don Luis de Requesens y Don Juan de Zúñiga*, CODOIN, cii (Madrid, 1892).

— 'Senato Mare: cose dell'Istria', *AMSIASP*, 11, for 1895 (1896), 37–96; 12, for 1896 (1897), 57–111, 397–453.

— 'Regesti di documenti dell'Archivio di Stato in Venezia riguardanti l'Istria: lettere segrete di Collegio (1308–1627)', *AMSIASP*, year 51, vol. 46 (1934), 65–105.

— ed., *Documente privind istoria României: veacul XVI. A: Moldova* , iii–iv (Bucharest, 1951–2).

— ed., *Documente privind istoria României: veacul XVII. A: Moldova*, ii (Bucharest, 1953).

Anselmi, S., 'Motivazioni economiche della neutralità di Ragusa nel cinquecento', in *MSMCLL*, 33–70.

Apostolescu, V., 'Un aventurier apusean la curtea lui Petru Şchiopul: Bartolomeo Brutti', *AIIAX*, 18 (1981), 567–74.

Appendini, F. M., *Notizie istorico-critiche sulle antichità, storia e letteratura de' Ragusei*, 2 vols. (Dubrovnik, 1803).

Arbel, B., 'Colonie d'oltremare', in A. Tenenti and U. Tucci, eds., *Storia di Venezia dalle origini alla caduta della Serenissima*, v (Rome, 1994), 947–85.

— 'Greek Magnates in Venetian Cyprus: The Case of the Synglitico Family', *Dumbarton Oaks Papers*, 49 (1995), 325–39.

— *Trading Nations: Jews and Venetians in the Early Modern Eastern Mediterranean* (Leiden, 1995).

Arcari, P. M., *Il pensiero politico di Francesco Patrizi da Cherso* (Rome, 1935).

Arce, A., 'Espionaje y ultima aventura de José Nasi (1569–1574)', *Sefarad*, 13 (1953), 257–86.

Armao, E., *Vende, kisha, lumenj, male e toponime të ndryshme të një harte të lashtë të Shqipërisë Veriore*, tr. A. Spathari (Tirana, 2006).

Asín, J. O., 'La hija de Agi Morato en la obra de Cervantes', *Boletin de la Real Academia Española*, 27 (1947–8), 245–339.

d'Atri, S., '"Adi 2 di marzo 1590 porta fornita": Rupe, il granaio di Ragusa (Dubrovnik)', *Mélanges de l'École Française de Rome: Italie et Méditerranée*, 120, no. 2 (2008), 569–80.

— '*Per conservare la città tributtaria et divota*: Ragusa (Dubrovnik) and the 1590–91 Crisis', *Dubrovnik Annals*, 14 (2010), 71–98.

Aymard, M., *Venise, Raguse et le commerce du blé pendant la seconde moitié du XVIe siècle* (Paris, 1966).

Babinger, F., *Die Geschichtsschreiber der Osmanen und ihre Werke* (Leipzig, 1927).

— *Das Ende der Arianiten*, Bayerische Akademie der Wissenschaften, philosophisch-historische Klasse, Sitzungsberichte, Jahrgang 1960, Heft 4 (Munich, 1960).

Bagi, Z. P., 'Esztergom 1595-ös ostroma', *Aetas: történettudomanyi folyóirat*, 4 (1999), 50–5.

Baiocchi, A., 'Contarini, Alessandro', in *DBI*, xxviii, 70–2.

Balbi di Correggio, F., *The Siege of Malta, 1565*, tr. E. Bradford, 2nd edn (London, 1965).

Balsamo, J., '*Il Turco vincibile*. Un "corpus turc" à la fin du XVIe siècle: La Noue, Naselli, Soranzo, Esprinchard', in Gruppo di studio sul cinquecento francese, *Scritture dell'impegno dal rinascimento all'età barocca* (Fasano, 1997), 205–16.

— '"Une parfaite intelligence de la raison d'estat": le *Trésor politique*, René de Lucinge et les Turcs (1588–1608)', in *DUSAL*, 297–321.

Barbarano de' Mironi, F., *Historia ecclesiastica della città, territorio, e diocese di Vicenza*, 6 vols. (Vicenza, 1649–1762).

Barbero, A., *La Bataille des trois empires: Lépante, 1571*, tr. P. Farazzi and M. Valensi (Paris, 2012).

Barbulescu, I., 'Relations entre les principautés roumaines, Raguse et les ragusains dans la période du slavonisme cultural [sic]', in V. Ćoralić *et al.*, eds., *Zbornik iz dubrovačke prošlosti Milanu Rešetaru o 70ᵒʲ godišnjici života* (Dubrovnik, 1931), 113–27.

de Barjavel, C.-F.-H., *Dictionnaire historique, biographique et bibliographique du Département de Vaucluse*, i (Carpentras, 1841).

Bârlea, O., *De confessione orthodoxa Petri Mohilae* (Frankfurt am Main, 1948).

Barleti, M., *The Siege of Shkodra*, tr. D. Hosaflook (Tirana, 2012).

Barozzi, N., and G. Berchet, eds., *Le relazioni degli stati europei letti al Senato dagli ambasciatori veneti nel secolo decimosettimo*, ser. 5, *Turchia* (Venice, 1866–72 [single vol., issued in fascicles]).

Bartl, P., '"Marciare verso Costantinopoli" – zur Türkenpolitik Klemens' VIII.', *Saeculum*, 20 (1969), 44–56.

— *Der Westbalkan zwischen spanischer Monarchie und Osmanischem Reich: zur Türkenkriegsproblematik an der Wende vom 16. zum 17. Jahrhundert* (Wiesbaden, 1974).

— 'Die Dulcignoten: Piraterie und Handelsschiffahrt im Adriaraum', in *SUH*, 17–27.

— ed., *Albania sacra: geistliche Visitationsberichte aus Albanien* (Wiesbaden, 2007–).

— 'Religion und Konfession im montenegrinisch-albanischen Raum im 16. und 17. Jahrhundert', in *BOAV*, 309–26.

Barwiński, E., ed., *Dyaryusze i akta sejmowe r. 1591–1592* (Kraków, 1911).

Bäumer, R., ed., *Concilium tridentinum* (Darmstadt, 1979).

Bayerle, G., *Ottoman Diplomacy in Hungary: Letters from the Pashas of Buda, 1590–1593* (Bloomington, IN, 1972).

— 'The Compromise at Zsitvatorok', *AO*, 6 (1980), 5–53.

Bazzano, N., *Marco Antonio Colonna* (Rome, 2003).

Beau ['Bellus'], L., *Consilia posthuma*, ed. J. Beau ['Bellus'] (Geneva, 1635).

Beduli, Dh., *Kishë dhe kulturë: studime* (Tirana, 2006).

Beldiceanu, N., 'La Moldavie ottomane à la fin du XV⁰ siècle et au début du XVI⁰', *REI*, 37 (1969), 239–66.

Belon, P., *Voyage au Levant: les observations de Pierre Belon du Mans*, ed. A. Merle (Paris, 2001).

Benda, K., ed., *Moldvai Csángó-Magyar okmánytár, 1467–1706* , 2nd edn, ed. L. Diószegi (Budapest, 2003).

van Beresteyn, E. A., *Geschiedenis der Johanniter-Orde in Nederland tot 1795: historische schets* (Assen, 1934).

Bertelè, T., *Il palazzo degli ambasciatori di Venezia a Costantinopoli e le sue antiche memorie* (Bologna, 1932).

Berthier, A., 'Turquerie ou turcologie? L'effort de traduction des Jeunes de Langues au XVII⁰ [*sic* – for 'XVIII⁰'] siècle d'après la collection de manuscrits conservée à la Bibliothèque nationale de France', in *ILO*, 283–317.

Bertoša, M., *Mletačka Istra u XVI i XVII stoljeću*, 2 vols. (Pula, 1986).

von Betzek, J., *Gesandtschaftsreise nach Ungarn und in die Türkei im Jahre 1564/65* (Munich, 1979).

Bicheno, H., *Crescent and Cross: The Battle of Lepanto, 1571* (London, 2003).

Biegman, N. H., 'Ragusan Spying for the Ottoman Empire: Some 16th-Century Documents from the State Archive at Dubrovnik', *Türk Tarih Kurumu belleten*, 27 (1963), 237–55.

— *The Turco-Ragusan Relationship according to the Firmans of Murad III (1575–1595) Extant in the State Archives of Dubrovnik* (The Hague, 1967).

Bielski, J., *Joachima Bielskiego dalszy ciąg Kroniki Polskiéj zawierającéj dzieje od 1587 do 1598 r.*, ed. F. M. Sobieszczański (Warsaw, 1851).

Binark, İ., ed., *5 Numaralı mühimme defteri (973/1565–1566)*, 2 vols. (Ankara, 1994).

— ed., *12 Numaralı mühimme defteri (978–979/1570–1572)*, 3 vols. (Ankara, 1996).

'Blessi, M.': *see* Molino.

Bojović, B., *Raguse (Dubrovnik) et l'Empire Ottoman (1430–1520): les actes impériaux ottomans en vieux-serbe de Murad II à Selim I⁰ʳ* (Paris, 1998).

Bolognetti, A., *Epistolae et acta 1581–1585*, ed. L. Boratyński, E. Kuntze and C. Nanke, 3 vols., *Monumenta poloniae vaticana*, v–vii (Krakow, 1923–50).

Bonin, F., *Solne poti: Le vie del sale: Salt Paths: Salzwege* (Piran, 2009).

Bonin, Z., ed., *Vodnik po fondih in zbirkah Pokrajinskega Arhiva Koper* (Koper, 2006).

Bono, S., *Schiavi musulmani nell'Italia moderna: galeotti, vu' cumprà, domestici* (Naples, 1999).

Börekçi, G., 'Factions and Favorites at the Courts of Sultan Ahmed I (r. 1603–1617) and his Immediate Predecessors', Ohio State University PhD thesis (2010).

Borghesi, V., *Il Mediterraneo tra due rivoluzioni nautiche (secoli XIV–XVIII)* (Florence, 1976).

Borino, G. B., A. Galieti and G. Navone, *Il trionfo di Marc'Antonio Colonna* (Rome, 1938).

Borretti, M., *Il S. M. Ordine di Malta in Calabria* (Messina, 1938).

Bosio, G., *Gli statuti della Sacra Religione di S. Giovanni Gierosolimitano* (Rome, 1589).

— *Li privilegii della Sacra Religione di S. Gio. Gierosolimitano* (Rome, 1589).

— *Dell'istoria della Sacra Religione et illustrissima militia di San Giovanni Gierosolimitano*, 3 vols. (Naples 1684).

Bošković, Dj., P. Mijović and M. Kovačević, *Ulcinj 1*, Arheološki Institut, posebna izdanja, xvi (Belgrade, 1981).

Botero, G., *Relationi universale*, 2 vols. (Vicenza, 1595).

Botteri, I., '"Buona vita, buona dottrina et buona creanza": i Gesuiti e il *Galateo*', in M. Hinz *et al.*, eds., *I Gesuiti e la Ratio Studiorum* (Rome, 2004), 21–41.

Bovill, E. W., *The Battle of Alcazar: An Account of the Defeat of King Sebastian of Portugal at El-Ksar el-Kebir* (London, 1952).

Boyar, E., 'Ottoman Expansion in the East', in *CHT*, 74–140.

— and K. Fleet, *A Social History of Ottoman Istanbul* (Cambridge, 2010).

Bracewell, C. W., *The Uskoks of Senj: Piracy, Banditry, and Holy War in the Sixteenth-Century Adriatic* (Ithaca, NY, 1992).

Bradford, E., *The Shield and the Sword: The Knights of St John* (London, 1972).

Braudel, F., *The Mediterranean and the Mediterranean World in the Age of Philip II*, tr. S. Reynolds, 2 vols. (London, 1972).

Brémond, J., *et al.*, *Le Collège des Jésuites à Avignon, 1565–1950* (Bellegarde, 1950).

Bressan, L., *Il canone tridentino sul divorzio per adulterio e l'interpretazione degli autori* (Rome, 1973).

Breuning, J. J., *Orientalische Reyss dess edlen unnd vesten Hanss Jacob Breuning von und zu Buochenbach ... under dess Türkischen Sultans Jurisdiction und Gebiet* (Strasbourg, 1612).

Brogini, A., *Malte, frontière de Chrétienté (1530–1670)* (Rome, 2006).

— 'Intermédiaires de rachat laïcs et religieux à Malte aux XVIe et XVIIe siècles', in *LCC*, 47–63.

Brookes, D. S., ed. and tr., *The Ottoman Gentleman of the Sixteenth Century: Mustafa Ali's Meva'idün-nefa'is fi kava'idi'l-mecalis, 'Tables of Delicacies concerning the Rules of Social Gatherings'* (Cambridge, MA, 2003).

Brown, H. F., *Studies in the History of Venice*, 2 vols. (London, 1907).

Brummett, P., *Ottoman Seapower and Levantine Diplomacy in the Age of Discovery* (Albany, NY, 1994).

— 'The Ottomans as a World Power: What we Don't Know about Ottoman Sea-Power', *OM*, n.s., 20 (2001), 1–21.

Brunelli, G., 'Poteri e privilegi: l'istituzione degli ordinamenti delle milizie nello Stato Pontificio tra cinque e seicento', *Cheiron: materiali e strumenti di aggiornamento storiografico*, year 12 (1995), no. 23, 105–29.

— 'Gallio (Galli), Tolomeo', in *DBI*, li, 685–90.

— *Soldati del papa: politica militare e nobiltà nello Stato della Chiesa (1560–1644)* (Rome, 2003).

Brunetti, M., and E. Vitale, eds., *La corrispondenza da Madrid dell'ambasciatore Leonardo Donà (1570–1573)*, 2 vols. (Venice, 1963).

Bulboacă, S., *Bartolomeo Brutti în Moldova: politică, diplomaţie şi religie* (Arad, 2006).

Burdelez, I., 'The Role of Ragusan Jews in the History of the Mediterranean Countries', in A. Meyuhas Ginio, ed., *Jews, Christians, and Muslims in the Mediterranean World after 1492* (London, 1992), 190–7.

[de Cadecombe, P.,] *Speculum illustriorum iuris interpretum qui publicè per quatuor saecula professi, vel interpretati sunt in celebri, ac famosa Universitate Avenionensi* (Avignon, 1712).

Caetani, O.: see Carinci.

Calendar of State Papers Relating to English Affairs in the Archives of Venice, 38 vols. (London, 1864–1937) [cited as *CSPVen.*].

Canosa, R., and I. Colonnello, *Spionaggio a Palermo* (Palermo, 1991).

Cantelli, G., *Albania propria overo superiore detta anche Macedonia occidentale* [engraved map, single sheet] (Rome, 1689).

Cantemir, D., *Descrierea Moldovei*, ed. and tr. G. Guţu (Bucharest, 1973).

Capponi, N., *Lepanto, 1571: la Lega Santa contro l'Imperio Ottomano* (Milan, 2010).

Caproşu, I., 'Creditul moldovenesc în timpul lui Petru Şchiopul', in *Stat, societate, naţiune: interpretări istorice*, ed. N. Edroiu, A. Răduţiu and P. Teodor (Cluj, 1982), 107–17.

Caracciolo, F., *I commentarii delle guerre fatte co' Turchi da D. Giovanni d'Austria, dopo che venne in Italia* (Florence, 1581).

Caracciolo, P., *La gloria del cavallo* (Venice, 1566).

Carinci, G. B., ed., *Lettere di Onorato Caetani Capitan General delle Fanterie Pontificie nella battaglia di Lepanto*, 2nd edn (Rome, 1893).

Carlier de Pinon, J., *Voyage en Orient*, ed. E. Blochet (Paris, 1920).

Carnicer, C., and J. Marcos, *Espías de Felipe II: los servicios secretos del Imperio español* (Madrid, 2005).

Caro Baroja, J., *Los moriscos del Reino de Granada*, 5th edn (Madrid, 2000).

Carr, M., *Blood and Faith: The Purging of Muslim Spain* (London, 2009).

Carrasco, R., 'L'Espionnage espagnol du Levant au XVIe siècle d'après la correspondance des agents espagnols en poste à Venise', in B. Perez, ed., *Ambassadeurs, apprentis espions et maîtres comploteurs: les systèmes de renseignement en Espagne à l'époque moderne* (Paris, 2010), 203–22.

Carter, F. W., *Trade and Urban Development in Poland: An Economic Geography of Cracow, from its Origins to 1795* (Cambridge, 1994).

Casale, G., *The Ottoman Age of Expansion* (Oxford, 2010).

Cascales, F., *Discursos historicos de la muy noble, y muy leal, ciudad de Murcia* (Murcia, 1775).

Cassar, C., *Society, Culture and Identity in Early Modern Malta* (Msida, 2000).

Cassola, A., ed., *The 1565 Ottoman Malta Campaign Register* (San Gwann, 1998).

de Castro, J., *O Prior do Crato* (Lisbon, 1942).

Căzan, I., 'Urmaşii lui Petru Şchiopul şi Casa de Austria: datorii şi procese', *Revista istorică*, 20 (2009), 261–76.

Cella, S., 'Documenti veneziani della fine del '500', *AMSIASP*, n.s. 26 (= 78) (1978), 229–54.

Cerezo Martínez, R., *Años cruciales en la historia del Mediterráneo (1570–1574)* (Madrid, 1971).

Cernovodeanu, P., 'An English Diplomat at War: Edward Barton's Attendance of the Ottoman Campaign in Central Europe (1596)', *RRH*, 28, no. 4 (1989), 429–49.

de Cervantes Saavedra, M., *The Adventures of Don Quixote*, tr. J. M. Cohen (Harmondsworth, 1950).

Charrière, E., ed., *Négociations de la France dans le Levant*, 4 vols. (Paris, 1848–60).

Chasiōtēs, I. K., *Makarios, Theodōros kai Nikēphoros oi Melissēnoi (Melizzourgoi) (160s–170s ai.)* (Salonica, 1966).

— *Oi Ellēnes stis paramones tēs naumachias tēs Naupaktou: ekklēseis, epanastatikes kinēseis kai exegerseis stēn ellēnikē Chersonēso apo tis paramones ōs to telos tou kupriakou polemou (1568–1571)* (Salonica, 1970).

Chatenay, L., *Vie de Jacques Esprinchard rochelais et journal de ses voyages au XVIᵉ siècle* (Paris, 1957).

Cherini, A., and P. Grio, *Le famiglie di Capodistria: notizie storiche ed araldiche* (Trieste, 1998).

Chetta-Schirò, F., *I Castriota principi d'Albania nell'ordine sovrano e militare di Malta (origine della famiglia Castriota)* (Valletta, 1929).

Chivu, G., *et al.*, eds., *Documente şi însemnări româneşti din secolul al XVI-lea* (Bucharest, 1979).

Chossat, M., *Les Jésuites et leurs oeuvres à Avignon, 1553–1768* (Avignon, 1896).

Cichowski, H., *Ks. Stanisław Sokołowski a kościół wschodni: studjum z dziejów teologji w Polsce w w. XVI* (Lwów, 1929).

Ciobanu, V., *La cumpănă de veacuri: Ţările Române în contextul politicii poloneze la sfirşitul secolului al XVI-lea şi începutul secolului al XVII-lea* (Iaşi, 1991).

Ciorănescu, A., ed., *Documente privitoare la istoria Românilor culese din arhivele din Simancas, Academia Română*, Studii şi cercetări, 43 (Bucharest, 1940).

Ciurea, D., 'Relaţii externe ale Moldovei', *AIIAX*, 10 (1973), 1–47.

Civale, G., *Guerrieri di Cristo: inquisitori, Gesuiti e soldati alla battaglia di Lepanto* (Milan, 2009).

Cleray, E., 'Le Voyage de Pierre Lescalopier "parisien" de Venise à Constantinople, l'an 1574', *Revue d'histoire diplomatique*, 35, no. 1 (1921), 21–55.

Cloulas, I., ed., *Correspondance du Nonce en France Anselmo Dandino (1578–1581)* (Rome, 1970).

Coco, C., and F. Manzonetto, *Baili veneziani alla Sublime Porta: storia e caratteristiche dell'ambasciata veneta a Costantinopoli* (Venice, 1985).

Codina, G., 'The "modus parisiensis"', in V. J. Duminuco, ed., *The Jesuit Ratio Studiorum: 400th Anniversary Perspectives* (New York, 2000), 28–49.

Coniglio, G., *Il regno di Napoli al tempo di Carlo V: amministrazione e vita economico-sociale* (Naples, 1951).

— *Il viceregno di Napoli e la lotta tra spagnoli e turchi nel Mediterraneo*, 2 vols. (Naples, 1987).

Conring, H., *De bello contra Turcas prudenter gerendo* (Helmstadt, 1664).

Contarini, G. B., *Della veneta historia*, 2 vols. (Venice, 1663–9).

Conti, N., *Delle historie de' suoi tempi*, tr. G. C. Saraceni, 2 vols. (Venice, 1589).

Čoralić, L., 'Iz prošlosti istočnoga Jadrana – tragom iseljenika iz grada Ulcinja u Mlecima', *PP*, 27 (2004), 37–56.

— 'Duhovne osobe iz grada Bara u Mlecima (XIV.–XVI. st.)', *PP*, 28 (2005), 45–70.

— 'Izbjeglištvo kao sudbina: Barani u Mlecima (XIV.–XVII. st.)', *ZOZPZ*, 23 (2005), 87–185.

— 'Iz prošlosti ulcinjske biskupije i barske nadbiskupije: tragom gradiva iz Mletačkog Državnog Arhiva (XVI. st.)', *CCP*, 30 (2006), 65–71.

— 'Staleški raskol – tragom gradje o društvenim sukobima u Baru u prvoj polovici XVI. stoljeća', *PP*, 32 (2007), 63–91.

— 'Od Ulcinja do Drača: albanski useljenici u Mlecima (14.–18. stoljeće)', *ZOZPZ*, 29 (2011), 39–82.

— and D. Karbić, *Pisma i poruke rektora Dalmacije i Mletačke Albanije*, i: *Pisma i poruke rektora Bara, Ulcinja, Budve i Herceg-Novog* (*MSHSM*, lv) (Zagreb, 2009).

Cordignano, F., 'Geografia ecclesiastica dell'Albania dagli ultimi decenni del secolo XVI° alla metà del secolo XVII°', *OC*, 36, no. 99 (1934), 229–94.

— ed., *Catasto veneto di Scutari e registrum concessionum, 1416–1417*, 2 vols. (Shkodër, Rome, 1940–2).

— *Onomasticon del catasto veneto di Scutari e registrum concessionum* (Tolmezzo, 1945).

— and G. Valentini, *Saggio di un regesto storico dell'Albania* (Shkodër, 1937–40).

Corfus, I., ed. and tr., *Documente privitoare la istoria României culese din arhivele polone: secolul al XVI-lea* (Bucharest, 1979).

Costantini, V., *Il sultano e l'isola contesa: Cipro tra eredità e potere ottomano* (Turin, 2009).

Cottier, C., *Notes historiques concernant les Recteurs du ci-devant Comté Venaissin* (Carpentras, 1808).

Coulter, L., 'An Examination of the Status and Activities of the English Ambassadors to the Ottoman Porte in the Late Sixteenth and Early Seventeenth Centuries', *RESEE*, 28 (1990), 57–87.

Crăciun, M., *Protestantism și ortodoxie în Moldova secolului al XVI-lea* (Cluj, 1996).

Crescentio, B., *Nautica mediterranea* (Rome, 1607).

Cristea, O., 'The Friend of my Friend and the Enemy of my Enemy: Romanian Participation in Ottoman Campaigns', in *ETSOE*, 253–74.

Crowley, R., *City of Fortune: How Venice Won and Lost a Naval Empire* (London, 2011).

Crusius, M., *Turcograeciae libri octo* (Basel, 1584).

Cucchetti, G., *Storia di Trento dalle origini al fascismo* (Palermo, 1939).

Cvetkova, B. A., 'Vie économique de villes et ports balkaniques aux XVᵉ et XVIᵉ siècles', *REI*, 38 (1970), 267–355.

Czubek, I., ed., *Stanislai Rescii diarium, 1583–1589*, Archiwum do dziejów literatury i oświaty w Polsce, xv, no. 1 (Kraków, 1915).

Danişmend, İ. H., *Osmanlı devlet erkânı* (= *İzahlı osmanlı tarihi kronolojisi*, v) (Istanbul, 1971).

Darovec, D., *Breve storia dell'Istria*, tr. M. Rebeschini (Udine, 2010).

David, G., *Petru Șchiopul (1574–1577; 1578–1579; 1582–1591)* (Bucharest, 1984).

Davies, B. L., *Warfare, State and Society on the Black Sea Steppe, 1500–1700* (London, 2007).

Davis, N. Z., *The Gift in Sixteenth-Century France* (Oxford, 2000).

Davis, R. C., *Christian Slaves, Muslim Masters: White Slavery in the Mediterranean, the Barbary Coast and Italy, 1500–1800* (Basingstoke, 2003).

De Caro, G., 'Basta, Giorgio', in *DBI*, vii, 154–7.

Decei, A., *Relații româno-orientale: culegere de studii* (Bucharest, 1978).

DeCoursey, C., 'Society of Antiquaries (*act.* 1586–1607)', in *ODNB*.

Demény, L., and P. Cernovodeanu, *Relațiile politice ale Angliei cu Moldova, Țara Românească și Transilvania în secolele XVI–XVIII* (Bucharest, 1974).

De Zanche, L., *Tra Costantinopoli e Venezia: dispacci di stato e lettere dei mercanti dal basso medioevo alla caduta della Serenissima*, Quaderni di storia postale, xxv (Prato, 2000).

Dilworth, M., 'Chisholm, William (*c.*1547–1629), Roman Catholic Bishop of Vaison', in *ODNB*.

Djuvara, T. G., *Cent projets de partage de la Turquie (1281–1913)* (Paris, 1914).

van der Does, J. ['Dousa, G.'], *De itinere suo constantinopolitano epistola* (Leiden, 1599).

Doglioni, G. N., *Historia venetiana* (Venice, 1598).

Dokle, N., *Sinan Pasha i Topojanit* (Tirana, 2006).

Dopierała, K., *Stosunki dyplomatyczne Polski z Turcją za Stefana Batorego* (Warsaw, 1986).

[pseudo-]Dorotheos of Monemvasia, *Vivlion istorikon periechon en synopsei diaphorous kai exochous istorias* (Venice, 1631).

Doumerc, B., *Venise et son empire en Méditerranée, IXᵉ–XVᵉ siècles* (Paris, 2012).

Draganović, K., 'Massenübertritte von Katholiken zur "Orthodoxie" im kroatischen Sprachgebiet zur Zeit der Türkenherrschaft', *Orientalia christiana periodica*, 3 (1937), 181–232.

Ducellier, A., *La Façade maritime de l'Albanie au moyen age: Durazzo et Valona du XIe au XVe siècle* (Salonica, 1981).

Dudek, L., and H. Kowalewicz, 'Przyczynek do zagadnienia działalności obcego wywiadu na ziemiach polskich w XVI wieku', *Studia i materiały do historii wojskowości* 15 (1969), no. 2, 197–207.

Duhamel, L., *Inventaire-sommaire des Archives Communales antérieures à 1790 de la ville d'Avignon* (Avignon, 1906).

Duka, F., 'Aspekte social-ekonomike dhe demografike të Himarës gjatë sundimit osman (shek. XV–XVI)', in L. Nasi *et al.*, eds., *Himara në shekuj* (Tirana, 2004), 62–95.

— 'Coast and Hinterland in the Albanian Lands (16th–18th Centuries)', in *BOAV*, 261–70.

Durham, M. E., *High Albania* (London, 1909).

— *Some Tribal Origins, Laws and Customs of the Balkans* (London, 1928).

Dursteler, E. R., 'Commerce and Coexistence: Veneto-Ottoman Trade in the Early Modern Era', *Turcica*, 34 (2002), 105–33.

— *Venetians in Constantinople: Nation, Identity and Coexistence in the Early Modern Mediterranean* (Baltimore, 2006).

— *Renegade Women: Gender, Identity, and Boundaries in the Early Modern Mediterranean* (Baltimore, 2011).

— 'Speaking in Tongues: Language and Communication in the Early Modern Mediterranean', *Past & Present*, no. 217 (Nov. 2012), 47–77.

Džaja, S., *et al.*, eds., *Austro-turcica, 1541–1552: diplomatische Akten des habsburgischen Gesandtschaftsverkehrs mit der Hohen Pforte im Zeitalter Süleymans des Prächtigen* (Munich, 1995).

Dziubiński, A., 'Drogi handlowe polsko-tureckie w XVI stuleciu', *Przegląd historyczny*, 56 (1965), 232–59.

— *Na szlakach Orientu. Handel między Polską a Imperium Osmańskim w XVI–XVIII wieku* (Wrocław, 1997).

Earle, P., *Corsairs of Malta and Barbary* (London, 1970).

Echevarría Bacigalupe, M. A., 'El espionaje y las rebeliones de los siglos XVI y XVII en la monarquía hispánica', in W. Thomas and B. de Groof, eds., *Rebelión y resistencia en el mundo hispánico del siglo XVII* (Leuven, 1992), 144–66.

Ehses, S., 'Bericht der Trienter Konzilskommission zur Residenz der Bischöfe', *Römische Quartalschrift für Altertumskunde und für Kirchengeschichte*, 30, for 1916–22 (1922), 54–75.

Elsie, R., *Early Albania: A Reader of Historical Texts, 11th–17th Centuries*, Balkanologische Veröffentlichungen, xxxix (Wiesbaden, 2003).

Ermeni, G., *Storia dell'Università di Perugia*, 2 vols. (Florence, 1971).

Esprinchard, J., *Histoire des Ottomans, ou empereurs des Turcs, iusques à Mahomet III*, 2nd edn (Paris, 1609).

Evans, R. J. W., *Rudolf II and his World*, 3rd edn (London, 1997).

Evliya Çelebi, *Evliya Çelebi in Albania and Adjacent Regions (Kosovo, Montenegro, Ohrid)*, ed. and tr. R. Dankoff and R. Elsie (Leiden, 2000).

Fabris, A., 'Hasan "Il veneziano" tra Algeri e Costantinopoli', in *VLMV*, 51–66.

Fantoni Castrucci, S., *Istoria della città d'Avignone, e del Contado Venesino stati della Sede Apostolica nella Gallia*, 2 vols. (Venice, 1678).

Farlati, D., *Illyrici sacri*, 8 vols. (Venice, 1751–1819).

Faroqhi, S., *Die Vorlagen (telhise) des Grosswesirs Sinan paša an Sultan Murad III.* (Hamburg, 1967).

— *The Ottoman Empire and the World around It* (London, 2004).

Farrell, A. P., *The Jesuit Code of Liberal Education: Development and Scope of the Ratio Studiorum* (Milwaukee, WI, 1938).

Fenicia, G., *Il regno di Napoli e la difesa del Mediterraneo nell'età di Filippo II (1556–1598): organizzazione e finanziamento* (Bari, 2003).

Fenlon, I., *The Ceremonial City: History, Memory and Myth in Renaissance Venice* (New Haven, CT, 2007).

Fermendžin, E., *Acta Bosnae potissimum ecclesiastica cum insertis editorum documentorum regestis ab anno 925 usque ad annum 1752* (Zagreb, 1892).

Fernández Collado, A., *Gregorio XIII y Felipe II en la nunciatura de Felipe Sega (1577–1581): aspectos político, jurisdiccional y de reforma* (Toledo, 1991).

Fernández Navarrete, M., M. Salvá and P. Sainz de Baranda, eds., *Correspondencia entre Don García de Toledo, cuarto Marques de Villafranca, y el Sr. D. Juan de Austria*, CODOIN, iii (Madrid, 1843).

Fetvacı, E., *Picturing History at the Ottoman Court* (Bloomington, IN, 2013).

Fichtner, P. S., *Emperor Maximilian II* (New Haven, CT, 2001).

Filitti, I. C., *Din arhivele Vaticanului*, 2 vols. (Bucharest, 1913–14).

Fine, J. V. A., *The Late Medieval Balkans: A Critical Survey from the Late Twelfth Century to the Ottoman Conquest* (Ann Arbor, MI, 1994).

— *When Ethnicity Did not Matter in the Balkans: A Study of Identity in Pre-Nationalist Croatia, Dalmatia, and Slavonia in the Medieval and Early-Modern Periods* (Ann Arbor, MI, 2005).

Finkel, C. B., 'The Provisioning of the Ottoman Army during the Campaigns of 1593–1606', in *HOB*, 107–23.

— *The Administration of Warfare: The Ottoman Military Campaigns in Hungary, 1593–1606* (Vienna, 1988).

Fisher, Sir Godfrey, *Barbary Legend: War, Trade, and Piracy in North Africa, 1415–1830* (Oxford, 1957).

Fleet, K., 'Ottoman Expansion in the Mediterranean', in *CHT*, 141–72.

Fleischer, C. H., *Bureaucrat and Intellectual in the Ottoman Empire: The Historian Mustafa Âli (1541–1600)* (Princeton, NJ, 1986).

Floristán Imízcoz, J. M., ed., *Fuentes para la política oriental de los Austrias: la documentación griega del Archivo de Simancas (1571–1621)*, 2 vols. (León, 1988).

— 'Los contactos de la Chimarra con el reino de Nápoles durante el siglo XVI y comienzos del XVII', *EREBN*, 11–12 (1990–1), 105–39; 13 (1992), 53–87.

— ['Floristán',] 'Felipe II y la empresa de Grecia tras Lepanto (1571–78)', *EREBN*, 15 (1994), 155–90.

— ['Floristán',] 'Los prolegómenos de la tregua hispano-turca de 1578', *SF*, 57 (1998), 37–72.

Fodor, P., *In Quest of the Golden Apple: Imperial Ideology, Politics, and Military Administration in the Ottoman Empire* (Istanbul, 2000).

— 'Prelude to the "Long War" (1593–1606): Some Notes on Ottoman Foreign Policy in 1591–1593', in *GOTC*, i, 297–301.

Foglietta, U., *Istoria della sacra lega contra Selim, e d'alcune altre imprese di suoi tempi*, tr. G. Guastavini (Genoa, 1598).

Fois, M., 'Carlo Borromeo Cardinale Nepote di Pio IV', *SB*, 3 (1989), 7–44.

de Foix, P., *Les Lettres de Messire Paul de Foix, archevesque de Tolose, & ambassadeur pour le Roy auprès du Pape Gregoire XIII* (Paris, 1628).

Fontenay, M., 'Corsaires de la foi ou rentiers du sol? Les chevaliers de Malte dans le "corso" méditerranéen au XVIIe siècle', *Revue d'histoire moderne et contemporaine*, 35 (1988), 361–84.

Foretić, V., 'Korčula, Dubrovnik, Boka Kotorska i Lepantska Bitka', *Adriatica maritima*, 1 (1974), 165–180.

Fornery, J., *Histoire du Comté Venaissin et de la ville d'Avignon*, 3 vols. (Avignon, n.d. [1909]).

Foster, Sir William, *The Travels of John Sanderson in the Levant, 1584–1602* (London, 1931).

Fournier, M., *Histoire de la science du droit en France*, iii (Paris, 1892).

Freidenberg, M. M., *Dubrovnik i Osmanskaia imperiia*, 2nd edn (Moscow, 1989).

Freller, T., *The German Langue of the Order of Malta: A Concise History* (Santa Venera, 2010).

du Fresne-Canaye, P., *Le Voyage du Levant*, ed. H. Hauser (Paris, 1897).

Galea, M., *Grand Master Jean Levesque de La Cassière* (San Gwann, 1994).

García Hernán, D., and E. García Hernán, *Lepanto: el dia después* (Madrid, 1999).

García Hernán, E., 'The Price of Spying at the Battle of Lepanto', *Eurasian Studies*, 11 (2003), 227–50.

García Martínez, S., *Bandolers, corsaris i moriscos* (Valencia, 1980).

Gattini, M., *I priorati, i baliaggi e le commende del sovrano militare ordine di S. Giovanni di Gerusalemme nelle provincie meridionali d'Italia prima della caduta di Malta* (Naples, 1928).

Gattoni, M., 'La spada della croce: la difficile alleanza ispano-veneto-pontificia nella guerra di Cipro. Politica estera e teoresi filosofica nei documenti pontifici', *Ricerche storiche*, 29 (1999), no. 3, 611–50.

Gegaj, A., *L'Albanie et l'invasion turque au XVe siècle* (Paris, 1937).

Gemil, T., *Românii şi otomanii în secolele XIV–XVI* (Bucharest, 1991).

Gennari, P., '"Milione", redazione *VB*: edizione critica commentata', Università Ca' Foscari, Venice, PhD thesis (2009).

Gentilezza, G., 'L'Albania, la Dalmazia e le Bocche di Cattaro negli anni 1570 e 1571, difese dai veneziani contro il Turco', *Bessarione*, year 19, vol. 31 (1915), 61–78.

Gentili, A., *Laudes academiae perusinae et oxoniensis* (Hanau, 1605).

Gerlach, S., *Stephan Gerlachs dess Aeltern Tage-Buch*, ed. S. Gerlach (Frankfurt am Main, 1674).

Gertwagen, R., 'The Venetian Colonies in the Ionian and Aegean Seas in Venetian Defense Policy in the Fifteenth Century', *Journal of Mediterranean Studies*, 12 (2002), 351–84.

Geuder von Heroltzberg, J. ['I.'], *Conclusiones de personis per quas cuique dominium acquiritur* (Strasbourg, 1592).

Ghinea, N., 'La Famille de la Princesse Cathérine Salvaressa: contribution à la connaissance des relations roumano-italiennes au XVIᵉ siècle', *RRH*, 22, no. 4 (1983), 391–9.

Giannelli, C., 'Documenti inediti sullo stato di alcune comunità catoliche della Serbia meridionale nel 1578', *Ricerche slavistiche*, 2 (1953), 29–59.

Giard, L., 'Le Devoir de l'intelligence ou l'insertion des Jésuites dans le monde du savoir', in L. Giard, ed., *Les Jésuites à la Renaissance: système éducatif et production du savoir* (Paris, 1995), xi–lxxix.

de Giorgio, R., *A City by an Order* (Valletta, 1985).

Giovio ['Iovius'], P., *Historiarum sui temporis tomus primus* (Venice, 1566).

Giurescu, C. C., *Tîrguri sau oraşe şi cetăţi moldovene din secolul al X-lea pînă la mijlocul secolului al XVI-lea* (Bucharest, 1967).

Glücklich, J., ed., *Václava Budovce z Budova, korrespondence z let 1579–1619* (Prague, 1908).

Gökbilgin, M. T., *Rumeli'de Yürükler, Tatarlar ve Evlâd-ı Fâtihân* (Istanbul, 1957).

Goldenberg, S., 'Le Pouvoir central et les villes des pays roumains aux XVᵉ–XVIIᵉ siècles', in M. Mollat, ed., *Le Pouvoir central et les villes en Europe de l'Est et du Sud-Est du XVᵉ siècle aux débuts de la révolution industrielle. Les Villes portuaires* (Sofia, 1985), 40–55.

Golobutskii, V. A., *Zaporozhskoe kazachestvo* (Kiev, 1957).

Gorfer, A., *Trento città del Concilio* (Trent, 1963).

Gorovei, Ş., 'Moldova în "Casa Păcii": pe marginea izvoarelor privind primul secol de relaţii moldo-otomane', *AIIAX*, 17 (1980), 629–77.

Gorris, R., 'Naviguer avec prudence: la politique éditoriale de Vittorio Baldini imprimeur-libraire ferrarais dans les années 1597–1607', in *DUSAL*, 323–43.

— '*Prudentia perpetuat*: Vittorio Baldini, editore ferrarese di Francesco Patrizi', in P. Castelli, ed., *Francesco Patrizi filosofo platonico nel crepuscolo del Rinascimento* (Florence, 2002), 219–52.

Graf, T., '"I am Still Yours": Christian-European Renegades in the Ottoman Elite during the Late Sixteenth and Early Seventeenth Centuries', Heidelberg University PhD thesis (2013).

Granucci, N., *L'eremita, il carcere, e 'l diporto, opera nella quale si contengono novelle, & altre cose morali; con un breve compendio de' fatti più notabili de' Turchi, sin' a tutto l'anno 1566* (Lucca, 1569).

Greene, M., 'Ruling an Island without a Navy: A Comparative View of Venetian and Ottoman Crete', *OM*, n.s., 20 (2001), 193–207.

— 'Trading Identities: The Sixteenth-Century Greek Moment', in A. A. Husain and K. E. Fleming, eds., *A Faithful Sea: The Religious Cultures of the Mediterranean, 1200–1700* (Oxford, 2007), 121–48.

— *Catholic Pirates and Greek Merchants: A Maritime History of the Mediterranean* (Princeton, NJ, 2010).

Grimaldi, D., *Copia di una lettera di Monsignor Grimaldo commissario di sua Santità . . . dove si narra la battaglia presentata à l'Occhiali Capitano Generale della armata turchesca, & la fuga di detto Occhialì* (Rome, n.d. [1572]).

Griswold, W. J., *The Great Anatolian Rebellion, 1000–1020/1591–1611* (Berlin, 1983).

Grmek, M. D., *Santorio Santorio i njegovi aparati i instrumenti* (Zagreb, 1952).

Groto, L., ed., *Trofeo della vittoria sacra, ottenuta dalla Christianiss. Lega contra Turchi nell'anno MDLXXI* (Venice, n.d. [1572]).

Grunebaum-Ballin, P., *Joseph Naci duc de Naxos* (Paris, 1968).

Guarnieri, G. G., *Cavalieri di Santo Stefano: contributo alla storia della marina militare italiana (1562–1859)* (Pisa, 1928).

de Gubernatis, D., and A. M. de Turre, *Orbis seraphicus: historia de tribus ordinibus . . . deque eorum progressibus per quatuor mundi partes . . . tomus secundus*, ed. M. a Civetia and T. Domenichelli (Quaracchi, 1886).

Guboglu, M., and M. Mehmet, *Cronici turceşti privind Ţările Române*, i (Bucharest, 1966).

Guerrini, P., *Una celebre famiglia lombarda, i Conti di Martinengo: studi e ricerche genealogiche* (Brescia, 1930).

Guglielmotti, A., *Storia della marina pontificia*, vi: *Marcantonio Colonna alla battaglia di Lepanto* (Rome, 1887).

Guilmartin, J. F., *Gunpowder and Galleys: Changing Technology and Mediterranean Warfare at Sea in the Sixteenth Century* (Cambridge, 1974).

— 'The Tactics of the Battle of Lepanto Clarified: The Impact of Social, Economic, and Political Factors on Sixteenth-Century Galley Warfare', in C. L. Symonds, ed., *New Aspects of Naval History* (Annapolis, MD, 1981), 41–65.

Gürçağlar, A., 'Patterns of Patronage: An Istrian Family of Dragomans as Patrons of Arts', *Across Languages and Cultures*, 14 (2013), 287–301.

Gürkan, E. S., 'The Efficacy of Ottoman Counter-Intelligence in the 16th Century', *Acta orientalia Academiae Scientiarum Hungaricae*, 65 (2012), 1–38.

— 'Espionage in the 16th-Century Mediterranean: Secret Diplomacy, Mediterranean Go-Betweens and the Ottoman Habsburg Rivalry', Georgetown University PhD thesis (2012).

György, L., 'A kolozsvári római katolikus Lyceum-könyvtár története (1579–1948)' (www.mek.oszk.hu/03100/03186/html/gyorgy13.htm).

'Haji Khalifeh': *see* Katib Çelebi.

Halecki, O., *From Florence to Brest (1439–1596)* (Rome, 1958).

von Hammer, J., *Geschichte des osmanischen Reiches*, 10 vols. (Pest, 1827–35).

Hanlon, G., *Twilight of a Military Tradition: Italian Aristocrats and European Conflicts, 1560–1800* (London, 1998).

Harris, R., *Dubrovnik: A History* (London, 2003).

Heberer, M., *Aegyptiaca servitus, das ist, Warhafte Beschreibung einer dreyjährigen Dienstbarkeit, so in Alexandrien in Egypten ihren Anfang, vnd zu Constantinopel ihr Endschafft genommen* (Heidelberg, n.d. [1610?]).

Heidenstein, R., *Rerum polonicarum ab excessu Sigismundi Augusti libri XII* (Frankfurt am Main, 1672).

Hernando Sánchez, C. J., *Castilla y Nápoles en el siglo XVI. El virrey Pedro de Toledo: linaje, estado y cultura (1532–1553)* (Valladolid, 1994).

Hess, A. C., 'The Moriscos: An Ottoman Fifth Column in Sixteenth-Century Spain', *American Historical Review*, 74 (1968), 1–25.

— *The Forgotten Frontier: A History of the Sixteenth-Century Ibero-African Frontier* (Chicago, 1978).

Hirn, [J.,] 'Das Exil des Moldauer Fürsten Peter Schiopul', *Historisches Jahrbuch*, 7 (1886), 434–41.

Hocquet, J.-C., *Le Sel et la fortune de Venise*, 2 vols. (Lille, 1982).

Hofmann, G., 'Griechische Patriarchen und römische Päpste: Untersuchungen und Texte', *OC*, 25, no. 2 (= no. 76) (1932), 221–304.

Holban, M., *et al.*, eds., *Călători străini despre Țările Române*, 8 vols. (Bucharest, 1968–83).

Holmes, P., 'Stucley, Thomas, *c.*1520–1578, Soldier', in *ODNB*.

Hoszowski, S., *Les Prix à Lwow (XVIᵉ–XVIIᵉ siècles)* (Paris, 1954).

Housley, N., *The Later Crusades: From Lyons to Alcazar, 1274–1580* (Oxford, 1992).

— *Crusading and the Ottoman Threat, 1453–1505* (Oxford, 2012).

Howard, D. A., 'Ottoman Historiography and the Literature of "Decline" of the Sixteenth and Seventeenth Centuries', *Journal of Asian History*, 22 (1988), 52–77.

Hoxha, Sh., *Shqiptari Sinan Pashë Topojani (qëmtime historiko-etnologjike për Lumën e Gorën)* (Tirana, 2007).

Hrabak, B., 'Kuga u balkanskim zemljama pod Turcima od 1450 do 1600 godine', *Istorijski glasnik* (1957), nos. 1–2, 19–37.

— *Izvoz žitarica iz Osmanlijskog Carstva u XIV, XV i XVI stoleću: udeo Dubrovčana u prometu 'turskim' žitom* (Prishtinë, 1971).

Hrushevsky, M., *History of Ukraine-Rus'*, vii, tr. B. Strumiński (Edmonton, Alberta, 1999).

Hunt, C., 'The Romanian Lands in the Sixteenth Century: Their Juridical Status according to Ottoman Law', in *EPEM*, 391–414.

Hupchick, D. P., *The Bulgarians in the Seventeenth Century: Slavic Orthodox Society and Culture under Ottoman Rule* (Jefferson, NC, 1993).

de Hurmuzaki, E., *et al.*, eds., *Documente privitóre la istoria Românilor*, 19 vols. (Bucharest, 1887–1938) [cited as '*HD*'].

Hurtubise, P., ed., *Correspondance du Nonce en France Antonio Maria Salviati (1572–1578)*, 2 vols. (Rome, 1975).

Hysi, Y., *Southern Albanian Riviere: Vlora – Saranda* (Tirana, 2010).

Imber, C. H., 'The Navy of Süleyman the Magnificent', *AO*, 6 (1980), 211–82.

— 'The Reconstruction of the Ottoman Fleet after the Battle of Lepanto, 1571–1572', in C. H. Imber, *Studies in Ottoman History and Law* (Istanbul, 1996), 85–101.

— *The Ottoman Empire, 1300–1650: The Structure of Power*, 2nd edn (London, 2009).

İnalcık, H., *The Ottoman Empire: The Classical Age, 1300–1600* (London, 1973).

— 'Lepanto in the Ottoman Documents', in *MSMCLL*, 185–92.

— 'The Question of the Closing of the Black Sea under the Ottomans', *Archeion Pontou*, 35 (1979), 74–110.

— *The Middle East and the Balkans under the Ottoman Empire: Essays on Economy and Society* (Bloomington, IN, 1993).

İnbaşı, M., 'Rumeli Yörükleri', in T. Gündüz, ed., *Anadolu'da ve Rumeli'de Yörükler ve Türkmenler sempozyumu bildirileri* (Tarsus, 2000), 145–82.

Ingegneri, A., *Del buon segretario libri tre* (Rome, 1594).

Ingegneri ['Ingegnere'], G., *Fisionomia naturale*, ed. A. Ingegneri (Milan, 1607).

Iorga, N., *Acte și fragmente cu privire la istoria Romînilor adunate din depozitele de manuscrise ale Apusuluĭ*, 2 vols. (Bucharest, 1895–6).

— 'Contribuţiuni la istoria Munteniei în a doua jumătate a secolului XVI-lea', *Analele Academiei Romane*, ser. 2, *Memoriile Secţiunii Istorice*, 18 (1896), 1–112.

— 'Documente noue, in mare parte românesci, relative la Petru Şchiopul şi Mihaiu Vitézul', *Analele Academiei Romane* [sic], ser. 2, *Memoriile Secţiunii Istorice*, 20 (1899), 435–502.

— *Studiĭ istorice asupra Chilieĭ şi Cetăţiĭ-Albe* (Bucharest, 1899).

— *Relaţiile comerciale ale ţerilor noastre cu Lembergul: regeste şi documente din archivele oraşului Lemberg* (Bucharest, 1900).

— *Geschichte des Osmanischen Reiches*, 5 vols. (Gotha, 1908–13).

— 'Les Premières Relations entre l'Angleterre et les pays roumains du Danube (1427 à 1611)', in *Mélanges d'histoire offerts à M. Charles Bémont par ses amis et ses élèves* (Paris, 1913), 559–80.

— *Notes et extraits pour servir à l'histoire des croisades au XVe siècle*, v (Bucharest, 1915).

— *Ospiti romeni in Venezia (1570–1610)* (Bucharest, 1932).

— *Byzance après Byzance: continuation de l'"Histoire de la vie byzantine'* (Bucharest, 1935).

— *Histoire des Roumains et de la romanité orientale*, 10 vols. (Paris, Bucharest, 1937–45).

Isom-Verhaaren, C., 'An Ottoman Report about Martin Luther and the Emperor: New Evidence of the Ottoman Interest in the Protestant Challenge to the Power of Charles V', *Turcica*, 28 (1996), 299–318.

— *Allies with the Infidel: The Ottoman and French Alliance in the Sixteenth Century* (London, 2011).

Isopescu, C., 'Alcuni documenti inediti della fine del Cinquecento', *Ephemeris dacoromana: annuario della Scuola Romena di Roma*, 2 (1924), 460–500.

Israel, J., *European Jewry in the Age of Mercantilism, 1550–1750*, 2nd edn (Oxford, 1989).

Ivanics, M., 'The Military Co-operation of the Crimean Khanate with the Ottoman Empire in the Sixteenth and Seventeenth Centuries', in *ETSOE*, 275–99.

Ivetić, E., *La popolazione dell'Istria nell'età moderna: lineamenti evolutivi* (Trieste, 1997).

Jačov, M., *Spisi tajnog vatikanskog arhiva, XVI–XVII veka* (Belgrade, 1983).

— *L'Europa tra conquiste ottomane e leghe sante* (Vatican City, 2001).

Jaitner, K., ed., *Die Hauptinstruktionen Clemens' VIII. für die Nuntien und Legaten an den europäischen Fürstenhöfen 1592–1605*, 2 vols. (Tübingen, 1984).

Jedin, H., *Geschichte des Konzils von Trient*, 4 vols. (Freiburg, 1949–75).

— *Kirche des Glaubens, Kirche der Geschichte: ausgewählte Aufsätze und Vorträge*, 2 vols. (Freiburg, 1966).

Jireček, K. ['C.'], 'Die Romanen in den Städten Dalmatiens während des Mittelalters', *Denkschriften der kaiserlichen Akademie der Wissenschaften in Wien, philosophisch-historische Classe*, (i): 48 (1902), no. 3; (ii–iii): 49 (1904), nos. 1–2.

Jouanna, A., *La Saint-Barthélemy: les mystères d'un crime d'état, 24 août 1572* (Paris, 2007).

Judde de Larivière, C., *Naviguer, commercer, gouverner: économie maritime et pouvoirs à Venise (XVe–XVIe siècles)* (Leiden, 2008).

Kafadar, C., 'A Death in Venice (1575): Anatolian Muslim Merchants Trading in the Serenissima', *Journal of Turkish Studies*, 10 (1986), 191–218.

Kahane, H., R. Kahane and A. Tietze, *The Lingua franca in the Levant: Turkish Nautical Terms of Italian and Greek Origin* (Urbana, IL, 1958).

Kaiser, W., 'Négocier la liberté: missions françaises pour l'échange et le rachat de captifs au Maghreb (XVIIe siècle)', in C. Moatti, ed., *La Mobilité des personnes en Méditerranée de l'Antiquité à l'époque moderne* (Rome, 2004), 501–28.

Kaleshi ['Kaleši'], H., 'Veliki vezir Kodža Sinan paša, njegove zadužbine i njegova vakufnama', *GjA*, 2 (1965), 105–44.

Karaiskaj, Gj., *Die spätantiken und mittelalterlichen Wehranlagen in Albanien: Städte, Burgen, Festungen und Kastelle*, ed. M. W. E. Peters (Hamburg, 2010).

Karalevskij ['Korolevskij'], 'La missione greco-cattolico della Cimarra nell'Epiro nei secoli XVI–XVII', *Bessarione*, year 15, ser. 3, vol. 8 (1910–11), fascs. 117–18, pp. 440–83; year 16, ser. 3, vol. 9 (1912), fasc. 120, pp. 183–99; year 17, vol. 29 (1913), pp. 170–97.

— 'Relaţiunile dintre Domnii români şi Sfântul Scaun în a doua jumătate a veacului al XVI-lea după documente inedite', *Revista catolică: publicaţiune trimestrială* (1913), 175–207, 411–26, 570–81; (1914), 46–60, 176–209.

Karapidakis, N., *Civis fidelis: l'avènement et l'affirmation de la citoyenneté corfiote (XVIème–XVIIème siècles)* (Frankfurt am Main, 1992).

Kármán, G., and L. Kunčević, eds., *The European Tributary States of the Ottoman Empire in the Sixteenth and Seventeenth Centuries* (Leiden, 2013).

Karttunen, L., *Grégoire XIII comme politicien et souverain* (Helsinki, 1911).

Kaser, K., *Hirten, Kämpfer, Stammeshelden: Ursprünge und Gegenwart des balkanischen Patriarchats* (Vienna, 1992).

Katib Çelebi [Hacı Kalfa; 'Haji Khalifeh'], *The History of the Maritime Wars of the Turks*, tr. J. Mitchell (London, 1831).

Kayapınar, A., 'Dobruca yöresinde XVI. yüzyılda gayr-i Sünni İslam'ın izleri', *Alevilik-Bektaşilik araştırmaları dergisi*, 1 (2009), 85–102.

Kesterčanek, F., 'Pad grada Bara u turske ruke 1571 god. prema mletačkim svjedočanstvima u Drž. notarijatu u Dubrovniku', *IZ*, year 13, vol. 17 (1960), 565–72.

Kiel, M., *Art and Society of Bulgaria in the Turkish Period* (Assen, 1985).

— *Ottoman Architecture in Albania, 1385–1912* (Istanbul, 1990).

Klarwill, V., ed., *Fugger-Zeitungen: ungedruckte Briefe an das Haus Fugger aus den Jahren 1568–1605* (Vienna, 1923).

Kolias, G. T., 'Epistolē tou mētropolitou Timotheou pros ton papan Pion E' (1572)', in *Eis mnēmēn K. Amantou, 1874–1960* (Athens, 1960), 391–412.

Kołodziejczyk, D., *Ottoman–Polish Diplomatic Relations (15th–18th Century): An Annotated Edition of* 'Ahdnames *and Other Documents* (Leiden, 2000).

— 'Inner Lake or Frontier? The Ottoman Black Sea in the Sixteenth and Seventeenth Centuries', in *EPEM*, 125–39.

Korade, M., 'Prijedlozi vizitatora Aleksandra Komulovića (1548.–1608.) za borbu protiv Osmanlija', in A. Ramaj, ed., *Poeta nascitur, historicus fit: ad honorem Zef Mirdita* (Sankt Gallen, 2013), 201–17.

Kortepeter, C. M., *Ottoman Imperialism during the Reformation: Europe and the Caucasus* (New York, 1972).

Kotarski, E., and B. Kumor, 'Solikowski, Jan Dymitr', in Polska Akademia Nauk, Polska Akademia Umiejętności, *Polski słownik biograficzny* (Kraków, 1935–) vol. 40(1), fasc. 164, 282–9.

Krajcar, J., *Cardinal Giulio Antonio Santoro and the Christian East*, Orientalia christiana analecta, clxxvii (Rome, 1966).

Krekić, B., 'Developed Autonomy: The Patricians in Dubrovnik and Dalmatian Cities', in B. Krekić, ed., *The Urban Society of Eastern Europe in Premodern Times* (Berkeley, CA, 1987), 185–215.

— 'On the Latino-Slavic Cultural Symbiosis in Late Medieval and Renaissance Dalmatia and Dubrovnik', *Viator*, 26 (1995), 321–32.

Krivošić, S., *Stanovništvo Dubrovnika i demografske promjene u prošlosti* (Dubrovnik, 1990).

Królikowska, N., 'Sovereignty and Subordination in Crimean–Ottoman Relations (Sixteenth–Eighteenth Centuries)', in *ETSOE*, 43–59.

Kruppa, T., 'Okmányok és iratok a tizenöt éves háború időszakából (1594–1597)', *Levéltári közlemények*, 76 (2005), no. 2, 51–92.

— 'Pasquale Bruti tolmács kalandos prágai követsége 1596-ban', *Lymbus* (2005), 27–47.

Kumrular, Ö., 'Ragusa: una fuente de información entre el Occidente y Oriente – Ragusa, Venecia y la Sublime Puerta', in *TDD*, 143–54.

Kunčević, L., 'Discourses on Liberty in Early Modern Ragusa', in Q. Skinner and M. van Gelderen, eds., *Freedom and the Construction of Europe*, 2 vols. (Cambridge, 2013), i, 195–214.

— 'Janus-Faced Sovereignty: The International Status of the Ragusan Republic in the Early Modern Period', in *ETSOE*, 91–121.

Kunt, M., 'Ethnic-Regional (*Cins*) Solidarity in the Seventeenth-Century Ottoman Establishment', *International Journal of Middle Eastern Studies*, 5 (1974), 233–9.

Kuntze, E., 'Les Rapports de la Pologne avec le Saint-Siège à l'époque d'Etienne Batory', in A. Áldásy *et al.*, *Etienne Báthory, Roi de Pologne, Prince de Transylvanie* (Kraków, 1935), 133–211.

Kütükoğlu, M. S., 'Narkh', in *EI2*.

Laiou, S., 'The Levends of the Sea in the Second Half of the 16th Century: Some Considerations', *AO*, 23 (2005–6), 233–47.

Lala, E., 'Violence and the Clergy in Late Medieval Albania: With and without the Penitentiary', in G. Jaritz and A. Marinković, eds., *Violence and the Medieval Clergy* (Budapest, 2011), 46–54.

Lamansky, V., 'L'Assassinat politique à Venise du XVe au XVIIIe siècle', *Revue historique*, 20 (1882), 105–20.

— *Secrets d'état de Venise: documents, extraits, notices et études servant à éclaircir les rapports de la Seigneurie avec les Grecs, les Slaves et la Porte Ottomane à la fin du XVe et au XVIe siècle* (St Petersburg, 1884).

Lane, F. C., *Venetian Ships and Shipbuilders of the Renaissance* (Baltimore, 1934).

— *Venice: A Maritime Republic* (Baltimore, 1973).

Languet, H., *Epistolae secretae*, 2 vols. (Halle, 1699).

Laskaris, M. T., 'Petros Lantzas, dioikētēs tēs Pargas (1573) kai organon tōn Ispanōn en Ēpeirō (1596–1608)', in *AEMCS*, 103–18.

— 'Sumplērōmatika peri Lantza klp', in *AEMCS*, 237–53.

de La Veronne, C., 'Giovanni Margliani et la trève de 1580 entre l'Espagne et la Turquie', *Arab Historical Review for Ottoman Studies*, nos. 3–4 (Dec. 1991), 67–78.

Lavrić, A., *Vizitacijsko poročilo Agostina Valiera o koprski škofiji iz leta 1579* (Ljubljana, 1986).

Lazari, V., ed., *Diario del viaggio da Venezia a Costantinopoli fatto da M. Jacopo Soranzo ambasciator straordinario della Serenissima Repubblica di Venezia al Sultano Murad III in compagnia di M. Giovanni Correr Bailo alla Porta Ottomana descritto da anonimo che fu al seguito del Soranzo* (Venice, 1856).

Lee, M., 'Seton, Alexander, first Earl of Dunfermline (1556–1622), Lord Chancellor of Scotland', in *ODNB*.

Lefaivre, A., *Les Magyars pendant la domination ottomane en Hongrie (1526–1722)*, 2 vols. (Paris, 1902).

Lepszy, K., ed., *Archiwum Jana Zamoyskiego, Kanclerza i Hetmana Wielkiego Koronnego*, iv (Kraków, 1948).

Lesure, M., *Lépante: la crise de l'Empire Ottoman* (Paris, 1972).

— 'Michel Černović "explorator secretus" à Constantinople (1556–1563)', *Turcica*, 15 (1983), 127–54.

Leunclavius, J. ['H. Lewenklaw', J. Löwenklau], ed., *Neuwe Chronica Türckischer Nation, von Türcken selbs* [sic] *beschrieben* (Frankfurt am Main, 1590).

de Leva, G., ed., *La legazione di Roma di Paolo Paruta (1592–1595)*, 3 vols. (Venice, 1887).

Levin, M. J., *Agents of Empire: Spanish Ambassadors in Sixteenth-Century Italy* (Ithaca, NY, 2005).

Ljubić, Š. ['S.'], ed., *Commissiones et relationes venetae*, ii: *(1525–1553)* (*MSHSM*, viii) (Zagreb, 1877).

— ed., *Commissiones et relationes venetae*, iii: *(1553–1571)* (*MSHSM*, xi) (Zagreb, 1880).

— 'Marijana Bolice kotoranina opis Sanžakata Skadarskoga od godine 1614', *SJAZU*, 12 (1880), 164–205.

— 'Poslanice dubrovačke na mletačku republiku', *SJAZU*, 15 (1883), 1–94.

Loebl, A. H., *Zur Geschichte des Türkenkriegs von 1593–1606*, 2 vols. (Prague, 1899–1904).

López Nadal, G., 'El corsarismo en las estructuras mercantiles: las fronteras del convencialismo', in G. López Nadal, ed., *El comerç alternatiu: corsarisme i contraban (ss. XV–XVIII)* (Palma, 1990).

Lubenau, R., *Beschreibung der Reisen des Reinhold Lubenau*, ed. W. Sahm, 2 vols. (Königsberg, 1914–30).

Luca, C., 'Veneziani, levantini e romeni fra prassi politiche e interessi mercantili nell'Europa sud-orientale tra cinque e seicento', in T. Ferro, ed., *Romania e Romània: lingua e cultura romena a fronte all'occidente* (Udine, 2003), 243–60.

— 'Associazionismo e individualismo nel commercio internazionale riguardante l'area del Basso Danubio fra XVI e XVII secolo', *QCRV*, 4 (2006), 151–66.

— 'Il patrizio veneto Polo Minio, viaggiatore in Moldavia nei primi decenni del Seicento', in G. Platania, ed., *Da Est ad Ovest, da Ovest ad Est: viaggiatori per le strade del mondo* (Viterbo, 2006), 81–98.

— 'Aspetti riguardanti i traffici mercantili e la circolazione del denaro tra Venezia, Costantinopoli e i Principati Romeni nei secoli XVI–XVIII', in C. Luca and G. Masi, eds., *L'Europa centro-orientale e la penisola italiana: quattro secoli di rapporti e influssi intercorsi tra stati e civiltà (1300–1700)* (Brăila, 2007), 247–84.

— *Ţările Române şi Veneţia în secolul al XVII-lea: din relaţiile politico-diplomatice, comerciale şi culturale ale Ţările Româneşti şi ale Moldovei cu Serenissima* (Bucharest, 2007).

— *Dacoromano-Italica: studi e ricerche sui rapporti italo-romeni nei secoli XVI–XVIII* (Cluj, 2008).

— 'Venetian Merchants in the Lower Danube Area and their Role in the Development of the International Trade Exchanges in the Seventeenth Century', *Český časopis historický*, 109 (2011), 294–328.

Lucchetta, F., 'La scuola dei "giovani di lingua" veneti nei secoli XVI e XVII', *QSA*, 7 (1989), 19–40.

— 'Il medico del bailaggio di Costantinopoli: fra terapie e politica (secc. XV–XVI)', in *VLMV*, 5–50.

Luciani, T., 'Notizie e documenti per la conoscenza delle cose istriane: i Bruti e i Borisi', *La provincia: giornale degli interessi civili, economici, amministrativi dell'Istria*, 7, no. 17 (1 Sept. 1873), 1303–5.

— 'Relazioni dei podestà e capitani di Capodistria', *AMSIASP*, 6 (1890), 45–103, 383–442; 7 (1891), 97–219, 279–353.

Ludolf, H., *De bello turcico feliciter conficiendo* (Frankfurt am Main, 1686).

Ludwig, G., and P. Molmenti, *Vittore Carpaccio: la vita e le opere* (Milan, 1906).

Luetić ['Luetiq'], J., 'Lundruesit detarë, marina tregtare dhe veprimtaria e porteve të Vlorës, Durrësit e Lezhës dhe lidhjet nautike-komerciale të shqiptarëve me dubrovnikasit në vitet 1566–1584', *GjA*, ser. shk. hist., 14, for 1984 (1985), 111–36.

Luglio, V., *L'antico vescovado giustinopolitano* (Trieste, 2000).

Lukács, L., ed., *Monumenta paedagogica Societatis Iesu*, 7 vols. (Rome, 1969–92).

— 'Introductio generalis', in L. Lukács, ed., *Monumenta paedagogica Societatis Iesu*, ii (Rome, 1974), 1*–59*.

— ed., *Monumenta antiquae Hungariae*, iii (Rome, 1981).

Lutrell, A., 'Late-Medieval Galley Oarsmen', in *LGMM*, i, 87–101.

McGowan, B., *Economic Life in Ottoman Europe: Taxation, Trade and the Struggle for Land, 1600–1800* (Cambridge, 1981).

McKee, S., *Uncommon Dominion: Venetian Crete and the Myth of Ethnic Purity* (Philadelphia, 2000).

MacLean, G., and N. Matar, *Britain and the Islamic World, 1558–1713* (Oxford, 2011).

Macůrek, J., 'Diplomatické poslání Jana Duckera v Polsku r. 1591', *Věstník Královské České Společnosti Nauk, třida filosoficko-historicko-jazykozpytná* (1929), item 3.

— *Zápas Polska a Habsburků o přístup k Černému Moři na sklonku 16. stol.* (Prague, 1931).

Madonia, C., *La Compagnia di Gesù e la riconquista cattolica dell'Europa orientale* (Genoa, 2002).

Maffei, G., *Degli annali di Gregorio XIII. Pontefice Massimo*, ed. C. Cocquelines, 2 vols. (Rome, 1742).

Mafrici, M., *Mezzogiorno e pirateria nell'età moderna (secoli XVI–XVIII)* (Naples, 1995).

Magdaleno, R., ed., *Papeles de Estado: Milan y Saboya*, Catalogo xxiii del Archivo de Simancas (Madrid, 1961).

Majda, T., 'L'École polonaise des langues orientales d'Istanbul au XVIIIᵉ siècle', in *ILO*, 123–8.

Majer, F., 'Gli ebrei feneratori a Capodistria', *Pagine istriane: periodico mensile*, 11, nos. 7–8 (July–Aug. 1913), 167–82.

Malcolm, N., *Bosnia: A Short History* (London, 1994).

— *Kosovo: A Short History* (London, 1998).

— 'The Kelmendi: Notes on the Early History of a Catholic Albanian Clan', *SF*, 59–60 (2000–1), 149–63.

— 'The Crescent and the City of the Sun: Islam and the Renaissance Utopia of Tommaso Campanella', *Proceedings of the British Academy*, 125 (2003), 41–67.

Małecki, J. M., 'Die Wandlungen im Krakauer und polnischen Handel zur Zeit der Türkenkriege des 16. und 17. Jahrhunderts', in O. Pickl, ed., *Die wirtschaftlichen Auswirkungen der Türkenkriege* (Graz, 1971), 145–51.

Mallett, M. E., and J. R. Hale, *The Military Organization of a Renaissance State* (Cambridge, 1984).

Mallia-Milanes, V., *Venice and Hospitaller Malta, 1530–1798: Aspects of a Relationship* (Marsa, 1992).

Malović-Djukić, M., 'Privredne veze Ulcinja i Dubrovnika krajem XIV i početkom XV veka', *Istorijski časopis*, 40–1 (1993–4), 57–70.

Manca, C., *Il modello di sviluppo economico delle città marittime barbaresche dopo Lepanto* (Naples, 1982).

Manfroni, C., 'La lega cristiana nel 1572, con lettere di M. Antonio Colonna', *ARSRSP*, 16 (1893), 347–445; 17 (1894), 23–67.

Manoussacas, M., 'Lepanto e i Greci', in *MSMCLL*, 215–41.

Mantran, R., 'L'Écho de la bataille de Lépante à Constantinople', in *MSMCLL*, 243–56.

Manzuoli, N., *Nova descrittione della provincia dell'Istria*, 2 parts (Venice, 1611).

— ed., *Rime, e prose di diversi autori in lode del sereniss. prencipe Nicolo Donato* (Venice, 1620).

March, J. M., *La batalla de Lepanto y Don Luis de Requeséns, Lugarteniente General de la Mar, con nuevos documentos históricos* (Madrid, 1944).

Marchand, J., *La Faculté des Arts de l'Université d'Avignon: notice historique accompagnée des statuts inédits de cette faculté* (Paris, 1897).

Marković, S., 'Benediktinska opatija Sv. Marije Ratačke kod Bara: acta diplomatica et iuridica', *CCP*, 28, no. 53 (2004), 183–234.

— 'Barski patricijski rod Borisi u prošlosti: Jadran, Evropa, Mediteran', *PP*, 28 (2005), 71–105.

Marmora, A., *Della historia di Corfù* (Venice, 1672).

Martinat, M., 'L'Annone romaine moderne entre contraintes morales et projet politique', in C. Virlouvet and B. Marin, eds., *Nourrir les cités de Méditerranée: antiquité – temps modernes* (Paris, 2003), 103–24.

Martínez Torres, J. A., *Prisioneros de los infieles: vida y rescate de los cautivos cristianos en el Mediterráneo musulmán (siglos XVI–XVII)* (Barcelona, 2004).

— 'Corso turco-berberisco y redenciones de cautivos en el Mediterráneo occidental (siglos XVI–XVII)', in *LCC*, 83–107.

Masiá, M. J. B., ed., *Cartas de un espía de Carlos V: la correspondencia de Jerónimo Bucchia con Antonio Perrenot de Granvela* (Valencia, 2005).

Matkovski, A., 'Kryengritje të panjohura në sanxhakun e Ohrit në vitet 1566–1574', *SH*, 27 (1973), no. 3, 53–66, 177–206.

de Mattei, R., 'Una "Orazione" di Scipione Ammirato alla Repubblica di Venezia, del 1595', *ASI*, 119 (1961), 91–104.

Matuz, J., 'Die Pfortendolmetscher zur Herrschaftszeit Süleymans des Prächtigen', *SF*, 34 (1975), 26–60.

Mavroeidē, Ph. ['Mavroidi, F.'], *Aspetti della società veneziana nel '500: la Confraternità di S. Nicolò dei Greci* (Ravenna, 1989).

— *O Ellēnismos sto Galata (1453–1600): koinōnikes kai oikonomikes pragmatikotētes* (Ioannina, 1992).

Maxim, M., 'Les Pays roumains et les relations habsbourg-ottomanes dans la seconde moitié du XVIe siècle', in *HOB*, 91–105.

— 'Haraciul Moldovei şi Ţării Româneşti în ultimul sfert al veacului XVI', *Studii şi materiale de istorie medie*, 12 (1994), 3–46.

— *L'Empire Ottoman au nord du Danube et l'autonomie des Principautés Roumaines au XVIe siècle* (Istanbul, 1999).

— *Noi documente turceşti privind Ţările Române şi Înalta Poartă (1526–1602)* (Brăila, 2008).

Mazziotti, I., *Immigrazioni albanesi in Calabria nel XV secolo e la colonia di San Demetrio Corone (1471–1815)* (Castrovillari, 2004).

Meier, A., 'The Charities of a Grand Vizier; Towards a Comparative Approach to Koca Sinân Pasha's Endowment Deeds (989–1004/1581–1596)', *Turcica*, 43 (2011), 309–43.

Ménage, V. L., 'Devshirme', in *EI2*.

Merkle, S., *et al.*, eds., *Concilium tridentinum: diariorum, actorum, epistularum, tractatuum nova collectio*, 10 vols. (Freiburg im Breisgau, 1901–80).

Mesrobeanu, A., 'Rolul politic al Movileştilor până la domnia lui Ieremia Vodă', *Cercetări istorice: buletinul seminarului de istoria Românilor al Universitaţii din Iaşi*, 1 (1925), 177–89.

— 'Nuovi contributi sul Vaivoda Gaspare Graziani e la guerra turco-polacca del 1621', in Şcoala Română din Roma, *Diplomatarium italicum: documenti raccolti negli archivi italiani*, 4 vols. (Rome, 1925–39), iii (1934), 126–239.

Michel, N., 'Chronologie', *Turcica*, 43 (2011), 261–2.

— 'Les *waqf*-s d'un homme d'état ottoman dans la seconde moitié du XVIe siècle: essai de synthèse', *Turcica*, 43 (2011), 269–308.

Mikov, L., *Izkustvoto na heterodoksnite miusiulmani v Bŭlgariia (XVI–XX vek): Bektaši i Kŭzŭlbaši/Alevii* (Sofia, 2005).

Milošević, M., 'Boka Kotorska, Bar i Ulcinj u kiparskom ratu (1570–1573)', *Boka: zbornik radova iz nauke kulture i umjetnosti*, 4 (1972), 17–32.

— *Boka Kotorska, Bar i Ulcinj od kraja XV do kraja XVIII vijeka* (Podgorica, 2008).

Minadoi, G. T., *The History of the Warres betweene the Turkes and the Persians*, tr. A. Hartwell (London, 1595).

Miović, V., *Dubrovačka diplomacija u Istambulu* (Zagreb, 2003).

— *Dubrovačka republika u spisima Osmanskih sultana* (Dubrovnik, 2005).

Molino, A. ['Manoli Blessi'], *Barzeletta de quattro compagni strathiotti de Albania, zuradi di andar per il mondo alla ventura* (Venice, 1570).

— *I fatti, e le prodezze di Manoli Blessi strathioto* (Venice, 1571).

— *Manoli Blessi sopra la presa de Margaritin, con un dialogo piaceuole di un Greco, & di un Fachino* (Venice, 1571).

— *Il vero successo della presa di Nicosia in Cipro* (Venice, 1572).

Mollat, M., 'Istanbul à la rencontre de la Mer Noire et de la Méditerranée', in H. Ahrweiler *et al.*, *Istanbul à la jonction des cultures balkaniques, méditerranéennes, slaves et orientales, aux XVIe–XIXe siècles* (Bucharest, 1977), 151–68.

Molmenti, P., *Sebastiano Veniero e la battaglia di Lepanto* (Florence, 1899).

— 'Sebastiano Veniero dopo la battaglia di Lepanto', *Nuovo archivio veneto*, n.s., 59 (1915), 5–146.

Monga, L., ed. and tr., *The Journal of Aurelio Scetti, a Florentine Galley Slave at Lepanto (1565–1577)* (Tempe, AZ, 2004).

de Montaigne, M., *Journal de voyage de Michel de Montaigne en Italie, par la Suisse & l'Allemagne en 1580 & 1581*, ed. [A. G. Meusnier] de Querlon, 3 vols. (Rome, 1774).

Moosa, M., *Extremist Shiites: The Ghulat Sects* (Syracuse, NY, 1988).

del Moral, J. M., *El virrey de Nápoles don Pedro de Toledo y la guerra contra el Turco* (Madrid, 1966).

Moretti, S., 'Gli albanesi a Venezia tra XIV e XVI secolo', in D. Calabi and P. Lanaro, eds., *La città italiana e i luoghi degli stranieri, XIV–XVIII secolo* (Rome, 1998), 5–20.

Mori Ubaldini, M., *La marina del sovrano militare ordine di San Giovanni di Gerusalemme di Rodi e di Malta* (Rome, 1971).

Morosini ['Maurocenus'], A., *Historia veneta ab anno M.D.XXI. usque ad annum M.DC.XV in quinque partes tributa* (Venice, 1623).

Morris, J., *The Venetian Empire: A Sea Voyage* (London, 1980).

da Mosto, A., 'Ordinamenti militari delle soldatesche dello stato romano nel secolo XVI', *Quellen und Forschungen aus italienischen Archiven und Bibliotheken*, 6 (1904), 72–133.

— *L'Archivio di Stato di Venezia: indice generale, storico, descrittivo ed analitico*, 2 vols. (Rome, 1937).

Moulierac-Lamoureux, R.-L., 'Le Comtat Venaissin pontifical: contribution à une histoire des institutions (1229–1791)', Université de Montpellier 1 thesis (1976).

Müller, R. C., *Franken im Osten: Art, Umfang, Struktur und Dynamik der Migration aus dem lateinischen Westen in das Osmanische Reich des 15./16. Jahrhunderts auf der Grundlage von Reiseberichten* (Leipzig, 2005).

— *Prosopographie der Reisenden und Migranten ins Osmanische Reich (1396–1611) (Berichterstatter aus dem Heiligen Römischen Reich, ausser burgundische Gebiete und Reichsromania)*, 10 vols. (Leipzig, 2006).

Mureşan, D. I., 'L'Émergence du sacre princier dans les Pays Roumains et son modèle impérial byzantin (XVᵉ–XVIᵉ siècles)', in M. Koumanoudi and C. Maltezou, eds., *Dopo le due cadute di Costantinopoli (1204, 1453): eredi ideologici di Bisanzio* (Venice, 2008), 57–126.

Murphey, R., 'Provisioning Istanbul: The State and Subsistence in the Early Modern Middle East', *Food & Foodways*, 2 (1988), 217–63.

— *Ottoman Warfare, 1500–1700* (London, 1999).

— 'Ottoman Imperial Identity in the Post-foundation Era: Coming to Terms with the Multiculturalism associated with the Empire's Growth and Expansion, 1450–1650', *AO*, 26 (2009), 83–108.

Murphy, P. V., 'Jesuit Rome and Italy', in T. Worcester, ed., *The Cambridge Companion to the Jesuits* (Cambridge, 2008), 71–87.

Muscat, J., 'Lepanto – One of the Greatest Naval Battles', in G. Cassar, ed., *From the Great Siege to the Battle of Lepanto* (n.p. [Valletta?], 2011), 99–166.

Mutafčieva ['Moutafchieva'], *Agrarian Relations in the Ottoman Empire in the 15th and 16th Centuries* (Boulder, CO, 1988).

Muzio, G., *Selva odorifera* (Venice, 1572).

Naldini, P., *Corografia ecclesiastica ò sia descrittione della città, e della diocesi di Giustinopoli detto volgarmente Capo d'Istria* (Venice, 1700).

Năsturel, P. Ş., 'Petru Vodă Şchiopul cel Milostiv şi mănăstirea Patmosului', in V. Barbu, ed., *In honorem Paul Cernovodeanu* (Bucharest, 1998), 117–28.

de Nicolay, N., *Dans l'Empire de Soliman le Magnifique*, ed. M.-C. Gomez-Géraud and S. Yerasimos (Paris, 1989).

Nicolescu, C., *Istoria costumului de curte în Ţările Române: secolele XIV–XVIII* (Bucharest, 1970).

Niederkorn, J. P., *Die europäischen Mächte und der 'Lange Türkenkrieg' Kaiser Rudolfs II (1593–1606)* (Vienna, 1993).

Nilles, N., *Symbolae ad illustrandam historiam ecclesiae orientalis in terris coronae S. Stephani*, 2 vols. (Innsbruck, 1885).

Nistor, I., *Handel und Wandel in der Moldau bis zum Ende des 16. Jahrhunderts* (Czernowitz, 1912).

Noflatscher, H., and E. Springer, 'Studien und Quellen zu den Beziehungen zwischen Rudolf II. und den bosnischen Christen', *MÖS*, 36 (1983), 31–82.

Novak, G., ed., *Commissiones et relationes venetae*, iv: *(1571–1590)* (*MSHSM*, xlvii) (Zagreb, 1964).

O'Connell, M., *Men of Empire: Power and Negotiation in Venice's Maritime State* (Baltimore, 2009).

O'Malley, J. W., *Trent: What Happened at the Council* (Cambridge, MA, 2013).

Ostapchuk, V., 'The Human Landscape of the Ottoman Black Sea in the Face of the Cossack Naval Raids', *OM*, n.s., 20 (2001), 23–95.

Özel, O., 'The Reign of Violence: The *celalis* c.1550–1700', in C. Woodhead, ed., *The Ottoman World* (Abingdon, 2012), 184–202.

Özgen, E., 'The Connected World of Intrigues: The Disgrace of Murad III's Favourite David Passi in 1591', *Leidschrift*, 27, no. 1 (April, 2012) (http:// media.leidenuniv.nl/legacy/elif-ozgen-leidschrift.pdf).

Padiglione, C., *Di Giorgio Castriota Scanderbech e de' suoi discendenti, narrazione* (Naples, 1879).

Pagès, J., *La Bataille de Lépante: traduction d'un texte anonyme* (Biarritz, 2011).

Pagkratēs, G. D., *Oi ektheseis tōn venetōn vailōn kai pronoētōn tēs Kerkuras (16os aiōnas)* (Athens, 2008).

Pagnol, J., *Valréas et 'l'enclave des papes' au fil des temps et des hommes depuis l'origine jusqu'à nos jours*, 2nd edn, i (Aubenais-en-Vivarais, 1979).

Palazzuolo, C., *Il soldato di Santa Chiesa* (Rome, 1606).

Palerne, J., *D'Alexandrie à Istanbul: pérégrinations dans l'Empire ottoman, 1581–1583*, ed. Y. Bernard (Paris, 1991).

von Palombini, B., *Bündniswerben abendländischer Mächte um Persien, 1453– 1600* (Wiesbaden, 1968).

Palumbo Fossati Casa, I., 'L'École vénitienne des "giovani di lingua"', in *ILO*, 109–22.

Pamuk, Ş., 'The Re-assessment of the Price Revolution in the Ottoman Empire', in *GOTC*, ii, 111–19.

Panaite, V., 'The Voivodes of the Danubian Principalities – as *harâcgüzarlar* of the Ottoman Sultans', *IJTS*, 9, nos. 1–2 (2003), 59–78.

— 'The *re'ayas* of the Tributary-Protected Principalities: The Sixteenth through Eighteenth Centuries', *IJTS*, 9, nos. 1–2 (2003), 79–104.

— 'From Allegiance to Conquest: Ottomans and Moldo-Wallachians from the Late Fourteenth to mid Sixteenth Centuries', *RESEE*, 48 (2010), 211–31; 49 (2011), 197–212.

— 'The Legal and Political Status of Wallachia and Moldavia in Relation to the Ottoman Porte', in *ETSOE*, 9–42.

Panciera, W., '"Tagliare i confini": la linea di frontiera Soranzo-Ferhat in Dalmazia (1576)', in A. Giuffrida, F. D'Avenia and D. Palermo, eds., *Studi storici dedicati a Orazio Cancila* (Palermo, 2011), 237–72.

Pantera, P., *L'armata navale* (Rome, 1614).

Panzac, D., *La Marine ottomane de l'apogée à la chute de l'Empire* (Paris, 2009).

Paoli ['Pauli'], S., *Codice diplomatico del sacro militare ordine Gerosolimitano oggi di Malta* (Lucca, 1737).

Papiu Ilarian, A., *Tesauru de monumente istorice pentru Romania*, 3 vols. (Bucharest, 1862–4).

Papoulia, B. D., *Ursprung und Wesen der 'Knabenlese' im osmanischen Reich* (Munich, 1963).

Parker, G., *The Grand Strategy of Philip II* (New Haven, CT, 1998).

— *Global Crisis: War, Climate Change, and Catastrophe in the Seventeenth Century* (New Haven, CT, 2013).

— and I. A. A. Thompson, 'The Battle of Lepanto, 1571: The Costs of Victory', *The Mariner's Mirror*, 64 (1978), 13–21.

Parrott, D., *The Business of War: Military Enterprise and Military Revolution in Early Modern Europe* (Cambridge, 2012).

Passerini, L., 'Malatesta da Rimini', in P. Litta, *Famiglie celebri italiane*, fasc. 162 (Milan, 1870), part 3.

Pastore, R., 'Costantino Castriota', in *DBI*, xxii, 219–21.

Patrizi, F., *Paralleli militari*, 2 vols. (Rome, 1594–5).

— *Lettere ed opuscoli inediti*, ed. D. Aguzzi Barbagli (Florence, 1975).

— ['Petrić'], *Izabrani politički spisi*, ed. Lj. Schiffler (Zagreb, 1998).

Păun, R. G., 'Enemies Within: Networks of Influence and the Military Revolts against the Ottoman Power (Moldavia and Wallachia, Sixteenth–Seventeenth Centuries)', in *ETSOE*, 209–49.

Pazzi, P., *I cavalieri di San Marco: storia documentata* (Perast, 2008).

Peçevi, İ ['I. Pečevija'], *Historija*, tr. F. Nametak, 2 vols. (Sarajevo, 2000).

Pedani, M. P., *In nome del Gran Signore: inviati ottomani a Venezia dalla caduta di Costantinopoli alla guerra di Candia* (Venice, 1994).

— ['Pedani-Fabris'], ed., *Relazioni di ambasciatori veneti al Senato*, xiv: *Costantinopoli: relazioni inedite (1512–1789)* (Padua, 1996).

— 'Safiye's Household and Venetian Diplomacy', *Turcica*, 32 (2000), 9–32.

— *Dalla frontiera al confine*, QSA, Studi e testi, v (Venice, 2002).

— 'Some Remarks upon the Ottoman Geo-Political Vision of the Mediterranean in the Period of the Cyprus War (1570–1573)', in C. Imber, K. Kiyotaki and R. Murphey, eds., *Frontiers of Ottoman Studies: State, Province, and the West*, 2 vols. (London, 2004–5), ii, 23–35.

— 'Sultans and Voivodas in the 16th C.: Gifts and Insignia', *Uluslararası sosyal araştırmalar dergisi: The Journal of International Social Research*, 1 (2007), 193–209.

— *Venezia, porta d'Oriente* (Bologna, 2010).

— ['Pedani Fabris'] and A. Bombaci, *I 'documenti turchi' dell'Archivio di Stato di Venezia* (Rome, 1994).

— *Inventory of the Lettere e scritture turchesche in the Venetian State Archives* (Leiden, 2009).

Pederin, I., 'Die venezianische Verwaltung Dalmatiens und ihre Organe (xv. und xvi. Jahrhundert)', *SV*, n.s., 12 (1986), 99–163.

— *Mletačka uprava, privreda i politika u Dalmaciji (1409–1797)* (Dubrovnik, 1990).

Pernice, A., 'Un episodio di valore toscano nelle guerre di Valacchia alla fine del secolo XVI.', *ASI*, ser. 7, 3 (1925), 249–97.

Perrin, C., *États pontificaux de France au seizième siècle* (Paris, 1847).

Personeni, A., *Notizie genealogiche storiche critiche e letterarie del Cardinale Cinzio Personeni da Ca Passero Aldobrandini nipote di Clemente VIII. S.P.* (Bergamo, 1786).

Pertusi, A., 'Per la storia di Dulcigno nei secoli XIV–XV e dei suoi statuti cittadini', *SV*, 15 (1973), 213–71.

— *Martino Segono di Novo Brdo, Vescovo di Dulcigno: un umanista serbo-dalmata del tardo Quattrocento* (Rome, 1981).

Petrosyan, I., 'The Janissary Corps in the Late 16th and Early 17th Century: The First Attempt at Military Reform in the Ottoman Empire', in *GOTC*, iii, 750–60.

Petrucci, F., 'Pompeo Colonna', in *DBI*, xxvii, 412–14.

Petta, P., *Stradioti: soldati albanesi in Italia (sec. XV–XIX)* (Lecce, 1996).

— *Despoti d'Epiro e principi di Macedonia: esuli albanesi nell'Italia del Rinascimento* (Lecce, 2000).

Pezzolo, L., *L'oro dello stato: società, finanza e fisco nella Repubblica veneta del secondo '500* (Venice, 1990).

Pierling, P., 'Novi izvori o L. Komuloviću', *SJAZU*, 16 (1884), 209–51.

— and F. Rački, 'L. Komulovića izvještaj i listovi o poslanstvu njegovu u Tursku, Erdelj, Moldavsku i Poljsku', *SJAZU*, 14 (1882), 83–124.

Pippidi, A., 'Les Pays danubiens et Lépante', in *MSMCLL*, 289–323.

— *Hommes et idées du Sud-Est européen à l'aube de l'âge moderne* (Bucharest, 1980).

— 'Drogmans et Enfants de langue: la France de Constantinople au XVIIe siècle', in *ILO*, 131–50.

— *Tradiţia politică bizantină în Ţările Române în secolele XVI–XVIII*, 2nd edn (Bucharest, 2001).

— *Byzantins, Ottomans, Roumains: le Sud-Est européen entre l'héritage impérial et les influences occidentales* (Paris, 2006).

— 'Cazacii navigatori, Moldova şi Marea Neagră la începutul secolului al XVII-lea', in O. Cristea, ed., *Marea Neagră. Puteri maritime, puteri terestre (sec.XIII–XVIII)* (Bucharest, 2006), 260–82.

— 'Tre antiche casate dell'Istria, esempi per lo sviluppo di un gruppo professionale: i dragomanni di Venezia presso la Porta', *QCRV*, 4 (2006), 61–76.

— *Visions of the Ottoman World in Renaissance Europe* (London, 2013).

Pittioni, M., *Korrespondenz mit dem Sultanshof: Dokumente genuesischer Gesandter des 16. Jahrhunderts* (Vienna, 2010).

Pllumi, Z., 'Pak histori mbi Shejtnoren e Shna Ndout në Sebaste-Laç' (http://www.forumikatolik.net/archive/index.php/t-13390.html).

Podea, I. I., 'A Contribution to the Study of Queen Elizabeth's Eastern Policy (1590–1593)', in *Mélanges d'histoire générale publiés par Constantin Marinescu* (Bucharest, 1938), 423–76.

Podhorodecki, L., *Chanat Krymski: państwo koczowników na kresach Europy*, 2nd edn (Warsaw, 2012).

Poggiani, G. ['Pogianus, J.'], *Epistolae, et orationes*, ed. A. M. Graziani ['Gratianus'], 4 vols. (Rome, 1756–62).

Poliakov, L., *Jewish Bankers and the Holy See from the Thirteenth to the Seventeenth Century*, tr. M. Kochan (London, 1977).

Polić Bobić, M., *Medju križom i polumjesecom: dubrovačke dojave španjolskome dvoru o Turcima u XVI. stoljeću* (Zagreb, 2000).

Pollo, S., and A. Buda, eds., *Historia e popullit shqiptar*, 2 vols. (Prishtinë, 1969).

Popescu, A., 'La Mer Noire ottomane: *mare clausum? Mare apertum?*', in *EPEM*, 141–70.

Popović, T., *Turska i Dubrovnik u XVI veku* (Belgrade, 1973).

— ed., *Pisma Bartolomeu Bordjanu (1593–1595)*, Srpska Akademija Nauka i Umetnosti, *Spomenik*, cxxiv (Odeljenje istorijskih nauka, iii) (Belgrade, 1984).

Possevino, A., *Il soldato christiano* (Venice, 1604).

Poullet, E., ed., *Correspondance du Cardinal de Granvelle, 1565–1586*, 12 vols. (Brussels, 1877–96).

Poumarède, G., *Pour en finir avec la Croisade: mythes et réalités de la lutte contre les Turcs aux XVIᵉ et XVIIᵉ siècles* (Paris, 2004).

Pozzi, M., *Filippo Pigafetta consigliere del principe*, 2 vols. (Vicenza, 2004).

dal Pozzo, B., *Historia della sacra religione militare di S. Giovanni gerosolimitano detta di Malta*, 2 vols. (Verona, 1703–15).

— and R. Solaro di Govone, *Ruolo generale de' cavalieri gerosolimitani della Veneranda Lingua d'Italia* (Turin, 1714).

Praga, G., *Storia di Dalmazia*, 3rd edn (Padua, 1954).

Predelli, R., *et al.*, eds., *I libri commemoriali della Repubblica di Venezia: registri*, 8 vols. (Venice, 1867–1914).

Preto, P., *I servizi segreti di Venezia* (Milan, 1994).

— 'La diplomazia segreta di Venezia e Ragusa', in *TDD*, 155–63.

Prifti, K., *et al.*, eds., *Historia e popullit shqiptar*, 4 vols. (Tirana, 2002–9).

de la Primaudaie, É., ed., 'Documents inédits sur l'histoire de l'occupation espagnole en Afrique (1506–1574)', *Revue africaine*, 21 (1877), 361–79.

Procházka-Eisl, G., 'Guild Parades in Ottoman Literature: The *Sûrnâme* of 1582', in S. Faroqhi and R. Deguilhem, eds., *Crafts and Craftsmen of the Middle East: Fashioning the Individual in the Muslim Mediterranean* (London, 2005), 41–54.

Promis, C., 'Biografie di ingegneri militari italiani dal secolo XIV alla metà del XVIII', in *Miscellanea di storia italiana edita per cura della Regia Deputazione di Storia Patria*, xiv (Turin, 1874), 208–388.

Pujeau, E., 'La Préveza (1538) entre idéologie et histoire', *SV*, n.s., 51 (2006), 155–204.

Pulaha, S., 'Krahinat e sanxhakut të Dukagjinit gjatë shekullit XVI', *SH*, 27 (1973), no. 3, 3–51; no. 4, 167–95.

— 'Formation des régions de selfgovernment [*sic*] dans les Malessies du sandjak de Shkodër aux XVᵉ–XVIIᵉ siècles', *Studia albanica*, 13 (1976), no. 2, 173–9.

— *Qëndresa e popullit shqiptar kundër sundimit osman nga shek. XVI deri në fillim të shek. XVIII: dokumente osmane* (Tirana, 1978).

Purchas, S., *Purchas his Pilgrimes in Five Bookes*, 5 vols. (London, 1625).

Puşcariu, S., *Studii istroromâne*, 3 vols. (Bucharest, 1906–29).

Quarantotti Gambini, P. A., 'I nobili di Rovigno e delle altre città istriane', *Archivio veneto*, ser. 5, 82 (1967), 61–85; 83 (1968), 41–101.

de Queiroz Velloso, J. M., *D. Sebastião, 1554–1578* (Lisbon, 1935).

— *O interregno dos governadores e o breve reinado de D. Antoño* (Lisbon, 1953).

Queller, D. E., *The Venetian Patriciate: Reality versus Myth* (Urbana, IL, 1986).

Raça, Sh., *Shtegtimet dhe ngulimet e shqiptarëve në Greqi shek. XIII–XVI* (Prishtinë, 2004).

Rački, F., 'Izvještaj barskoga nadbiskupa Marina Bizzia o svojem putovanju god. 1610 po Arbanaskoj i staroj Srbiji', *SJAZU*, 20 (1880), 50–156.

Radojčić, S., *Mileševa* (Belgrade, 1963).

Radonić, J., ed., *Dubrovačka akta i povelje*, ii, part 2 (Belgrade, 1938).

Radossi, G., with S. Žitko, *Monumenta heraldica iustinopolitana: stemmi di rettori, di famiglie notabili, di vescovi e della città di Capodistria* (Rovigno, 2003).

Rainer, J., H. Noflatscher and C. Rainer, eds., *Nuntiatur des Girolamo Portia und Korrespondenz des Hans Kobenzl, 1592–1595 (Grazer Nuntiatur*, iii) (Vienna, 2001).

Randa, A., *Pro republica christiana: die Walachei im 'langen' Türkenkrieg der katholischen Universalmächte (1593–1606)* (Munich, 1964).

Rangoni Machiavelli, L., 'L'Ordine di Malta', in Paolo Cherubelli, ed., *Il contributo degli ordini religiosi al Concilio di Trento* (Florence, 1946), 361–78.

Raukar, T., 'La Dalmazia e Venezia nel basso medioevo', in *VED*, 63–87.

— et al., *Zadar pod mletačkom upravom* (Zadar, 1987).

Rawlinson, H. G., 'The Embassy of William Harborne to Constantinople, 1583–8', *Transactions of the Royal Historical Society*, ser. 4, 5 (1922), 1–28.

Razzi, S., *La storia di Raugia* (Lucca, 1595).

Reindl-Kiel, H., 'Power and Submission: Gifting at Royal Circumcision Festivals in the Ottoman Empire (16th–18th Centuries)', *Turcica*, 41 (2009), 37–88.

Reinhard, W., *Die Reform in der Diözese Carpentras unter den Bischöfen Jacopo Sadoleto, Paolo Sadoleto, Jacopo Sacrati und Francesco Sadoleto, 1517–1596* (Münster, 1966).

Reusner, N., *Operis collectanei epistolarum turcicarum liber XII. XIII. & XIV.* (Frankfurt am Main, 1600) [the 3rd supplementary volume to his *Epistolarum turcicarum variorum et diversorum authorum libri V* (Frankfurt am Main, 1598)].

Rheubottom, D., *Age, Marriage, and Politics in Fifteenth-Century Ragusa* (Oxford, 2000).

Ritig, S., 'Primacijalni naslov splitske i barske metropolije', *Bogoslovska smotra*, 11 (1923), 89–95.

Rivero Rodríguez, M., *La batalla de Lepanto: cruzada, guerra santa e identidad confesional* (Madrid, 2008).

Rodgers, W. L., *Naval Warfare under Oars, 4th to 16th Centuries: A Study of Strategy, Tactics and Ship Design* (Annapolis, MD, 1939).

Rodríguez Salgado, M. J., *Felipe II, el 'Paladín de la Cristianidad' y la paz con el Turco* (Valladolid, 2004).

Rosaccio, G., *Viaggio da Venetia, a Costantinopoli per mare, e per terra, & insieme quello di Terra Santa* (Venice, 1598).

Rosi, M., 'Alcuni documenti relativi alla liberazione dei principali prigionieri turchi presi a Lepanto', *ARSRSP*, 21 (1898), 141–220.

— 'Nuovi documenti relativi alla liberazione dei principali prigionieri turchi presi a Lepanto', *ARSRSP*, 24 (1901), 5–47.

Rothenberg, G., *The Austrian Military Border in Croatia, 1522–1747* (Urbana, IL, 1960).

Rothman, E.-N., 'Between Venice and Istanbul: Trans-Imperial Subjects and Cultural Mediation in the Early Modern Mediterranean', University of Michigan PhD thesis (2006).

— ['E. N.',] 'Interpreting Dragomans: Boundaries and Crossings in the Early Modern Mediterranean', *Comparative Studies in Society and History*, 51 (2009), 771–800.

Rudt de Collenberg, W. H., *Esclavage et rançons des chrétiens en Méditerranée (1570–1600)* (Paris, 1987).

Rybarski, R., *Handel i polityka handlowa Polski w XVI stuleciu*, 2 vols. (Warsaw, 1958).

Sahillioğlu, H., ed., *Koca Sinan Paşa'nın telhisleri* (Istanbul, 2004).

Salerno, M., *L'Ordine di Malta in Calabria e la commenda di San Giovanni Gerosolimitano di Cosenza (secc. XII–XVI)* (Cosenza, 2010).

Salimei, A., *Gli italiani a Lepanto, 7 ottobre 1571* (Rome, 1931).

Salimei, F., 'La nobiltà pontificia alla battaglia di Lepanto', *Revista araldica*, 70 (1972), 13–16.

Salinerio, G. ['I. Salinerius'], *Annotationes Iulii Salinerii iureconsul. savonensis ad Cornelium Tacitum* (Genoa, 1602).

Samardžić, R., *Mehmed Sokolović*, 2nd edn (Belgrade, 1975).

Sanderson, J.: *see* Foster.

da Sanseverino, R., *Viaggio in Terra Santa*, ed. G. Maruffi (Bologna, 1888).

Santorio, S., *La medicina statica*, ed. G. Ongaro (Florence, 2001).

Sanuto [Sanudo], M., *I diarii*, ed. R. Fulin *et al.*, 58 vols. (Venice, 1879–1903).

Sardella, P., *Nouvelles et spéculations à Venise au début du XVIe siècle* (Paris, n.d. [c.1947]).

Sariyannis, M., 'Ottoman Critics of Society and State, Fifteenth to Early Eighteenth Centuries: Toward a Corpus for the Study of Ottoman Political Thought', *AO*, 26 (2009), 127–50.

von Saurau, M., *Orttenliche Beschreybung der Rayss gehen Constantinopel, mit der Pottschaft von Kaysser maxmillian dem anderen in die dürgkey abgeferdigt, anno im 15:67*, ed. K. Wickert (Erlangen, 1987).

Scetti, A.: *see* Monga.

Schmidt, J., 'The Egri Campaign of 1596: Military History and the Problem of Sources', in *HOB*, 125–44.

— *Catalogue of Turkish Manuscripts in the Library of Leiden University and Other Collections in the Netherlands*, 4 vols. (Leiden, 2000–12).

Schmidt, P., *Das Collegium Germanicum in Rom und die Germaniker* (Tübingen, 1984).

Schmitt, O. J., *Das venezianische Albanien (1392–1479)* (Munich, 2001).

— *Skanderbeg: der neue Alexander auf dem Balkan* (Regensburg, 2009).

— *Südosteuropa und die Adria im späten Mittelalter* (Bucharest, 2012).

— 'Storie d'amore, storie di potere: la tormentata integrazione dell'isola di Curzola nello Stato da mar in una prospettiva microstorica', in *VED*, 89–109.

Scholem, G., *Sabbatai Ṣevi: The Mystical Messiah, 1626–1676* (London, 1973).

Schutte, A. J., *Pier Paolo Vergerio: The Making of an Italian Reformer* (Geneva, 1977).

Schweigger, S., *Ein newe Reyssbeschreibung auss Teutschland nach Constantinopel und Jerusalem*, ed. R. Neck (Graz, 1964).

Seidel, F., *Denckwürdige Gesandtschafft an die Ottomanische Pforte* (Görlitz, 1711).

Sękowski, J. J. S., ed., *Collectanea z dziejopisów tureckich: rzeczy do historyi polskiey służących*, 2 vols. (Warsaw, 1824–5).

Selaniki Mustafa Efendi, *Tarih-i Selaniki*, ed. M. İpşirli, 2 vols. (Istanbul, 1989).

Seneca, F., *Il Doge Leonardo Donà: la sua vita e la sua preparazione politica prima del dogado* (Padua, 1959).

Seng, Y., 'A Liminal State: Slavery in Sixteenth-Century Istanbul', in S. E. Marmon, ed., *Slavery in the Islamic Middle East* (Princeton, NJ, 1999), 25–42.

Séraphin-Vincent, D., 'Du drogman barataire au drogman français (1669–1793): contexte et application de la réforme de Colbert', in *ILO*, 141–52.

Serassi, P., *La vita di Torquato Tasso*, 2nd edn, 2 vols. (Bergamo, 1790).

Sereno, B., *Commentari della guerra di Cipro e della lega dei principi cristiani contro il Turco* (Montecassino, 1845).

Šerović, P. S., 'Paštrovići, njihovo plemensko uredjenje i pomorska tradicija', *Godišnjak pomorskog muzeja u Kotoru*, 5 (1956), 25–37.

Serrano, L., ed., *Correspondencia diplomatica entre España y la Santa Sede durante el pontificado de S. Pio V.*, 4 vols. (Madrid, 1914).

— *La liga de Lepanto entre España, Venecia y la Santa Sede (1570–1573): ensayo historico a base de documentos diplomaticos*, 2 vols. (Madrid, 1918–20).

Setton, K. M., *The Papacy and the Levant (1204–1571)*, iii: *The Sixteenth Century to the Reign of Julius III* (Philadelphia, 1984).

— *The Papacy and the Levant (1204–1571)*, iv: *The Sixteenth Century from Julius III to Pius V* (Philadelphia, 1984).

Sferra, D., *et al.*, *L'Albania veneta: la Serenissima e le sue popolazioni nel cuore dei Balcani* (Milan, 2012).

Sforza, G., 'Un libro sfortunato contro i Turchi (documenti inediti)', in C. Cipolla *et al.*, *Scritti storici in memoria di Giovanni Monticolo* (Venice, 1922), 207–19.

Shaw, S., and E. K. Shaw, *History of the Ottoman Empire and Modern Turkey*, 2 vols. (Cambridge, 1976–7).

Shmurlo, E., *Rossiia i Italiia: sbornik istoricheskikh materialov i izsledovanii, kasaiushchikhsia snoshenii Rossii s Italiei*, 4 vols. (St Petersburg, 1907–27).

Simon, B., 'Contribution à l'étude du commerce dans l'Empire Ottoman au milieu du XVIᵉ siècle (1558–1560)', *Mélanges de l'École Française de Rome, moyenâge, temps moderne*, 96 (1984), 973–1020.

— 'Les Dépêches de Marin Cavalli Bayle à Constantinople, 1558–1560', École Pratique des Hautes Études, Paris, thesis, 3 vols. (1985).

Šimunković, Lj., 'La politica linguistica della Serenissima verso i possedimenti "di là da mar": il caso della Dalmazia', in S. Graciotti, ed., *Mito e antimito di Venezia nel bacino adriatico (secoli XV–XIX)* (Rome, 2001), 95–104.

Sirdani, M., 'Per historín kombëtare: "Dulcigno secondo l'antica descrizione"', *Hylli i dritës*, 12 (1936), nos. 5, 227–34; 6, 294–9; 7–8, 343–50.

Sire, H. J. A., *The Knights of Malta* (New Haven, CT, 1994).

Skilliter, S. A., 'The Turkish Documents relating to Edward Barton's Embassy to the Porte (1588–1598)', University of Manchester PhD thesis (1965).

— 'The Hispano-Ottoman Armistice of 1581', in C. E. Bosworth, ed., *Iran and Islam: In Memory of the Late Vladimir Minorsky* (Edinburgh, 1971), 491–515.

— *William Harborne and the Trade with Turkey, 1578–1582: A Documentary Study of the First Anglo-Ottoman Relations* (London, 1977).

— 'An Ambassador's *ta'yin*: Edward Barton's Ration on the Eğri Campaign, 1596', *Turcica*, 25 (1993), 153–63.

Smith, C. K., *Lightning over Yemen: A History of the Ottoman Campaign (1569–71), being a Translation from the Arabic of Part III of al-Barq al-Yamani fi al-Fath al-'Uthmani* (London, 2002).

Smith, J., *The Generall Historie of Virginia, New England & the Summer Isles, together with the True Travels, Adventures and Observations, and a Sea Grammar*, 2 vols. (Glasgow, 1907).

Šmitran, S., *Gli uscocchi: pirati, ribelli, guerrieri tra gli imperi ottomano e asburgico e la Repubblica di Venezia* (Venice, 2008).

Snŭgarov, I., *Istorija na ohridskata arhiepiskopija-patriaršija ot padaneto i pod Turčitŭ do neinoto uništoženie (1394–1767 g.)* (Sofia, 1932).

Sohrweide, H., 'Der Sieg der Safaviden in Persien und seine Rückwirkungen auf die Schiiten Anatoliens im 16. Jahrhundert', *Der Islam: Zeitschrift für Geschichte und Kultur des islamischen Orients*, 41 (1965), 95–223.

Sokołowski ['Socolovius'], S., ed. and tr., *Censura orientalis ecclesiae* (Kraków, 1582).

Sola, E., 'La frontera mediterránea y la información: claves para el conocimiento del turco a mediados del siglo XVI', in A. Servantie and R. Puig de la Bellacasa, eds., *L'Empire ottoman dans l'Europe de la Renaissance* (Leuven, 2005), 297–316.

— *Los que van y vienen: información y fronteras en el Mediterráneo clásico del siglo XVI* (Alcalá de Heneres, 2005).

— ['Sola Castaño',] *Uchalí: el Calabrés Tiñoso, o el mito del corsario muladí en la frontera* (Barcelona, 2010).

— and J. F. de la Peña, *Cervantes y la Berbería: Cervantes, mundo turco-berberisco y servicios secretos en la epóca de Felipe II* (Mexico City, 1995).

Šopova, D., ed. and tr., *Makedonija vo XVI i XVII vek: dokumenti od Carigradskite arhivi (1557–1645)* (Skopje, 1955).

Soranzo, L., *Carmen pythium Lazari Superantij Benedicti f. ad illustriss. equitem Ioannem Superantium, Brixiae praetorem, patruumq. amplissimum* (Venice, 1578).

— *Oratione del Sig. Lazaro Soranzo ad Henrico Quarto christianissimo rè di Francia e di Nauarra, nell'assolutione data à Sua Maestà da Clemente VIII. Sommo Pontefice* (Bergamo, 1596).

— *L'Ottomanno* (Ferrara, 1598).

— *Ottomanus, sive de rebus Turcicis*, tr. J. Geuder von Heroltzberg (Hanau, 1600).

— *Ottomanus: von Zustand, Macht und Gewalt . . . des Ottomannischen Türckischen Reichs*, tr. C. Cresse (Magdeburg, 1601).

— et al., *Turca nikētos, hoc est, de Imperio Ottomannico evertendo, et bello contra Turcas prospere gerendo consilia tria*, tr. J. Geuder von Heroltzberg (Frankfurt, 1601).

— *The Ottoman of Lazaro Soranzo*, tr. A. Hartwell (London, 1603).

Spissarevska, I. D., 'Alcuni problemi del traffico marittimo tra la costa bulgara del Mar Nero ed i porti mediterranei nella seconda metà del XVI secolo', in *LGMM*, ii, 715–24.

Springer, E., 'Kaiser Rudolf II., Papst Clemens VIII. und die bosnischen Christen: Taten und Untaten des Cavaliere Francesco Antonio Bertucci in kaiserlichen Diensten in den Jahren 1594 bis 1602', *MÖS*, 33 (1980), 77–105.

Stancovich, P., *Biografia degli uomini distinti dell'Istria*, 2nd edn (Koper, 1888).

Stanojević, G., 'Naseljavanje Istre u XVII vijeku s osvrtom na iseljavanje iz Crne Gore i crnogorskog primorja', *IZ*, year 18, vol. 22 (1965), 429–67.

— *Jugoslovenske zemlje u mletačko-turskim ratovima XVI–XVIII vijeka* (Belgrade, 1970).

Stefani, F., ed., 'Viaggio a Costantinopoli di Sier Lorenzo Bernardo per l'arresto del bailo Sier Girolamo Lippomano Cav. 1591 aprile', in R. Deputazione Veneta sopra gli Studi di Storia Patria, *Miscellanea*, 4 (Venice, 1887), 1st pagination, 1–47.

Steinhuber, A., *Geschichte des Collegium Germanicum Hungaricum in Rom*, 2 vols. (Freiburg im Breisgau, 1895).

Stella, Aldo, 'Lepanto nella storia e nella storiografia alla luce di nuovi documenti', *SV*, n.s., 51 (2006), 205–78.

Stella, Alessandro, *Histoires d'esclaves dans la péninsule ibérique* (Paris, 2000).

Stoicescu, N., *Dicţionar al marilor dregători din Ţara Românească şi Moldova, sec. XIV–XVII* (Bucharest, 1971).

Stoy, M., 'Das Wirken Gaspar Gracianis (Graţianis) bis zu seiner Ernennung zum Fürsten der Moldau am 4. Februar 1619', *SF*, 43 (1984), 49–122.

von Šufflay, M., 'Die Kirchenzustände im vortürkischen Albanien: die orthodoxe Durchbruchszone im katholischen Damme', in L. von Thallóczy, ed., *Illyrisch-albanische Forschungen*, 2 vols. (Munich, 1916), i, 188–281.

— 'Povijest sjevernih Arbanasa (sociološka študija)', *Arhiv za arbanasku starinu, jezik i etnologiju*, 2, for 1924 (1925), 193–242.

— ['Shuflaj'], *Qytetet dhe kështjellat e Shqipërisë, kryesisht në mesjetë*, tr. L. Malltezi (Tirana, 2009).

Sugar, P. F., 'The Ottoman "Professional Prisoner" on the Western Borders of the Empire in the Sixteenth and Seventeenth Centuries', *Études balkaniques*, 7, no. 2 (1971), 82–91.

Šundrica, Z., *Tajna kutija dubrovačkog arhiva*, 2 vols. (Zagreb, 2008–9).

Šusta, J., ed., *Die römische Kurie und das Konzil von Trient unter Pius IV: Akten-stücke zur Geschichte des Konzils von Trient*, 4 vols. (Vienna, 1904–14).

Szakály, F., 'Grenzverletzer: zur Geschichte der protestantischen Mission in Osteuropa', in *ETR*, 283–306.

Tabak, F., *The Waning of the Mediterranean, 1550–1870: A Geohistorical Approach* (Baltimore, 2008).

Tacchella, L., and M. M. Tacchella, *Il Cardinale Agostino Valier e la riforma tridentina nella diocesi di Trieste* (Udine, 1974).

Tadić, J., *Španja i Dubrovnik u XVI v.*, Srpska Kraljevska Akademija, posebna izdanja, xciii; društveni i istoriski spisi, xli (Belgrade, 1932).

— *Dubrovački portreti* (Belgrade, 1948).

Talbot, C. H., ed., *Elementa ad fontium editiones IV: res polonicae Elisabetha I Angliae regnante conscriptae ex archivis publicis Londoniarum* (Rome, 1961).

Tallett, F., *War and Society in Early-Modern Europe, 1495–1715* (London, 1992).

Tamaro, A., *Storia di Trieste*, 2nd edn, 2 vols. (Trieste, 1976).

et-Tamgrouti, Abou-l-Hasan Ali ben Mohammed, *En-nafhat el-miskiya fi-s-sifarat et-tourkiya. Relation d'une ambassade marocaine en Turquie, 1589–1591*, ed. and tr. H. de Castries (Paris, 1929).

Tappe, E. D., ed., *Documents concerning Rumanian History (1427–1601) collected from British Archives* (The Hague, 1964).

Tarducci, A., *Il Turco vincibile in Ungaria, con mediocri aiuti di Germania* (Ferrara, 1597).

Tasso, T., *Gerusalemme liberata* (Casalmaggiore, 1581).

Tenenti, A., *Cristoforo da Canal: la marine vénitienne avant Lépante* (Paris, 1962).

— *Piracy & the Decline of Venice, 1580–1615*, tr. B. Pullan and J. Pullan (London, 1967).

Testa, C., *Romegas* (Santa Venera, 2002).

Testa, L., 'Dalla fondazione alla visita apostolica sotto Clemente XIV (1565–1772)', in L. Mezzadri, ed., *Il Seminario Romano: storia di un'istituzione di cultura e di pietà* (Cinisello Balsamo, 2001), 15–65.

— *Fondazione e primo sviluppo del Seminario Romano (1565–1608)* (Rome, 2002).

de Teule, E., *Chronologie des docteurs en droit civil de l'Université d'Avignon (1303–1791)* (Paris, 1887).

Tezcan, B., *The Second Ottoman Empire: Political and Social Transformation in the Early Modern World* (Cambridge, 2010).

Theiner, A., ed., *Annales ecclesiastici*, 3 vols. (Rome, 1856).

— ed., *Vetera monumenta Poloniae et Lithuaniae gentiumque finitimarum historiam illustrantia*, 4 vols. (Rome, 1860–4).

Thëngjilli, P., *Renta feudale dhe evoluimi i saj në vise shqiptare (shek. XVII – mesi i shek. XVIII)* (Tirana, 1990).

— *Shqiptarët midis Lindjes dhe Perëndimit*, 2 vols. (Tirana, 2002–6).

Theunissen, H., 'Ottoman–Venetian Diplomatics: The 'Ahd-names. The Historical Background and the Development of a Category of Political-Commercial Instruments together with an Annotated Edition of a Corpus of Relevant Documents', University of Utrecht PhD thesis (1991).

de Thou ['Thuanus'], J.-A., *Historiarum sui temporis ... libri CXXXVIII*, 7 vols. (London, 1733).

Tomić, J. N., *Gradja za istoriju pokreta na Balkanu protiv Turaka krajem XVI. i početkom XVII. veka* (Belgrade, 1933).

de Torres y Aguilera, G. ['H.'], *Chronica, y recopilacion de varios successos de guerra que ha acontescido en Italia y partes de Levante y Berberia* (Saragossa, 1579).

Trisco, R., 'Carlo Borromeo and the Council of Trent: The Question of Reform', in J. M. Headley and J. B. Tomaro, eds., *San Carlo Borromeo: Catholic Reform and Ecclesiastical Politics in the Second Half of the Sixteenth Century* (Washington, DC, 1988), 47–66.

Truhelka, Ć., 'Über die Balkan-Yürüken', *Revue internationale des études balkaniques*, 1 (1934), 89–99.

Tucci, U., 'Marinai e galeotti nel Cinquecento veneziano', in *LGMM*, ii, 677–92.

Tudoran, P., *Domnii trecătoare – domnitori uitaţi* (Timişoara, 1983).

Uluç, L., 'Vezir-i Azam Sinan Paşa'dan gelen kitabdır – sene 999', in Z. Y. Yaman and S. Bağcı, eds., *Gelenek, kimlik, bireşim: kültürel kesişmeler ve sanat; Günsel Renda'ya armağan / Tradition, Identity, Synthesis: Cultural Crossings and Art; in Honor of Günsel Renda* (Ankara, 2011), 245–53.

Uluçay, Ç., 'Yavuz Sultan Selim nasıl padişah oldu?', *Tarih dergisi*, 6 (1954), no. 9, 53–90.

Ureche, G., *Letopiseţul Ţării Moldovei*, ed. P. P. Pănăitescu (Bucharest, 1955).

Ursu, J., *La Politique orientale de François Ier (1515–1547)* (Paris, 1908).

Ushaku, R., *Ulqini në gjurmët e shekujve* (Ulcinj, 1991).

— *Ulqini në përmasa kërkimi dhe frymëzimi* (Ulcinj, 2010).

Valdera, M. A., *Epistole d'Ovidio di nuovo tradotte in ottava rima da Marc'Antonio Valdera medico fisico* (Venice, 1604).

Valente, G., *Il Sovrano Militare Ordine di Malta e la Calabria* (Reggio Calabria, 1996).

Valentianus, C., *Panegyricus funebris habitus in exequiis illustrissimi & reverendissimi D. Dominici de Grimaldis in avenionensi legatione prolegati, & eiusdem civitatis Archiepiscopi religiosissimi* (Avignon, 1592).

Valentini, G., 'Perpjekje per lirim të Shqipnís 1593–1621: documenta de liberatione Albaniae a jugo Turcarum', *Leka: revistë muejore kulturale*, 10, no. 6 (June 1937), 251–5.

— ['J.'], ed., *Acta Albaniae veneta saeculorum XIV et XV*, 25 vols. (Munich, Palermo, Milan, 1967–75).

— 'L'elemento *vlah* nella zona scutarina nel sec. XV', in *SUH*, 269–74.

Vanino, M., *Isusovci i hrvatski narod*, 2 vols. (Zagreb, 1969–87).

Vargas-Hidalgo, R., *La batalla de Lepanto según cartas inéditas de Felipe II, Don Juan de Austria y Juan Andrea Doria e informes de embajadores y espías* (Santiago, 1998).

Vatin, N., *L'Ordre de Saint-Jean-de-Jérusalem, l'Empire ottoman et la Méditerranée orientale entre les deux sièges de Rhodes, 1480–1522* (Louvain, 1994).

— 'Une affaire interne: le sort et la libération des personnes de condition libre illégalement retenues en esclavage sur le territoire ottoman (XVIᵉ siècle)', *Turcica*, 33 (2001), 149–90.

— 'L'Empire Ottoman et la piraterie en 1559–1560', in E. Zachariadou, ed., *The Kapudan Pasha: His Office and his Domain* (Rethymnon, 2002), 371–408.

Vatova, G., *La colonna di Santa Giustina eretta dai capodistriani ad onore del loro podestà Andrea Giustinian ed a ricordo della vittoria di Lepanto* (Capodistria, 1884).

Veinstein, G., 'Un achat français de blé dans l'Empire Ottoman au milieu du XVIᵉ siècle', in H. Batu and J.-L. Bacqué-Grammont, eds., *L'Empire Ottoman, la République de Turquie et la France* (Istanbul, 1986), 15–36.

— 'Some Views on Provisioning in the Hungarian Campaigns of Suleyman the Magnificent', in H. G. Maier, ed., *Osmanistische Studien zur Wirtschafts- und Sozialgeschichte: in memoriam Vančo Boškov* (Wiesbaden, 1986), 177–85.

— 'Une communauté ottomane: les Juifs d'Avlonya (Valona) dans la deuxième moitié du XVIᵉ siècle', in G. Cozzi, ed., *Gli Ebrei e Venezia, secoli XIV–XVIII* (Milan, 1987), 781–828.

— 'Marchands ottomans en Pologne-Lituanie et en Moscovie sous le règne de Soliman le Magnifique', *Cahiers du monde russe*, 35 (1994), 713–38.

— 'Avlonya (Vlorë), une étape de la Voie Egnatia dans la seconde moitié du XVIᵉ siècle?', in E. Zachariadou, ed., *The Via Egnatia under Ottoman Rule, 1380–1699* (Rethymnon, 1996), 217–25.

Vekarić, N., *Pelješki rodovi*, 2 vols. (Dubrovnik, 1995–6).

Vella, A. P., *An Elizabethan–Ottoman Conspiracy* ('Malta' [Valletta], 1972).

Venard, M., 'L'Université d'Avignon et la ville au XVIᵉ siècle', in C. Haut *et al.*, *L'Université d'Avignon: naissance et renaissance, 1303–2003* (n.p., 2003), 131–4.

Ventura, A., *Nobiltà e popolo nella società veneta del Quattrocento e Cinquecento*, 2nd edn (Milan, 1993).

Venturini, D., 'La famiglia albanese dei conti Bruti', *AMSIASP*, 20 (1905), 346–419.

Veress, A., ed., *Documente privitoare la istoria Ardealului, Moldoviei și Țării-Românești*, 5 vols. (Bucharest, 1929–32).

de Vertot, R. A., *Histoire des chevaliers hospitaliers de S. Jean de Jérusalem, appellez depuis Chevaliers de Rhodes, et aujourd'hui Chevaliers de Malthe*, 6 vols. (Paris, 1726).

Vida, G., *Il Sileno: dialogo di Hieronimo Vida iustinopolitano, nel quale si discorre della felicità de' mortali … Insieme con le sue rime, & conclusioni amorose* (Vicenza, n.d. [1590]).

— *De' cento dubbi amorosi di Hieronimo Vida iustinopolitano*, ed. A. Vida (Padua, 1621).

Villain-Gandossi, C., 'Contribution à l'étude des relations diplomatiques et commerciales entre Venise et la Porte ottomane au XVIᵉ siècle', *SF*, 26 (1967), 22–45; 28 (1969), 13–47; 29 (1970), 290–301.

— 'Notes sur la terminologie turque de la course', in Commission Internationale d'Histoire Maritime, *Course et piraterie*, 2 vols. (Paris, 1975), i, 137–45.

— '*Giovani di lingua*, drogmans auprès du baile de Venise et la Porte ottomane au XVIᵉ siècle', in G. Buti, M. Janin-Thivos and O. Raveux, eds., *Langues et langages du commerce en Méditerranée et en Europe à l'époque moderne* (Paris, 2013), 33–56.

Villani, P., ed., *Nunziature di Napoli*, i *(1570–1577)* (Rome, 1962).

— and D. Veneruso, eds., *Nunziature di Napoli*, ii *(1577–87)* (Rome, 1969).

Villoslada, R. G., *Storia del Collegio Romano dal suo inizio (1551) alla soppressione della Compagnia di Gesù (1773)*, Analecta gregoriana, lxvi (Rome, 1954).

Vinaver, V. 'Dubrovačko-albanski ekonomski odnosi krajem XVI veka', *Anali Historijskog Instituta u Dubrovniku*, 1 (1952), 207–31.

Viscovich, F., *Storia di Perasto (raccolta di notizie e documenti) dalla caduta della Repubblica Veneta al ritorno degli austriaci* (Trieste, 1898).

Voinovich, L. Graf, 'Depeschen des Francesco Gondola Gesandten der Republik Ragusa bei Pius V. und Gregor XIII. (1570–1573)', *Archiv für österreichische Geschichte*, 98 (1909), 495–653.

Völkl, E., *Das rumänische Fürstentum Moldau und die Ostslaven im 15. bis 17. Jahrhundert* (Wiesbaden, 1975).

Voltaire [F.-M. Arouet], *Collection complette* [sic] *des oeuvres de Mr. de Voltaire*, 17 vols. (n.p. [Geneva], 1756–7).

Vrandečić, J., 'Islam immediately beyond the Dalmatian Coast: The Three Reasons for Venetian Success', in *BOAV*, 287–307.

— 'La Dalmazia nell'età moderna: l'influsso della "rivoluzione militare" sulla società dalmata', in *VED*, 151–63.

Vratislav, V. ['Baron Wenceslas Wratislaw'], *The Adventures of Baron Wenceslas Wratislaw of Mitrowitz*, tr. A. H. Wratislaw (London, 1862).

Waldstein-Wartenberg, B., *Rechtsgeschichte des Malteserordens* (Vienna, 1969).

Weczerka, H., *Das mittelalterliche und frühneuzeitliche Deutschtum im Fürstentum Moldau von seinen Anfängen bis zu seinem Untergang (13.–18. Jahrhundert)* (Munich, 1960).

Werner, E., 'Yürüken und Wlachen', *Wissenschaftliche Zeitschrift der Karl-Marx-Universität Leipzig, Gesellschafts- und Sprachwissenschaftliche Reihe*, 15 (1966), 471–8.

Wettinger, G., *Slavery in the Islands of Malta and Gozo, ca. 1000–1812* (San Gwann, 2002).

White, S., *The Climate of Rebellion in the Early Modern Ottoman Empire* (Cambridge, 2011).

Wild, J., *Reysbeschreibung eines Gefangenen Christen Anno 1604*, ed. G. A. Narciss and K. Teply (Stuttgart, 1964).

Williams, P., *Empire and Holy War in the Mediterranean: The Galley and Maritime Conflict between the Habsburgs and Ottomans* (London, 2014).

Wojtyska, H. D., 'Carlo Borromeo e il Concilio di Trento', *SB*, 3 (1989), 45–63.

Wood, A. C., *A History of the Levant Company* (Oxford, 1935).

— ed., 'Mr. Harrie Cavendish his Journey to and from Constantinople, 1589, by Fox, his Servant', *Camden Miscellany*, xvii (Camden ser. 3, lxiv) (London, 1940), 1–29.

Woodhead, C., ed., *Ta'liki-zade's şehname-i hümayun: A History of the Ottoman Campaign into Hungary, 1593–94* (Berlin, 1983).

— 'Barton, Edward (1562/3–1598), Diplomat', in *ODNB*.

Woolfson, J., *Padua and the Tudors: English Students in Italy, 1485–1603* (Cambridge, 1998).

Woś, J. W., *Annibale di Capua, nunzio apostolico e arcivescovo di Napoli (1544 c. –1595): materiali per una biografia* (Rome, 1984).

Xhufi, P., 'La Population des villes côtières albanaises du XIIᵉ au XVᵉ siècle', *Studia albanica*, 19 (1982), 149–59.

Yerasimos, S., *Les Voyageurs dans l'Empire Ottoman (XIVᵉ–XVIᵉ siècles): bibliographie, itinéraires et inventaire des lieux habités* (Ankara, 1991).

Yıldırım ['Yildirim'], O., 'The Battle of Lepanto and its Impact on Ottoman History and Historiography', in R. Cancila, ed., *Mediterraneo in armi (secc. XV–XVIII)*, 2 vols. (Palermo, 2007), ii, 533–56.

Yıldırım, R., 'Turkomans between Two Empires: The Origins of the Qizilbash Identity in Anatolia (1447–1514)', Bilkent University PhD thesis (2008).

Yotopoulou Sicilianou, E., 'Alcune considerazioni sulle classi sociali corfiotte e sulla politica veneta nei loro confronti in base a quanto risulta dalle fonti e in modo particolare dai teste delle ambasciate', in M. Costantini and A. Nikiforou, eds., *Levante veneziano: aspetti di storia delle Isole Ionie al tempo della Serenissima* (Rome, 1996), 97–121.

Yriarte, C., *La Vie d'un patricien de Venise au XVIᵉ siècle d'après les papiers d'état des Frari* (Paris, 1874).

Zach, C. R., 'Bemerkungen über das Verhältnis von Staat und Kirche in der Walachei und Moldau des 16. und 17. Jahrhunderts', *SF*, 43 (1984), 21–47.

Zamputi, I., 'Disa fletë të historisë së Shqipnisë në periudhën 1506–1574', *Buletin i Universitetit Shtetëror të Tiranës: seria shkencat shoqërore*, 14 (1960), no. 2, 3–31.

— ed., *Dokumente të shekujve XVI–XVII për historinë e Shqipërisë*, vols. 1–2 (Tirana, 1989).

Zapperi, R., 'Michele Bonelli', in *DBI*, xi, 774–5.

Ziliotto, B., *Capodistria* (Trieste, 1910).

— *Accademie ed accademici di Capodistria (1478–1807)* (Trieste, 1944).

Zinkeisen, J. W., *Geschichte des osmanischen Reiches in Europa*, 6 vols. (Hamburg and Gotha, 1840–59).

Zirojević, O., *Ulcinj u prošlosti* (Podgorica, 2009).

Žitko, S., *Koper: The Town and its Heritage* (Koper, 2011).

Zlatar, Z., *Our Kingdom Come: The Counter-Reformation, the Republic of Dubrovnik, and the Liberation of the Balkan Slavs* (Boulder, CO, 1992).

Žontar, J., 'Michael Černović, Geheimagent Ferdinands I. und Maximilians II., und seine Berichterstattung', *MÖS*, 24 (1971), 169–222.

— *Obveščevalna služba in diplomacija avstrijskih Habsburžanov v boju proti Turkom v 16. stoletju* (Ljubljana, 1973).

Index